SPECULATIONS

SPECULATIONS

Readings in Culture, Identity, and Values

EDITED BY

CHARLES I. SCHUSTER
University of Wisconsin—Milwaukee

WILLIAM V. VAN PELT
University of Wisconsin—Milwaukee

A BLAIR PRESS BOOK

PRENTICE HALL, ENGLEWOOD CLIFFS, NJ 07632

Library of Congress Cataloging-in-Publication Data

Speculations / edited by Charles I. Schuster, William V. Van Pelt.
    p.   cm.
    "A Blair Press book."
    Includes index.
    1. Readers—United States. 2. United States—Civilization—
Problems, exercises, etc. 3. English language—Rhetoric.
4. College readers. I. Schuster, Charles I. II. Van Pelt, William V.
PE1127.H5S77 1993
808'.0427—dc20   92-36802
                                                 CIP

Cover design: Richard Stalzer Associates, Ltd.
Cover photo: Carla A. Sansone © 1992
Photo credits: John Griffin/The Image Works, p. 1; Al Pereira/Star File, p. 129;
  © Douglas Kent Hall, p. 359; Kenneth Murray/Photo Researchers, p. 403;
  Barbara Alper/Stock Boston, p. 509
Prepress buyer: Herb Klein
Manufacturing buyers: Robert Anderson/Patrice Fraccio

Acknowledgments appear on pages 655–657, which constitute a continuation of the copyright page.

Blair Press
The Statler Building
20 Park Plaza, Suite 1113
Boston, MA 02116-4399

© 1993 by Prentice-Hall, Inc.
A Simon & Schuster Company
Englewood Cliffs, NJ 07632

Printed in the United States.
10 9 8 7 6 5 4 3 2 1

ISBN 0-13-827064-3

Prentice-Hall International (UK) Limited, *London*
Prentice-Hall of Australia Pty., Limited, *Sydney*
Prentice-Hall of Canada Inc., *Toronto*
Prentice-Hall of Hispanoamerica, S. A., *Mexico*
Prentice-Hall of India Private Limited, *New Dehli*
Prentice-Hall of Japan, Inc., *Tokyo*
Simon & Schuster Asia Pte. Ltd., *Singapore*
Editora Prentice-Hall do Brasil, Ltda., *Rio de Janeiro*

PREFACE

Speculations was born within the freshman writing program of the University of Wisconsin—Milwaukee, where it took the form of a homegrown reader. Even though it originally included only fifteen or so selections, our intent then, as now, was to put together a book that reflected a cultural studies perspective. For us, cultural studies tapped directly into students' experience and critical consciousness so as to move them from one way of knowing to another. This philosophy remains in the five themes that give focus to our current sections: Growing Up, Music and Morality, Crime and Punishment, Self and Society, and Work and Wealth.

During the three years that we worked on *Speculations*, we discovered other important objectives as well. First, we wanted to create a book that offered fundamental critiques of society; hence our subtitle: "Readings in Culture, Identity, and Values." We believe that the social, political, economic, and educational values that have gained ascendancy over the past twenty-five years need to be reassessed. Clearly there is a powerful sense among Americans of all ages that something is wrong with 1990s America, that we have lost our way. Without getting too evangelical, our view is that college education needs to return to a consideration of fundamental issues: morality, values, family, the social nature of crime, the meaning of work and wealth. We want students to think about gender, race, and class, about their own histories and possible futures. Although such topics are clearly polemical and potentially divisive, we worked hard to contextualize these issues, to find selections that were thoughtful and exploratory rather than hysterical and hortatory. In our view, there is no way to sweep such issues under the rug of academe.

In putting together *Speculations*, we looked for selections—essays primarily, but also stories and poems—that engage readers with the issues, that cry out to be read and reread. We tried hard to select works that have broad appeal, that capture the interests of undergraduates and faculty, majority and minority students, men and women, theorists and practitioners. We hope that the choices in *Speculations* reward first reading, but even more importantly we hope that they reward subsequent readings. There isn't a selection included that we haven't read at least four or five times, discussed, debated, argued through. That, in fact, was our main test for including a work; if it sustained itself over multiple readings, arguments, and conversations—then it was something we wanted to share with students.

We wanted, too, to create a book that was eminently teachable. To that end, we decided to concentrate on just five themes, thereby giving students and instructors the opportunity for substantive investigation and analysis without loss of focus. The twelve to fifteen selections included within each thematic section offer a series of interlocking perspectives. As with any book, the organizing principles are somewhat arbitrary: for example, we could have included Léon Bing's "When You're a Crip (or a Blood)" under Crime and Punishment, Martin Luther King, Jr.'s "Letter from Birmingham Jail" under Self and Society, Zora Neale Hurston's "How It Feels to Be Colored Me" under Growing Up. Frankly, some selections shifted as we moved from section to section, but we ultimately felt that the essays, stories, and poems within each thematic section informed each other in the most effective way.

We feel positive as well about the apparatus. The headnotes that introduce selections are as full and informative as we could make them. Because many of the authors included in this book are likely to be unfamiliar to instructors as well as to students, we worked doubly hard to provide biographical, historical, and bibliographic information. We also wanted the headnotes to function as windows that open onto the selections that follow. In describing the openings of his own literary journalistic essays, John McPhee had said that a lead should shine a light into the piece. We have similarly tried to shine such a light with our headnotes.

The questions and assignment sequences offer a substantial departure from those in more typical composition anthologies. The questions that accompany selections focus primarily on structure, argument, style, and content. We struggled to articulate fundamental issues, as often as possible formulating questions that do not have simple or correct answers, so as to invite discussion and debate. The end-of-chapter assignment sequences represent the kind of pedagogy that we have used for years. "Situational sequencing," as we refer to it, forces students to situate themselves within a specific rhetorical context, to engage with the text through role playing and imaginative speculation. For virtually all students, such serious but playful writing is powerful and productive. It forces them to experiment with styles and voices, to write from someone else's point of view, to explore alternative perspectives. As they work their way through a sequence, students engage in what might best be described as conceptual revision; that is, they write an essay and then write on the same subject but from a different perspective or for a different audience, or they work their way through one argument and then apply that same argument to a different text. Given the richness of the selections in this book, we felt that assignment sequences offered the greatest potential for students and instructors to mine the depths.

Ultimately, it is you and your students who will tell us whether we have succeeded, whether we have made the kind of pedagogical and intellectual difference that we intended. Thus we would like to receive your responses, suggestions, critiques. And we definitely would like to receive your students' essays if you think they belong in a subsequent edition of this anthology. Our hope is to include student essays along with those by professional writers in the next edition of *Speculations*. We can only do this if you send us those essays care of our publisher, Blair Press.

When we began this project, it felt completely out of reach. There was so much to do—the reading, selecting, teaching, writing, editing, experimenting—and so little time. Thank goodness for long distance lines, fax machines, and overnight express service. But we have other, more important debts to acknowledge, individuals who have helped us far beyond the call of duty. First of all, we want to thank Nancy Perry, publisher of Blair Press, who believed in this book even before we did. We greatly appreciate her work—and the work of Leslie Cavaliere and LeeAnn Einert, her assistants at Blair Press, who kept us organized and on-task. We want to thank the dedicated graduate students and staff in the English and Comparative Literature Department at the University of Wisconsin—Milwaukee who provided much-needed support, especially Mary Cyrulik, Donna DeWitt, Johanna Atwood, Matt Matcuk, Kristi Yager, Eileen Schell, and Marguerite Helmers. Matt and Kristi in particular contributed a great deal of research that was especially valuable in the writing of headnotes. We also want to thank our reviewers, who helped give the book shape and definition: Nancy Barry, Luther College; Judith Goleman, University of Massachusetts, Boston; Thomas Recchio, University of Connecticut; Melita Schaum, University of Michigan, Dearborn; Lucille Schultz, University of Cincinnati; Mark Wiley, California State University, Long Beach; Randy Woodland, University of California, Los Angeles. We owe a great debt as well to the freshmen and sophomores at UWM who inspired us always to rethink our assignments and return one more time to the library to find that elusive essay we needed to complete one thematic section or another. And finally we want to thank our families: Patricia Ellis and Jacob Schuster, and Mary Mullins. Anyone who has completed a book knows how all-enveloping the work can be. Our wives and son had to suffer weeks and months of long absences and vacant stares on the part of their husbands and father. Perhaps more significantly, they were our first audience, our primary support staff. And they were our inspiration. Without them, *Speculations* would have remained a bunch of scattered pages sitting on a back table.

Charles I. Schuster
William V. Van Pelt

CONTENTS

2
MUSIC AND MORALITY   129

3
CRIME AND PUNISHMENT   259

4

SELF AND SOCIETY   403

5

WORK AND WEALTH   509

INTRODUCTION

Speculations provides a diverse collection of readings for students who want to learn more about themselves, their culture, and the changing values of the 1990s. In creating this anthology, our first goal was to find selections that you would enjoy reading and that you would want to read more than once. We tried to create an anthology that would make you want to read and keep reading, a book that you would keep on your bookshelf long after completing the course for which it is required. Our second goal was to include readings that would challenge you intellectually and stimulate you to think critically about your own cultural history, social background, and personal identity. Many of the ideas presented in this book are controversial and intended to provoke argument and debate. The selections, then, should give you not only pleasure in reading but also pleasure in debating and writing about ideas and issues you care about. We believe that you and your classmates will have a lot to say about the five areas of modern life that the readings address: growing up, music and morality, crime and punishment, self and society, and work and wealth.

For example, the opening section, Growing Up, presents teenage as well as adult perspectives on how and why parents and children have trouble getting along. Many of you will identify with the stories of resistance to parental and social domination told by writers like Jamaica Kincaid and Amy Tan, both of whom display strong egos and strong wills to succeed on their own. Other selections may reflect experiences different from yours, but they deal with subjects that you have heard or seen a good deal about, such as Léon Bing's "When You're a Crip (or a Blood)," which vividly describes, in their own words, the lives of gang members in Los Angeles, or Elizabeth Marek's "The Lives of Teenage Mothers," which provides a real sense of how difficult it is to be a parent and finish high school at the same time. In the Music and Morality section, you may reject Allan Bloom's argument that rock ruins the moral education of modern youth, or you may take sides for or against the censorship of obscene lyrics in rap music as discussed by Barbara Dority in her essay "The War on Rock and Rap." Or you may find something in this section that strikes a chord with your own love of music, such as the essays on folk music, the great jazz musicians, the evolution of the blues, the myths surrounding Elvis Presley, or the feminist critique of Madonna's music. We hope you come to such selections with your own opinions and preferences and that you engage them critically and thoughtfully.

The Crime and Punishment section looks at our national obsession with the problems of crime and its consequences: How effective are prisons? What causes white-collar crime? How can we deal with rape and other forms of physical violence? Jessica Mitford's "The Criminal Type," for example, examines our perceptions of who criminals are and how they are created within our society: Are the causes biological, behavioral, economic, or social? In "Senseless Crimes," Rick Telander looks at teenage murderers and asks us to ponder difficult questions: Why do kids kill for sports clothes? Should professional athletes promote such products? What is the role of advertising in a society where kids kill for clothes? In a much different essay, Ellen Sweet examines "Date Rape," which occurs frequently on college campuses; she looks at the startling facts, stereotypes, and misconceptions that men and women have about date rape. We think you'll have something to say about these issues; moreover, you'll probably want to know more about them, which will encourage you to do further reading and writing.

The selections in Self and Society address the problems of difference, diversity, and the identity of the "self" versus "others" in our society. They explore how we see others and how we are shaped by our vision of them. For example, Gretel Ehrlich's "Other Lives," Richard Selzer's "Imelda," and Ernest Hemingway's "Indian Camp" all deal with death and renewal, revealing how we are changed through our intimacy with others, their lives and their deaths. Zora Neale Hurston's "How It Feels to Be Colored Me" gives powerful expression to how she came to terms with her "otherness" in a white culture. In "Complexion," Richard Rodriguez explores how his and others' awareness of skin color affected his growing up, manhood, education, work experience, and eventual assimilation into the larger culture of the United States.

In the final section, Work and Wealth, the readings examine work-related issues that concern all college students. This section asks you to think about the nature not only of work but of wealth and success. What are the pleasures as well as the material gains to be derived from work? How does one find a good job? What is the relation among education, employment, and wealth? What is the future of work for young people in the United States? Is there an invisible cultural barrier that holds back women, blacks, and other minorities? You'll find many opportunities for discussing these and other questions as you read such selections as Wendell Berry's "The Profit in Work's Pleasure," Barbara Garson's "McDonald's—We Do It All for You," Studs Terkel's "Mike LeFevre, Steelworker," Susan Fraker's "Why Women Aren't Getting to the Top," and Maxine Lipner's "Ben and Jerry's: Sweet Ethics Evince Social Awareness."

In addition to the rich diversity of perspectives on American culture in *Speculations*, you will find writing that speaks from within several different genres and styles of writing: personal essays, scholarly essays, newspaper articles, sermons, interviews, speeches, short stories, song lyrics, and poems. We chose these diverse forms of writing not just to enhance your pleasure in reading but because each form has its own way of communicating and making its point. Similarly, the writing sequences at the end of each section of the book invite you to write your thoughts and responses in several different forms and styles. Our intention here is to encourage you to look at a variety of ways of thinking and writing.

Thus we have created a variety of assignments in the writing sequences. They build on specific themes which we think you will find absorbing and important. In the Growing Up section, for example, we invite you to explore specific themes such as "family life," "using language," "parent and child," "the search for identity," and "family values." The Music and Morality section asks you to evaluate your own relation to music and culture, to write a review of a musical performance, or to compile your own anthology of music lyrics and write an interpretive introduction for it. Work and Wealth has assignments that ask you to explore values in the workplace, to evaluate your own experience with gender difference at work, or to interview a professional in your community and write a profile of that professional for your peers. Most of the writing suggestions in the sequences build on issues, ideas, or points of view first articulated in the "Speculations" questions that follow each reading selection. Therefore, you may find it useful to return to the "Speculations" questions when considering specific readings that you want to write about.

As with the reading selections, the writing sequences in this book are designed to encourage you to respond critically to issues and ideas that you already know something about. *Speculations* seeks to connect your personal knowledge and personal voice to a new experience of academic writing and a new understanding of your identity within the changing values and culture of our society. We encourage you to draw on your personal experience to voice your own opinion, enter the debate, and learn more about what others have to say. Most importantly, we hope you enjoy reading and speculating about the ideas and perspectives you encounter in this book.

SPECULATIONS

1

GROWING UP

If family life were subject to "truth in advertising" regulations, every marriage ceremony might be required to carry the following warning to prospective parents: "Growing up in America can be dangerous to your children's health." This has often been true in America, at least for certain segments of the population, but there is an increasing perception that the difficulties of growing up—poverty, drugs, AIDS, crime, suicide, stress—now reach into virtually every community, regardless of race, color, or socioeconomic character. Thus, with all the wealth and technological advances in America, there is considerable evidence just from a daily reading of the newspaper that families—children and their parents—face significant problems as they negotiate their way through the 1990s.

While concern about the social crises in American life is the main theme of this section and of this entire collection of readings, there is much to celebrate: the richness of America's resources and the resiliency of the American people are qualities recognized all over the world. Americans believe in themselves and have always had an optimism about themselves and their country. For the first time in the history of the United States, however, our standard of living is at best precarious; children today may not be able to achieve the same standard of living as their parents. Additionally, health care is in crisis and children increasingly live in single-parent families or are born to teenage mothers barely able to take care of themselves let alone their babies. As drugs and poverty erode city life, urban children often find themselves tempted by gangs and a culture of casual violence.

To offer such a stark picture is not to engage in hopelessness. The problems of growing up are real, but so are the solutions. The selections in this section address both the challenges we face and the means by which we can improve the quality of life for one of America's most important natural resources: our future generations.

With a range of topics from growing up as an African-American woman, confronting the horror of homelessness, living in hotel warehouses, feeling suffocated by the overwhelming affluence of upper-middle-class life, struggling to achieve independence, or coming to terms with the effects of alcoholism, the writers included here powerfully and eloquently inspire readers to react, respond, and reconsider values and assumptions. Our hope is that they provide a forum for active reading and writing—and perhaps a little public "doing" as well.

Girl

JAMAICA KINCAID

Antigua, a small Caribbean island that remained a British colony until 1967, is a sun-drenched exotic locale visited by rich tourists but inhabited by impoverished black families. Jamaica Kincaid described it as "a small place" in her defiant book by that title (1988), one of four that she has published since 1983. Her books offer a collection of brilliantly evoked impressions—of an angry childhood in Antigua, a young girl's sense of betrayal, the relationship between mother and daughter, the experiences of a young black woman hired into a wealthy family in New York City as a live-in housekeeper and child-sitter.

Although Kincaid publishes her work as fiction, much of it closely follows the outlines of her own life. As described in a 1990 article in *The New York Times Sunday Magazine*, Kincaid "was born into tropical poverty. Her father was a carpenter and her mother kept house. They had no electricity, no bathroom, no running water. Every Wednesday he registered their outhouse at the Public Works Department so that the 'night soil men,' as they were called, would take away their full tub and replace it with a clean one. And every morning she went to a public pipe and drew four pails of water for her mother—more if it was a washday." These and other duties occupied much of Kincaid's life, even during her school years when she learned to love to read, pursuing her desire to own books past the point of recklessness. "Books," she said, "brought me the greatest satisfaction . . . I stole books, and I stole money to buy them."

In her writing, Kincaid manages to be defiant and outraged about life's injustices and yet celebratory and lyrical. A meticulous stylist who may spend hours choosing the right word, Kincaid has crafted some of the most beautiful sentences in the English language. "Girl," set in Antigua, is the first piece Jamaica Kincaid ever published; it appeared in *The New Yorker*, which has published her work ever since.

Wash the white clothes on Monday and put them on the stone heap; wash the color clothes on Tuesday and put them on the clothesline to dry; don't walk barehead in the hot sun; cook pumpkin fritters in very hot sweet oil; soak your little cloths right after you take them off; when buying cotton to make yourself a nice blouse, be sure that it doesn't have gum on it, because that way it won't hold up well after a wash; soak salt fish overnight before you cook it; is it true that you sing benna in Sunday school?; always eat your food in such a way that it won't turn someone else's stomach; on Sundays try to walk like a lady and not like the slut you are so bent on becoming; don't sing benna in Sunday school; you mustn't speak to wharf-rat boys, not even to give directions; don't eat fruits on the street—flies will follow you; *but I don't sing benna on Sundays at all and never in Sunday school;*

this is how to sew on a button; this is how to make a button-hole for the button you have just sewed on; this is how to hem a dress when you see the hem coming down and so to prevent yourself from looking like the slut I know you are so bent on becoming; this is how you iron your father's khaki shirt so that it doesn't have a crease; this is how you iron your father's khaki pants so that they don't have a crease; this is how you grow okra—far from the house, because okra tree harbors red ants; when you are growing dasheen, make sure it gets plenty of water or else it makes your throat itch when you are eating it; this is how you sweep a corner; this is how you sweep a whole house; this is how you sweep a yard; this is how you smile to someone you don't like too much; this is how you smile to someone you don't like at all; this is how you smile to someone you like completely; this is how you set a table for tea; this is how you set a table for dinner; this is how you set a table for dinner with an important guest; this is how you set a table for lunch; this is how you set a table for breakfast; this is how to behave in the presence of men who don't know you very well, and this way they won't recognize immediately the slut I have warned you against becoming; be sure to wash every day, even if it is with your own spit; don't squat down to play marbles—you are not a boy, you know; don't pick people's flowers—you might catch something; don't throw stones at blackbirds, because it might not be a blackbird at all; this is how to make a bread pudding; this is how to make doukona; this is how to make pepper pot; this is how to make a good medicine for a cold; this is how to make a good medicine to throw away a child before it even becomes a child; this is how to catch a fish; this is how to throw back a fish you don't like, and that way something bad won't fall on you; this is how to bully a man; this is how a man bullies you; this is how to love a man, and if this doesn't work there are other ways, and if they don't work don't feel too bad about giving up; this is how to spit up in the air if you feel like it, and this is how to move quick so that it doesn't fall on you; this is how to make ends meet; always squeeze bread to make sure it's fresh; *but what if the baker won't let me feel the bread?*; you mean to say that after all you are really going to be the kind of woman who the baker won't let near the bread?

SPECULATIONS

1.   In "Girl," Jamaica Kincaid presents a relationship between a mother and daughter. How does she accomplish this portrayal? Why do you think Kincaid chooses this particular form to express this relationship? Who do you think is speaking? Who is the listener?

2. What kind of a life is being described here? What is the scene that is described? How important is the locale to "Girl"?

3. Do you think "Girl" offers good advice? Why or why not?

4. What do you think is intended by the words in italics? Why do you think Kincaid wrote "Girl" all as one sentence, using italics, not using any paragraphs? What is the effect of this form on you as a reader?

5. What genre do you think best describes "Girl"? That is, is "Girl" an essay, a story, a prose poem? Is it fiction or nonfiction? Does its form influence the way you read and understand it?

The Lesson

TONI CADE BAMBARA

A distinguished writer, lecturer, and civil rights activist, Toni Cade Bambara is perhaps best known for her collections of short stories, *Gorilla, My Love* (1972) and *The Sea Birds Are Still Alive* (1977), vignettes of African-American life in the North and the South. *The Salt Eaters* (1980), a dream-like novel, explores a developing relationship between two women who suffer intense emotional turmoil. The critic John Leonard described it as "an incantation, poem-drunk, myth-happy, mud-caked, jazz-ridden, prodigal in meanings, a kite and a mask. . . . It is as if she jived the very stones to groan." This comment captures the rich blend of inspirational, political, and street-smart colloquial talk that characterizes Bambara's prose.

Unlike many writers, Bambara has not been content to lead the quiet life of the writer in her study. Since the urban turmoil and civil rights struggles of the 1960s, Bambara has worked to promote equal rights for blacks. Born in New York City in 1939, she began her professional life as a social investigator for the New York State Department of Welfare where she gained many insights concerning poverty and possibility. It is clear that her experiences in that job influenced "The Lesson."

Bambara has worked tirelessly with community centers, local writers in cities across the country, and public service organizations. She has lectured and read her work in museums, prisons, libraries, and universities. Winner of numerous awards including the Black Rose Award from *Encore* and *Ebony*'s Achievement in the Arts Award, Bambara has been described in *The New York Times Book Review* as able to tell "more about being black through her quiet, proud, silly, tender, hip, acute, loving stores than any amount of literary polemicizing could hope to do. She writes about love: a love for one's family, one's friends, one's race, one's neighborhood and it is the sort of love that comes with maturity and inner peace." Much of that love is in evidence in "The Lesson," a story of discovery by a young, poor, black girl in New York City who takes a trip to the most famous toy store in the world.

Back in the days when everyone was old and stupid or young and foolish and me and Sugar were the only ones just right, this lady moved on our block with nappy hair and proper speech and no makeup. And quite naturally we laughed at her, laughed the way we did at the junk man who went about his business like he was some big-time president and his sorry-ass horse his secretary. And we kinda hated her too, hated the way we did the winos who cluttered up our parks and pissed on our handball walls and stank up our hallways and stairs so you couldn't halfway play hide-and-seek without a god-damn gas mask. Miss Moore was her name. The only woman on the block with no first name. And she was black as hell, cept for her feet, which were fish-white and spooky. And she was always planning these boring-ass things for us to do, us being my cousin, mostly, who lived on the block cause we all moved North the same time and to the same apartment then spread out gradual to breathe. And our parents would yank our heads into some kinda shape and crisp up our clothes so we'd be presentable for travel with Miss Moore, who always looked like she was going to church, though she never did. Which is just one of things the grown-ups talked about when they talked behind her back like a dog. But when she came calling with some sachet she'd sewed up or some gingerbread she'd made or some book, why then they'd all be too embarrassed to turn her down and we'd get handed over all spruced up. She'd been to college and said it was only right that she should take responsibility for the young ones' education, and she not even related by marriage or blood. So they'd go for it. Specially Aunt Gretchen. She was the main gofer in the family. You got some ole dumb shit foolishness you want somebody to go for, you send for Aunt Gretchen. She been screwed into the goalong for so long, it's a blood-deep natural thing with her. Which is how she got saddled with me and Sugar and Junior in the first place while our mothers were in a la-de-da apartment up the block having a good ole time.

So this one day Miss Moore rounds us all up at the mailbox and it's puredee hot and she's knocking herself out about arithmetic. And school suppose to let up in summer I heard, but she don't never let up. And the starch in my pinafore scratching the shit outta me and I'm really hating this nappy-head bitch and her goddamn college de-gree. I'd much rather go to the pool or to the show where it's cool. So me and Sugar leaning on the mailbox being surly, which is a Miss Moore word. And Flyboy checking out what everybody brought for lunch. And Fat Butt already wasting his peanut-butter-and-jelly sand-wich like the pig he is. And Junebug punchin on Q.T.'s arm for potato chips. And Rosie Giraffe shifting from one hip to the other waiting for somebody to step on her foot or ask her if she from Georgia so she can kick ass, preferably Mercedes's. And Miss Moore asking us do we know what money is, like we a bunch of retards. I mean real money, she say, like it's only poker chips or monopoly papers we lay on the grocer. So right away I'm tired of this and say so. And would much rather snatch Sugar and go to the Sunset and terrorize the West Indian kids and take their hair ribbons and their money too. And Miss Moore files that remark away for next week's lesson on brotherhood, I can tell. And finally I say we oughta get to the subway cause it's cooler and besides we might meet some cute boys. Sugar done swiped her mama's lipstick, so we ready.

So we heading down the street and she's boring us silly about what things cost and what our parents make and how much goes for rent and how money ain't divided up right in this country. And then she gets to the part about we all poor and live in the slums, which I don't feature. And I'm ready to speak on that, but she steps out in the street and hails two cabs just like that. Then she hustles half the crew in with her and hands me a five-dollar bill and tells me to calculate 10 percent tip for the driver. And we're off. Me and Sugar and Junebug and Flyboy hangin out the window and hollering to everybody, putting lipstick on each other cause Flyboy a faggot anyway, and making farts with our sweaty armpits. But I'm mostly trying to figure how to spend this money. But they all fascinated with the meter ticking and Junebug starts laying bets as to how much it'll read when Flyboy can't hold his breath no more. Then Sugar lay bets as to how much it'll be when we get there. So I'm stuck. Don't nobody want to go for my plan, which is to jump out at the next light and run off to the first bar-b-que we can find. Then the driver tells us to get the hell out cause we there already. And the meter reads eight-five cents. And I'm stalling to figure out the tip and Sugar say give him a dime. And I decide he don't need it bad as I do, so later for him. But then he tries to take off with Junebug's foot still in the door so we talk about his mama something ferocious. Then we check out that we on Fifth Avenue and everybody dressed up in stockings. One lady in a fur coat, hot as it is. White folks crazy.

"This is the place," Miss Moore say, presenting it to us in the voice she uses at the museum. "Let's look in the windows before we go in."

"Can we steal?" Sugar asks very serious like she's getting the ground rules squared away before she plays. "I beg your pardon," say Miss Moore, and we fall out. So she leads us around the windows of the toy store and me and Sugar screamin, "This is mine, that's mine, I gotta have that, that was made for me, I was born for that," till Big Butt drowns us out.

"Hey, I'm going to buy that there."

"That there? You don't even known what it is, stupid."

"I do so," he say punchin on Rosie Giraffe. "It's a microscope."

"Whatcha gonna do with a microscope, fool?"

"Look at things."

"Like what, Ronald?" ask Miss Moore. And Big Butt ain't got the first notion. So here go Miss Moore gabbing about the thousands of bacteria in a drop of water and the somethinorother in a speck of blood and the million and one living things in the air around us is invisible to the naked eye. And what she say that for? Junebug go to town on that "naked" and we rolling. Then Miss Moore ask what it cost. So we all jam into the window smudgin it up and the price tag say three hundred dollars. So then she ask how long'd take for Big Butt and Junebug to save up their allowances. "Too long," I say. "Yeh," adds Sugar, "outgrown it by that time." And Miss Moore say no, you never outgrow learning instruments. "Why, even medical students and interns and," blah, blah, blah. And we ready to choke Big Butt for bringing it up in the first damn place.

"This here costs four hundred eighty dollars," say Rosie Giraffe. So we pile up all over her to see what she pointin out. My eyes tell me it's a chunk of glass cracked with something heavy, and different-color inks dripped into the splits, then the whole thing put into a oven or something. But for $480 it don't make sense.

"That's a paperweight made of semi-precious stones fused together under tremendous pressure," she explains slowly, with her hands doing the mining and all the factory work.

"So what's a paperweight?" asks Rosie Giraffe.

"To weigh paper with, dumbbell," say Flyboy, the wise man from the East.

"Not exactly," say Miss Moore, which is what she say when you warm or way off too. "It's to weigh paper down so it won't scatter and make your desk untidy." So right away me and Sugar curtsy to each other and then to Mercedes who is more the tidy type.

"We don't keep paper on top of the desk in my class," say Junebug, figuring Miss Moore crazy or lyin one.

"At home, then," she say. "Don't you have a calendar and a pencil case and a blotter and a letter-opener on your desk at home where you do your homework?" And she know damn well what our homes look like cause she nosys around in them every chance she gets.

"I don't even have a desk," say Junebug, "Do we?"

"No. And I don't get no homework neither," says Big Butt.

"And I don't even have a home," say Flyboy like he do at school to keep the white folks off his back and sorry for him. Send this poor kid to camp posters, is his specialty.

"I do," says Mercedes. "I have a box of stationery on my desk and a picture of my cat. My godmother bought the stationery and the desk. There's a big rose on each sheet and the envelopes smell like roses."

"Who wants to know about your smelly-ass stationery," say Rosie Giraffe fore I can get my two cents in.

"It's important to have a work area all your own so that . . ."

"Will you look at this sailboat, please," say Flyboy, cuttin her off and pointin to the thing like it was his. So once again we tumble all over each other to gaze at this magnificent thing in the toy store which is just big enough to maybe sail two kittens across the pond if you strap them to the posts tight. We all start reciting the price tag like we in assembly. "Handcrafted sailboat of fiberglass at one thousand one hundred ninety-five dollars."

"Unbelievable," I hear myself say and am really stunned. I read it again for myself just in case the group recitation put me in a trance. Same thing. For some reason this pisses me off. We look at Miss Moore and she lookin at us, waiting for I dunno what.

"Who'd pay all that when you can buy a sailboat set for a quarter at Pop's, a tube of glue for a dime, and a ball of string for eight cents? It must have a motor and a whole lot else besides," I say. "My sailboat cost me about fifty cents."

"But will it take water?" say Mercedes with her smart ass.

"Took mine to Alley Pond Park once," say Flyboy. "String broke. Lost it. Pity."

"Sailed mine in Central Park and it keeled over and sank. Had to ask my father for another dollar."

"And you got the strap," laugh Big Butt. "The jerk didn't even have a string on it. My old man whaled on his behind."

Little Q.T. was staring hard at the sailboat and you could see he wanted it bad. But he too little and somebody'd just take it from him. So what the hell. "This boat for kids, Miss Moore?"

"Parents silly to buy something like that just to get all broke up," say Rosie Giraffe.

"That much money it should last forever," I figure.

"My father'd buy it for me if I wanted it."

"Your father, my ass," say Rosie Giraffe getting a chance to finally push Mercedes.

"Must be rich people shop here," say Q.T.

"You are a very bright boy," say Flyboy. "What was your first clue?" And he rap him on the head with the back of his knuckles, since Q.T. the only one he could get away with. Though Q.T. liable to come up behind you years later and get his licks in when you half expect it.

"What I want to know is," I says to Miss Moore though I never talk to her, I wouldn't give the bitch that satisfaction, "is how much a real boat costs? I figure a thousand'd get you a yacht any day."

"Why don't you check that out," she says, "and report back to the group?" Which really pains my ass. If you gonna mess up a perfectly good swim day least you could do is have some answers. "Let's go in," she say like she got something up her sleeve. Only she don't lead the way. So me and Sugar turn the corner to where the entrance is, but when we get there I kinda hang back. Not that I'm scared, what's there to be afraid of, just a toy store. But I feel funny, shame. But what I got to be shamed about? Got as much right to go in as anybody. But somehow I can't seem to get hold of the door, so I step away for Sugar to lead. But she hangs back too. And I look at her and she looks at me and this is ridiculous. I mean, damn, I have never ever been shy about doing nothing or going nowhere. But then Mercedes steps up and then Rosie Giraffe and Big Butt crowd in behind and shove, and next thing we all stuffed into the doorway with only Mercedes squeezing past us, smoothing out her jumper and walking right down the aisle. Then the rest of us tumble in like a glued-together jigsaw done all wrong. And people lookin at us. And it's like the time me and Sugar crashed into the Catholic church on a dare. But once we got in there and everything so hushed and holy and the candles and the bowin and the handkerchiefs on all the drooping heads, I just couldn't go through with the plan. Which was for me to run up to the altar and do a tap dance while Sugar played the nose flute and messed around in the holy water. And Sugar kept givin me the elbow. Then later teased me so bad I tied her up in the shower and turned it on and locked her in. And she'd be there till this day if Aunt Gretchen hadn't finally figured I was lying about the boarder takin a shower.

Same thing in the store. We all walkin on tiptoe and hardly touchin the games and puzzles and things. And I watched Miss Moore who is steady watchin us like she waiting for a sign. Like Mama Drewery watches the sky and sniffs the air and takes note of just how much slant is in the bird formation. Then me and Sugar bump smack into each other, so busy gazing at the toys, 'specially the sailboat. But we don't laugh and go into our fat-lady bump-stomach routine. We just stare at that price tag. Then Sugar ran a finger over the whole boat. And I'm jealous and want to hit her. Maybe not her, but I sure want to punch somebody in the mouth.

"Whatcha bring us here for, Miss Moore?"

"You sound angry, Sylvia. Are you mad about something?" Givin me one of them grins like she tellin a grown-up joke that never turns out to be funny. And she's lookin very closely at me like maybe she plannin to do my portrait from memory. I'm mad, but I won't give her that satisfaction. So I slouch around the store bein very bored and say, "Let's go."

Me an Sugar at the back of the train watchin the tracks whizzin by large then small then gettin gobbled up in the dark. I'm thinkin about this tricky toy I saw in the store. A clown that somersaults on a bar then does chin-ups just cause you yank lightly at his leg. Cost $35. I could see me askin my mother for a $35 birthday clown. "You wanna who that costs what?" she'd say, cocking her head to the side to get a better view of the hole in my head. Thirty-five dollars could buy new bunk beds for Junior and Gretchen's boy. Thirty-five dollars and the whole household could go visit Granddaddy Nelson in the country. Thirty-five dollars would pay for the rent and the piano bill too. Who are these people that spend that much for performing clowns and $1,000 for toy sailboats? What kinda work they do and how they live and how come we ain't in on it? Where we are is who we are, Miss Moore always pointin out. But it don't necessarily have to be that way, she always adds then waits for somebody to say that poor people have to wake up and demand their share of the pie and don't none of us know what kind of pie she talkin about in the first damn place. But she ain't so smart cause I still got her four dollars from the taxi and she sure ain't getting it. Messin up my day with this shit. Sugar nudges me in my pocket and winks.

Miss Moore lines us up in front of the mailbox where we started from, seem like years ago, and I got a headache for thinkin so hard. And we lean all over each other so we can hold up under the draggy-ass lecture she always finishes us off with at the end before we thank her for borin us to tears. But she just looks at us like she readin tea leaves. Finally she say, "Well, what do you think of F.A.O. Schwarz?"

Rosie Giraffe mumbles, "White folks crazy."

"I'd like to go there again when I get my birthday money," says Mercedes, and we shove her out the pack so she has to lean on the mailbox by herself.

"I'd like a shower. Tiring day," says Flyboy.

Then Sugar surprises me by sayin, "You know, Miss Moore, I don't think all of us here put together eat in a year what that sailboat costs." And Miss Moore lights up like somebody goosed her. "And?" she say, urging Sugar on. Only I'm standin on her foot so she don't continue.

"Imagine for a minute what kind of society it is in which some people can spend on a toy what it would cost to feed a family of six or seven. What do you think?"

"I think," say Sugar pushing me off her feet like she never done before, cause I whip her ass in a minute, "that this is not much of a democracy if you ask me. Equal chance to pursue happiness means an equal crack at the dough, don't it?'' Miss Moore is besides herself and I am disgusted with Sugar's treachery. So I stand on her foot one more time to see if she'll shove me. She shuts up, and Miss Moore looks at me, sorrowfully I'm thinkin. And somethin weird is goin on. I can feel it in my chest.

"Anybody else learn anything today?'' lookin dead at me. I walk away and Sugar has to run to catch up and don't even seem to notice when I shrug her arm off my shoulder.

"Well, we got four dollars anyway,'' she says.

"Uh-hunh.''

"We could go to Hascombs and get half a chocolate layer and then go to the Sunset and still have plenty money for potato chips and ice cream sodas.''

"Uh-hunh.''

"Race you to Hascombs,'' she say.

We start down the block and she gets ahead which is OK by me cause I'm going to the West End and then over to the Drive to think this day through. She can run if she want to and even run faster. But ain't nobody gonna bet me at nuthin.

SPECULATIONS

1. This story appears as if it is spoken by one person in a literary form known as a dramatic monologue. How would you characterize the speaker? How would you describe her value system, her neighborhood, her attitudes toward herself and her culture?

2. Why does Miss Moore take the kids to F.A.O. Schwarz on Fifth Avenue in New York City, the most expensive toy store in America if not the world? What is "the lesson?''

3. When you see "things'' that you want in stores, magazines, or on television that you cannot afford, what is your response? How do you work through your frustration at not being able to attain something you want very much?

4. This is a first person narrative written in black dialect or black English vernacular. What grammatical and stylistic differences do you see between the dialect in which this story is written and edited American English, the standard dialect of writing and publishing? Why do you think Bambara chose to tell this story using black dialect? What kind of effect does it create?

5. Once in F.A.O. Schwarz, the narrator and Sugar bump into each other while staring at the sailboat. The narrator says:

> We just stare at that price tag. Then Sugar ran a finger over the whole boat. And I'm jealous and want to hit her. Maybe not her, but I sure want to punch somebody in the mouth.

Why is the narrator angry? Who does she want to punch?

The 10 Biggest Myths About the Black Family

LERONE BENNETT, JR.

The heroism and cultural contributions of black Americans through-out American history—from the Colonial period to the present—are the main focus of Lerone Bennett, Jr.'s work. Author of several historical studies that combine vivid journalistic reporting with a commitment to telling stories accurately, Bennett has dedicated his writing to celebrating black accomplishments. That is part of the mission of *Ebony*, a national magazine based in Chicago that publishes articles largely of interest to black readers, where Bennett has served as senior editor since 1958.

Born in Clarksdale, Mississippi, in 1928, Lerone Bennett, Jr., earned a bachelor's degree from Morehouse College and has been awarded honorary degrees from numerous colleges and universities including Morgan State University, Marquette University, and the University of Illinois. Author of *Before the Mayflower: A History of the Negro in America, 1619–1966*, 5th edition; *Confrontation: Black and White*; *Black Power U.S.A.: The Human Side of Reconstruction, 1867–1877*; and *What Manner of Man*, he served as a reporter and city editor for the *Atlanta Daily World* and an associate editor for *Jet*, a magazine that also claims a large black readership. He has lived in Chicago since the early 1950s.

Bennett's essay "The 10 Biggest Myths About the Black Family" was first published in *Ebony* in 1986 and then republished in 1989. In it, Bennett challenges the mainstream view of black family life, attacking commonly held ideas as "myths" rather than based in fact and reality.

"In propaganda against the Negro since emancipation in this land," W. E. B. Du Bois said, "we face one of the most stupendous efforts the world ever saw to discredit human beings, an effort involving universities, history, science, social life and religion."

Nowhere is this more clearly visible than in the pervasive and continuing effort to discredit black fathers, mothers, and children. And it is scarcely possible to understand the problems and enduring strengths of the black family if we do not at the least make an effort to understand and dispel the misconceptions, myths and outright lies men and women have invented to hide themselves from black reality and American racism. There are, of course, scores of misconceptions about black sexuality and black kinship networks, but the vast propaganda campaign against the black family is generally organized around ten major myths.

1. Raw and uncontrolled sex, according to the biggest and most pervasive myth, is at the root of the black family problem.

This is the most enduring of all lies about blacks, and sociologists and historians froth at the mouth and strain at the leash of synonymity ("riotous debauchery," "unbridled passions," "wild and primitive emotions") in passionate attempts to express this academic and political voyeurism. For most, if not almost all, critics of the black family, there is always at the back of the mind this myth, this image of black America as Babylon, where the Studs and Sapphires are *always* making babies, where—in the words of the myth—"They do it, honey, right out in the middle of the streets." And one of the most challenging problems we face is confronting scholars, journalists and politicians, who have repeatedly used the black family to exorcise the demons of their own sexuality and the guilt of their complicity in oppression. What makes this so difficult is that we are dealing here with a magical idea that is impervious to "facts." There are, in fact, no facts in this area, for there has never been a systematic analysis of the sexual differences between American blacks and American whites. And the few facts we have (see Robert Staples, "Black Male Sexuality," EBONY, August 1983) contradict the supersex theory of black history and suggest that the differences between racial groups are relatively small, especially when you correct for economic and historical differences. More to the point, blacks, according to the statistics, are not even in the running in the areas of wife-swapping and other experiments of the Sexual Revolutions.

2. The root cause of the problem, according to the second most widely disseminated myth, is loose morals.

This myth has a thousand lives and has surfaced repeatedly in the last 300 years. It has even seduced some black writers, male and female, who have created a new and curiously popular literature based on the idea that black America is a vast emotional wasteland populated by hustlin' men and maimed women.

In this instance, as in the preceding one, we are dealing with explosive emotions that exist in areas of the psyche that cannot be reached by the light of evidence. Some blacks, for example, have children out of wedlock, but so do millions of whites, including stars who are celebrated by the same media which browbeat and humiliate poor blacks. The mythmakers know this, but they cannot be convinced by "facts," for their knowledge precedes the facts and makes the facts. And when they say that blacks are immoral, they mean that there is a black way and a white way of making babies and a black way and a white way of being immoral.

A case in point is the controversy over illegitimacy. For a common impression to the contrary notwithstanding, black America has always condemned unrestrained sexual expression and has insisted—with a singular lack of support from the American government and white institutions—on stable and responsible mating patterns between knowledgeable and economically qualified parents. But black America has refused to follow white America in the barbarous practice of condemning infants. It has said, to its credit, that there are no illegitimate children, only illegitimate parents and, it must be added, illegitimate societies which make it impossible for parents to find the work and wherewithal (the day-care centers and the network of supporting images and institutions) to become responsible parents.

Another important point is that there have been marked changes in the last 15 years in the marriage and childbearing patterns of *both* black and white young women in the United States. In a letter to the *New York Times*, Constance A. Nathanson, a professor of population dynamics in the Johns Hopkins University School of Hygiene and Public Health, said: "These changes, however, have been more profound among whites than among blacks; in 1983 there were, for the first time, more births to single white than to single black teenagers." She added: "The tradition of finding the causes of social ills in the victims of those ills, and particularly in their supposed inadequacies as spouses and parents, has a long history in America. The true causes, however, lie deeply imbedded in our social and economic structure."

Assuredly, and this is the point we want to make: the real moral problem is our failure to deal with those causes and not some mysterious self-perpetuating "pathology" in the black family or the black community.

3. Blacks lack a family tradition and came to America without a sense of morality and a background of stable sexual relationships.

Far from harming blacks, this myth maintains, whites did them a favor by transporting them from an oversexed land to a hospitable climate of cottonfields, chastity, and nuclear families. Cottonfields apart, there is not a word of truth in this. In fact, blacks came from an ancient culture where there were stable and non-European marriage patterns and where men and women were not cursed by the sexual demons that pursued the Puritans and the sexual demons that pursue the sons and daughters of the Puritans. Two other points are relevant. The first is that polygamy was sanctioned in some of these cultures, although in practice the poor, like the poor everywhere, contented themselves with monogamy. The second is that this non-Puritan, non-uptight ethos was the basis of the great synthesis Africans made of African and European forms. This synthesis began with a revealing family pact that seems to have bound together all slaves who came over on the same ship. For, according to scholar Orlando Patterson, "it was customary for children to call their parents' shipmates 'uncle' and 'aunt,' " and for men and women to *"look upon each other's children mutually as their own* [my emphasis]."

Thus contrary to the myth, the African-American adventure began not in chaos, but in love and in a *higher* morality. And it began in a way with the story of Antoney and Isabell, two of the first black immigrants to English America, who married in Virginia in 1623 or 1624. Isabell was soon brought to bed with what was probably the first black child born in English America. In 1624, the child, a boy named William, was baptized in Jamestown. And since his parents were for all practical purposes free, the black family in America was born not in slavery but in freedom.

From all this it is clear that the black American family is the product of a particular history and that *we must explain the family by the history and not the history by the family*.

4. The bonds of the black family were destroyed in slavery.

Certain scholars, Daniel Patrick Moynihan in particular, have argued that the problems of the black family are rooted in the slave experience and a 300-year "cycle of self-perpetuating pathology." But Moynihan and his followers misread the plantation records and the tracks of the black spirit, and pathfinding studies by Herbert G. Gutman (*The Black Family in Slavery and Freedom*) and other scholars, black and white, have destroyed that myth and established three major points:

1. Most slaves lived in families headed by a father and a mother and "large numbers of slave couples lived in long marriages," some for 30 years or more.

2. In slavery (and afterward), blacks were more open and honest about sex, but they did not condone indiscriminate mating and begetting. And although premarital sex was fairly common, the slave community expected a pregnancy to be followed by marriage.

3. In slavery (and afterwards), slave marriages were buttressed by extended family groupings that seemed to include most members of Slave Row. Slave children, according to numerous sources, were taught to respect and revere older persons whom they called "aunt" and "uncle." It was customary for adult slaves to call each other "brother" and "sister."

The implications of Gutman's massively documented study are extensive and require a total revision of the traditional picture of matriarchal families and unstructured sexual relationships. Gutman's data also demolish superficial "cycle of pathology" studies which say that the "problem" of the black family—the "problem," to be precise, is not the black family but the society that oppresses the black family—is almost insoluble. For, as Professor Gutman said, "a vast difference exists in dealing with a problem rooted in 'three centuries of exploitation' and one caused by massive structural unemployment."

5. The black family collapsed after Emancipation.

In dealing with this myth, we have to notice first that it offers a theory of history and a theory of race. For we are asked to believe that the "fragile" roots of black familyhood, nourished by nearness to ol' marsa and Scarlett O'Hara ("Lawdy, Miss Scarlett, I don't know nothin' 'bout birthin' no babies.") withered and almost died after the "mean" Northerners separated blacks from the guiding model of white families and the guiding light of white morality. This, of course, is preposterous, for white morality *was* the problem; and once that obstacle was removed blacks exploded in a post-Emancipation festival of family building. According to almost all witnesses, the roads of the South were clogged in 1865 with black men and women searching for long-lost wives, husbands, children, brothers, and sisters. The ingathering continued for several years and began in most communities with mass marriage ceremonies that legalized the slave vows. This was a voluntary process, for husbands and wives were free to renounce slave vows and search for new mates. Significantly, most freedmen, some of them 80 and 90 years old, decided to remain with their old mates, thereby giving irrefutable testimony on the meaning of their love. No one understood this better than Albion Tourgee, a North Carolina Reconstruction judge, who said: "Let the marriage bond be dissolved throughout the state of New York today, and it may be doubted if as large a proportion of the intelligent white citizens would choose again their old partners."

6. The black family collapsed after the Great Migration to the North.

According to this myth, urbanization and the defiling lights of Chicago and Harlem destroyed the last vestiges of black institutional life and doomed the black family. The evidence does not support this view. The hard fact is that the black family was an unusually strong institution for several decades after the Great Migration. According to Gutman and others, the overwhelming majority of black households (85 percent in New York City in 1925) were headed by fathers and mothers until the 1930s. It has also been established that black families were at least as stable as the households of Northern white ethnics.

7. The black family is a product of white paternalism and government welfare.

This theory turns black history upside out, like a glove, and gives missionaries and government agencies credit for the heroic efforts of black men and women. For it was internal giving, it was communal sharing the caring, that ensured the survival of black America. From the very beginning of the black American adventure, black people, slaves and quasi-free people, assumed responsibility for one another and for the young, the weak, the halt and the blind. After Emancipation, the first black schools and welfare institutions were founded not by white missionaries, as we have been told, but by black men and women. Many, perhaps most, of the large number of black orphans, were taken in by black families, and black churches and lodges raised thousands of dollars for indigents. The most significant fact about this period is that the Freedmen's Bureau assisted only 0.5 percent of the four million freed blacks. The black tradition of self-help spilled over into the 20th century with the work of black club women and black churches and fraternal organizations. If blacks are alive and reasonably well today, it is not because of missionaries and welfare agents—it is because of the extended black family and house rent parties and church suppers and black schools and black churches.

8. The black family has always been a matriarchy characterized by strong and domineering women and weak and absent men.

This is a half-truth which hides and distorts and lies. For it is true that black America has produced a long line of strong and beautiful black women, and there is no need for anyone to apologize for it. Because of repeated and continuing attempts to destroy the economic foundations of black manhood, these women played crucial and pioneering roles in the history of black people and *the history of women*. But all this must be seen in proper perspective. For black America has also produced a long life of extraordinary fathers, and black fathers and mothers working together and loving and living together ensured the survival of black people. Anyone who doubts this need only read the records (plantation records, Freedmen's Bureau records, census records) which tell us that the black family was a whole in spirit and in fact until the beginning of the fifty-year Depression (except for World War II and the Korean War) in the 1930s. For some reason, it is not fashionable to celebrate that wholeness in popular plays and movies. Among the notable exceptions are *Sounder* and *Nothing But a Man*. Nor can we overlook the great scene in *A Raisin In The Sun*, when the allegedly matriarchal Mama Lena Younger remembers the strong black man, now dead, who gave the family the Dream.

9. Black men cannot sustain stable relationships.

In simple and insulting terms, this myth asserts that black men are no-good philanderers who were not made for monogamy. Although the factual lies of the present may appear to give some validity to some aspects of this myth, it is a perversion of the truth. What is so egregiously lacking in these assertions is a sense of social structure and a sense of the dynamics of oppression. For in every oppressed group, certain men (and women) destroy themselves—with drugs, with knives, with guns, with impotent rage—in vain attempts to destroy the loathsome images the oppressors have installed within them. In other cases, in every oppressed group, certain men (and women) use alienating means, including sex, to affirm themselves and to make themselves real in their own eyes and in the eyes of others. These aberrations, inevitable in any situation of oppression, are expressions not of black sexuality but of *oppressed* black sexuality. And it should be borne in mind, in dealing with this myth, that although enforced unemployment and lives of harrowing insecurity have corrupted some men and reduced others to despair and macho futility, most black fathers are still in their homes, and the black center is still holding, despite poverty, despite drugs, *despite everything*. There is additional evidence which seems to indicate that middle-class black fathers are often-times more family-oriented than middle-class white fathers.

10. The history of the black family is a history of fussin' and fightin' by hard-hearted men and heartless women.

The images and tones of this myth are part of the national fantasy life. In movies, books and plays, in newspaper stories and TV documentaries. Blacks made in the image of this fantasy are always screeching at each other and playing the marital fool. Rarely if ever do they speak in civil and loving tones. Like archetypes, frozen in time, they seem to be destined to play prefabricated roles in portable and prefabricated Catfish Rows.

"For the vast majority of Negroes," author Charles Keil wrote, "the battle of the sexes is no mere figure of speech. In the ghetto, men and women are considered to be separate and antagonistic species. . . ."

Common sense, the black birthrate, and census figures contradict this idea, which would be funny if it did not carry so much weight in the myth of the black love deficit.

So persuasive is this myth, so intimidating are its constantly repeated themes, that even blacks who know better, even blacks who were raised in the center of an overpowering love, are apologetic and say that there must be something wrong with us.

There is nothing wrong with us. And we must avoid the hyperempiricist fallacy of constructing theories of black biology and black history on the basis of the economic dislocations of today. For when all is said and done the most significant social and sexual fact of our history is that we survived and that the overwhelming majority of black men and women lived and loved in two-parent households until the 1930s and 1940s. There can be no understanding of the character of black men and black women without some understanding of this crucial and still undefined moment in their adventure together. For if, as the statistics say, the overwhelming majority of black men and women were still living in double-headed households after 200 years of slavery and 80 years of segregation, if after all that time, after the hunger and the cotton and the lies and the blood, they were still together in their hearts and in their homes, then the true story of the black family is the precise opposite of the myth, and black men and women deserve credit for creating one of the great love stories of our era.

Far from being ciphers, then, we are and always have been dreamers, witnesses, and *lovers*. The most persuasive evidence on this score is that we endured and created out of the miracle of our survival jazz and the blues and the cakewalk and "Little Sally Walker" and "For Once In My Life" and "Fine and Mellow" and "Satin Doll" and "When Malindy Sings" and "When Sue Wears Red".

> *When Susanna Jones wears red*
> *A queen from some time-dead*
> *Egyptian night*
> *Walks once again.*
>
> *Blow trumpets, Jesus!*
>
> *And the beauty of Susanna Jones*
> *in red*
> *Burns in my heart a love-fire*
> *sharp like pain.*
>
> *Sweet silver trumpets,*
> *Jesus!*

These and other pieces of evidence, conventional and unconventional, tell us that we have been sold a false bill of goods in this country and that we are greater, more loving and more giving than white media say. And to understand the trumpets and the love-fire of our experience, to understand how we got over and what we must do now to overcome, we must forget everything we think we know about black women and black men and go back to the rich soil of our tradition and *dig* there for the spreading roots of a love that slavery and segregation couldn't kill.

It is on this deep level, and in the context of personal family responsibilities, that the crisis of the black family assumes its true meaning. For given the 300-year war against black manhood and black womanhood, and given the circumstances under which most black fathers and mothers are forced to live the mystery is not that some have failed—the mystery is that so many still stand and love.

Sweet silver trumpets,
    Jesus!

SPECULATIONS

1.   Why do you think Lerone Bennett, Jr., wrote this essay? How does this approach accomplish his goal?
2.   Do you think one's own racial identification as a reader makes a major difference to how one responds to this essay?
3.   Bennett chooses to consider the black family in terms of myths rather than truths or insights. Why do you think he chose to structure his essay around the notion of myths? Whose myths are they? What is a myth anyway—as opposed to a lie, a belief, an opinion? Why does he structure his essay around ten myths rather than five or seven or twelve?
4.   How would you characterize Bennett's tone in myth 3: "Blacks lack a family tradition and came to America without a sense of morality and a background of stable sexual relationships"? How is the tone sustained as he proceeds through his analysis? How did you respond to this tone as a reader?
5.   How important is family life to you? Describe some family experiences that have helped you. Do you think of your family as friends and neighbors rather than people related to you by birth? How does Bennett's essay relate to your own views about family and family relationships?

Rachel and Her Children

JONATHAN KOZOL

"I'm not a violent person," Jonathan Kozol remarked during an interview in 1985 with the *Chicago Tribune* about the growing problems of illiteracy and poverty in America, "but I do think we will be faced with some form of extraordinary upheaval in our society, possibly extremely violent, if we let this go another fifteen years. If we allow this to smolder, there will simply not be enough people earning money to support those who can't."

Born into an affluent family in Boston in 1936, Kozol grew up as the son of a physician in a neighborhood devoid of crime, drugs, and poverty. His only contact with poor and black America was in the car with his father when driving their live-in maid back to Roxbury, Boston's black ghetto. Only much later did he realize, as he writes in his introduction to *Illiterate America* (1985), "with a wave of shame and fear," that the maid's children "had been denied the childhood and happiness and care that had been given to me by their mother."

The main theme to Kozol's writing is his outrage at the injustices that exist within our society. In 1964–65, his social conscience awakened while he worked as a permanent substitute fourth-grade teacher in an elementary school in Roxbury. There, he heard white teachers describe their black pupils as "animals" and then saw black children whipped for failing to show those same teachers proper "respect." In defiance of the Boston School Committee, Kozol introduced his students to the black poet Langston Hughes. Fired for "curriculum deviation," he was told that he would never again work in the Boston public school system.

Kozol described this experience in *Death at an Early Age: The Destruction of the Hearts and Minds of Negro Children in the Boston Public Schools* (1967), which won the 1968 National Book Award. He donated the $1,000 prize to Roxbury's community leaders. Kozol went on to write *The Night is Dark and I am Far from Home* (1975), an indictment of middle-class American values; *Illiterate America* (1985), an account of the plight of millions of Americans who cannot read; and *Savage Inequalities* (1991), in which he argues that America denies education to the poor.

Rachel and her Children (1988) is a study of the homeless in America. Like Kozol's other work, the theme of injustice is eloquently invoked.

Houses can be built without a number of ingredients that other ages viewed as indispensable. Acrylics, plastics, and aluminum may substitute for every substance known to nature. Parental love cannot be synthesized. Even the most earnest and methodical foster care demonstrates the limits of synthetic tenderness and surrogate emotion. So it seems of keen importance to consider any ways, and *every* way, by which a family, splintered, jolted and imperiled though it be by loss of home and subsequent detention in a building like the Martinique, may nonetheless be given every possible incentive to remain together.

The inclination to judge harshly the behavior of a parent under formidable stress seems to be much stronger than the willingness to castigate the policies that undermine the competence and ingenuity of many of these people in the first place.

"Men can be unequal in their needs, in their honor, in their possessions," writes historian Michael Ignatieff, "but also in their rights to judge others." The king's ultimate inequality, he says, "is that he is never judged." An entire industry of scholarship and public policy exists to judge the failing or defective parent; if we listen to some of these parents carefully we may be no less concerned by their impaired abilities, but we may be less judgmental or, if we remain compelled to judge, we may redirect our energies in more appropriate directions.

New Year's Eve.

She stalks into the room. He eyes are reddened and her clothes in disarray. She wears a wrinkled and translucent nightgown. On her feet: red woolen stockings. At her throat: a crucifix. Over her shoulders is a dark and heavy robe. Nothing I have learned in the past week prepares me for this apparition.

She cries. She weeps. She paces left and right and back and forth. Pivoting and turning suddenly to face me. Glaring straight into my eyes. A sudden halt. She looks up toward the cracked and yellowish ceiling of the room. Her children stand around her in a circle. Two little girls. A frightened boy. They stare at her, as I do, as her arms reach out—for what? They snap like snakes and coil back. Her hair is gray—a stiff and brushlike Afro.

Angelina is twelve years old, Stephen is eleven, Erica is nine. The youngest child, eleven months, is sitting on the floor. A neighbor's child, six years old, sits in my lap and leans her head against my chest; she hold her arms around my neck. Her name or nickname (I do not know which) is Raisin. When she likes she puts her fingers on my mouth and interrupts the conversation with a tremolo of rapid words. There are two rooms. Rachel disappears into the second room, then returns and stands, uneasy, by the door.

ANGIE: "Ever since August we been livin' here. The room is either very hot or freezin' cold. When it be hot outside it's hot in here. When it be cold outside we have no heat. We used to live with my aunt but then it got too crowded there so we moved out. We went to welfare and they sent us to the shelter. Then they shipped us to Manhattan. I'm scared of the elevators. 'Fraid they be stuck. I take the stairs."

RAISIN: "Elevator might fall down and you would die."

RACHEL: "It's unfair for them to be here in this room. They be yellin'. Lots of times I'm goin' to walk out. Walk out on the street and give it up. No, I don't do it. BCW [Bureau of Child Welfare] come to take the children. So I make them stay inside. Once they walk outside that door they are in danger."

ANGIE: "I had a friend Yoki. They was tryin' to beat her. I said: 'Leave her.' They began to chase me. We was runnin' to the door. So we was runnin'. I get to the door. The door was stuck. I hit my eye and it began to bleed. So I came home and washed the blood. Me and my friends sat up all night and prayed. Prayin' for me. 'Dear Lord, can you please help me with my eye? If you do I promise to behave.' I was askin' God why did this happen. I wish someone in New York could help us. Put all of the money that we have together and we buy a building. Two or three rooms for every family. Everybody have a kitchen. Way it is, you frightened all the time. I think this world is coming to the end."

STEPHEN: "This city is rich."

ANGIE: "Surely is!"

ERICA: "City and welfare, they got something goin'. Pay $3,000 every month to stay in these here rooms . . ."

RACHEL: "I believe the City Hall got something goin' here. Gettin' a cut. They got to be. My children, they be treated like chess pieces. Send all of that money off to Africa? You hear that song? They're not thinking about people starvin' here in the United States. I was thinkin': Get my kids and all the other children here to sing, 'We are the world. We live here too.' How come do you care so much for people you can't see? Ain't we the world? Ain't we a piece of it? We are so close they be afraid to see. Give us a shot at something. We are something! Ain't we *something*? I'm depressed. But we are *something!* People in America don't want to see."

ANGIE: "Christmas is sad for everyone. We have our toys. That's not the reason why. They givin' you toys and that do help. I would rather that we have a place to be."

ERICA: "I wrote a letter to Santa Claus. Santa say that he don't have the change."

RAISIN: "I saw Santa on the street. Then I saw Santa on another street. I pulled his beard and he said something nasty."

ANGIE: "There's one thing I ask: a home to be in with my mother. That was my only wish for Christmas. But it could not be."

RAISIN: "I saw Mr. Water Bug under my mother's bed. Mr. Rat be livin' with us too."

ANGIE: "It's so cold right now you got to use the hot plate. Plug it in so you be warm. You need to have a hot plate. Are you goin' to live on cold bologna all your life?"

RAISIN: "Mr. Rat came in my baby sister's crib and bit her. Nobody felt sorry for my sister. Then I couldn't go to sleep. I started crying. All of a sudden I pray and went to sleep and then I woke up in the mornin', make my bed, and took a bath, and ate, and went to school. So I came back and did my homework. And all of a sudden there was something *irritatin'* at my hand. I looked out the window and the moon was goin' up. And then—I had a dream. I went to sleep and I was dreamin' and I dreamed about a witch that bit me. I felt *dead*. When I woke back up I had a headache."

ANGIE: "School is bad for me. I feel ashamed. They know we're not the same. My teacher do not treat us all the same. They know which children live in the hotel."

ERICA: "My teacher isn't like that. She treats all of us the same. We all get smacked. We all get punished the same way."

STEPHEN: "I'm in sixth grade. When I am a grown-up I be a computer."

ERICA: "You're in the fifth. You lie."

RAISIN: "When I grow up I want to be multiplication and subtraction and division."

ANGIE: "Last week a drug addict tried to stab me. With an ice pick. Tried to stab my mother too. Older girls was botherin' us. They try to make us fight. We don't fight. We don't start fires. They just pickin' on us. We ran home and got our mother. They ran home and got their mother."

RAISIN: "Those girls upstairs on the ninth floor, they be bad. They sellin' crack."

ERICA: "Upstairs, ninth floor, nine-o-five, they sellin' crack."

RAISIN: "A man was selling something on the street. He had some reefers on him and the po-lice caught him and they took him to the jail. You know where the junkies put the crack? Put the crack inside the pipe. Smoke it like that. They take a torch and burn the pipe and put it in their mouth. They go like this." [Puffs.]

I ask: "Why do they do it?"

ERICA: "Feel good! Hey! Make you feel fine!"

ANGIE: "This girl I know lives in a room where they sell drugs. One day she asks us do we want a puff. So we said: 'No. My mother doesn't let us do it.' One day I was walkin' in the hall. This man asked me do I want some stuff. He said: 'Do you want some?' I said no and I ran home."

RAISIN: "One day my brother found these two big plastic bags inside his teddy bear. Po-lice came up to my room and took that teddy bear." She's interrupted. "I ain't finished! And they took it. One day we was by my uncle's car and this man came and he said: 'Do you want some?' We said no. We told my uncle and he went and found the man and he ran to the bar and went into the women's bathroom in the bar. And so we left."

ANGIE: "I think this world is ending. Yes. Ending. Everybody in this city killin' on each other. Countries killin' on each other. Why can't people learn to stick together? It's no use to fightin'. Fightin' over nothin'. What they fightin' for? A flag! I don't know what we are fightin' for. President Reagan wants to put the rockets on the moon. What's he doin' messin' with the moon? If God wanted man and woman on the moon He would of put us there. They should send a camera to the moon and feed the people here on earth. Don't go messin' there with human beings. Use that money to build houses. Grow food! Buy seeds! Weave cloth! Give it to the people in America!"

ERICA: "When we hungry and don't have no food we borrow from each other. Her mother [Raisin's] give us food. Or else we go to Crisis. In the mornin' when we wake up we have a banana or a cookie. If the bus ain't late we have our breakfast in the school. What I say to President Reagan: Give someone a chance! I believe he be a selfish man. Can't imagine how long he been president."

RAISIN: "Be too long."

ANGIE: "Teacher tell us this be a democracy. I don't know. I doubt it. Rich people, couldn't they at least give us a refund?"

RAISIN: "This man say his son be gettin' on his nerves. He beat his little son 'bout two years old. A wooden bat. He beat him half to death. They took him to the hospital and at five-thirty he was dead. A little boy." [Interrupted.] "Let me talk!"

ERICA: "The little boy. He locked himself into the bathroom. He was scared. After he died police came and his father went to jail. His mother, she went to the store."

RAISIN, in a tiny voice: "People fight in here and I don't like it. Why do they do it? 'Cause they're sad. They fight over the world. I ain't finished!"

ERICA: "One time they was two cops in the hall. One cop pulled his gun and he was goin' shoot me. He said did I live there? I said no. So I came home."

RAISIN: "I was in this lady room. She be cryin' because her baby died. He had [mispronounced] pneumonia. He was unconscious and he died." Soft voice: "Tomorrow is my birthday."

The children are tended by a friend. In the other bedroom, Rachel, who is quieter now, paces about and finally sits down.

"Do you know why there's no carpet in the hall? If there was a carpet it would be on fire. Desperate people don't have no control. You have to sleep with one eye open. Tell the truth, I do not sleep at night.

"Before we lived here we were at the Forbell shelter [barracks shelter on Forbell Street in Brooklyn]. People sleep together in one room. You sleep across. You have to dress in front of everybody. Men and women. When you wake, some man lookin' at you puttin' on your clothes. Lookin' at your children too. Angelina, she be only twelve years old. . . .

"There's one thing. My children still are pure. They have a concept of life. Respect for life. But if you don't get 'em out of here they won't have anything for long. If you get 'em out right now. But if you don't . . . My girls are innocent still. They are unspoiled. Will they be that way for long? Try to keep 'em in the room. But you can't lock 'em up for long.

"When we moved here I was forced to sign a paper. Everybody has to do it. It's a promise that you will not cook inside your room. So we lived on cold bologna. Can you feed a child on that? God forgive me but nobody shouldn't have to live like this. I can't even go downstairs and get back on the elevator. Half the time it doesn't work. Since I came into this place my kids begun to get away from me."

There's a crucifix on the wall. I ask her: "Do you pray?"

"I don't pray! Pray for what? I been prayin' all my life and I'm still here. When I came to this hotel I still believed in God. I said: 'Maybe God can help us to survive.' I lost my faith. My hopes. And everything. Ain't nobody—no God, no Jesus—gonna help us in no way.

"God forgive me. I'm emotional. I'm black. I'm in a blackness. Blackness is around me. In the night I'm scared to sleep. In the mornin' I'm worn out. I don't eat no breakfast. I don't drink no coffee. If I eat, I eat one meal a day. My stomach won't allow me. I have ulcers. I stay in this room. I hide. This room is safe to me. I am afraid to go outside.

"If I go out, what do I do? People drink. Why do they drink? A person gets worn out. They usin' drugs. Why they use drugs? They say: 'Well, I won't think about it now.' Why not? You ain't got nothin' else to do, no place to go. 'Where I'm gonna be tomorrow or the next day?' They don't know. All they know is that they don't have nothin'. So they drink. And some of them would rather not wake up. Rather be dead. That's right.

"Most of us are black. Some Puerto Rican. Some be white. They suffer too. Can you get the government to know that we exist? I know that my children have potential. They're intelligent. They're smart. They need a chance. There's nothin' wrong with them for now. But not for long. My daughter watches junkies usin' needles. People smokin' crack in front a them. Screwin' in front a them. They see it all. They see it everywhere. What is a man and woman gonna do when they are all in the same room?

"I met a girl the other day. She's twelve years old. Lives on the fourteenth floor. She got a baby the same age as mine. Her mother got five children of her own. I don't want my daughter havin' any baby. She's a child. Innocent. Innocent. No violence. She isn't bitter. But she's scared. You understand? This is America. These children growin' up too fast. We have no hope. And you know why? Because we all feel just the same way deep down in our hearts. Nowhere to go . . . I'm not a killer. My kids ain't no killers. But if they don't learn to kill they know they're goin' to die.

"They didn't go to school last week. They didn't have clean clothes. Why? Because the welfare messed my check. It's supposed to come a week ago. It didn't come. I get my check today. I want my kids to go to school. They shouldn't miss a day. How they gonna go to school if they don't got some clothes? I couldn't wash. I didn't have the money to buy food.

"Twice the welfare closed my case. When they do it you are s'posed to go for a fair hearing. Take some papers, birth certificates. So I went out there in the snow. Welfare worker wasn't there. They told me to come back. Mister, it ain't easy to be beggin'. I went to the Crisis. And I asked her, I said, 'Give me somethin' for the kids to eat. Give me *somethin'*! Don't turn me away when I am sittin' here in front of you and askin' for your help!' She said she had nothin'. So my kids went out into the street. That's right! Whole night long they was in Herald Square panhandlin'. Made five dollars. So we bought bologna. My kids is good to me. We had bread and bologna.

"Welfare, they are not polite. They're personal. 'Did you do this? Did you do that? Where your husband at?' Understand me? 'Cause they sittin' on the other side of this here desk, they think we're stupid and we do not understand when we're insulted. 'Oh, you had another baby?' Yeah! I had another baby! What about it? Are you goin' to kill that baby? I don't say it, but that's what I feel like sayin'. You learn to be humble.

"I'm here five miserable months. So I wonder: Where I'm goin'? Can't the mayor give us a house? A part-time job? I am capable of doin' *somethin'*.

"You go in the store with food stamps. You need Pampers. You're not s'posed to use the stamps for Pampers. Stores will accept them. They don't care about the law. What they do is make you pay a little extra. They know you don't have no choice. So they let you buy the Pampers for two dollars extra.

"Plenty of children livin' here on nothin' but bread and bologna. Peanut butter. Jelly. Drinkin' water. You buy milk. I bought one gallon yesterday. Got *this* much left. They drink it fast. Orange juice, they drink it fast. End up drinkin' Kool Aid.

"Children that are poor are used like cattle. Cattle or horses. They are owned by welfare. They know they are bein' used—for what? Don't *use* them! Give 'em somethin'!

"In this bedroom I'm not sleepin' on a bed. They won't give me one. You can see I'm sleepin' on a box spring. I said to the manager: 'I need a bed instead of sleepin' on a spring.' Maid give me some blankets. Try to make it softer."

The Bible by her bed is opened to the Twenty-third Psalm.

"I do believe. God forgive me. I believe He's there. But when He sees us like this, I am wonderin' where is He? I am askin': Where the hell He gone?

"Before they shipped us here we lived for five years in a basement. Five years in a basement with no bathroom. One small room. You had to go upstairs two floors to use the toilet. No kitchen. It was fifteen people in five rooms. Sewer kept backing up into the place we slept. Every time it flooded I would have to pay one hundred dollars just to get the thing unstuck. There were all my children sleepin' in the sewage. So you try to get them out and try to get them somethin' better. But it didn't get no better. I came from one bad place into another. But the difference is this is a place where I cannot get out.

"If I can't get out of here I'll give them up. I have asked them: 'Do you want to go away?' I love my kids and, if I did that, they would feel betrayed. They love me. They don't want to go. If I did it, I would only do it to protect them. They'll live anywhere with me. They're innocent. Their minds are clean. They ain't corrupt. They have a heart. All my kids love people. They love life. If they got a dime, a piece of bread, they'll share it. Letting them panhandle made me cry. I had been to welfare, told the lady that my baby ain't got Pampers, ain't got nothin' left to eat. I got rude and noisy and it's not my style to do that but you learn that patience and politeness get you nowhere.

"When they went out on the street I cried. I said: 'I'm scared. What's gonna happen to them?' But if they're hungry they are goin' to do *something*. They are gonna find their food from somewhere. Where I came from I was fightin' for my children. In this place here I am fightin' for my children. I am tired of fightin'. I don't want to fight. I want my kids to live in peace.

"I was thinkin' about this. If there was a place where you could sell part of your body, where they buy an arm or somethin' for a thousand dollars, I would do it. I would do it for my children. I would give my life if I could get a thousand dollars. What would I lose? I lived my life. I want to see my children grow up to live theirs.

"A lot of women do not want to sell their bodies. This is something that good women do not want to do. I will sell mine. I *will*. I will solicit. I will prostitute if it will feed them."

I ask: "Would you do it?"

"Ain't no 'would I?' I would do it." Long pause . . . "Yes. I *did*.

"I had to do it when the check ain't come. Wasn't no one gonna buy my arm for any thousand dollars. But they's plenty gonna pay me twenty dollars for my body. What was my choice? Leave them out there on the street, a child like Angelina, to panhandle? I would take my life if someone found her dead somewhere. I would go crazy. After she did it that one time I was ashamed. I cried that night. All night I cried and cried. So I decided I had one thing left. In the mornin' I got up out of this bed. I told them I was goin' out. Out in the street. Stand by the curb. It was a cold day. Freezin'! And my chest is bad. I'm thirty-eight years old. Cop come by. He see me there. I'm standin' out there cryin'. Tells me I should go inside. Gives me three dollars. 'It's too cold to be outside.' Ain't many cops like that. Not many people either. . . .

"After he's gone a man come by. Get in his car. Go with him where he want. Takin' a chance he crazy and he kill me. Wishin' somehow that he would.

"So he stop his car. And I get in. I say a price. That's it. Go to a room. It's some hotel. He had a lot of money so he rented a deluxe. Asked me would I stay with him all night. I tell him no I can't 'cause I have kids. So, after he done . . . whatever he did . . . I told him that I had to leave. Took out a knife at me and held it at my face. He made me stay. When I woke up next day I was depressed. Feel so guilty what I did. I feel real scared. I can understand why prostitutes shoot drugs. They take the drugs so they don't be afraid.

"When he put that knife up to my throat, I'm thinkin' this: What is there left to lose? I'm not goin' to do any better in this life. If I be dead at least my kids won't ever have to say that I betrayed them. I don't like to think like that. But when things pile up on you, you do. 'I'm better if I'm dead.'

"So I got me twenty dollars and I go and buy the Pampers for the baby and three dollars of bologna and a loaf of bread and everyone is fed.

"That cross of Jesus on the wall I had for seven years. I don't know if I believe or not. Bible say that Jesus was God's son. He died for us to live here on this earth. See, I believe—Jesus was innocent. But, when He died, what was it for? He died for nothin'. Died in vain.

He should a let us die like we be doin'—we be dyin' all the time. We dyin' every day.

"God forgive me. I don't mean the things I say. God had one son and He gave His son. He gave him up. I couldn't do it. I got four. I could not give any one of them. I couldn't do it. God could do it. Is it wrong to say it? I don't know if Jesus died in vain."

She holds the Bible in her hands. Crying softly. Sitting on the box spring in her tangled robe.

"They laid him in a manger. Right? Listen to me. I didn't say that God forsaken us. I am confused about religion. I'm just sayin' evil overrules the good. So many bad things goin' on. Lot of bad things right here in this buildin'. It's not easy to believe. I don't read the Bible no more 'cause I don't find no more hope in it. I don't believe. But yet and still . . . I know these words." She reads aloud: "'Lie down in green pastures . . . leadeth me beside still waters . . . restores my soul . . . I shall not want.'

"All that I want is somethin' that's my own. I got four kids. I need four plates, four glasses, and four spoons. Is that a lot? I know I'm poor. Don't have no bank account, no money, or no job. Don't have no nothin'. No foundation. Then and yet my children have a shot in life. They're innocent. They're pure. They have a chance." She reads: "'I shall not fear . . .' I fear! A long, long time ago I didn't fear. Didn't fear for nothin'. I said God's protectin' me and would protect my children. Did He do it?

"Yeah. I'm walkin'. I am walkin' in the wilderness. That's what it is. I'm walkin'. Did I tell you that I am an ex-drug addict? Yeah. My children know it. They know and they understand. I'm walkin'. Yeah!"

The room is like a chilled cathedral in which people who do not believe in God ask God's forgiveness. "How I picture God is like an old man who speaks different languages. His beard is white and He has angels and the instruments they play are white and everything around is white and there is no more sickness, no more hunger for nobody. No panhandlin'. No prostitutes. No drugs. I had a dream like that.

"There's no beauty in my life except two things. My children and"—she hesitates—"I write these poems. How come, when I write it down, it don't come out my pencil like I feel? I don't know. I got no dictionary. Every time I read it over I am finding these mistakes.

> Deep down in my heart
> I do not mean these things I said.
> Forgive me. Try to understand me.
> I love all of you the same.
> Help me to be a better mother.

"When I cry I let 'em know. I tell 'em I was a drug addict. They know and they try to help me to hold on. They helpin' me. My children is what's holdin' me together. I'm not makin' it. I'm reachin'. And they see me reachin' out. Angelina take my hand. They come around. They ask me what is wrong. I do let them know when I am scared. But certain things I keep inside. I try to solve it. If it's my department, I don't want them to be sad. If it be too bad, if I be scared of gettin' back on drugs, I'll go to the clinic. They have sessions every other night.

"Hardest time for me is night. Nightmares. Somethin's grabbin' at me. Like a hand. Some spirit's after me. It's somethin' that I don't forget. I wake up in a sweat. I'm wonderin' why I dream these dreams. So I get up, turn on the light. I don't go back to sleep until the day is breakin'. I look up an' I be sayin': 'Sun is up. Now I can go to sleep.'

"After the kids are up and they are dressed and go to school, then I lay down. I go to sleep. But I can't sleep at night. After the sun go down makes me depressed. I want to turn the light on, move around.

"Know that song—'Those Monday Blues'? I had that album once."

I say the title: "'Monday Blues'?"

"I got 'em every day. Lots of times, when I'm in pain, I think I'm goin' to die. That's why I take a drink sometimes. I'm 'fraid to die. I'm wonderin': Am I dying?"

SPECULATIONS

1.   "Rachel and Her Children" is the title both of one chapter and of the entire book. Obviously, the title carries great significance for Jonathan Kozol. What is the significance of the title, and how does it relate to the subject of children, families, and homelessness in America?

2.   Kozol says that "the inclination to judge harshly the behavior of a parent under formidable stress seems to be much stronger than the willingness to castigate the policies that undermine the competence and ingenuity of many of these people in the first place." What does he mean by this analysis? What is your opinion? What policies is he referring to?

3.   Kozol presents Rachel and her children through the use of dialogue and monologue, as if they were characters in a play. Why do you think Kozol chooses this way of presenting them? What other ways could he have told their story?

4.   Homeless people are part of many cities and towns. What is your reaction to them? How do you identify with them? Would you react differently if you knew that it was children who were homeless rather than adults?

5.   Rachel confesses that she engages in prostitution in order to support her

children. She also states that she has a problem with alcohol and that she is an ex-drug addict. Why do you think Kozol includes those statements in this section when he could have ended it a few paragraphs earlier? Who are the victims in this story?

The Lives of Teenage Mothers: Schoolbooks, Boyfriends, and Babies

ELIZABETH MAREK

At the end of her junior year in 1982 at Harvard College, Elizabeth Marek had reached a crisis point. She had broken up with her boyfriend of six years and lost her sense of academic mission. As she puts it in *The Children of Santa Clara*:

> . . . I had lost my self, submerged it in a sea of demands and expectations. I had made myself up according to too many scripts. I was the understanding girlfriend for my lover; the cheerful friend for Rachael and Eve; the sane, successful daughter for my parents. If I stopped playing any of those roles—there, at Harvard, at home—I risked losing the love I knew in my heart was based on their convincing enactment. But if I could get away, go somewhere that no one knew me, I would be free to invent for myself, to make myself over, at last, in my own image.

Her solution was to drop out of college for a year. She found a job working at a home for emotionally disturbed adolescents in the mountains of the Southwest, in Santa Clara, California.

From that experience and after graduating from Harvard, Marek wrote *The Children of Santa Clara*, a book about young people teetering on the edge of failure and hopelessness, anguish and rejection. Published in 1987, writer Cynthia Ozick described it as an "illuminating narrative about love and salvation among the wounded young—and [Marek] discovers that she too is one of those whom she has learned to heal."

Marek currently works at a school for emotionally disturbed children in New York City.

The essay, "The Lives of Teenage Mothers: Schoolbooks, Boyfriends, and Babies," depicts Marek's concern for at-risk adolescents and the factors that lead young girls into early motherhood.

At 2:30 on a Thursday afternoon in June, when most teenagers, done with school for the day, are hanging out with their friends, the girls I have come to meet are seated in a small office, reaching for cookies with one hand as they settle their babies on their laps with the other. We are at the Kingsbridge Heights Community Center in the Bronx. The center sits at the crossroads of several worlds. The spacious homes of Riverdale dot the rolling green hills to the west; to the south rise the housing projects that cast their shadow on the lower-middle-class single-family homes and the shops which line the blocks closest to the center. The Teen Parenting Program, which provides counseling, education, and health care to teenage parents and soon-to-be parents throughout the Bronx, was started in 1986 with a group of girls from the projects. Once a week the girls in the program, along with their babies and sometimes their boyfriends, crowd into a simply furnished room to drink Coke, munch on snacks, and talk about the difficulties of being a teenage parent.

On this particular Thursday, I have come too. For years I've read about the "problem of teenage parenthood"—children having children. In New York City, teen pregnancies make up 15 percent of all pregnancies and account for more than 13,000 births each year. Sociologists and psychologists speculate about social pressures and individual motivation. President George Bush, in his inaugural address, spoke of the need to help young women "who are about to become mothers of children they can't care for and might not love."

But despite the concern voiced by others, we've heard very little from the young women themselves. Are they ignorant about birth control, or are they choosing to get pregnant? What are the conditions of loneliness, poverty, and hopelessness in which having a baby might make sense? What happens to these girls and their babies? How does having a baby affect their lives? Where do the fathers fit in?

I've come to Kingsbridge because I want to get to know the mothers, most of whom are not much younger than I am. Sophie-Louise, the social worker in charge of the group, introduces me, and the room falls silent. "Well," she laughs, "here we are. Ask away." Looking at the girls, as they tug at a baby's diaper to straighten a barrette, I am not sure where to begin.

"Tell me what it's like, having a baby at your age," I ask at last. As if on cue, all heads turn toward Janelle,[1] a heavyset black girl with short, blown-straight hair, who sits in an overstuffed chair with her three-month-old son, Marc, draped across her lap. The baby, dressed in a pale green sleeper embroidered with a blue bunny, is drooling onto her stylish black skirt. She is eating a chocolate cookie and begins to talk about the logistical problems involved in getting to and from high school with an infant. She has just started summer school to make up credits from the classes she missed during her pregnancy. She is seventeen.

"Let's see," she begins. "I get myself up and get the baby up and get myself dressed and get the baby dressed, get my books, get the baby's bag, get the stroller. . . ." She laughs. "Do you know how

---

[1] The names of the young women and their boyfriends and some identifying details have been changed.

hard it is to get a stroller on the bus? That first day of school, I thought I wasn't going to make it."

Newspaper accounts of teen pregnancy tend to dwell on girls from welfare families. Janelle, however, is the daughter of a retired postal-service clerk and grew up in a small, one-family house in a lower-middle-class neighborhood in the North Bronx. Her childhood was relatively secure: Her parents were together and could afford to send her to a Catholic school, where she made friends, got good grades, and dreamed about what she would be when she grew up. "I was gonna finish high school," she says. "Gonna go on to college, like my cousins did. I wanted to get married and have a baby some-day, but, really, not now. All through high school I never cut classes, hardly was sick even. . . ."

The turning point came when Janelle was fifteen and her parents divorced. "When my parents split, my family just fell apart. My mother only wanted my little sister, so she took her, and then my older sister, she left, too, so it was just me and my father all alone in the house." Feeling unwanted and unloved, Janelle moved into a room in the basement, and her father took over the upstairs. Some-times they met at breakfast, but other times Janelle went for days without seeing him. "So I started hanging out with a bad bunch of kids," she says, "and cutting classes—I went through an entire year and only got three credits. And then I got pregnant and dropped out." She laughs bitterly. "One thing they don't teach you in high school is how to get a stroller on the bus."

Lynda, at twenty the mother of a three-year-old girl, nods sympa-thetically. She is a pretty, young Hispanic woman with long hair pulled away from her face in a ponytail. Three weeks earlier she had graduated from high school, having gone to classes in the evening and worked during the day as a cashier in a small store in Manhattan. Her daughter, Danielle, a small child with blonde hair and a dirty face, walks unsmiling around the edge of the room. There is little interaction between mother and daughter. They neither look at nor speak to each other.

Lynda's father, like Janelle's, could be classified as lower middle class. Unlike Janelle's, Lynda's parents are strict Roman Catholics. On the day Lynda told her father that she was pregnant, he left home. "I guess it was either that or throw me out," she says. A few months later he moved back, but even now, although he allows her to live at home, she feels that he has not forgiven her. Lynda believes that her father, having worked hard to provide the best for her and her sib-lings, took her pregnancy as a slap in the face.

Leaning back in the circle of her boyfriend's arms, Lynda's large black eyes are ringed with dark circles. "My mother still talked to me, like, at the table, pass the salt and stuff. I think my father blamed her—'If you had brought her up right, this wouldn't have happened.' "

Janelle nods. "My father blamed my mother, too. I don't understand that, though, because he didn't even know that I was pregnant. Now he thinks it's my fault that he didn't know, and I think it's his fault. He was always telling me to stay downstairs, and we never talked. We never did anything. Now all he does is compare me to his sister's children, who are much older. They got jobs, finished college, and he says you make me look so bad, having babies, dropping out of school. But he didn't want to come back to my mother, he didn't want to try to help me. It was all just, 'Don't make me look bad. Don't make me look bad.' "

"So what did he do when he found out you were pregnant?" asks Lynda.

"He never found out! Not until I came home from the hospital. He found out when the baby was a week old."

Lynda's boyfriend, Tony, a construction worker in his early thirties, joins the discussion. "Maybe it's more that he didn't want to know. He wanted to keep it from himself." Tony is not Danielle's father, although he too was a teenage parent and has two boys of his own. He and Lynda have been going out for almost a year. "You know the parents, they blame themselves," he says. "Like maybe they did something wrong with your upbringing."

Janelle lets out her breath in a snort. "Yeah, well now he tells all his friends, 'She's so sneaky.' But I think that if he was really interested, he would have known. I mean, the last day, the day that I gave birth, he went out to the store and said, 'I'll be right back.' And I said, 'Fine, but I won't be here.' But he didn't hear me."

Later, riding home on the subway, I wonder whether, in part, Janelle got pregnant to get her father's attention. Or, perhaps, as one social worker I spoke with earlier suggested, part of the motivation for teenage girls to have babies is a wish to be reborn themselves, to re-create themselves as children, so they can get the love and attention they feel they were denied.

Nine girls, their babies, and a few of their boyfriends are officially enrolled in Sophie-Louise's group, but since the school year ended, only Janelle and Lynda have been coming regularly. The others, Sophie-Louise explains, have drifted away—to the beach, to parties—or are staying home, too overwhelmed by their lives as mothers to make the trip to the center. Janelle and Lynda represent what Sophie-Louise calls the "cream of the crop": the only ones able to structure their lives sufficiently to attend a regular weekly meeting. The others fade in and out.

At the next meeting, I notice that Lynda's boyfriend is missing. Sophie-Louise explains to me privately that Tony and Lynda have been having problems lately. Two new people are present, however: Janelle's boyfriend, Eron, and a new girl, April, a sad-looking black teenager, who brings her five-month-old daughter. April is thin, her ribs just out below the orange halter top she wears. In contrast to the Calvin Klein jeans Lynda wears, April's jeans are frayed and stained. She sits with her shoulders hunched, as though shielding herself from the vagaries of life. Glancing up, she notices my tape recorder on the table, and she stares at me for a moment before busying herself with the baby on her lap. The baby's dark eyes flicker across her mother's face, but neither of them registers a smile. Sophie-Louise has told me a few facts about April's life: She is the oldest child and lives with her mother, her two siblings, and her baby in a two-room apartment in a housing project in the East Bronx. Seemingly the least equipped to care for an infant, April appears to have been the most determined to have a baby: Kisha was the result of her third pregnancy, the other two having ended in abortions.

As the meeting starts, Janelle reaches across the table with one hand to grab some potato chips, while her other hand effortlessly settles baby Marc in a sitting position on her leg. April, sitting alone at the far end of the couch, shakes off Sophie-Louise's offer of a Coke and, grabbing a handful of Cheez Doodles, drapes a towel over her shoulder so that Kisha can nurse quietly at her breast. April seems to hover on the periphery of the discussion, offering tangential comments or staring fixedly at a spot on the wall. Sophie-Louise finds some rubber cows for Danielle to play with, but the little girl is more interested in building towers of checkers in the corner and knocking them down with excited squeals. Over the din, I ask the girls whether they had planned their pregnancies, and how they felt when they discovered they were pregnant.

As usual, Janelle begins. "At first, you know, I was real scared. I didn't want to have the baby," she says, smoothing her hand over Marc's diaper. "I was dead set against it. 'Cause you know, I'm just seventeen, and I didn't want to have a baby. I wanted to still go out and have fun with my friends and stuff. But now, you know, it's been three months, and I'm used to it." She pauses. "Of course, I haven't had too much time to myself. Just twice, in three months. I counted it. Twice. The father's family took care of him for a whole day. I couldn't believe it. I was outside and everything was so much fun. But I like being a mom now. I can handle it. All my friends keep telling me, 'Janelle, you're in a closet!' But I'm not in no closet. And if I am, well, they should leave me alone. It's fun in this closet now that I know what I'm doing and everything."

Lynda's mother takes care of Danielle during the day, when she is at work, and again in the evenings, when she attends classes. But Lynda also complains about a lack of freedom. "My mom says, 'Now you are a mother, you have responsibilities.' She will babysit when I go to work or to school, but otherwise, anywhere I go, Danielle goes."

"Did either of you ever think about having an abortion?" I ask.

"Abortion," muses Janelle. "Well, by the time I knew I was pregnant, I was already six months pregnant."

I wonder whether she has misspoken. Surely she can't mean that she had a baby growing inside her for six months before she was aware of its presence. But, shaking her head, she assures me that it was six months.

"Before that, I had no idea," she says.

Lynda backs her up. "By the time I knew I was pregnant, I was five months."

"Maybe," Sophie-Louise says, "it goes back to what we talked about before. Not knowing because you really didn't want to know."

Lynda is adamant. "No. There was no way I could know. I still had my regular monthly period until I was five months, and that's when I found out. And by then I didn't have much choice because they told me they only did abortions until twelve weeks, and I was way past that. And besides, I don't believe in doing abortions at five months. They say that at three months the baby is still not really formed into a baby, but after that the baby starts forming, and then I feel that it's killing. . . ."

April reaches down to straighten Kisha's dress. She speaks for the first time, her voice so soft and low that the rest of us have to strain to hear her. "I didn't know I was pregnant until I was three months. I jumped in a pool and felt something move inside me, and that's when I knew." She pulls her daughter to a sitting position on her lap, pushing a Cheez Doodle into the baby's flaccid mouth.

Janelle pauses and then says quietly, "I don't think I knew, but then I wonder. Maybe somewhere in me I knew, but it was like I was saying, no, I'm not pregnant, I'm not pregnant . . . I was living day-to-day, one day at a time. I would just get up in the morning and do what I needed to do, and not think about it."

As the girls speak, their words reflect their sense of powerlessness. Even their bodies rebel, growing alien creatures without their knowledge, the awareness of their pregnancy dawning only after the possibility for abortion has passed. Does this reflect a yearning for a child? Or is it only a child's way of coping with something too terrifying to acknowledge?

Lynda glances at Danielle, who is still amusing herself with the checkers. She brings the group back to the abortion question. "I think that the girl should just make up her own mind, and then that's it," she says. "Because even if you don't let your boyfriend go, you are still going to get left."

"What do you mean?" Sophie-Louise asks. Like many working mothers, Lynda has an air of perpetual exhaustion. "Sometimes, if you're in love with a guy, and 'I love you' comes up, that's the one thing that always makes you weak. You say, 'Oh, I love you too.' But then it's time for you both to sit down and talk about the situation, you know, after you say, 'Well, I'm pregnant,' and he says, 'Oh, you are?' and he gets happy and everything. This happened to me. And I said, 'I want an abortion.' Then the brainwash would begin, the 'I love you and it's our baby and I'll give you support.' It was like, if I had an abortion, then I didn't love him. I feel that the woman should just make up her own mind, make her own decision. But he said, 'Oh, I love you, and I'll do this for you, I'll do that for you, and our baby will have this, and our baby will have that.' Now she's two and a half years old, and all he ever got her was a big box of Pampers and socks and T-shirts and $20 and that was it." Suddenly, the resentment in her voice changes to wistfulness. "She's two and a half. And he was going to buy her a baby crib and a bassinet and clothes. Everything. . . ."

I have heard stories like this from other girls I talked with and from social workers as well. One fifteen-year-old mother told me that her boyfriend said that if she really loved him, she would have his baby. Despite her mother's urging, she decided against having an abortion. But by the time the baby was born, she and her boyfriend had broken up, and he was expecting another child by another girl in her school. As Sophie-Louise puts it, the guys like to have three or four "pots on different stoves" at the same time—visible proof of their virility.

Sophie-Louise turns to Eron, Janelle's boyfriend. He is seventeen and works two jobs, one in a garage and the other as an attendant at Rye Playland. She asks him how he felt when he found out that Janelle was pregnant. He laughs, "I was scared."

"More scared than me!" Janelle adds. "I mean, you were chicken!" "Well my life was changing, too," says Eron. "I mean, I know guys who just say, oh no, a baby, and then walk off, but I'm not that type of person. My father was never there for me when I was little, so, you know, I don't want that to happen to my son. I don't want him to grow up and hate me and all that. I want to have somebody to love me. Even if me and Janelle don't end up together, I got him to remind me of her."

It interests me that Eron wants the baby as someone to love him. When I ask the girls what they think of this, April rejoins the discussion. Without raising her eyes from her baby, she says, "When my boyfriend found out I was pregnant, he just played it off. He would always play at my stomach, sort of punch me in the stomach.

"Now I don't even let him see her anymore. All he wants to do is play with her, and then give her back when it's time for changing."

"That's tough," Sophie-Louise says. "It takes two to make a baby, but then one of the two doesn't want any of the responsibility. Do you think you can talk to him about it?"

"I don't want to," April says. "I don't even want him to see her. Ever since I was pregnant, he kept saying that he was going to get me some stuff. He lied to his mother, saying that he was going to get me a carriage for the baby, but he didn't get me nothing. I had to do it all. And then I found out that he had some kind of drug addict, some girl in his house, some Puerto Rican girl, and his mother went on vacation and she came back and seen all these suitcases in her room, and she seen this Puerto Rican girl in the house with him. They just did it, right there."

As she clutches Kisha to her breast, I see how absorbed they are in each other. With no job, no boyfriend, nothing to fill her days, the baby is her life. Yet both mother and daughter seem drained.

Janelle looks concerned. "But aren't you worried that she might grow up without having a relationship with her father?"

"Well, I don't even want to see her father anymore," April says. "Her father is crazy! He busted my window one time. I tell you about that? He wanted to see the baby so bad and he was drunk one night, four-thirty in the morning, and he came banging on my door, saying, 'I'm not going nowhere until I see my baby.' So then I brought the baby into my mother's room, because he had cracked the window with a rock and he was making a lot of noise. And then he just left. . . . Besides, I don't want him taking her to his house, 'cause his mother is a crack-head."

April falls silent. Sophie-Louise asks her whether her role in her own family has changed since she got pregnant.

"Oh yeah," April says. "Now, my mother thinks that I have to do everything. You know, when I was pregnant, she tried to make me do more than I was supposed to, more than I did before I was pregnant. Now she says, 'You're no more teenager. You're an adult.' But before that, before I had the baby, I wasn't classified as no adult. So what makes us having a baby be an adult?"

During the next session, the last before the August recess, there is a small "graduation" party for Eron. He feels confident about passing his summer-school course, and when he does, he will officially become a high-school graduate. After the cake is cut and the group settles down, the talk turns to peer pressure. Sophie-Louise has been telling the story of a fourteen-year-old girl she counseled at a local high school. Although the girl had been taught about birth control and abortion and warned about the difficulties facing teen mothers, she became pregnant midway through eighth grade. Speaking with the girl later, Sophie-Louise asked her why, after all they had talked about, had she let this happen. "I don't know," she said. "All my friends have babies. I was beginning to wonder what was wrong with me that I didn't have one too."

The girls in the group laugh at the story. "I don't know about her," Janelle says, "but I knew that seventeen was too young to have a baby. None of my friends have babies. My sister, she just had a baby . . . but it wasn't like I wanted to get pregnant."

"Were you using birth control?" I ask.

Janelle's cheeks flush.

"I gotta tell you," she says. "I never used birth control. I mean, now I do, but before, well, I just never thought I would get pregnant. I was like, that can't happen to me. I thought that only happened to the bad girls across town. Who do drugs and stuff. But I didn't do none of that, so I thought I was safe. You know, like when you think it just can't happen to you. To other people *yes*, but not to you."

"I can believe that," Lynda says. "Like, I used to think that if the guy didn't come in you, then you couldn't get pregnant."

"Well," says Janelle, "my friend told me once that if you took a bath afterward, then you were safe."

"Or if you do it standing up!"

I could add to the list. A social worker I spoke with said that most of the girls use the chance method. And each month that they don't get pregnant reinforces their belief that they are safe.

The existence of these myths may reflect denial rather than ignorance. As the girls talk, I begin to see why the idea of having a baby might be compelling. There is a sense of loneliness eased, of purpose granted, of a glimmering of hope.

Janelle smiles. "But now that I am a mother, I do enjoy it. I mean, he keeps me company all the time, so I never have to be bored or lonely. He's my friend, this little guy. He keeps me so busy that I never have time to get into trouble. And before, I never really had a reason to get up in the morning, to go to school, whatever. But now, because of him, I do."

In Janelle's words, I hear the unspoken wish that, through the baby, the mothers may get a second chance at childhood, that in loving their babies they may almost be loving themselves.

Sophie-Louise asks whether, perhaps, Janelle had some of those thoughts before getting pregnant, whether on some level part of the reason that she did not use birth control was because somewhere inside her she wished for a baby.

Janelle pauses to consider the question. "Well, I don't know. Maybe. You know, I was lonely. My parents had split, and I really didn't have anyone, just me and my father together in the house."

Sophie-Louise turns to April. Despite the fact that Kisha was the result of her third pregnancy, April is unwilling to admit that she had wanted the baby. "It was an accident," she insists. "I mean, I said that this isn't going to happen to me. I was using all kinds of protection. Most times I even had him use protection."

Sophie-Louise seems surprised. "You were using protection?" she asks. "What kind?"

Indignantly, April answers, "Well, I was taking the pill. I mean, I wasn't taking it all the time, but I was taking it. But I missed a couple of days, I guess. I think I took it on the day before my birthday, but not on my birthday, I don't think. . . ."

"So for you it really was an accident," I say. I am surprised when she contradicts me.

"No. I wouldn't really say it was an accident. See, all the other times I got pregnant, my mother made me get rid of it. So I guess part of it was revenge against my mother, like I was gonna get pregnant but not let her know until she couldn't do nothing."

"Not with me," says Lynda. "With me it was just a pure accident. Just a pure accident. I wanted to get an abortion. I said that I was going to have one. But my boyfriend and my parents, my father especially . . . they wanted me to have it. That's when the brainwash began."

It occurs to me that I've been looking for a motivation, a reason why these girls, and others like them, might *choose* to become pregnant. But the more I listen, the more I wonder whether the question of choice is relevant. In all their stories, I hear again and again how little volition these girls feel they have, how little control over the events of their lives. The deadline for school admission passes and April shrugs. Sophie-Louise makes an appointment for Lynda with a job counselor, but Lynda forgets to go. Janelle knows about birth control but doesn't believe "it" will happen to her. Sophie-Louise told me once that these girls exert no more control over their lives than a "leaf falling from a tree." Perhaps having a baby is less a question of ignorance or choice than one of inevitability. Once a girl is sexually active, it is not *having* a baby that requires choice and conscious action, but *not* having one.

Eron shifts in his chair. "You know, all this talk about we didn't want to have the baby, or it was an accident, or whatever . . . I just think it's a waste of time. I mean, now we have the baby. The question is, what are we going to do now?''

Sophie-Louise asks him what he means, and he explains that the cycle of babies having babies, single parents raising single parents, has haunted him as it has haunted most of the teens in the room, and that he feels it can end with them, but only if they are willing to face the realities of their situation. ''My father was never there when I was little,'' he says, ''but I don't want that to happen to my son. I don't want him to grow up and hate me and all that . . . That's why I'm going to finish school and do whatever I need to do.''

His eyes shine as he speaks of his ambition, but he looks down shyly, as if afraid that someone will mock him. Janelle, however, backs him up with pride and speaks of her own ambition to become a social worker. ''It's so easy to go on welfare,'' she says. ''You just sit home and cash a check. But I'm not going to get on welfare, 'cause it makes you lazy. It's addictive.''

''I couldn't do that,'' Eron says. ''I'm the kind of person who needs to work.'' But then the realities of fatherhood seem to descend upon him. ''I don't know, though. See, 'cause with a baby, it takes all the money that you don't even have. . . .''

At the end of the session, the discussion shifts back to the problems that the girls will encounter when they return to school in the fall. Janelle is telling April that summer school really wasn't so bad. ''It was hard leaving him at first,'' she says, ''but I tried not to think about it. And I didn't think about it, because the classes were hard. And I was usually really tired. But I was happy. I just thought about the work, and the time flew by, and I was picking up the baby before I knew it.''

Sophie-Louise presses April to consider how she will feel when she is separated from her daughter for the first time. ''Have you thought at all about what it's going to be like?'' Sophie-Louise asks. ''How it's going to feel, emotionally, to be separated?''

April ignores her at first, and then shakes her head no. Sophie-Louise encourages her, suggesting she might feel relief or worry or sadness, but April clearly does not want to pursue the issue. Finally, in frustration, April says, ''Look, I haven't thought about it yet. I haven't thought about it because it hasn't happened.''

With that, the session ends. Having missed the deadline for entrance to summer school, April stays behind to talk to Sophie-Louise about starting a diploma-geared class in the fall. Danielle tugs at Lynda's arm, asking whether they can finally go to the zoo as she promised. I hear Eron and Janelle bickering about whose turn it is to buy diapers. And I head down the steep hill to the subway that will take me back downtown.

SPECULATIONS

1.   In this essay, Elizabeth Marek undergoes a significant change in her views about teenage pregnancy. How would you describe that change? What questions and concerns does she start out with? What insights and conclusions does she end with?

2.   Marek offers us multiple perspectives on teenage pregnancy: the voices of young women, of at least one young man, of Sophie-Louise (the social worker), of Marek herself. What would the effect have been if Marek had written an analysis focusing on her own perceptions and conclusions, leaving out the other voices? Explain your response.

3.   Why do you think Marek draws attention to Eron's statement that he wants "to have somebody to love me"?

4.   Based on your own experience during adolescence, what do you think teenagers want and need? Do these insights help explain why there is such a significant increase in teenage pregnancies?

5.   The last paragraph is a descriptive account of what happens at the end of the session with Sophie-Louise, but it implies Marek's perspective concerning the likely fates of Janelle, April, Lynda, and their respective boyfriends and children. What do you think Marek is suggesting here? What evidence can you find in the text to support your conclusions?

When You're a Crip (or a Blood)
LÉON BING

The author of *Do or Die*, a gripping study of the teenage culture of gangs and violence in America, Léon Bing is a writer compelled by the teenage subculture, the "disenfranchised kids of America."

A Californian by birth, Bing's interest in American youth originates from her view that "the way we treat our kids in this country is clearly the way we treat our future, and that treatment seems to me to be the trashing of the American dream. I wrote *Do or Die* to focus attention on the African-American gangs because it doesn't get much more disenfranchised than to grow up black in America."

Bing's writing drew notice in 1985 with an article entitled "Slow Death in Venice" in the *L.A. Weekly*. Her career launched, Bing continued to research and write essays about teenage gangs. Her next essay, entitled "Caged Kids," (*L.A. Weekly*, 1985) was nominated for the H.L. Mencken award; it offered a warning to teenagers that they had "better behave or Mom and Dad will put you in the nuthouse." She followed up with pieces on the Crips and the Bloods, street gangs in Los Angeles. *Harper's* asked to reprint her work and requested the Forum piece, "When You're a Crip (or a Blood)," which appeared in 1989. This in turn led to a book contract for *Do or Die*, which won the American Library Award in 1992.

Bing loves to work with children and teenagers because "Kids tell you the truth. What they say is not filtered through the layers of calluses that build up with adults; kids are much less self-serving—and even when they are, you are going to get an extraordinary answer." A good bit of that unfiltered honesty is present in "When You're a Crip (or a Blood)."

The drive-by killing is the sometime sport and occasional initiation rite of city gangs. From the comfort of a passing car, the itinerant killer simply shoots down a member of a rival gang or an innocent bystander. Especially common among L.A.'s Bloods and Crips, the drive-by killing is the parable around which every telling of the gang story revolves. Beyond that lies a haze of images: million-dollar drug deals, ominous graffiti, and colorfully dressed marauders armed with Uzis. The sociologists tell us that gang culture is the flower on the vine of single-parent life in the ghetto, the logical result of society's indifference. It would be hard to write a morality play more likely to strike terror into the hearts of the middle class.

Many questions, though, go unasked. Who, really, are these people? What urges them to join gangs? What are their days like? To answer these questions, *Harper's Magazine* recently asked Léon Bing, a journalist who has established relations with the gangs, to convene a meeting between two Bloods and two Crips and to talk with them about the world in which the drive-by killing is an admirable act.

> The following forum is based on a discussion held at the Kenyon Juvenile Justice Center in south central Los Angeles. Parole Officer Velma V. Stevens assisted in the arrangements. Léon Bing served as moderator.
>
> LÉON BING is a Los Angeles-based journalist. She is currently writing a book about teenage life in Los Angeles.
>
> LI'L MONSTER was a member of the Eight-Trey Gangsters set of the Crips. He is twenty-three years old and currently on probation; he has served time for first-degree murder, four counts of attempted murder, and two counts of armed robbery.
>
> RAT-NECK was a member of the 107-Hoover Crips. He is twenty-eight years old and currently on probation after serving time for attempted murder, robbery with intent to commit grave bodily harm, assault and battery, burglary, and carrying concealed weapons.
>
> TEE RODGERS founded the first Los Angeles chapter of the Chicago-based Blackstone Rangers, affiliated with the Bloods. He is currently

the resident "gangologist" and conflict specialist at Survival Education for Life and Family, Inc., and an actor and lecturer.

B-DOG is a pseudonym for a twenty-three-year-old member of the Van Ness Gangsters set of the Bloods. After this forum was held, his telephone was disconnected, and he could not be located to supply biographical information.

Getting Jumped In

LEON BING: Imagine that I'm a thirteen-year-old guy, and I want to get into a gang. How do I go about it? Am I the right age?

LI'L MONSTER: There's no age limit. It depends on your status coming into it. It's like, some people get jumped in, some people don't.

BING: Jumped in?

LI'L MONSTER: Beat up.

B-DOG: Either beat up or put some work in.

RAT-NECK: Put some work in, that's mandatory, you know, a little mis [misdemeanor]—small type of thing, you know.
It's like this: say I get this guy comin' up and he says, "Hey, Cuz, I wanna be from the set." Then I'm like, "Well, what you *about*, man? I don't know you—you might be a punk." So I might send him somewhere, let him go and manipulate, send him out on a burg' or—

BING:—is that a burglary?

LI'L MONSTER: Yeah. But then, you might know some person who's got a little juice, and, like, I might say, "You don't got to go through that, come on with me. You *from* the set."

TEE RODGERS: If you click with somebody that's already from a set, then you clicked up, or under his wing, you his protégé, and you get a ride in. Now, even though you get a ride in, there's gonna come a time when you got to stand alone and hold your own.

BING: Stand alone and hold your own? Does that mean I might have to steal a car or beat up somebody or commit a burglary?

RAT-NECK: Right.

BING: Is there another way?

RAT-NECK: You can be good from the shoulders.

LI'L MONSTER: Yeah. Fighting.

TEE: That's one of *the* best ways. A homeboy says:

I'm young and mean and my mind's more keen
And I've earned a rep with my hands
And I'm eager to compete with the bangers on the street
'Cause I've got ambitious plans.

LI'L MONSTER: See, when Tee was comin' up—he's *first* generation and we *second* generation. Now, if he saw me, he wouldn't be comin' from the pants pocket with a gat or a knife, he'd be comin' from his shoulders like a fighter. That's what it was established on. Then, later on, come a whole bunch of cowards that *can't* come from the shoulders, so they come from the pocket—

RAT-NECK:—he unloads!

BING: What's the most popular weaponry?

B-DOG: Whatever you get your hands on.

TEE: Keep in mind we don't have no target ranges and shit where we get prolific with these guns.

B-DOG: Shoot 'til you out of bullets, then back up.

RAT-NECK: Bullet ain't got no name, hit whatever it hit.

TEE: Wait a minute! That was a hell of a question, 'cause the mentality of the people that gonna read this be thinkin'—

LI'L MONSTER:—every gang member walks around with that type of gun—

TEE:—and I can hear the police chief saying, "That's why we need bazookas!" Look, put it on the record that everybody ain't got a mother-fuckin' bazooka—or an Uzi. Okay?

BING: It's all on the record.

B-DOG: There *are* some people still believe in .22s.

TEE: Or ice picks. And don't forget the bat.

RAT-NECK: And the lock in the sock!

BING: Are there little peewees, say, nine- to ten-year-olds, in the sets?

RAT-NECK: Yeah, but we say "Li'l Loc" or "Li'l Homie" or "Baby Homie." We never use "peewee" because then people think you're a Mexican. Mexicans say "peewee."

TEE: If it's a Blood set, they use a *k* instead of a *c*. Li'l lok with a *k*. See, Bloods don't say *c*'s and Crips don't say *b*'s. To a Blood, a cigarette is a "bigarette." And Crips don't say "because," they say "cecause."

BING: What prompted you to join, Li'l Monster?

LI'L MONSTER: Say we're white and we're rich. We're in high school and we been buddies since grammar school. And we all decide to go to the same *college*. Well, *we* all on the same street, all those years, and we all just decide to—

RAT-NECK:—join the gang.

TEE: What I think is formulating here is that human nature wants to be accepted. A human being gives less of a damn what he is accepted into. At that age—eleven to seventeen—all kids want to belong. They are un-people.

BING: If you move—can you join another set?

LI'L MONSTER: A couple weeks ago I was talking to a friend 'bout this guy—I'll call him "Iceman." He used to be from Eight-Trey, but he moved to Watts. Now he's a Bounty Hunter.

B-DOG: Boy, that stinks, you know?

BING: He went from the Crips to the Bloods!

LI'L MONSTER: Yeah. And he almost lost his life.

TEE: When you switch sets, when you go from Cuz to Blood, or Blood to Cuz, there's a jacket on you, and you are really pushed to prove yourself for that set. Sometimes the set approves it, and other times they cast you out. If you don't have loyalty to the *first* set you belong to, what the fuck makes us think that you gonna be loyal to us? That's just too much *information*. Shit, we kickin' it, we hangin', bangin', and slangin'. But who the fuck are you, and where are you *really* at? Where your *heart* at?

B-DOG: Perpetrated is what he is!

BING: What does that mean?

TEE: A perpetrator is a fraud, a bullshitter.

BING: How can someone prove himself?

LI'L MONSTER: All right, like the cat Iceman. They might say, "To prove yourself as a Bounty Hunter you go hit somebody from Eight-Trey."

B-DOG: If you got that much love.

BING: Hit somebody from the very set he was in?

RAT-NECK: Yeah. Then his loyalty is there.

BING: But is it really? Wouldn't someone say, "Hey, he hit his homeboy, what's to say he won't hit us if he changes his mind again?"

TEE: Look, when he changes sets, he's already got a jacket on his ass. And when he goes back and takes somebody else out, that cuts all ties, all love.

B-DOG: Can't go to no 'hood. Can't go nowhere.

RAT-NECK: There it is.

TEE: The highest honor you can give for your set is death. When you die, when you go out in a blaze of glory, you are respected. When you kill for your set, you earn your stripes—you put work in.

RAT-NECK: But once you a Crip—no matter what—you can't get out. No matter what, woo-wah-wham, you still there. I can leave here for five years. Then I get out of jail, I gets a new haircut, new everything. Then, "Hey, there goes Rat-Neck!" You can't hide your face. You can't hid nothin'! All that immunity stuff—that's trash. Nobody forgets you.

TEE: That's how it goes. Just like L.A.P.D.—once he retire and shit, that fool still the police! He's still strapped, carrying a gun. He's *always* a cop. Same with us. If you know the words, sing along: "When you're a Jet, you're a Jet all the way, from your first cigarette to your last dying day."

LI'L MONSTER: There you go.

Hangin', Bangin', Slangin'

BING: Once you're a Blood or a Crip, do you dress differently? We hear about guys with their jeans riding low, their underwear showing up top, wearing colors, and having a certain attitude.

TEE: See, a lot of that is media shit. A brother will get up, take his time, spray his hair, put his French braids in, fold his rag, press his Pendleton or his khaki top, put creases in his pants, lace his shoes, and hit the streets.

LI'L MONSTER: He's dressed to go get busy!

TEE: He's dressed, pressed, he's down!

BING: Is that the way you dress after you're in?

TEE: The reason a lot of brothers wear khaki and house slippers and shit like that is because it's cheap and comfortable.

B-DOG: Ain't no dress code nowadays.

LI'L MONSTER: Look, Rat-Neck got on a blue hat, I got on this hat, we Crips. B-Dog's a Blood: he got red stripes on his shoes, and *that* is that. Now I can be in the mall, look at his shoes, and know he's a Blood. He can look at *my* shoes—these B-K's I got on—and say, "He's a Crip."

RAT-NECK: But then again, might be none of that. Might just be ordinary guys.

BING: I've always thought that B-K stands for "Blood Killers" and that's why Crips wear them.

LI'L MONSTER: It stands for British Knights. I don't buy my clothes because they blue. My jacket and my car is red and white. I wear the colors I want to wear. I don't have no blue rag in my pocket. I don't have no blue rubber bands in my hair. But I can be walking down the street and, nine times out of ten, the police gonna hem me up, label me a gangbanger—

RAT-NECK:—or a dope dealer.

LI'L MONSTER: There's only one look at that you got to have. Especially to the police. You got to look black. *That's* the look. Now B-Dog here's a Blood, and he doesn't even have to be gangbanging because if I'm in a mall with some of my homeboys, nine times out of ten we gonna look at him *crazy*. That's how you know. He don't have to have no red on, we gonna look at him crazy. *That's* the mentality.

TEE: Let me give up this, and you correct me if I'm wrong: police officers can recognize police officers, athletes can recognize athletes, gay people can recognize gay people. Well, we can recognize each other. It's simple.

BING: When someone insults you, what happens?

LI'L MONSTER: Depends on what he saying.

BING: Say he calls you "crab" or "E-ricket." Or, if you're a Blood, he calls you a "slob." These are fighting words, aren't they?

RAT-NECK: It's really just words. Words anybody use. But really, a lot of that word stuff don't get people going nowadays.

LI'L MONSTER: That's right.

TEE: There was a time when you could say something about somebody's mama, and you got to fight. Not so anymore.

LI'L MONSTER: Now just ignore the fool.

TEE: But if somebody say, "Fuck your dead homeboys," oh, *now* we got a problem.

LI'L MONSTER: Yeah, that's right.

TEE: Somebody call me "oo-lah" or "slob," fuck 'em. My rebuttal to that is "I'm a super lok-ed out Blood." There's always a cap back, see what I'm saying? But when you get down to the basics, like, "Fuck your dead homeboy," and you *name* the homeboy, that is death. Oh man, we got to take *this* to the grave.

BING: Well, let's say you're with your homeboys and someone does say, "Fuck your dead homeboys." What happens then?

B-DOG: That's it. The question of the matter is on, right there, *wherever* you at.

LI'L MONSTER: He's dead. And if he's not, he's gonna—

B-DOG:—wish he was.

BING: What does that mean?

TEE: I cannot believe the readers of this magazine are that naive. The point of the matter is, if he disrespects the dead homeboys, his ass is gonna get got. Period. Now let your imagination run free; Steven Spielberg does it.

BING: Why this intensity?

TEE: Because there's something called dedication that we got to get into—dedication to the gang mentality—and understanding where it's coming from. It's like this: there's this barrel, okay? All of us are in it together, and we all want the same thing. But some of us are not so highly motivated to be educated. So we have to get ours from the blood, the sweat, and the tears of the street. And if a homeboy rises up—and it is not so much jealousy as it is the fear of him *leaving* me—I want to come up *with* him, but when he reaches the top of the barrel, I grab him by the pants leg and I—

TEE and LI'L MONSTER:—pull him back down.

TEE: It's not that I don't want to see you go home, but *take me with you!* As a man, I'm standing alone as an individual. But I can't say that to him! I got that manly pride that won't let me break down and say, "Man, I'm scared! Take me with you—I want to go with you!" Now, inside this barrel, we are in there so tight that every time we turn around we are smelling somebody's ass or somebody else's stinky breath. There's so many people, I got to leave my community to change my fuckin' mind!

RAT-NECK: Yeah!

TEE: That's how strong peer pressure is! It's that crab-in-the-barrel syndrome. We are just packed in this motherfucker, but I want to feel good. So how? By bustin' a nut. So I fuck my broad, she get pregnant, and now I got *another* baby. So we in there even tighter. In here, in this room, we can relax, we can kick it, we can laugh, we can say, "Well, shit—homeboy from Hoover's all right." Because we in a setting now, and nobody's saying, "FUCK HIM UP, BLOOD! FUCK HIS ASS! I DON'T LIKE HIM—*KICK* HIS ASS!" You know what I'm saying? That's *bullshit!* We can't just sit down and enjoy each other and say, "Are you a man? Do you wipe your ass like I wipe my ass? Do you cut? Do you bleed? Do you cry? Do you die?" There's nowhere where we can go and just experience each other as *people*. And then, when we *do* do that, everybody's strapped.

RAT-NECK: Seems like nothin' else . . .

BING: You make it sound inescapable. What would you tell someone coming along? What would you tell a younger brother?

RAT-NECK: I had a younger brother, fourteen years old. He's dead now, but we never did talk about it. He was a Blood and I am a Crip, and I *know* what time it is. I couldn't socialize with him on what he do. All he could do is ask me certain things, like, "Hey, bro, do you think I'm doing the right thing?" And, well, all I could say is, "Hey, man, choose what you wanna be. What can I do? I love you, but what do I look like, goin' to my mama, tellin' her I *smoked* you, *smoked* my brother? What I look like? But why should I neglect you because you from there? Can't do that. You my love." And if I don't give a fuck about my love, and I don't give a fuck about my brother, then I don't give a fuck about my mama. And then your ass out, when you don't give a fuck about your mama.

Like some people say, "I don't give a fuck, I'll *smoke* my mama!" Well, you know, that's stupidity shit.

BING: I realize that loyalty is paramount. But what I want to know is, if a rival set has it out for someone, does it always mean death?

LI'L MONSTER: Before anybody go shooting, it's going to be, "What is the problem?" Then we are going to find the root of the problem. "Do you personally have something against Eight-Trey?" You say, "No, I just don't like what one of your homeboys did." Then you all beat him up.

B-DOG: Beat him up, yeah.

LI'L MONSTER: Just head it up. Ain't nobody else going to get in this.

BING: Head it up?

LI'L MONSTER: Fight. One on one. You know, head up. And then it's over.

BING: Are you friends after that?

LI'L MONSTER: Well, you not sending each other Christmas cards.

BING: What if you just drive through another gang's turf? Are you in danger?

LI'L MONSTER: Yeah. I mean, I could be sitting at a light, and somebody say, "That's that fool, Li'l Monster," and they start shooting. That could be anywhere. Bam! Bam! Bam!

BING: Are you targeted by reputation?

LI'L MONSTER: Yeah. That's my worst fear, to be sitting at a light.

B-DOG: That's one of mine, too.

LI'L MONSTER: So I don't stop. I don't pull up right behind a car. And I am always looking around.

B-DOG: Always looking.

LI'L MONSTER: That's my worst fear because *we* did so much of it. You know, you pull up, man, block him in, and—

B-DOG:—that was it.

LI'L MONSTER: They put in work. That is my worst fear. And if you ever ride with me, you notice I always position myself where there is a curb. That middle lane is no-man's land.

B-DOG: That's dangerous.

LI'L MONSTER: You know how they say, "Look out for the other guy?" Well, I *am* the other guy. Get out of my way. Give me the starting position. You know, because I can—phew! Claustrophobia. I see that shit happenin', man. I *be* that shit happenin', man, and I don't *never* want that to happen to me, just to be sitting at the light and they take your whole head off.

BING: Say everybody's fired up to get somebody from an enemy set, but there's this young kid who says, "I can't do that. I don't feel right about it—this is a friend of mine." What's going to happen?

LI'L MONSTER: There's many ways that it can be dealt with. Everybody can disown him, or everybody can just say, "Okay, *fine*, but you gotta do something else." See what I'm saying?

B-DOG: But he's gonna be disciplined one way or the other.

RAT-NECK: 'Cause he know everything, man, and he think he gonna ride on up outta here?

LI'L MONSTER: So you go home and say, "Yeah, mama. I got out, mama. Everything's cool." And mama looking at *you* like—"Son, are you sure?" 'Cause she knows damn well those motherfuckers ain't gonna let you go that easy.

TEE: Now that's the flip side to those motherfuckers who say, "I smoke *anybody*—I'll smoke my mama!" We, as homeboys, look at him and say, "Your mama carried you nine months and shitted you out, and if you'll kill your mama, I know you don't give two shakes of a rat's rectum about me!"

RAT-NECK: He'll kill me. He'll smoke me.

BING: What's going to happen in 1989? Los Angeles has the highest body count ever. More deaths than in Ireland.

RAT-NECK: Not more than New York. In New York they kill you for just a penny. I took a trip to New York one time. This guy wanted me to see what it was like.

BING: You mean gang life in New York City?

RAT-NECK: No, to see how people live—gang life, the whole environment, the whole everything. I was there for two days, right? He took us to Queens, Harlem, the Bronx—everywhere. We talked about going out strapped. He said, "What the fuck, you can't go out there strapped! What's wrong with you?" But I say I gotta let 'em know what time it is and carry *something*, you know, 'cause we don't really know what's going on in New York. But we hear so *much* about New York, how they operate, how rough it's supposed to be. So, okay, we decide we gonna carry a buck knife—something. So we kickin', walkin', cruisin' the street, everything. And then I see a homeboy standin' right here next to me.

And he come up to us and do some shit like this: he take three pennies, shake 'em, and throw 'em down in front of his shoe. We, like, what the fuck is this? Is it, you got a beef? Like, he knew we weren't from there. So we not lookin' at him, but, like, why the fuck he throw three pennies down there? Like, was it, "Get off our turf"? But we didn't understand his language. Out here, it's like, "What's happenin'? What's up, Cuz? What's up, Blood?" But in New York, you lookin' at the damn pennies, and maybe he come back and hit you. Maybe if you pick up the pennies, then you got a beef with him. Maybe if you don't pick 'em up, then you supposed to walk off. But shit, we lookin' at the pennies, and lookin' at him, and it's like god-*damn!* So we walks off and leaves the Bronx and goes to Harlem.

Oh, man—*that's* what you call a gutter. You get to lookin' around there and thinking, "God*damn*, these my people? Livin' like *this?* Livin' in a cardboard box?" I mean, skid row got it goin' *on* next to Harlem. Skid row look like *Hollywood* to them.

Kickin' It

BING: Did you vote in the last election?

TEE: Yeah, I voted. But look at the choice I had: Bush bastard and Dumb-kakis.

RAT-NECK: A bush and a cock.

BING: Why didn't you vote for Jesse in the primary?

TEE: I truly believe that shit rigged. Everybody I know voted for Jesse, but—

B-DOG:—Jesse was out.

RAT-NECK: It's different for us. Like, what's that guy's name shot President Reagan? What happened to that guy? *Nothin'!*

BING: He's in prison.

LI'L MONSTER: Oh no he's not. He's in a *hospital.*

TEE: They're *studyin'* him.

RAT-NECK: See, they did that to cover his ass. They say he retarded or something.

B-DOG: See, if I had shot Reagan, would they have put *me* in a mental facility?

RAT-NECK: They would have put you away right there where you shot him. Bam—judge, jury, executioner.

TEE: Why is it they always study white folks when they do heinous crimes, but they never study us? *We* got black psychiatrists.

BING: What about all this killing, then?

TEE: I'm gonna shut up now, because the way the questions are coming, you portray us as animals. Gangbanging is a way of life. You got to touch it, smell it, feel it. Hearing the anger, the frustration, and the desperation of all of us only adds to what the media's been saying—and it's worse, coming out of *our* mouths. There has to be questions directed with an understanding of our point of view. Sorry.

BING: All right. Ask one.

TEE: It's not my interview.

BING: I'm trying to understand your motives. Let me ask a different question: If a homeboy is killed, how is the funeral conducted?

TEE: You got four different sets here in this room, and each set has its own rules and regulations.

RAT-NECK: Okay, like, my little brother just got killed. You talkin' funeralwise, right? At this funeral, Bloods *and* Crips was there. But didn't nobody wear nothin', just suits. *Every* funeral you go to is not really colors.

TEE: Thank you! Yeah!

RAT-NECK: You just going to give your last respect. Like my little brother, it really tripped me out, the way I seen a big "B" of flowers with red roses in it, and one tiny *blue* thing they brought. And these were *Bloods!*—goddamn! Like one of my homeboys asked me, "What's happenin', Rat?" and I said, "Hey, man—you tell *me*." And I looked around, saw some other guys there, you know? They ain't *us*, but they came and showed respect, so—move back. Couple of them walked by us, looked at us, and said, "That's our homeboy, that's Rat-Neck's brother."

When he got killed, you know, I had a whole lot of animosity. I'd smoke any damn one of 'em, but one thing—one thing about it—*it wasn't black people who did it.* That's the one thing that didn't make me click too much. Now, if a black person woulda did it, ain't no tellin' where I'd be right now, or what I'd do, or how I'd feel. I'd be so confused I might just straight out fuck my job, my wife, my kid, whatever, and say, "I don't give a fuck about you—bro got killed!"

BING: How did he get killed?

RAT-NECK: I don't really know the whole rundown.

TEE: What Rat-Neck's saying is the respect. We buried three of our own yesterday, and for each one we went to the mother to see how *she* wanted it—

LI'L MONSTER:—how she wanted it! That's it!

TEE: 'Cause the mother carried that baby for nine months—that's her *child*. It's *her* family, and we're the extended family. She got the first rights on what goes on there. It's the respect factor that lies there, and if the mother says there's no colors, you better believe ain't no colors!

Rat-Neck: And no cartridges in the coffin.

Tee: If he went out in a blaze of glory, and his mama say, "You all bury him like you want to bury him"—oh, then we *do* it."

Bing: How would that be?

Tee: If he was a baller—you know what I'm saying—then everybody get suited and booted.

Bing: Do you mean a sea of colors?

Everyone: *NO!* Suits and ties! Shined shoes!

Li'l Monster: Jump in the silk!

Tee: We own suits, you know. Brooks Brothers, C and R Clothiers! And some of the shit is tailored!

Bing: You mention your mothers a lot, and I sense a love that's very real. If you do love your moms so much and you kill each other, then it has to be the mothers who ultimately suffer the worst pain. How do you justify that?

B-Dog: Your mother gonna suffer while you living, anyway. While you out there gangbanging, she's suffering. My mother's suffering right now. All my brothers in jail.

Rat-Neck: My mother's sufferin', sittin' in her living room, and maybe there's a bullet comin' in the window.

Bing: What do you say to your mother when she says, "All your brothers are in jail, and you're out there in danger"?

B-Dog: We don't even get *into* that no more.

Rat-Neck: She probably don't think about that at all—just so she can cope with it.

B-Dog: Me and my mother don't discuss that no more, because I been into this for so long, you know. When me and my mother be together, we try to be happy. We don't talk about the gang situation.

Li'l Monster: Me and my mother are real tight, you know? We talk like sister and brother. I don't try to justify myself to her—any more than she tries to justify *her* work or how she makes her money to me. What I do *may* come back to hurt her, but what *she* does may also come back to hurt me. Say I'm thirteen and I'm staying with my mother, and she goes off on her boss and loses her job—how does she justify that to *me*?

BING: Well, the loss of a job is not quite the same as an actively dangerous life-style in the streets, wouldn't you agree?

TEE: "An actively dangerous life-style"—that really fucks me up. Okay, here we go. "Woman" is a term that means "of man." Wo-*man*. My mother raised me, true enough. Okay? And she was married. There was a male figure in the house. But I never accepted him as my father. My mother can only teach me so much 'bout being a man-child in the Promised Land. If, after that, there is nothing for me to take pride in, then I enter into manhood asshole backwards, and I stand there, a warrior strong and proud. But there is no outlet for that energy, for me or my brothers, so we *turn on each other*.

So, Mom sends us to the show, and all we get is Clint Eastwood, *Superfly*, and *Sweet Sweet Bad Ass*. Now what goes up on the silver screen comes down into the streets, and now you got a homeboy. And mama says, "I don't want you to go to your grave as a slave for the minimum wage." So you say, "I am going to go get us something, make this better, pay the rent."

The first thing a successful athlete does—and you can check me out—is buy his mama a big-ass house. That's what we want. And if we have to get it from the streets, that's where we go.

BING: Why?

TEE: It's the same *everywhere*. A sorority, a fraternity, the Girl Scouts, camping club, hiking club, L.A.P.D., the Los Angeles Raiders, are all the same. Everything that you find in those groups and institutions you find in a gang.

BING: So are you saying there's no difference between the motives of you guys joining a gang and, say, a young WASP joining a fraternity?

RAT-NECK: You got a lot of gangbangers out there who are smart. They want it. They *got* what it takes. But the difference is they got no money.

TEE: I know a homie who had a scholarship to USC. But he left school because he found prejudice *alive* in America, and it cut him out. He said, "I don't have to stand here and take this. As a matter of fact, you owe my great-grandfather forty acres and a mule."

LI'L MONSTER: Forget the mule, just give me the forty acres.

TEE: So he took to the streets. He got a Ph.D. from SWU. That's a Pimp and Hustler Degree from Sidewalk University.

BING: If it went the other way, what would your life be like?

RAT-NECK: I'm really a hardworking man. I make bed mattresses now, but I would like to straight out be an engineer, or give me a day-care center with little kids coming through, and get me the hell away as far as I can. All I want to do is be myself and not perpetrate myself, try not to perpetrate my black people. Just give me a job, give me a nice house—everybody dream of a nice home—and just let me deal with it.

BING: And how do drugs figure into this?

LI'L MONSTER: Wait a minute. I just want to slide in for a minute. I want to set the record straight. People think gangs and drugs go hand in hand, but they don't. If I sell drugs, does that make me a gangbanger? No. If I gangbang, does that make me sell drugs? No. See, for white people—and I am not saying for all white people, just like what I say about black people is not for all black people—they go for college, the stepping-stone to what they want to get. And some black people look to drugs as a stepping-stone to get the same thing.

B-DOG: They want to live better. To buy what they want. To get a house.

RAT-NECK: Not worry about where the next meal come from.

TEE: To live comfortable and get a slice of American Pie, the American Dream.

B-DOG: There it is.

TEE: The Army came out with a hell of a slogan: "Be all you can be." And that's it. We all want the same thing. We've been taught by television, the silver screen, to grow up and have a chicken in every pot, two Chevys, 2.3 kids in the family. So we have been taught the same thing that you have been taught, but there is certain things that we can hold on to and other things that—we see them, but we just cannot reach them. Most of us are dealing with the reality of surviving as opposed to, "Well, my dad will take care of it."

BING: Are you saying that gangbanging is just another version of the American Dream?

LI'L MONSTER: It's like this. You got the American Dream over there, and you reaching for it. But you can't get it. And you got dope right here, real close. You can grab it easy. Dealing with the closer one, you might possibly make enough money to grab the other one. Then you throw away the dope. That's a big *if* now.

BING: Seriously, does anybody every stop dealing?

B-DOG: If you was making a million dollars off of drugs, you know what I'm saying, are you gonna give that up for a legitimate business?

TEE: This goes back to it. You started out for need, and now you stuck in it because of greed. That's when you play your life away. There comes a time when you have to stop playing, but as far as the streets go, you are a *street player*. Now there may come a time when you say, all right, I've played. I've had time in the gang, now I got to raise up. But if you is so greedy that you cannot smell the coffee, then you're cooked.

BING: But if you do get out, do you always have to come back when your homeboys call?

LI'L MONSTER: It ain't like you gonna be called upon every month.

B-DOG: But if you gets called, then you must be needed, and you must come.

LI'L MONSTER: It's like this—and I don't care who you are, where you started, or how far you got—you *never* forget where you come from.

TEE: That's it.

B-DOG: You *never* forget where you come from.

A Gangbanger's Glossary

Baller: a gangbanger who is making money; also *high roller*

Cap: a retort

Click up: to get along well with a homeboy

Crab: insulting term for a Crip; also *E-ricket*

Cuz: alternative name for a Crip; often used in a greeting, e.g., "What's up, Cuz?"

Down: to do right by your homeboys; to live up to expectations; to protect your turf, e.g., "It's the job of the homeboys to be down for the 'hood"

Gangbanging: the activities of a gang

Gat: gun

Give it up: to admit to something

Hangin', bangin', and slangin': to be out with the homeboys, talking the talk, walking the walk; slangin' come from "slinging" or selling dope

Head up: to fight someone one-on-one

Hemmed up: to be hassled or arrested by the police

'Hood: neighborhood; turf

Homeboy: anyone from the same

neighborhood or gang; a friend or an accepted person; in a larger sense, a person from the inner city; also *homie*

Jacket: a record or a reputation, both within the gang and at the police station

Jumped in: initiated into a gang; getting jumped in typically entails being beaten up by the set members

Kickin' it: kicking back, relaxing with your homeboys

Loc-ed out: also *lok-ed out*; from "loco," meaning ready and willing to do anything

Make a move: commit a crime; also *manipulate*

Mark: someone afraid to commit a crime; also *punk*

O.G.: an abbreviation for Original Gangster; i.e., a gang member who has been in the set for a long time and has made his name

Oo-lah: insulting term for a Blood; also *slob*

Perpetrate: betray your homeboys; bring shame on yourself and your set

Put in work: any perilous activity from fighting to murder that benefits the set or the gang

Set: any of the various neighborhood gangs that fit within the larger framework of Bloods and Crips

Smoke: to kill someone

Top it off: to get along well with someone; reach an understanding

SPECULATIONS

1. According to this article, why do kids join gangs? What do they receive from gangs that they need—and otherwise would be lacking?

2. The language in this selection can be described as offensive. What would have been lost if the swearing and expletives had been deleted? What would have been gained in terms of the reader's response? Aside from the coarseness of the language, evaluate what is said and the ability of the gang members to communicate.

3. The gang members are well aware that their conversation is being recorded by *Harper's Magazine* and that it will be published. Where do you detect evidence of this awareness? How you think it influences what they say and how they say it? How do you think the gang members are responding to Bing? What is her interest in what they have to say?

4. What parallels, if any, would you draw between your own experiences growing up and those of gang members as represented in this essay? What kind of rapport would you have with the Crips and Bloods? What are your "gang" or group experiences as far as loyalty to the group and respect for your family?

5. Li'l Monster, B-Dog, Rat-Neck, and Tee all talk about the relationship between gangs, drugs, television, and images of success. How have these elements influenced your goals and future plans? Why do you think these elements were particularly influential on the Crips and Bloods?

Childhood's End

DAVID ELKIND

A specialist in child development, David Elkind is a professor of psychology and chair of the Department of Child Study at Tufts University. Educated at UCLA, Elkind is a member of the American Psychological Association and other professional organizations, including the Society for the Scientific Study of Religion.

Born in Michigan in 1931, David Elkind has devoted his professional life to the study of children. His list of publications includes translating and editing the work of famed child researcher Jean Piaget and authoring books of his own such as *Exploitation in Middle Class Delinquency: Issues in Human Development* (1971), *Child Development and Education* (1976), *The Child and Society* (1979), and *Mis-Education: Preschoolers at Risk* (1987).

The selection reprinted here is an excerpt from *The Hurried Child*, a book published in 1989 that analyzes the American family's obsession with pushing children headlong into adulthood without taking the necessary time to allow children to enjoy childhood for its own sake.

The concept of childhood, so vital to the traditional American way of life, is threatened with extinction in the society we have created. Today's child has become the unwilling, unintended victim of overwhelming stress—the stress borne of rapid, bewildering social change and constantly rising expectations. The contemporary parent dwells in a pressure-cooker of competing demands, transitions, role changes, personal and professional uncertainties, over which he or she exerts slight direction. We seek release from stress whenever we can, and usually the one sure ambit of our control is the home. Here, if nowhere else, we enjoy the fact (or illusion) of playing a determining role. If child-rearing necessarily entails stress, then by hurrying children to grow up, or by treating them as adults, we hope to remove a portion of our burden of worry and anxiety and to enlist our children's aid in carrying life's load. We do not mean our children harm in acting thus—on the contrary, as a society we have come to imagine that it is good for young people to mature rapidly. Yet we do our children harm when we hurry them through childhood.

The principal architect of our modern notion of childhood was the French philosopher Jean-Jacques Rousseau. It was he who first criticized the educational methods for presenting materials from a uniquely adult perspective, reflecting adult values and interests. Classical *paideia*—that is, the value of transmitting a cultural-social heritage—was a good thing, said Rousseau, but the learning process must take the child's perceptions and stage of development into account. In his classic work *Emile*, Rousseau wrote, "Childhood has its own way of seeing, thinking, and feeling, and nothing is more foolish than to try to substitute ours for theirs." More specifically, he observed that children matured in four stages, and just as each stage had its own characteristics, it should also have a corresponding set of appropriate educational objectives.[1]

This idea of childhood as a distinct phase preceding adult life became inextricably interwoven with the modern concepts of universal education and the small, nuclear family (mother, father, children—not the extended family of earlier eras) in the late eighteenth and early nineteenth centuries, the heyday of the original Industrial Revolution. The transition is well explained by futurologist Alvin Toffler: "As work shifted out of the fields and the home, children had to be prepared for factory life. . . . If young people could be prefitted in the industrial system, it would vastly ease the problems of industrial discipline later on. The result was another central structure of all [modern] societies: mass education."[2]

In addition to free, universal, public education, the emergent society tended to create smaller family units. Toffler writes, "To free workers for factory labor, key functions of the family were parcelled out to new specialized institutions. Education of the child was turned over to schools. Care of the aged was turned over to the poor houses or old-age homes or nursing homes. Above all, the new society required mobility. It needed workers who would follow jobs from place to place. . . . Torn apart by migration to the cities, battered by economic storms, families stripped themselves of unwanted relatives, grew smaller, more mobile, more suited to the needs of the [work place].[3]

Miniature Adults

Today's pressures on middle-class children to grow up fast begin in early childhood. Chief among them is the pressure for early intellectual attainment, deriving from a changed perception of precocity. Several decades ago precocity was looked upon with great suspicion. The child prodigy, it was thought, turned out to be a neurotic adult; thus the phrase "early ripe, early rot!" Trying to accelerate children's acquisition of academic skills was seen as evidence of bad parenting.

A good example of this type of attitude is provided by the case of William James Sidis, the son of a psychiatrist. Sidis was born at the turn of the century and became a celebrated child prodigy who entered Harvard College at the age of eleven. His papers on higher

---

[1] J.-J. Rousseau, *Emile*. New York: Dutton, 1957.
[2] A. Toffler, *The Third Wave*. New York: Bantam, 1980.
[3] *Ibid.*

mathematics gave the impression that he would make major contributions in this area. Sidis soon attracted the attention of the media, who celebrated his feats as a child. But Sidis never went further and seemed to move aimlessly from one job to another. In 1930 James Thurber wrote a profile of Sidis in the *New Yorker* magazine entitled "Where Are They Now?"; he described Sidis's lonely and pitiful existence in which his major preoccupation was collecting streetcar transfers from all over the world.

Such attitudes, however, changed markedly during the 1960s when parents were bombarded with professional and semiprofessional dicta on the importance of learning in the early years. If you did not start teaching children when they were young, parents were told, a golden opportunity for learning would be lost. Today, tax-supported kindergartens are operating in almost every state, and children are admitted at increasingly earlier ages. (In many cities a child born before January 1 can enter kindergarten the preceding September, making his or her effective entrance age four.) Once enrolled in kindergarten, children are now often presented with formal instruction in reading and math once reserved for the later grades.

How did this radical turnabout in attitudes happen? There are probably many reasons, but a major one was the attack on "progressive" education that occurred in the fifties and that found much education material dated. The Russian launching of the Sputnik in 1957 drove Americans into a frenzy of self-criticism about education and promoted the massive curriculum movement of the 1960s that brought academics from major universities into curriculum writing. Unfortunately, many academics knew their discipline but didn't know children and were unduly optimistic about how fast and how much children could learn. This optimism was epitomized in Jerome Bruner's famous phrase. "That any subject can be taught effectively in some intellectually honest form to any child at any stage of development."[4] What a shift from "early ripe, early rot"!

The trend toward early academic pressure was further supported by the civil rights movement, which highlighted the poor performance of disadvantaged children in our schools. Teachers were under attack by avant-garde educators such as John Holt,[5] Jonathan Kozol,[6] and Herbert Kohl,[7] and they were forced to defend their lack of success by shifting the blame. Their children did not do well because they came inadequately prepared. It was not what was going on in the

---

[4] J. Bruner, *The Process of Education*. Cambridge, Massachusetts: Harvard University Press, 1960.

[5] J. C. Holt, *How Children Fail*. New York: Pitman, 1964.

[6] J. Kozol, *Death at an Early Age*. Boston: Houghton Mifflin, 1967.

[7] H. R. Kohl, *36 Children*. New York: New American Library, 1967.

classroom but what had not gone on at home that was the root of academic failure among the disadvantaged; hence Headstart, hence busing, which by integrating students would equalize background differences.

One consequence of all this concern for the early years was the demise of the "readiness" concept. The concept of readiness had been extolled by developmental psychologists such as Arnold Gesell who argued for the biological limitations on learning.[8] Gesell believed that children were not biologically ready for learning to read until they had attained a Mental Age (a test score in which children are credited with a certain number of months for each correct answer) of six and one-half years. But the emphasis on early intervention and early intellectual stimulation (even of infants) made the concept of readiness appear dated and old-fashioned. In professional educational circles readiness, once an honored educational concept, is now in disrepute.

The pressure for early academic achievement is but one of many contemporary pressures on children to grow up fast. Children's dress is another. Three or four decades ago, prepubescent boys wore short pants and knickers until they began to shave; getting a pair of long pants was true rite of passage. Girls were not permitted to wear makeup or sheer stockings until they were in their teens. For both sexes, clothing set children apart. It signaled adults that these people were to be treated differently, perhaps indulgently; it made it easier for children to act as children. Today even preschool children wear miniature versions of adult clothing. From overalls to LaCoste shirts to scaled-down designer fashions, a whole range of adult costumes is available to children. (Along with them is a wide choice of corresponding postures such as those of young teenagers modeling designer jeans.) Below is an illustration from a recent article by Susan Ferraro entitled "Hotsy Totsy."

> It was a party like any other; ice cream and cake, a donkey poster and twelve haphazard tails, and a door prize for everyone including Toby, the birthday girl's little brother who couldn't do anything but smear icing.
>
> "Ooh," sighed seven-year-old Melissa as she opened her first present. It was Calvin Klein jeans. "Aah," she gasped as the second box revealed a bright new top from Gloria Vanderbilt. There were Christian Dior undies from grandma—a satiny little chemise and matching bloomer bottoms—and mother herself had fallen for a marvelous party outfit from Yves St. Laurent. Melissa's best friend gave her an Izod sports shirt, complete with alligator emblem. Added to that a couple of books were, indeed, very nice and predictable—ex-

---

[8] Arnold L. Gesell, Louise B. Ames, and Frances L. Ilg, *Infant and Child in the Culture of Today.* New York: Harper & Row, 1943.

cept for the fancy doll one guest's eccentric mother insisted on bringing.[9]

When children dress like adults they are more likely to behave as adults do, to imitate adult actions. It is hard to walk like an adult male wearing corduroy knickers that make an awful noise. But boys in long pants can walk like men, and little girls in tight jeans can walk like women. It is more difficult today to recognize that children are children and not miniature adults, because children dress and move like adults.

Another evidence of the pressure to grow up fast is the change in the programs of summer camps for children. Although there are still many summer camps that offer swimming, sailing, horseback riding, archery, and camp fires—activities we remember from our own childhood—an increasing number of summer camps offer specialized training in many different areas, including foreign languages, tennis, baseball, dance, music, and even computers.

Among such camps the most popular seem to be those that specialize in competitive sports: softball, weight training, tennis, golf, football, basketball, hockey, soccer, lacrosse, gymnastics, wrestling, judo, figure skating, surfing. "Whatever the sport there's a camp (or ten or a hundred of them) dedicated to teaching the finer points. Often these camps are under the direction, actual or nominal, of a big name in a particular sport, and many have professional athletes on their staffs. The daily routine is rigorous, with individual and/or group lessons, practice sessions and tournaments, complete with trophies. And, to cheer the athletes on with more pep and polish, cheerleaders and song girls can also attend."[10]

The change in the programs of summer camps reflects the new attitude that the years of childhood are not to be frittered away by engaging in activities merely for fun. Rather, the years are to be used to perfect skills and abilities that are the same as those of adults. Children are early initiated into the rigors of adult competition. Competitive sports for children are becoming ever more widespread and include everything from Little League to Pee Wee hockey. The pressure to engage in organized, competitive sports at camp and at home is one of the most obvious pressures on contemporary children to grow up fast.

There are many other pressures as well. Many children today travel across the country, and indeed across the world, alone. The so-called unaccompanied minor has become so commonplace that air-

---

[9] S. Ferraro, "Hotsy Totsy," *American Way Magazine*, April, 1981, p. 61.
[10] C. Emerson, "Summer Camp, It's Not the Same Anymore," *Sky*, March 1981, 29–34.

lines have instituted special rules and regulations for them. The phenomenon is a direct result of the increase in middle-class divorces and the fact that one or the other parent moves to another part of the country or world. Consequently, the child travels to visit one parent or the other. Children also fly alone to see grandparents or to go to special camps or training facilities.

Other facets of society also press children to grow up fast. Lawyers, for example, are encouraging children to sue their parents for a variety of grievances. In California, four-and-one-half-year-old Kimberely Ann Alpin, who was born out of wedlock, is suing her father for the right to visit with him. The father, who provides support payments, does not want to see Kimberely. Whatever the decision, or the merits of the case, it illustrates the tendency of child-advocates to accord adult legal rights to children. In West Hartford, Connecticut, David Burn, age 16, legally "divorced" his parents under a new state law in 1980. While such rights may have some benefits, they also put children in a difficult and often stressful position vis-à-vis their parents.

The media too, including music, books, films, and television, increasingly portray young people as precocious and present them in more or less explicit sexual or manipulative situations. Such portrayals force children to think they should act grown up before they are ready. In the movie *Little Darlings* the two principals—teenage girls—are in competition as to who will lose her virginity first. Similarly, teen music extols songs such as "Take Your Time (Do It Right)" and "Do That to Me One More Time," which are high on the charts of teen favorites. Television also promotes teenage erotica with features detailing such themes as teenage prostitution. According to some teenagers, the only show on television where playing hard to get is not regarded as stupid is "Laverne and Shirley."

The media promote not only teenage sexuality but also the wearing of adult clothes and the use of adult behaviors, language, and interpersonal strategies. Sexual promotion occurs in the context of other suggestions and models for growing up fast. A Jordache jean commercial, which depicts a young girl piggyback on a young boy, highlights clothing and implicit sexuality as well as adult expressions, hairstyles, and so on. Likewise, in the film *Foxes*, four teenage girls not only blunder into sexual entanglements but also model provocative adult clothing, makeup, language, and postures. Thus the media reinforce the pressure on children to grow up fast in their language, thinking, and behavior.

But can young people be hurried into growing up fast emotionally as well? Psychologists and psychiatrists recognize that emotions and feelings are the most complex and intricate part of development. Feelings and emotions have their own timing and rhythm and cannot be hurried. Young teenagers may look and behave like adults but they usually don't feel like adults. (Watch a group of teenagers in a children's playground as they swing on the swings and teeter on the teeter-totters.) Children can grow up fast in some ways but not in others. Growing up emotionally is complicated and difficult under any circumstances but may be especially so when the children's behavior and appearance speak "adult" while their feelings cry "child."

The Child Inside

Some of the more negative consequences of hurrying usually become evident in adolescence, when the pressures to grow up fast collide with institutional prohibitions. Children pushed to grow up fast suddenly find that many adult prerogatives—which they assumed would be their prerogative—such as smoking, drinking, driving, and so on, are denied them until they reach a certain age. Many adolescents feel betrayed by a society that tells them to grow up fast but also to remain a child. Not surprisingly, the stresses of growing up fast often result in troubled and troublesome behavior during adolescence.

In a recent article, Patricia O'Brien gave some examples of what she called "the shrinking of childhood." Her examples reflect a rush to experiment that is certainly one consequence of growing up fast:

> Martin L (not his real name) confronted his teenager who had stayed out very late the night before. The son replied, "Look, Dad, I've done it all—drugs, sex, and booze, there is nothing left I don't know about." This young man is twelve years old!
>
> In Washington, D.C. area schools administrators estimate that many thousands of teenagers are alcoholics, with an estimated 30,000 such young people in Northern Virginia alone.[11]

The rush to experiment is perhaps most noticeable in teenage sexual behavior. Although survey data are not always as reliable as one might wish, the available information suggests that there has been a dramatic increase in the number of sexually active teenage girls in the last decade. Melvin Zelnick and John F. Kanther, professors of public health at Johns Hopkins University in Baltimore, conclude that nearly 50 percent of the total population of teenage girls between the ages of fifteen and nineteen (about 10.3 million females) have had

---

[11] Patricia O'Brien, "Dope, Sex, Crime, What Happened to Childhood," *Chicago Tribune*, March 8, 1981.

premarital sex. The percentage has nearly doubled since the investigators first undertook their study in 1971. "Things that supported remaining a virgin in the past—the fear of getting pregnant, being labelled the 'town pump,' or whatever have disappeared," observes Zelnick.[12]

Young people themselves are very much aware of this trend. "I'd say half the girls in my graduating class are virgins," says an eighteen-year-old high school senior from New Iberia, Louisiana. "But you wouldn't believe those freshmen and sophomores. By the time they graduate there aren't going to be any virgins left."[13]

There are a number of disturbing consequences of this sexual liberation. The number of teenage pregnancies is growing at a startling rate. About 10 percent of all teenage girls, one million in all, get pregnant each year and the number keeps increasing. About 600,000 teenagers give birth each year, and the sharpest increase in such births is for girls under fourteen! In addition, venereal disease is a growing problem among teenagers, who account for 25 percent of the one million or so cases of gonorrhea each year.

The causes of this enhanced sexual activity among young people today are many and varied. The age of first menstruation, for example, has dropped from age seventeen about a century ago to age twelve and a half today. Fortunately this seems to be the lower limit made possible by good health care and nutrition. However, this age of first menstruation has remained stable over the past decade, so it cannot account for the increased sexual activity of young women during this period. Other contributing factors include rapid changes in social values, women's liberation, the exploding divorce rate, the decline of parental and institutional authority, and the fatalistic sense, not often verbalized, that we are all going to die in a nuclear holocaust anyway, so "what the hell, have a good time."

Although the media are quick to pick up these sexual trends and exploit them for commercial purposes (for example, the cosmetics for girls four to nine years old currently being marketed by toy manufacturers), the immediate adult model is perhaps the most powerful and the most pervasive. Married couples are generally discreet about their sexuality in front of their offspring—in part because of a natural tendency to avoid exposing children to what they might not understand, but also because by the time the children are born, much of the romantic phase of the relationship for many couples is in the past.

But single parents who are dating provide a very different model for children. Quite aside from confrontations such as that in *Kramer*

---

[12] The Games Teen Agers Play," *Newsweek*, September 1, 1980.
[13] *Ibid.*

vs. Kramer wherein the son encounters the father's naked girlfriend, single parents are likely to be much more overtly sexual than married couples. With single parents, children may witness the romantic phase of courtship—the hand-holding, the eye-gazing, the constant touching and fondling. This overt sexuality, with all the positive affection it demonstrates, may encourage young people to look for something similar.

It is also true, as Professor Mavis Hetherington of the University of Virginia has found in her research, that daughters of divorced women tend to be more sexually oriented, more flirtatious with men than daughters of widowed mothers or daughters from two-parent homes.[14] Because there are more teenage daughters from single-parent homes today than ever before, this too could contribute to enhanced sexual activity of contemporary teenage girls.

While it is true that some young people in every past generation have engaged in sex at an early age, have become pregnant, contracted venereal disease, and so on, they were always a small proportion of the population. What is new today are the numbers, which indicate that pressures to grow up fast are social and general rather than familial and specific (reflecting parental biases and needs). The proportion of young people who are abusing drugs, are sexually active, and are becoming pregnant is so great that we must look to the society as a whole for a full explanation, not to just the parents who mirror it.

Paralleling the increased sexuality of young people is an increase in children of what in adults are known as stress diseases. Pediatricians report a greater incidence of such ailments as headaches, stomachaches, allergic reactions, and so on in today's youngsters than in previous generations. Type A behavior (high-strung, competitive, demanding) has been identified in children and associated with heightened cholesterol levels. It has also been associated with parental pressure for achievement.

Another negative reflection of the pressure to grow up fast is teenage (and younger) crime. During 1980, for example, New York police arrested 12,762 children aged sixteen and under on felony charges. In Chicago the figure for the same period was 18,754 charges. Having worked for juvenile courts, I am sure that these figures are underestimated. Many children who have committed felonies are released without a formal complaint so that they will not have a police record. The children who are "booked" have usually had several previous encounters with the law.

---

[14] E. M. Hetherington, M. Cos, and R. Cox, "The Aftermath of Divorce." In J. H. Stevens, Jr. & M. Mathews (Eds.) *Mother-child, father-child relations.* Washington, D.C.: NAEYC, 1978.

The following examples, recent cases from the New York Police Department, illustrate the sort of activities for which children get arrested:

- On 27 February 1981, a boy who had to stand on tiptoes to speak to the bank teller made off with $118 that he had secured at gunpoint. He was nine years old, the youngest felon ever sought by the F.B.I.
- A ten-year-old Brooklyn girl was apprehended in December after she snatched a wallet from a woman's purse. Police said it was the girl's nineteenth arrest.
- One of four suspects captured in the murder of a policeman in Queens on 12 January 1981 was a fifteen-year-old youth.
- A thirteen-year-old Bronz boy was arrested in March 1981 on charges that he killed two elderly women during attempted purse snatchings.
- Another thirteen-year-old boy had a record of thirty-two arrests when seized last year on a charge of attempted murder. He later confessed to an incredible 200 plus felonies.[15]

Such crimes are not being committed just by poor disadvantaged youth who are acting out against a society prejudiced against them. Much teenage crime is committed by middle-class youngsters. However, it tends to be concealed because police and parents try to protect the children; but sometimes this is not possible. One case involved a thirteen-year-old Long Island boy who was killed by three teenagers who stomped on him and strangled him by stuffing stones down his throat. He was attacked because he accidentally discovered that the other boys had stolen an old dirt bike worth only a couple of dollars. It was one of the most brutal and gruesome murders to be committed on Long Island.

. . . There are many . . . solutions to [the] pressure to achieve early. One such solution is to join a cult, such as the "Moonies." What characterizes such cults is that they accept young people unconditionally, regardless of academic success or failure. The cults, in effect, provide an accepting family that does not demand achievement in return for love, although cults do demand obedience and adherence to a certain moral ethic. Even rebellious young people find it easy to adhere to these rules in the atmosphere of acceptance and lack of

[15] Michael Coakley, "Robert, a Robber at Age 9, and Just One of Thousands," *Chicago Tribune*, March 8, 1981.

pressure and competition offered by the cult group. Cult membership is [a] form of negative identity in which young people adopt a group identity rather than an individual one.

A case in point is the Christ Commune (a pseudonym), a branch of the best-organized and most rapidly growing sect of what has been called the Jesus movement. The Commune is a summer camp where members come from their homes for a few months each year. The population (about one hundred) consists of young adults between the ages of fifteen and thirty (average age twenty-one) who are white and come from large (four to eight children), middle-class families. Most have completed high school and some have done college work. One gets the impression they are young people who have not distinguished themselves socially, academically, or athletically and who have held boring, low-paying jobs.

The group offers a strict moral code, a rigid behavioral program, and a sense of mission, of being chosen by and working for God through the mediation of Christ. The members work hard—they get up at 4:30 A.M. and go to sleep at 11:00 P.M. They seem happy with simple food (little meat, water to drink, peanut butter sandwiches for lunch) and strenuous work six days a week. Entertainment and recreation are limited to sitting in a common room, talking, singing spirituals, and engaging in spontaneous prayer.

Such communes, the Jesus movement, and other religious groups are attractive to young people whose personal styles are at variance with those of the larger society. Such groups offer recognition and status to young people who tend to be noncompetitive, anti-intellectual, and spiritual in orientation. Thus the groups provide a needed haven from the pressure to grow up fast, to achieve early, and to make a distinctive mark in life.

The last phenomenon in relation to hurrying to be discussed here is teenage suicide. Currently, suicide is the third leading cause of death during the teen years—preceded only by death via accidents and homicide. An American Academy of Pediatrics report on teenage suicide indicates a large increase in the number of suicides by adolescents in the last decade—the number is now about 5000 per year. For young people between the ages of fifteen to nineteen, the number of suicides per year doubled during the period from 1968 to 1976. The data for young adolescents of ages ten to fourteen are even more distressing: The number of suicides was 116 in 1968 and rose to 158 by 1976.

For every suicide completed, some 50 to 200 are attempted but not successful. Adolescents from all walks of life, all races, religions, and ethnic groups commit or attempt to commit suicide. Boys are generally more successful than girls because they use more lethal methods—boys tend to shoot or hang themselves whereas girls are more likely to overdose on pills or to cut their wrists. "For most adolescents," the pediatric report concludes, "suicide represents an attempt to resolve a difficult conflict, escape an intolerable living arrangement, or punish important individuals in their lives."

To illustrate how hurrying can contribute to teenage suicide, consider the data from the most affluent suburbs of Chicago, a ten-mile stretch of communities along Chicago's northside lakefront that is one of the richest areas in the country. It is the locale chosen by director Robert Redford for the movie *Ordinary People*. The median income per family is about $60,000. Children in these areas attend excellent schools, travel about the world on vacations, are admitted to the best and most prestigious private colleges, and often drive their own cars (which can sometimes be a Mercedes). These are children of affluence who would seem to have it made.

And yet, this cluster of suburbs has the highest number of teenage suicides per year in the state, and almost in the nation. There has been a 250 percent increase in suicides per year over the past decade. These figures are dismaying not only in and of themselves but because the community has made serious efforts at suicide prevention, including the training of teachers in suicide detection and the provision of a twenty-four-hour hot line. One hot line, provided by Chicago psychoanalyst Joseph Pribyl, receives some 150 calls per month. But the suicides continue.

A nineteen-year-old from Glencoe, Illinois, says, "We have an outrageous number of suicides for a community our size." One of this teenager's friends cut her wrist and two others drove their cars into trees. "Growing up here you are handed everything on a platter, but something else is missing. The one thing parents don't give is love, understanding, and acceptance of you as a person." And Isadora Sherman, of Highland Park's Jewish Family and Community Service says, "People give their kids a lot materially, but expect a lot in return. No one sees his kids as average, and those who don't perform are made to feel like failures."[16]

Chicago psychiatrist Harole Visotsky succinctly states how pressure to achieve at an early age, to grow up and be successful fast can contribute to teenage suicide: "People on the lower end of the social scale expect less than these people. Whatever anger the poor experience is acted out in antisocial ways—vandalism, homicide, riots—and the sense of shared misery in the lower income groups prevents people from feeling so isolated. With well-to-do kids, *the rattle goes in the*

---

[16] "Suicide Belt," *Time* Magazine, September 1, 1980.

mouth and the foot goes on the social ladder. The competition ethic takes over, making a child feel even more alone. He's more likely to take it out on himself than society.[17]

Adolescents are very audience conscious. Failure is a public event, and the adolescent senses the audience's disapproval. It is the sense that "everyone knows" that is so painful and that can lead to attempted and successful suicides in adolescents who are otherwise so disposed. Hurrying our children has, I believe, contributed to the extraordinary rise in suicide rates among young people over the past decade.

All Grown Up and No Place to Go

Sigmund Freud was once asked to describe the characteristics of maturity, and he replied: *lieben und arbeiten* ("loving and working"). The mature adult is one who can love and allow himself or herself to be loved and who can work productively, meaningfully, and with satisfaction. Yet most adolescents, and certainly all children, are really not able to work or to love in the mature way that Freud had in mind. Children love their parents in a far different way from how they will love a real or potential mate. And many, probably most, young people will not find their life work until they are well into young adulthood.

When children are expected to dress, act, and think as adults, they are really being asked to playact, because of the trappings of adulthood do not in any way make them adults in the true sense of *lieben und arbeiten.* It is ironic that the very parents who won't allow their children to believe in Santa Claus or the Easter Bunny (because they are fantasy and therefore dishonest) allow their children to dress and behave as adults without any sense of the tremendous dishonesty involved in allowing children to present themselves in this grown-up way.

It is even more ironic that practices once considered the province of lower-class citizens now have the allure of middle-class chic. Divorce, single parenting, dual-career couples, and unmarried couples living together were common among the lower class decades ago. Such arrangements were prompted more often than not by economic need, and the children of low-income families were thus pressured to grow up fast out of necessity. They were pitied and looked down upon by upper- and middle-class parents, who helped provide shelters like the Home for Little Wanderers in Boston.

Today the middle class has made divorce its status symbol. And

---

[17] *Ibid.*

single parenting and living together without being married are increasingly commonplace. Yet middle-class children have not kept pace with the adjustments these adult changes require. In years past a child in a low-income family could appreciate the need to take on adult responsibilities early; families needed the income a child's farm or factory labor would bring, and chores and child-rearing tasks had to be allocated to even younger members of the family. But for the middle-income child today, it is hard to see the necessity of being relegated to a baby sitter or sent to a nursery school or a day care center when he or she has a perfectly nice playroom and yard at home. It isn't the fact of parents being divorced that is so distressing to middle-class children, but rather that often it seems so unnecessary, so clearly a reflection of parent and not child need. . . . It is the feeling of being used, of being exploited by parents, of losing the identity and uniqueness of childhood without just cause that constitutes the major stress of hurrying and accounts for so much unhappiness among affluent young people today.

It is certainly true that the trend toward obscuring the divisions between children and adults is part of a broad egalitarian movement in this country that seeks to overcome the barriers separating the sexes, ethnic and racial groups, and the handicapped. We see these trends in unisex clothing and hairstyles, in the call for equal pay for equal work, in the demands for affirmative action and in the appeals and legislation that provide the handicapped with equal opportunities for education and meaningful jobs.

From this perspective, the contemporary pressure for children to grow up fast is only one symptom of a much larger social phenomenon in this country—a movement toward true equality, toward the ideal expressed in our Declaration of Independence. While one can only applaud this movement with respect to the sexes, ethnic and racial groups, and the handicapped, its unthinking extension to children is unfortunate.

Children need time to grow, to learn, and to develop. To treat them differently from adults is not to discriminate against them but rather to recognize their special estate. Similarly, when we provide bilingual programs for Hispanic children, we are not discriminating against them but are responding to the special needs they have, which, if not attended to, would prevent them from attaining a successful education and true equality. In the same way, building ramps for handicapped students is a means to their attaining equal opportunity. Recognizing special needs is not discriminatory; on the contrary, it is the only way that true equality can be attained.

All children have, vis-à-vis adults, special needs—intellectual, social, and emotional. Children do not learn, think, or feel in the same way as adults. To ignore these differences, to treat children as adults, is really not democratic or egalitarian. If we ignore the special needs of children, we are behaving just as if we denied Hispanic or Indian children bilingual programs, or denied the handicapped their ramps and guideposts. In truth, the recognition of a group's special needs and accommodation to those needs are the only true ways to ensure equality and true equal opportunity.

SPECULATIONS

1. Elkind argues that children are different from adults. In what ways do you think he means this? What should children be doing—and not doing—that is different from adults?
2. What does Elkind mean by "the child inside"? What does he think happens to that child as young people grow up? In what ways do you support his argument? Express your point of view in terms of the "child" inside you.
3. Elkind's first sentence argues that "the concept of childhood, so vital to the traditional American way of life, is threatened with extinction in the society we have created." What parts of this statement do you agree with? In what ways do you think childhood has changed?
4. Elkind illustrates his argument with numerous examples drawn from cases of teenage suicide, violent crime, litigation, films, television, music, etc. Which examples are persuasive? Since most of them are over ten years old, are they too out-of-date to provide useful support for his argument?
5. Based on Elkind's assumptions, how would you characterize the difference between a "child" and an "adult"?

Two Kinds

AMY TAN

Amy Tan was born in 1952 in Oakland, California, shortly after her parents arrived in the United States from China. Like the children of most immigrants to America, Tan had to come to terms with living on the outside of two cultures—that is, being neither Chinese nor American—and yet identifying strongly with both. Typically, Tan's mother held high aspirations for her daughter: she wanted her to become a neurosurgeon. Instead, Tan, who resides in San Francisco, has become one of the brightest stars on the literary horizon.

During her adolescence, Tan discovered that she had two half-sisters, left behind, by her mother, in China, after the Red Army invaded Beijing. Twenty-two years later, Amy Tan wrote about her family in *The Joy Luck Club*. Through sixteen interconnected stories told by four Chinese-born mothers and their four American-born daughters, Tan presents two generations of tough, intelligent, resourceful women trying to come to terms with their identifies, aspirations, losses, and successes.

The central character of *The Joy Luck Club* is Jing-mei (June) Woo, who closely resembles Amy Tan. Ultimately June must travel to Shanghai to meet with her half-sisters and answer their inevitable questions about their mother—about June's mother. In the following selection from the book, Jing-mei Woo and her mother struggle over their conflicting notions of identity, ambition, success, and selfhood.

My mother believed you could be anything you wanted to be in America. You could open a restaurant. You could work for the government and get good retirement. You could buy a house with almost no money down. You could become rich. You could become instantly famous.

"Of course you can be prodigy, too," my mother told me when I was nine. "You can be best anything. What does Auntie Lindo know? Her daughter, she is only best tricky."

America was where all my mother's hopes lay. She had come here in 1949 after losing everything in China: her mother and father, her family home, her first husband, and two daughters, twin baby girls. But she never looked back with regret. There were so many ways for things to get better.

We didn't immediately pick the right kind of prodigy. At first my mother thought I could be a Chinese Shirley Temple. We'd watch Shirley's old movies on TV as though they were training films. My mother would poke my arm and say, *"Ni kan"*—You watch. And I would see Shirley tapping her feet, or singing a sailor song, or pursing her lips into a very round O while saying, "Oh my goodness."

"Ni kan," said my mother as Shirley's eyes flooded with tears. "You already know how. Don't need talent for crying!"

Soon after my mother got this idea about Shirley Temple, she took me to a beauty training school in the Mission district and put me in the hands of a student who could barely hold the scissors without shaking. Instead of getting big fat curls, I emerged with an uneven mass of crinkly black fuzz. My mother dragged me off to the bathroom and tried to wet down my hair.

"You look like Negro Chinese," she lamented, as if I had done this on purpose.

The instructor of the beauty training school had to lop off these soggy clumps to make my hair even again. "Peter Pan is very popular these days," the instructor assured my mother. I now had hair the length of a boy's, with straight-across bangs that hung at a slant two inches above my eyebrows. I liked the haircut and it made me actually look forward to my future fame.

In fact, in the beginning, I was just as excited as my mother, maybe even more so. I pictured this prodigy part of me as many different images, trying each one on for size. I was a dainty ballerina girl standing by the curtains, waiting to hear the right music that would send me floating on my tiptoes. I was like the Christ child lifted out of the straw manger, crying with holy indignity. I was Cinderella stepping from her pumpkin carriage with sparkly cartoon music filling the air.

In all of my imagingings, I was filled with a sense that I would soon become *perfect*. My mother and father would adore me. I would be beyond reproach. I would never feel the need to sulk for anything.

But sometimes the prodigy in me became impatient. "If you don't hurry up and get me out of here, I'm disappearing for good," it warned. "And then you'll always be nothing."

Every night after dinner, my mother and I would sit at the Formica kitchen table. She would present new tests, taking her examples from stories of amazing children she had read in *Ripley's Believe It or Not*, or *Good Housekeeping, Reader's Digest*, and a dozen other magazines she kept in a pile in our bathroom. My mother got these magazines from people whose houses she cleaned. And since she cleaned many houses each week, we had a great assortment. She would look through them all, searching for stories about remarkable children.

The first night she brought out a story about a three-year-old boy who knew the capitals of all the states and even most of the European countries. A teacher was quoted as saying the little boy could also pronounce the names of the foreign cities correctly.

"What's the capital of Finland?" my mother asked me, looking at the magazine story.

All I knew was the capital of California, because Sacramento was the name of the street we lived on in Chinatown. "Nairobi!" I guessed, saying the most foreign word I could think of. She checked to see if that was possibly one way to pronounce "Helsinki" before showing me the answer.

The tests got harder—multiplying numbers in my head, finding the queen of hearts in a deck of cards, trying to stand on my head without using my hands, predicting the daily temperatures in Los Angeles, New York, and London.

One night I had to look at a page from the Bible for three minutes and then report everything I could remember. "Now Jehosphaphat had riches and honor in abundance and . . . that's all I remember, Ma," I said.

And after seeing my mother's disappointed face once again, something inside of me began to die. I hated the tests, the raised hopes and failed expectations. Before going to bed that night, I looked in the mirror above the bathroom sink and when I saw only my face staring back—and that it would always be this ordinary face—I began to cry. Such a sad, ugly girl! I made high-pitched noises like a crazed animal, trying to scratch out the face in the mirror.

And then I saw what seemed to be the prodigy side of me—because I had never seen that face before. I looked at my reflection, blinking so I could see more clearly. The girl staring back at me was angry, powerful. This girl and I were the same. I had new thoughts, willful thoughts, or rather thoughts filled with lots of won'ts. I won't let her change me, I promised myself. I won't be what I'm not.

So now on nights when my mother presented her tests, I performed listlessly, my head propped on one arm. I pretended to be bored. And I was. I got so bored I started counting the bellows of the foghorns out on the bay while my mother drilled me in other areas. The sound was comforting and reminded me of the cow jumping over the moon. And the next day, I played a game with myself, seeing if my mother would give up on be before eight bellows. After a while I usually counted only one, maybe two bellows at most. At last she was beginning to give up hope.

Two or three months had gone by without any mention of my being a prodigy again. And then one day my mother was watching "The Ed Sullivan Show" on TV. The TV was old and the sound kept shorting out. Every time my mother got halfway up from the sofa to adjust the set, the sound would go back on and Ed would be talking. As soon as she sat down, Ed would go silent again. She got up, the TV broke into loud piano music. She sat down. Silence. Up and down, back and forth, quiet and loud. It was like a stiff embraceless dance between her and the TV set. Finally she stood by the set with her hand on the sound dial.

She seemed entranced by the music, a little frenzied piano piece with this mesmerizing quality, sort of quick passages and then teasing lilting ones before it returned to the quick playful parts.

"*Ni kan,*" my mother said, calling me over with hurried hand gestures. "Look here."

I could see why my mother was fascinated by the music. It was being pounded out by a little Chinese girl, about nine years old, with a Peter Pan haircut. The girl had the sauciness of a Shirley Temple. She was proudly modest like a proper Chinese child. And she also did this fancy sweep of a curtsy, so that the fluffy skirt of her white dress cascaded slowly to the floor like the petals of a large carnation.

In spite of these warning signs, I wasn't worried. Our family had no piano and we couldn't afford to buy one, let alone reams of sheet music and piano lessons. So I could be generous in my comments when my mother bad-mouthed the little girl on TV.

"Play note right, but doesn't sound good! No singing sound," complained my mother.

"What are you picking on her for?" I said carelessly. "She's pretty good. Maybe she's not the best, but she's trying hard." I knew almost immediately I would be sorry I said that.

"Just like you," she said. "Not the best. Because you not trying." She gave a little huff as she let go of the sound dial and sat down on the sofa.

The little Chinese girl sat down also to play an encore of "Anitra's Dance" by Grieg. I remember the song, because later on I had to learn how to play it.

Three days after watching "The Ed Sullivan Show," my mother told me what my schedule would be for piano lessons and piano practice. She had talked to Mr. Chong, who lived on the first floor of our apartment building. Mr. Chong was a retired piano teacher and my mother had traded housecleaning services for weekly lessons and a piano for me to practice on every day, two hours a day, from four until six.

When my mother told me this, I felt as though I had been sent to hell. I whined and then kicked my foot a little when I couldn't stand it anymore.

"Why don't you like me the way I am? I'm *not* a genius! I can't play the piano. And even if I could, I wouldn't go on TV if you paid me a million dollars!" I cried.

My mother slapped me. "Who ask you be genius?" she shouted. "Only ask you be your best. For you sake. You think I want you be genius? Hnnh! What for! Who ask you!"

"So ungrateful," I heard her mutter in Chinese. "If she had as much talent as she has temper, she would be famous now."

Mr. Chong, whom I secretly nicknamed Old Chong, was very strange, always tapping his fingers to the silent music of an invisible orchestra. He looked ancient in my eyes. He had lost most of the hair on top of his head and he wore thick glasses and had eyes that always looked tired and sleepy. But he must have been younger than I thought, since he lived with his mother and was not yet married.

I met Old Lady Chong once and that was enough. She had this peculiar smell like a baby that had done something in its pants. And her fingers felt like a dead person's, like an old peach I once found in the back of the refrigerator; the skin just slid off the meat when I picked it up.

I soon found out why Old Chong had retired from teaching piano.

He was deaf. "Like Beethoven!" he shouted to me. "We're both listening only in our head!" And he would start to conduct his frantic silent sonatas.

Our lessons went like this. He would open the book and point to different things, explaining their purpose: "Key! Treble! Bass! No sharps or flats! So this is C major! Listen now and play after me!"

And then he would play the C scale a few times, a simple chord, and then, as if inspired by an old, unreachable itch, he gradually added more notes and running trills and a pounding bass until the music was really something quite grand.

I would play after him, the simple scale, the simple chord and then I just played some nonsense that sounded like a cat running up and down on top of garbage cans. Old Chong smiled and applauded and then said, "Very good! But now you must learn to keep time!"

So that's how I discovered that Old Chong's eyes were too slow to keep up with the wrong notes I was playing. He went through the motions in half-time. To help me keep rhythm, he stood behind me, pushing down on my right shoulder for every beat. He balanced pennies on top of my wrists so I would keep them still as I slowly played scales and arpeggios. He had me curve my hand around an apple and keep that shape when playing chords. He marched stiffly to show me how to make each finger dance up and down, staccato like an obedient little solider.

He taught me all these things, and that was how I also learned I could be lazy and get away with mistakes, lots of mistakes. If I hit the wrong notes because I hadn't practiced enough, I never corrected myself. I just kept playing in rhythm. And Old Chong kept conducting his own private reverie.

So maybe I never really gave myself a fair chance. I did pick up the basics pretty quickly, and I might have become a good pianist at that young age. But I was so determined not to try, not to be anybody different that I learned to play only the most ear-splitting preludes, the most discordant hymns.

Over the next year, I practiced like this, dutifully in my own way. And then one day I heard my mother and her friend Lindo Jong both talking in a loud bragging tone of voice so others could hear. It was after church, and I was leaning against the brick wall wearing a dress with stiff white petticoats. Auntie Lindo's daughter, Waverly, who was about my age, was standing farther down the wall about five feet away. We had grown up together and shared all the closeness of two sisters squabbling over crayons and dolls. In other words, for the most part, we hated each other. I thought she was snotty. Waverly Jong had gained a certain amount of fame as "Chinatown's Littlest Chinese Chess Champion."

"She bring home too many trophy," lamented Auntie Lindo that Sunday. "All day she play chess. All day I have no time do nothing but dust off her winnings." She threw a scolding look at Waverly, who pretended not to see her.

"You lucky you don't have this problem," said Auntie Lindo with a sigh to my mother.

And my mother squared her shoulders and bragged: "Our problem worser than yours. If we ask Jing-mei wash dish, she hear nothing but music. It's like you can't stop this natural talent."

And right then, I was determined to put a stop to her foolish pride.

A few weeks later, Old Chong and my mother conspired to have me play in a talent show which would be held in the church hall. By then, my parents had saved up enough to buy me a secondhand piano, a black Wurlitzer spinet with a scarred bench. It was the showpiece of our living room.

For the talent show, I was to play a piece called "Pleading Child" from Schumann's *Scenes from Childhood*. It was a simple, moody piece that sounded more difficult than it was. I was supposed to memorize the whole thing, playing the repeat parts twice to make the piece sound longer. But I dawdled over it, playing a few bars and then cheating, looking up to see what notes followed, I never really listened to what I was playing. I daydreamed about being somewhere else, about being someone else.

The part I liked to practice best was the fancy curtsy: right foot out, touch the rose on the carpet with a pointed foot, sweep to the side, left leg bends, look up and smile.

My parents invited all the couples from the Joy Luck Club to witness my debut. Auntie Lindo and Uncle Tin were there. Waverly and her two older brothers had also come. The first two rows were filled with children both younger and older than I was. The littlest ones got to go first. They recited simple nursery rhythms, squawked out tunes on miniature violins, twirled Hula Hoops, pranced in pink ballet tutus, and when they bowed or curtsied, the audience would sigh in unison, "Awww," and then clap enthusiastically.

When my turn came, I was very confident. I remember my childish excitement. It was as if I knew, without a doubt, that the prodigy side of me really did exist. I had no fear whatsoever, no nervousness. I remember thinking to myself, This is it! This is it! I looked out over the audience, at my mother's blank face, my father's yawn, Auntie Lindo's stiff-lipped smile, Waverly's sulky expression. I had on a white dress layered with sheets of lace, and a pink bow in my Peter

Pan haircut. As I sat down I envisioned people jumping to their feet and Ed Sullivan rushing up to introduce me to everyone on TV.

And I started to play. It was so beautiful. I was so caught up in how lovely I looked that at first I didn't worry how I would sound: So it was a surprise to me when I hit the first wrong note and I realized something didn't sound quite right. And then I hit another and another followed that. A chill started at the top of my head and began to trickle down. Yet I couldn't stop playing, as though my hands were bewitched. I kept thinking my fingers would adjust themselves back, like a train switching to the right track. I played this strange jumble through two repeats, the sour notes staying with me all the way to the end.

When I stood up, I discovered my legs were shaking. Maybe I had just been nervous and the audience, like Old Chong, had seen me go through the right motions and had not heard anything wrong at all. I swept my right foot out, went down on my knee, looked up and smiled. The room was quiet, except for Old Chong, who was beaming and shouting, "Bravo! Bravo! Well done!" But then I saw my mother's face, her stricken face. The audience clapped weakly, and as I walked back to my chair, with my whole face quivering as I tried not to cry, I heard a little boy whisper loudly to his mother, "That was awful," and the mother whispered back, "Well, she certainly tried."

And now I realized how many people were in the audience, the whole world it seemed. I was aware of eyes burning into my back. I felt the shame of my mother and father as they sat stiffly throughout the rest of the show.

We could have escaped during intermission. Pride and some strange sense of honor must have anchored my parents to their chairs. And so we watched it all: the eighteen-year-old boy with a fake mustache who did a magic show and juggled flaming hoops while riding a unicycle. The breasted girl with white makeup who sang from *Madama Butterfly* and got honorable mention. And the eleven-year-old boy who won first prize playing a tricky violin song that sounded like a busy bee.

After the show, the Hsus, the Jongs, and the St. Clairs from the Joy Luck Club came up to my mother and father.

"Lots of talented kids," Auntie Lindo said vaguely, smiling broadly.

"That was somethin' else," said my father, and I wondered if he was referring to me in a humorous way, or whether he even remembered what I had done.

Waverly looked at me and shrugged her shoulders. "You aren't a genius like me," she said matter-of-factly. And if I hadn't felt so bad, I would have pulled her braids and punched her stomach.

But my mother's expression was what devastated me: a quiet, blank look that said she had lost everything. I felt the same way, and it seemed as if everybody were now coming up, like gawkers at the scene of an accident, to see what parts were actually missing. When we got on the bus to go home, my father was humming the busy-bee tune and my mother was silent. I kept thinking she wanted to wait until we got home before shouting at me. But when my father unlocked the door to our apartment, my mother walked in and then went to the back, into the bedroom. No accusations. No blame. And in a way, I felt disappointed. I had been waiting for her to start shouting, so I could shout back and cry and blame her for all my misery.

I assumed by talent-show fiasco meant I never had to play the piano again. But two days later, after school, my mother came out of the kitchen and saw me watching TV.

"Four clock," she reminded me as if it were any other day. I was stunned, as though she were asking me to go through the talent-show torture again. I wedged myself more tightly in front of the TV.

"Turn off TV," she called from the kitchen five minutes later.

I didn't budge. And then I decided. I didn't have to do what my mother said anymore. I wasn't her slave. This wasn't China. I had listened to her before and look what happened. She was the stupid one.

She came out from the kitchen and stood in the arched entryway of the living room. "Four clock," she said once again, louder.

"I'm not going to play anymore," I said nonchalantly. "Why should I? I'm not a genius."

She walked over and stood in front of the TV. I saw her chest was heaving up and down in an angry way.

"No! " I said, and I now felt stronger, as if my true self had finally emerged. So this was what had been inside me all along.

"No! I won't!" I screamed.

She yanked me by the arm, pulled me off the floor, snapped off the TV. She was frighteningly strong, half pulling, half carrying me toward the piano as I kicked the throw rugs under my feet. She lifted me up and onto the hard bench. I was sobbing by now, looking at her bitterly. Her chest was heaving even more and her mouth was open, smiling crazily as if she were pleased I was crying.

"You want me to be someone that I'm not!" I sobbed. "I'll never be the kind of daughter you want me to be!"

"Only two kinds of daughters," she shouted in Chinese. "Those who are obedient and those who follow their own mind! Only one kind of daughter can live in this house. Obedient daughter!"

"Then I wish I wasn't your daughter. I wish you weren't my

mother," I shouted. As I said these things I got scared. I felt like worms and toads and slimy things were crawling out of my chest, but it also felt good, as if this awful side of me had surfaced, at last.

"Too late change this," said my mother shrilly.

And I could sense her anger rising to its breaking point. I wanted to see it spill over. And that's when I remembered the babies she had lost in China, the ones we never talked about. "Then I wish I'd never been born!" I shouted. "I wish I were dead! Like them."

It was as if I had said the magic words. Alakazam!—and her face went blank, her mouth closed, her arms went slack, and she backed out of the room, stunned, as if she were blowing away like a small brown leaf, thin, brittle, lifeless.

It was not the only disappointment my mother felt in me. In the years that followed, I failed her so many times, each time asserting my own will, my right to fall short of expectations. I didn't get straight A's. I didn't become class president. I didn't get into Stanford. I dropped out of college.

For unlike my mother, I did not believe I could be anything I wanted to be. I could only be me.

And for all those years, we never talked about the disaster at the recital or my terrible accusations afterward at the piano bench. All that remained unchecked, like a betrayal that was now unspeakable. So I never found a way to ask her why she had hoped for something so large that failure was inevitable.

And even worse, I never asked her what frightened me the most: Why had she given up hope?

For after our struggle at the piano, she never mentioned my playing again. The lessons stopped. The lid to the piano was closed, shutting out the dust, my misery, and her dreams.

So she surprised me. A few years ago, she offered to give me the piano, for my thirtieth birthday. I had not played in all those years. I saw the offer as a sign of forgiveness, a tremendous burden removed.

"Are you sure?" I asked shyly. "I mean, won't you and Dad miss it?"

"No, this your piano," she said firmly. "Always your piano. You only one can play."

"Well, I probably can't play anymore," I said. "It's been years."

"You pick up fast," said my mother, as if she knew this was certain. "You have natural talent. You could been genius if you want to."

"No I couldn't."

"You just not trying," said my mother. And she was neither angry nor sad. She said it as if to announce a fact that could never be disproved. "Take it," she said.

But I didn't at first. It was enough that she had offered it to me. And after that, every time I saw it in my parents' living room, standing in front of the bay windows, it made me feel proud, as if it were a shiny trophy I had won back.

Last week I sent a tuner over to my parents' apartment and had the piano reconditioned, for purely sentimental reasons. My mother had died a few months before and I had been getting things in order for my father, a little bit at a time. I put the jewelry in special silk pouches. The sweaters she had knitted in yellow, pink, bright orange—all the colors I hated—I put those in moth-proof boxes. I found some old Chinese silk dresses, the kind with little slits up the sides. I rubbed the old silk against my skin, then wrapped them in tissue and decided to take them home with me.

After I had the piano tuned, I opened the lid and touched the keys. It sounded even richer than I remembered. Really, it was a very good piano. Inside the bench were the same exercise notes with handwritten scales, the same secondhand music books with their covers held together with yellow tape.

I opened up the Schumann book to the dark little piece I had played at the recital. It was on the left-hand side of the page. "Pleading Child." It looked more difficult than I remembered. I played a few bars, surprised at how easily the notes came back to me.

And for the first time, or so it seemed, I noticed the piece on the right-hand side. It was called "Perfectly Contented." I tried to play this one as well. It had a lighter melody but the same flowing rhythm and turned out to be quite easy. "Pleading Child" was shorter but slower; "Perfectly Contented" was longer but faster. And after I played them both a few times, I realized they were two halves of the same song.

SPECULATIONS

1.   Why is the mother in this story so determined to make her daughter into a prodigy? What attitudes are typical of immigrants? of Chinese parents? of most or all parents?

2.   Tan uses a lot of detail in this story: Shirley Temple, the Formica kitchen table, "The Ed Sullivan Show," magazine titles, descriptions of various characters, titles of musical compositions. Why do you think she does this? What effects do these kinds of details have on you as you read?

3.   Throughout "Two Kinds," there is a debate between mother and daughter as to whether the daughter is trying hard enough. How would you analyze

her motivations, seriousness, willingness to please her mother? What are her qualifications to be a genius as the mother tells her long after she has grown up? Do you believe that the narrator at the end of the story was actually able to play "Pleading Child" and "Perfectly Contented"—and what does she mean by saying that "they were two halves of the same song?"

4. The narrator's mother states that there are two kinds of daughters: "Those who are obedient and those who follow their own mind!" How does the narrator react? How would you react? When the daughter retorts, "I wish I were dead! Like them," why is the mother stunned, silenced, defeated?

5. Can you describe your own relation to what your parent(s) want(s) for you? How do you sort out what you want for yourself from what your mother or father wants for you?

Shopping

JOYCE CAROL OATES

In a 1987 interview with *Contemporary Authors*, Joyce Carol Oates remarked, "Writers are always under attack, usually for not being 'moral' enough. There is insufficient recognition of the fact that one of the traditional roles of the writer is to bear witness—not simply to the presumably good things in life, the uplifting, life-enhancing, *happy* things, but to their polar opposites as well." The short story "Shopping," included here, illuminates one of the dark corners of family life—namely, the relationship of a particular mother and daughter as expressed through the material culture that surrounds them. The story originally appeared in *Ms.* in 1987.

Born in 1938, Joyce Carol Oates is a gifted and prolific writer. She has authored over twenty novels, sixteen anthologies of short stories, nine collections of poetry, several plays, three books of essays, and considerable literary criticism. Winner of many awards and honors, including grants from the National Endowment for the Arts and the Guggenheim Foundation, as well as prizes from the O. Henry competition and the National Book Award, Oates continues to dazzle readers with both her insights and her narrative genius. Some of her best known works include *A Garden of Earthly Delights* (1967), *Expensive People* (1967), *them* (1969), *Women Whose Lives Are Food, Men Whose Lives Are Money* (1978), *Unholy Loves (1979)*, and *Bellefleur* (1980).

Oates, who teaches writing at Princeton University, is, essentially, a writer concerned with social and moral issues, with societal conflicts and debates about nature, religion, history, individual choice, and responsibility. She sees the world as a place of difficulty and violence. "Uplifting endings and resolutely cheery world views," she stated in the *New York Times Book Review*, "are appropriate to television commercials but insulting elsewhere. It is not only wicked to pretend otherwise, it is futile."

An old ritual, Saturday morning shopping. Mother and daughter. Mrs. Dietrich and Nola. Shops in the village, stores and boutiques at the splendid Livingstone Mall on Route 12. Bloomingdale's, Saks, Lord & Taylor, Bonwit's, Neiman-Marcus: and the rest. Mrs. Dietrich would know her way around the stores blindfolded but there is always the surprise of lavish seasonal displays, extraordinary holiday sales, the openings of new stores at the Mall like Laura Ashley, Paraphernalia. On one of their Mall days Mrs. Dietrich and Nola would try to get there at midmorning, have lunch around 1 P.M. at one or another of their favorite restaurants, shop for perhaps an hour after lunch, then come home. Sometimes the shopping trips were more successful than at other times but you have to have faith, Mrs. Dietrich tells herself. Her interior voice is calm, neutral, free of irony. Ever since her divorce her interior voice has been free of irony. You have to have faith.

Tomorrow morning Nola returns to school in Maine; today will be a day at the Mall. Mrs. Dietrich has planned it for days. At the Mall, in such crowds of shoppers, moments of intimacy are possible as they rarely are at home. (Seventeen-year-old Nola, home on spring break for a brief eight days, seems always to be *busy*, always out with her *friends*—the trip to the Mall has been postponed twice.) But Saturday, 10:30 A.M., they are in the car at last headed south on Route 12, a bleak March morning following a night of freezing rain, there's a metallic cast to the air and no sun anywhere in the sky but the light hurts Mrs. Dietrich's eyes just the same. "Does it seem as if spring will ever come?—it must be twenty degrees colder up in Maine," she says. Driving in heavy traffic always makes Mrs. Dietrich nervous and she is overly sensitive to her daughter's silence, which seems deliberate, perverse, when they have so little time remaining together—not even a full day.

Nola asks politely if Mrs. Dietrich would like her to drive and Mrs. Dietrich says no, of course not, she's fine, it's only a few more miles and maybe traffic will lighten. Nola seems about to say something more, than thinks better of it. So much between them that is precarious, chancy—but they've been kind to each other these past seven days. Mrs. Dietrich loves Nola with a fierce unreasoned passion stronger than any she felt for the man who had been her husband for thirteen years, certainly far stronger than any she ever felt for her own mother. Sometimes in weak despondent moods, alone, lonely, self-pitying, when she has had too much to drink, Mrs. Dietrich thinks she is in love with her daughter—but this is a thought she can't contemplate for long. And how Nola would snort in amused contempt, incredulous, mocking—"Oh *Mother!*"—if she were told.

Mrs. Dietrich tries to engage her daughter in conversation of a harmless sort but Nola answers in monosyllables, Nola is rather tired from so many nights of partying with her friends, some of whom attend the local high school, some of whom are home for spring break from prep schools—Exeter, Lawrenceville, Concord, Andover, Portland. Late nights, but Mrs. Dietrich doesn't consciously lie awake waiting for Nola to come home: they've been through all that before. Now Nola sits beside her mother looking wan, subdued, rather melancholy. Thinking her private thoughts. She is wearing a bulky quilted jacket Mrs. Dietrich has never liked, the usual blue jeans, black calfskin boots zippered tightly to mid-calf. Mrs. Dietrich must resist the temptation to ask, "Why are you so quiet, Nola? What are you thinking?" They've been through all that before.

Route 12 has become a jumble of small industrial parks, high-rise office and apartment buildings, torn-up landscapes—mountains of raw earth, uprooted trees, ruts and ditches filled with muddy water. There is no natural sequence to what you see—buildings, construction work, leveled woods, the lavish grounds owned by Squibb. Though she has driven this route countless times, Mrs. Dietrich is never quite certain where the Mall is and must be prepared for a sudden exit. She remembers getting lost the first several times, remembers the excitement she and her friends felt about the grand opening of the Mall, stores worthy of serious shopping at last. Today is much the same. No, today is worse. Like Christmas when she was a small child, Mrs. Dietrich thinks. She'd hoped so badly to be happy she'd felt actual pain, a constriction in her throat like crying.

"*Are* you all right, Nola?—you've been so quiet all morning," Mrs. Dietrich asks, half-scolding. Nola stirs from her reverie, says she's fine, a just perceptible edge to her reply, and for the remainder of the drive there's some stiffness between them. Mrs. Dietrich chooses to ignore it. In any case she is fully absorbed in driving—negotiating a tricky exit across two lanes of traffic, then the hairpin curve of the ramp, the numerous looping drives of the Mall. Then the enormous parking lot, daunting to the inexperienced, but Mrs. Dietrich always heads for the area behind Lord & Taylor on the far side of the Mall, Lot D; her luck holds and she finds a space close in. "Well—we made it," she says, smiling happily at Nola. Nola laughs in reply—what does a seventeen-year-old's laughter *mean*?—but she remembers, getting out, to lock both doors on her side of the car. The smile Nola gives Mrs. Dietrich across the car's roof is careless and beautiful and takes Mrs. Dietrich's breath away.

The March morning tastes of grit with an undercurrent of something acrid, chemical; inside the Mall, beneath the first of the elegant brass-buttressed glass domes, the air is fresh and tonic, circulating from invisible vents. The Mall is crowded, rather noisy—it *is* Saturday morning—but a feast for the eyes after that long trip on Route 12. Tall slender trees grow out of the mosaic-tiled pavement, there are beds of Easter lilies, daffodils, jonquils, tulips of all colors. Mrs. Dietrich smiles with relief. She senses that Nola too is relieved, cheered. It's like coming home.

The shopping excursions began when Nola was a small child but did not acquire their special significance until she was twelve or thirteen years old and capable of serious, sustained shopping with her mother. This was about the time when Mr. Dietrich moved out of the house and back into their old apartment in the city—a separation, he'd called it initially, to give them perspective—though Mrs. Dietrich had no illusions about what "perspective" would turn out to entail—so the shopping grips were all the more significant. Not that Mrs. Dietrich and Nola spent very much money—they really didn't, *really* they didn't, when compared to friends and neighbors.

At seventeen Nola is shrewd and discerning as a shopper, not easy to please, knowledgeable as a mature woman about certain aspects of fashion, quality merchandise, good stores. Her closets, like Mrs. Dietrich's, are crammed, but she rarely buys anything that Mrs. Dietrich thinks shoddy or merely faddish. Up in Portland, at the Academy, she hasn't as much time to shop but when she is home in Livingstone it isn't unusual for her and her girlfriends to shop nearly every day. Like all her friends she has charge accounts at the better stores, her own credit cards, a reasonable allowance. At the time of their settlement Mr. Dietrich said guiltily that it was the least he could do for them—if Mrs. Dietrich wanted to work part-time, she could (she was trained, more or less, in public relations of a small-scale sort); if not, not. Mrs Dietrich thought, It's the most you can do for us too.

Near Bloomingdale's entrance mother and daughter see a disheveled woman sitting by herself on one of the benches. Without seeming to look at her, shoppers are making a discreet berth around her, a stream following a natural course. Nola, taken by surprise, stares. Mrs. Dietrich has seen the woman from time to time at the Mall, always alone, smirking and talking to herself, frizzed gray hair in a tangle, puckered mouth. Always wearing the same black wool coat, a garment of fairly good quality but shapeless, rumpled, stained, as if she sleeps in it. She might be anywhere from forty to sixty years of age. Once Mrs. Dietrich saw her make menacing gestures at children who were teasing her, another time she'd seen the woman staring belligerently at *her*. A white paste had gathered in the corners of her mouth. . . . "My God, that poor woman," Nola says. "I didn't think there were people like her here—I mean, I didn't think they would allow it."

"She doesn't seem to cause any disturbance," Mrs. Dietrich says. "She just sits—Don't stare, Nola, she'll see you."

"You've seen her here before? Here?"

"A few times this winter."

"Is she always like that?"

"I'm sure she's harmless, Nola. She just *sits*."

Nola is incensed, her pale blue eyes like washed glass. "I'm sure *she's* harmless, Mother. It's the harm the poor woman has to endure that is the tragedy."

Mrs. Dietrich is surprised and a little offended by her daughter's passionate tone but she knows enough not to argue. They enter Bloomingdale's, taking their habitual route. So many shoppers!—so much merchandise! Nola speaks of the tragedy of women like that woman—the tragedy of the homeless, the mentally disturbed—bag ladies out on the street—outcasts of an affluent society—but she's soon distracted by the busyness on all sides, the attractive items for sale. They take the escalator up to the third floor, to the Juniors department where Nola often buys things. From there they will on to Young Collector, then to New Impressions, then to Petites, then one or another boutique and designer—Liz Claiborne, Christian Dior, Calvin Klein, Carlos Falchi, and the rest. And after Bloomingdale's the other stores await, to be visited each in turn. Mrs. Dietrich checks her watch and sees with satisfaction that there's just enough time before lunch but not *too* much time. She gets ravenously hungry, shopping at the Mall.

Nola is efficient and matter-of-fact about shopping, though she acts solely upon instinct. Mrs. Dietrich likes to watch her at a short distance—holding items of clothing up to herself in the three-way mirrors, modeling things she thinks especially promising. A twill blazer with rounded shoulders and blouson jacket, a funky zippered jumpsuit in white sailcloth, a pair of straight-leg Evan-Picone pants, a green leather vest: Mrs. Dietrich watches her covertly. At such times Nola is perfectly content, fully absorbed in the task at hand; Mrs. Dietrich knows she isn't thinking about anything that would distress her. (Like Mr. Dietrich's betrayal. Like Nola's difficulties with her friends. Like her difficulties at school—as much as Mrs. Dietrich knows of them.) Once, at the Mall, perhaps in this very store in this very department, Nola saw Mrs. Dietrich watching her and walked away angrily and when Mrs. Dietrich caught up with her she said, "I can't stand it, Mother." Her voice was choked and harsh, a vein prominent in her forehead. "Let me go. For Christ's sake will you let me go." Mrs. Dietrich didn't dare touch her though she could see Nola was trembling. For a long terrible moment mother and daughter stood side by side near a display of bright brash Catalina beachwear while Nola whispered, "Let me go. *Let me go.*"

Difficult to believe that girl standing so poised and self-assured in front of the three-way mirror was once a plain, rather chunky, unhappy child. She'd been unpopular at school. Overly serious. Anxious. Quick to tears. Aged eleven she hid herself away in her room for hours at a time, reading, drawing pictures, writing little stories she could sometimes be prevailed upon to read aloud to her mother, sometimes even to her father, though she dreaded his judgment. She went through a "scientific" phase a while later—Mrs. Dietrich remembers an ambitious bas-relief map of North America, meticulous illustrations for "photosynthesis," a pastel drawing of an eerie ball of fire labeled "Red Giant" (a dying star?) which won a prize in a state competition for junior high students. Then for a season it was stray facts Nola confronted them with, often at the dinner table. Interrupting her parents' conversation to say brightly: "Did you know that Nero's favorite color was green?—he carried a giant emerald and held it up to his eye to watch Christians being devoured by lions." And once at a large family gathering: "Did you know that last week downtown a little baby's nose was chewed off by rats in his crib?—a little *black* baby?" Nola meant only to call attention to herself but you couldn't blame her listeners for being offended. They stared at her, not knowing what to say. What a strange child! What queer glassy-pale eyes! Mr. Dietrich told her curtly to leave the table—he'd had enough of the game she was playing and so had everyone else.

Nola stared at him, her eyes filling with tears. Game?

When they were alone Mr. Dietrich said angrily to Mrs. Dietrich: "Can't you control her in front of other people, at least?" Mrs. Dietrich was angry too, and frightened. She said "I *try.*"

They sent her off aged fourteen to the Portland Academy up in Maine and without their help she matured into a girl of considerable beauty. A heart-shaped face, delicate features, glossy red-brown hair scissor-cut to her shoulders. Five feet seven inches tall, weighing less than one hundred pounds—the result of constant savage dieting. (Mrs. Dietrich, who has weight problems herself, doesn't dare to inquire as to details. They've been through that already.) Thirty days after they'd left her at the Portland Academy Nola telephoned home at 11:00 P.M. one Sunday giggly and high telling Mrs. Dietrich she adored the school she adored her suite mates she adored most of her teachers particularly her riding instructor Terri, Terri the Terrier they called the woman because she was so fierce, such a character, eyes that bore right through your skull, wore belts with the most amazing silver buckles! Nola loved Terri but she wasn't *in* love—there's a difference!

Mrs. Dietrich broke down weeping, *that* time.

Now of course Nola has boyfriends. Mrs. Dietrich has long since given up trying to keep track of their names. There is even one "boy"—or young man—who seems to be married: who seems to be, in fact, one of the junior instructors at the school. (Mrs. Deitrich does not eavesdrop on her daughter's telephone conversations but there are things she cannot help overhearing.) Is your daughter on the Pill? the women in Mrs. Dietrich's circle asked one another for a while, guiltily, surreptitiously. Now they no longer ask.

But Nola has announced recently that she loathes boys—she's fed up.

She's never going to get married. She'll study languages in college, French, Italian, something exotic like Arabic, go to work for the American foreign service. Unless she drops out of school altogether to become a model.

"Do you think I'm fat, Mother?" she asks frequently, worriedly, standing in front of the mirror twisted at the waist to reveal her small round belly which, it seems, can't help being round: she bloats herself on diet Cokes all day long. "Do you think it *shows*?"

When Mrs. Dietrich was pregnant with Nola she'd been twenty-nine years old and she and Mr. Dietrich had tried to have a baby for nearly five years. She'd lost hope, begun to despise herself, then suddenly it happened: like grace. Like happiness swelling so powerfully it can barely be contained. I can hear its heartbeat! her husband exclaimed. He'd been her lover then, young, vigorous, dreamy. Caressing the rock-hard belly, splendid white tight-stretched skin. Mr. Dietrich gave Mrs. Dietrich a reproduction on stiff glossy paper of Dante Gabriel Rossetti's *Beata Beatrix*, embarrassed, apologetic, knowing it was sentimental and perhaps a little silly but that was how he thought of her—so beautiful, rapturous, pregnant with their child. She told no one but she knew the baby was to be a girl. It would be herself again, reborn and this time perfect.

"Oh, Mother—isn't it *beautiful*?" Nola exclaims.

It is past noon. Past twelve-thirty. Mrs. Dietrich and Nola have made the rounds of a half-dozen stores, traveled countless escalators, one clothing department has blended into the next and the chic smiling saleswomen have become indistinguishable and Mrs. Dietrich is beginning to feel the urgent need for a glass of white wine. Just a glass. "Isn't it beautiful?—it's *perfect*," Nola says. Her eyes glow with pleasure, her smooth skin is radiant. As Nola models in the three-way mirror a queer little yellow-and-black striped sweater with a ribbed waist, punk style, mock-cheap, Mrs. Dietrich feels the motherly obligation to register a mild protest, knowing that Nola will not hear. She must have it and will have it. She'll wear it a few times, then retire it to the bottom of a drawer with so many other novelty sweaters, accumulated since sixth grade. (She's like her mother in that regard—can't bear to throw anything away.)

"*Isn't* it beautiful?" Nola demands, studying her reflection in the mirror.

Mrs. Dietrich pays for the sweater on her charge account.

Next, they buy Nola a good pair of shoes. And a handbag to go with them. In Paraphernalia, where rock music blasts overhead and Mrs. Dietrich stands to one side, rather miserable, Nola chats companionably with two girls—tall, pretty, cutely made up—she'd gone to public school in Livingstone with, says afterward with an upward rolling of her eyes, "God, I was afraid they'd latch on to us!" Mrs. Dietrich has seen women friends and acquaintances of her own in the Mall this morning but has shrunk from being noticed, not wanting to share her daughter with anyone. She has a sense of time passing ever more swiftly, cruelly.

She watches Nola preening in a mirror, watches other shoppers watching her. My daughter. Mine. But of course there is no connection between them—they don't even resemble each other. A seventeen-year-old, a forty-seven-year-old. When Nola is away she seems to forget her mother entirely—doesn't telephone, certainly doesn't write. It's the way all their daughters are, Mrs. Dietrich's friends tell her. It doesn't *mean* anything. Mrs. Dietrich thinks how when she was carrying Nola, those nine long months, they'd been completely happy—not an instant's doubt or hesitation. The singular weight of the body. A trancelike state you are tempted to mistake for happiness because the body is incapable of thinking, therefore incapable of anticipating change. Hot rhythmic blood, organs, packed tight and moist, the baby upside down in her sac in her mother's belly, always present tense, always *now*. It was a shock when the end came so abruptly but everyone told Mrs. Dietrich she was a natural mother, praised and pampered her. For a while. Then of course she'd had her baby, her Nola. Even now Mrs. Dietrich can't really comprehend the experience. *Giving birth. Had a baby. Was born.* Mere words, absurdly inadequate. She knows no more of how love ends than she knew as a child, she knows only of how love begins—in the belly, in the womb, where it is always present tense.

The morning's shopping has been quite successful but lunch at La Crêperie doesn't go well for some reason. La Crêperie is Nola's favorite Mall restaurant—always amiably crowded, bustling, a simulated sidewalk café with red-striped umbrellas, wrought-iron tables and chairs, menus in French, music piped in overhead. Mrs. Dietrich's nerves are chafed by the pretense of gaiety, the noise, the openness onto one of the Mall's busy promenades where at any minute a familiar face might emerge, but she is grateful for her glass of chilled white wine. She orders a small tossed salad and a creamed-chicken crepe and devours it hungrily—she *is* hungry. While Nola picks at her seafood crepe with a disdainful look. A familiar scene: mother watching while daughter pushes food around on her plate. Suddenly Nola is tense, moody, corners of her mouth downturned. Mrs. Dietrich wants to ask, What's wrong? She wants to ask, Why are you unhappy? She wants to smooth Nola's hair back from her forehead, check to see if her forehead is overly warm, wants to hug her close, hard. Why, why? What did I do wrong? Why do you hate me?

Calling the Portland Academy a few weeks ago Mrs. Dietrich suddenly lost control, began crying. She hadn't been drinking and she hadn't known she was upset. A girl unknown to her, one of Nola's suite mates, was saying, "Please, Mrs. Dietrich, it's all right, I'm sure Nola will call you back later tonight, or tomorrow, Mrs. Dietrich?—I'll tell her you called, all right?— Mrs. Dietrich?" as embarrassed as if Mrs. Dietrich had been her own mother.

How love begins. How love ends.

Mrs. Dietrich orders a third glass of wine. This is a celebration of sorts isn't it?—their last shopping trip for a long time. But Nola resists, Nola isn't sentimental. In casual defiance of Mrs. Dietrich she lights up a cigarette—yes, Mother, Nola has said ironically, since *you* stopped smoking *everybody* is supposed to stop—and sits with her arms crossed, watching streams of shoppers pass. Mrs. Dietrich speaks lightly of practical matters, tomorrow morning's drive to the airport, and will Nola telephone when she gets to Portland to let Mrs. Dietrich know she has arrived safely?

Then with no warning—though of course she'd been planning this all along—Nola brings up the subject of a semester in France, in Paris and Rouen, the fall semester of her senior year it would be; she has put in her application, she says, and is waiting to hear if she's been accepted. She smokes her cigarette calmly, expelling smoke from her nostrils in a way Mrs. Dietrich thinks particularly coarse. Mrs. Dietrich, who believed that particular topic was finished, takes care to speak without emotion. "I just don't think it's a very practical idea right now, Nola," she says. "We've been through it haven't we? I—"

"I'm going," Nola says.

"The extra expense, for one thing. Your father—"

"If I get accepted, I'm going."

"Your father—"

"The hell with him too."

Mrs. Dietrich would like to slap her daughter's face. Bring tears to those steely eyes. But she sits stiff, turning her wine glass between her fingers, patient, calm, she's heard all this before; she says, "Surely this isn't the best time to discuss it, Nola."

Mrs. Dietrich is afraid her daughter will leave the restaurant, simply walk away, that has happened before and if it happens today she doesn't know what she will do. But Nola sits unmoving; her faced closed, impassive. Mrs. Dietrich feels her quickened heartbeat. Once after one of their quarrels Mrs. Dietrich told a friend of hers, the mother too of a teenage daughter, "I just don't know her any longer, how can you keep living with someone you don't know?" and the woman said, "Eventually you can't."

Nola says, not looking at Mrs. Dietrich: "Why don't we talk about it, Mother?"

"Talk about what?" Mrs. Dietrich asks.

"You know."

"The semester in France? Again?"

"No."

"What, then?"

"You *know*."

"I don't know, really. Really!" Mrs. Dietrich smiles, baffled. She feels the corners of her eyes pucker white with strain.

Nola says, sighing, "How exhausting it is."

"How *what*?"

"How exhausting it is."

"What is?"

"You and me—"

"What?"

"Being together—"

"Being together how—?"

"The two of us, like this—"

"But we're hardly ever together, Nola," Mrs. Dietrich says.

Her expression is calm but her voice is shaking. Nola turns away, covering her face with a hand, for a moment she looks years older than her age—in fact exhausted. Mrs. Dietrich sees with pity that her daughter's skin is fair and thin and dry—unlike her own, which tends to be oily—it will wear out before she's forty. Mrs. Dietrich reaches over to squeeze her hand. The fingers are limp, ungiving. "You're going back to school tomorrow, Nola," she says. "You won't come home again until June 12. And you probably will go to France—if your father consents."

Nola gets to her feet, drops her cigarette to the flagstone terrace and grinds it beneath her boot. A dirty thing to do, Mrs. Dietrich thinks, considering there's an ashtray right on the table, but she says nothing. She dislikes La Crêperie anyway.

Nola laughs, showing her lovely white teeth. "Oh, the hell with him," she says. "Fuck Daddy, right?"

They separate for an hour, Mrs. Dietrich to Neiman-Marcus to buy a birthday gift for her elderly aunt, Nola to the trendy new boutique Pour Vous. By the time Mrs. Dietrich rejoins her daughter she's quite angry, blood beating hot and hard and measured in resentment, she has had time to relive old quarrels between them, old exchanges, stray humiliating memories of her marriage as well, these last-hour disagreements are the cruelest and they are Nola's specialty. She locates Nola in the rear of the boutique amid blaring rock music, flashing neon lights, chrome-edged mirrors, her face still hard, closed, prim, pale. She stands beside another teenage girl looking in a desultory way through a rack of blouses, shoving the hangers roughly along, taking no care when a blouse falls to the floor. As Nola glances up, startled, not prepared to see her mother in front of her, their eyes lock for an instant and Mrs. Dietrich stares at her with hatred. Cold calm clear unmistakable hatred. She is thinking, Who are *you*? What have I to do with *you*? I don't know *you*, I don't love *you*, why should I?

Has Nola seen, heard?—she turns aside as if wincing, gives the blouses a final dismissive shove. Her eyes look tired, the corners of her mouth downturned. Anxious, immediately repentant, Mrs. Dietrich asks if she has found anything worth trying on. Nola says with a shrug, "Not a thing, Mother."

On their way out of the Mall Mrs. Dietrich and Nola see the disheveled woman in the black coat again, this time sitting prominently on a concrete ledge in front of Lord & Taylor's busy main entrance. Shopping bag at her feet, shabby purse on the ledge beside her. She is shaking her head in a series of annoyed twitches as if arguing with someone but her hands are loose, palms up, in her lap. Her posture is unfortunate—she sits with her knees parted, inner thighs revealed, fatty, dead white, the tops of cotton stockings rolled tight cutting into the flesh. Again, streams of shoppers are making a careful berth around her. Alone among them Nola hesitates, seems about to approach the woman—Please don't, Nola! please! Mrs. Dietrich thinks—then changes her mind and keeps on walking. Mrs. Dietrich murmurs isn't it a pity, poor thing, don't you wonder where she lives, who her family is, but Nola doesn't reply. Her pace through the first door of Lord & Taylor is so rapid that Mrs. Dietrich can barely keep up.

But Nola's upset. Strangely upset. As soon as they are in the car, packages and bags in the backseat, she begins crying.

It's childish helpless crying, as though her heart is broken. But Mrs. Dietrich knows it isn't broken, she had heard these very sobs before. Many times before. Still she comforts her daughter, embraces her, hugs her hard, hard. A sudden fierce passion. Vehemence. "Nola honey. Nola dear, what's wrong, dear, everything will be all right, dear," she says, close to weeping herself. She would embrace Nola even more tightly except for the girl's quilted jacket, that bulky L. L. Bean thing she has never liked, and Nola's stubborn lowered head. Nola has always been ashamed, crying, frantic to hide her face. Strangers are passing close by the car, curious, staring. Mrs. Dietrich wishes she had a cloak to draw over her daughter and herself, so that no one else would see.

SPECULATIONS

1.   Examine closely the first two paragraphs of this story—the abbreviated, choppy fragments in the opening sentences; the list of stores followed by "and the rest"; the daughter's name, "Nola," coupled with the choice of using "Mrs. Dietrich" to describe the mother; the parenthetical statement with its use of italicized words; the long sentences with their run-on clauses. How do these stylistic and structural choices by the author affect you as a reader? What do they tell you about Mrs. Dietrich and her daughter?

2.   We know that Joyce Carol Oates is the author of this story, but who is the speaker? That is, from whose point of view is the story told? What is gained by such a decision? What is lost?

3.   What is the implication of the statement:

> Mrs. Dietrich checks her watch and sees with satisfaction that there's just enough time before lunch but not *too* much time. She gets ravenously hungry, shopping at the Mall.

Why does Oates include the detail of a woman who becomes hungry while shopping? What is Oates saying about Mrs. Dietrich?

4.   Nola has a troubled relationship with her mother. How would you describe the problem, particularly in relation to their Mall experience? That is, although they go to the same Mall to shop, they respond differently to what they see. How would you describe those differences? Why do you think Oates set this story in a mall anyway?

5.   At the end of the story, Nola sees the disheveled woman in the black coat, hesitates, then walks quickly to the car. As Oates tell us: ". . . Nola's upset. Strangely upset. As soon as they are in the car, packages and bags in the backseat, she begins crying."

Why is she upset? What's bothering Nola? And what does Mrs. Dietrich's embarrassment tell us about her?

My Papa's Waltz
THEODORE ROETHKE

While professor of English at Michigan State University, Theodore Roethke wanted to encourage his students to describe physical action vividly. After telling them to describe what they were about to see, he crawled out a classroom window and inched himself along the ledge, making faces into each of the windows he passed. One can only imagine the shocked faces of the students inside. The story illustrates some of Roethke's essential qualities: his devotion to teaching, his willingness to be outrageous and to take risks, his precarious stance somewhere between security and catastrophe.

Roethke could also surprise readers with his poetry. "The Greenhouse Poems," probe the darkness of his childhood as the son of a greenhouse owner. His poems frequently depict the pain of growing up, of loneliness, of struggling to achieve some kind of love and self-affirmation. Such peace was to elude Roethke, however, even after he became a distinguished Professor of English and Creative Writing at the University of Washington beginning in 1947. Roethke suffered numerous emotional breakdowns over the years, but he continued to teach and to write throughout his life until his untimely death of a heart attack in 1963.

The poem included here, "My Papa's Waltz," expresses the ambivalent feelings in many father–son relationships.

The whiskey on your breath
Could make a small boy dizzy;
But I hung on like death:
Such waltzing was not easy.

We romped until the pans
Slid from the kitchen shelf;
My mother's countenance
Could not unfrown itself.

The hand that held my wrist
Was battered on one knuckle;
At every step you missed
My right ear scraped a buckle.

You beat time on my head
With a palm caked hard by dirt,
Then waltzed me off to bed
Still clinging to your shirt.

SPECULATIONS

1. Why do you think Roethke titles this poem a "waltz" and not some other kind of dance? What details and use of language create a feeling of a waltz? What details contradict that impression?

2. How would you describe the relationship between the young boy and his father? the young boy and his mother?

3. How old do you think Roethke was when he wrote this poem?

Under the Influence: Paying the Price of My Father's Booze

SCOTT RUSSELL SANDERS

A thumbnail sketch of Scott Russell Sanders might well include the organizations which he belongs to: Friends of the Earth, Sierra Club, Society of Friends, Science Fiction Writers of America, Phi Beta Kappa. He also is a family man with two children; a writer of essays, stories, and novels; and a professor of English at the University of Indiana. Concerning his writing, Sanders has stated to *Contemporary Authors*:

> I am concerned with the ways in which human beings come to terms with the practical problems of living on a small planet, in nature and in communities. I am concerned with the life people make together, in marriages and families and towns, more than with the life of isolated individuals.

Born in Memphis, Tennessee, in 1945, Sanders holds a Ph.D. from Cambridge University (England). His published work includes *Wilderness Plots: Tales about the Settlement of the American Land* (1983), *Fetching the Dead* (1984), *Stone Country* (1985), and *Paradise of Bombs* (1987). In the latter book, in an essay entitled "Inheritance of Tools," Sanders evokes a loving portrait of his father as a master workman who taught his small son how to hammer, saw, and work with wood:

> Looming as huge as a colossus, my father worked over and around me, now and again bending down to inspect my work, careful not to trample my creations. It was a landscape that smelled dizzyingly of wood. Even after a bath my skin would carry the smell, and so would my father's hair, when he lifted me for a bedtime hug.

A much more disturbing view emerges from "Under the Influence," an essay Sanders published two years later in *Harper's Magazine*.

My father drank. He drank as a gut-punched boxer gasps for breath, as a starving dog gobbles food—compulsively, secretly, in pain and trembling. I use the past tense not because he ever quit drinking but because he quit living. That is how the story ends for my father, age sixty-four, heart bursting, body cooling, slumped and forsaken on the linoleum of my brother's trailer. The story continues for my brother, my sister, my mother, and me, and will continue as long as memory holds.

In the perennial present of memory, I slip into the garage or barn to see my father tipping back the flat green bottles of wine, the brown cylinders of whiskey, the cans of beer disguised in paper bags. His

Adam's apple bobs, the liquid gurgles, he wipes the sandy-haired back of a hand over his lips, and then, his bloodshot gaze bumping into me, he stashes the bottle or can inside his jacket, under the workbench, between two bales of hay, and we both pretend the moment has not occurred.

"What's up, buddy?" he says, thick-tongued and edgy.

"Sky's up," I answer, playing along.

"And don't forget prices," he grumbles. "Prices are always up. And taxes."

In memory, his white 1951 Pontiac with the stripes down the hood and the Indian head on the snout lurches to a stop in the driveway; or it is the 1956 Ford station wagon, or the 1963 Rambler shaped like a toad, or the sleek 1969 Bonneville that will do 120 miles per hour on straightaways; or it is the robin's-egg-blue pickup, new in 1980, battered in 1981, the year of his death. He climbs out, grinning dangerously, unsteady on his legs, and we children interrupt our game of catch, our building of snow forts, our picking of plums, to watch in silence as he weaves past us into the house, where he drops into his overstuffed chair and falls asleep. Shaking her head, our mother stubs out a cigarette he has left smoldering in the ashtray. All evening, until our bedtimes, we tiptoe past him, as past a snoring dragon. Then we curl fearfully in our sheets, listening. Eventually he wakes with a grunt, Mother slings accusations at him, he snarls back, she yells, he growls, their voices clashing. Before long, she retreats to their bedroom, sobbing—not from the blows of fists, for he never strikes her, but from the force of his words.

Left alone, our father prowls the house, thumping into furniture, rummaging in the kitchen, slamming doors, turning the pages of the newspaper with a savage crackle, muttering back at the late-night drivel from television. The roof might fly off, the walls might buckle from the pressure of his rage. Whatever my brother and sister and mother may be thinking on their own rumpled pillows, I lie there hating him, loving him, fearing him, knowing I have failed him. I tell myself he drinks to ease the ache that gnaws at his belly, an ache I must have caused by disappointing him somehow, a murderous ache I should be able to relieve by doing all my chores, earning A's in school, winning baseball games, fixing the broken washer and the burst pipes, bringing in the money to fill his empty wallet. He would not hide the green bottles in his toolbox, would not sneak off to the barn with a lump under his coat, would not roar and fume, would not drink himself to death, if only I were perfect.

I am forty-four, and I know full well now that my father was an alcoholic, a man consumed by disease rather than by disappointment. What had seemed to me a private grief is in fact, of course, a public scourge. In the United States alone, some ten or fifteen million people share his ailment, and behind the doors they slam in fury or disgrace, countless other children tremble. I comfort myself with such knowledge, holding it against the throb of memory like an ice pack against a bruise. Other people have keener sources of grief: poverty, racism, rape, war. I do not wish to compete to determine who has suffered most. I am only trying to understand the corrosive mixture of helplessness, responsibility, and shame that I learned to feel as the son of an alcoholic. I realize now that I did not cause my father's illness, nor could I have cured it. Yet for all this grown-up knowledge, I am still ten years old, my own son's age, and as that boy I struggle in guilt and confusion to save my father from pain.

Consider a few of our synonyms for *drunk*: tipsy, tight, pickled, soused, and plowed; stoned and stewed, lubricated and inebriated, juiced and sluiced; three sheets to the wind, in your cups, out of your mind, under the table; lit up, tanked up, wiped out; besotted, blotto, bombed, and buzzed; plastered, polluted, putrefied; loaded or looped, boozy, woozy, fuddled, or smashed; crocked and shit-faced, corked and pissed, snockered and sloshed.

It is a mostly humorous lexicon, as the lore that deals with drunks—in jokes and cartoons, in plays, films, and television skits—is largely comic. Aunt Matilda nips elderberry wine from the sideboard and burps politely during supper. Uncle Fred slouches to the table glassy-eyed, wearing a lampshade for a hat and murmuring, "Candy is dandy, but liquor is quicker." Inspired by cocktails, Mrs. Somebody recounts the events of her day in a fuzzy dialect, while Mr. Somebody nibbles her ear and croons a bawdy song. On the sofa with Boyfriend, Daughter Somebody giggles, licking gin from her lips, and loosens the bows in her hair. Junior knocks back some brews with his chums at the Leopard Lounge and stumbles home to the wrong house, wonders foggily why he cannot locate his pajamas, and crawls naked into bed with the ugliest girl in school. The family dog slurps from a neglected martini and wobbles to the nursery, where he vomits in Baby's shoe.

It is all great fun. But if in the audience you notice a few laughing faces turn grim when the drunk lurches on-stage, don't be surprised, for these are the children of alcoholics. Over the grinning mask of Dionysus, the leering face of Bacchus, these children cannot help seeing the bloated features of their own parents. Instead of laughing, they wince, they mourn. Instead of celebrating the drunk as one freed from constraints, they pity him as one enslaved. They refuse to believe *in vino veritas*, having seen their befuddled parents skid away from truth toward folly and oblivion. And so these children bite their lips until the lush staggers into the wings.

My father, when drunk, was neither funny nor honest; he was pathetic, frightening, deceitful. There seemed to be a leak in him somewhere, and he poured in booze to keep from draining dry. Like a torture victim who refuses to squeal, he would never admit that he had touched a drop, not even in his last year, when he seemed to be dissolving in alcohol before our very eyes. I never knew him to lie about anything, ever, except about this one ruinous fact. Drowsy, clumsy, unable to fix a bicycle tire, balance a grocery sack, or walk across a room, he was stripped of his true self by drink. In a matter of minutes, the contents of a bottle could transform a brave man into a coward, a buddy into a bully, a gifted athlete and skilled carpenter and shrewd businessman into a bumbler. No dictionary of synonyms for *drunk* would soften the anguish of watching our prince turn into a frog.

Father's drinking became the family secret. While growing up, we children never breathed a word of it beyond the four walls of our house. To this day, my brother and sister rarely mention it, and then only when I press them. I did not confess the ugly, bewildering fact to my wife until his wavering and slurred speech forced me to. Recently, on the seventh anniversary of my father's death, I asked my mother if she ever spoke of his drinking to friends. "No, no, never," she replied hastily. "I couldn't bear for anyone to know."

The secret bores under the skin, gets in the blood, into the bone, and stays there. Long after you have supposedly been cured of malaria, the fever can flare up, the tremors can shake you. So it is with the fevers of shame. You swallow the bitter quinine of knowledge, and you learn to feel pity and compassion toward the drinker. Yet the shame lingers and, because of it, anger.

For a long stretch of my childhood we lived on a military reservation in Ohio, an arsenal where bombs were stored underground in bunkers and vintage airplanes burst into flames and unstable artillery shells boomed nightly at the dump. We had the feeling, as children, that we played within a minefield, where a heedless footfall could trigger an explosion. When Father was drinking, the house, too, became a minefield. The least bump could set off either parent.

The more he drank, the more obsessed Mother became with stopping him. She hunted for bottles, counted the cash in his wallet, sniffed at his breath. Without meaning to snoop, we children blundered left and right into damning evidence. On afternoons when he came home from work sober, we flung ourselves at him for hugs and felt against our ribs the telltale lump in his coat. In the barn we tumbled on the hay and heard beneath our sneakers the crunch of broken glass. We tugged open a drawer in his workbench, looking for screwdrivers or crescent wrenches, and spied a gleaming six-pack among the tools. Playing tag, we darted around the house just in time to see him sway on the rear stoop and heave a finished bottle into the woods. In his good-night kiss we smelled the cloying sweetness of Clorets, the mints he chewed to camouflage his dragon's breath.

I can summon up that kiss right now by recalling Theodore Roethke's lines about his own father:

> The whiskey on your breath
> Could make a small boy dizzy;
> But I hung on like death:
> Such waltzing was not easy

Such waltzing was hard, terribly hard, for with a boy's scrawny arms I was trying to hold my tipsy father upright.

For years, the chief source of those incriminating bottles and cans was a grimy store a mile from us, a cinder-block place called Sly's, with two gas pumps outside and a mangy dog asleep in the window. Inside, on rusty metal shelves or in wheezing coolers, you could find pop and Popsicles, cigarettes, potato chips, canned soup, raunchy postcards, fishing gear, Twinkies, wine, and beer. When Father drove anywhere on errands, Mother would send us along as guards, warning us not to let him out of our sight. And so with one or more of us on board, Father would cruise up to Sly's, pump a dollar's worth of gas or plump the tires with air, and then, telling us to wait in the car, he would head for the doorway.

Dutiful and panicky, we cried, "Let us go with you!"

"No," he answered. "I'll be back in two shakes.'

"Please!"

"No!" he roared. "don't you budge or I'll jerk a knot in your tails!"

So we stayed put, kicking the seats, while he ducked inside. Often, when he had parked the car at a careless angle, we gazed in through the window and saw Mr. Sly fetching down from the shelf behind the cash register two green pints of Gallo wine. Father swigged one of them right there at the counter, stuffed the other in his pocket, and then out he came, a bulge in his coat, a flustered look on his reddened face.

Because the mom and pop who ran the dump were neighbors of ours, living just down the tar-blistered road, I hated them all the more for poisoning my father. I wanted to sneak in their store and smash the bottles and set fire to the place. I also hated the Gallo brothers, Ernest and Julio, whose jovial faces beamed from the labels of their wine, labels I would find, torn and curled, when I burned the trash.

I noted the Gallo brothers' address in California and studied the road atlas to see how far that was from Ohio, because I meant to go out there and tell Ernest and Julio what they were doing to my father, and then, if they showed no mercy, I would kill them.

While growing up on the back roads and in the country schools and cramped Methodist churches of Ohio and Tennessee, I never heard the word *alcoholic*, never happened across it in books or magazines. In the nearby towns, there were no addiction-treatment programs, no community mental-health centers, no Alcoholics Anonymous chapters, no therapists. Left alone with our grievous secret, we had no way of understanding Father's drinking except as an act of will, a deliberate folly or cruelty, a moral weakness, a sin. He drank because he chose to, pure and simple. Why our father, so playful and competent and kind when sober, would choose to ruin himself and punish his family we could not fathom.

Our neighborhood was high on the Bible, and the Bible was hard on drunkards. "Woe to those who are heroes at drinking wine and valiant men in mixing strong drink," wrote Isaiah. "The priest and the prophet reel with strong drink, they are confused with wine, they err in vision, they stumble in giving judgment. For all tables are full of vomit, no place is without filthiness." We children had seen those fouled tables at the local truck stop where the notorious boozers hung out, our father occasionally among them. "Wine and new wine take away the understanding," declared the prophet Hosea. We had also seen evidence of that in our father, who could multiply seven-digit numbers in his head when sober but when drunk could not help us with fourth-grade math. Proverbs warned: "Do not look at wine when it is red, when it sparkles in the cup and goes down smoothly. At the last it bites like a serpent and stings like an adder. Your eyes will see strange things, and your mind utter perverse things." Woe, woe.

Dismayingly often, these biblical drunkards stirred up trouble for their own kids. Noah made fresh wine after the flood, drank too much of it, fell asleep without any clothes on, and was glimpsed in the buff by his son Ham, whom Noah promptly cursed. In one passage—it was so shocking we had to read it under our blankets with flashlights—the patriarch Lot fell down drunk and slept with his daughters. The sins of the fathers set their children's teeth on edge.

Our ministers were fond of quoting St. Paul's pronouncement that drunkards would not inherit the kingdom of God. These grave preachers assured us that the wine referred to in the Last Supper was in fact grape juice. Bible and sermons and hymns combined to give us the impression that Moses should have brought down from the mountain another stone tablet, bearing the Eleventh Commandment: Thou shalt not drink.

The scariest and most illuminating Bible story apropos of drunkards was the one about the lunatic and the swine. We knew it by heart: When Jesus climbed out of his boat one day, this lunatic came charging up from the graveyard, stark naked and filthy, frothing at the mouth, so violent that he broke the strongest chains. Nobody would go near him. Night and day for years, this madman had been wailing among the tombs and bruising himself with stones. Jesus took one look at him and said, "Come out of the man, you unclean spirits!" for he could see that the lunatic was possessed by demons. Meanwhile, some hogs were conveniently rooting nearby. "If we have to come out," begged the demons, "at least let us go into those swine." Jesus agreed, the unclean spirits entered the hogs, and the hogs raced straight off a cliff and plunged into a lake. Hearing the story in Sunday school, my friends thought mainly of the pigs. (How big a splash did they make? Who paid for the lost pork?) But I thought of the redeemed lunatic, who bathed himself and put on clothes and calmly sat at the feet of Jesus, restored—so the Bible said—to "his right mind."

When drunk, our father was clearly in his wrong mind. He became a stranger, as fearful to us as any graveyard lunatic, not quite frothing at the mouth but fierce enough, quick-tempered, explosive; or else he grew maudlin and weepy, which frightened us nearly as much. In my boyhood despair, I reasoned that maybe he wasn't to blame for turning into an ogre: Maybe, like the lunatic, he was possessed by demons.

If my father was indeed possessed, who would exorcise him? If he was a sinner, who would save him? If he was ill, who would cure him? If he suffered, who would ease his pain? Not ministers or doctors, for we could not bring ourselves to confide in them; not the neighbors, for we pretended they had never seen him drunk; not Mother, who fussed and pleaded but could not budge him; not my brother and sister, who were only kids. That left me. It did not matter that I, too, was only a child, and a bewildered one at that. I could not excuse myself.

On first reading a description of delirium tremens—in a book on alcoholism I smuggled from a university library—I thought immediately of the frothing lunatic and the frenzied swine. When I read stories or watched films about grisly metamorphoses—Dr. Jekyll becoming Mr. Hyde, the mild husband changing into a werewolf, the kindly neighbor inhabited by a brutal alien—I could not help but see my own father's mutation from sober to drunk. Even today, knowing better, I am attracted by the demonic theory of drink, for when I recall my father's transformation, the emergence of his ugly second self, I find it easy to believe in being possessed by unclean spirits. We never knew which version of Father would come home from work, the true or the tainted, nor could we guess how far down the slope toward cruelty he would slide.

How far a man *could* slide we gauged by observing our back-road neighbors—the out-of-work miners who had dragged their families to our corner of Ohio from the desolate hollows of Appalachia, the tightfisted farmers, the surly mechanics, the balked and broken men. There was, for example, whiskey-soaked Mr. Jenkins, who beat his wife and kids so hard we could hear their screams from the road. There was Mr. Lavo the wino, who fell asleep smoking time and again, until one night his disgusted wife bundled up the children and went outside and left him in his easy chair to burn; he awoke on his own, staggered out coughing into the yard, and pounded her flat while the children looked on and the shack turned to ash. There was the truck driver, Mr. Sampson, who tripped over his son's tricycle one night while drunk and got mad, jumped into his semi, and drove away, shifting through the dozen gears, and never came back. We saw the bruised children of these fathers clump onto our school bus, we saw the abandoned children huddle in the pews at church, we saw the stunned and battered mothers begging for help at our doors.

Our own father never beat us, and I don't think he beat Mother, but he threatened often. The Old Testament Yahweh was not more terrible in His rage. Eyes blazing, voice booming, Father would pull out his belt and swear to give us a whipping, but he never followed through, never needed to, because we could imagine it so vividly. He shoved us, pawed us with the back of his hand, not to injure, just to clear a space. I can see him grabbing Mother by the hair as she cowers on a chair during a nightly quarrel. He twists her neck back until she gapes up at him, and then he lifts over her skull a glass quart bottle of milk, the milk spilling down his forearm, and he yells at her, "Say just one more word, one goddam word, and I'll shut you up!" I fear she will prick him with her sharp tongue, but she is terrified into silence, and so am I, and the leaking bottle quivers in the air, and milk seeps through the red hair of my father's uplifted arm, and the entire scene is there to this moment, the head jerked back, the club raised.

When the drink made him weepy, Father would pack, kiss each of us children on the head, and announce from the front door that he was moving out. "Where to?" we demanded, fearful each time that he would leave for good, as Mr. Simpson had roared away for good in his diesel truck. "Someplace where I won't get hounded every minute," Father would answer, his jaw quivering. He stabbed a look at Mother, who might say, "Don't run into the ditch before you get there," or "good riddance," and then he would slink away. Mother watched him go with arms crossed over her chest, her face closed like the lid on a box of snakes. We children bawled. Where could he go? To the truck stop, that den of iniquity? To one of those dark, ratty flophouses in town? Would he wind up sleeping under a railroad bridge or on a park bench or in a cardboard box, mummied in rags like the bums we had seen on our trips to Cleveland and Chicago? We bawled and bawled, wondering if he would ever come back.

He always did come back, a day or a week later, but each time there was a sliver less of him.

In Kafka's *Metamorphosis*, which opens famously with Gregor Samsa waking up from uneasy dreams to find himself transformed into an insect, Gregor's family keep reassuring themselves that things will be just fine again "when he comes back to us." Each time alcohol transformed our father we held out the same hope, that he would really and truly come back to us, our authentic father, the tender and playful and competent man, and then all things would be fine. We had grounds for such hope. After his tearful departures and chapfallen returns, he would sometimes go weeks, even months, without drinking. Those were glad times. Every day without the furtive glint of bottles, every meal without a fight, every bedtime without sobs encouraged us to believe that such bliss might go on forever.

Mother was fooled by such a hope all during the forty-odd years she knew Greeley Ray Sanders. Soon after she met him in a Chicago delicatessen on the eve of World War II and fell for his butter-melting Mississippi drawl and his wavy red hair, she learned that he drank heavily. But then so did a lot of men. She would soon coax or scold him into breaking the nasty habit. she would point out to him how ugly and foolish it was, this bleary drinking, and then he would quit. He refused to quit during their engagement, however, still refused during the first years of marriage, refused until my older sister came along. The shock of fatherhood sobered him, and he remained sober through my birth at the end of the war and right on through until we moved in 1951 to the Ohio arsenal. The arsenal had more than its share of alcoholics, drug addicts, and other varieties of escape artists. There I turned six and started school and woke into a child's flickering awareness, just in time to see my father begin sneaking swigs in the garage.

He sobered up again for most of a year at the height of the Korean War, to celebrate the birth of my brother. But aside from that dry spell, his only breaks from drinking before I graduated from high school were just long enough to raise and then dash our hopes. Then during the fall of my senior year—the time of the Cuban Missile Crisis, when it seemed that the nightly explosions at the munitions dump and the nightly rages in our household might spread to engulf the globe—Father collapsed. His liver, kidneys, and heart all conked out. The doctors saved him, but only by a hair. He stayed in the hospital for weeks, going through a withdrawal so terrible that Mother would not let us visit him. If he wanted to kill himself, the doctors solemnly warned him, all he had to do was hit the bottle again. One binge would finish him.

Father must have believed them, for he stayed dry the next fifteen years. It was an answer to prayer, Mother said, it was a miracle. I believe it was a reflex of fear, which he sustained over the years through courage and pride. He knew a man could die from drink, for his brother Roscoe had. We children never laid eyes on doomed Uncle Roscoe, but in the stories Mother told us he became a fairy-tale figure, like a boy who took the wrong turn in the woods and was gobbled up by the wolf.

The fifteen-year dry spell came to an end with Father's retirement in the spring of 1978. Like many men, he gave up his identity along with his job. One day he was a boss at the factory, with a brass plate on his door and a reputation to uphold; the next day he was a nobody at home. He and Mother were leaving Ontario, the last of the many places to which his job had carried them, and they were moving to a new house in Mississippi, his childhood stomping ground. As a boy in Mississippi, Father sold Coca-Cola during dances while the moonshiners peddled their brew in the parking lot; as a young blade, he fought in bars and in the ring, winning a state Golden Gloves championship; he gambled at poker, hunted pheasant, raced motorcycles and cars, played semiprofessional baseball, and, along with all his buddies—in the Black Cat Saloon, behind the cotton gin, in the woods—he drank hard. It was a perilous youth to dream of recovering.

After his final day of work, Mother drove on ahead with a car full of begonias and violets, while Father stayed behind to oversee the packing. When the van was loaded, the sweaty movers broke open a six-pack and offered him a beer.

"Let's drink to retirement!" they crowed. "Let's drink to freedom! to fishing! hunting! loafing! Let's drink to a guy who's going home!"

At least I imagine some such words, for that is all I can do, imagine, and I see Father's hand trembling in midair as he thinks about the fifteen sober years and about the doctors' warning, and he tells himself, *Goddamnit, I am a free man,* and *Why can't a free man drink one beer after a lifetime of hard work?* and I see his arm reaching, his fingers closing, the can tilting to his lips. I even supply a label for the beer, a swaggering brand that promises on television to deliver the essence of life. I watch the amber liquid pour down his throat, the alcohol steal into his blood, the key turn in his brain.

Soon after my parents moved back to Father's treacherous stomping ground, my wife and I visited them in Mississippi with our four-year-old daughter. Mother had been too distraught to warn me about the return of the demons. So when I climbed out of the car that bright July morning and saw my father napping in the hammock, I felt uneasy, and when he lurched upright and blinked his bloodshot eyes and greeted us in a syrupy voice, I was hurled back into childhood.

"What's the matter with Papaw?" our daughter asked.

"Nothing," I said. "Nothing!"

Like a child again, I pretended not to see him in his stupor, and behind my phony smile I grieved. On that visit and on the few that remained before his death, once again I found bottles in the workbench, bottles in the woods. Again his hands shook too much for him to run a saw, to make his precious miniature furniture, to drive straight down back roads. Again he wound up in the ditch, in the hospital, in jail, in the treatment center. Again he shouted and wept. Again he lied. "I never touched a drop," he swore. "Your mother's making it up."

I no longer fancied I could reason with the men whose names I found on the bottles—Jim Beam, Jack Daniel's—but I was able now to recall the cold statistics about alcoholism: ten million victims, fifteen million, twenty. And yet, in spite of my age, I reacted in the same blind way as I had in childhood, by vainly seeking to erase through my efforts whatever drove him to drink. I worked on their place twelve and sixteen hours a day, in the swelter of Mississippi summers, digging ditches, running electrical wires, planting trees, mowing grass, building sheds, as though what nagged at him was some list of chores, as though by taking his worries upon my shoulders I could redeem him. I was flung back into boyhood, acting as though my father would not drink himself to death if only I were perfect.

I failed of perfection; he succeeded in dying. To the end, he considered himself not sick but sinful. "Do you want to kill yourself?" I asked him. "Why not?" he answered. "Why the hell not? What's there to save?" To the end, he would not speak about his feelings, would not or could not give a name to the beast that was devouring him.

In silence, he went rushing off the cliff. Unlike the biblical swine, however, he left behind a few of the demons to haunt his children. Life with him and the loss of him twisted us into shapes that will be familiar to other sons and daughters of alcoholics. My brother became a rebel, my sister retreated into shyness, I played the stalwart and dutiful son who would hold the family together. If my father was unstable, I would be a rock. If he squandered money on drink, I would pinch every penny. If he wept when drunk—and only when drunk—I would not let myself weep at all. If he roared at the Little League umpire for calling my pitches balls, I would throw nothing but strikes. Watching him flounder and rage, I came to dread the loss of control. I would go through life without making anyone mad. I vowed never to put in my mouth or veins any chemical that would banish my everyday self. I would never make a scene, never lash out at the ones I loved, never hurt a soul. Through hard work, relentless work, I would achieve something dazzling—in the classroom, on the basketball court, in the science lab, in the pages of books—and my achievement would distract the world's eyes from his humiliation. I would become a worthy sacrifice, and the smoke of my burning would please God.

It is far easier to recognize these twists in my character than to undo them. Work has become an addiction for me, as drink was an addiction for my father. Knowing this, my daughter gave me a placard for the wall: WORKAHOLIC. The labor is endless and futile, for I can no more redeem myself through work than I could redeem my father. I still panic in the face of other people's anger, because his drunken temper was so terrible. I shrink from causing sadness or disappointment even to strangers, as though I were still concealing the family shame. I still notice every twitch of emotion in those faces around me, having learned as a child to read the weather in faces, and I blame myself for their least pang of unhappiness or anger. In certain moods I blame myself for everything. Guilt burns like acid in my veins.

I am moved to write these pages now because my own son, at the age of ten, is taking on himself the griefs of the world, and in particular the griefs of his father. He tells me that when I am gripped by sadness, he feels responsible; he feels there must be something he can do to spring me from depression, to fix my life. And that crushing sense of responsibility is exactly what I felt at the age of ten in the face of my father's drinking. My son wonders if I, too, am possessed. I write, therefore, to drag into the light what eats at me—the fear, the guilt, the shame—so that my own children may be spared.

I still shy away from nightclubs, from bars, from parties where the solvent is alcohol. My friends puzzle over this, but it is no more peculiar than for a man to shy away from the lions' den after seeing his father torn apart. I took my own first drink at the age of twenty-one, half a glass of burgundy. I knew the odds of my becoming an alcoholic were four times higher than for the children of nonalcoholic fathers. So I sipped warily.

I still do—once a week, perhaps, a glass of wine, a can of beer, nothing stronger, nothing more. I listen for the turning of a key in my brain.

SPECULATIONS

1.   Sanders chooses to begin this essay with the straightforward statement:

> My father drank. He drank as a gut-punched boxer gasps for breath, as a starving dog gobbles food—compulsively, secretly, in pain and trembling.

What effect does such a strong opening have on the reader? Why do you think Sanders chooses to open in this dramatic fashion?

2.   Sanders states that he is "still ten years old, my own son's age, and as that boy I struggle in guilt and confusion to save my father from pain." What does he mean by saying that he is "ten years old"? Why is it significant that his son is also ten years old?

3.   Sanders' essay makes us reconsider our own relation to drinking. How would you describe your own values in regard to the consumption of alcohol? Does drinking make you feel mature, depressed, foolish, elated, excited? Why do you drink—or why do you not—and how do your actions affect those around you?

4.   As Sanders points out, alcoholics tend to be figures of humor and good cheer in our culture. What do you think of that idea? Do you think that the values of our culture encourage alcoholism?

5.   In another essay by Sanders about his father, he describes a certain kind of "inheritance" from his father. What kind of inheritance has he received from his father according to this essay?

Beauty: When the Other Dancer Is the Self

ALICE WALKER

"I have come to understand my work as prayer," Alice Walker has said, and a strong spiritual element illumines virtually all of her poetry, fiction, and essays. Perhaps her common theme is the search for a love that transcends race, gender, and societal prejudices, a love that ultimately includes a sense of one's intense and personal relation to all living beings, human and nonhuman, that make up our planet.

This is not to say that Walker's work lacks anger and outrage. Her novel *The Color Purple*, for which she won the Pulitzer Prize and the American Book Award, emphasizes the cruel and oppressive nature of the relationship between men, black men in particular, and black women. Walker has stated, "The cruelty of the black man to his wife and family is one of the greatest [American] tragedies. It has mutiliated the spirit and body of the black family and of most black mothers." Although attacked for her anti-male views, Walker clearly believes in the powers of reformation and redemption, for men and women of all races.

Born in Eatonton, Georgia, in 1944, Walker has written about her childhood frequently in essays like "Beauty: When the Other Dancer is the Self." After attending Spelman College and graduating from Sarah Lawrence with a B.A., Walker for many years dedicated herself to the civil rights movement and social causes—serving as a voter registration worker in Georgia, a Head Start worker in Mississippi, and a welfare worker in New York City. She is almost singlehandedly responsible for resurrecting the work of another great black woman writer, Zora Neale Hurston.

Walker's published works include *Once: Poems* (1968), *You Can't Keep a Good Woman Down* (1981) and *The Color Purple* (1982), *In Search of Our Mother' Gardens: Womanist Prose* (1983), *Living by the Word* (1988), and *Possessing the Secret of Joy* (1992).

In a letter to an imaginary black woman named Joanna (*Living by the Word*), Walker wrote:

> Inner beauty, an irrepressible music, certainly courage to say No or Yes, dedication to one's own Gods, affection for one's own spirit(s), a simplicity of approach to life, will survive all of us, through your own will.
>
> You are, perhaps, the last unconquered resident on this earth. And must live, in any case, as if it *must* be so.

She explores a similar theme in the following essay.

It is a bright summer day in 1947. My father, a fat, funny man with beautiful eyes and a subversive wit, is trying to decide which of his eight children he will take with him to the county fair. My mother, of course, will not go. She is knocked out from getting most of us ready: I hold my neck stiff against the pressure of her knuckles as she hastily completes the braiding and then beribboning of my hair.

My father is the driver for the rich old white lady up the road. Her name is Miss Mey. She owns all the land for miles around, as well as the house in which we live. All I remember about her is that she once offered to pay my mother thirty-five cents for cleaning her house, raking up piles of her magnolia leaves, and washing her family's clothes, and that my mother—she of no money, eight children, and a chronic earache—refused it. But I do not think of this in 1947. I am two and a half years old. I want to go everywhere my daddy goes. I am excited at the prospect of riding in a car. Someone has told me fairs are fun. That there is room in the car for only three of us doesn't faze me at all. Whirling happily in my starchy frock, showing off my biscuit-polished patent-leather shoes and lavender socks, tossing my head in a way that makes my ribbons bounce, I stand, hands on hips, before my father. "Take me, Daddy," I say with assurance; "I'm the prettiest!"

Later, it does not surprise me to find myself in Miss Mey's shiny black car, sharing the back seat with the other lucky ones. Does not surprise me that I thoroughly enjoy the fair. At home that night I tell the unlucky ones all I can remember about the merry-go-round, the man who eats live chickens, and the teddy bears, until they say: that's enough, baby Alice. Shut up now, and go to sleep.

It is Easter Sunday, 1950. I am dressed in a green, flocked, scalloped-hem dress (handmade by my adoring sister, Ruth) that has its own smooth satin petticoat and tiny hot-pink roses tucked into each scallop. My shoes, new T-strap patent leather, again highly biscuit-polished. I am six years old and have learned one of the longest Easter speeches to be heard that day, totally unlike the speech I said when I was two: "Easter lilies / pure and white / blossom in / the morning light." When I rise to give my speech I do so on a great wave of love and pride and expectation. People in the church stop rustling their new crinolines. They seem to hold their breath. I can tell they admire my dress, but it is my spirit, bordering on sassiness (womanishness), they secretly applaud.

"That girl's a little *mess*," they whisper to each other, pleased.

Naturally I say my speech without stammer or pause, unlike those who stutter, stammer, or, worst of all, forget. This is before the word "beautiful" exists in people's vocabulary, but "Oh, isn't she the *cutest* thing!" frequently floats my way. "And got so much sense!" they gratefully add . . . for which thoughtful addition I thank them to this day.

It was great fun being cute. But then, one day, it ended.

I am eight years old and a tomboy. I have a cowboy hat, cowboy boots, checkered shirt and pants, all red. My playmates are my brothers, two and four years older than I. Their colors are black and green, the only difference in the way we are dressed. On Saturday nights we all go to the picture show, even my mother; Westerns are her favorite kind of movie. Back home, "on the ranch," we pretend we are Tom Mix, Hopalong Cassidy, Lash LaRue (we've even named one of our dogs Lash LaRue); we chase each other for hours rustling cattle, being outlaws, delivering damsels from distress. Then my parents decide to buy my brothers guns. These are not "real" guns. They shoot "BBs," copper pellets my brothers say will kill birds. Because I am a girl, I do not get a gun. Instantly I am relegated to the position of Indian. Now there appears a great distance between us. They shoot and shoot at everything with their new guns. I try to keep up with my bow and arrows.

One day while I am standing on top of our makeshift "garage"—pieces of tin nailed across some poles—holding my bow and arrow and looking out towards the fields, I feel an incredible blow in my right eye. I look down just in time to see my brother lower his gun.

Both brothers rush to my side. My eye stings, and I cover it with my hand. "If you tell," they say, "we will get a whipping. You don't want that to happen, do you?" I do not. "Here is a piece of wire," says the older brother, picking it up from the roof; "say you stepped on one end of it and the other flew up and hit you." The pain is beginning to start. "Yes," I say. "Yes, I will say that is what happened." If I do not say this is what happened, I know my brothers will find ways to make me wish I had. But now I will say anything that gets me to my mother.

Confronted by our parents we stick to the lie agreed upon. They place me on a bench on the porch and I close my left eye while they examine the right. There is a tree growing from underneath the porch that climbs past the railing to the roof. It is the last thing my right eye sees. I watch as its trunk, its branches, and then its leaves are blotted out by the rising blood.

I am in shock. First there is intense fever, which my father tries to break using lily leaves bound around my head. Then there are chills: my mother tries to get me to eat soup. Eventually, I do not know how, my parents learn what has happened. A week after the "accident" they take me to see a doctor. "Why did you wait so long to come?" he asks, looking into my eye and shaking his head. "Eyes are sympathetic," he says. "If one is blind, the other will likely become blind too."

This comment of the doctor's terrifies me. But it is really how I look that bothers me most. Where the BB pellet struck there is a glob of whitish scar tissue, a hideous cataract, on my eye. Now when I stare at people—a favorite pastime, up to now—they will stare back. Not at the "cute" little girl, but at her scar. For six years I do not stare at anyone, because I do not raise my head.

Years later, in the throes of a mid-life crisis, I ask my mother and sister whether I changed after the "accident" "No," they say, puzzled. "What do you mean?"

What do I mean?

I am eight, and, for the first time, doing poorly in school, where I have been something of a whiz since I was four. We have just moved to the place where the "accident" occurred. We do not know any of the people around us because this is a different county. The only time I see the friends I knew is when we go back to our old church. The new school is the former state penitentiary. It is a large stone building, cold and drafty, crammed to overflowing with boisterous, ill-disciplined children. On the third floor there is a huge circular imprint of some partition that has been torn out.

"What used to be here?" I ask a sullen girl next to me on our way past it to lunch.

"The electric chair," says she.

At night I have nightmares about the electric chair, and about all the people reputedly "fried" in it. I am afraid of the school, where all the students seem to be budding criminals.

"What's the matter with your eye?" they ask, critically.

When I don't answer (I cannot decide whether it was an "accident" or not), they shove me, insist on a fight.

My brother, the one who created the story about the wire, comes to my rescue. But then brags so much about "protecting" me, I become sick.

After months of torture at the school, my parents decide to send me back to our old community, to my old school. I live with my grandparents and the teacher they board. But there is no room for Phoebe, my cat. By the time my grandparents decide there *is* room, and I ask for my cat, she cannot be found. Miss Yarborough, the boarding teacher, takes me under her wing, and begins to teach me to play the piano. But soon she marries an African—a "prince," she says—and is whisked away to his continent.

At my old school there is at least one teacher who loves me. She is the teacher who "knew me before I was born" and bought my first baby clothes. It is she who makes life bearable. It is her presence that finally helps me turn on the one child at the school who continually calls me "one-eyed bitch." One day I simply grab him by his coat and beat him until I am satisfied. It is my teacher who tells me my mother is ill.

My mother is lying in bed in the middle of the day, something I have never seen. She is in too much pain to speak. She has an abscess in her ear. I stand looking down on her, knowing that if she dies, I cannot live. She is being treated with warm oils and hot bricks held against her check. Finally a doctor comes. But I must go back to my grandparents' house. The weeks pass but I am hardly aware of it. All I know is that my mother might die, my father is not so jolly, my brothers still have their guns, and I am the one sent away from home.

"You did not change," they say.

Did I imagine the anguish of never looking up?

I am twelve. When relatives come to visit I hide in my room. My cousin Brenda, just my age, whose father works in the post office and whose mother is a nurse, comes to find me. "Hello," she says. And then she asks, looking at my recent school picture, which I did not want taken, and on which the "glob," as I think of it, is clearly visible, "You still can't see out of that eye?"

"No," I say, and flop back on the bed over my book.

That night, as I do almost every night, I abuse my eye. I rant and rave at it, in front of the mirror. I plead with it to clear up before morning. I tell it I hate and despise it. I do not pray for sight. I pray for beauty.

"You did not change," they say.

I am fourteen and baby-sitting for my brother Bill, who lives in Boston. He is my favorite brother and there is a strong bond between us. Understanding my feelings of shame and ugliness he and his wife take me to a local hospital, where the "glob" is removed by a doctor named O. Henry. There is still a small bluish crater where the scar tissue was, but the ugly white stuff is gone. Almost immediately I become a different person from the girl who does not raise her head. Or so I think. Now that I've raised my head I win the boyfriend of my dreams. Now that I've raised my head I have plenty of friends. Now that I've raised my head classwork comes from my lips as faultlessly as Easter speeches did, and I leave high school as valedictorian, most popular student, and *queen*, hardly believing my luck. Ironically, the girl who was voted most beautiful in our class (and was) was later shot twice through the chest by a male companion, using a "real" gun, while she was pregnant. But that's another story in itself. Or is it?

"You did not change," they say.

It is now thirty years since the "accident." A beautiful journalist comes to visit and to interview me. She is going to write a cover story for her magazine that focuses on my latest book. "Decide how you want to look on the cover," she says. "Glamorous, or whatever."

Never mind "glamorous," it is the "whatever" that I hear. Suddenly all I can think of is whether I will get enough sleep the night before the photography session; if I don't my eye will be tired and wander, as blind eyes will.

At night in bed with my lover I think up reasons why I should not appear on the cover of a magazine. "My meanest critics will say I've sold out," I say. "My family will now realize I write scandalous books."

"But what's the real reason you don't want to do this?" he asks.

"Because in all probability," I say in a rush, "my eye won't be straight."

"It will be straight enough," he says. Then, "Besides, I thought you'd made your peace with that."

And I suddenly remember that I have.

I remember:

I am talking to my brother Jimmy, asking if he remembers anything unusual about the day I was shot. He does not know I consider
that day the last time my father, with his sweet home remedy of cool
lily leaves, chose me, and that I suffered and raged inside because of
this. "Well," he says, "all I remember is standing by the side of the
highway with Daddy, trying to flag down a car. A white man stopped,
but when Daddy said he needed somebody to take his little girl to the
doctor, he drove off."

I remember:

I am in the desert for the first time. I fall totally in love with it. I
am so overwhelmed by its beauty, I confront for the first time, consciously, the meaning of the doctor's words years ago: "Eyes are sympathetic. If one is blind, the other will likely become blind too." I
realize I have dashed about the world madly, looking at this, looking
at that, storing up images against the fading of the light. *But I might
have missed seeing the desert!* The shock of that possibility—and gratitude for over twenty-five years of sight—sends me literally to my
knees. Poem after poem comes—which is perhaps how poets pray.

ON SIGHT

I am so thankful I have seen
The Desert
And the creatures in the desert
And the desert Itself.

The desert has its own moon
Which I have seen
With my own eye.

There is no flag on it.

Trees of the desert have arms
All of which are always up
That is because the moon is up
The sun is up
Also the sky
The stars
Clouds
None with flags.

If there *were* flags, I doubt
the trees would point.
Would you?

But mostly, I remember this:

I am twenty-seven, and my baby daughter is almost three. Since
her birth I have worried about her discovery that her mother's eyes
are different from other people's. Will she be embarrassed? I think.
What will she say? Every day she watches a television program called
"Big Blue Marble." It begins with a picture of the earth as it appears

from the moon. It is bluish, a little battered-looking, but full of light, with whitish clouds swirling around it. Every time I see it I weep with love, as if it is a picture of Grandma's house. One day when I am putting Rebecca down for her nap, she suddenly focuses on my eye. Something inside me cringes, gets ready to try to protect myself. All children are cruel about physical differences, I know from experience, and that they don't always mean to be is another matter. I assume Rebecca will be the same.

But no-o-o-o. She studies my face intently as we stand, her inside and me outside her crib. She even holds my face maternally between her dimpled little hands. Then, looking every bit as serious and law-yerlike as her father, she says, as if it may just possibly have slipped my attention: "Mommy, there's a *world* in your eye." (As in, "Don't be alarmed, or do anything crazy.") And then, gently, but with great interest: "Mommy, where did you *get* that world in your eye?"

For the most part, the pain left then. (So what, if my brothers grew up to buy even more powerful pellet guns for their sons and to carry real guns themselves. So what, if a young "Morehouse man" once nearly fell off the steps of Trevor Arnett Library because he thought my eyes were blue.) Crying and laughing I ran to the bathroom, while Rebecca mumbled and sang herself off to sleep. Yes indeed, I realized, looking into the mirror. There *was* a world in my eye. And I saw that it was possible to love it: that in fact, for all it had taught me of shame and anger and inner vision, I *did* love it. Even to see it drifting out of orbit in boredom, or rolling up out of fatigue, not to mention floating back at attention in excitement (bearing witness, a friend has called it), deeply suitable to my personality, and even characteristic of me.

That night I dream I am dancing to Stevie Wonder's song "Always" (the name of the song is really "As," but I hear it as "Always"). As I dance, whirling and joyous, happier than I've ever been in my life, another bright-faced dancer joins me. We dance and kiss each other and hold each other through the night. The other dancer has obviously come through all right, as I have done. She is beautiful, whole and free. And she is also me.

SPECULATIONS

1. Do you think Alice Walker blames her brother for her eye injury? Describe her tone toward the injury.
2. In what way is gender a key element in what happens to Alice Walker, both as a contributing factor in her injury and afterward in the ways she—and others—react to it?
3. What is the effect of this essay being written in more or less discontinuous

chunks? Why do you think Alice Walker chose to tell her story this way?
Within those sections, Walker includes quite a few italicized words and sentences. Why do you think Walker chose to set them apart this way? What is
she after?

4.   Have you ever felt "disfigured" in some way, however insignificant or
temporary that change was? How did it make you feel? Were you concerned
about the impression you were making on other people? How important is it
to you to look your best whenever you are out among relative strangers?

5.   Why does Rebecca's comment mean so much to Walker? And what is the
meaning of the dancing image in the last paragraph?

Time-Travel

SHARON OLDS

A writer who transforms the personal into the poetic, Sharon Olds
is the author of two volumes of poetry, *Satan Says* (1980) and *The
Dead and the Living* (1984), as well as numerous poems that have
appeared in many anthologies. A Californian by birth, Olds earned
a B.A. from Stanford in 1964 and a Ph.D. from Columbia in 1972.
She resides in northern California.

Olds's work might best be described, as one critic put it, as "poems
of extreme emotions." Her writing is filled with feelings of anger,
betrayal, pain, love, anxiety, and loss. She transforms private experiences into metaphors of universal understanding. According to critic
Lisel Mueller, Olds explores "the roles in which she experiences
herself, 'Daughter,' 'Woman,' and 'Mother.'" She is a poetic chron-
icler of growing up.

Olds's work has been nationally recognized. Recipient of a Guggenheim fellowship and a grant from the National Endowment for
the Arts, she has also received the San Francisco Poetry Center
Award and the National Book Critics Circle Award. She has read her
work at numerous colleges, libraries, and museums.

The death of Olds's father has been the subject of many poems,
and each one, like "Time-Travel," creates a vivid world within reach.

I have learned to go back and walk around
and find the windows and doors. Outside
it is hot, the pines are black, the lake
laps. It is 1955 and I am
looking for my father.
I walk from a small room to a big one
through a doorway. The walls and floors are pine,
full of splinters.
I come upon him.

I can possess him like this, the funnies
rising and falling on his big stomach,

his big solid secret body
where he puts the bourbon.
He belongs to me forever like this,
the red plaid shirt, the baggy pants,
the long perfectly turned legs,
the soft padded hands folded across his body,
the hair dark as a burnt match,
the domed, round eyes closed,
the firm mouth. Sleeping it off
in the last summer the family was together.
I have learned to walk

so quietly into that summer
no one knows I am there. He rests
easy as a baby. Upstairs
mother weeps. Out in the tent
my brother reads my diary. My sister
is changing boyfriends somewhere in a car
and down by the shore of the lake there is a girl
twelve years old, watching the water
fold and disappear. I walk up behind her,
I touch her shoulder, she turns her head—

I see my face. She looks through me
up at the house. This is the one I have
come for. I gaze in her eyes, the waves,
thick as the air in hell, curling in
over and over. She does not know
any of this will ever stop.
She does not know she is the one
survivor.

SPECULATIONS

1.   What does Olds mean by:

> I have learned to go back and walk around
> and find the windows and doors.

Walk around what? Find the windows and doors into where? Out of what?
2.   How do you explain the last two lines of the poem? When Olds writes,
"She does not know any of this will ever stop," to what does the "this" refer?
What does the twelve-year-old girl survive?

ASSIGNMENT SEQUENCES

Sequence One: Family Life

1. You are a researcher, interested in discovering and collecting data about college students and their family experiences. You job is to develop a questionnaire that you can give to 15 to 20 college students, from which you will draw some conclusions about the family experiences of those particular students.

Creating a questionnaire is not easy; you will need to develop a clear sense of purpose, focus on just one or two specific areas of interest, and write questions that are clear and unambiguous. Such work might best be done in teams, with lots of in-class workshopping, sharing, and revising. You will want to make sure that your questionnaire is complete enough to provide you the information you want, yet short enough that students not known to you will be willing to fill it out easily and completely.

Once you have developed this questionnaire, give it to at least 15 to 20 college students whom you do not know. You might simply find students in another class, in the student union, in the cafeteria, and the like. Make sure that you get full responses.

2. Now that you have responses to your questionnaire, the next step is to compile the data and draw some conclusions in a thoughtful, well-reasoned report. Your assignment, either individually or in groups (as designated by your instructor), is to draft a report on "the family experience of college students" based on the data from your questionnaire.

3. In *Rachel and Her Children*, Jonathan Kozol writes:

> It is a commonplace that a society reveals its reverence or contempt for history by the respect or disregard that it displays for older people. The way we treat our children tells us something of our moral disposition too.

Making use of the insights from the selections by Kozol, Elizabeth Marek, and Léon Bing, write an essay that analyzes societal values in terms of the ways the United States treats families in general and young people in particular.

In your essay, you might want to focus on the particular problems of teenagers, single-parent families, gangs, or the homeless, drawing upon the works that you have read in *Speculations* as well as additional research that you do outside of class. Once you have analyzed your subject closely, draw some conclusions about the general "moral disposition" of society, based on what you discover.

4. Elizabeth Marek offers various hypotheses explaining why teenage girls become mothers. In an essay drawing on Marek and Kozol, speculate as to possible social remedies that might discourage or prevent teenage pregnancy. Would you want to propose psychological counseling, free medical help, classes on sexuality, some other form of intervention? What do you think should be done—and how do you think your solutions would best be implemented?

5. What is it that enables successful families to thrive? What is a successful family? Based on selections by Lerone Bennett, Jr., David Elkind, and Amy Tan, offer your own view of what it takes to create successful family life. What central principles do you think families should adhere to? How should inevitable problems and disagreements be resolved? Can successful families consist of only one child? Only one parent? Various adults and children living together within a collective? Gay or lesbian parents who have adopted a child? Parents of one race adopting a child of another? Offer your views, making sure that you remain aware that other readers may hold views very strongly opposed to your own.

6. You are now an expert on the particular subject you have just written about in Assignment 5. Write an editorial comment for your local newspaper on the Op-Ed page.
 Before you write your editorial comment, make sure that you have a strong commitment toward a specific position. You will also need to make sure that you have enough facts, data, and information to be persuasive. You will also need to consider factors such as potential audience, appropriate tone, desirable length, etc. You might share drafts of this comment in class before handing in the final copy—which should go not only to your instructor but in the mail to your local newspaper as well.

Sequence Two: Using Language

1. In "Girl," Jamaica Kincaid explores what it means to be a particular girl in a particular family and culture. Taking this selection as your inspiration and model, write your own account of what it means to be a child in a specific family or culture. Entitle your essay "Girl" or "Boy" as appropriate. Although you do not have to imitate Kincaid's "Girl," do your best to emulate its sense of style, coherence, voice, and drama.

2. The experience of language that one has in families, neighborhoods, and among friends can make a major difference in the ways one perceives and uses words. We see such language use in selections by Kincaid, Bing, Bambara, and others. After brainstorming about the different contexts and uses of language in your own life, write an essay which describes some specific words, phrases, or usages that you remember with great pleasure and affection. They might have been words expressed by grandparents, parents, siblings, friends, neighbors. In your essay, consider as well why words/phrases/language usage are so important to you. What kinds of values do they represent?

3.   Toni Cade Bambara's story "The Lesson" is notable for its use of black dialect or black English vernacular. As a research project, investigate dialect in American society. What effect does dialect, black dialect in particular, have upon its audience? How did such a dialect develop in America? In what ways does it differ from the dialect known as edited American English? Is one dialect "superior" or "inferior" to another? What is the relation between dialect and class? Dialect and influence? Dialect and the speaker's place in society? Any one of these topics—when researched—can provide material for a thoughtful and substantial essay.

4.   "When You're a Crip (or a Blood)" presents an entirely different kind of language use. How do you explain the idiomatic and frequently profane use of language by Li'l Monster, Rat-Neck, Tee Rodgers, and B-Dog? Why do you think they speak the way they do? In a short essay, present your analysis; be prepared to share your essay with the rest of the class.

5.   The previous questions focus on the relationship between language and reality. They suggest that language does not simply describe reality but actually gives shape to it. Thus the words people use influence what they see—and what they don't see. Drawing upon at least three of the selections in "Growing Up," explore the relationship between words and perception. Include your own personal insights and experiences as well.

Sequence Three: Parent and Child

1.   In "Time-Travel," Sharon Olds uses the technique of moving backward through time to observe herself during her own childhood—and then using her observations to draw out certain truths and feelings about her family experience. In an exploratory essay, use that same technique to write about a feeling, an experience, an event, a truth that has meaning for you. Remember that the past event or experience that you revisit does not have to be anything momentous, although it can be. It can, however, also be a time which is representative of some experience, or a seemingly insignificant moment during which you achieved some important insight, or a time when you were oblivious to the significance of what was going around you but which you know now was important. Remember that you will want to write about that "you" of the past as if she/he were someone else, yet you will also want to establish for the reader a deep psychic connection between that "you" of the past and yourself as the author of this essay.

2.   Many of the essays in this section focus on the relation between parents and children. What are the responsibilities that parents have in relation to their children? What should parents do to help their children? What must they do? Look particularly at the selections by Elizabeth Marek, David Elkind, and Alice Walker. What kinds of issues are raised by the way the parents in these selections relate to their children? What insights or comments would you want to offer them?

3.   Now consider the same question from the other vantage point—namely, what are the responsibilities that children have in relation to their parents? In this case, look specifically at selections by Toni Cade Bambara, Amy Tan, Joyce Carol Oates, and Scott Russell Sanders. Do children owe their parents anything? If so, in what ways are they obligated to their parents? How would you describe a healthy child-parent relationship?

4.   Lerone Bennett, Jr., describes the "Ten Biggest Myths About the Black Family." Using a similar format, write your own "Ten Biggest Myths." For your subject, choose one of the following: "The Ten Biggest Myths About Growing Up in a . . . (Single-Parent Family, Only Child Family, "Typical" Family, Asian or Hispanic, or White, or Native American Family)."
   Consider your audience to be the students and instructor in your class—and that your essay is likely to be published so that everyone in the class will read it. As you work through your ten myths, consider the kind of "ten myths" essay that you want to write: do you want it to be informative, outraged, poignant, sensitive, funny, argumentative?

5.   For the purposes of this assignment, assume that the mother in "Two Kinds" knows the mother in "Shopping." They get together at a meeting of "Mothers Anonymous," a self-help group that has recently formed in their community. The two women begin to discuss a subject of great importance to them—namely, mother-daughter relationships.

Based on a close reading of the two selections, record the discussion as a narrative or as a dialogue. In particular, you might want to focus on the themes of responsibility, guilt, and caring.

Sequence Four: The Search for Identity

1. In "Beauty: When the Other Dancer Is the Self," Alice Walker struggles to come to terms with her own disfigurement. In an essay, show why the eye injury she suffered became so important to her, way beyond physical appearance. Relate the disfigurement to family relations between herself and her father, race, and gender. In your essay, explain her repeated insistence that her family said she did not change. Why does Walker keep repeating that?

2. Compare Alice Walker's sense of her own identity to Zora Neale Hurston's view of herself in "How It Feels to Be Colored Me" (in the Self and Society section). What are the causes and conditions that create these two black women artists? In an essay based on your reading of the two selections, describe what these two writers hold in common.

3. In "Ten Biggest Myths About the Black Family," Lerone Bennett, Jr., states:

> [Black America] has said, to its credit, that there are no illegitimate children, only illegitimate parents and, it must be added, illegitimate societies which make it impossible for parents to find the work and wherewithal (the day-care centers and the network of supporting images and institutions) to become responsible parents.

Bennett is arguing here that the problem of teen-age pregnancy, especially among black Americans, has a root cause in what might be called institutional racism. That is, the ways the United States allocates its social, cultural, and financial resources exacerbates the unfortunate consequences of black illegitimacy.

Consider Bennett's argument in the context of selections by Jonathan Kozol, Toni Cade Bambara, and Elizabeth Marek in this section. (You might also want to read the selections by Clarence Darrow, Nathan McCall, and Donna Gaines elsewhere in this reader.) Then assess the ways American society defines illegitimacy—and the ways it chooses some values over others through allocation of tax dollars; depictions of black and white families on television and in the movies; the treatment of kids in our schools, etc. Is the United States, at least to some extent, an "illegitimate society"?

4. Imagine that one or two of the young women featured in "The Lives of Teenage Mothers" goes to a nearby mall and meets Nola, the character in "Shopping." Create the conversation that you think would occur, basing it on a close reading of the two selections. If you wish, you may include other voices from the two selections.

5.   David Elkind argues that:

> . . . the trend toward obscuring the divisions between children and adults is part of a broad egalitarian movement in this country that seeks to overcome the barriers separating the sexes, ethnic and racial groups, and the handicapped. . . . From this perspective, the contemporary pressure for children to grow up fast is only one symptom of a much larger social phenomenon in this country—a movement toward true equality, toward the ideal expressed in our Declaration of Independence. While one can only applaud this movement with respect to the sexes, ethnic and racial groups, and the handicapped, its unthinking extension to children is unfortunate.

In a carefully reasoned essay, analyze this statement and the various assumptions that Elkind makes. Is there a movement toward equality? How so? Does such a movement include the collapse of difference between child and adult? How do children's rights compare to those of an adult? In your essay, attempt to formulate a set of principles that govern the rights of children without forcing them, in Elkind's terms, to forsake their childhoods.

Sequence Five: Family Values

1.   Selections by Theodore Roethke, Scott Russell Sanders, Amy Tan, and Joyce Carol Oates focus on parent-child relationships, but there is a difference. Roethke, Sanders, and Tan write about those relationships from the child's point of view, while Oates for the most part writes about them from the parent's point of view. Choosing one of these four selections, write the opposite account. That is, if you choose Roethke, Sanders, or Tan, write an essay from the perspective of the parent; if you choose Oates, write from the perspective of the daughter. Base your account on your interpretation of the selection in this book, and focus on the same central themes as the original work from which your character derives.

2.   Both "The Lesson" and "Shopping" focus on that "quintessential" American experience—looking at and buying things in stores. Based on your reading of these two stories, what is the political and cultural significance of going to stores, whether they are toy stores or shopping malls? What do stores offer us? What kinds of values are embodied in them? What do they tell us about American society—both good and bad? What do they tell us about families?

3. In "Under the Influence," Scott Russell Sanders makes an open and painful confession about his father being an alcoholic—and the effect this had upon himself, his brother, his sister, and his mother. Theodore Roethke, in "My Papa's Waltz," focuses on a similar theme. In an essay, examine alcoholism and offer an explanation of what it is. Consult at least two outside sources. In your essay consider whether you think alcoholism is a disease, a character flaw, or an inherited tendency. What makes people drink? What specific and positive steps would you recommend to try to reduce the problem? Prohibition obviously won't work; America tried that in the 1920s. But are there strategies that will help? As part of this essay, you might want to investigate what alcohol treatment centers and Alcoholics Anonymus actually do to help people stop drinking.

4. As a second stage in your analysis of "My Papa's Waltz," "Under the Influence," or texts of your choice discuss the effect that alcoholism has on families—and what you think ought to be done about it. What are the consequences of alcoholism within a family? How do families cope and compensate when a mother or father (or son or daughter) becomes an alcoholic? What kinds of intervention would you recommend to prevent the kinds of difficulties the Roethke and the Sanders families experienced?

5. If you are interested in doing some outside reading, you might want to get a copy of Sanders's other essay on his father, "The Inheritance of Tools." It can be found in *Paradise of Bombs* as well as in *Best American Essays of 1987* (ed. Gay Talese). When you compare "The Inheritance of Tools" to "Under the Influence," you will see two dramatically different views of Sanders's father.

Assume that you are Scott Russell Sanders, and that a publisher wants to print both essays in a little book—along with an introductory essay that explains the apparent inconsistencies between the two portraits and adds to the father-son relationship described in these two works. Write the introduction, drawing as much as you can on the two essays by Scott Russell Sanders for your inspiration.

6. National leaders often call for Americans to return to traditional family values, especially during election years. Basing your views on the selections in Growing Up, write an essay that explores contemporary family values. What do the families of 1990s America believe in? What's right—and what's wrong—with family life?

2

MUSIC AND MORALITY

Music is as old as history. Human beings sang, danced, and played instruments long before they wrote books or watched NFL football on Super Sunday. The ancient Greeks understood that music embodies *ethos*, the fundamental character and values of a people, and that music possesses the power to influence the listener's emotions, behavior, and morals. At the same time, music is perhaps the most pervasive of the arts, permeating all levels of culture. It plays an essential role in celebrations, dance, and worship; it can be heard in virtually every aural medium—radio, television, film, or theater. Clearly, the human psyche has some need to move to instrumentation, rhythm, and beat, and to marry words to musical notes. The explosion of musical genres in the twentieth century alone testifies to music's universal appeal: ballads, folk music, blues, jazz, big band, rock 'n' roll, pop, punk, heavy metal, and rap, to mention only a few.

Music is an idiom that speaks to virtually everyone who hears it. Rock 'n' roll, for example, appeals strongly to rebellious teenagers. Jazz is an expression for playful sophisticates. Rap music tests the boundaries of middle-class conventions. Folk music fuels the muscle underlying political struggle. Country music tells life stories and appeals to the audience's emotions. Although such statements are broad generalizations, they reflect perceptions shared by many within our culture.

Because music is such a broad subject, this section of *Speculations* focuses on only a few key themes and individuals that intersect music, culture, and the politics of expression. In particular, the real and presumed dangers of music and their significance as cultural and political markers are examined. For many critics, music is a clear and present danger to society, something that needs to be regulated, supervised, and occasionally banned. Such responses are nothing new; over 2,000 years ago in Book III of the *Republic*, Plato warned that "innovations in music" could corrupt "the fundamental political and social conventions" of his idealized Republic. Philosophers, politicians, educators, parents—they all have expressed strong concerns about the nature and role of music within society.

The selections that follow illustrate the complexity of our view of music. Is its current formulation within culture destructive? Does it isolate individuals and make its listeners into cultural zombies or defiant outlaws? How can the genius of certain forms of music be explained? Is music sexist, racist, ageist? What roles, positive or negative, do musical icons play within youth culture? What does it mean to be a fan or a groupie, transfixed within a mindless gaze toward an adored object? The writers included here raise these kinds of questions as they speculate on the relations between music and morality.

130

Music

ALLAN BLOOM

Allan Bloom described his childhood the following way in an interview with *Contemporary Authors*: "I was a kind of intellectual kid. . . . Self-understanding was always my goal, a scholarly goal, even when I was little." Born in 1930 in Indiana, Bloom entered college after his second year of high school and went on to earn B.A., M.A., and Ph.D. degrees at the University of Chicago, where he now teaches political philosophy. He has taught at Yale, Cornell, Toronto, and Tel Aviv universities, and has published several books, including translations of Plato's *Republic* and two books by Rousseau, a co-authored book on *Shakespeare's Politics* (1964), and *The Closing of the American Mind: How Higher Education Has Failed Democracy and Impoverished the Souls of Today's Students* (1987), which contains the chapter "Music," reprinted here.

Throughout his career, Bloom has expressed strong concern about what he considers irresponsible politics and policies in education. In 1969, two years after winning the Clark Distinguished Teaching Award at Cornell University, he resigned his position in protest of Cornell's failure to protect teachers' academic freedoms and their right to teach unpopular views. His resignation came in the wake of a campus uprising in which a group of rifle-wielding students took over the administration building. Bloom felt strongly that administrators had acted cowardly by giving in to the students' radical demands and by failing to protect professors who had received death threats for opposing them.

In 1987, Bloom provoked an intense debate with the publication of *The Closing of the American Mind*, a critique of the way American universities are educating students. According to Bloom, tolerance has become an end in itself, which means accepting everything and denying reason's power to make distinctions between important and superficial ideas. Bloom believes that a philosophy of complete equality and openness may limit learning by undermining traditional educational values. He favors a "Great Books" approach to education, which focuses on human questions formulated by such authors as Plato, Shakespeare, Rousseau, Hegel, and others in the Western tradition.

Many critics of *The Closing of the American Mind* charged Bloom with elitism and antiquarianism, while others celebrated its message as a return to fundamental American values. As one critic said, this book "will provoke nearly everyone." "Music" focuses on one aspect of American culture—rock music—as an example of how modern culture undermines our intellectual foundations, and may prevent young people from developing insights into a fuller life.

Though students do not have books, they most emphatically do have music. Nothing is more singular about this generation than its addiction to music. This is the age of music and the states of soul that accompany it. To find a rival to this enthusiasm, one would have to go back at least a century to Germany and the passion for Wagner's operas. They had the religious sense that Wagner was creating the meaning of life and that they were not merely listening to his works but experiencing that meaning. Today, a very large proportion of young people between the ages of ten and twenty live for music. It is their passion; nothing else excites them as it does; they cannot take seriously anything alien to music. When they are in school and with their families, they are longing to plug themselves back into their music. Nothing surrounding them—school, family, church—has anything to do with their musical world. At best that ordinary life is neutral, but mostly it is an impediment, drained of vital content, even a thing to be rebelled against. Of course, the enthusiasm for Wagner was limited to a small class, could be indulged only rarely and only in a few places, and had to wait on the composer's slow output. The music of the new votaries, on the other hand, knows neither class nor nation. It is available twenty-four hours a day, everywhere. There is the stereo in the home, in the car; there are concerts; there are music videos, with special channels exclusively devoted to them, on the air nonstop; there are the Walkmans so that no place—not public transportation, not the library—prevents students from communing with the Muse, even while studying. And, above all, the musical soil has become tropically rich. No need to wait for one unpredictable genius. Now there are many geniuses, producing all the time, two new ones rising to take the place of every fallen hero. There is no dearth of the new and the startling.

The power of music in the soul—described to Jessica marvelously by Lorenzo in the *Merchant of Venice*—has been recovered after a long period of desuetude. And it is rock music alone that has effected this restoration. Classical music is dead among the young. This assertion will, I know, be hotly disputed by many who, unwilling to admit tidal changes, can point to the proliferation on campuses of classes in classical music appreciation and practice, as well as performance groups of all kinds. Their presence is undeniable, but they involve not more than 5 to 10 percent of the students. Classical music is now a special taste, like Greek language or pre-Columbian archeology, not a common culture of reciprocal communication and psychological shorthand. Thirty years ago, most middle-class families made some of the old European music a part of the home, partly because they liked it, partly because they thought it was good for the kids. University students usually had some early emotive association with Beethoven, Chopin and Brahms, which was a permanent part of their makeup and to which they were likely to respond throughout their lives. This was probably the only regularly recognizable class distinction between educated and uneducated in America. Many, or even most, of the young people of that generation also swung with Benny

Goodman, but with an element of self-consciousness—to be hip, to prove they weren't snobs, to show solidarity with the democratic ideal of a pop culture out of which would grow a new high culture. So there remained a class distinction between high and low, although private taste was beginning to create doubts about whether one really liked the high very much. But all that has changed. Rock music is as unquestioned and unproblematic as the air the students breathe, and very few have any acquaintance at all with classical music. This is a constant surprise to me. And one of the strange aspects of my relations with good students I come to know well is that I frequently introduce them to Mozart. This is a pleasure for me, inasmuch as it is always pleasant to give people gifts that please them. It is interesting to see whether and in what ways their studies are complemented by such music. But this is something utterly new to me as a teacher; formerly my students usually knew much more classical music than I did.

Music was not all that important for the generation of students preceding the current one. The romanticism that had dominated serious music since Beethoven appealed to refinements—perhaps overrefinements—of sentiments that are hardly to be found in the contemporary world. The lives people lead or wish to lead and their prevailing passions are of a different sort than those of the highly educated German and French bourgeoisie, who were avidly reading Rousseau and Baudelaire, Goethe and Heine, for their spiritual satisfaction. The music that had been designed to produce, as well as to please, such exquisite sensibilities had a very tenuous relation to American lives of any kind. So romantic musical culture in America had had for a long time the character of a veneer, as easily susceptible to ridicule as were Margaret Dumont's displays of coquettish chasteness, so aptly exploited by Groucho Marx in *A Night At The Opera*. I noticed this when I first started teaching and lived in a house for gifted students. The "good" ones studied their physics and then listened to classical music. The students who did not fit so easily into the groove, some of them also serious, were looking for things that really responded to their needs. Almost always they responded to the beat of the newly emerging rock music. They were a bit ashamed of their taste, for it was not respectable. But I instinctively sided with this second group, with real, if coarse, feelings as opposed to artificial and dead ones. Then their musical sans-culotteism won the revolution and reigns unabashed today. No classical music has been produced that can speak to this generation.

Symptomatic of this change is how seriously students now take the famous passages on musical education in Plato's *Republic*.[1] In the

---

[1] See Book III of Plato's *Republic*, paragraphs 397 through 404. [Eds.]

past, students, good liberals that they always are, were indignant at the censorship of poetry, as a threat to free inquiry. But they were really thinking of science and politics. They hardly paid attention to the discussion of music itself and, to the extent that they even thought about it, were really puzzled by Plato's devoting time to rhythm and melody in a serious treatise on political philosophy. Their experience of music was as an entertainment, a matter of indifference to political and moral life. Students today, on the contrary, know exactly why Plato takes music so seriously. They know it affects life very profoundly and are indignant because Plato seems to want to rob them of their most intimate pleasure. They are drawn into argument with Plato about the experience of music, and the dispute centers on how to evaluate it and deal with it. This encounter not only helps to illuminate the phenomenon of contemporary music, but also provides a model of how contemporary students can profitably engage with a classic text. The very fact of their fury shows how much Plato threatens what is dear and intimate to them. They are little able to defend their experience, which had seemed unquestionable until questioned, and it is most resistant to cool analysis. Yet if a student can—and this is most difficult and unusual—draw back, get a critical distance on what he clings to, come to doubt the ultimate value of what he loves, he has taken the first and most difficult step toward the philosophic conversion. Indignation is the soul's defense against the wound of doubt about its own; it reorders the cosmos to support the justice of its cause. It justifies putting Socrates to death. Recognizing indignation for what it is constitutes knowledge of the soul, and is thus an experience more philosophic than the study of mathematics. It is Plato's teaching that music, by its nature, encompasses all that is today most resistant to philosophy. So it may well be that through the thicket of our greatest corruption runs the path to awareness of the oldest truths.

Plato's teaching about music is, put simply, that rhythm and melody, accompanied by dance, are the barbarous expression of the soul. Barbarous, not animal. Music is the medium of the *human* soul in its most ecstatic condition of wonder and terror. Nietzsche, who in large measure agrees with Plato's analysis, says in *The Birth of Tragedy* (not to be forgotten is the rest of the title, *Out of the Spirit of Music*) that a mixture of cruelty and coarse sensuality characterized this state, which of course was religious, in the service of gods. Music is the soul's primitive and primary speech and it is *alogon*,[2] without articulate speech or reason. It is not only not reasonable, it is hostile to reason.

---

[2] *Alogon* is the Greek word for that which is beyond or without words or rational thought. [Eds.]

Even when articulate speech is added, it is utterly subordinate to and determined by the music and the passions it expresses.

Civilization or, to say the same thing, education is the taming or domestication of the soul's raw passions—not suppressing or excising them, which would deprive the soul if its energy—but forming and informing them as art. The goal of harmonizing the enthusiastic part of the soul with what develops later, the rational part, is perhaps impossible to attain. But without it, man can never be whole. Music, or poetry, which is what music becomes as reason emerges, always involves a delicate balance between passion and reason, and, even in its highest and most developed forms—religious, warlike and erotic—that balance is always tipped, if ever so slightly, toward the passionate. Music, as everyone experiences, provides an unquestionable justification and a fulfilling pleasure for the activities it accompanies: the solider who hears the marching band is enthralled and reassured; the religious man is exalted in his prayer by the sound of the organ in the church; and the lover is carried away and his conscience stilled by the romantic guitar. Armed with music, man can damn rational doubt. Out of the music emerge the gods that suit it, and they educate men by their example and their commandments.

Plato's Socrates disciplines the ecstasies and thereby provides little consolation or hope to men. According to the Socratic formula, the lyrics—speech and, hence, reason—must determine the music—harmony and rhythm. Pure music can never endure this constraint. Students are not in a position to know the pleasures of reason; they can only see it as a disciplinary and repressive parent. But they do see, in the case of Plato, that that parent has figured out what they are up to. Plato teaches that, in order to take the spiritual temperature of an individual or a society, one must "mark the music." To Plato and Nietzsche, the history of music is a series of attempts to give form and beauty to the dark, chaotic, premonitory forces in the soul—to make them serve a higher purpose, an ideal, to give man's duties a fullness. Bach's religious intentions and Beethoven's revolutionary and humane ones are clear enough examples. Such cultivation of the soul uses the passions and satisfies them while sublimating them and giving them an artistic unity. A man whose noblest activities are accompanied by a music that expresses them while providing a pleasure extending from the lowest bodily to the highest spiritual, is whole, and there is no tension in him between the pleasant and the good. By contrast a man whose business life is prosaic and unmusical and whose leisure is made up of coarse, intense entertainments, is divided, and each side of his existence is undermined by the other.

Hence, for those who are interested in psychological health, music is at the center of education, both for giving the passions their due and for preparing the soul for the unhampered use of reason. The centrality of such education was recognized by all the ancient educators. It is hardly noticed today that in Aristotle's *Politics* the most important passages about the best regime concern musical education, or that the Poetics is an appendix to the *Politics*. Classical philosophy did not censor the singers. It persuaded them. And it gave them a goal, one that was understood by them, until only yesterday. But those who do not notice the role of music in Aristotle and despise it in Plato went to school with Hobbes, Locke and Smith, where such considerations have become unnecessary. The triumphant Enlightenment rationalism thought that it had discovered other ways to deal with the irrational part of the soul, and that reason needed less support from it. Only in those great critics of Enlightenment and rationalism, Rousseau and Nietzsche, does music return, and they were the most musical of philosophers. Both thought that the passions—and along with them their ministerial arts—had become thin under the rule of reason and that, therefore, man himself and what he sees in the world have become correspondingly thin. They wanted to cultivate the enthusiastic states of the soul and to re-experience the Corybantic possession deemed a pathology by Plato. Nietzsche, particularly, sought to tap again the irrational sources of vitality, to replenish our dried-up stream from barbaric sources, and thus encouraged the Dionysian and the music derivative from it.

This is the significance of rock music. I do not suggest that it has any high intellectual sources. But it has risen to its current heights in the education of the young on the ashes of classical music, and in an atmosphere in which there is no intellectual resistance to attempts to tap the rawest passions. Modern-day rationalists, such as economists, are indifferent to it and what it represents. The irrationalists are all for it. There is no need to fear that "the blond beasts" are going to come forth from the bland souls of our adolescents. But rock music has one appeal only, a barbaric appeal, to sexual desire—not love, not *eros*, but sexual desire undeveloped and untutored. It acknowledges the first emanations of children's emerging sensuality and addresses them seriously, eliciting them and legitimating them, not as little sprouts that must be carefully tended in order to grow into gorgeous flowers, but as the real thing. Rock gives children, on a silver platter, with all the public authority of the entertainment industry, everything their parents always used to tell them they had to wait for until they grew up and would understand later.

Young people know that rock has the beat of sexual intercourse. That is why Ravel's *Bolero* is the one piece of classical music that is commonly known and liked by them. In alliance with some real art and a lot of pseudo-art, an enormous industry cultivates the taste for the orgiastic state of feeling connected with sex, providing a constant flood of fresh material for voracious appetites. Never was there an art form directed so exclusively to children.

Ministering to and according with the arousing and cathartic music, the lyrics celebrate puppy love as well as polymorphous attractions, and fortify them against traditional ridicule and shame. The words implicitly and explicitly describe bodily acts that satisfy sexual desire and treat them as its only natural and routine culmination for children who do not yet have the slightest imagination of love, marriage or family. This has a much more powerful effect than does pornography on youngsters, who have no need to watch others do grossly what they can so easily do themselves. Voyeurism is for old perverts; active sexual relations are for the young. All they need is encouragement.

The inevitable corollary of such sexual interest is rebellion against the parental authority that represses it. Selfishness thus becomes indignation and then transforms itself into morality. The sexual revolution must overthrow all the forces of domination, the enemies of nature and happiness. From love comes hate, masquerading as social reform. A worldview is balanced on the sexual fulcrum. What were once unconscious or half-conscious childish resentments become the new Scripture. And then comes the longing for the classless, prejudice-free, conflictless, universal society that necessarily results from liberated consciousness—"We Are the World," a pubescent version of *Alle Menschen werden Brüder*,[3] the fulfillment of which has been inhibited by the political equivalents of Mom and Dad. These are the three great lyrical themes: sex, hate and a smarmy, hypocritical version of brotherly love. Such polluted sources issue in a muddy stream where only monsters can swim. A glance at the videos that project images on the wall of Plato's cave since MTV took it over suffices to prove this. Hitler's image recurs frequently enough in exciting contexts to give one pause. Nothing noble, sublime, profound, delicate, tasteful or even decent can find a place in such tableaux. There is room only for the intense, changing, crude and immediate, which Tocqueville warned us would be the character of democratic art, combined with a pervasiveness, importance and content beyond Tocqueville's wildest imagination.

Picture a thirteen-year-old boy sitting in the living room of his family home doing his math assignment while wearing his Walkman headphones or watching MTV. He enjoys the liberties hard won over centuries by the alliance of philosophic genius and political heroism,

---

[3] All Men Are Brothers. [Eds.]

consecrated by the blood of martyrs; he is provided with comfort and leisure by the most productive economy ever known to mankind; science has penetrated the secrets of nature in order to provide him with the marvelous, lifelike electronic sound and image reproduction he is enjoying. And in what does progress culminate? A pubescent child whose body throbs with orgasmic rhythms; whose feelings are made articulate in hymns to the joys of onanism or the killing of parents; whose ambition is to win fame and wealth in imitating the drag-queen who makes the music. In short, life is made into a non-stop, commercially prepackaged masturbational fantasy.

This description may seem exaggerated, but only because some would prefer to regard it as such. The continuing exposure to rock music is a reality, not one confined to a particular class or type of child. One need only ask first-year university students what music they listen to, how much of it and what it means to them, in order to discover that the phenomenon is universal in America, that it begins in adolescence or a bit before and continues through the college years. It is *the* youth culture and, as I have so often insisted, there is now no other countervailing nourishment for the spirit. Some of this culture's power comes from the fact that it is so loud. It makes conversation impossible, so that much of friendship must be without the shared speech that Aristotle asserts is the essence of friendship and the only true common ground. With rock, illusions of shared feelings, bodily contact and grunted formulas, which are supposed to contain so much meaning beyond speech, are the basis of association. None of this contradicts going about the business of life, attending classes and doing the assignments for them. But the meaningful inner life is with the music.

This phenomenon is both astounding and indigestible, and is hardly noticed, routine and habitual. But it is of historic proportions that a society's best young and their best energies should be so occupied. People of future civilizations will wonder at this and find it as incomprehensible as we do the caste system, witch-burning, harems, cannibalism and gladiatorial combats. It may well be that a society's greatest madness seems normal to itself. The child I described has parents who have sacrificed to provide him with a good life and who have a great stake in his future happiness. They cannot believe that the musical vocation will contribute very much to that happiness. But there is nothing they can do about it. The family spiritual void has left the field open to rock music, and they cannot possibly forbid their children to listen to it. It is everywhere; all children listen to it; forbidding it would simply cause them to lose their children's affection and obedience. When they turn on the television, they will see President Reagan warmly grasping the daintily proffered gloved hand of

Michael Jackson and praising him enthusiastically. Better to set the faculty of denial in motion—avoid noticing what the words say, assume the kid will get over it. If he has early sex, that won't get in the way of his having stable relationships later. His drug use will certainly stop at pot. School is providing real values. And popular historicism provides the final salvation: there are new life-styles for new situations, and the older generation is there not to impose its values but to help the younger one to find its own. TV, which compared to music plays a comparatively small role in the formation of young people's character and taste, is a consensus monster—the Right monitors its content for sex, the Left for violence, and many other interested sects for many other things. But the music has hardly been touched, and what efforts have been made are both ineffectual and misguided about the nature and extent of the problem.

The result is nothing less than parents' loss of control over their children's moral education at a time when no one else is seriously concerned with it. This has been achieved by an alliance between the strange young males who have the gift of divining the mob's emergent wishes—our versions of Thrasymachus, Socrates' rhetorical adversary—and the record-company executives, the new robber barons, who mine gold out of rock. They discovered a few years back that children are one of the few groups in the country with considerable disposable income, in the form of allowances. Their parents spend all they have providing for the kids. Appealing to them over their parents' heads, creating a world of delight for them, constitutes one of the richest markets in the postwar world. The rock business is perfect capitalism, supplying to demand and helping to create it. It has all the moral dignity of drug trafficking, but it was so totally new and unexpected that nobody thought to control it, and now it is too late. Progress may be made against cigarette smoking because our absence of standards or our relativism does not extend to matters of bodily health. In all other things the market determines the value. (Yoko Ono is among America's small group of billionaires, along with oil and computer magnates, her late husband having produced and sold a commodity of worth comparable to theirs.) Rock is very big business, bigger than the movies, bigger than professional sports, bigger than television, and this accounts for much of the respectability of the music business. It is difficult to adjust our vision to the changes in the economy and to see what is really important. McDonald's now has more employees than U.S. Steel, and likewise the purveyors of junk food for the soul have supplanted what still seem to be more basic callings.

This change has been happening for some time. In the late fifties, De Gaulle gave Brigitte Bardot one of France's highest honors. I could not understand this, but it turned out that she, along with Peugeot, was France's biggest export item. As Western nations became more prosperous, leisure, which had been put off for several centuries in favor of the pursuit of property, the means to leisure, finally began to be of primary concern. But, in the meantime, any notion of the serious life of leisure, as well as men's taste and capacity to live it, had disappeared. Leisure became entertainment. The end for which they had labored for so long has turned out to be amusement, a justified conclusion if the means justify the ends. The music business is peculiar only in that it caters almost exclusively to children, treating legally and naturally imperfect human beings as though they were ready to enjoy the final or complete satisfaction. It perhaps thus reveals the nature of all our entertainment and our loss of a clear view of what adulthood or maturity is, and our incapacity to conceive ends. The emptiness of *values* results in the acceptance of the natural *facts* as the ends. In this case infantile sexuality is the end, and I suspect that, in the absence of other ends, many adults have come to agree that it is.

It is interesting to note that the Left, which prides itself on its critical approach to "late capitalism" and is unrelenting and unsparing in its analysis of our other cultural phenomena, has in general given rock music a free ride. Abstracting from the capitalist element in which it flourishes, they regard it as a people's art, coming from beneath the bourgeoisie's layers of cultural repression. Its antinomianism and its longing for a world without constraint might seem to be the clarion of the proletarian revolution, and Marxists certainly do see that rock music dissolves the beliefs and morals necessary for liberal society and would approve of it for that alone. But the harmony between the young intellectual Left and rock is probably profounder than that. Herbert Marcuse appealed to university students in the sixties with a combination of Marx and Freud. In *Eros and Civilization* and *One Dimensional Man* he promised that the overcoming of capitalism and its false consciousness will result in a society where the greatest satisfactions are sexual, of a sort that the bourgeois moralist Freud called polymorphous and infantile. Rock music touches the same chord in the young. Free sexual expression, anarchism, mining of the irrational unconscious and giving it free rein are what they have in common. The high intellectual life . . . and the low rock world are partners in the same entertainment enterprise. They must both be interpreted as parts of the cultural fabric of late capitalism. Their success comes from the bourgeois' need to feel that he is not bourgeois, to have undangerous experiments with the unlimited. He is willing to pay dearly for them. The Left is better interpreted by Nietzsche than by Marx. The critical theory of late capitalism is at once late capitalism's subtlest and crudest expression. Anti-bourgeois ire is the opiate of the Last Man.

This strong stimulant, which Nietzsche called Nihiline, was for a very long time, almost fifteen years, epitomized in a single figure, Mick Jagger. A shrewd, middle-class boy, he played the possessed lower-class demon and teen-aged satyr up until he was forty, with one eye on the mobs of children of both sexes whom he stimulated to a sensual frenzy and the other eye winking at the unerotic, commercially motivated adults who handled the money. In his act he was male and female, heterosexual and homosexual; unencumbered by modesty, he could enter everyone's dreams, promising to do everything with everyone; and, above all, he legitimated drugs, which were the real thrill that parents and policemen conspired to deny his youthful audience. He was beyond the law, moral and political, and thumbed his nose at it. Along with all this, there were nasty little appeals to the suppressed inclinations toward sexism, racism and violence, indulgence in which is not now publicly respectable. Nevertheless, he managed not to appear to contradict the rock ideal of a universal classless society founded on love, with the distinction between brotherly and bodily blurred. He was the hero and the model for countless young persons in universities, as well as elsewhere. I discovered that students who boasted of having no heroes secretly had a passion to be like Mick Jagger, to live his life, have his fame. They were ashamed to admit this in a university, although I am not certain that the reason has anything to do with a higher standard of taste. It is probably that they are not supposed to have heroes. Rock music itself and talking about it with infinite seriousness are perfectly respectable. It has proved to be the ultimate leveler of intellectual snobbism. But it is not respectable to think of it as providing weak and ordinary persons with a fashionable behavior, the imitation of which will make others esteem them and boost their own self-esteem. Unaware and unwillingly, however, Mick Jagger played the role in their lives that Napoleon played in the lives of ordinary young Frenchmen throughout the nineteenth century. Everyone else was so boring and unable to charm youthful passions. Jagger caught on.

In the last couple of years, Jagger has begun to fade. Whether Michael Jackson, Prince or Boy George can take his place is uncertain. They are even weirder than he is, and one wonders what new strata of taste they have discovered. Although each differs from the others, the essential character of musical entertainment is not changing. There is only a constant search for variations on the theme. And this gutter phenomenon is apparently the fulfillment of the promise made by so much psychology and literature that our weak and exhausted Western civilization would find refreshment in the true source, the unconscious, which appeared to the late romantic imagination to be identical to Africa, the dark and unexplored continent. Now all has been explored; light has been cast everywhere; the unconscious has been made conscious, the repressed expressed. And what have we found? Not creative devils, but show business glitz. Mick Jagger tarting it up on the stage is all that we brought back from the voyage to the underworld.

My concern here is not with the moral effects of this music—whether it leads to sex, violence or drugs. The issue here is its effect on education, and I believe it ruins the imagination of young people and makes it very difficult for them to have a passionate relationship to the art and thought that are the substance of liberal education. The first sensuous experiences are decisive in determining the taste for the whole of life, and they are the link between the animal and spiritual in us. The period of nascent sensuality has always been used for sublimation, in the sense of making sublime, for attaching youthful inclinations and longings to music, pictures and stories that provide the transition to the fulfillment of the human duties and the enjoyment of the human pleasures. Lessing, speaking of Greek sculpture, said "beautiful men made beautiful statues, and the city had beautiful statues in part to thank for beautiful citizens." This formula encapsulates the fundamental principle of the esthetic education of man. Young men and women were attracted by the beauty of heroes whose very bodies expressed their nobility. The deeper understanding of the meaning of nobility comes later, but is prepared for by the sensuous experience and is actually contained in it. What the senses long for as well as what reason later sees as good are thereby not at tension with one another. Education is not sermonizing to children against their instincts and pleasures, but providing a natural continuity between what they feel and what they can and should be. But this is a lost art. Now we have come to exactly the opposite point. Rock music encourages passions and provides models that have no relation to any life the young people who go to universities can possibly lead, or to the kinds of admiration encouraged by liberal studies. Without the cooperation of the sentiments, anything other than technical education is a dead letter.

Rock music provides premature ecstasy and, in this respect, is like the drugs with which it is allied. It artificially induces the exaltation naturally attached to the completion of the greatest endeavors—victory in a just war, consummated love, artistic creation, religious devotion and discovery of the truth. Without effort, without talent, without virtue, without exercise of the faculties, anyone and everyone is accorded the equal right to the enjoyment of their fruits. In my experience, students who have had a serious fling with drugs—and gotten over it—find it difficult to have enthusiasms or great expectations. It is as though the color has been drained out of their lives and they see everything in black and white. The pleasure they experienced in the beginning was so intense that they no longer look for it at the end, or as the end. They may function perfectly well, but dryly, routinely. Their energy has been sapped, and they do not expect their life's activity to produce anything but a living, whereas liberal education is supposed to encourage the belief that the good life is the pleasant life and that the best life is the most pleasant life. I suspect that the rock addiction, particularly in the absence of strong counterattractions, has an effect similar to that of drugs. The students will get over this music, or at least the exclusive passion for it. But they will do so in the same way Freud says that men accept the reality principle—as something harsh, grim and essentially unattractive, a mere necessity. These students will assiduously study economics or the professions and the Michael Jackson costume will slip off to reveal a Brooks Brothers suit beneath. They will want to get ahead and live comfortably. But this life is as empty and false as the one they left behind. The choice is not between quick fixes and dull calculation. This is what liberal education is meant to show them. But as long as they have the Walkman on, they cannot hear what the great tradition has to say. And, after its prolonged use, when they take it off, they find they are deaf.

SPECULATIONS

1.   Allan Bloom writes: "Today, a very large portion of young people between the ages of ten and twenty live for music. It is their passion; nothing else excites them as it does; they cannot take seriously anything alien to music." Discuss this opinion. What do you think he means by "music" as young people's "passion"?

2.   What is extraordinary about music for you? How do you compare the importance and value of music to other daily activities such as school, work, watching television, dating?

3.   Consider the kinds of music you like and listen to the most. How would you describe the benefits, educational qualities, and entertainment value of your music? Or put another way, how does music affect you and your peers?

4.   Notice that Bloom refers to Richard Wagner's operas, the classical music of Beethoven, Chopin, and Brahms, the philosophy of Plato and Nietzsche, and many other literary figures in our culture. Why does he do this? How do these figures illustrate present-day culture?

5.   What is Bloom's attitude toward students in this essay? How does he talk about them? What tone does he use? How do you feel about his attitude toward "today's students"? Would you take a class from this teacher? Why or why not?

6.   Assume you are a parent of a teenage daughter and a teenage son: How would you respond to the effects of rock music on teenagers described by Bloom? Are these effects that you would want your own teenage son and daughter to experience? Why or why not?

Urban Spaceman

JUDITH WILLIAMSON

Judith Williamson's prose shows a remarkable talent for combining the personal, the political, the theoretical, and the practical in a fluent and accessible writing style. Born in 1954 in England, Williamson recounts how she struggled with her own passions during her teenage years, torn between the desire for "magazine glamour" and the knowledge that she would never achieve it. Ultimately, she set out on an intellectual quest to discover how she could be so drawn to this pop-concept of "beauty," a desire sustained by its own inevitable unfulfillment. After continuing avidly to read both Karl Marx and *Honey* glamour magazine as a teenager, she arrived at the University of California in Berkeley with a bulging file of advertisements clipped out of magazines over many years. There she began her analysis of popular culture by analyzing how and why these advertisements had such powerful effects on her. The result was her first book, *Decoding Advertisements: Ideology and Meaning in Advertising*, which has been a tremendous success since its publication in 1978. In the Preface to *Decoding Advertisements*, she describes her goals as follows: "We should be trying to see new things both in society and in our own feelings and reactions. . . . My interest has never been so much in adverts [advertisements] as in what they show about our society and ways of seeing ourselves."

"Urban Spaceman" is from Judith Williamson's second book, *Consuming Passions*, which opens with the following insight: "We are consuming passions all the time—at the shops, at the movies, in the streets, in the classroom: in the old familiar ways that no longer seem passionate because they are the shared paths of our social world, the known shapes of our waking dreams." According to Williamson, wearing and listening to a Walkman in public is not just a simple act of pleasure; it defines a relationship between the private and public, between the individual and public communion. This kind of rich insight is characteristic of the way Williamson takes the ordinary and helps us understand its deeper significance.

A vodka advertisement in the London underground shows a cartoon man and woman with little headphones over their ears and little cassette players over their shoulders. One of them holds up a card which asks, "Your place or mine?"—so incapable are they of communicating in any other way. The walkman has become a familiar image of modern urban life, creating troops of sleep-walking space-creatures, who seem to feel themselves invisible because they imagine that what they're listening to is inaudible. It rarely is: nothing is more irritating than the gnats' orchestra which so frequently assails the fellow-passenger of an oblivious walk-person—sounding, literally, like a flea in your ear. Although disconcertingly insubstantial, this phantom music has all the piercing insistency of a digital watch alarm;

it is your request to the headphoned one to turn it down that cannot be heard. The argument that the walkman protects the *public* from hearing one person's sounds, is back-to-front: it is the walk-person who is protected from the outside world, for whether or not their music is audible they are shut off as if by a spell.

The walkman is a vivid symbol of our time. It provides a concrete image of alienation, suggesting an implicit hostility to, and isolation from, the environment in which it is worn. Yet it also embodies the underlying values of precisely the society which produces that alienation—those principles which are the lynchpin of Thatcherite Britain: individualism, privatization and "choice." The walkman is primarily a way of escaping from a *shared* experience or environment. It produces a privatized sound, in the public domain; a weapon of the individual against the communal. It attempts to negate *chance:* you never know what you are going to hear on a bus or in the streets, but the walk-person is buffered against the unexpected—an apparent triumph of individual control over social spontaneity. Of course, *what the walk person controls* is very limited; they can only affect their *own* environment, and although this may make the individual *feel* active (or even rebellious) in social terms they are absolutely passive. The wearer of a walkman states that they expect to make no input into the social arena, no speech, no reaction, no intervention. Their own body is the extent of their domain. The turning of desire for control inwards towards the body has been a much more general phenomenon of recent years; as if one's muscles or jogging record were all that one *could* improve in this world. But while everyone listens to whatever they want within their "private" domestic space, the peculiarity of the walkman is that it turns the inside of the head into a mobile home—rather like the building society image of the couple who, instead of an umbrella, carry a tiled roof over their heads (to protect them against hazards created by the same system that provides their mortgage).

This interpretation of the walkman may seem extreme, but only because first, we have become accustomed to the privatization of social space, and second, we have come to regard sound as secondary to sight—a sort of accompaniment to a life which appears as essentially visual. Imagine people walking round the streets with little TVs strapped in front of their eyes, because they would rather watch a favorite film or program than see where they were going, and what was going on around them. (It could be argued that this would be too dangerous—but how about the thousands of suicidal cyclists who prefer taped music to their own safety?) This bizarre idea is no more extreme in principle than the walkman. In the visual media there has already been a move from the social setting of the cinema, to the privacy of the TV set in the living room, and personalized mobile viewing would be the logical next step. In all media, the technology of this century has been directed towards a shift, first from the social to the private—from concert to record player—and then of the private *into* the social—exemplified by the walkman, which, paradoxically, allows someone to listen to a recording of a public concert, in public, completely privately.

The contemporary antithesis to the walkman is perhaps the appropriately named ghetto blaster. Music in the street or played too loud indoors *can* be extremely anti-social—although at least its perpetrators can hear you when you come and tell them to shut up. Yet in its current use, the ghetto blaster stands for a shared experience, a communal event. Outdoors, ghetto blasters are seldom used by only their individual owners, but rather act as the focal point for a group, something to gather around. In urban life "the streets" stand for shared existence, a common understanding, a place that is owned by no one and used by everyone. The traditional custom of giving people the "freedom of the city" has a meaning which can be appropriated for ourselves today. There *is* a kind of freedom about *chance* encounters, which is why conversations and arguments in buses and bus queues are often so much livelier than those of the wittiest dinner party. Help is also easy to come by on urban streets, whether with a burst shopping bag or a road accident.

It would be a great romanticization not to admit that all these social places can also hold danger, abuse, violence. But, in both its good and bad aspects, urban space is like the physical medium of society itself. The prevailing ideology sees society as simply a mathematical sum of its individual parts, a collection of private interests. Yet social life demonstrates the transformation of quantity into quality: it has something extra, over and above the characteristics of its members in isolation. That "something extra" is unpredictable, unfixed, and resides in interaction. It would be a victory for the same forces that have slashed public transport and privatized British Telecom, if the day were to come when everyone walked the street in headphones.

SPECULATIONS

1. We have all observed people using walkmans in public. What seems different or odd about people's behavior when they have walkmans on? How does the walkman change your relation to these people or theirs to you?

2. What is striking about the vocabulary Williamson uses to describe the effects of the walkman on society? What specific words does she use to describe the individual versus the social effects of the walkman? How would you characterize her tone, her voice, her identity as an author?

3. When Williamson says "There *is* a kind of freedom about *chance* encounters, which is why conversations and arguments in buses and bus queues are so much livelier than at the wittiest dinner party," what is she driving at? What kind of human interaction does she see threatened by the walkman?

4. If you went to a party or street dance and wore a walkman the whole time, how would it change your interactions with your peers? How does the walkman affect your view of the music you listen to?

5. Imagine that you were told that you could not use a walkman in a public space for safety reasons. How would you argue for or against your right to privacy in a public space?

What Pop Lyrics Say to Us

ROBERT PALMER

No one understands music like a musician. Robert Palmer first established his credentials as a professional saxophonist and clarinetist who played in jazz groups, rock bands, and country music combos for five years before he became a freelance music writer in 1970. Six years later he assumed the position of contemporary music critic for *The New York Times*, a position he has held ever since. Palmer has recorded jazz, popular, contemporary, and experimental music with a variety of labels including Capitol, Atco, and A&M. He has also worked as a professor of vernacular music at Bowdoin College, Yale University, and the Smithsonian Institution.

Born in Little Rock, Arkansas, in 1945, Palmer earned a B.A. at the University of Arkansas in 1967. A member of the American Folklore Society and the Society for Ethnomusicology, Palmer has written five books, including *Baby, That Was Rock & Roll* (1978), *Jerry Lee Lewis Rocks!* (1981), and *The Rolling Stones* (1983). Perhaps his best known book is *Deep Blues* (1981), which traces the history of the blues from its West African origins through the Mississippi Delta to Chicago and the northern cities of the United States. Winner of the ASCAP-Deems Taylor Award, the book was described by Charles Keil in his August 7, 1981 *New York Times Book Review* as a "storehouse of black history, filled with rich detail and dialogue, wonderful memories of recording sessions, parties and performances and, most important, crucial information about the precise point at which deep blues became the high profitable commodity called rock."

The essay included here first appeared in the *New York Times* in 1985. In it, Palmer traces the cultural echoes, the popular attitudes, and the political messages embedded in the popular music of three decades, from the 1960s through the 1980s. Although Palmer provides insights in terms of evolutionary history, his most important question remains only partially answered: What do pop lyrics say to us? In asking and trying to answer this question, Palmer returns to the basic question that Judith Williamson asked about our consuming passions for music and advertising; that is, how does our popular music show us who we are—and what we desire to be?

Bruce Springsteen became the first rock lyricist to be courted by both of the major candidates in a Presidential election last fall. First Ronald Reagan singled him out as an artist whose songs instill pride in America. Walter Mondale retaliated, asserting that *he* had won the rock star's endorsement. "Bruce may have been born to run," Mr. Mondale quipped, quoting the title of a Springsteen hit, "but he wasn't born yesterday."

Rock is part of adult culture now, to an extent that would have been unthinkable as recently as a decade ago. It is no longer the exclusive reserve of young people sending messages to each other. But pop music has always reflected and responded to the currents of its own time, and today's pop music is no exception. What does it seem to be telling us about our own time? Part of the message is in the music itself—in the insistence of the beat, the shriek of heavily amplified guitars. But lyrics remain the most accurate barometer of what makes *these* times different from, for example, the 1960s and '70s.

Today's pop music is sending several dominant messages. Material values are on the ascendant, but idealism is by no means a spent force. Most pop songs are love songs, as always, but today's versions try to look at relationships without rose-colored glasses. Romantic notions are viewed with some suspicion; so are drugs. And important rock artists and rappers, while no longer anticipating radical change, are addressing issues, and challenging their listeners to actively confront the world around them. There have probably been more angry protest lyrics written and recorded in the last three or four years than in any comparable period of the '60s.

In the '60s, it would have been unthinkable for a politician to seek endorsements from rock musicians; rock was rebel music. Stars like Bob Dylan and the Rolling Stones wrote and recorded outspoken lyrics that urged sweeping social change and an end to war, and flirted with the rhetoric revolution. They sang openly about sex and drugs. The music was the voice of a new generation and a constant reminder of the generation gap. The battle lines were drawn.

The rock lyricists of the '60s were fond of talking about "love." To the Beatles, "love" was transcendent, an irresistible force for good that could accomplish practically anything. ("All You Need is Love," for example.)

Love is still something one hears a great deal about in pop lyrics, but the contemporary version is more hard-headed and down-to-earth than the cosmic, effulgent Love of the '60s. Many of today's songwriters argue that romance isn't as important as material values or sex. "What's love go to do with it?" Tina Turner asked in her recent heavy-breathing hit of the same title. And Madonna, whose come-hither pout and undulating style have made her pop's hottest video star, serves notice in her hit "Material Girl" (written by Peter Brown and Robert Rans) that she won't worry much about love as long as there's money in the bank. . . .[1]

Madonna's carefully calculated image has struck a chord among many of today's more affluent young listeners, though she is perhaps too one-dimensional to be Queen of the Yuppies. And she will never be the darling of the feminists.

Nevertheless, during the past decade, the hue and cry against rock lyrics that demeaned women seemed to have a broad and salutary effect. One didn't here many songs of the sort the Rolling Stones and other '60s bands used to perform, songs like the Stones' "Under My Thumb."

> Under my thumb her eyes are just kept to herself
> Under my thumb, well, I can still look at someone else
> It's down to me, the way she talks when she's spoken to
> Down to me, the change has come, she's under my thumb.[2]

The title tune from Mick Jagger's new solo album, "She's The Boss," is sung like a taunt or a tease, but that doesn't disguise its message; Mr. Jagger seems to have experienced a shift in values since he wrote "Under My Thumb."

> She's the boss! She's the boss!
> She's the boss in bed, she's the boss in my head
> She's got the pants on, now she's the boss.[3]

Still, many of today's pop lyrics continue to celebrate male dominance. Aggressively macho rock has been making a comeback. Heavy metal rock, which appeals almost exclusively to white male teen-agers and tends to treat women as either temptresses or chattel, is more popular than ever. Women like Tina Turner and Cyndi Lauper, who project a certain independence and strength, are helping to counter this trend, but sometimes one can't hear them very well over heavy metal's sexist thunder.

---

[1] Permission to reprint four lines here from Madonna's "Material Girl" was denied by Jack Rosner at Warner/Chappel Music in Los Angeles, California. [Eds.]
[2] From "Under My Thumb" by Mick Jagger and Keith Richards. © 1966 by ABCKO Music, Inc. All rights reserved. Reprinted by permission.
[3] From "She's the Boss" by Mick Jagger. All rights reserved. Reprinted by permission of Promopub B. V.

Amid these changes in attitude, the old-fashioned romantic love song, always the staple of pop lyrics, continues to flourish. Prince, another of today's biggest-selling artists, has progressed from early songs that dealt explicitly with various sexual situations and permutations to love lyrics of a more conventional sort. "Take Me With U" (sic), a song from his phenomenally successful album "Purple Rain," could have been written decades ago or yesterday.

Pop songs can do more than chart changing attitudes toward love and romance; they can address topical issues and appeal to our social conscience. In the 60's, Bob Dylan and other songwriters composed anthems that were sung by civil rights workers as they headed south, and by hundreds of thousands demonstrating for peace and equal rights. "How many deaths will it take till we know that too many people have died," Dylan asked. "The answer, my friend, is blowin' in the wind."[4] And, he added, in a line in another song that provided a name for the radical faction within Students for a Democratic Society, "You don't need a weatherman to tell which way the wind blows."

By the late '60s, the peace and civil rights movements were beginning to splinter. The assassinations of the Kennedys and Martin Luther King had robbed a generation of its heroes, the Vietnam war was escalating despite the protests, and at home, violence was on the rise. Young people turned to rock, expecting it to ask the right questions and come up with answers, hoping that the music's most visionary artists could somehow make sense of things. But rock's most influential artists—Bob Dylan, the Beatles, the Rolling Stones—were finding that serving as the conscience of a generation exacted a heavy toll. Mr. Dylan, for one, felt the pressures becoming unbearable, and wrote about his predicament in songs like "All Along the Watchtower."

> "There must be some way out of here," said the joker to the thief.
> "There's too much confusion, I can't get no relief.
> "Businessmen they drink my wine, plowmen dig my earth.
> "None of them along the line knows what any of it is worth."[5]

Many rock artists of the '60s turned to drugs before the decade ended. For a while, songs that were thought to be about drugs, whatever their original intentions (Bob Dylan's "Mr. Tambourine Man," the Byrds' "Eight Miles High," the Rolling Stones' "Get Off My Cloud"), were widely heard. Bob Dylan sang that "everybody must

---

[4] From "Blowin' in the Wind" by Bob Dylan. © 1962 (Renewed) Warner Bros. Inc. All rights reserved. Used by permission.

[5] From "All Along the Watchtower" by Bob Dylan. Copyright © 1968 by Dwarf Music. All rights reserved. International copyright secured. Reprinted by permission.

get stoned," and many young people seemed to agree. But the fad for drug lyrics was short-lived. They were never again as prevalent as during that brief Indian summer of the counter-culture. One hears few drug references in today's pop lyrics, and when drugs *are* mentioned, listeners are usually advised to stay away from them; "Don't do it," Grandmaster Flash and the Furious Five cautioned listeners about to experiment with drugs in their rap hit "White Lines."

The mainstream rock of the 1970s produced little in the way of socially relevant lyrics. But toward the end of that decade a change began to be felt. The rise of punk rock in Britain brought to the country's pop charts angry songs about unemployment and nuclear Armageddon. In America, the issue of nuclear energy and the threat of nuclear war enlisted the sympathies of many prominent rock musicians. But attempts by Graham Nash, John Hall, and other anti-nuclear activists to turn their concerns into anthems were too self-conscious; the songs were quickly forgotten.

Rap, the new pop idiom that exploded out of New York's black and Latin neighborhoods in the late 70s, seemed to concern itself mostly with hedonism and verbal strutting—at first. Then, in the early 80's, came "The Message," the dance-single by Grandmaster Flash and the Furious Five that provided listeners with an angry, eye-witness account of inner-city neighborhoods and people abandoned to rot, prey to crime, poverty, and disease. "It's like a jungle/Sometimes it makes me wonder/How I keep from going under,"[6] chanted the group's champion rapper, Melle Mel.

The rap records of the last several years have confronted similar issues head-on, and they have been danceable enough to attract a sizable audience. Run-D.M.C.'s recent his single "It's Like That" ticked off a list of some of the daily horrors many black Americans have to contend with. But you can't give up, Run-D.M.C. insisted to their young, predominantly black and urban audience. You have to make something of yourself, to rise above "the way it is."

Bruce Springsteen's recent songs have also been topical and deeply felt. They have also been the most popular music of his career. He is writing for and about the America of his dreams and the America he sees around him, and his lyrics are followed closely by a huge audience, as last year's [1984] Presidential campaign references made abundantly clear.

The narrator of Mr. Springsteen's recent hit "Born in the U.S.A." is a Vietnam veteran who returns home to confront harsh realities.

---

[6] From "The Message." © 1983 Sugar Hill Music, Inc. Used with permission.

> Went down to see my V.A. man
> He said "Son don't you understand now"
> Had a brother at Khe Sahn fighting off the Viet Cong
> They're still there he's all gone[7]

Other songs on Mr. Springsteen's most recent album suggest that there is a pervasive gloom hanging over the country's decaying inner cities and factory towns. But their message is a positive one. "Hold on," the songs seem to say, "you've got to have something to believe in." The laborer in "Working on the Highway" is certainly hanging on to *his* dream:

> I work for the county out on 95
> All day I hold a red flag and watch the traffic pass me by
> In my head I keep a picture of a pretty little miss
> Someday mister I'm gonna lead a better life than this.[7]

Mr. Springsteen's songs look at America and find both despair and hope. And like Chuck Berry and so many other rock and roll lyricists, past and present, he finds a source of strength and inspiration in rock itself. Singing of his schooldays, he captures rock and roll's heart:

> We learned more from a three-minute record than we
> ever learned in school
> Tonight I hear the neighborhood drummer sound
> I can feel my heart begin to pound
> We made a promise we swore we'd always remember
> No retreat, no surrender.[7]

SPECULATIONS

1. What is Robert Palmer's thesis about pop lyrics and their message? What do pop lyrics tell us?
2. Give several specific examples of how Palmer's ideas about music lyrics apply to songs you know, and describe how the message in those lyrics resembles or differs from specific lyrics Palmer talks about.
3. What is Palmer's argument about feminist views and the lyrics used by the Rolling Stones and by heavy metal rock bands? Explain why you agree or disagree with his argument and give specific examples from rock music.
4. What changes does Palmer describe from the music of the 1950s to the music of the early 1980s? How do these changes relate to a social awareness and how have these changes continued or faltered, in your opinion, in the 1990s?
5. Why do you think Palmer ends with several selected lyrics from the music of Bruce Springsteen? What kind of final message do these lyrics project?

---

[7] From "Born in the U.S.A.," "Working on the Highway," and "No Surrender" by Bruce Springsteen. Reprinted by permission of Jon Landau Management.

Born to Run

BRUCE SPRINGSTEEN

Born in Freehold, New Jersey, in 1949, rock singer and songwriter Bruce Springsteen began playing his guitar at the age of thirteen. He joined a band called the Castiles and was writing songs for them by the age of eighteen. Springsteen's lyrics are carefully crafted and his image is that of a romantic, working-class man. His exuberant performances on stage are considered by many to be the high point of rock; it was rumored that one NBA basketball star demanded that tickets to Springsteen concerts be written into his Portland Trail-blazers' contract.

Springsteen's lyrics often speak to the darker side of American culture: shattered dreams, racial conflicts, sexual passion that can never quite find its fulfillment. He may be best known for his best-selling album *Born in the U.S.A.* and his extremely popular video "Dancing in the Dark," which highlights Springsteen's performing prowess. "Born to Run," from the album of the same name (1975), contains some of his most allegorical lyrics.

In the day we sweat it out on the streets
   of a runaway American dream
At night we ride through mansions
   of glory in suicide machines
Sprung from cages on Highway 9
Chrome wheeled, fuel injected
And steppin' out over the line
Oh, Baby this town rips the bones from your back
It's a death trap, it's a suicide rap
We gotta get out while we're young
'Cause tramps like us, baby we were born to run

Wendy, let me in, I wanna be your friend
I wanna guard your dreams and visions
Just wrap your legs round these velvet rims
And strap your hands 'cross my engines
Together we could break this trap
We'll run till we drop and, baby, we'll never go back
Oh, Will you walk with me out on the wire?
'Cause baby I'm just a scared and lonely rider
But I gotta know how it feels
I want to know if love is wild, babe,
I want to know if love is real

Beyond the Palace hemi-powered drones
   scream down the boulevard
Girls comb their hair in rear-view mirrors
And the boys try to look so hard

The amusement park rises bold and stark
As kids are huddled on the beach in a mist
I wanna die with you, Wendy, on the streets tonight
In an everlasting kiss

The highways jammed with broken heroes
On a last chance power drive
Everybody's out on the run tonight
But there's no place left to hide
Together, Wendy, we can live with the sadness
I'll love you with all the madness in my soul
Oh, someday girl, I don't know when,
   we're gonna get to that place
Where we really wanna go
And we'll walk in the sun
But till then tramps like us
Baby we were born to run

Ah, honey, tramps like us
Baby, we were born to run!
Come on, Wendy
Tramps like us, baby, we were born to run!

SPECULATIONS

1.   How would you describe the speaker of these lines? What is bothering him? What does he want to do and to change about his life?
2.   This song is now over fifteen years old. How would you relate to the song if you heard it for the first time today? Relate the song to some of the other essays that you have read in this book.

The Rap Attitude

JERRY ADLER

Jerry Adler's stance in "The Rap Attitude" might best be described as hard-hitting, a kind of "frontal assault–take no prisoners" approach to argument. This strategy can be effective, but Adler does more than just slash and burn. His considerable understanding of the arts can be seen from his informed allusions to opera, jazz artist Jelly Roll Morton, and folk singer Woody Guthrie. This depth of knowledge establishes Adler as someone who knows his subject, an authority worth listening to. What characterizes his point of view is his abiding concern for the moral impact of music on youth, similar in some ways to the concerns expressed by Allan Bloom.

Well known in the New York theater community, Jerry Adler is a
graduate of Syracuse University and has spent most of his career as
a director, stage manager, and producer of Broadway musical theater
and television, including *My Fair Lady, Camelot, California Suite,* and
Little Murders.

To his credit, Adler's commentary on rap and heavy metal music,
originally published in *Newsweek* magazine, takes into account both
sides of the story behind the recent evolution of negative attitudes
in our society. He presents the conservative reactions of organizations such as the Parents' Music Resource Center and the FBI as well
as the liberal sentiments of the American Civil Liberties Union and
the rap groups' own attempts to defend themselves against criticism.
Perhaps the most telling and disturbing aspect of his indictment,
however, is his analysis of the band members' public statements and
his close readings of the song lyrics themselves.

Let's talk about "attitude." And I don't mean a good attitude,
either. I mean "attitude" by itself, which is always bad, as in, you'd
better not be bringing any attitude around here, boy, and, when that
bitch gave me some attitude, I cut her good. I mean attitude as a
cultural style, marrying the arrogance of Donald Trump to the vulgarity of Roseanne Barr. Comedians have attitude, rock bands have attitude, in America today even *birthday cards* have attitude. In the rap-
music group N.W.A, which stands for Niggas With Attitude, you
don't have to guess what kind of attitude they mean: jaunty and sullen
by turns; showy but somehow furtive, in glasses as opaque as a limousine window and sneakers as white as a banker's shirt. Their music
is a rhythmic chant, a rhyme set to a drum solo, a rant from the streets
about gunning down cops. Now *that's* attitude.

OK, here it is: the first important cultural development in America
in 25 years that the baby-boom generation didn't pioneer: The Culture
of Attitude. It is heard in the thundering cacophony of heavy metal
and the thumping, clattering, scratching assault of rap—music so
postindustrial it's mostly not even *played*, but pieced together out of
prerecorded sound bites. It is the culture of American males frozen in
various stages of adolescence: their streetwise music, their ugly macho
boasting and joking about anyone who hangs out on a different
block—cops, other races, women and homosexuals. Its most visible
contribution has been the disinterment of the word nigger, a generation after a national effort to banish it and its ugly connotations from
the American language. Now it is back, employed with savage irony
by black rappers and dumb literal hostility by their white heavy-metal
counterparts. *Nigger! Faggot!* What ever happened to the idea that
rock and roll would make us free?

Although most Americans may never have heard of them, these
are not obscure bands playing in garages and afterhours clubs. In the
'70s, urban rappers performed in parks, plugging loudspeakers into

lampposts. Now they fill major arenas—although more and more arenas won't have rap concerts any longer, because of fear that the violence can spill over from the stage to the crowd. Public Enemy, a
rap group caught up in a protracted anti-Semitic controversy, and
N.W.A., have had platinum albums, with more than a million in sales.
The heavy-metal group Guns N' Roses sold more than 4 million copies
worldwide of the "G N' R Lies" record, whose lyrics insult blacks,
homosexuals and "immigrants" inside 10 lines. Major companies are
behind them: Public Enemy's releases for the Def Jam label are distributed by CBS/Columbia Records; Guns N' Roses parades its prejudices
on Geffen Records, headed by the noted AIDS philanthropist David
Geffen.

Attitude! Civilized society abhors attitude, and perpetuates itself
by keeping it under control. There are entire organizations devoted
to this job, most notably the Parents' Music Resource Center in Arling-
ton, Va. The center has an extensive file of lyrics in rap and heavy-
metal music, describing every imaginable perversity from unsafe sex
to Devil worship. (The Satanist influence on heavy metal called down
a condemnation last week from New York's Cardinal John O'Connor
as well.) But executive director Jennifer Norwood is careful to point
out that the center takes "no position on any specific type of music."
There are rap ballads whose sentiments would not have brought a
blush to the cheek of Bing Crosby, and rap acts that promote an antidrug message. The center does support printing song lyrics on album
jackets for the information of parents—although such a step might
also make it easier for kids to learn them—and a warning label, which
some record companies already apply voluntarily, about "explicit
lyrics."

Others who stand against attitude include Florida Gov. Bob Martinez, who asked the statewide prosecutor to investigate the Miami rap
group The 2 Live Crew for alleged violations of obscenity laws in the
album "As Nasty as They Want to Be." "If you answer the phone one
night and the voice on the other end begins to read the lyrics of one of
those songs, you'd say you received an obscene phone call," reasoned
Martinez. This proved to be outside the governor's jurisdiction. But a
Broward County judge last week cleared the way for prosecutors to
charge record-shop owners who *sell* the album; courts would then
rule on whether the material was obscene. And the Kentucky-based
chain that operates 121 Disc Jockey record stores announced that it
would no longer carry records with warning stickers. In part, says
company executive Harold Guilfoil, this is a move to preempt manda-
tory-labeling and sales-restriction laws under consideration in at least
10 states. A Pennsylvania bill that has already passed in one House
would require labels for lyrics describing or advocating suicide, incest,

sodomy, morbid violence or several other things. "That about takes care of every opera in the world," observes Guilfoil.

Particularly concerned is the Anti-Defamation league, whose civil-rights director, Jeffrey Sinensky, sees evidence in popular music that "hatred is becoming hip." The rap group Public Enemy was the most notorious offender, not even for anything in their music, but for remarks by a nonsinging member of the group, Professor Griff, a hanger-on and backup dancer with the grandiloquent but meaningless title of Minister of Information. Griff, a follower of Louis Farrakhan's Nation of Islam, gave an interview last spring in which he parroted some Farrakhanesque nonsense about Jews being behind "the majority of wickedness that goes on across the globe." After the predictable outcry Griff was fired and the group disbanded; but soon it re-formed, and Griff came back as "Supreme Allied Chief of Community Relations," a position in which he is not allowed to talk to the press. And Public Enemy proceeded to discuss the episode in ominous, if somewhat obscure, terms in "Welcome to the Terrordome," a single prereleased from its forthcoming album, "Fear of a Black Planet". . . .

"I mean, I made the apology, but people are still trying to give me hell," elaborates Public Enemy's lead rapper, Chuck D. "The media crucified me, comparable to another brother who caught hell." If you add up all the Jewish blood that has been spilled over the slander of deicide, it makes Chuck D's sufferings at the hands of his critics seem mild by comparison. The ADL reacted swiftly to what appeared to be a gratuitous incitement to anti-Semitism, and took its protest to where it would do the most good, CBS Records. CBS Records Inc. president Walter Yetnikoff responded with a commitment to police future releases for "bigotry and intolerance." While "it goes without saying that artists have the right of freedom of expression," Yetnikoff wrote in a memo to the rest of the company, "when the issue is bigotry, there is a fine line of acceptable standards which no piece of music should cross." And once again, Chuck D is saying that Professor Griff will leave the group . . . maybe later this year.

N.W.A.'s attitude even got it into trouble with the FBI. In a letter last summer to N.W.A.'s distributor, FBI Assistant Director Milt Ahlerich observed that the groups' album "Straight Outta Compton" "encourages violence against and disrespect for the law-enforcement officer." But Ahlerich couldn't do much more than make the company "aware of the FBI's position" on lyrics in a song ("F--- Tha Police") he couldn't bring himself to name:

> Pullin' out a silly club so you stand
>   With a fake-ass badge and a gun in your
>   hand
> Take off the gun so you can see what's up

> And we'll go at it, punk, and I'm 'a f--- you
>   up . . .
> I'm a sniper with a hell of a 'scope . . .
>   Takin' out a cop or two . . .

Are even such appalling expressions of attitude protected by the First Amendment? Yes, according to an American Civil Liberties Union official, who told *The Village Voice* that "the song does not constitute advocacy of violence as that has been interpreted by the courts." (Although in plain English, it's hard to imagine what else it might be advocating.) Asked whether his music doesn't give the impression that the gang culture in the sorry Los Angeles slum of Compton is fun, Eazy-E, the groups coleader, replied, "It *is* fun," "'F--- tha police' was something people be wanting to say for years but they were too scared to say it," he says. "The next album might be 'F--- tha FBI'".

Yes, having an attitude means it's always someone else's fault: cops who disrespect (or "dis") you when you walk through a housing project with a gold chain that could lock up a motorcycle, immigrants so dumb they can't speak the language, women who are just asking for it anyway. The outrageous implication is that to *not* sing about this stuff would be to do violence to an artistic vision as pure and compelling as Bach's. The viler the message, the more fervent the assertion of honesty that underlies it. Eazy sometimes calls himself a "street historian" to deflect the charge that he is a rabble-rouser. "We're like underground reporters," he says; "We just telling it like it is, we don't hold back." The fact is, rap grows out of a violent culture in which getting shot by a cop is a real fear. But music isn't reportage, and the way to deal with police brutality is not to glorify "taking out a cop or two." By way of self-exculpation, Eazy denies any aspirations toward being a role model. As he puts it, "I don't like anybody want to look at me and stop being theyself."

Even so, Eazy sounds like Edmund Wilson, compared with Axl Rose of Guns N' Roses trying to explain the lyrics to "One in a Million." He says he's mad at immigrants because he had a run-in with a Middle Eastern clerk at a 7-Eleven. He hates homosexuals because one once made advances to him while he was sleeping. This is a textbook definition of bigotry. "I used words like . . . niggers because you're not allowed to use the word nigger," he told his "authorized biographer," Del James, in an interview printed in *Rolling Stone*. "I don't like being told what I can and what I can't say. I used the word *nigger* because it's a word to describe somebody that is basically a pain in your life, a problem. The word nigger doesn't necessarily mean black."

Oh, no? This is an example of what Todd Gitlin, director of the mass-communications program at the University of California, Berkeley, calls the "free-floating rancor" of the youth culture, the "tribal acrimony" that leads to fights over turf, real and psychic. Attitude primarily is a working-class and underclass phenomenon, a response to the diminishing expectations of the millions of American youths who forgot to go to business school in the 1980s. *If* they had ever listened to anything except the homeboys talking trash, *if* they had ever studied anything but the strings of a guitar, they might have some more interesting justifications to offer. They could quote the sainted Woody Guthrie about "Pretty Boy Floyd," who "laid [a] deputy down" (for disrespecting his wife, as it happened in the song). Apropos of their penchant for exaggerated sexual braggadocio, they could point out that the great jazz pianist Jelly Roll Morton didn't get his nickname because he liked pastry. They could point out that as recently as a generation ago, racial epithets that today would make Morton Downey, Jr., swoon with embarrassment came tripping innocently off the tongues of educated, decent people. *Then* we might have a sensible discussion with them; but they haven't, so we can't.

But of course attitude resists any such attempt at intellectualizing. To call it visceral is to give it the benefit of the doubt. It has its origins in parts of the body even less mentionable, as the pioneering California rapper Ice-T puts it: "Women have some eerie connection with gangsters. They always want the rebel more than the brain. Girls want somebody who can beat everybody up." . . .

This is the height of gallantry for Ice-T: no one gets killed. More often, when attitude meets woman, woman is by far the worse for it. If she's lucky, she gets made love to with a flashlight ("Shut Up, Be Happy" by Ice-T). Otherwise, she finds herself in the even less healthy company of Eazy-E:

> Now back on the street and
>   my records are clean
> I creeped on my bitch with my
>   Uzi machine
> Went to the house and kicked
>   down the door
>   Unloaded like hell, cold
>   smoked the ho'.

It is not just that romance has gone out of music—attitude has done the seemingly impossible and taken sex out of teenage culture, substituting brutal fantasies of penetration and destruction. Girls who want to have fun this way need to have their heads examined.

But that's the point. The end of attitude is nihilism, which by definition leads nowhere. The culture of attitude is repulsive, but it's mostly empty of political content. As Gitlin puts it, "There's always a population of kids looking to be bad. As soon as the establishment tells them what's bad this season, some of them are going to go off and do it." And that's not good, but it's probably not a case for the FBI, either. If we learned one thing from the '60s, it's how *little* power rock and roll has to change the world.

SPECULATIONS

1.   In "The Rap Attitude," Adler makes the argument that in much of today's music, particularly rap music, it is acceptable and even desirable to be offensive and insulting. Can you provide examples beyond the article? Is this a new phenomenon or do we find similar instances in the history of popular music, such as Elvis, the Beatles, and the Rolling Stones?

2.   Why does Adler assert that "civilized society abhors attitude, and perpetuates itself by keeping it under control. There are entire organizations devoted to this job, most notably the Parents' Music Resource Center. . . ."? Why should attitude be kept under control? What do you think "civilized society" is afraid of here? Discuss Adler's "attitude" in this essay.

3.   What does Adler's analysis of Ice-T's music say about this kind of rap music and sexuality? What attitude toward women and sex does this music express and what lies behind that attitude? Discuss whether this attitude is appropriate and realistic or dangerous?

4.   How have you been frightened or threatened by other people's strongly expressed feelings or "attitudes"? Draw on your own personal experiences to explain what you think people should be free to say and what you think the limits of free expression are. Who gets hurt when such limits are either imposed or violated?

5.   Adler finally argues that rock and roll has "little power" to change the world. Why does he make this final argument? Do you agree or disagree? What specific examples from your own experience or observations about rock and roll support your view?

The War on Rock and Rap Music
BARBARA DORITY

Barbara Dority is a committed activist in politics and social reform. President of the Humanists of Washington, Executive Director of the Washington Coalition Against Censorship, and a member of the Washington Board of the American Civil Liberties Union, she is familiar with the legal ramifications of censorship and its history in the popular music world. Writing for *The Humanist* magazine, Dority upholds an unequivocal stand in defense of "intellectual freedom and free speech." Her activism also extends to the feminist movement and the terminally ill as co-chair of the Northwest Feminists Anti-Censorship Taskforce and board member of the Hemlock Society—a nonprofit organization which seeks "to promote a climate of public opinion which is tolerant of the right of people who are terminally ill to end their own lives in a planned manner."

Dority's article pinpoints specific legal actions and political figures responsible for the war against rock and rap. Like Jerry Adler in "The Rap Attitude," she identifies the FBI's criticism of the rap group N.W.A.'s album *Straight Outta Compton* as a response to specific musical lyrics—something worthy of our analysis and attention. But unlike Adler, Dority sees the powerful force of rap music among young people as "a new form of communication and protest" by the disenfranchised. She and Adler offer a kind of point and counterpoint debate about the complex issue surrounding free speech as guaranteed by the First Amendment of the Bill of Rights.

All music lovers, including those who prefer classical music and opera to more modern sounds, should be vitally concerned about the censorship of rock and rap music. As a long-time anti-censorship activist, I am alarmed by recent events which make a mockery of our Bill of Rights. I am convinced that we must take a stand against this strong-arm suppression of intellectual freedom and free speech.

A nationwide movement to restrict access to music began in 1985 with the founding of the Parents' Music Resource Center by Susan Baker, wife of Secretary of State James Baker, and Tipper Gore, wife of Senator Albert Gore. After a series of sensational congressional hearings failed to convince Congress to pass legislation mandating government labeling of "objectionable" music, the PMRC shifted its pressure tactics to the record companies. Insisting that rock and rap lyrics cause violence and sexual irresponsibility, the PMRC demanded that record producers institute a system of "voluntary" labeling.

Persistence pays off. On May 9, 1990, the Recording Industry Association of America announced the coming of a uniform warning label system on "all possibly objectionable materials" beginning in July.

This alarming concession, however, still falls woefully short of what pro-censorship activists really want. Many states are considering repressive legislation that would ban the sale of recordings containing lyrics about adultery, incest, illicit drug or alcohol use, murder, or suicide. Opera lovers will note that such works as *Madame Butterfly*, *Tosca*, *Carmen*, *La Traviata*, and many others would fall victim to these standards.

In Missouri, Representative Jean Dixon, with help from Phyllis

Schlafly's Eagle Forum, has fashioned a model anti-rock-and-rap bill that would make labeling mandatory for music containing "unsuitable" lyrics. Proposed measures in 20 other states would prohibit the sale of stickered recordings to those under 18. Some would prohibit minors from attending live concerts by the targeted groups. Many would provide for awarding damages to persons injured by someone "motivated" by a recording.

Such proposals have frightened retailers into requiring proof of age for purchases, puling labeled recordings altogether, or applying their own stickers. (Meyer Music Markets have gone so far as to apply a warning label to Frank Zappa's *Jazz from Hell*, an all-instrumental album.)

This year we witnessed the first two music obscenity trials ever held in the United States. In February, an Alabama retailer was arrested and charged for selling a purportedly obscene rap album by the group 2 Live Crew to a police officer. An Alabama jury acquitted him after a four-day trial in which experts traced the musical and cultural developments of rap music. The high cost of defending against such prosecutions has, of course, created a chilling effect on the content of creative works.

After a grand jury in Volusia County, Florida, declared 2 Live Crew's best-selling *As Nasty As They Wanna Be* obscene, another record store clerk in Sarasota was arrested for selling the album to a minor. He faces up to five years in prison and a $5,000 fine. At least six other Florida counties have banned 2 Live Crew's recordings.

In June, a U.S. district court judge in Fort Lauderdale ruled that a second 2 Live Crew album was obscene. The ruling was followed within days by the arrest of a record shop owner and the Gestapo-style arrest of two members of the band. That picture is engraved forever behind my eyes: two young black musicians being led away in handcuffs in the middle of the night. As Frank Zappa says, "Is this really the Land of the Free and the Home of the Brave? Then where the hell are we, Wanda?"

Meanwhile, the Federal Communications Commission is cracking down on what it calls "indecency" in broadcast music. Last October, KLUC in Las Vegas was fined $2,000 for playing Prince's "Erotic City"; WTZA in Miami was fined $2,000 for playing "Penis Envy" by the folk group Uncle Bonsai; and WIOD in Miami was fined $10,000 for various broadcast music infractions.

Late last year, the FBI became a formidable rock critic when its chief spokesperson, Milt Ahlerich, sent a letter on Department of Justice stationery to the president of Priority Records, which had just released the million-selling album *Straight Outta Compton* by the rap group N.W.A. The letter, referring to a song from the album called "----tha police" (dashes in the official title), states that the song "encourages violence against and disrespect for law enforcement officers. I wanted you to be aware of the FBI's position. . . . I believe my views reflect the opinion of the entire law enforcement community."

The FBI's letter is historic; the bureau has never before taken an official position on a work of art. Although direct FBI action wasn't specifically threatened, it was hardly necessary. Local police departments faxed a version of the song from city to city. When N.W.A. attempted to perform the song at a concert in Detroit, police moved toward the stage and ended the set.

Rap music is a powerful force for young people. This new form of communication and protest is the voice of the disenfranchised. N.W.A. and other rap groups—almost exclusively young black musicians—are deliberately provocative. These people are expressing the reality of their lives and their culture, which includes drug use, sexual activity, and violence. In today's climate of hostility and violence between police and the black community, these songs illuminate a harsh reality—a reality we must confront. This cannot be accomplished by silencing bands. In fact, this draconian suppression will only further enflame the situation.

"----tha police" is part of a long tradition of literature and art that question authority. So far, the FBI seems concerned only when those expressing anti-authority sentiments are young, black, and amplified. Certainly this music from the streets and ghettos of America makes many people uncomfortable. That's what it's supposed to do. The First Amendment itself makes many people uncomfortable. But it doesn't exist to promote comfort. It exists to promote freedom.

Rockers, rappers, and free speech advocates are organizing to fight back. Music in Action, a coalition of artists, retailers, fans, and concerned citizens, is forming local affiliates and has held several rallies in Washington, D.C. At one rally, rock critic and journalist Dave Marsh told the crowd, "It's shameful that on this day we live in a climate of fear. We are here to serve notice that free speech is for everyone, not just the elite." You can contact MA at 705 President Street, Brooklyn, NY 11215. Rock & Roll Confidential, another group keeping members informed and fighting music censorship, can be contacted at Box 15052, Long Beach, CA 90815.

If the state is given license to require producers and retailers to label and restrict access to commercial recordings, it's a small step to requiring publishers and booksellers to label and restrict access to books. New forms of music have always served as the cutting-edge voice of youth and have long been attacked due to sex, drugs, and obscenity. But the current campaign goes beyond past efforts and involves many powerful people. Why? I believe, along with Dave Marsh, that suppression tactics have increased because of the explosion of social and political comment in pop music and the growing social and political involvement of musicians and their audiences.

These heavy-handed attacks on the freedom of expression of young musicians are direct assaults on everyone's First Amendment rights of free speech and political dissent. We *must not tolerate* government censorship. We must stand together against this tyranny!

SPECULATIONS

1. What parts of Dority's argument that we should be concerned about the censorship of rock and rap music affect you? Describe her assertion that we must take a stand against this strong-arm suppression of intellectual freedom and censorship.

2. Compare rap music with other art forms. How do the lyrics represent artistic self-expression and social commentary? Cite examples that support your answers.

3. What political, cultural, or social assumptions support Dority's assertion that the FBI's letter condemning *Straight Outta Compton* by the rap group N.W.A. is "historic" because "the bureau has never before taken an official position on a work of art"? Why do you think the FBI took action now?

4. Why is it important to Dority's argument for us to understand rap music as a form of "protest" and "political comment" voiced by "the disenfranchised"? Who are these disenfranchised? In what ways does rap music communicate a statement? Based on this article, who listens to rap? Explain why rap does or does not cause you discomfort.

They Had a Right to Sing the Blues

TOM BETHELL

Tom Bethell has described himself as a political conservative and a practicing Roman Catholic. He also admits that he has "spent a fourth of his life listening to music." He displays a remarkable range in his knowledge and appreciation of music, from Gregorian Chants and Beethoven to Jelly Roll Morton and the gospel singing of Mahalia Jackson. However, Bethell once informed an interviewer that he detested all modern and experimental music.

Born in London in 1940, Bethell attended the Royal Naval College and received his Masters of Arts from Oxford University. He moved to the United States and became a naturalized citizen in 1974. He lives in Washington, D. C. and has worked as an editor for *Harper's* magazine since 1976. Bethell started as a mathematics teacher, but moved on to jazz research and then joined District Attorney Jim Garrison's investigative team in their work on the assassination of President John F. Kennedy.

His interest in researching jazz culminated in his scholarly book, *George Lewis: A Jazzman From New Orleans* (1977). "They Had a Right to Sing the Blues" offers a thoughtful and provocative argument about the roots and context of blues music.

It's difficult to go to a large music store these days without being bombarded by this insistent doggerel called rap music. "I could do that when I was ten years old," said Ray Charles, capturing in his comment the mood of triumphant mockery that characterizes rap. As in a bad dream, words and phrases turn over and repeat restlessly. At times we seem to be in the midst of a convention of imps hopping about on pogo sticks.

Some are eager to deny that this is decadence. Invoking the Progressive Myth as though we had not heard it a thousand times, a *New York Times* editorial writer found something very familiar in these sounds: the history of music has been one of "innovative, even outrageous styles" that eventually "became mainstream." And so it will be, no doubt, with rap. (Beethoven, too, wasn't appreciated in his own day.) *Newsweek* referred to rap as "the next evolutionary step."

I'm not here concerned about the immorality of what used to be called the "lyrics," or the general air of triumphant badness. It is the musical decline, reflecting a more general change in the culture, that concerns me here. How are we to account for it?

The evidence of this decline is readily at hand. "Next to the nettle lies the rose," and next to rap there lies, in the music-store racks, a great treasure trove of American music, reissued on compact disc. The "hot" collectors of the 1930s would be dumbfounded: their long-sought "wants" on such labels as Okeh and Vocalion not only copiously available but complete, in many cases, with second takes, unissued masters, and archival photographs.

Musical Paradise Regained

We've heard about the Robert Johnson reissue, with every known take of this Mississippi Delta blues singer recently released by Columbia. It sold 325,000 copies and made the *Billboard* charts. What I want to draw attention to here is a new issue of (I believe) even greater musical merit, which has so far received no attention. I refer to some recordings made in 1944 by the great trumpeter Bunk Johnson and the clarinetist George Lewis, in an old dance hall in New Orleans. The sessions (which lasted for a week) were recorded by William Russell, as it happens one of those old "hot" collectors himself. Now 86, and living in New Orleans, Russell has been supervising the release of the material.

Bunk Johnson was discovered in the late 1930s when a number of people did the first research into early jazz history. Several New Orleans musicians said that Bunk had been among the best trumpeters in the early days. He had "the most beautiful tone, the best imagination," Louis Armstrong said. It turned out that Bunk, then 59, was working in a rice mill in New Iberia, Louisiana. He claimed he could still play. The story of his being equipped with false teeth and a new trumpet has been often told.

The band that Russell brought together to play with Bunk was probably the best then available in New Orleans. The drummer, Baby Dodds, was brought down from Chicago, where he had earlier recorded with Armstrong. Columbia's famous talent scout, John Hammond, who signed up everyone from Bessie Smith to Count Basie to Bob Dylan, happened to be in New Orleans that summer. He heard about Russell's session and showed up one night as the band was playing. He remarked to Russell that these would be the best recordings ever made in the city. Time proved Hammond right. Nothing since has come close.

Russell returned to New Orlean the following year and recorded more bands, including a brass band with Bunk, and a great session with the old-time trumpeter Wooden Joe Nicholas and Albert Burbank, the clarinetist much admired by Woody Allen.

However, few people ever heard these wonderful recordings. Finally, in 1988, Russell concluded that the time was right, and he sold them to a local record producer (Audiophile, 1206 Decatur, New Orleans, La. 70116). Recently I spent some time with Russell in New Orleans, and he told me that one of the things that encouraged him to sell was the quality of sound on compact discs.

Three CDs have been issued ($15 each), two of Bunk at his best, and the third including perhaps the best George Lewis sides ever recorded ("High Society," "Ice Cream," "Burgundy Street Blues," and others).

From Bunk to Junk

In fifty years, the history of jazz uncannily recapitulated the history of European music: from classical to avant garde, with an intermediate romantic phase. With Bunk's band the idiom is classical, yet amazingly relaxed. Trumpet, trombone, and clarinet create an interweaving polyphony comparable in complexity to parts of the Brandenburg Concertos. In the long, nine-minute "Midnight Blues" Jim Robinson's glissando and George Lewis's poignant soaring provide a nonchalant counterpoint to Bunk's endlessly inventive melodic line. I don't know anything else quite like it in American music. But Bunk, always ready with a putdown for those who admired the Art of it, cruelly remarked as it ended: "There's a record Bill Colburn is going to put under his arm and carry all over San Francisco." One of his greatest admirers, Colburn had put Bunk up in his apartment the year before.

Bunk, nonetheless, had unerring musical taste. Hearing him in San Francisco in 1943, the composer Virgil Thomson wrote in the *Herald Tribune*: "Bunk is an artist of delicate imagination, meditative in style rather than flashy, and master of the darkest trumpet tone I have ever heard." His tone and "his melodic invention are at all times expressive, at all times reasonable, and at all times completely interesting. His work takes on, in consequence, depth, ease, and lucidity. Nothing could be less sentimental, or speak more seriously from the heart."

In a new and excellent book about Preservation Hall, the writer and photographer William Carter points out the irony that when these recordings were made the local studios refused to record blacks. So Russell did the job himself, capturing with a single microphone these "old black men" sitting "in rickety chairs in old wooden halls that possessed a beautiful natural resonance." Many have since felt, he adds, that "those resonant woods and cavernous, humid spaces provided an ideal sonority for the stripped-down, spacious sounds, which seemed to evoke days beyond recall."

The only word I disagree with is "old." Bunk (who died in 1949) was admittedly 63 when these recordings were made, but Lewis was 44, and the rest of the band in either their forties or their early fifties. They were no doubt in their prime. But at the time, Russell later remarked, jazzman were thought of as equivalent to baseball players: their legs gave out at forty.

Years later I went to live in New Orleans. Preservation Hall had recently opened, and a remnant from the great earlier period played there. The music had declined considerably, however. George Lewis & Co. went through their paces, but the creative spark had gone. Mere routine survived. I spent some time with Lewis (who died in 1968) and wrote a book about him. He never analyzed the music he played—didn't even have his own records in the house. The contrapuntal style of the New Orleans tradition? George either didn't know what you were talking about or pretended not to. He and the other musicians thought of music in wholly functional terms. Music was something that was "furnished"—for weddings, funerals, and dances. Such notions as "black culture" were too abstract by half. Then, trying to please, he would tell you about a musician he *did* admire . . . and it would be someone he had just heard on the Johnny Carson show.

The Moving Spotlight

The whole history of American music has been one of abrupt appearance, followed by decline—almost the opposite of "evolution." Mysteriously, an energetic spotlight of creativity is focused at a point. It diffuses and wanes. Then (until recently?) it has equally mysteriously reappeared somewhere else. Around 1900 there was an explosive burst of creativity, with the simultaneous and geographically separate appearances of jazz, blues, and ragtime. I agree with Russell Banks's observation, in his recent essay on Robert Johnson, that the blues "suddenly appeared in a specific region in a fully articulated and evolved form." The same was true of jazz in New Orleans. There's no evidence of an antecedent, "primitive" period. The earliest jazzmen could read music. It was the later ones who didn't bother to learn.

Within the lifetime of some of its earliest practitioners, the jazz tradition, like the European one before it, succumbed to an experimental avant garde. Every new experiment was praised by critics who noted that European innovators, too, had "freed" music from its shackles. (But they failed to note its subsequent decline.) In 1945 Louis Armstrong remarked that bebop, then the rage in New York, was "filled with malice," a daring criticism. The music had degenerated into empty displays of technique.

But the decline didn't matter, because new forms appeared; the spotlight moved on. They may not have had the sophistication of Jelly Roll Morton, but Jimmy Yancey and Meade Lux Lewis were playing some wonderful boogie-woogie piano in Chicago. Guitars were electrified, and soon there was another, although lesser, peak with the performances of blues singers like John Lee Hooker in the late Fifties. The music was popularized in Memphis, prettified in Liverpool, and presented, finally, by Ed Sullivan.

The English groups who played before mass audiences in the Sixties and Seventies were candid enough to feature the bands whose recordings they had faithfully imitated. But the musicians so honored—B. B. King and Howlin' Wolf, for example—were rapidly reduced by the exposure to a stale repertoire of mannerisms. Here we come to something that has been peculiar to American music. It is almost a law that the early recordings of a given musician will turn out to be his best. There are exceptions, but mostly we find this familiar pattern of discovery, peak, and prolonged decline. The market may be the problem. Old hits are demanded by new audiences, so that crowd-pleasing tricks are repeated *ad nauseam*. Resort to the tried-and-true guarantees a certain success, but artistic maturation must have been thwarted time and again as a result. George Lewis may have been fortunate not to be discovered until his forties.

The market has also made possible the constant renewal of American music. There was always a way out of the cul de sac, sparing us the European fate of a dead form ruled by an academy. Just when one style was beginning to suffer from overexposure or die of tedium, something new and unexpected would appear. Well into the 1970s, one heard it through the grapevine, Marvin Gaye and others were producing some wonderful stuff in Motown. That, too, will live—on disc.

Listening for the Sound

What's happening now? Not much, I fear; a matter for concern if we regard the genius of American popular music as a proxy for the vitality of society as a whole. In particular there doesn't seem to be much from the black community, other than this hip-hopping. Maybe I'm missing something important, and I hope so. I twist the radio dial in search of some new burst of energy (and it would be easy to recognize, contrary to the easy assumption of bourgeois insensibility). Wynton Marsalis, a young trumpeter from New Orleans, was praised in a *Time* cover story. I bought a couple of his albums but what I heard was lugubrious cocktail-lounge noodling in the expressionless tone patented by Miles Davis.

If we use foreign taste as a fairly reliable listening post, Nashville may now be the most important center of American musical influence. Which seems reasonable to my ears. Country music never soars to the heights, but it doesn't descend to the depths either. Mostly it's fair-to-middling stuff—amiable without being soul-stirring. Reba McEntire and Waylon Jennings aim to please, and they never resort to aural ugliness as an attention-getting device. Country music, of course, is white.

Jazz is sometimes represented as a black art form, but it is more accurate to think of it as American. As with ragtime, its earliest practitioners were both black and white. But the best ones were black—to an overwhelming extent. How are we to explain this? It was not a superiority of musicianship. The mellifluous cornetist Bix Beiderbecke, the leading white jazzman of the "classical" period, was technically the superior of Louis Armstrong, but Louis was the greater player, for artistic reasons that are as hard to deny as they are to define.

No doubt a measure of adversity and tension with his environment is advantageous to the creative artist. Without it, he may get along perfectly well without the subterfuges of art. The blues contain much aesthetically coded protest, making the music seem to express private sorrow, not potential insurrection. The coding also enables us to enjoy the blues today purely as music, and it ensures that others will still be doing so a hundred years from now. Protest songs from the civil-rights movement face a less certain future. Mahalia Jackson was a great gospel singer in the 1940s and '50s. Artistically, she did not survive co-optation by the civil-rights movement.

If people are too comfortable, the creative juices are unlikely to flow. No doubt this is another reason why, so often, commercial success has been followed by artistic decline—for whites as well as blacks. A really big commercial success will bring with it a permanent change, possibly a disorienting one. Listen to Fats Domino, probably the most successful vocalist from New Orleans since World War II. His early records have a very appealing, lightly lilting quality. One can see why he became a big hit. Then came the golden discs and Las Vegas—forget it.

The level of adversity encountered by blacks in New Orleans was noticeable but not disabling. They were better off than most people in most centuries. Compared to most Irishmen in the nineteenth century, for example, most black musicians in New Orleans lived in comfort, even in the "Jim Crow" years. They had musical instruments, the leisure to learn how to play them, music teachers to patronize, social clubs they could join, and above all an economy productive enough to keep literally hundreds of them in work. Is a man oppressed if he can support himself and his family by going off to work every day—clarinet in hand (as George Lewis did in the 1920s)? Tell it to the ditch-digger. When I asked Lewis about segregation, incidentally, what still rankled with him was the memory of discrimination at the hands of light-skinned blacks—so-called "Creoles of color." They had their own social clubs, and sometimes George was hired to play at them. "They would look at you hard if your hair wasn't silky," he recalled.

Not that this should be construed as an argument for adversity. In return for an end to segregation, George Lewis and the others would have gladly surrendered any artistic residue; especially as they didn't recognize its existence.

The most erroneous idea about popular culture is that we can subtract the all-important functional setting (the dance, wedding, funeral) that gave purpose to the original creation, and still somehow preserve these distilled aesthetic drops in the cultural centers: art furnished for art's sake, with the help of educational programs, community input, "outreach," national endowments, and dedicated funds. It won't work.

San Jacinto Hall, where the Bunk Johnson recordings were made, survived until 1967. Then it was torn down as part of an urban-renewal program. A cultural center was to replace it. "Louis Armstrong Park," it was called. When I was in New Orleans recently I thought I might go there; it is only a block from William Russell's apartment. But I was told that it is not safe, even in daytime. And when I left Russell's apartment late one night, after he had played me some of those beautiful old recordings, some of which will be coming out on later CDs (there may be as many as 12), he gave me a little palm-of-the-hand tear-glass container to carry—just to be on the safe side.

SPECULATIONS

1.   Tom Bethell believes that rap music is part of a general decline in culture, particularly in the culture of popular music. According to Bethell, what are the reasons for that decline? What is your assessment of rap music?

2.   Bethell argues that "a measure of adversity and tension with his environment is advantageous to the creative artist," and then adds, "if people are too comfortable, the creative juices are unlikely to flow." What kind of theory of artistic creation does this suggest? How does it relate to the title of his essay "They Had a Right to Sing the Blues"? Explain your point of view.

3.   Why does Bethell tell us the story of Bunk Johnson in such detail? What is the point of this story and what does Bunk represent for Bethell? What does Bunk represent to you? Explain your point by comparing Bunk to musicians with whom you are familiar.

4.   What is the logic of Bethell's argument about the history of American music? How does he present this history as a natural law that always favors one period over another and what claims does this enable him to make?

5.   Consider the music of a musician or musical group that you have enjoyed or greatly admired and consider musicians and groups that have imitated the music you admired or have been strongly influenced by that music: How would you describe the relationship of the original music and the music that follows it? Give examples of how that relationship represents a decline or an improvement in comparison with the original.

6.   What role does nostalgia play in Bethell's depiction of past musical greatness and in his comparison of today's popular music with the music of the past? Why do you think Bethell can't find great music today? Why should it exist only in the past? Is he right?

Swing—From Verb to Noun

AMIRI BARAKA (LeROI JONES)

Born in Newark, New Jersey, in 1934 as Everett LeRoi Jones, Amiri Baraka holds a major place in the American literary scene. As a critic of American civilization, he has been compared to Allen Ginsberg, Norman Mailer, and Ezra Pound. Baraka continues to be an irritant to the literary establishment because of his radical politics and inflammatory style. A poet, dramatist, essayist, fiction writer, religious leader, and founder of black American aesthetic and political movements, Baraka has provoked both criticism and high artistic praise.

Baraka attended Rutgers and Columbia Universities and the New School for Social Research and has taught Afro-American literature at several universities, including Buffalo, Columbia, George Washington, and San Francisco State. He currently teaches at the State University of New York, Stony Brook. The winner of many awards, including a Guggenheim fellowship and the American Book Award, Baraka's most notable works include the play "Dutchman" (1964) which won the Obie Award, *Tales* (1967), and *The Autobiography of LeRoi Jones/Amiri Baraka* (1983).

In 1960, Baraka traveled to Cuba, a trip which was a turning point in his life because the experience politicized his art. Later, in response to the assassination of Malcolm X, he moved to Harlem where he established the Black Arts Repertory Theatre/School which inspired many black theaters throughout the country. In 1967, as confirmation of his pride in black culture, Baraka changed his name to the Bantuized Muslim name Imamu ("spiritual leader") Ameer ("blessed") Baraka ("prince"), later shortened to Amiri Baraka.

In 1963, Baraka wrote *Blues People: Negro Music in White America*, about the social and aesthetic history of black music in America. Beginning with slavery, the book argues that since the Emancipation, the blues have come to represent a union of American and African cultural experience. In many ways, this fusion of two very different traditions speaks to the genius and enduring artistry to be found in Baraka's work.

The blues was conceived by freedmen and ex-slaves—if not as the result of a personal or intellectual experience, at least as an emotional confirmation of, and reaction to, the way in which most Negroes were still forced to exist in the United States. The blues impulse was a psychological correlative that obscured the most extreme ideas of *assimilation* for most Negroes, and made any notion of the complete abandonment of the traditional black culture an unrealizable possibility. In a sense, the middle-class spirit could not take root among most Negroes because they sensed the final fantasy involved. Besides, the pay check, which was the aspect of American society that created a modern black middle class, was . . . also available to what some of my mother's friends would refer to as "low-type coons." And these "coons" would always be unavailable both socially and culturally to any talk of assimilation from white man or black. The Negro middle class, always an exaggeration of its white model, could include the professional men and educators, but after the move north it also included men who worked in stores and as an added dig, "sportsmen," i.e., gamblers and numbers people. The idea of Negro "society," as E. Franklin Frazier pointed out, is based only on acquisition, which, as it turns out, makes the formation of a completely parochial meta-society impossible. Numbers bankers often make as much money as doctors and thereby are part of Negro "society." And even if the more formal ("socially responsible") Negro middle class wanted to become simply white Americans, they were during the late twenties and thirties merely a swelling minority.

The two secularities I spoke of are simply the ways in which the blues was beginning to be redistributed in black America through these years. The people who were beginning to move toward what they could think of as citizenship also moved away from the older blues. The unregenerate Northerners already had a music, the thin-willed "society" bands of Jim Europe, and the circus as well as white rag had influenced the "non-blues" bands of Will Marion Cook and Wilbur Sweatman that existed before the migration. But the huge impact the Southerners made upon the North changed that. When the city blues began to be powerful, the larger Negro dance bands hired some of the emigrants as soloists, and to some degree the blues began to be heard in most of the black cabarets, "dance schools," and theaters. The true jazz sound had moved north, and even the blackest blues could be heard in the house parties of Chicago and New York. But for most of America by the twenties, jazz (or *jass*, the noun, not the verb) meant the Original Dixieland Jazz Band (to the hip) and Paul Whiteman (to the square). Whiteman got rich; the O.D.J.B. never did.

The O.D.J.B. was a group of young white men who had been deeply influenced by the King Oliver band in New Orleans: they moved north, and became the first jazz band to record. They had a profound influence upon America, and because they, rather than the actual black innovators, were heard by the great majority of Americans *first*, the cultural lag had won again.

A Negro jazz band, Freddie Keppard's Original Creoles, turned down an invitation to record a few months before the O.D.J.B.; Keppard (myth says) didn't accept the offer because he thought such a project would merely invite imitation of his style! This is probably true, but it is doubtful that Keppard's band would have caught as much national attention as the smoother O.D.J.B. anyway, for the same reason the O.D.J.B. could never have made as much money as Whiteman.

It is significant that by 1924, when Bessie Smith was still causing riots in Chicago and when young Louis Armstrong was on his way to New York to join the Fletcher Henderson band—and by so doing, to create the first really swinging *big* jazz band, the biggest names in "jazz" were Whiteman and the Mound City Blue Blowers, another white group. Radio had come into its own by 1920, and the irony is that most Negroes probably thought of jazz, based on what they had heard, as being a white dilution of older blues forms! It was only after there had been a few recordings sufficiently distributed through the black Northern and urban Southern neighborhoods, made by Negro bands like King Oliver's (Oliver was then in Chicago with his historic Creole Jazz Band, which featured Louis Armstrong, second cornet), Fletcher Henderson's and two Kansas City bands—Bennie Moten's and Clarence Williams's, that the masses of Negroes became familiar with jazz. At Chicago's Lincoln Gardens Cafe, Oliver first set the Northern Negro neighborhoods on fire, and then bands like Moten's and Williams's in the various clubs around Kansas City; but Henderson reached his Negro audience mostly via records because even when he got his best band together (with Coleman Hawkins, Louis Armstrong, Don Redman, etc.) he was still playing at Roseland, which was a white club.

The earliest jazz bands, like Buddy Bolden's, were usually small groups. Bolden's instrumentation was supposed to have been cornet, clarinet, trombone, violin, guitar, bass (which was one of the first instrumental innovations for that particular group since most bands of that period and well after used the tuba) and drums. These groups were usually made up of musicians who had other jobs (like pre-classic blues singers) since there was really no steady work for them. And they played most of the music of the time: quadrilles, schottisches, polkas, ragtime tunes, like many of the other "cleaner" groups around New Orleans. But the difference with the Bolden band was the blues quality, the Uptown flavor, of all their music. But this music still had the flavor of the brass marching bands. Most of the musicians of that period had come through those bands; in fact, probably still marched with them when there was a significant funeral. Another quality that must have distinguished the Bolden band was the improvisational character of a good deal of their music. Charles Edward Smith remarks that "the art of group improvisation—like the blues, the life blood of jazz—was associated with this uptown section of New Orleans in particular. As in folk music, two creative forces were involved, that of the group and that of the gifted individual."[1]

---

[1] "New Orleans and Traditions in Jazz," in *Jazz*, p. 39.

Most of the Uptown bands were noted for their "sloppy ensemble styles." The Bolden band and the other early jazz groups must have sounded even sloppier. The music was a raw mixture of march, dance, blues, and early rag rhythm, with all the players improvising simultaneously. It is a wonderful concept, taking the unison tradition of European march music, but infesting it with teeming improvisations, catcalls, hollers, and the murky rhythms of the ex-slaves. The Creoles must have hated that music more than anything in life.

But by the time the music came upriver along with the fleeing masses, it had changed a great deal. Oliver's Creole Band, the first really influential Negro jazz band in the North, had a much smoother ensemble style than the Bolden band: the guitar and violin had disappeared, and a piano had been added. In New Orleans, pianists had been largely soloists in the various bawdy houses and brothels of Storyville. In fact, pianists were the only Negro musicians who worked steadily and needed no other jobs. But the early New Orleans jazz groups usually did not have pianos. Jelly Roll Morton, one of the first jazz pianists, was heavily influenced by the ragtime style, though his own rags were even more heavily influenced by blues and that rougher rag style called "barrelhouse." As Bunk Johnson is quoted as saying, Jelly played music "the whores liked." And played in a whorehouse, it is easy to understand how functional that music must have been. But the piano as part of a jazz ensemble was something not indigenous to earlier New Orleans music. The smoother and more clearly polyphonic style of Oliver's band, as opposed to what must have been a veritable heterophony of earlier bands like Bolden's—Kid Ory's Sunshine Orchestra, the first black jazz band to record (Los Angeles, 1921), gives us some indication—showed a discipline and formality that must certainly have been imposed to a large degree by ragtime and the more precise pianist techniques that went with it.

Oliver's band caused a sensation with audiences and musicians alike and brought the authentic accent of jazz into the North. Garvin Bushell remembers: "We went on the road with Mamie Smith in 1921. When we got to Chicago, Bubber Miley and I went to hearing Oliver at the Dreamland every night. [This was before Armstrong joined the band and they moved to Lincoln Gardens.] It was the first time I'd heard New Orleans jazz to any advantage and I studied them every night for the entire week we were in town. I was very much impressed with their blues and their sound. The trumpets and clarinets in the East had a better 'legitimate' quality, but their [Oliver's band's] sound touched you more. It was less cultivated but more expressive of how the people felt. Bubber and I sat there with our mouths open."[2]

---

[2] "Garvin Bushell and New York Jazz in the 1920's," *Jazz Review* (February 1959), p. 9.

Louis Armstrong's arrival at twenty-two with Oliver's band had an even more electrifying effect on these Northern audiences, which many times included white jazz musicians. Hoagy Carmichael went to the Lincoln Gardens with Bix Beiderbecke in 1923 to hear that band:

"The King featured two trumpets, a piano, a bass fiddle and a clarinet . . . a big black fellow . . . slashed into 'Bugle Call Rag.'

"I dropped my cigarette and gulped my drink. Bix was on his feet, his eyes popping. For taking the first chorus was that second trumpet, Louis Armstrong.

"Louis was taking it fast. Bob Gillette slid off his chair and under the table.

"Every note Louis hit was perfection."[3]

This might seem amusing if it is noted that the first and deepest influences on most white Northern and Midwestern jazz musicians were necessarily the recordings of the O.D.J.B., who were imitating the earlier New Orleans styles, and Oliver, who had brought that style to its apex. Thus, this first hearing of the genuine article by these white musicians must have been much like tasting real eggs after having been brought up on the powdered variety. (Though, to be sure, there's no certainty that a person will like the original if he has developed a taste for the other. So it is that Carmichael can write that he still preferred Beiderbecke to Armstrong, saying, "Bix's breaks were not as wild as Armstrong's but they were hot and he selected each note with musical care."[4])

Blues as an autonomous music had been in a sense inviolable. There was no clear way into it, *i.e.*, its production, not its appreciation, except as concomitant with what seems to me to be the peculiar social, cultural, economic, and emotional experience of a black man in America. The idea of a white blues singer seems an even more violent contradiction of terms than the idea of a middle-class blues singer. The materials of blues were not available to the white American, even though some strange circumstance might prompt him to look for them. It was as if these materials were secret and obscure, and blues a kind of ethno-historic rite as basic as blood.

The classic singers brought this music as close to white America as it could ever get and still survive. W. C. Handy, with the publication of his various "blues compositions," *invented* it for a great many Americans and also showed that there was some money to be made from it. Whiteman, Wilbur Sweatman, Jim Europe, all played Handy's com-

---

[3] *The Stardust Road* (1946) (New York: Rinehart), p. 53.
[4] As quoted in *The Story of Jazz*, p. 128.

positions with success. There was even what could be called a "blues craze" (of which Handy's compositions were an important part) just after the ragtime craze went on the skids. But the music that resulted from the craze had little, if anything, to do with legitimate blues. That could not be got to, except as the casual expression of a whole culture. And for this reason, blues remained, and remains in its most moving manifestations, obscure to the mainstream of American culture.

Jazz made it possible for the first time for something of the legitimate feeling of Afro-American music to be imitated successfully. (Ragtime had moved so quickly away from any pure reflection of Negro life that by the time it became popular, there was no more original source to imitate. It was, in a sense, a premature attempt at the sociocultural merger that later produced jazz.) Or rather, jazz enabled separate and *valid* emotional expressions to be made that were based on older traditions of Afro-American music that were clearly not a part of it. The Negro middle class would not have a music if it were not for jazz. The white man would have no access to blues. It was a music capable of reflecting not only the Negro and a black America but a white America as well.

During the twenties, serious young white musicians were quick to pick up more or less authentic jazz accents as soon as they had some contact with the music. The O.D.J.B., who came out of a parallel tradition of white New Orleans marching bands, whizzed off to Chicago and stunned white musicians everywhere as well as many Negro musicians in the North who had not heard the new music before. Young white boys, like Beiderbecke, in the North and Midwest were already forming styles of their own based on the O.D.J.B.'s records and the playing of another white group, the New Orleans Rhythm Kings, before Joe Oliver's band got to Chicago. And the music these boys were making, or trying to make, had very little to do with Paul Whiteman. They had caught the accent, understood the more generalized emotional statements, and genuinely moved, set out to involve themselves in this music as completely as possible. They hung around the Negro clubs, listening to the newly employed New Orleans musicians, and went home and tried to play their tunes.

The result of this cultural "breakdown" was not always mere imitation. As I have said, jazz had a broadness of emotional meaning that allowed many separate ways into it, not all of them dependent on the "blood ritual" of blues. Bix Beiderbecke, as a mature musician, was even an innovator. But the real point of this breakdown was that it reflected not so much the white American's increased understanding of the Negro, but rather the fact that the Negro had created a music that offered such a profound reflection of America that it could attract white Americans to want to play it or listen to it for exactly that reason. The white jazz musician was even a new *class* of white American. Unlike the earlier blackface acts and the minstrels who sought to burlesque certain facets of Negro life (and, superficially, the music associated with it), there were now growing ranks of white jazz musicians who wanted to play the music because they thought it emotionally and intellectually fulfilling. It made a common cultural ground where black and white America seemed only day and night in the same city and at their most disparate, proved only to result in different *styles*, a phenomenon I have always taken to be the whole point (and value) of divergent cultures.

It is interesting that most of these young white musicians who emerged during the early twenties were from the middle class and from the Middle West. Beiderbecke was born in Davenport, Iowa: that town, however, at the turn of the century was a river port, and many of the riverboats docked there—riverboats whose staffs sometimes included bands like Fate Marable's, Dewey Jackson's, and Albert Wynn's, and musicians like Jelly Roll Morton and Louis Armstrong. Beiderbecke's first group, the Wolverines, played almost exclusively at roadhouses and colleges in the Midwest, most notably at Indiana University.

A few years after the Wolverines had made their reputation as what George Hoefer calls "the first white band to play the genuine Negro style of jazz," another group of young white musicians began to play jazz "their own way." They were also from the Midwest, but from Chicago. Eddie Condon, Jimmy McPartland, Bud Freeman, PeeWee Russell, Dave Tough, and some others, all went to Austin High School and became associated with a style of playing known as "Chicago jazz," which took its impetus from the records of the O.D.J.B. and the New Orleans Rhythm Kings dates on the North Side of Chicago.

Chicago and nearby parts of the Midwest were logically the first places where jazz could take root in the North (although there were some parallel developments in New York). In a sense Chicago was, and to a certain extent is now, a kind of frontier town. It sits at the end of the riverboat runs, and it was the kind of industrial city that the first black emigrants were drawn to. It had many of the heavy industries that would employ Negroes, whereas New York's heaviest industry is paperwork. And in Chicago, during what was called the "Jazz Age," there was an easiness of communication on some levels between black and white that was not duplicated in New York until some time later. Chicago at this time was something like the musical capital of America, encompassing within it black emigrants, white emigrants, country blues people, classic stylists, city house-party grinders, New Orleans musicians, and young Negro musicians and younger white musicians listening and reacting to this crush of cultures that so clearly typified America's rush into the twentieth century.

The reaction of young white musicians to jazz was not always connected directly to any *"understanding* of the Negro." In many cases, the most profound influence on young white musicians was the music of other white musicians. Certainly this is true with people like Beiderbecke and most of the Chicago-style players. But the entrance of the white man into jazz at this level of sincerity and emotional legitimacy did at least bring him, by implication, much closer to the Negro; that is, even if a white trumpet player were to learn to play "jazz" by listening to Nick LaRocca and had his style set (as was Beiderbecke's case) *before* he ever heard black musicians, surely the musical debt to Negro music (and to the black culture from which it issued) had to be understood. As in the case of LaRocca's style, it is certainly an appropriation of black New Orleans brass style, most notably King Oliver's; though the legitimacy of its deviation can in no way be questioned, the fact that it is a deviation must be acknowledged. The serious white musician was in a position to do this. And this acknowledgment, whether overt or tacit, served to place the Negro's culture and Negro society in a position of intelligent regard it had never enjoyed before.

This acknowledgment of a developed and empirical profundity to the Negro's culture (and as the result of its separation from the mainstream of American culture) also caused the people who had to make it to be separated from this mainstream themselves. Any blackness admitted within the mainstream existed only as it could be shaped by the grimness of American sociological (and political) thought. There was no life to Negroes in America that could be understood by America, except negatively or with the hopeless idealism of impossible causes. During the Black Renaissance the white liberal and sensual dilettante "understood" the Negro. During the Depression, so did the Communist Party. The young white jazz musicians at least had to face the black American head-on and with only a very literal drum to beat. And they could not help but do this with some sense of rebellion or separateness from the rest of white America, since white America could have no understanding of what they were doing, except perhaps in the terms that Whiteman and the others succeeded in doing it, which was not at all—that is, explaining a bird by comparing it with an airplane.

"Unlike New Orleans style, the style of these musicians—often and confusingly labeled 'Chicago'—sacrificed ease and relaxation for tension and drive, perhaps because they were mastering a new idiom in a more hectic environment. They had read some of the literature of the 20s—drummer Dave Tough loved Mencken and the *American Mercury*—and their revolt against their own middle-class background tended to be conscious. The role of the improvising—and usually non-reading—musician became almost heroic."[5]

Music, as paradoxical as it might seem, is the result of thought. It is the result of thought perfected at its most empirical, *i.e.*, as *attitude*, or *stance*. Thought is largely conditioned by reference; it is the result of consideration or speculation against reference, which is largely arbitrary.

There is no *one* way of thinking, since reference (hence value) is as scattered and dissimilar as men themselves. If Negro music can be seen to be the result of certain attitudes, certain specific ways of thinking about the world (and only ultimately about the *ways* in which music can be made), then the basic hypothesis of this book is understood. The Negro's music changed as he changed, reflecting shifting attitudes or (and this is equally important) *consistent attitudes within changed contexts*. And it is *why* the music changed that seems most important to me.

When jazz first began to appear during the twenties on the American scene, in one form or another, it was introduced in a great many instances into that scene by white Americans. Jazz as it was originally conceived and in most instances of its most vital development was the result of certain attitudes, or empirical ideas, attributable to the Afro-American culture. Jazz as played by white musicians was not the same as that played by black musicians, nor was there any reason for it to be. The music of the white jazz musician did not issue from the same cultural circumstance; it was, at its most profound instance, a learned art. The blues, for example, which I take to be an autonomous black music, had very little weight at all in pre-jazz white American culture. But blues is an extremely important part of jazz. However, the way in which jazz utilizes the blues "attitude" provided a musical analogy the white musician could understand and thus utilize in his music to arrive at a style of jazz music. The white musician understood the blues first as music, but seldom as an attitude, since the attitude, or world-view, the white musician was responsible to was necessarily quite a different one. And in many cases, this attitude, or world-view, was one that was not consistent with the making of jazz.

There should be no cause for wonder that the trumpets of Bix Beiderbecke and Louis Armstrong were so dissimilar. The white middle-class boy from Iowa was the product of a culture which could *place*

[5] *The Story of Jazz*, p. 129.

Louis Armstrong, but could never understand him. Beiderbecke was also the product of a subculture that most nearly emulates the "official" or formal culture of North America. He was an instinctive intellectual who had a musical taste that included Stravinsky, Schoenberg, and Debussy, and had an emotional life that, as it turned out, was based on his conscious or unconscious disapproval of most of the sacraments of his culture. On the other hand, Armstrong was, in terms of emotional archetypes, an honored priest of his culture—one of the most impressive products of his society. Armstrong was not *rebelling* against anything with his music. In fact, his music was one of the most beautiful refinements of Afro-American musical tradition, and it was immediately recognized as such by those Negroes who were not busy trying to pretend that they had issued from Beiderbecke's culture. The incredible irony of the situation was that both stood in similar places in the superstructure of American society: Beiderbecke, because of the isolation any deviation from mass culture imposed upon its bearer; and Armstrong, because of the socio-historical estrangement of the Negro from the rest of America. Nevertheless, the music the two made was as dissimilar as is possible within jazz. Beiderbecke's slight, reflective tone and impressionistic lyricism was the most impressive example of "the artifact given expression" in jazz. He played "white jazz" in the sense I am trying to convey, that is, as a music that is the product of attitudes expressive of a peculiar culture. Armstrong, of course, played jazz that was securely within the traditions of Afro-American music. His tone was brassy, broad, and aggressively dramatic. He also relied heavily on the vocal blues tradition in his playing to amplify the expressiveness of his instrumental technique.

I am using these two men as examples because they were two early masters of a developing *American* music, though they expressed almost antithetical versions of it. The point is that Afro-American music did not become a completely American expression until the white man could play it! Bix Beiderbecke, more than any of the early white jazzmen, signified this development because he was the first white jazz musician, the first white musician who brought to the jazz he created any of the *ultimate concern* Negro musicians brought to it as a casual attitude of their culture. This development signified also that jazz would someday have to contend with the idea of its being an art (since that was the white man's only way into it). The emergence of the white player meant that Afro-American culture had already become the expression of a particular kind of American experience, and what is most important, that this experience was available intellectually, that it could be learned.

Louis Armstrong's departure from the Oliver Creole Jazz Band is more than an historical event; given further consideration, it may be seen as a musical and socio-cultural event of the highest significance. First, Armstrong's departure from Chicago (as well as Beiderbecke's three years later, in 1927, to join the Goldkette band and then Paul Whiteman's enterprise) was, in a sense, symbolic of the fact that the most fertile period for jazz in Chicago was finished and that the jazz capital was moving to New York. It also meant that Louis felt mature enough musically to venture out on his own without the presence of his mentor Joe Oliver. But most important, Armstrong in his tenure with Fletcher Henderson's Roseland band was not only responsible to a great degree for giving impetus to the first big jazz band, but in his capacity as one of the hot soloists in a big dance (later, jazz) band, he moved jazz into another era: the ascendancy of the soloist began.

Primitive jazz, like most Afro-American music that preceded it, was a communal, collective music. The famous primitive ensemble styles of earlier jazz allowed only for "breaks," or small solo-like statements by individual players, but the form and intent of these breaks were still dominated by the form and intent of the ensemble. They were usually just quasi-melodic punctuations at the end of the ensemble chorus. Jazz, even at the time of Oliver's Creole Band, was still a matter of *collective improvisation*, though the Creole Band did bring a smoother and more complex polyphonic technique to the ensemble style. As Larry Gushee remarked in a review of a recent LP of the Creole Band (Riverside 12-122) ". . . the Creole Jazz Band . . . sets the standard (possibly, who knows, only because of an historical accident) for all kinds of jazz that do not base their excellence on individual expressiveness, but on form and *shape* achieved through control and balance."[6]

The emergence of this "individual expressiveness" in jazz was signaled impressively by Armstrong's recordings with a small group known as the Hot Five. The musicians on these recordings, made in 1925 and 1926, were Kid Ory, trombone; Johnny Dodds, clarinet and *alto saxophone*; Lil Hardin, now Mrs. Armstrong, piano; and Johnny St. Cyr, banjo. On these sides, Armstrong clearly dominates the group, not so much because he is the superior instrumentalist, but because rhythmically and harmonically the rest of the musicians followed where Louis led, sometimes without a really clear knowledge of where that would be. The music made by the Hot Five is Louis Armstrong music: it has little to do with collective improvisation.

"The 1926 Hot Five's playing is much less purely collective than King Oliver's. In a sense, the improvised ensembles are cornet solos

---

[6] *Jazz Review* (November 1958), p. 37.

accompanied by *impromptu countermelodies* [my italics], rather than true collective improvisation. This judgment is based on the very essence of the works, and not merely on the cornet's closeness to the microphone. Listen to them carefully. Isn't it obvious that Armstrong's personality absorbs the others? Isn't your attention spontaneously concentrated on Louis? With King Oliver, you listen to the *band*, here, you listen first to *Louis*."[7]

The development of the soloist is probably connected to the fact that about this time in the development of jazz, many of the "hot" musicians had to seek employment with larger dance bands of usually dubious quality. The communal, collective improvisatory style of early jazz was impossible in this context, though later the important big jazz bands and big "blues bands" of the Southwest solves this problem by "uniting on a higher level the individual contribution with the entire group."[8]

The isolation that had nurtured Afro-American musical tradition before the coming of jazz had largely disappeared by the mid-twenties, and many foreign, even debilitating, elements drifted into this broader instrumental music. The instrumentation of the Henderson Roseland band was not chosen initially for its jazz possibilities, but in order to imitate the popular white dance bands of the day. The Henderson band became a jazz band because of the collective personality of the individual instrumentalists in the band, who were stronger than any superficial forms that might be imposed upon them. The saxophone trio, which was a clichéed novelty in the large white dance bands, became something of remarkable beauty when transformed by Henderson's three reeds, Buster Bailey, Don Redman, and Coleman Hawkins. And just as earlier those singular hollers must have pierced lonely Southern nights after the communal aspect of the slave society had broken down and had been replaced by a pseudoautonomous existence on many tiny Southern plots (which represented, however absurd it might seem, the widest breadth of this country for those Negroes, and their most exalted position in it), so the changed society in which the large Negro dance bands existed represented, in a sense, another post-communal black society. The move north, for instance, had broken down the old communities (the house parties were one manifestation of a regrouping of the newer communities: the Harlems and South Chicagos). Classic blues, the public face of a changed Afro-American culture, was the solo. The blues that developed at the house parties was the collective, communal music. So the jam sessions of the late twenties and thirties became the musicians' collective communal

[7] André Hodeir, *Jazz: Its Evolution and Essence* (1956) New York: Grove Press, pp. 50–51.
[8] *Jazz: A People's Music*, p. 206.

expression, and the solo in the large dance bands, that expression as it had to exist to remain vital outside its communal origins. The dance bands or society orchestras of the North replaced the plot of land, for they were the musician's only means of existence, and the solo, like the holler, was the only link with an earlier, more intense sense of the self in its most vital relationship to the world. The solo spoke singly of a collective music, and because of the emergence of the great soloists (Armstrong, Hawkins, Hines, Harrison), even forced the great bands (Henderson's, Ellington's, and later Basie's) into wonderfully extended versions of that communal expression.

The transformation of the large dance bands into jazz bands was in good measure the work of the Fletcher Henderson orchestra, aided largely by the arrangements of Don Redman, especially his writing for the reed section which gave the saxophones in the Henderson band a fluency that was never heard before. The reeds became the fiery harmonic and melodic imagination of the big jazz bands. And it was the growing prominence of the saxophone in the big band and the later elevation of that instrument to its fullest expressiveness by Coleman Hawkins that planted the seed for the kind of jazz that is played even today. However, it was not until the emergence of Lester Young that jazz became a saxophone or reed music, as opposed to the brass music it had been since the early half-march, half-blues bands of New Orleans.

Louis Armstrong had brought *brass jazz* to its fullest flowering and influenced every major innovation in jazz right up until the forties, and bebop. Earl Hines, whose innovations as a pianist began a new, single-note line approach to the jazz piano, was merely utilizing Armstrong's trumpet style on a different instrument, thereby breaking out of the ragtime-boogie-stride approach to piano that had been predominant since that instrument was first used in jazz bands. Coleman Hawkins's saxophone style is still close to the Armstrong-perfected brass style, and of course, all Hawkins's imitators reflect that style as well. Jimmy Harrison, the greatest innovator on the trombone, was also profoundly influenced by Armstrong's brass style.

With the emergence of many good "hot" musicians from all over the country during the mid-twenties, the big jazz bands continued to develop. By the late twenties there were quite a few good jazz bands all over the country. And competent musicians "appeared from everywhere, from 1920 on: by 1930 every city outside the Deep South with a Negro population (1920 census) above sixty thousand except Philadelphia had produced an important band: Washington, Duke Ellington; Baltimore, Chick Webb; Memphis, Jimmie Lunceford; St. Louis, the Missourians; Chicago, Luis Russell and Armstrong; New York, Henderson, Charlie Johnson, and half a dozen more."[9]

So an important evolution in Afro-American musical form had occurred again and in much the same manner that characterized the many other changes within the tradition of Negro music. The form can be called basically a Euro-American one—the large (sweet) dance band, changed by the contact with Afro-American musical tradition into another vehicle for that tradition. Just as the Euro-American religious song and ballad had been used, so with the transformation of the large dance band into the jazz band and the adaptation of the thirty-two-bar popular song to jazz purposes, the music itself was broadened and extended even further, and even more complex expressions of older musical traditions were made possible.

By the late twenties a great many more Negroes were going to high school and college, and the experience of an American "liberal" education was bound to leave traces. The most expressive big bands of the late twenties and thirties were largely middle-class Negro enterprises. The world of the professional man had opened up, and many scions of the new Negro middle class who had not gotten through professional school went into jazz "to make money." Men like Fletcher Henderson (who had a chemistry degree), Benny Carter, Duke Ellington, Coleman Hawkins, Jimmie Lunceford, Sy Oliver, and Don Redman, for example, all went to college: "They were a remarkable group of men. Between 1925 and 1935 they created, in competition, a musical tradition that required fine technique and musicianship (several of them were among the earliest virtuosi in jazz); they began to change the basis of the jazz repertory from blues to the wider harmonic possibilities of the thirty-two-bar popular song; they created and perfected the new ensemble-style big-band jazz; they kept their groups together for years, working until they achieved a real unity. They showed that jazz could absorb new, foreign elements without losing its identity, that it was in fact capable of evolution."[10]

These men were all "citizens," and they had all, to a great extent, moved away from the older *lowdown* forms of blues. Blues was not so *direct* to them, it had to be utilized in other contexts. Big show-band jazz was a music of their own, a music that still relied on older Afro-American musical tradition, but one that had begun to utilize still greater amounts of popular American music as well as certain formal European traditions. Also, the concept of making music as a means of making a living that had developed with the coming of classic blues

---

[9] Hsio Wen Shih, "The Spread of Jazz and the Big Bands," in *Jazz*, p. 161.
[10] *Ibid.*, p. 164.

singers was now thoroughly a part of the constantly evolving Afro-American culture. One did not expect to hear Bessie Smith at a rent party, one went to the theater to hear her. She was, at all levels, a *performer*. The young middle-class Negroes who came into jazz during the development of the show bands and dance bands all thought of themselves as performers as well. No matter how deeply the music they played was felt, they still thought of it as a public expression.

"If so many musicians came to jazz after training in one of the professions, it was because jazz was both more profitable and safer for a Negro in the 1920s; it was a survival of this attitude that decided Ellington to keep his son out of M.I.T. and aeronautical engineering in the 1930s."[11]

Just as Bessie Smith perfected vocal blues style almost as a Western artifact, and Louis Armstrong perfected the blues-influenced brass style in jazz (which was a great influence on all kinds of instrumental jazz for more than two decades), so Duke Ellington perfected the big jazz band, transforming it into a highly expressive instrument. Ellington, after the Depression had killed off the big theater-band "show-biz" style of the large jazz bands, began to create a personal style of jazz expression as impressive as Armstrong's innovation as a soloist (if not more so). Ellington replaced a "spontaneous collective music by a worked-out orchestral language."[12]

Ellington's music (even the "jungle" bits of his twenties show-band period, which were utilized in those uptown "black and tan" clubs that catered largely to sensual white liberals) was a thoroughly American music. It was the product of a native American mind, but more than that, it was a music that *could* for the first time exist within the formal boundaries of American culture. A freedman could not have created it, just as Duke could never have played like Peatie Wheatstraw. Ellington began in much the same way as a great many of the significant Northern Negro musicians of the era had begun, by playing in the ragtime, show-business style that was so prevalent. But under the influence of the Southern styles of jazz and with the growth of Duke as an orcnestra leader, composer, and musician, the music he came to make was as "moving" in terms of the older Afro-American musical tradition as it was a completely American expression. Duke's sophistication was to a great extent the very quality that enabled him to integrate so perfectly the older blues traditions with the "whiter" styles of big-band music. But Ellington was a "citizen," and his music, as Vic Bellerby has suggested, was "the detached impressionism of a sophisticated Negro city dweller."

---

[11] *Ibid.*, p. 164.
[12] *Jazz: Its Evolutions and Essence*, p. 33.

Even though many of Ellington's compositions were "hailed as uninhibited jungle music," the very fact that the music was so much an American music made it cause the stir it did: "Ellington used musical materials that were familiar to concert-trained ears, making jazz music more listenable to them. These, however, do not account for his real quality. . . . In his work all the elements of the old music may be found, but each completely changed because it had to be changed. . . . Ellington's accomplishment was to solve the problem of form and content for the large band. He did it not by trying to play pure New Orleans blues and stomp music rearranged for large bands, as Henderson did, but by re-creating all the elements of New Orleans music in new instrumental and harmonic terms. What emerged was a music that could be traced back to the old roots and yet sounded fresh and new."[13]

For these reasons, by the thirties the "race" category could be dropped from Ellington's records. Though he would quite often go into his jungle things, faking the resurrection of "African music," the extreme irony here is that Ellington was making "African sounds," but as a sophisticated American. The "African" music he made had much less to do with Africa than his best music, which . . . can be seen as a truly Afro-American music, though understandable only in the context of a completely American experience. This music could, and did, find a place within the main culture. Jazz became more "popular" than ever. The big colored dance bands of the thirties were a national entertainment and played in many white night clubs as well as the black clubs that had been set up especially for white Americans. These bands were also the strongest influence on American popular music and entertainment for twenty years.

The path of jazz and the further development of the Afro-American musical tradition paradoxically had been taken over at this level to a remarkable degree by elements of the Negro middle class. Jazz was their remaining connection with blues; a connection they could make, at many points, within the mainstream of American life.

The music had moved so far into the mainstream that soon white "swing" bands developed that could play with some of the authentic accent of the great Negro bands, though the deciding factor here was the fact that there were never enough good white jazz musicians to go around in those big bands, and most of the bands then were packed with a great many studio and section men, and perhaps one or two "hot" soloists. By the thirties quite a few white bands had mastered the swing idiom of big-band jazz with varying degrees of authenticity.

---

[13] *Jazz: A People's Music*, p. 192.

One of the most successful of these bands, the Benny Goodman orchestra, even began to buy arrangements from Negro arrangers so that it would have more of an authentic tone. The arranger became one of the most important men in big-band jazz, demonstrating how far jazz had gotten from earlier Afro-American musical tradition. (Fletcher Henderson, however, was paid only $37.50 per arrangement by Goodman before Goodman actually hired him as the band's chief arranger.)

The prominence of radio had also created a new medium for this new music, and the growing numbers of white swing bands automatically qualified for these fairly well paying jobs: "The studio work was monopolized by a small group of musicians who turn up on hundreds of records by orchestras of every kind. One of the least admirable characteristics of the entire arrangement was that it was almost completely restricted to white musicians and it was the men from the white orchestras who were getting the work. The Negro musicians complained bitterly about the discrimination, but the white musicians never attempted to help them, and the contractors hired the men they wanted. At the Nest Club or the Lenox Club the musicians were on close terms, but the relationship ended when the white musicians went back to their Times Square hotels. A few of them, notably Goodman, were to use a few of the Harlem musicians, but in the first Depression years the studio orchestras were white."[14]

So the widespread development of the swing style produced yet another irony—when the "obscurity" of the Negro's music was lessened with the coming of arranged big-band jazz, and the music, in effect, did pass into the mainstream of American culture, in fact, could be seen as an integral part of that culture, it not only ceased to have meaning for a great many Negroes but also those Negroes who were most closely involved with the music were not even allowed to play it at the highest salaries that could be gotton. The spectacle of Benny Goodman hiring Teddy Wilson and later Lionel Hampton, Charlie Christian, and Cootie Williams into his outrageously popular bands and thereby making them "big names" in the swing world seems to me as fantastically amusing as the fact that in the jazz polls during the late thirties and early forties run by popular jazz magazines, almost no Negro musicians won. Swing music, which was the result of arranged big-band jazz, as it developed to a music that had almost nothing to do with blues, had very little to do with black America, though that is certainly where it had come from. But there were now more and more Negroes like that, too.

---

[14] Samuel Charters and Leonard Kunstadt, *Jazz: A History of the New York Scene* (New York, Doubleday, 1962), p. 262.

SPECULATIONS

1. Why did Amiri Baraka title this essay "Swing—From Verb to Noun"? Is that change (from verb to noun) a positive one?

2. In the middle of his essay, Baraka makes the following assertion: "Music, as paradoxical as it might seem, is the result of thought. It is the result of thought perfected at its most empirical, i.e., as *attitude*, or *stance*." How is music the result of thinking or of "attitude"? How does the change in black music parallel a change in black thinking and black attitudes? Give your own examples of how today's music parallels specific changes in thinking and attitudes.

3. What does the "blood ritual" of blues mean in this essay and how does it represent the fate of black culture for Baraka?

4. How are blues, jazz, and swing different from each other? How does Baraka structure this essay around the development and exchange of black and white attitudes about these three forms of music? How do your own ideas and attitudes towards these forms of music differ from or resemble the attitudes described in this essay?

5. Why does Baraka insist on claiming every form of music he discusses as a "distinctly American experience," even when he identifies its relation to European or African roots? Identify which forms you value most and explain why you value them.

6. What roles do race and class play in his essay? Do you agree with the importance that Baraka assigns to them? In what ways does the history of jazz, as stated by Baraka, parallel the history of black Americans? In what ways do you think it does not?

Woody Guthrie: "Shakespeare in Overalls"

RAY PRATT

Ray Pratt was born in Detroit, Michigan, the center of the industrial heartland, and grew up in Lansing, Michigan, where he studied history and sociology at Michigan State University. Pratt completed a Master of Arts in political science at Michigan State, and a Ph.D. in political science at the University of Oregon. He has taught at several universities, including the University of California at Santa Barbara, the University of Michigan, and Washington University. Since 1971, he has been teaching political science at Montana State University.

"Woody Guthrie: 'Shakespeare in Overalls'" is a selection from Pratt's 1990 book, *Rhythm and Resistance: Explorations in the Political Uses of Popular Music*. As the subtitle of the book suggests, Pratt is interested in the ways that politics, history, and popular music combine to create folk heroes such as Joe Hill and Woody Guthrie. Their song lyrics and music created a political message of protest that began in the early 1900s and continued to carry hope for American workers throughout the bleak years of the Great Depression. Pratt shows that even today, a "people's music" taken from utopian politics, hero worship, and popular legend reaffirms our romantic longings for a lifestyle of freedom, the open road, and "authentic self-creation."

In the early 1940s the arrival in New York City of Woody Guthrie, a "Shakespeare in overalls" from the dust bowl of Oklahoma, amazed many progressive intellectuals searching for the authentic anticapitalist voice of the real America, who found his native populist radicalism almost too good to be true. One Communist writer, Mike Gold, had previously discoursed at length on folk and popular song, expressing the need for a "Communist Joe Hill" in his column in *The Daily Worker*.[1]

Joe Hill (born Joseph Hillstrom in Sweden in 1879) had been an itinerant laborer and an organizer for the old Industrial Workers of the World (IWW), known as "the Wobblies."[2] He wrote over 25 songs in wide use in the pre-World War I period of radical labor activism in which the IWW played the central role before succumbing to massive government and "patriotic" citizen vigilante repression during the war.[3] Hill's songs, collected in a small booklet designed to fit into a worker's pocket and popularly known as *The Little Red Songbook*, were in wide circulation.[4] Tens of thousands were printed and each new IWW member got a copy with the membership card. Guthrie had acquired a copy in his travels in the early 1930s as he became acquainted with older radicals, particularly among the hoboes and itinerant workers, who had been one of the significant social bases of IWW support.[5]

Joe Hill's career,[6] while fascinating, was secondary to the role he subsequently played as a character in novels and plays and film from the 1930s on as the preeminent labor folk hero and martyr, assuming the status of myth-hero in the radical pop culture of the 1960s. Arrested on a robbery-murder charge in Salt Lake City in 1914, Hill was tried and convicted on very questionable (largely circumstantial) evidence.[7] A major campaign to have a new trial or at least a stay of execution failed to have any impact on the Utah authorities.

Joe Hill was executed by firing squad by his own command to fire on November nineteenth, 1915, in the face of massive international protests. Hill's exuberance and humor as a writer of popular and widely used labor songs,[8] which now sound rather quaint and very dated in their rigid class-consciousness and especially in their utopian optimism concerning the future, as do many of Guthrie's songs from 30 years later, was perhaps exceeded by the skillful manner in which he directed his own performance as a martyr. Hill was a master of melodramatic eloquence, never bending in his public statements. He is perhaps best remembered for his final words in a telegram to IWW leader Big Bill Haywood urging him not to waste time mourning but to "organize!"

Hill's canonization and elevation to mythic status, beyond the narrow subculture of old-time socialists and labor radicals who knew his story well, was aided by his appearance as a character in John Dos Passos's 1932 novel *Nineteen Nineteen* and the wide circulation of the 1938 Alfred Hayes and Earl Robinson song "Joe Hill" with its famous line saying the singer dreamed he saw Joe Hill last night.[9] Pete Seeger has sung the song in his performances for almost half a century. Probably the song's greatest exposure came with Joan Baez's performance before half a million people at Woodstock in 1969 and subsequent recordings, establishing a link between the counterculture of the 1960s and an earlier generation of radicalism. A 1971 Swedish film directed by Bo Widerberg, though limited in circulation to art houses and campuses, effectively portrayed an accurate version of what is known of Hill's life, though it was not the pop culture artifact that the movie life of Woody Guthrie became a few years later.

Symbolizing the incredible, often naive revolutionary zeal of the anarchosyndicalist IWW with its almost mystical faith in the innate creative ability of workers to build a new world "within the shell of the old," Joe Hill became the first and greatest radical culture hero, largely through the way he seems to have masterminded the symbolism around his own death. He became the man who "never dies" in leftist political culture because virtually all the public has ever known about him originated in his songs and the heroic myth he was able to create from his cell with the aid of thousands of leftist supporters across the country and in Europe. Sending out telegrams and letters with lines like "I have lived like an artist, and I shall die like an artist" and "I'm going to get a new trial or die trying," Hill became a figure still well known in leftist political culture around the world. Indeed, U.S. students, who know little of his life, report being asked about him in places as far away as Finland. The Hill legend has apparently become a part of worldwide leftist political cultural images concerning the suppression of native radicalism in the United States. This is understandable in terms of the theoretical functions of such images, as noted earlier.[10] Like the Mexican revolutionary Emiliano Zapata,* lured into a carefully planned assassination four years after Hill's death, Hill represents an idealized, even utopian, wish-image of the kind of clear-eyed and fearless radical who never sold out his convic-

---

* Zapata (1877?–1917); agrarian reformer; guerilla leader 1911–1916. [Eds.]

tions or his cause, a model needed both by individual radicals and movements in struggle against the often seemingly insurmountable power of existing authorities. Because Hill's image so effectively represents and contains the hopes and anxieties of rebels against the American "Eden," he truly will be the man who "never died." Musical references have played the most significant role in the maintenance of his image.

The Arrival of Woody Guthrie

Though it took perhaps four decades for its significance to be fully evident, the arrival of Woodrow Wilson Guthrie in New York in 1940 was possibly the single most significant moment in the history of folk music and one of the pivotal moments in the growth of an oppositional popular political culture in the United States.[11] Woody Guthrie was just one of the many great individuals who collectively make up any movement of popular culture. The details of his life have become familiar to folk music buffs and scholars interested in popular folk music, or "people's music," but assumed mythic proportions in the 1960s with Bob Dylan and other singers acknowledging him as their hero, becoming a celluloid fantasy in the 1970s with Hal Ashby's 1976 film *Bound for Glory* released by United Artists and starring David Carradine as Guthrie. Loosely based on Guthrie's own autobiography of the same title, the film contained some beautiful photography but failed to say anything concerning Guthrie's Communist organizational commitments, further obscuring the popular myth and further (a more serious omission) contributing to the denial of the significance of the party in U.S. life that has become an element of the dominant political cultural consensus.

Born in Okemah, Oklahoma, on July 14, 1912, of an essentially downwardly mobile family, an itinerant ramblin' man, hobo, songwriter, and country singer in the Depression years, Woodrow Wilson Guthrie roamed across the nation absorbing the sounds and soul of a rural America economically disintegrating in the "hard times" and experiencing a massive flight of population off the land. But Woody Guthrie encountered another side of Depression-era America, one demonstrating the tough and gritty resilience of hundreds of thousands of displaced "Okies" and other poor ordinary people who fought for and maintained a measure of dignity whether on the road, in migrant workers' camps, or as new arrivals in a number of major cities—a comforting finding, affirming important elements of U.S. culture and institutions that led many to a more conservative view of what the country needed.[12] Guthrie early on, while thoroughly "American" in cultural origins, had apparently concluded traditional two-party, "free enterprise" politics did not provide the answers to the problems he had seen and lived in his journeys across the country. No more authentically native American leftist has ever existed. But his story has had to be rescued from a continuing process of mythologizing. Anyone with more than a passing interest in the social history or popular music of the United States should read Joe Klein's *Woody Guthrie: A Life*, which deals with this period with acute sensitivity and sympathy and does more than any work this writer has encountered to recapture the essence of a time whose memories have been suppressed by over four decades of cold war denial. Klein's book is, for anyone interested in popular music or oppositional political culture, quite simply one of the most instructive and informative works on twentieth-century America—a biography and a social history of an era.[13]

The United States had a vitally significant left political subculture in the 1930s and 1940s that exercised a very significant influence in popular culture, not through some sort of insidious "infiltration," as hysterical government Communist hunters and Congressional investigators of the 1950s might have imagined, but because it was grounded in some of the economic and social realities that the nation has often seen fit to forget, deny, or censor. Only recently, with commercial films such as Warren Beatty's *Reds* (1981) and documentary films such as Julia Reichert's *Seeing Red* (1983) has an effort been made to begin to counteract the decades of suppression and denial of this part of our history.

It would be grossly inaccurate to identify the leftist counterculture of the half century of United States political history preceding the conformist and paranoid 1950s exclusively with the experience of those who were members of the American Communist party; nonetheless that group, Joseph Starobin pointed out in his appraisal of the party's declining years, involved "several hundred thousand Americans who gave the attempt to build a revolutionary community in a nonrevolutionary situation their best years, their immense energies, and highest hopes."[14] The music of Woody Guthrie should be understood in the context of the experience of a community of men and women who in Starobin's terms by "trying to fuse the experience of a rich past and confront the urgent issues of their times, . . . built what was by far the most powerful and pervasive radical movement in American life and then helped to shatter it."[15] Their community was, Starobin suggested, a political party

> which they tried to make into a fraternity of comrades, animated by the great ideal of human brotherhood and the aim of making the whole society conform to such brotherhood. It was a community that went beyond national boundaries and differences of race and creed:

it was driven by the certainty that man's sojourn on earth could be happier if only . . . social relations were transformed from competition to cooperation. These Americans were sure that a universal strategy for creating a new society had been found in the experience of Russia and China.[16]

That virtually all political persuasions from left to right now recognize how shortsighted and wrong their strategy was for the United States does not detract from the fact that their hopes and immense energies powered many movements for change in the twentieth century and that many of the individuals within or close to the Communist party made important and enduring contributions to our popular culture. Woody Guthrie himself always denied any formal membership in the party and authorities are conflicting in the evidence concerning the fact, but much of his work was done for the community of people centered around that organization.[17]

Guthrie's Significance

So much has been written and said and sung about Guthrie, and so many individuals have tried to emulate what they thought his lifestyle was, that his life has become something of a myth beyond explication. Yet given the distortions of his film biography, and the naive efforts to gloss over the complexities of the history of communism in the United States, there are several things that must be reemphasized concerning his contribution to popular culture and music in the country.

Guthrie's significance, musically speaking, is that he virtually *reinvented* a traditional form, the folk ballad, transforming it into a powerful instrument of political cultural commentary. In the over 1,000 songs he wrote, he chronicled an era. Indeed, through some of those songs, such as "So Long, It's Been Good to Know Ya," "Pastures of Plenty," and "This Land Is Your Land" (the latter sometimes mentioned as a new national anthem), he transcended time and place to originate new and subsequently enduring elements of a national popular political culture.

His music fuses some of the best raw materials of traditional grass roots regional musical culture with an insight and human concern for the ordinary person, the underdog, and the dispossessed that was utterly unique at the time and remains so. Such composer-singers as Bob Dylan in his 1963 album *The Times They Are A-Changin'* and Bruce Springsteen in his 1982 album *Nebraska* and in both earlier and later songs such as "The River" (1979) and "Seeds" (1985), among many, have tried to emulate Guthrie's thematic concern with the lives of ordinary people and the spirit of his identification with the nation. However, because the precise historical circumstances of disintegration of a widely shared rural life experience that provided Guthrie with his opportunities will not be repeated, the character of their contributions remains of a different kind, though still significant.

If Woody Guthrie had a kind of genius that included a devastatingly critical eye combined with a wry wit and humor that only rarely appears, he was also a product of a rural regional subculture that he clearly tried to escape but that somehow also must have engendered and nurtured these very qualities. His vivid figures of speech and turns of phrase remind me of some of the sparkling similes I heard from former in-laws during journeys through rural Missouri, a corner of Oklahoma, and Kentucky over a quarter century ago (one example of an expression that sticks in my mind: "He was as fat as a town dog!"). Guthrie was unique, and although clearly a leftist intellectual in spite of his efforts to create a folksy identity, he assumed at times (such as his month of writing songs about the Columbia River region[18]) an almost Whitmanesque quality—he *was* grass roots America. His native folk radicalism is typified by his definition of folk music in a letter to Alan Lomax:

> I think real folk stuff scares most of the boys around Washington. A folk song is what's wrong and how to fix it, or it could be whose hungry and where their mouth is, or whose out of work and where the job is or whose broke and where the money is or whose carrying a gun and where the peace is—that's folk lore and folks made it up because they seen that the politicians could find nothing to fix or nobody to feed or give a job of work. We don't aim to hurt you or scare you when we get to feeling sorta folksy and make up some folk lore, we're doing all we can to make it easy on you. I can sing all day and all night sixty days and sixty nights but of course I ain't got enough wind to be in office.[19]

That Woody Guthrie and his songs continue to inspire the admiration of some of the greatest popular artists would by itself constitute sufficient judgment of his importance. From Bob Dylan, whose unique self-creation was modeled after Guthrie (and also "Ramblin Jack" Elliott, who himself affected an almost uncanny vocal resemblance to Guthrie over a decade before Dylan), Phil Ochs, and Tom Paxton through Bruce Springsteen (who sang "This Land Is Your Land" consistently during his 1980–81 and 1984–85 tours, introducing it as "the greatest song ever written about America"), there has been a consistently recurring recognition of Guthrie's qualities. Descriptions like "artless," "simple," "direct," and "eloquent" are frequently applied to his songs and style.[20] Woody Guthrie clearly remains a "culture hero."[21]

An additional dimension exists that might help explain the Guthrie appeal. In the images that come down to the present of his detached, rambling existence, he touches deeper sources of romantic individual longings to break free and "hit the road." His lifestyle provides a model of freedom, an alternative model of existence when the chains of civilization and the daily grind begin to chafe. Lee Hays found, working at a resort in the Adirondacks, that young people had a tremendous interest in Guthrie. One expressed what seems to be the persisting appeal: "Most kids reach a point where they really want their freedom. You had school, your parents—anything that stands in the way. All you can think about is getting *out*. You want to hitch a ride, hop a freight, go wherever you want. Woody, I guess, represents that kind of freedom for me."[22]

This myth of radical, authentic self-creation resonates within many Americans. It is a central element in the promise of American life, to the American Dream, that *here* one can become whatever one wants to be. If most find themselves eventually trapped on webs of their own devising, that prevent them from getting away, the Guthrie myth may embody that escape. Elements are evident (with a greater sense of the ambiguities and ultimate deception in the promise), in the work of Springsteen in such songs as "Born to Run" and "Thunder Road," and especially from the songs of *Darkness on the Edge of Town* (1978) onward through the album *Nebraska* (clearly inspired by Guthrie) to the powerful social criticism of "Seeds."

This first period of folk revival contained little of the microscopic examination among fans of style and technique that would emerge in the second stage of the 1950s and1960s. Indeed, during this first stage some urban folk proponents tended to regard integral aspects of traditional style such as vocal timbre, phrasing, diction, and metrical "irregularities" as mere "embarrassing mistakes" caused by poor education.[23] That, of course, was not the case with most of those around Guthrie—professionals such as Alan Lomax, and especially Pete Seeger.

Notes

1. See Joe Klein, *Woodie Guthrie: A Life*. New York Ballantine Books: p. 145, on Mike Gold; more generally, see Richard A. Reuss, "The Roots of American Left-Wing Interest in Folksong," *Labor History* 17 (1971):259–79.

2. The major historical treatment of the IWW is Melvyn Dubovsky, *We Shall Be All: A History of the Industrial Workers of the World* (Chicago: Quadrangle Books, 1969).

3. On the repression against the IWW see the good brief account in Wayne Hampton's *Guerilla Minstrels*, (Knoxville: University of Tennessee Press, 1986), pp. 83–85. Also, Dubovsky, *We Shall Be All*. More generally concerning repression of radicalism as a recurrent phenomenon see Alan Wolfe's provocative work, *The Seamy Side of Democracy: Repression in America*, 2nd ed. (New York and London: Longman, 1978).

4. Richard Brazier, "The Story of the IWW's 'Little Red Songbook,'" *Labor History* 9 (Winter 1968):91–105.

5. See the account of Hill's influence on Guthrie in Klein, *Woody Guthrie*, pp. 82–85.

6. Hill's career is profiled briefly and concisely in Hampton, *Guerilla Minstrels*, pp. 60–92, under the chapter title "Joe Hill: The Man Who Never Died."

7. A good overview of the evidence in the case was presented by historian Philip S. Foner, *The Case of Joe Hill* (New York: International Publishers, 1965). Novelist Wallace Stegner, who wrote a novel on Hill, *The Preacher and the Slave* (Boston: Houghton Mifflin, 1950), was convinced of his guilt. See Wallace Stegner, "Joe Hill: The Wobblies' Troubadour," *New Republic*, January 5, 1948, pp. 20–24, and the reply by IWW veteran Fred Thompson in a *New Republic* letter of February 9, 1948. A longer IWW view was in the November 15, 1948, *New Republic*.

8. Two good albums of "Joe Hill" and other IWW songs are Utah Phillips, *We Have Fed You All a Thousand Years*, Philo Records 1076 (distributed by Rounder Records), and Joe Glazer, *Songs of the Wobblies*, Collector Records 1927 (P.O. Box 1143, Columbia, MD 21044).

9. Complete lyrics and music to "Joe Hill" appeared in *The People's Song Book* (New York: Oak Publications, 1948; and many subsequent editions).

10. Especially in Fredric Jameson, "Reification and Utopia in Mass Culture," *Social Text*, I, 1979.

11. There is no better introduction to the spirit of the time than Klein's chapter "American Spirit" in *Woody Guthrie*.

12. See the numerous esentially conservative, affirmative reactions discussed by Stott, *Documentary Expression*, pp. 238–57.

13. Klein's *Woody Guthrie* was discussed repeatedly by Bruce Springsteen during his 1980–81 tour as part of his introduction to singing "This Land Is Your Land." Hear the introduction to the performance on *Bruce Springsteen and the E-Street Band Live, 1975–85*, Columbia Records.

14. Joseph Starobin, *American Communism in Crisis, 1943–1957* (Cambridge, Mass.: Harvard University Press, 1972), p. ix.

15. Ibid.

16. Ibid.

17. On Guthrie's associations with the party see Klein, *Woody Guthrie*, pp. 156–57; Hampton, *Guerilla Minstrels*, p. 95, cites as evidence of formal membership a *Broadside* magazine statement of Gordon Friesen, who knew Guthrie well: "When I knew him he was a full-fledged member of the village branch of the Communist Cultural Section, and proud of it."

18. Klein, *Woody Guthrie*, p. 195.

19. Cited by ibid., p. 168–69.

20. See the extensive list of bibliographical material in Hampton's *Guerilla Minstrels* and the bibliographical notes in Klein, *Woody Guthrie*, pp. 451–57.

21. Much of his recorded work has been reissued in compact disc format, and a new celebration of his and Leadbelly's songs, *A Vision Shared*, was issued by CBS in 1988 featuring contributions by Dylan, Springsteen, U2, Taj Mahal, Arlo Guthrie, and others.

Two interesting works on folk-protest music utilize the concept of culture hero: Jerome L. Rodnitzky, *Minstrels of the Dawn* (Chicago: Nelson-Hall, 1976), and Hampton, *Guerilla Minstrels*. Hampton's work is the more substantial of the two in terms of the depth of inquiry into similar subject matter and individuals (Joe Hill, Woody Guthrie, Bob Dylan, John Lennon) but, curiously, fails even to mention the Rodnitzky work, which is certainly worth examination and would seem to be the source of the conception.

22. Klein, *Woody Guthrie*, p. 421.

23. Sandberg and Weissman, *The Folk Music Source Book*, p. 100.

SPECULATIONS

1.   Ray Pratt repeatedly uses terms like "myth-hero," "folk hero," "martyr," "greatest radical culture hero," and "heroic myth" to describe Joe Hill and Woody Guthrie. How do you regard Hill and Guthrie? What values, if any, do such figures have for us today?

2.   What are the essential differences between Joe Hill and Woody Guthrie as described in this article? In your mind, which one is a more enduring mythic figure?

3.   What does Pratt mean when he describes Joe Hill as "an idealized, even utopian, wish-image of the kind of clear-eyed and fearless radical who never sold out his convictions or his cause, a model needed by both individual radicals and movements in struggle against the often seemingly insurmountable power of existing authorities"? Explain why you agree or disagree that this kind of model is needed by people.

4.   Pratt writes that "It is a central element in the promise of American life, to the American Dream, that *here* one can become whatever one wants to be." Explain how you agree or disagree with this statement by describing your own idea of the "American Dream" and how it differs from or resembles Pratt's idea. Provide examples of popular music that help articulate or represent your idea of the "American Dream."

5.   What is Pratt's major point in writing about Joe Hill and Woody Guthrie? Why does he say that Woody Guthrie's "story has had to be rescued from a continuing process of mythologizing"? What kind of rhetorical move is Pratt making here?

Joe Hill

PHIL OCHS

Folk singer and songwriter Philip David Ochs was born in El Paso, Texas, in 1940. Early in his career, he was influenced by Johnny Cash and Elvis Presley. He later studied at Ohio State University, where he was influenced by the folk music of Woody Guthrie and Pete Seeger. Ochs's first two albums, *All the News That's Fit to Sing* and *I Ain't Marchin' Anymore*, contain songs of protest that grew out of his opposition to the war in Vietnam; they include songs such as "Draft Dodger Rag" and "Talking Vietnam," which established him as a powerful and colorful voice during the political and social protest of the sixties. His ballad "Joe Hill" first appeared in the Industrial Workers of the World (IWW)'s 35th edition of *The Little Red Songbook*, now officially titled *Songs of the Workers: To Fan the Flames of Discontent*.

Oh, his clothes were coarse, and his hopes were high,
As he headed for the Promised Land.
And it took a few weeks on the out-of-work streets
Before he began to understand, before he began to
    understand.

So he headed out for the California shore.
There things were just as bad.
So he joined the Industrial Workers of the World,
'Cause the Union was the only friend he had,
  'cause The Union was the only friend he had.

The strikes were bloody; the strikes were black,
As hard as they were long.
In the dark of the night, Joe would stay awake and write.
In the morning he would wake them with a song,
  in the morning he would wake them with a song.

He wrote his words to the tunes of the day,
To be passed along the union vine.
And the strikes were led; and the songs were spread.
And Joe Hill was always on the line,
  and Joe Hill was always on the line.

Then in Salt Lake City, a murder was made.
There was hardly a clue to find.
Yes, the proof was poor but the sheriff was sure
That Joe was the killer of the crime,
  that Joe was the killer of the crime.

Strange are the ways of the western law;
Strange are the ways of fate.
For the government crawled to the mine owners call,
And the judge was appointed by The State,
  and the judge was appointed by The State.

Now Utah justice can be had,
But not for a Union Man.
And Joe was warned by some early morn
There'd be one less singer in the land,
  there'd be one less singer in the land.

For thirty-six years he lived out his days,
And he more than played his part.
For the songs that he made, he was carefully paid
By a rifle bullet buried in his heart,
  by a rifle bullet buried in his heart.

Yes, they lined Joe Hill up against the wall,
Blindfold over his eyes.
It's the life of the rebel that he chose to live;
It's the death of the rebel that he died,
  It's the death of the rebel that he died.

Joe Hill's Last Will (Written in his cell November 18, 1915, on the eve of his execution.)

JOE HILL

Joseph Hillstrom, better known as "Old Joe Hill," was born in Galve, Sweden, in 1879, and immigrated to the United States in 1902. He worked as a piano player in a saloon in New York's Bowery district and as a manual laborer on the West coast, where he began writing songs about workers and became a leader in the labor movement. He joined the Industrial Workers of the World (IWW) in 1910 and contributed many songs to *The Little Red Songbook*. Joe Hill's reputation for courage and his selfless contributions to the American labor movement are part of labor history—he was a zealous spokesperson for union causes and the rights of "the working man." His organizing made him unpopular with the authorities, and he was convicted of murder and robbery in Utah under what many claim to have been false charges. He wrote his "Last Will" the night before he was executed by a firing squad.

My will is easy to decide,
For there is nothing to divide.
My kin don't need to fuss and moan—
"Moss does not cling to a rolling stone."
My body? Ah, if I could choose,
I would to ashes it reduce,
And let the merry breezes blow
My dust to where some flowers grow.
Perhaps some fading flower then
Would come to life and bloom again.
This is my last and final will,
Good luck to all of you.

—Joe Hill

SPECULATIONS

1. Based on these lyrics, do you think Joe Hill is an American hero? Why do you think he was so popular? Explain your response.
2. Why do you think Phil Ochs, a folk singer active in the 1960s, chose to write about Joe Hill?

The Degradation of Women

MARION MEADE

Marion Meade in an interview with *Contemporary Authors* confessed: "I am a feminist and my writings reflect a feminist point of view." As a novelist and biographer, her published works reflect that ideological commitment; they focus on famous women and their places in history: *Bitching* (1973), *Free Woman: The Life and Times of Victoria Woodhull* (1976), *Eleanor of Aquitaine* (1977), *Stealing Heaven: The Love Story of Héloïse and Abélard* (1979), and *Madame Blavatsky: The Woman Behind the Myth* (1980).

Born in Pittsburgh in 1934, Meade earned a bachelor's degree at Northwestern University and a master's at Columbia University. She currently resides and works in New York City.

The following selection, taken from an article entitled "Does Rock Degrade Women?", was written for the *New York Times* in 1971. Her indictment of rock music's misogynist lyrics, attitudes, and politics echoes many similar remarks from other writers in this section, including Jerry Adler, Robert Palmer, Sheryl Garratt, and Susan McClary. Meade's position sees through the allure of rebellion and social protest that is sometimes attributed to rock music, and she condemns male rock musicians for their unrelenting reinforcement of "old-fashioned sex-role stereotypes." At the same time, she refuses to indulge in endless diatribe and pessimism. The women's movement represents to her signs of hope.

Last spring I sat through three hours of the film *Woodstock* alternating between feelings of enchantment and repulsion. Sure, there was all that magnificent music, along with the generous helpings of peace and love and grass. And yet I found something persistently disturbing about the idyllic spectacle on the screen.

For one thing, with the exception of a pregnant Joan Baez who couldn't seem to stop talking about her husband, all the musicians were men. Sweaty, bearded men were busy building the stage, directing traffic, shooting the film, and running the festival. *Brother*hood was repeatedly proclaimed, both on stage and off. Woodstock Nation was beginning to look ominously like a fantasyland which only welcomed men. How about the women? Barefooted and sometimes barebreasted, they sprawled erotically in the grass, looked after their babies, or dished up hot meals. If this was supposed to be the Aquarian Utopia,[1] it reminded me more of a Shriners' picnic at which the wife and kiddies are invited to participate once a year.

---

[1] *Aquarian Utopia* refers to the notion that the earth is passing under the influence of Aquarius, the eleventh sign of the zodiac, which will bring about a new age of love, peace, harmony, and understanding as proclaimed in the song "Aquarius" from the popular 1968 rock musical "Hair" [Eds.]

Looking back, I think the movie confirmed an uneasiness I'd felt for some time but had refused to admit: Rock music, in fact the entire rock "culture," is tremendously degrading to women. I reached this conclusion reluctantly and with a good deal of sadness because rock has been important to me. And while I still dig the vitality of the sound, I find myself increasingly turned off in nearly every other respect.

Stokely Carmichael[2] recalls that as a child he loved Westerns and always cheered wildly for the cowboys to triumph over the Indians until one day he realized *he* was an Indian. All along he'd been rooting for the wrong side. More and more, women rock fans are discovering themselves in the same curiously surprised position. For those who have taken the trouble to listen carefully, rock's message couldn't be clearer. It's a man's world, baby, and women have only one place in it. Between the sheets or, if they're talented like Arlo Guthrie's Alice, in the kitchen.

The paradox is that rock would appear to be an unlikely supporter of such old-fashioned sex-role stereotypes. In fact, its rebellion against middle-class values, its championing of the unisex fashions and long hair styles for men seem to suggest a blurring of the distinctions between male and female. But for all the hip camouflage sexism flourishes.

The clearest indication of how rock music views womankind is in its lyrics. Women certainly can't complain that the image presented there is one-dimensional. On the contrary, the put-downs are remarkably multifaceted, ranging from open contempt to sugar-coated condescension. Above all, however, women are always-available sexual objects whose chief function is to happily accommodate any man who comes along. This wasn't always the case. Elvis's pelvis notwithstanding, the popular songs of the fifties and early sixties explored such innocuous adolescent pastimes as dancing around the clock, the beach, going steady, and blue suede shoes. In those days before the so-called sexual revolution, the typical woman portrayed in rock was the nice girl next door with whom the Beatles only wanted to hold hands. Then suddenly came the nice girl's metamorphosis into "groovy chick," the difference being that a groovy chick is expected to perform sexually. In rock songs, she never fails.

The worst picture of women appears in the music of the Rolling Stones, where sexual exploitation reaches unique heights. A woman is a "Stupid Girl" who should be kept "Under My Thumb," a "Honky Tonk Woman" who gives a man "Satisfaction." In "Yesterday's Pa-

---

[2] Stokely Carmichael (b. 1942) is a black political activist. [Eds.]

pers,'' where women are equated with newspapers, the dehumanization is carried to an extreme. Who wants yesterday's papers, the song arrogantly demands, who wants yesterday's girl? The answer: Nobody. Once used, a woman is as valuable as an old newspaper, presumably good only for wrapping garbage.

But the Stone's album *Let It Bleed* is surely unrivaled when it comes to contempt for women, as well as lewdness in general. One cut in particular, "Live With Me," is explicit about woman's proper place:

Doncha' think there's a place for you in-between the sheets?

And only an extraordinarily masochistic woman could listen to the album's title song with any sense of pleasure whatsoever. There a woman is represented as a drive-in bordello, a one-stop sexual shopping center offering all the standard services plus a few extras casually thrown in as a kind of shopper's Special of the Day.

The Stone's next album has been tentatively titled "Bitch." It figures.

Misogyny is only slightly more disguised in the music of Bob Dylan who, in his early work at least, tended to regard nearly every female as a bitch. For example, in "Like a Rolling Stone," Dylan apparently feels so threatened by Miss Lonely (whose only sin as far as I can tell is that she has a rather shallow life style) that he feels compelled to destroy her. First he takes away her identity, then he puts her out on the street without shelter or food, and in the end—obliteration, as he makes her invisible. "How does it feel?" he asks.

There's no more complete catalogue of sexist slurs than Dylan's "Just Like a Woman," in which he defines woman's natural traits as greed, hypocrisy, whining, and hysteria. But isn't that cute, he concludes, because it's "just like a woman." For a finale, he throws in the patronizing observation that adult women have a way of breaking "just like a little girl."

These days a seemingly mellowed Dylan has been writing about women with less hatred, but the results still aren't especially flattering. Now he calls his females ladies and invites them to lay across his big brass bed. In short, he has more or less caught up with Jim Morrison's request to "Light my fire" and with John Lennon's suggestion, "Why don't we do it in the road?"

Again and again throughout rock lyrics women emerge either as insatiable, sex-crazed animals or all-American emasculators. Although one might think these images indicate a certain degree of aggressiveness in women, oddly enough they still wind up in a servile position where they exist only to enhance the lives of men.

As for romance, rock hasn't rejected it entirely. Rock love songs exhibit a regular gallery of passive, spiritless women, sad-eyed ladies propped on velvet thrones as the private property of a Sunshine Superman. From the Beatles we get motherly mandonnas whispering words of wisdom ("Let it be, let it be") or pathetic spinsters like Eleanor Rigby who hang around churches after weddings to collect the rice. Leonard Cohen's romantic ideal is the mystical Suzanne who wears rags from the Salvation Army and acts, the composer asserts, "half crazy." Seldom does one run across a mature, intelligent woman or, for that matter, a woman who is capable enough to hold a job (one exception is the Beatles' meter maid, Rita). Only the Stones' Ruby Tuesday insists on an independent life of her own.

Since rock is written almost entirely by men, it's hardly surprising to find this frenzied celebration of masculine supremacy. But it's also understandable in terms of the roots from which rock evolved. In both blues and country music, attitudes toward women reflected a rabid machismo: men always dominated and women were fickle bitches who ran off with other men. Often they were seen in relationship to the wandering superstud who recounts his conquests in every town along the road, a fantasy which remains fashionable in rock today.

Apart from the myths of female inferiority proclaimed by rock lyricists, the exploitation and dehumanization of women also extends into the off-stage rock scene. How else can one account for a phenomenon like the groupies? That these aggressive teenage camp followers could possibly be regarded as healthy examples of sexual liberation is certainly a cruel joke. In fact, groupies service the needs of the male musicians and further symbolize rock's impersonal view of women as cheap commodities which can be conveniently disposed of after use. The Stones said it: nobody in the world wants yesterday's papers.

Finally, rock is a field from which women have been virtually excluded as musicians. Not only is it rare to find an integrated band, but the few all-female groups have been notably unsuccessful. The very idea of a women's rock band is looked upon as weird, in the same category as Phil Spitalny's all-girl orchestra, a freak show good for a few giggles.

The problem is that women have been intimidated from even attempting a career in rock. Women, the myth says, aren't smart enough to understand the complexities of electronics or tough enough to compose music of sufficient intensity or physically strong enough to play drums. The guitar is acceptable but the electric guitar is unfeminine.

As for female rock singers, you can count them on a few fingers. We did have Janis Joplin, a blueswoman in the finest tradition of Bessie Smith and Billie Holiday. When Janis wailed about love as a ball and chain and women being losers, now there were ideas with which women could identify. At least we knew what she meant. The soul sounds of Tina Turner and Laura Nyro also radiate the feeling that they know what it's like to be a woman. Otherwise, just about the only rock queen left is Grace Slick. Although some may regard her private life as liberated in that she decided to have an illegitimate child and generally appears to care little for society's conventions, even her work with the Jefferson Airplane is hardly oriented toward women.

Which leaves us with Joan Baez, Judy Collins and Joni Mitchell, who specialize in the bland folk-rock deemed appropriate for a delicate sex.

At this point, what does rock offer women? Mighty little.

Recently, however, rock bands have reported strange happenings at concerts. Instead of the usual adoring screams from the women, every so often they've been hearing boos and unladylike shouts of "male chauvinist pigs." Because the bands tend to regard these disturbances as a puzzling but passing phenomenon, they've made little effort so far to understand the changes taking place in their audience. What they fail to recognize is that the condescending swaggering which worked for Elvis in the fifties and the sadistic, anti-woman sneers of Mick Jagger in the sixties are no longer going to make it in the seventies.

There's no question that rock is already in trouble. The current spiritual and economic malaise has been variously attributed to the Hendrix-Joplin deaths, the general tightness of money, as well as lackluster albums and tired performances from the popular stars. Whatever the reasons, rock listeners today are plainly bored. Does anyone really care if John, Paul, Ringo, and George ever get together again? Not me.

On the other hand, isn't it about time for women to band together and invade the chauvinistic rock scene? Only then will the vicious stereotypes be eliminated and, one hopes, some fresh energy generated as well. For too long we've sat wistfully on the sidelines, acting out our expected roles as worshipful groupies.

Women have always constituted an important segment of the rock audience. Unless the industry is willing to alienate us completely, they'd better remember what Bob Dylan said about not needing a weatherman to know which way the wind blows. For the times they are a-changin', eh, fellas?

SPECULATIONS

1. In what ways do you agree or disagree with Marion Meade's basic thesis that "rock music, in fact the entire rock 'culture,' is tremendously degrading to women"? What specific examples support your view?

2.   Meade's essay first appeared in the *New York Times*, one of America's greatest newspapers. What parts of her essay are characteristic of a newspaper column? Describe the aspects of her style, tone, form, and argument that suggest she wrote it for a newspaper audience.

3.   How does Meade's use of specific words and detailed examples support her argument? What effect do these examples have on you? In what ways are you surprised by them? What additional examples would you add to the argument?

4.   What is Meade's point when she recalls Stokely Carmichael's account of how he had always rooted for the cowboys as a child until one day he realized he was an Indian himself and had been rooting for the wrong side all along? Have you ever cheered the wrong side? When it comes to rock music, are you rooting for the "wrong" side or "right" side now? Explain your side of the female rock musician issue and how you got there.

5.   Meade's article was published in 1971, and she concludes by saying "the times they are a-changin'." How has rock music and your perception of its treatment of women changed or not changed since 1971? What specific examples and images of female or male rock musicians since 1971 support your view on this issue?

Teenage Dreams

SHERYL GARRATT

Sheryl Garratt has long been a devoted music fan. When she was in school in Birmingham, England, she was involved in an organization called Rock Against Racism. She also helped to organize musical productions and wrote magazine articles on music and politics. Garratt moved to London to continue her education, and has continued to work as a freelance journalist, publishing in journals such as *The Face*, *Collusion*, and New York's *NY Rocker*. She is currently the editor of *The Face*, one of Great Britain's most influential magazines about youth culture. In 1985, she co-authored, with Sue Steward, *Signed, Sealed, and Delivered: True Life Stories of Women in Pop*, a book whose title demonstrates Garratt's sense of humor and understanding of the many contradictions and confusions surrounding the question of women and pop music. Similarly, in the essay below, "Teenage Dreams," she pursues an open-ended and motivated inquiry into the complexities of music and sexuality faced by teenagers in today's pop culture.

It's a teenage dream to be seventeen
And to find you're all wrapped up in love.

"GIVE A LITTLE LOVE,"
Bay City Rollers

One of my clearest memories is of a bus ride from my housing estate in Birmingham into the city center. An atmosphere like a cup final coach, but with all of us on the same side and with one even more radical difference—there were no boys. At every stop, more and more girls got on, laughing, shouting, singing the songs we all knew off by heart. We compared the outfits and banners we had spent hours making, swapped jokes and stories, and talked happily to complete strangers because we all had an interest in common: we were about to see the Bay City Rollers.

That was 5 May 1975. I know the exact date because the ticket stub was carefully preserved in my scrapbooks, along with every one of that year's press cuttings to refer to the Rollers. And they were mentioned a lot. Tartan was the year's most fashionable accessory; you could buy Bay City socks, knickers, watches, shoes, lampshades, and countless other fetish objects to fantasize over. For a while at least, the Rollers were big business. Yet nine years later, I see that they didn't even play on their early records; the songs that reached the Top 10 on advance orders alone were weak and sloppily made, with words so wet they almost dripped off the vinyl. Considering that we were supposedly driven into a frenzy the second they walked on stage, they weren't even that pretty.

So what *was* the appeal? Johnny Ray, Sinatra, Billy Fury, Cliff Richard, the Beatles, Bolan, the Osmonds, Duran Duran, Nik Kershaw . . . the names have changed, the process of capitalizing on the phenomenon may have become more efficient and calculated, but from my mother to my younger cousin, most women go through "that phase." Most of us scream ourselves silly at a concert at least once, although many refuse to admit it later, because like a lot of female experience, our teen infatuations have been trivialized, dismissed, and so silenced. Wetting your knickers over a pop group just isn't a hip thing to have done, much better to pretend you spent your formative years listening to Northern soul or Billie Holiday.

Even the artists making money out of girls' fantasies are usually embarrassed and at pains to point out that they have *male* fans, too; to get out of the teeny trap and aim their music at a more "mature" or serious audience seems to be their general ambition. Once they've attained those heights, they're quick to sneer at the girls who helped make them in the first place. Of course, the serious, thinking rock audience they want is mainly male. In spite of a number of women journalists (and some men do make the effort), the music press is mainly written by men for other men. "Primarily for men" is a message that permeates the ads and the way they use women's bodies to shift product, and that informs the casual sexism of articles on women artists (the references to "dogs" and "boilers" in *Sounds*, for example).

As part of the same bias, "teenybop" music is either ignored or made into a joke. Often with justice, of course: the Rollers may have been atrocious, but later bands have plumbed depths that my little Scots boys couldn't have dreamed of.

But no matter how bad the music, what the press or any of the self-appointed analysts of "popular culture" fail to reflect is that the whole pop structure rests on the backs of these "silly, screaming girls." They bought the records in millions and made a massive contribution to the early success of Elvis, the Beatles, the Stones, Marc Bolan, Michael Jackson, and many of the others who have since been accepted by the grownups and become monuments, reference points in the rock hierarchy. Before you sneer again, boys, remember that it's often their money that allows you your pretensions.

But the real question is, of course, why? Why do adolescent girls go loopy over gawky, sometimes talentless young men? The answer lies partly in the whole situation of adolescent women in our society. We live in a world where sex has become a commodity—used to sell everything from chocolate to cars, sold in films and magazines, and shown everywhere to be a wonderful, desirable ideal that is central to our lives. The pages of *Jackie*, *My Guy*, and countless other magazines have a clear message: look good, shape up, and flaunt it. Yet hand in glove with this dictum there goes another: *nice girls don't do it*—or at least not until they're 16/married/going steady (and even then, they don't take the initiative). Sex is the sweetest con-trick of our time, a candy-coated sweetie with a guilt-filled center. At adolescence, we start to realize that this magic/punishment may actually apply to us, too.

A confusing and often traumatic time for everyone. For girls, however, these new expectations, the new rules and roles they have to conform to, are even more perplexing. Growing aware of our bodies and needs is alarming, because while male sexuality is exaggerated by society—portrayed as insatiable and uncontrollable—ours has been virtually obliterated. It is men who *need* sex; women supply it (though it is our responsibility to keep them at bay until the time is right). With double standards, feelings we aren't supposed to *have*—let alone enjoy—and a body or ambitions that may not fit the acceptable stereotypes, it can be a pretty tough time. Falling in love with posters can be a way of excluding real males and of hanging on to that ideal of "true love" for just a little longer. It is a safe focus for all that newly discovered sexual energy, and a scream can often be its only release. It is the sound of young women, not "hysterical schoolgirls" as one reporter would have it—a scream of defiance, celebration, and excitement.

"When their fans are old enough to start looking for *real* boyfriends," sneered a *Birmingham Evening Mail* review of that May 1975 show, "the Rollers will soon be forgotten." But it's not that simple: some of us were lesbians, some of us *did* have boyfriends. In any case, girls mature earlier than boys, so it was more a question of us waiting for *them* grow up than the other way round.

Carol Bedford, who wrote *Waiting for the Beatles* about her experiences as an avid Beatles follower, firmly dismissed the idea that their obsession was due to any fear of sex. In an interview in the *News of the World's* Sunday magazine (5 April 1984), she says:

> We weren't neurotic and we weren't all virgins. I knew what sex was, I'd lived with a man—so it can't be true. And I didn't get afraid or hysterical when George [Harrison, her favorite] did touch me. I didn't want to go further because if he did have a "stable," I didn't want to be one of a crowd. Of course, it must have been an escape from reality into an idealized relationship. But that's wonderful and I wish I had an escape now. I knew what was important then—seeing George. Today, I couldn't answer that. I keep in touch with the other Scruffs [the name adopted by the gang of women who sat outside the band's offices all day]. We remember it as a giggling and happy time. Life is much harder now.

Part of the appeal is desire for comradeship. With the Rollers at least, many became involved not because they particularly liked the music, but because they didn't want to miss out. We were a gang of girls having fun together, able to identify each other by tartan scarves and badges. Women are in the minority on demonstrations, in union meetings, or in the crowd at football matches: at the concerts, many were experiencing mass power for the first and last time. Looking back now, I hardly remember the gigs themselves, the songs, or even what the Rollers looked like. What I *do* remember are the bus rides, running home from school together to get to someone's house in time to watch "Shang-a-Lang" on TV, dancing in lines at the school disco, and sitting in each others' bedrooms discussing our fantasies and compiling our scrapbooks. Our real obsession was with ourselves; in the end, the actual men behind the posters had very little to do with it at all.

But why those particular men? It is interesting to note that although many of their lyrics tell how girls continually lust over their irresistible bodies, Rainbow, Whitesnake, or even the more enlightened, younger heavy metal bands just don't get women screaming at them. The people most attracted to the ideal of the hard, hairy, virile hunk of male are, in fact, other men, who form the majority of the audience at any heavy metal gig. Women seem far more excited by slim, unthreatening, baby-faced types who act vulnerable and who resemble them. Androgyny is what they want: men they can dress like and identify with, as well as drool over. With so few women performers to use as models, perhaps girlish boys are the next best thing. There's no way you could imitate Whitesnake's David Coverdale; a Rollers loo-brush haircut or a Brian Jones pageboy, on the other hand, was easy. Furthermore you, too, could wear the same clothes as those slim-hipped, pretty young boys. It is easy to forget that even the Rolling Stones—now Real Men without question—were once condemned for their effeminancy and implied to be gay.

A touch of homosexuality seems to *enhance* a male star's popularity with women, in fact—especially if it is carefully denied elsewhere. When Marc Bolan's former manager, Simon Napier–Bell, took on Wham! after seeing them on "Top of the Pops," he knew that their exclusive, buddy-boy act would go down as well with a young female audience as it had with the clientele of Bolts, a North London gay club. Many stars are openly bisexual, knowing that it adds to their infamy and appeal. Even Frankie Goes to Hollywood—whose first record was banned from the BBC due to its gay overtones—found they had attracted a teen audience. This success caused them to consider toning down their act, they said in the gay magazine *Square Peg*:

> I think we are paddling backwards, because we've realized that there's a lot of money to be made out of 13-year-old girls, which is sad. But we've been told by people in office buildings that we're treading on thin ice now, to be careful—not that we're going to be that careful. I'm not singing for 13-year-olds, I'm still singing for men.

Roxy Music, Bowie, Bolan, the Sweet, Adam Ant, and Boy George have all used camp presentation to advantage; one of the Bay City Rollers had formerly posed for gay porn magazines (which, of course, says more about his financial state than his sexuality). Even cuddly Barry Manilow, the aural equivalent of Mills and Boon, began his career playing the gay clubs with Bette Midler. This isn't to say that all of the people mentioned here *are* gay—but the notion that they *may* be somehow enhances their appeal to women. Perhaps it makes them safer. Or perhaps this hint of deviancy titillates. Maybe even women feel that they would be the one to mother the boy, to love him and set him back on the right path.

The idea of the hero as an outsider is very important. After all, young women are having problems adapting to that same alienating society themselves. This "bad boy" image has been a powerful theme for pop heroes. It links together groups like the Stones and early Wham!—who are otherwise very far apart. These boys are the ones your parents definitely wouldn't like—nor, for that matter, would your straight and prissy classmates. They, like you, don't fit in. But they're rebels not rejects, and by liking them, you too become a rebel.

A lifetime of suppression means that few girls dream of themselves becoming exceptional—instead, they fantasize about having boyfriends who do it for them, projecting their desires yet again onto men. With songs such as "He's a Rebel," "Home of the Brave," and, of course, "Leader of the Pack," the Crystals and the Shangri-Las built careers around the contradictions that male stars often pander to. Rebels by proxy, girls envied for their associations with wild men, they were still ultimately safe, took mom's advise, and snuggled sadly back into the family fold.

Most groups choose a safer path, and are at pains to present a reassuringly wholesome image for parents and the media. Girls' magazines are usually happy to help, as in this conversation overheard in a record company office:

> REPORTER: What do you eat for breakfast?
> SINGER: Fried eggs, bacon, beans, and tea.
> REPORTER: Isn't that a bit lumpen?
> SINGER: How about champagne and kippers, then?
> REPORTER: A little too exotic, I think.
> SINGER: OK. Coffee, toast, and marmalade?
> REPORTER: Great. What's your favorite drink?

And a thousand 12-year-olds cut it out and put it in their scrapbooks, knowing they'll be able to cook him what he wants when he comes to stay.

Even with the sickeningly wholesome Osmonds or the Rollers, however, the feeling of going against normal society, of rebellion, persisted. One of the most important points about most teeny groups is that almost everyone else hates them. With the Rollers, everyone but the fans continually made fun of us, insisting that the band was stupid and couldn't play. They were right, of course, but that wasn't the point. It was us against the world—and, for a while at least, we were winning.

For the girls' magazines, the band meant big circulation. When guitarist Alan Longmuir tried to escape from the band pleading old age (probably yet another publicity stunt), many even printed petition forms. Presumably in exchange for the endless color posters and the fawning coverage they gave the band, *Mirabelle* and *Fab 208* were allowed to print weekly "letters" from the boys. I hardly missed a copy. The few brave souls who did dare to criticize were usually forced to retract due to the sheer volume of abuse; next to each of these apologies, I lovingly drew a little skull-and-crossbones victory sign. We were invincible, a tartan army defying critics, DJs, newspapers, and everyone else who spoke against "our boys."

In the end, media attention was so focused on the fans and the mass hysteria that the music itself was forgotten altogether. The Rollers were accused of engineering their first U.S. TV appearance so that fans surged forward and knocked two of them unconscious minutes into their act. The estimated 50 million viewers of the satellite broadcast didn't get to *hear* much, but they saw what manager Tam Paton wanted them to see: Rollermania. It meant that when they made their first visit to the United States a week later, there were already tartan hordes waiting at the airport, ready to join the fun. It takes an efficient publicity machine to escalate one single teeny band into a mass phenomenon, and Tam Paton was a slick manipulator of the media and pop. As he trumpeted in a *Daily Mirror* piece.:

> I used to pick Rollers on personality rather than on skill. I felt you could take someone who had an image and teach him to play. You can have the most fantastic musician in the world, but what's the point if you have to spend a fortune in plastic surgery to get him right as far as image is concerned?

The ultimate in this selection process is perhaps the New York/Puerto Rican Group, Menudo, whose members have to be under 16, and good looking. They are unceremoniously sacked on their sixteenth birthday, and replaced.

It is looks that attract the magazines that tell young women how to look and what to buy. "Personality" is what these magazines promote: they will interview stars about food, pets, or (clean) funny stories about life on the road. They are not interested in music: how or what the artists play—lyrics aside—is usually irrelevant; even the inevitable color posters rarely show the band actually performing. What girls are sold is a catchy hook, and an image and lyrics they can identify with. Fantasy fodder. This is the male as sex object, posed, airbrushed, and marketed just like any female model. He, however, is usually imperfect and ordinary enough for the fans to believe that, one day, he could be theirs.

That myth, the illusion of accessibility, is essential—and artists aiming for this market are careful never to mention a girlfriend or even the type of woman they prefer in any but the vaguest terms. Once again, the Rollers had the routine down to perfection: "It's not looks that count, it's personality," said Les McKeowan, giving hope to plain girls everywhere, while forgetting to mention his friendships with women like Britt Ekland.

A fan's mind is a curious thing, though. It picks and chooses from the information available, giving credence only where it wants to, and even managing to retain and believe quite contradictory facts simultaneously. Fantasy, unlike reality, isn't binding, which is the big advantage pop heroes have over real men. You can turn Boy George into your gentle, cuddly, funny, dream romance and still enjoy your father turning purple with anger over his effeminacy.

In every interview there's an endless litany of "no permanent girl at the moment . . . someday I'll find the right girl . . . believe in ro-

mance . . . we love all our fans." You know it's you he's really waiting
for. But you also know he's unavailable. And there's the crunch. Normally, even the most obsessive fan knows that her chances are so
slight as to be negligible. Jona MacDonald first saw Chris Hughes on
"Top of the Pops" in 1979, drumming with Adam and the Ants. She
went on to follow him with an energy, persistence, and ingenuity that
begs admiration in spite of its being so pointless and oppressive. In
1983, she sat on the steps of the Abbey Road Studios morning and
night for a total of 110 days (she counted), while he produced Wang
Chung's first album, *Points on a Curve*. Years before, Beatles fan Jill
Pitchard sat waiting outside those same studios for so long that she
was eventually made the receptionist: she is still there, and when EMI
[Recording Studios] opened the room in which the Beatles recorded
to the public, Jona was offered a job alongside Jill, ushering in awe-
struck fans.

So what's the appeal of famous men?

> I don't look on him as being famous now that he's not in the Ants
> anymore. I just think he's really good looking. I'd like to be a friend
> of his. Well, I'd like to go out with him, that's my ambition. But then
> there's somebody else, isn't there? I know deep down I'll never get
> anywhere with him. I just wish it wasn't true, I'm going out with
> someone now, but I still keep in contact with Chris. And if I go off
> him, I won't forget him: I've still got my scrapbooks and everything.

And so have I. Four volumes of carefully pasted cuttings and pictures.
It is this retentiveness that makes teenage girls such a lucrative market. And how exploitable is this urge to collect not only the records,
but the posters, tour programs, fan club specials, books, magazines,
and any other product companies wish to foist on them! Birthdays,
names, measurements, likes, and dislikes are all learned by heart, and
fans can often relate more statistical information about an artist than
he could himself, offhand. Yet the picture they build up is the one
they want to believe, with faults rationalized or glossed over, and
virtues often invented. It is easy to create an idealized fantasy man
with none of the flaws of real men, and to transfer those attributes on
to an inaccessible, but real, star. For most, it's just a way of brightening
up dull, ordinary lives: the cynical comments written in my scrapbooks show that even at my most infatuated, I knew half of what was
written was lies. For a minority, though, the dream can become an
obsession. It happens gradually, as Carol Bedford explained:

> You realize that you could ask for an autograph, and then you start
> to think, "Wouldn't it be nice if he knew my name?" I've tried to
> understand why that is important. Perhaps it's an inferiority complex
> . . . you got special status for length of service. When he singled you
> out, all those hours of waiting didn't seem to exist.

Carol's waiting ended after a record company Christmas party in 1971, when George Harrison asked her to stop wasting her life in such a way:

> It was a very moving conversation because it showed he cared. It was also a low point because I realized I would have to quit. If that was the only thing I could give to him, then I would. It took two months to build up courage to even ask myself if I could survive without seeing him: could I go through a week without the most important thing in the world to me—watching George Harrison walk out of the building?

Carol had come to England from Dallas to follow her band. "Polythene" Pat Dawson, on the other hand, was a fan in Liverpool before the Beatles became famous. She recounted her memories to Mike Evans in *Let It Rock* (July 1975):

> There was a hierarchy of people who'd been watching them for a long time, and they were quite matey with us—they used to pull birds from this group but when the newer fans arrived, they were already beginning to get "distanced." The older fans tended to like them for their music, and as fellas in the personal sense, whereas the newer ones liked them because they were the Beatles. This was long before they made records or anything, but they were already a big cult in Liverpool. It wasn't like seeing people who were stars. You still saw them as a bunch of lads you might get off with.

As they became better known, many of the early fans refused to buy the records, not wanting their boys to leave them. Pat clearly recalls her sadness at their success:

> The night Bob Wooler [the Cavern DJ] announced as they were going on stage that "Please Please Me" had reached number one, it was awful, because the reaction was the opposite to what they expected. Everyone was stunned. That was the end of it as far as we were concerned.

Men become obsessed, too, of course. But the difference between, say, the man who changes his name to Elvis and the woman who spends all her savings following Spandau Ballet to the United States is that, for her, a close, socially acceptable relationship—marriage—is at least a possibility, no matter how remote. It is also difficult for a woman to actually fantasize about *being* her hero in the same way as a man could. With so few role models to follow, to fantasize about being on stage as a *female* performer may be almost a contradiction in terms. Instead most of us dream of being a pop star's girlfriend: fame and recognition by proxy. Girls are taught to wait for men to give us what we want, rather than to get it ourselves. In the world of the Mills and Boon, romance, passion, wealth, status, and excitement are conferred on the passive heroine by the men who come into her life.

That idea is a persistent one. My favorite daydream in boring classes at school was of a famous star suddenly walking into the room to take me away, leaving my classmates sighing in regret that they hadn't realized I was so wonderful. I felt that my lover could actually transform me, and many of my friends have confessed to similar Cinderella fantasies.

While women are judged—and taught to value themselves—by the status of their men, they will continue to follow personable young groups. Perhaps, even, the most obsessive are also the most ambitious. Most of the fans I have met waiting outside studios and concert halls have been bright, energetic, articulate young women—hardly the stereotypical "groupie" described in the songs, videos, and fantasies of the Real Men of rock 'n' roll.

The term "groupie" is a dangerous one, for it is often used as a putdown for *any* woman involved in the industry. In February 1969, the newly formed *Rolling Stone* magazine devoted a whole issue to "Groupies: The Girls of Rock," explaining to the reader that "some of the girls of rock, girls who are very much part of the scene—everybody knows them—never were groupies in the strict sense, but are somehow cut from the same fabric. Like Trixie, the girl bass-player, and Dusty, the girl recording engineer." Pauline Black told of similar false assumptions being made by men when she was the singer in the Selecter, on the 2-Tone national tour:

> Guys, when they're on the road, have a different attitude to when they're at home, and invariably I'd find myself with a whole load of young girls outside my door saying, "Oh, so-and-so's thrown me out of his room because I won't do whatever." Really young, naive girls who were just into the whole thing and had come back to the hotel expecting to have a bit of a drink and a good time without thinking of the consequences of hanging around hotels with loads of guys.

If a woman wishes to be involved in any way, it is often assumed that she is only there ultimately because she is attracted to the man. It is worth bearing this in mind whenever the term "groupie" is used. And then there's the question of how "groupies" see themselves. Pat Hartley, an American woman involved in the New York–Andy Warhol music scene, when interviewed by *Spare Rib* (1974), saw it as a form of autonomous female activity:

> The whole groupie thing turned itself around. It used to be that the guys could pick and choose. Well, after the first three years it was us choosing, the guys had no choice. In the end, when the groups came to town, the girls would decide whether . . . I mean, after having Stevie Winwood, was it worth it to have anyone less? And for the groups, in a way it was part and parcel of selling the albums.

It was 1964 that the Beatles first came to the States, and around that year the groupies started. It was a different kind of thing then: the place was littered with 14-year-old girls, and there were people like me, Jenny Dean, Devon and others who were going into it from an intelligent point of view. We'd just find out who was in town and what hotel they were in. It's not that difficult, if one decided to put a little effort behind it. It's a society of a kind, the way it functions, it has its own strange rules. A lot of it is women dressing for women; a lot of it had to do with the competition between the chicks. We paired off in twos and there were always couples who were like married couples. Very few chicks would go in one at a time. Going in twos was sort of an adventure and it was fun. It was a weird thing. When it started, it started like a teenage sex vibe . . . all those women standing outside the Plaza Hotel screaming our knickers down for these incredible pop groups, and at the time, it really was the girls after the boys.

The freedom to be used by the consumer of your choice. But what happens when the stars themselves are women? Girls scream at girls, too. When the Ronettes or the Shangri-Las played to a live audience, the front rows were full of young women screaming, reaching, and hand-dancing in their seats. The girl-group era told women that they could be stars, that they could dress up and look strong and sexy, get up there with the boys. "I knew I was going to sing," says Ronnie Spector firmly on the video of Alan Betrock's "Girl Groups." "I knew, I had no qualms, nothing. I was going to sing, and I was going to sing rock 'n' roll." For Ronnie it was 13-year-old Frankie Lymon, a boy with a girl's high voice, who showed the way. For the girls watching her, Ronnie herself was opening up new possibilities. The girl groups told young women that their dreams were possible, and even as their songs reinforced the most reactionary ideas of love and marriage ("He Hit Me, and It Felt Like a Kiss"), they were showing that it *was* possible to be something more than somebody's girlfriend: a singer and a star.

In the August 1982 issue of *Ms.* magazine, Marcia Gillespie talks of the significance for black girls of one of the few groups to survive the Beatles and the British invasion that followed:

The Supremes were important—symbols of the idea that integration could happen, that we could make it and still have the dream. That black girls could be glamorous and beautiful and celebrated for it—at home and abroad. . . . The idea that black managers and recording companies could take three girls from the ghetto, take rhythm and blues, and move it and them from the back of the bus and to a limousine was daring and visonary for its time.

Women have continued to idolize women, to pin them up and objec-tify them in just the way any boy would. In the late 70s, the most popular pinup in girls' bedrooms was not John Travolta or Johnny Rotten, but Debbie Harry. It's often hard to tell if they just want to *be* them, or if they are in love with them. In adolescence, the line is thin between admiration and lust (*boys* screamed at both Bolan and Bowie)—although, with a little help, most of us grow out of it and become as anti-gay as the society which raised us. Helen Terry describes her relationship with her Culture Club fans:

> I get loads of letters, and the other day I met two girls with "I Love Helen Terry" scratched on their arm. That's really beyond me—all these girls screaming, "I really love you!" It's so unreal. I think half of it is that they'd like to be me, they'd like to be close to George, to be able to sing, maybe. The other half is that, basically, I'm very safe: I'm like everyone's best mate, I talk to anyone. I'm fairly low-key.

On the whole, the word "fans," when applied to women, is derogatory. It is always assumed that they are attracted to a person for the "wrong" reasons, that they are uncritical and stupid. As an audience, they are usually treated with contempt by both bands and record companies. The "real" audience is assumed to be male, and advertisements, record sleeves, and even stage presentation are nearly always aimed at men. Yet a substantial majority of women own a stereo, and music is a constant background to our lives—on the radio at home, piped into supermarkets and factories, in the disco, records played while we do our chores. And in the brief time when the majority of girls *are* actively involved as fans, the fun and the thrills are unlike anything most men will ever experience. For us, in 1975, the real excitement had little to do with the Bay City Rollers: it was about ourselves.

SPECULATIONS

1. According to Sheryl Garratt's essay, what does it mean to be "a fan"? What are the main qualities that define fans? Expand on your definition.

2. Explain in your own terms Sheryl Garratt's statement that "we live in a world in which sex has become a commodity . . . . Sex is the sweetest contrick, a candy-coated sweetie with a guilt-filled center. At adolescence, we start to realize that this magic/punishment may actually apply to us, too." How does this statement relate to your experience of popular music?

3. What does Garratt mean when she sums up her attraction and other young women's attraction to male singers by saying "our real obsession was with ourselves"? Do you agree with this assertion?

4. What is the "bad boy" image that Garratt talks about and how does it work psychologically for young women? How would you characterize specific rock stars you know as fitting the "bad boy" image? What kind of appeal do you think this image possesses for you or young people in our culture?

5. Garratt provides many examples of young women's "groupie" activities and relates their stories of admiration for famous popular singers by quoting

the women's own words and descriptions of events. What impact do these personal stories have on you as a reader? Do they support Garratt's argument?
6.   Why does Garratt keep switching male and female gender roles, sexual preferences, and audience versus performer perspectives back and forth throughout the piece? How does this switching affect your reading of her argument?

Elvis, or the Ironies of a Southern Identity

LINDA RAY PRATT

Linda Ray Pratt was born in New Orleans in 1943 and grew up in Mississippi and Florida. She received an M.A. and Ph.D. in English Literature from Emory University in Atlanta, Georgia. A Professor of English at the University of Nebraska in Lincoln, she teaches courses on Victorian and early modern poetry and the novels of the Brontë sisters. Pratt has published many scholarly articles on such writers as Arnold, the Brontës, Yeats, and Eliot.

A long-standing fan of Elvis and his music, Pratt was inspired to write this article in 1978, the year after Elvis died, when she saw the remarkable ways in which the media had begun to capitalize on the myths that survived him. Her most recent article, entitled "Speaking in Tongues: Dead Elvis and the Greil Quest" is a review of Greil Marcus's book, *The Dead Elvis: A Chronicle of a Cultural Obsession*. In this review Pratt suggests that our recreation of the dead Elvis is an on-going cultural production. As Pratt sees it, this project of keeping Elvis alive is part of our country's quest "not to understand 'the reality' of its idols but to make them up to fit its needs. Perhaps the quest is about not wanting to know who the real Elvis was . . ." (*Postmodern Culture*, volume 2, number 3, May 1992).

About her own writing, Pratt says, "I write best when I write about something I love, a subject that unlocks my imagination and vocabulary. I am happiest with my writing when the topic or argument is something that I care about; words come to me suddenly when I'm fired up in the act of writing—words that I didn't even know I had" (interview with editor, July 2, 1992).

Elvis was the most popular entertainer in the world, but nowhere as popular as in his native South. In the last years of his career, his audience in other parts of the country was generally centered in the original "fifties" fans whose youth and music were defined by Elvis, and in the lower or working class people who saw in Elvis some glamorized image of their own values. In the South, however, the pattern of Elvis's popularity tended to cut across age barriers and class lines which were themselves a less recognizable thing in a region in which almost no one is more than a generation or two away from poverty, and where "class" in small communities might have more to do with family and past status than with money. Among Southern youth, Elvis was not a relic from a musical past; he was still one of the vital forces behind a Southern rock, which though different now from his, still echoes the rhythms which his music had fused out of the region. His numerous concerts in the South could not exhaust the potential audience. At his death, leading politicians and ministers from the South joined the people on the street in eulogizing him. Local radio and television stations ran their own specials in addition to the syndicated or national programs. Halftime ceremonies at the Liberty Bowl were in tribute to him. When someone commented on national TV that the Presleys were "white trash," it was a regional slur, not just a personal one. The white South expressed love, grief, and praise for Elvis from all age groups at virtually every level of the social, intellectual, and economic structures.

The phenomenon of such widespread sectional regard and emotional intensity went beyond the South's usual pride in the success of "one of our own." The emotion became more puzzling if one listened to some of the reasons offered to explain it: Elvis loved his mother; Elvis's heart was broken; Elvis loved Jesus; Elvis was the American Dream. Such reasons for loving and mourning Elvis seemed strange because, on the surface at least, they were so tangential to Elvis himself or to the musical or cultural impact he unquestionably did have. How, in the face of his vitality and defiance of convention, could one love Elvis because he loved Jesus? And how, in a man expressing nothing if not undisguised sexuality, could one love Elvis because he was so good to his mother? But people, especially those beyond the age group of his original teen fans, often did say such things. Merle Haggard's "From Graceland to the Promised Land," with its emphasis on Elvis's mother's death and his faith in Jesus, is, after all, the perfect Southern folk song about Elvis. The South's involvement with Elvis is sincere, but most of the expressed reasons for it do not reach very far, and some of them seem patently false. They are the myths sent up to justify the emotion and to obscure its source. The emotions spring from associations with a reality the South collectively prefers to conceal and yet constantly experiences. The paradox of Elvis was that he was able simultaneously to reveal the reality of the modern South while concealing it in a myth of the American Dream. He was at once both "King" and outsider.

The myth of Elvis which the South voices is in part very familiar. He is the sharecropper's son who made millions, the Horatio Alger story in drawl. Almost everyone who knew him assured us that, despite the money and fame, "he never changed" (no one remarks how tragic such a static condition would be, were it possible). He never got over his mother's death (in 1958); he was humble and polite; he doted on his little girl; he loved his home town; he never forgot where he came from. He had wealth, yes; but in the tradition of those who love Jesus, he was uncomfortable with riches when others were poor and so gave millions of dollars away to the less fortunate. The American success story turned to altruism. Even his money was not tainted, just dollars freely given in exchange for entertainment so good it always seemed a bargain. Unlike some others whose success was a ticket out of the South and into the broader, happier American identity, Elvis remained in Memphis. His regional loyalty when he could have lived anywhere deeply complimented the South. Graceland was a new image of the Southern plantation, this time free from associations with slavery and a guilt-ridden past. The very gates had musical notes on them. He was a good boy and a good ole boy. Elvis himself seemed to believe this vision; certainly he played to it in his "family" movies, his sacred music, and in his "American Trilogy" dominated by "Dixie." It was a sentimental myth, but, then, W. J. Cash has called Southerners "the most sentimental people in history" (*The Mind of the South*, p. 130).

Elvis's fame initially grew out of an image in opposition to the one the myth attempts to disguise. He was scandalous, sexual, defiant of all authority. He was preached against from the pulpit as an immoral force. In a blackboard jungle, he was the juvenile delinquent. On the streets, he was a hood. Socially, he was a "greaser." Economically, he was "poor white," a gentler rendition of "white trash." Maybe he loved Jesus, but even his Christmas songs could be dirty. In songs like "Santa Clause Is Back In Town" he played with the conventions of Christmas music in order to startle and subvert.

This image of Elvis, the rocker with "a dirty, dirty feeling," "born standing up and talking back," never fully disappeared. His last few movies, like a lot of the lyrics he improvised in concert, were sprinkled with off-color jokes and plays on words. His 1976 image was as excessive and extravagant as his 1956 image, though not in the same ways. The violence still flowed out of the karate movements, the sexuality in such songs as "Burning Love." In concert, his emotional passion sometimes transfigured such schmaltzy songs of lost love and broken hearts as "Hurt" or "You Gave Me a Mountain" into rich autobiographical moments. Even the obscene subversion of Christmas showed up again in "Merry Christmas, Baby."

The Elvis of the sentimental myth would never have changed musical or cultural history, but the authentic Elvis who did so was transformed into a legend obscuring what the man, the music, or the image really meant. Although some elements of the myth were commonly associated with Elvis throughout the country, in the South—particularly the white South—the myth was insisted upon and pushed to its extremes. The question is why. Jimmy Carter loves his mother and Jesus, too, but the South has not rewarded him with uncritical devotion. The real Elvis, both early and late, might have been severely criticized, but even his drug-involved death is called a "heart attack," the ten drugs the autopsy found in his body merely the "prescription medicines" of a sick and heartbroken man who kept pushing himself because he did not want to disappoint the fans. Those who have argued that people projected onto Elvis anything they liked because his image was essentially vacuous are mistaken; if anything, the image is too rich in suggestion to be acknowledged fully or directly.

Some critics attribute the sentimental myth of Elvis to the cleverness of Colonel Parker and the cooperation of Elvis himself. To do so is to oversimplify a complex phenomenon and to misread a generation's genuine mythmaking as merely another shrewd "sell" campaign. For anyone less significant than Elvis, the path that Colonel Parker apparently advised by way of numbingly stupid movies and empty music would have been the path to sure oblivion. The 1968 Black Leather television special saved Elvis from that, but allegedly against the advice of Parker who wanted the show to be all Christmas music. Elvis, pursued by the myth and under pressure to confirm it, kept to himself and never told the public anything. The Colonel was smart enough to promote the myth, but it was the authentic handiwork of a society that needed a legend to justify the identification it felt with such a figure. After Elvis died, the Brentwood, Tennessee, Historical Society even supplied the Presley genealogy. The family was, of course, completely respectable, producing "renowned professors, doctors, judges, ministers" in every generation until poverty overcame them during Reconstruction.

C. Vann Woodward has said that the South's experience is atypical of the American experience, that where the rest of America has known innocence, success, affluence, and an abstract and disconnected sense of place, the South has known guilt, poverty, failure, and a concrete sense of roots and place ("The Search for Southern Identity" in *The Burden of Southern History*). These myths collide in Elvis. His American success story was always acted out within its Southern limitations. No matter how successful Elvis became in terms of fame and money, he remained fundamentally disreputable in the minds of many Americans. Elvis had rooms full of gold records earned by million-copy sales, but his best rock and roll records were not formally honored by the people who control, if not the public taste, the rewarding of the public taste. Perhaps this is always the fate of innovators; awards are created long after the form is created. His movies made millions but could not be defended on artistic grounds. The *New York Times* view of his fans was "the men favoring leisure suits and sideburns, the women beehive hairdos, purple eyelids and tight stretch pants" (*New York Times* story by Wayne King, 8 Jan. 1978). Molly Ivins, trying to explain in the *New York Times* the crush of people and "genuine emotion" in Memphis when Elvis died would conclude, "It is not required that love be in impeccable taste." Later, in the year after his death, Mike Royko would sarcastically suggest that Elvis's body and effects be sent to Egypt in exchange for the King Tut exhibit. ("So in terms of sheer popularity, no other American dead body can stand up to Presley's.") The "Doonesbury" cartoon strip would see fit to run a two-week sequence in which "Boopsie" would go visit Elvis's grave. Her boyfriend puts her down with, "2,000,000 necrophiliacs can't be wrong." Elvis's sheer commercial value commanded respect, but no amount of success could dispel the aura of strangeness about him. He remained an outsider in the American culture that adopted his music, his long hair, his unconventional clothes, and his freedom of sexual movement.

Although he was the world's most popular entertainer, to like Elvis a lot was suspect, a lapse of taste. It put one in beehives and leisure suits, in company with "necrophiliacs" and other weird sorts. The inability of Elvis to transcend his lack of reputability despite a history-making success story confirms the Southern sense that the world outside thinks Southerners are freaks, illiterates, Snopeses, sexual perverts, lynchers. I cannot call this sense a Southern "paranoia" because ten years outside the South has all too often confirmed the frequency with which non-Southerners express such views. Not even the presidency would free LBJ and Jimmy Carter from such ridicule. At the very moment in which Southerners proclaim most vehemently the specialness of Elvis, the greatness of his success, they understand it to mean that no Southern success story can ever be sufficient to satisfy a suspicious America.

And Elvis was truly different, in all those tacky Southern ways one is supposed to rise above with money and sophistication. He was a pork chops and brown gravy man. He liked peanut butter and banana sandwiches. He had too many cars, and they were too pink. He liked guns, and capes, and a Venus de Milo water fountain in the entry at Graceland. I once heard about 1958 that he had painted the ceiling at Graceland dark blue with little silver stars that twinkled in the dark. His taste never improved, and he never recanted anything. He was the sharecropper's son in the big house, and it always showed.

Compounding his case was the fact that Elvis didn't always appear fully white. Not sounding white was his first problem, and white radio stations were initially reluctant to play his records. Not to be clearly white was dangerous because it undermined the black–white rigidities of a segregated society, and to blur those definitions was to reveal the falseness at the core of segregation. Racial ambiguity is both the internal moral condemnation and the social destruction of a racist society which can only pretend to justify itself by abiding by its own taboos. Yet all Southerners know, despite the sternest Jim Crow laws, that more than two hundred years of racial mixing has left many a Southerner racially ambiguous. White Southerners admit only the reality of blacks who have some white blood, but, of course, the knife cuts both ways. Joe Christmas and Charles Bon. Désirée's Baby. In most pictures, Elvis might resemble a blue-eyed Adonis, but in some of those early back and white photographs, his eyes sultry, nostrils flared, lips sullen, he looked just that—black and white. And he dressed like blacks. His early wardrobe came from Lansky Brothers in Memphis. Maybe truck drivers wore greasy hair and long side-burns, but only the blacks were wearing zoot suits and pegged pants with pink darts in them. Country singers might sequin cactus and saddles on satin shirts, Marty Robbins would put a pink carnation on a white sport coat, and Johnny Cash would be the man in black. Only Elvis would wear a pink sport coat with a black velvet collar. "The Memphis Flash," he was sometimes called.

The music was the obvious racial ambiguity. Elvis's use of black styles and black music angered many Southern blacks who resented the success he won with music that black artists had originated but could not sell beyond the "race record" market of a segregated commercial world. In interviews today, these black blues musicians usually say that Elvis stole everything from them, an understandable complaint but one that nevertheless ignores his fusion of black music with white country to create a genuinely new sound. He was the Hillbilly Cat singing "Blue Moon of Kentucky" and "That's All Right (Mama)." Elvis's role in fusing the native music of poor Southern whites and poor Southern blacks into rock and roll is the best known aspect of his career and his greatest accomplishment.

Students of rock always stress this early music, but the sentimental myth gives it less attention, though the records always sold better in the South than in any other region. The music in the myth is more often the love ballads and the Protestant hymns. Yet the music that was in reality most important to Southerners was the music most closely tied to Southern origins. Elvis himself seemed to understand this; compare, for example, his 1974 concert album from Memphis's Mid-South Coliseum (the "Graceland" album) with any other concert album. The music I remember hearing most was music like "Mystery Train," "One Night," "Lawdy Miss Clawdy," "Heartbreak Hotel,"

"Peace in the Valley," "Blue Christmas," and "American Trilogy." For Southerners, this fusion of "Dixie," "All My Trials," and "The Battle Hymn of the Republic" has nothing to do with the rest of America, although its popularity around the country suggests that other Americans do relate it to their own history. The trilogy seems to capture Southern history through the changes of the civil rights movement and the awareness of black suffering which had hitherto largely been excluded from popular white images of Southern history. The piece could not have emerged before the seventies because only then had the "marching" brought a glimmer of hope. Even Elvis could not have sung this trilogy in New York's Madison Square Garden before there was some reason for pride and hope in the South. Elvis was right to make the song his; it is an appropriate musical history from one whose music moved always in the fused racial experiences of the region's oppressed. Rock and roll, taking inside it rhythm and blues and country, was the rhythm of Southern life, Southern problems, and Southern hopes. It is not coincidence that rock and roll emerged almost simultaneously with the civil rights movement, that both challenged the existing authority, and that both were forces for "integration."

The most stunning quality about Elvis and the music was the sexuality, yet the sentimental myth veers away from this disturbing complexity into the harmlessly romantic. Elvis might be "nice looking" or "cute" or perhaps "sexy," but not sexual. The sexuality he projected was complicated because it combined characteristics and appeals traditionally associated with both males and females. On one hand, he projected masculine aggression and an image of abandoned pleasure, illicit thrills, back alley liaisons and, on the other hand, a quality of tenderness, vulnerability, and romantic emotion. Andy Warhol captured something of this diversified sexuality in his portrait of Elvis, caught in a threatening stance with a gun in his hand but with the face softened in tone and line. The image made Elvis the perfect lover by combining the most appealing of male and female characteristics and satisfying both the physical desire for sensual excitement and the emotional need for loving tenderness. The music echoed the physical pleasure in rhythm and the emotional need in lyrics that said "Love Me," "Love Me Tender," "Don't," "I Want You I Need You I Love You," and "Don't Be Cruel." Unlike many later rock stars whose music would voice an assault on women, Elvis's music usually portrayed an emotional vulnerability to what women could do *to* him, as well as what he could do *for* them. When the public's notion of his heartbroken private life confirmed this sense of vulnerability, the image took on renewed power. Despite the evidence in the music or the long hair and lashes and full, rounded features, most Elvis fans would deny that his appeal is vaguely androgynous. Many male and female fans talk about Elvis as an ideal male image but would probably find it threatening to traditions of sexual identity to admit that the ideal male figure might indeed combine traditional male characteristics with some which are freely admitted only in women. In the South where sex roles are bound up with the remnants of a chivalric "way of life," open sexuality was allowable only in the "mysterious" lives of blacks, and permissible sexual traits in whites were rigidly categorized by sex. But the image of Elvis goes behind these stereotypes to some ideal of sexuality that combines the most attractive elements in each of them.

Women's sexual imaginations of Elvis have rarely been openly expressed, in part because women weren't supposed to have any explicit sexual fantasies and in part because those who did were perhaps least likely, because of the cultural and regional prohibitions, to admit them. Despite the mass of published material about Elvis, almost nothing of a serious nature by women has been printed. One remarkable exception is a short story by Julie Hecht, "I Want You I Need You I Love You" in *Harper's* (May 1978). Hecht's story makes the only serious effort I have seen to reveal those characteristics which gave Elvis's sexual appeal such complexity and power. The woman in the story remembers first imagining his kiss when she was twelve and didn't know what came after the kiss. Twenty years later in her fantasy of August 1977, she is able to "save" Elvis's life by getting him on a good health food diet. They become "best of friends," and she has her moment of tenderness: "I did get to touch him. I touched his hands, I touched his face, we hugged, we kissed, I kissed his hands, I kissed his face, I touched his face, I touched his arms, I touched his eyes, I touched his hair, I saw his smile, I heard his voice, I saw him move, I heard him laugh, I heard him sing" (*Harper's*, p. 67). This passage illustrates the obsessive physical attraction that combined with the illusion that Elvis was really sweet, tender, and in need of loving care. Seeing or hearing Elvis was never enough; one had to try to touch him. In life, such fans tore at his clothes and his person; in death, they visit his grave. Does any woman really care whether or not Elvis loved his mother or Jesus? But I never met a female fan who did not detest Priscilla. "Somebody ought to put a bullet through her," a pleasant faced middle-aged saleswoman in a bookstore once told me.

Elvis said he grew sideburns because he wanted to look like truck drivers, and many such men would later want to look like him. One important element in Elvis's sexual appeal for men seemed to be the acting out of the role of the "hood" who got the girl, won the fight, and rose above all the economic powerlessness of real hoods. Men who because of class and economic binds knew their own limitations seemed especially attracted to this aspect of the image. They wore their hair like his, affected his mannerisms, sang with his records. Men too sophisticated to betray themselves in such overt ways betrayed themselves in other ways. I remember a highly educated man rhapsodizing about how phallic the black leather suit was that Elvis wore in his 1968 television appearance. When Elvis aged and put on weight, men were his cruelest detractors. They seemed to take his appearance as a personal offense.

Beyond the money, the power, the fame, there was always at some level this aspect of Elvis, the American Dream in its Southern variation. Like other great Southern artists, Elvis revealed those characteristics of our culture which we know better than outsiders to be part of the truth. In Elvis was also the South that is bizarre, or violent, or darkly mysterious, the South called the grotesque in Faulkner or O'Connor. Perhaps this is why a book like *Elvis: What Happened?* could not damage the appeal. The hidden terrors, pain, and excesses of the private life which the book reveals, despite its mean-spirited distortions, only make the image more compelling in its familiarity. Even his drug problem had a familiar Southern accent—prescription medicines, cough syrups, diet pills.

Elvis's South is not the old cotton South of poor but genteel aristocrats. His Mississippi is not that of Natchez. Elvis is the Mississippi of pulpwood, sharecroppers, small merchants. His Memphis had nothing to do with riverboats or the fabled Beale Street. Elvis's Memphis was the post-World War II city of urban sprawl, racial antagonism, industrial blight, slums, Humes High. He walked the real Beale Street. Despite Graceland, and "Dixie" in Madison Square Garden, Elvis was the antithesis of the Rhett and Scarlett South. But no one living in the South today ever knew the Rhett and Scarlett South. Southerners themselves go to Natchez as to a tourist attraction. Elvis's South was the one that most Southerners really experience, the South where not even the interstate can conceal the poverty, where industrial affluence threatens the land and air which have been so much a part of our lives, where racial violence touches deep inside the home, where even our successes cannot overcome the long reputation of our failures. Even Graceland is not really beautiful. Squeezed in on all sides by the sprawl of gas stations, banks, shopping plazas, and funeral homes, Elvis's beloved home is an image of the South that has been "new" now for over fifty years.

Elvis evoked the South of modern reality with a fidelity he could not himself escape. The South rewarded him with its most cherished myths, but Elvis's tragedy was that he got caught in the contradictions. We only wanted to be able to claim that he was a good boy who loved Jesus. He apparently needed to become that, to live out the mythic expectations. He hungered for approval. The problem was that most of what Elvis really was could never be so transmogrified. He *was* the king of rock and roll, but he was uncomfortable with what the title implied. Linda Thompson has said that in his later years he hated hard rock. The further he moved from the conventions of the romantic myth, the more he proclaimed them. The more drugs he sued, the more he supported law and order. When the counter culture he helped to usher in became widespread, he thought of helping the FBI as an undercover agent. How could he not be schizophrenic at the end, balancing the rock myth he created, the sentimental myth he adopted, and the emotional needs that made him like anyone else? He was destroyed by having to be what he was and wanting to be what he thought he ought to be. The Jesus-loving boy singing dirty Christmas songs. "One Night" and "How Great Thou Art."

After Elvis died, it was necessary to deify him. It isn't, after all, very becoming to grieve for a rock idol who died, as the *New York Times* once put it, "puffy and drug-wasted." But saying what and why one grieved was difficult. The South has had a lot of practice mythologizing painful and ambiguous experiences into glamorous and noble abstractions. So it was from Graceland to the Promised Land. Rex Humbard told us that Elvis found peace in Jesus, and Billy Graham assured us that Elvis was in Heaven. Billy was even looking forward to visiting him there. A disc jockey playing "How Great Thou Art" reflects at the end of the record, "And he certainly was." In Tupelo the Elvis Presley Memorial Foundation is building a $125,000 Chapel of Inspiration in his memory. Memphis will put a 50-ton bronze statue on a river bluff. Priscilla wants their daughter to remember, most of all, his humbleness. He loved his Jesus, his daughter, his lost wife. He loved his daddy. He loved the South. He was a great humanitarian. "God saw that he needed some rest and called him home to be with Him," the tombstone reads. Maybe all of this is even true. The apotheosis of Elvis demands such perfection because his death confirmed the tragic frailty, the violence, the intellectual poverty, the extravagance of emotion, the loneliness, the suffering, the sense of loss. Almost everything about his death, including the enterprising cousin who sold the casket pictures to *National Enquirer*, dismays; but nothing can detract from Elvis himself. Even this way, he is as familiar as next door, last year, the town before.

Greil Marcus wrote in his book *Mystery Train: Images of America in Rock 'n' Roll Music* that Elvis created a beautiful illusion, a fantasy that shut nothing out. The opposite was true. The fascination was the reality always showing through the illusion—the illusion of wealth and the psyche of poverty; the illusion of success and the pinch of ridicule; the illusion of invincibility and the tragedy of frailty; the illusion of complete control and the reality of inner chaos. In Faulkner's *Absalom, Absalom!* Shreve thinks that Quentin hates the South. He does not understand that Quentin is too caught in it ever to have thought of such a question, just as Elvis was and just as we were in Elvis. Elvis had all the freedom the world can offer and could escape nothing. What chance that the South could escape him, reflecting it as he did?

Southerners do not love the old Confederacy because it was a noble ideal, but because the suffering of the past occasioned by it has formed our hearts and souls, both good and evil. But we celebrate the past with cheap flags, cliché slogans, decorative license plates, decaled ash trays, and a glorious myth of a Southern "way of life" no one today ever lived. And Southerners do not love Elvis because he loved Jesus or anyone else. The Elvis trinkets, his picture on waste cans or paperweights or T-shirts or glowing in the dark from a special frame, all pay the same kind of homage as the trinkets in worship of the past. People outside the Elvis phenomenon may think such commercialization demeans the idol and the idolater. But for those who have habitually disguised the reality of their culture from even themselves, it is hard to show candidly what and why one loves. In impeccable taste. By the most sentimental people in history.

SPECULATIONS

1.   How does Pratt's depiction of the South and Elvis represent a culture and a set of values different from those of the rest of the United States? How does this representation coincide with or differ from your own perceptions of the South and its people?

2.   Pratt describes Elvis as both a "king" and an outsider; as someone who was perceived ambiguously; as someone who blurred racial distinctions between blacks and whites; as someone whose sexual appeal combined elements attributed to both men and women; and as a "Jesus-loving boy singing dirty Christmas songs." What does Pratt's essay gain by developing these paradoxes and contradictions as part of the Elvis myth? How does this depiction of Elvis confirm, alter, or recreate your image of him and the myths that surround him?

3.   What does Pratt mean when she says: "After Elvis died, it was necessary to deify him" and that "for those who have habitually disguised their culture from even themselves, it is hard to show candidly what and why one loves"?

4.   According to Pratt, what special relationships and bonds exist between Elvis and his fans? What relationships exist between the illusions of Elvis as a star and the realities of Elvis as a man?

5.   Although Elvis achieved tremendous popularity, wealth, and fame, he died tragically. How do you account for this?

6.   What kind of American dream does Pratt's account of Elvis create or suggest to you? How does this dream differ from or resemble your idea of the American dream?

7.   According to Pratt's essay, what myths surrounded Elvis at the beginning of his career and what myths came out of the end of his career? How do these myths explain Elvis's career and our culture? Why do you think the myths changed over time?

Living to Tell: Madonna's Resurrection of the Fleshly

SUSAN McCLARY

With a bachelor's of music in piano from Southern Illinois University and a Ph.D. in musicology from Harvard University, Susan McClary brings to her work a strong music background. Her essays and books span 400 years of musical history. She is as comfortable writing about Renaissance madrigals as she is writing about Madonna and the rock scene. A professor of musicology at the University of Minnesota, McClary is active in the experimental arts scene and has co-written musical theater pieces entitled "Susanna Does the Elders" and "Hildegard." In 1992, McClary accepted a new position on the music faculty at McGill University.

Her published work includes *Music and Society: The Politics of Composition, Performance, and Reception* (1987, co-edited with Richard Leppert) and a book entitled *George Bizet's Carmen* (1992). She is working on three other books: *Power and Desire in 17th Century Music, DeTonations: Narrative and Signification in Absolute Music,* and an untitled book about "content and musical form."

Her best known work is *Feminine Endings: Music, Gender, and Sexuality* (1991), a theoretical analysis of the ways we construct music and the ways we construct ourselves sexually within society. In the introduction to *Feminine Endings*, McClary describes how what she wanted to understand most about music was "always missing from classrooms, textbooks, or music research. . . . I was drawn to music because it is the most compelling cultural form I know. I wanted evidence that the overwhelming responses I experience with music are not just in my own head, but rather are shared." McClary felt that the academic study of music ignored the emotional effects and social meanings of music.

It was finally feminism that helped her understand what was missing. The selection from the final chapter of *Feminine Endings* represents the cultural significance of the pop phenomenon Madonna. McClary describes how Madonna creates and speaks for a "whole new set of possible feminine subject positions," by which she means a new set of roles, identities, and perspectives from which women can see themselves as meaningful participants and creative individuals in the world of music and modern culture.

A great deal of ink has been spilled in the debate over pop star Madonna's visual image and the narratives she has enacted for music video. Almost every response in the spectrum has been registered, ranging from unambiguous characterizations of her as "a porn queen in heat"[1] or "the kind of woman who comes into your room at three A.M. and sucks your life out,"[2] to formulations that view her as a kind of organic feminist whose image "enables girls to see that the meanings of feminine sexuality *can* be in their control, *can* be made in their interests, and that their subjectivities are not necessarily totally determined by the dominant patriarchy."[3]

What most reactions to Madonna share, however, is an automatic dismissal of her music as irrelevant. The scorn with which her ostensible artistic focus has been trivialized, treated as a conventional backdrop to her visual appearance, often is breathtaking. For example, John Fiske's complex and sympathetic discussion of the struggle over meaning surrounding Madonna begins, "Most critics have nothing good to say about her music, but they have a lot to say about her image."[4] He then goes on to say a lot about her image, and he too has nothing whatsoever to say about the music. E. Ann Kaplan's detailed readings of Madonna's music videos likewise push the music to the side and treat the videos strictly through the techniques of film criticism.[5]

This essay will concentrate on Madonna, the musician. First, I will locate her within a history of gender relationships in the music world: I hope to demonstrate that Madonna has served as a lightning rod to make only slightly more perceptible the kinds of double binds always presented to a woman who attempts to enter Western music. Second, I will turn to her music and examine some of the ways she operates within a persistently repressive discourse to create liberatory musical images. Finally I will present a brief discussion of the music videos "Open Your Heart" and "Like a Prayer," in which I consider the interactions between musical and visual components.

Throughout this essay, I will be writing of Madonna in a way that assigns considerable credit and responsibility to her as a creator of texts. To be sure, the products ascribed to Madonna are the result of complex collaborative processes involving the input of co-writers, co-producers, studio musicians, video directors, technicians, marketing specialists, and so forth. As is the case in most pop, there is no single originary genius for this music.

Yet the testimonies of co-workers and interviewers indicate that Madonna is very much in control of almost every dimension of her media persona and her career. Even though certain components of songs or videos are contributed by other artists, she has won and fiercely maintains the right to decide finally what will be released under her name. It may be that Madonna is best understood as head of a corporation that produces images of her self-representation, rather than as the spontaneous, "authentic" artist of rock mythology. But a puppet she's not. As she puts it:

> People have this idea that if you're sexual and beautiful and provocative, then there's nothing else you could possibly offer. People have *always* had that image about women. And while it might have seemed like I was behaving in a stereotypical way, at the same time, I was also masterminding it. I was in control of everything I was doing, and I think that when people realized that, it confused them.[6]

I am stressing Madonna's agency in her own self-representation in part because there is such a powerful tendency for her agency to be erased completely—for her to be seen as just a mindless doll fulfilling male fantasies of anonymous puppeteers. This particular strategy for dismissing Madonna has always seemed odd to me because the fantasies she enacts are not very successful at being male fantasies, if that is their objective: they often inspire discomfort and anxiety among men who wish to read her as a genuine "Boy Toy."[7] And I am rather amused when men who are otherwise not conspicuously concerned with feminist issues attack Madonna for setting the cause of women back twenty years—especially because so many girls and women (some of them feminist theorists, including even Betty Friedan)[8] perceive her music and videos as articulating a whole new set of possible feminine subject positions. Furthermore, her spirited, self-confident statements in interviews (several of which are sprinkled liberally throughout this essay) tend to lend support to the interpretations of female fans.

Yet Madonna's agency is not hers alone: even if she wrote everything she performs all by herself, it would still be important to remember that her music and personae are produced within a variety of social discursive practices. Her style is assembled from the musics of many different genres, and her visual images draw upon the conventions of female representation that circulate in film, advertisements, and stage shows. Indeed, in order to be as effective as she unquestionably is, she has to speak intelligibly to the cultural experiences and perceptions of her audience. Her voices are credible precisely because they engage so provocatively with ongoing cultural conversations about gender, power, and pleasure.

Moreover, as will be demonstrated throughout this essay, Madonna's art itself repeatedly deconstructs the traditional notion of the unified subject with finite ego boundaries. Her pieces explore—sometimes playfully, sometimes seriously—various ways of constituting identities that refuse stability, that remain fluid, that resist definition. This tendency in her work has become increasingly pronounced: for instance, in her recent, controversial video "Express Yourself" (which borrows its imagery from Fritz Lang's *Metropolis*), she slips in and out of every subject position offered within the video's narrative context—including those of the cat and the tyrannical master of industry—refusing more than ever to deliver the security of a clear, unambiguous message or an "authentic" self.

Thus I do not want to suggest that she (of all artists!) is a solitary creator who ultimately determines fixed meanings for her pieces. But I will focus on how a woman artist can make a difference within discourse. To strip Madonna of all conscious intention in her work is to reduce her once again to a voiceless, powerless bimbo. In a world in which many people assert that she (along with most other women artists) can't have meant what one sees and hears because she isn't smart enough, claims of intentionality, agency, and authorship become extremely important strategically.

Although there are some notable exceptions, women have traditionally been barred from participating in Western music. The barriers that have prevented them from participation have occasionally been formal: in the seventeenth century there were even papal edicts proscribing women's musical education.[9] More often, however, women are discouraged through more subtle means from considering themselves as potential musicians. As macho rock star David Lee Roth (rarely accused of being an ardent feminist) observes: "What if a little girl picked up a guitar and said 'I wanna be a rock star.' Nine times out of ten her parents would never allow her to do it. We don't have so many lead guitar women, not because women don't have the ability to play the instrument, but because they're kept locked up, taught to be something else. I don't appreciate that."[10]

Women have, of course, been discouraged from writing or painting as well, and feminist scholars in literary and art history have already made the barriers hindering women in those areas familiar. But there are additional factors that still make female participation in music riskier than in either literature or the visual arts. First, the charismatic performance of one's music is often crucial to its promotion and transmission. Whether Liszt in his matinee-idol piano recitals, Elvis on "The Ed Sullivan Show," or the aforementioned David Lee Roth, the composer–performer often relies heavily on manipulating audience response through his enactments of sexual power and desire.[11]

However, for a man to enact his sexuality is not the same as for a woman: throughout Western history, women musicians have usually been assumed to be publicly available, have had to fight hard against pressures to yield, or have accepted the granting of sexual favors as one of the prices of having a career. The seventeenth-century composer Barbara Strozzi—one of the very few women to compete successfully in elite music composition—may have been forced by her agent–pimp of a father to pose for a bare-breasted publicity portrait as part of his plan for launching her career.[12] Women on the stage are viewed as sexual commodities regardless of their appearance or seriousness. Brahms pleaded with the aging Clara Schumann (provocatively dressed, to be sure, in widow's weeds) to leave off her immodest composition and concertizing.[13] One of Madonna's principal accomplishments is that she brings this hypocrisy to the surface and problematizes it.

Second, musical discourse has been carefully guarded from female participation in part because of its ability to articulate patterns of desire. Music is an extremely powerful medium, all the more so because most listeners have little rational control over the way it influences them. The mind/body split that has plagued Western culture for centuries shows up most paradoxically in attitudes toward music: the most cerebral, nonmaterial of media is at the same time the medium most capable of engaging the body. This confusion over whether music belongs with mind or with body is intensified when the fundamental binary opposition of masculine/feminine is mapped onto it.[14] To the very large extent that mind is defined as masculine and body as feminine in Western culture, music is always in danger of being perceived as a feminine (or effeminate) enterprise altogether.[15] And one of the means of asserting masculine control over the medium is by denying the very possibility of participation by women. For how can an enterprise be feminine if actual women are excluded?

Women are not, of course, entirely absent from traditional music spectacle: women characters may even be highlighted as stars in operas. But opera, like the other genres of Western music, is an almost exclusively male domain in that men write both libretti and music, direct the stage action, and interpret the scores. Thus it is not surprising that operas tend to articulate and reinforce precisely the sexual politics just described. The proceedings are controlled by a discourse organized in accordance with masculine interests—a discourse that offers up the female as spectacle while guaranteeing that she will not step out of line. Sometimes desire is articulated by the male character while the passive, domesticated female simply acquiesces. In such instances, the potential violence of male domination is not necessarily in evidence: the piece seems to unfold in accordance with the "natural" (read: patriarchal) sexual hierarchy.

But a kind of desire-dread-purge mechanism prevails in operas in which the tables are turned and a passive male encounters a strong, sexually aggressive female character. In operas such as *Carmen, Lulu,* and *Salome*, the "victimized male" who has been aroused by the temptress finally must kill her in order to reinstate social order.[16] Even in so-called absolute music (instrumental music in which there is no explicit extramusical or programmatic component), the themes conventionally designated as "feminine" must be domesticated or eradicated for the sake of narrative closure.[17]

The ways in which fear of female sexuality and anxiety over the body are inscribed in the Western music tradition are obviously very relevant for the would-be (wannabe?) woman musician. First, women are located within the discourse in a position of both desire and dread—as that which must reveal that it is controlled by the male or which must be purged as intolerable. Many male attacks on Madonna unselfconsciously locate their terror in the fact that she is not under masculine control. Like Carmen or Lulu, she invokes the body and feminine sexuality; but unlike them, she refuses to be framed by a structure that will push her back into submission or annihilation. Madonna interprets the problem as follows:

> I think for the most part men have always been the aggressors sexually. Through time immemorial they've always been in control. So I think sex is equated with power in a way, and that's scary in a way. It's scary for men that women would have that power, and I think it's scary for women to have that power—or to have that power and be sexy at the same time.[18]

Second, the particular popular discourse within which Madonna works—that of dance—is the genre of music most closely associated with physical motion. The mind/body-masculine/feminine problem places dance decisively on the side of the "feminine" body rather than with the objective "masculine" intellect. It is for this reason that dance music in general usually is dismissed by music critics, even by "serious" rock critics. Recall the hysterical scorn heaped upon disco when it emerged, and recall also that disco was the music that underwrote the gay movement, black urban clubs, *Saturday Night Fever*'s images of working-class leisure, and other contexts that did not conform to the cherished ideal of (white, male, heterosexual, middle-class) rebel rock.[19] Similar dismissals of dance music can be found throughout the critical history of Western "serious" music. To the extent that the appeal is to physicality rather than abstracted listening, dance music is often trivialized at the same time that its power to distract and arouse is regarded with anxiety.[20]

Madonna works out of a discursive tradition that operates according to premises somewhat different from those of mainstream Western music. Her musical affiliations are with African-American music, with a culture that places great value on dance and physical engagement in music. It also is a culture that has always had prominent female participants: there are no white equivalents of Bessie Smith or Aretha Franklin—women who sing powerfully of both the spiritual and the erotic without the punitive, misogynist frame of European culture.[21] In critiquing Madonna's music, Dave Marsh (usually a defender of Madonna) once wrote, "A white Deniece Williams we don't need."[22] But perhaps that is precisely what we *do* need: a white woman musician who can create images of desire without the demand within the discourse itself that she be destroyed.

Madonna writes or co-writes most of her own material. Her first album was made up principally of her tunes. She surrendered some of the writing responsibility on *Like a Virgin* (interestingly, two of the songs that earned her so much notoriety—"Material Girl" and "Like a Virgin"—were written by men). But in her third album, *True Blue*, she is credited (along with her principal collaborators, Stephen Bray and Patrick Leonard) with co-production and with the co-writing of everything except "Papa Don't Preach." She co-wrote and co-produced (with Bray, Leonard, and Prince) all of the songs on her . . . album, *Like a Prayer*. It is quite rare for women singers to contribute so much to the composition of their materials, and it is almost unheard of for them to acquire the skills required for production. Indeed, very few performers of either sex attain sufficient prestige and power within the recording business to be able to demand that kind of artistic control.

Madonna's music is deceptively simple. On one level, it is very good dance music: inevitably compelling grooves, great energy. It is important to keep in mind that before she even presented her scandalous video images to the public, she had attracted a sizable following among the discerning participants of the black and gay disco scenes through her music alone. She remains one of the few white artists (along with George Michael) who regularly show up on the black charts.

Her music deliberately aims at a wide popular audience rather than at those who pride themselves on their elite aesthetic discrimination. Her enormous commercial success is often held against her, as evidence that she plays for the lowest common denominator—that she prostitutes her art (and, by extension, herself).[23] Moreover, the fact that her music appeals to masses of young girls is usually taken as proof that the music has absolutely no substance, for females in our culture are generally thought to be incapable of understanding music on even a rudimentary level. But surely Madonna's power as a figure in culture politics is linked to her ability to galvanize that particular audience—among others.[24]

To create music within a male-defined domain is a treacherous task. As some women composers of so-called serious or experimental music are discovering, many of the forms and conventional procedures of presumably value-free music are saturated with hidden patriarchal narratives, images, agendas.[25] The options available to a woman musician in rock music are especially constrictive, for this musical discourse is typically characterized by its phallic backbeat. It is possible to try to downplay that beat, to attempt to defuse its energy—but this strategy often results in music that sounds enervated or stereotypically "feminine." It is also possible to appropriate the phallic energy of rock and to demonstrate (as Chrissie Hynde, Joan Jett, and Lita Ford do so very well) that boys don't have any corner on that market. But that beat can always threaten to overwhelm: witness Janet Jackson's containment by producers Jimmy Jam and Terry Lewis in (ironically) her song "Control."[26]

Madonna's means of negotiating for a voice in rock resemble very much the strategies of her visual constructions; that is, she evokes a whole range of conventional signifiers and then causes them to rub up against each other in ways that are open to a variety of divergent readings, many of them potentially empowering to girls and women. She offers musical structures that promise narrative closure, and at the same time she resists or subverts them. A traditional energy flow is managed—which is why to many ears the whole complex seems always already absorbed—but that flow is subtly redirected.

The most obvious of her strategies is irony: the irony of the little-girl voice in "Like a Virgin" or of fifties girl-group sentiment in "True Blue." Like her play with the signs of famous temptresses, bustiers, and pouts, her engagement with traditional musical signs of childish vulnerability projects her knowledge that this is what the patriarchy expects of her and also her awareness that this fantasy is ludicrous. Her unsupervised parody destroys a much-treasured male illusion: even as she sings . . .* she becomes a disconcerting figure—the woman who knows too much, who is not at all the blank virginal slate she pretends to present. But to her female audience, her impersonation of these musical types is often received with delight as a knowing wink, a gesture of empowerment.[27]

Madonna's engagement with images of the past is not always to be understood as parody, however. Some of the historical figures she impersonates are victims of traditions in opera and popular culture that demand death as the price for sexuality.[28] Principal among the victims she invokes are Carmen and Marilyn Monroe, both highly desired, sexual women who were simultaneously idolized and casti-

---

* Permission to reprint Madonna's song lyrics in this sentence and elsewhere throughout this article was denied by Warner/Chappel Music in Los Angeles, California. [Eds.]

gated, and finally sacrificed to patriarchal standards of behavior. It is in her explicit acknowledgment of the traditional fate of artistic women who dare be erotic and yet in her refusal to fall likewise a victim that Madonna becomes far more serious about what have been referred to as "sign crimes."[29] If the strategy of appropriating and redefining conventional codes is the same in these more serious pieces as in the "True Blue" parody, the stakes are much, much higher.

. . . Tonal music is narratively conceived at least to the extent that the original key area—the tonic—also serves as the final goal. Tonal structures are organized teleologically, with the illusion of unitary identity promised at the end of each piece. But in order for pieces to have any narrative content, they must depart from the tonic and enact an adventure in which other key areas are visited (theorists sometimes say "conquered") and in which the certainty of tonal identity is at least temporarily suspended. Otherwise there is no plot. Yet with the exception of a few pieces in the nineteenth century and early twentieth that deliberately call into question the premises of this narrative schema, the outcome—the inevitable return to tonic—is always known in advance. To the extent that "Other" keys stand in the way of unitary identity, they must finally be subdued for the sake of narrative closure.[30] They serve as moments both of desire (because without the apparent longing to approach these other keys, there is only stagnation) and of dread (because they threaten identity).

As we have already seen, such narratives can easily be observed in nineteenth-century symphonies, in which lyrical "feminine" themes are encountered and then annexed (for the sake of closure and generic convention) to the key of the "masculine" theme. The more seductive or traumatic the encounter with the Other, the more violent the "necessary" heroic reaction. Beethoven's symphonies are especially telling in this regard: in the *Eroica*, an unprecedented level of dissonant bashing seems "required" to maintain thematic, rhythmic, and tonal identity. The struggle appears justified in the end, however, when we get to hear the uninterrupted transcendence of the theme in its tonic homeland.[31] In the Ninth Symphony, in which identity is marked as far more tentative, the violence levels are even higher. The arcadian third movement (a rare moment in which Beethoven permits dialogue and freedom of movement without the suggestion of overt anxiety) is self-consciously obliterated by the crashing dissonance introducing the finale's so-called "Ode to Joy."[32]

Most popular music avoids this schema, for songs typically are content with the sustaining of harmonic identity. There is usually no implied Other within these musical procedures, no structural obstacle or threat to overcome. However, all that is required to transform these stable procedures into narratives is for a detail to be problematized—to be construed as Other and as an obstacle to the configuration defined as Self or identity. In such songs, time becomes organized around the expectation of intensified conflict, climax, and eventual resolution. They adopt, in other words, the same desire-dread-purge sequence that characterizes the narratives of so much classical music and literature.

Rock songs that work on the basis of this sequence can be found from Led Zeppelin to The Cult's "Fire Woman [you're to blame]" or Dokken's "Kiss of Death.". . . .

In the stage performance of "Live to Tell," the backdrop of the stage is filled with a huge projection of Madonna as Monroe, the quintessential female victim of commercial culture. The instrumental introduction sets up a bass pedal on D, performed by an inert synthesizer sonority utterly lacking in warmth. Over the pedal, a series of bleak open fifths mechanically marks the pulses of the metric order as through they are inevitable. This stark image alternates with an energetic pattern that emerges suddenly in the area of the relative major, F. The second sound-image differs from the opening sonority in part because the major key is semiotically associated with hope. Moreover, the bass is active rather than static, and it resists the apparent inevitability of the opening meter by anticipating slightly each of its changes: it seems to possess freedom of motion. However, just as this passage seems on the brink of establishing F major as the principal point of reference, it is recontained by the clanging fifths and the empty pedal on D. A traditional reading would understand D (with its pedal and fifths) as fundamental (as that which defines identity) and F major as the "feminine" region, which—even if it offers the illusion of hope, escape, and freedom—must be contained and finally purged for the sake of satisfactory closure.[33]

When she begins singing the verse, Madonna steps temporarily outside of this dichotomy of D-versus-F to sing over a new pedal on C. As she sings, her voice repeatedly falls lethargically back to the void of the C-pedal, as though she cannot overcome the gravitational pull it and the meter exert. Her text suggests that she has a weighty, long-buried "tale to tell," and her language . . . resonates with biblical references. If she as a woman is necessarily identified as the Other, as she who is held responsible for "the Fall," how is she to enter into narrative? How to step into a musical procedure in which the choices are already so loaded?

With the chorus . . . , she opts for the warmer major key of F, her momentum picks up, and she begins to sound as though she will establish this more affirmative region as her tonic or point of reference.

However, to close in this second region—conventionally the "feminine" position—is to accept as identity the patriarchal definition of femininity. Moreover, to the extent that F major is not the opening key, to cadence here is to choose fantasy; for while this key is reassuring and nurturing, it is not "reality" as the piece defines it initially. And formal convention would dictate that this second key area must eventually be absorbed and purged. Thus closure here is revealed as perilous. At the last moment before the implied cadence . . . , she holds to a pitch incompatible with harmonic closure. The age-old contrapuntal norm would dictate that her melodic pitch . . . must resolve down to conform with the bass. Instead, her melodic pitch and the harmonic backdrop hold in a standoff until the bass—not the melody—moves to conform to the melody's (that is, to *her*) will.

The pitch cadenced on, however, is D; and while it defies immediate closure, it also strikes the common tone that permits the pitiless pedal of the beginning to return. As before, Madonna steps outside the dilemma to C for a verse in which she wearily comments on her subjective knowledge of beauty, warmth, truth, light even in the face of this apparent no-win situation. But eventually she must rejoin the world in which she has to engage with the choice between F and D, and once again she works to avoid closure in either.

Finally, after this escape–recontainment process has occurred a couple of times, the bottom suddenly drops out. It sounds as though the piece has ended in the foreordained defeat of the victim—she who is offered only the second-position slot in the narrative schema. In her live performance, at this point Madonna sinks to the floor and lies motionless for what seems an interminable length of time. There is silence except for the low, lifeless synthesizer drone on D. For someone like myself who is used to this scenario as the inevitable end of my heroines, witnessing this moment from a performer who has been so brash, so bursting with erotic energy and animation, is bitter indeed. But then she rises from the floor, bearing with her the ghosts of all those victims—Marilyn most explicitly, but also Carmen, barebreasted Barbara Strozzi, and all the others who were purged for the sake of social order and narrative closure—and begins singing again.

In order to take charge of the narrative procedure, Madonna begins to oscillate strategically between the two tonal poles on D and F. As she sings . . . , she sings over a bass that moves up and down indecisively between D and A (mediant of F, but dominant of D), suggesting a blurred region in which both keys cohabit. When the opening dilemma returns, she prevents the recontainment gesture of the fifths by anticipating their rhythmic moment of reentry and jumping in to interpose the F-major refrain instead. So long as she manages thus to switch back and forth, she can determine the musical discourse. To settle for an option—either option—is to accept a lie, for it is flexibility in identity rather than unitary definition that permits her to "live to tell." The piece ends not with definitive closure but with a fade. As long as we can hear her, she continues to fluctuate.

This extraordinary song finally is not about unambiguous triumph: triumph would be easy to simulate, since this is what tonal pieces conventionally do. Yet given the premises of this song, triumphant closure would be impossible to believe. Moreover, it would merely reproduce the structure of oppression that informs narrative convention. Rather it is about staying in motion for the sake of survival, resisting closure wherever it lies in wait.[34]

By thus creating songs that refuse to choose between identity and Other—that invoke and then reject the very terms of this schema of narrative organization—Madonna is engaged in rewriting some very fundamental levels of Western thought. In "Live to Tell," the two clear regions of the traditional narrative schema seem to be implied. Semiotically, the unyielding fifths are "masculine," the lyrical, energetic refrain, "feminine," and the early part of the piece revels that the fifths are formally designed to contain the excess and relative freedom of the refrain. But to the extent that identification with the feminine moment in the narrative spells death, the piece cannot embrace this space as reality without losing strategic control. Thus the singer risks resisting identification with "her own" areas, even if it means repeated encounters with that which would contain her. In a sense, she sets up residence on the moments of the harmonic context that fluctuate between desire and dread on the one hand and resolution on the other. Rather than deciding for the sake of secure identity (a move that would lapse back into the narrative of masculine subjectivity), she inhabits both and thus refuses closure.

Formulations such as this are all the more remarkable because the ideological implications of musical narratives are only now beginning to be analyzed by cultural critics. The fact that some of Madonna's music enacts models of organization that correspond to formulations of critics such as Teresa de Lauretis need not suggest that Madonna is a connoisseur of critical theory. Yet to the extent that de Lauretis and Madonna inhabit the same historical world and grapple with the same kinds of problems with respect to feminine identity, their similarities are not entirely coincidental either. And Madonna is as much an expert in the arena of musical signification as de Lauretis is in theoretical discourse. It seems clear that she has grasped the assumptions embedded within these basic musical mechanisms and is audaciously redirecting them.

It must be conceded that male musicians could construct forms along these lines if they wanted to do so—there is nothing essentially feminine about what Madonna is doing in this piece. But most men would not perceive that there was a problem in the standard narrative, would not enact struggles that involve resistance to purging the alien element.[35] The strategies of Madonna's songs are those of one who has radically conflicting subject positions—one who has been taught to cheer for resolutions in cultural narratives, but who also realizes that she is of the sort that typically gets purged for the sake of that resolution. Madonna's refusal of definition (which infuriates many a critic) goes beyond the paradox of her name, her persona, her visual imagery. It also produces brave new musical procedures. These themes—survival, pleasure, resistance to closure—are reengaged most dramatically in Madonna's song and video, "Like a Prayer." In contrast to the relationship between sight and sound in "Open Your Heart," the tensions she is putting into play in this music video are virtually all audible within the music itself, prior to the visual images. Moreover, many of the tensions that have always surrounded her personae are here made explicit.

The central dichotomy she inevitably invokes is that of the virgin and the whore.[36] Her name (actually, fortuitously, her given name: Madonna Louise Veronica Ciccone), her apparently casual flaunting of crucifixes and rosaries as accessories, and her overtly erotic dress and behavior have consistently thrown into confusion the terms of that standard binary opposition; but what precisely she means by this play of signs has never been obvious. Indeed, many critics have taken her use of religious imagery to be a prime example of what Fredric Jameson calls "blank pastiche": the symbols are seen as detached from their traditional context and thus as ceasing to signify.[37] However, Madonna's insistence on the codes of Catholic iconography has always at least potentially engaged with the sedimented memory of that tradition, even if only negatively—as blasphemy. In "Like a Prayer," the religious connotations of her entire project are reactivated and reinterpreted. But although this set of issues is finally foregrounded, her treatment of these highly sensitive themes is quite unexpected and, as it turns out, highly controversial.

The song draws upon two very different semiotic codes associated with two very different forms of Christianity: Catholicism and the black Gospel church. These codes would seem at first glance to be incompatible. But Madonna is tapping into a tradition of Catholicism that has long been suppressed: that of the female mystics such as Saint Teresa who claimed to have experienced mystical union with Christ.[38] In Saint Teresa's writings, religious ecstasy is described through images of sexual ecstasy, for the intensity of her relationship with the deity could only be expressed verbally to other human beings through metaphors of submission, penetration, even orgasm. In the seventeenth century, composers of sacred music freely borrowed images of desire and eroticism from the steamy operatic stage for purposes of their devotionals and worship services, for these experiences were thought to be relevant to the new forms of personalized faith encouraged by both the Reformation and the Counter-Reformation.[39]

After the seventeenth century, this strain of religious erotic imagery was purged from most mainstream Christian denominations, only to reemerge occasionally during moments of intense emotional revivalism. Certain forms of charismatic fundamentalism since the eighteenth century have employed erotic imagery for purposes of inducing personalized meditation or even trance states and speaking in tongues. Both Bach's pietistic bride-and-groom duets (see Cantata 140) and Jerry Lew Lewis's evangelical rock 'n' roll ("Whole Lot of Shakin' Goin' On") testify to this phenomenon. However, the semiotic connections between religious and sexual ecstasy are most consistently apparent in the black Gospel churches. Throughout its history (as preserved on recordings), Gospel has freely borrowed musical and poetic styles from the secular music of its day: witness, for instance, the mergers with jazz, blues, funk, and rap evident on present-day Gospel radio stations—or, for that matter, the entire career of Aretha Franklin. Moreover, the Gospel church continually produces new generations of black pop musicians whose music is fueled by the fervent energy of that spiritual context.

"Like a Prayer" opens with an invocation of stereotyped mystical Catholicism: with the halo of a wordless (heavenly) choir and the fundamental accompaniment of a "timeless" pipe organ as she sings. . . . Madonna breaks into ecstatic, funky, Gospel-flavored dance music. These two moments are distinguished for narrative purposes through the same harmonic contrast between D minor and F major as in "Live to Tell." What seems to be a struggle between mystical timelessness on D minor and exuberant, physical celebration on F major ensues. This time, however, she is not afraid to embrace F as tonic, especially when halfway through, on the words . . . , she lands decisively on that pitch.

But D minor does not disappear entirely—it reenters for a long, rather sinister return of the beginning material in the middle of the song. Eventually, however, the music is channeled back to F major for more celebration. Gradually D minor comes to serve only for "deceptive" cadences. Traditionally deceptive cadences spell disappointment, a jarring intervention at the promised moment of identity. But in "Like a Prayer," they provide the means of avoiding closure and maintaining the dance. Finally, in the long, ecstatic coda to the song, F major and D minor at cadences become in a sense interchangeable: no longer self and Other, they become two flickering moments in a flexible identity that embraces them both, that remains constant only insofar as both continue to be equally present.

This is similar to the strategy of "Live to Tell," except that here the music itself does not involve the suggestion of threatened annihilation. But the controversial video released with the album sets up something like the external threats of containment articulated in "Live to Tell." The video is organized in terms of an inside and an outside. Outside the church is the world of Ku Klux Klan cross-burnings, of rape and murder, of racist authority. One of the most striking moments in the video occurs when Madonna dances provocatively in front of the burning crosses, aggressively defying those who burn crosses to contain her and her sexuality as well. And, indeed, Madonna has testified to having planned originally to present an even more extreme scenario: "I had all these ideas about me running away with the black guy and both of us getting shot by the KKK."[40] Video director Mary Lambert says of the segment with the burning crosses: "That's an ecstatic vision. The cross is a cautionary symbol and Madonna's performance throughout has been tortured and emotional. The inference of Ku Klux Klan racism is there, but the burning cross is an older symbol than the Klan. Saints had it. It symbolizes the wrath of God."[41]

But inside the church is the possibility of community, love, faith, and interracial bonding. The references to Catholic mysticism and the black Gospel church are made explicit in the visuals, with a heady mixture of a miraculously weeping statue, the stigmata, the Saint Teresa-like union between the saint and the believer, and the highly physical musical performance by the Andraé Crouch choir. Within the security of the church, difference can be overcome and the boundless joy of the music can become reality.[42] As in "Live to Tell," this song is about survival rather than simple triumph. And it is about the possibility of creating musical and visual narratives that celebrate multiple rather than unitary identities, that are concerned with ecstatic continuation rather than with purging and containment.[43]

In a world in which the safe options for women musicians seem to be either denying gender difference or else restricting the expression of feminine pleasure to all-women contexts, Madonna's counternarratives of female heterosexual desire are remarkable. The intelligence with which she zeroes in on the fundamental gender tensions in culture and the courage with which she takes them on deserve much greater credit than she usually is given. That she manages both to outrage those who would have her conform and to delight those who are still trying to puzzle out their own future options within this society indicates that her strategies are by and large successful. If

Madonna does, in fact, "live to tell"—that is, survive as a viable cultural force—an extraordinarily powerful reflex action of patriarchy will have been successfully challenged.*

Notes

1. J. D. Considine, "That Girl: Madonna Rolls Across America," *BuZZ* 2, no. 11 (September 1987): "According to the PMRC's Susan Baker, in fact, Madonna taught little girls how to act 'like a porn queen in heat'" (17). E. Ann Kaplan describes her image as a combination of bordello queen and bag lady. See *Rocking Around the Clock: Music Television, Postmodernism, and Consumer Culture* (New York: Methuen, 1987), 126.

2. Milo Miles, music editor of *Boston Phoenix*, as quoted in Dave Marsh, "Girls Can't Do What the Guys Do: Madonna's Physical Attraction," *The First Rock & Roll Confidential Report* (New York: Pantheon, 1985), 161. Compare the imagery in Considine, "That Girl": "By some accounts—particularly a notorious *Rolling Stone* profile—Madonna slept her way to the top, sucking her boyfriends dry, then moving on to the next influential male" (16). Both Marsh and Considine refute this image, but it is a fascinating one that combines the predatory sexuality of the vampire and succubus with the servile masochism of the female character in *Deep Throat*. For a reasonably detailed (if positively slanted) account of Madonna's early career, see Debbi Voller, *Madonna: The Illustrated Biography* (London: Omnibus Press, 1988).

3. John Fiske, "British Cultural Studies and Television," *Channels of Discourse*, ed. Robert C. Allen (Chapel Hill: University of North Carolina Press, 1987), 297.

4. Ibid., 270.

5. See Kaplan, *Rocking Around the Clock*, especially 115–27; and "Feminist Criticism and Televsion," *Channels of Discourse*, 211–53.

6. Mikal Gilmore, "The Madonna Mystique," *Rolling Stone* 508 (September 10, 1987): 87. I wish to thank Ann Dunn for this citation.

7. In his interview with Madonna in *Rolling Stone* 548 (March 28, 1989), Bill Zehme says: "Maybe you noticed this already, but a number of songs on the new album [*Like a Prayer*] have sort of antimale themes." Her response: "[*Surprised*] Well, gee, I never thought of that. This album definitely does have a very strong feminine point of view. Hmmm. I've had some painful experiences with men in my life, just as I've had some incredible experiences. Maybe I'm representing more of the former than the latter. I certainly don't hate men. No, no, no! Couldn't live without them!" (180). Madonna is caught typically in a double bind in which she is chastised at the same time for being a passive doll and for being an aggressive man-hater. See again the citations in note 1.

8. On a special MTV broadcast called "Taboo Videos" (March 26, 1988), Betty Friedan states in an interview: "I tell you, Madonna—in contrast to the image of women that you saw on MTV—at least she had spirit, she had guts,

---

* Ironically, the vice president of Warner/Chappel Music reproduced his own version of what McClary calls the "reflex action of the patriarchy" when he denied our request to reprint Madonna's lyrics to "Live to Tell" as the next selection in this book. Explaining that he did not understand McClary's commentary and could not condone what it says, he denied Madonna one more opportunity to tell her story. [Eds.]

she had vitality. She was in control of her own sexuality and her life. She was a relatively good role model, compared with what else you saw."

9. Jane Bowers, "Women Composers in Italy, 1566–1700," *Women Making Music: The Western Art Tradition, 1150–1950*, ed. Jane Bowers and Judith Tick (Urbana: University of Illinois Press, 1986): "On 4 May 1686 Pope Innocent XI issued an edict which declared that 'music is completely injurious to the modesty that is proper for the [female] sex, because they become distracted from the matters and occupations most proper for them.' Therefore, 'no unmarried woman, married woman, or widow of any rank, status, condition, even those who for reasons of education or anything else are living in convents or conservatories, under any pretext, even to learn music in order to practice it in those convents, may learn to sing from men, either laymen or clerics or regular clergy, no matter if they are in any way related to them, and to play any sort of musical instrument'" (139–40).

An especially shocking report of the silencing of women performers is presented in Anthony Newcomb, *The Madrigal at Ferrara, 1579–1597* (Princeton: Princeton University Press, 1980). The court at Ferrara had an ensemble with three women virtuoso singers who became internationally famous. Duke Alfonso of Ferrara had the "three ladies" sing for Duke Guglielmo of Mantua and expected the latter to "praise them to the skies." "Instead, speaking loudly enough to be heard both by the ladies and by the Duchesses who were present [Duke Guglielmo] burst forth, 'ladis are very impressive indeed—in fact, I would rather be an ass than a lady.' And with this he rose and made everyone else do so as well, thus puting an end to the singing" (24).

See also the examinations of the restrictions placed on women as musicians and performers in Richard Leppert, *Music and Image: Domesticity, Ideology and Socio-cultural Formation in Eighteenth-Century England* (Cambridge: Cambridge University Press, 1988); and Julia Kosa, "Music and References to Music in *Godey's Lady's Book*, 1830–77" (Ph.D. dissertation, University of Minnesota, 1988).

10. David Lee Roth, cited in Marsh, "Girls Can't Do," 165. I might add that this is a far more liberal attitude than that of most academic musicians.

11. This is not always an option socially available to male performers, however. The staged enactment of masculine sensuality is problematic in Western culture in which patriarchal rules of propriety dictate that excess in spectacles be projected onto women. Thus Liszt, Elvis, and Roth can be understood as effective in part because of their transgressive behaviors. This distinction in permissible activities in music theater can be traced back to the beginnings of opera in the seventeenth century. . . . See also Robert Walser, "Running with the Devil: Power, Gender, and Madness in Heavy Metal Music" (Ph.D. dissertation, University of Minnesota, forthcoming).

12. Ellen Rosand, "The Voice of Barbara Strozzi," *Women Making Music*, 185. See also Anthony Newcomb, "Courtesans, Muses, or Musicians? Professional Women Musicians in Sixteenth-Century Italy," *Women Making Music*, 90–115; and Linda Phyllis Austern, "'Sing Againe Syren': The Female Musician and Sexual Enchantment in Elizabethan Life and Literature," *Renaissance Quarterly* 42, no. 3 (Autumn 1989): 420–48. For more on the role of Renaissance courtesans in cultural production, see Ann Rosalind Jones, "City Women and Their Audiences: Louise Labé and Veronica Franco," *Rewriting the Renaissance: The Discourses of Sexual Difference in Early Modern Europe*, ed. Margaret W. Ferguson, Maureen Quilligan, and Nancy J. Vickers (Chicago: University of Chicago Press, 1986), 299–316.

13. See the exerpts from Clara's diary entries and her correspondences with Robert Schumann and Brahms in Carol Neuls-Bates, ed., *Women in Music: An Anthology of Source Readings from the Middle Ages to the Present* (New York: Harper & Row, 1982), 92–108; and Nancy B. Reich, *Clara Schumann: The Artist and the Woman* (Ithaca: Cornell University Press, 1985). *Women in Music* contains many other documents revealing how women have been discouraged from participating in music and how certain of them persisted to become productive composers nonetheless.

14. For examinations of how the mind/body split intersects with gender in Western culture see Genevieve Lloyd, *The Man of Reason: "Male" and "Female" in Western Philosophy* (Minneapolis: University of Minnesota Press, 1984); Susan Bordo, "The Cartesian Masculinization of Thought," *Signs* 11, no. 3 (1986): 439–56; and Evelyn Fox Keller, *Reflections on Gender and Science* (New Haven: Yale University Press, 1985).

For discussions of how these slipping binary oppositions inform music, see Geraldine Finn, "Music, Masculinity and the Silencing of Women," *New Musicology*, ed. John Shepherd (New York: Routledge, forthcoming); and my "Agenda for a Feminist Criticism of Music," *Canadian University Music Review*, forthcoming.

15. This binary opposition is not, of course, entirely stable. Imagination for instance, is an attribute of the mind, though it was defined as "feminine" during the Enlightenment and consequently becomes a site of contestation in early Romanticism. See Jochen Schulte-Sasse, "Imagination and Modernity: Or the Taming of the Human Mind," *Cultural Critique* 5 (Winter 1986–87): 23–48. Likewise, the nineteenth-century concept of "genius" itself was understood as having a necessary "feminine" component, although actual women were explicitly barred from this category. See Christine Battersby, *Gender and Genius* (London: Women's Press, 1989).

The common association of music with effeminacy is only now being examined in musicology. See Leppert, *Music and Image*; Linda Austern, "'Alluring the Auditorie to Effeminacie': Music and the English Renaissance Idea of the Feminine," paper presented to the America Musicological Society, Baltimore (November 1988); Jeffrey Kallberg, "Genre and Gender: The Nocturne and Women's History," unpublished paper; and Maynard Solomon, "Charles Ives: Some Questions of Veracity," *Journal of the American Musicological Society* 40 (1987): 466–69.

16. See Catherine Clément, *Opera, or the Undoing of Women*, trans. Betsy Wing (Minneapolis: University of Minnesota Press, 1988). . . .

17. See Chapter 3 of Susan McClary's *Feminine Endings*, University of Minnesota Press, 1991.

18. Quoted in Gilmore, "The Madonna Mystique," 87. Nevertheless, Madonna is often collapsed back into the stereotype of the *femme fatale* of traditional opera and literature. See the comparison between Madonna and Berg's Lulu in Leo Treitler, "The Lulu Character and the Character of *Lulu*," *Music and the Historical Imagination* (Cambridge, Mass.: Harvard University Press, 1989), 272–75.

19. See Richard Dyer, "In Defense of Disco," *On Record: Rock, Pop, and the Written Word*, ed. Simon Frith and Andrew Goodwin (New York: Pantheon Press, 1990), 410–18.

20. See, for instance, Theodor W. Adorno's hysterical denouncements of jazz in "Perennial Fashion—Jazz," *Prisms*, trans. Samuel Weber and Shierry Weber (Cambridge, Mass.: MIT Press, 1981), 121–32: "They [jazz fans] call

themselves 'jitterbugs,' bugs which carry out reflex movements, performers of their own ecstasy" (128). . . .

21. However, I have often encountered hostile reactions on the part of white middle-class listeners to Aretha Franklin's frank sensuality, even when (particularly when) it is manifested in her sacred recordings such as "Amazing Grace." The argument is that women performers ought not to exhibit signs of sexual pleasure, for this invariably makes them displays for male consumption. See the discussion in John Shepherd, "Music and Male Hegemony," *Music and Society: The Politics of Composition, Performance and Reception*, ed. Richard Leppert and Susan McClary (Cambridge: Cambridge University Press, 1987), 170–72.

22. Marsh, "Girls Can't Do," 162.

23. See Mary Harron's harsh and cynical critique of rock's commercialism in general and Madonna in particular in "McRock: Pop as a Commodity," *Facing the Music*, ed. Simon Frith (New York: Pantheon Books, 1988), 173–220. At the conclusion of a reading of Madonna's "Open Your Heart" video, Harron writes: "The message is that our girl [Madonna] may sell sexuality, but she is free" (218). See also Leslie Savan, "Desperately Selling Soda," *Village Voice* (March 14, 1989): 47, which critiques Madonna's decision to make a commercial for Pepsi. Ironically, when her video to "Like a Prayer" (discussed later in this essay) was released the day after the first broadcast of the commercial, Pepsi was pressured to withdraw the advertisement, for which it had paid record-high fees. Madonna had thus maintained her artistic control, even in what had appeared to be a monumental sellout.

24. See the discussion of the responses to Madonna of young girls in Fiske, "British Cultural Studies," 269–83. See also the report of responses of young Japanese fans in Gilmore, "The Madonna Mystique," 38. Madonna's response: "But mainly I think they feel that most of my music is really, really positive, and I think they appreciate that, particularly the women. I think I stand for everything that they're really taught to *not* be, so maybe I provide them with a little bit of encouragement." Considine, "That Girl," quotes her as saying: "Children always understand. They have open minds. They have built-in shit detectors" (17).

25. See Chapter 5.

26. When Jackson first signed on with Jam and Lewis, the music for this song was already "in the can" awaiting an appropriate signer. The mix throughout highlights the powerful beats, such that Jackson constantly seems thrown off balance by them. At one point the sound of a car collision punctuates her words, "I never knew what hit me"; and the ironic conclusion depicts the crumbling of her much-vaunted control. Not only was Jackson in a more dependent position with respect to production than Madonna, but the power relations *within the song itself* are very different from those Madonna typically enacts.

27. "There is also a sense of pleasure, at least for me and perhaps a large number of other women, in Madonna's defiant look or gaze. In 'Lucky Star' at one point in the dance sequence Madonna dances side on to the camera, looking provocative. For an instant we glimpse her tongue: the expectation is that she is about to lick her lips in a sexual invitation. The expectation is denied and Madonna appears to tuck her tongue back into her cheek. This, it seems, is how most of her dancing and groveling in front of the camera is meant to be taken. She is setting up the sexual idolization of women. For a woman who has experienced this victimization, this setup is most enjoyable

and pleasurable, while the male position of voyeur is displaced into uncertainty." Robyn Blair, quoted in Fiske, "British Cultural Studies," 283.

28. For the ways women performers have been seen as inviting tragic lives, see Robyn Archer and Diana Simmonds, *A Star Is Torn* (New York: E. P. Dutton, 1986); Gloria Steinem, *Marilyn* (New York: Henry Holt, 1986). For an analysis of Hitchcock's punishments of sexual women, see Tania Modleski, *The Women Who Knew Too Much: Hitchcock and Feminist Theory* (New York: Methuen, 1988). For treatments of these issues in classical music, see my "The Undoing of Opera: Toward a Feminist Criticism of Music," foreword to Clément, *Opera*, ix–xviii; and Chapter 3 in this volume.

29. In Gilmore, "Madonna Mystique," Madonna states: "I do feel something for Marilyn Monroe. A sympathy. Because in those days, you were really a slave to the whole Hollywood machinery, and unless you had the strength to pull yourself out of it, you were just trapped. I think she didn't know what she was getting herself into and simply made herself vulnerable, and I feel a bond with that. I've certainly felt that at times—I've felt an invasion of privacy and all that—but I'm determined never to let it get me down. Marilyn Monroe was a victim, and I'm not. That's why there's really no comparison" (87). The term "sign crimes" is from Arthur Kroker and David Cook, *The Postmodern Scene: Excremental Culture and Hyper-Aesthetics* (New York: St. Martin's Press, 1986), 21.

30. All previous chapters have dealt extensively with these mechanisms.

31. For an excellent narrative account of the *Eroica*, see Philip Downs, "Beethoven's 'New Way' and the Eroica," *The Creative World of Beethoven*, ed. Paul Henry Lang (New York: W.W. Norton, 1970), 83–102. Downs's interpretation is not inflected, however, by concerns of gender or "extramusical" notions of alterity.

32. See the discussion in Chapter 5. For other readings of the Ninth Symphony, see Leo Treitler, "History, Criticism, and Beethoven's Ninth Symphony" and "'To Worship That Celestial Sound': Motives for Analysis," *Music and the Historical Imagination*, 19–66; and Maynard Solomon, "Beethoven's Ninth Symphony: A Search for Order," *19th-Century Music* 10 (Summer 1986): 3–23.

33. Compare, for example, the opening movement of Schubert's "Unfinished" Symphony, in which the tune we all know and love is in the second position and is accordingly quashed. George Michael's "Hand to Mouth" (on the *Faith* album) is a good example of the same imperatives at work in popular music. In both the Schubert and Michael, the pretty tune represents illusion up against harsh reality. My thanks to Robert Walser for bringing the Michael song to my attention.

34. This strategy of always staying in motion is advocated in Teresa de Lauretis, "The Technology of Gender," especially 25–26. See also Denise Riley, *"Am I That Name?": Feminism and the Category of "Women" in History* (Minneapolis: University of Minnesota Press, 1988); and Kaja Silverman, "Fragments of a Fashionable Discourse," in *Studies in Entertainment: Critical Approaches to Mass Culture*, ed. Tania Modleski (Bloomington: Indiana University Press, 1986), 150–51. I discuss Laurie Anderson's "O Superman" or "Langue d'amour" in terms of these strategies in Chapter 6.

35. Some of the so-called Minimalist composers such as Philip Glass and Steve Reich also have called the conventions of tonal closure into question, as did Debussy at an earlier moment. See my "Music and Postmodernism," *Contemporary Music Review*, forthcoming. And see the discussions of Schoen-

berg's (very different) strategies for resisting the narrative schemata of tonality and sonata in Chapters 1 and 4.

36. In the souvenir program book from her 1987 tour, Madonna is quoted as saying: "Madonna is my real name. It means a lot of things. It means virgin, mother, mother of earth. Someone who is very pure and innocent but someone who's very strong." Needless to say, this is not how the name has always been received.

37. For a cynical interpretation, see Steve Anderson, "Forgive Me, Father," *Village Voice*, April 4, 1989: "Madonna snags vanguard attention while pitching critics into fierce Barthesian discussions about her belt buckles. Certainly she's an empire of signs, but the trick behind the crucifixes, opera gloves, tulle, chains, and the recent rosary-bead girdle is that they lead only back to themselves, representing *nothing*" (68).

But see also the complex discussion in Fiske, "British Cultural Studies," 275–76, which quotes Madonna as saying: "I have always carried around a few rosaries with me. One day I decided to wear [one] as a necklace. Everything I do is sort of tongue in cheek. It's a strong blend—a beautiful sort of symbolism, the idea of someone suffering, which is what Jesus Christ on a crucifix stands for, and then not taking it seriously. Seeing it as an icon with no religiousness attached. It isn't sacrilegious for me." Fiske concludes that "her use of religious iconography is neither religious nor sacrilegious. She intends to free it from this ideological opposition and to enjoy it, use it, for the meanings and pleasure that it has for *her* and not for those of the dominant ideology and its simplistic binary thinking."

38. For excellent discussions of the Catholic tradition of female saints and erotic imagery, see Caroline Walker Bynum, "The Female Body and Religious Practice in the Later Middle Ages," *Zone: Fragments for a History of the Human Body*, ed. Michel Feher et al. (New York: Zone, 1989), 160–219; and Julia Kristeva, *Tales of Love*, trans. Leon S. Roudiez (New York: Columbia Unviersity Press, 1987), especially 83–100 and 297–317.

This association is in line with many of Madonna's statements concerning Catholicism, such as her claim that "nuns are sexy" (Fiske, "British Cultural Studies," 275). However, she need not be aware of Saint Teresa in order for these kinds of combinations of the sacred and erotic to occur to her. Once again, her experiences as a woman in this culture mesh in certain ways with the traditional symbolism of holy submission in Christianity, and thus her metaphors of spirituality are similar in many ways to Saint Teresa's. She also intends to create this collision in the song and video. In Armond White, "The Wrath of Madonna," *Millimeter*, June 1989, Mary Lambert (director of the "Like a Prayer" video) states: "Madonna and I always work together on a concept. We both felt the song was about sexual and religious ecstasy" (31). The black statue in the church is identified as Saint Martin de Porres. I wish to thank Vaughn Ormseth for bringing this article to my attention.

39. See the many settings of texts from the Song of Songs by composers such as Alessandro Grandi and Heinrich Schütz. The sacred erotic likewise influenced the literary and visual arts. See Bernini's sculpture of, or Richard Crashaw's poem concerning, Saint Teresa. I am at the moment writing a book, *Power and Desire in Seventeenth-Century Music* (Princeton: Princeton University Press, forthcoming), that examines this phenomenon.

40. Quoted in Liz Smith's column, *San Francisco Chronicle*, April 19, 1989, E1. I wish to thank Greil Marcus for bringing this to my attention. Lydia Hamessley first pointed out to me the significance of inside and outside in the organization of the video.

41. White, "The Wrath of Madonna," 31.

42. For an excellent discussion of the political strength of the music, rhetoric, and community of the black church today, see the interview of Cornel West by Anders Stephanson in *Universal Abandon? The Politics of Postmodernism*, ed. Andrew Ross (Minneapolis: University of Minnesota Press, 1988), 227–86. Madonna speaks briefly about her identification with black culture in Zehme, "Madonna," 58.

43. For another sympathetic discussion of the politics of this video, see Dave Marsh, "Acts of Contrition," *Rock & Roll Confidential* 67 (May 1989): 1–2.

SPECULATIONS

1.   At the beginning of this selection, McClary characterizes other writers' responses to Madonna. How does her treatment of Madonna differ from these other writers? How effective is her argument? Why do you think she wants us to know about other points of view; why does she mention them at all?

2.   McClary claims at one point that female participation in rock music is riskier than in arts such as literature or painting. What is her evidence and how does she support this view?

3.   What is the significance of the song title "Live to Tell" in McClary's argument? Why do you think she chose to illustrate her essay with this song?

4.   Why do you think Madonna uses religious imagery in her music, videos, and self-promotions? How does this use of traditional religion affect you?

5.   What is your own response to Madonna, that is, to the image of Madonna that you hear and see? Has your response changed over the years, and if so, in what ways?

6.   It is probably fair to say that the most famous rock stars and pop musicians in the United States have been men: Bruce Springsteen, Michael Jackson, James Brown, the Rolling Stones, Elvis, the Beatles. The only current pop icon that contradicts this statement is Madonna. How do you explain this? How does Madonna play off the male stereotypes in her music and her performances? What are the differences between Madonna's public image and the public image of male rock stars? What difference does it make to you whether a musician is male or female? How does your own experience as a man or as a women influence your response to this issue?

Fast Car

TRACY CHAPMAN

Tracy Chapman was born in Cleveland, Ohio, in 1964, and was raised by her mother, a part-time church and club singer who separated from her father when Chapman was four. She attended the progressive Wooster school in Connecticut and then Tufts University, where she studied West African culture while majoring in anthropology. Writing songs since age twelve, Chapman started her music career by performing in Boston-area folk clubs and on the streets in Harvard Square in Cambridge. In 1988 she cut her first album with Elektra Records and has since written and produced several albums.

Chapman's style is independent, undiluted, and uncompromising. Her songs combine narrative lyricism with a heartfelt political message delivered in a powerfully emotive voice. With songs that cry out for social change such as "Talkin' 'Bout a Revolution" and the blues lament of "Subcity," she combines 1960s political protest with the 1980s folk revival. But Chapman is quick to point out that hers is not the Anglo-American tradition most Americans think about when they think "folk music," but a combination of black and white folk traditions. Like Bruce Springsteen's "Born to Run," Chapman's "Fast Car" uses the metaphor of flight along the open road combined with images of escape from oppressive conditions and the search for the American dream.

You got a fast car
I want a ticket to anywhere
Maybe we make a deal
Maybe together we can get somewhere
Anyplace is better
Starting from zero got nothing to lose
Maybe we make something
But me myself I got nothing to prove
You got a fast car
And I got a plan to get us out of here
I been working at the convenience store
Managed to save just a little bit of money
We won't have to drive too far
Just 'cross the border and into the city
You and I can both get jobs
And finally see what it means to be living

You see my old Man's got a problem
He live with the bottle that's the way it is
He says his body's too old for working
I say his body's too young to look like his
My mamma went off and left him
She wanted more from life than he could give
I said somebody's got to take care of him
So I quit school and that's what I did
You got a fast car
But is it fast enough so we can fly away
We gotta make a decision
We leave tonight or live and die this way

I remember we were driving driving in your car
The speed so fast I felt like I was drunk
City lights lay out before us
And your arm felt nice wrapped 'round my shoulder
And I had a feeling that I belonged
And I had a feeling that I could be someone, be someone, be
    someone

You got a fast car
And we go cruising to entertain ourselves
You still ain't got a job
And I work in a market as a checkout girl
I know things will get better
You'll find work and I'll get promoted
We'll move out of the shelter
Buy a big house and live in the suburbs

You got a fast car
And I got a job that pays all our bills
You stay out drinking late at the bar
See more of your friends than you do of your kids
I'd always hoped for better
Thought maybe together you and me would find it
I got no plans I ain't going nowhere
So take your fast car and keep on driving

You got a fast car
But is it fast enough so you can fly away
You gotta make a decision
You make a decision or live and die this way

SPECULATIONS

1.   What does the "fast car" represent in this song? If taken metaphorically, how could other words, images, or ideas could take the place of the "fast car" in this song as a vehicle for change, escape, or potential self-destruction?
2.   How would you compare the message of Chapman's "Fast Car" to Bruce Springsteen's "Born to Run"? What do each of these songs say to you, and how are their messages similar or different?
3.   What is happening in the relationship between the speaker and the person addressed in this song and what are the difficulties they face? In what ways are the problems of the female protagonist in this song different from her male partner's problems? Why does the speaker say near the end "So take your fast car and keep on driving"?

ASSIGNMENT SEQUENCES

Sequence One: Music and Value

1. Write an essay in which you agree or disagree with the position put forth by Allan Bloom's "Music." Consider your own experience of music and how it corresponds to or contradicts Bloom's main points about the effects of rock music. Consider, for example, his statements that "When [young people] are in school and with their families, they are longing to plug themselves back into their music. Nothing surrounding them—school, family, church—has anything to do with their musical world. At best that ordinary life is neutral, but mostly it is an impediment, drained of vital content, even a thing to be rebelled against." What do you think? As you consider this quotation, analyze what you think Bloom considers to be the effects of rock music, how these effects differ from the effects of other forms of music, and why Bloom associates rock music with escape, rebellion against parental authority, and premature sexuality. Use specific examples of music that illustrate your views and build your own idea of music's place among young people today.

2. Assume you are a parent of a teenage daughter and a teenage son. How would you respond to Bloom's arguments? Would you find yourself in agreement with the negative effects rock music has on teenagers as described by Bloom? What effects do you believe your own teenage son and daughter would experience? Write an essay from the point of view of a parent concerned about music and your own children. Try not to create a stereotype of a parent; to prevent this, you might want to speak to some parents or read some "letters to the editor" or other statements written by parents about music and music lyrics.

3. Select a piece of music that illustrates, responds to, contradicts, or adds something new to one or more of the positions articulated in the essays in this section. Write your own essay in which you identify the message, values, and effects of the piece of music you have selected on young people today. You may consider the examples of rap music in relation to issues of freedom of expression, or the way the blues represents a specific attitude or view of life, or a song that expresses a specific political message as suggested in Jerry Adler's, Amiri Baraka's, or Ray Pratt's essays, or you may explore a song that speaks to differences between men and women as in Marion Meade's, Sheryl Garratt's, or Susan McClary's essays. Or you may choose a piece of music that represents a worthwhile perspective you think has been neglected in these essays altogether. Your job is to write an

essay that presents your chosen piece of music to your classmates as representative of some meaningful idea, value, or experience in our culture. After completing the essay, you should be prepared to play a taped selection of the music for class and to summarize orally the arguments in your paper.

4. You are Bruce Springsteen. You have recently been compared to a modern combination of Woody Guthrie and Bob Dylan. The *Los Angeles Times* Sunday music section is doing a retrospective on recent rock music and has asked you to write about what you were driving at in the lyrics for "Born to Run" (or another lyric of your own choosing). Write a short piece that explains or comments on your intentions—what you were striving to say and how well you said it.

5. Imagine that you have been selected as a student representative on the Chancellor's Committee for Improving Undergraduate Curriculum at your university. Allan Bloom has been acting as an advisor to the committee and has strongly recommended a course in the great musical culture of the West that would include many of the philosophers, operas, and musicians mentioned in his article and would, in his view, remedy the negative influence of rock music. He concludes his argument with the statement that "My concern here is not with the moral effects of rock music—whether it leads to sex, violence or drugs. The issue here is its effect on education, and I believe it ruins the imagination of young people and makes it very difficult for them to have a passionate relationship to the art and thought that are the substance of liberal education . . . . [A]s long as they have the Walkman on, they cannot hear what the great tradition has to say. And, after its prolonged use, when they take it off, they find they are deaf." Susan McClary, who wrote the essay "Living to Tell: Madonna's Resurrection of the Fleshly," is also on the committee. She responds that such a course should include a final unit on popular culture which critically examines rock music as a real and vital part of the Western cultural tradition. The chancellor responds to this debate by saying that such a course should revitalize and reinvigorate the liberal education of students, and that the committee wants to hear what students think will help most in this regard. Since you are the student member of the committee, the chancellor asks you to write a statement of several paragraphs that would examine this issue from the students' perspective and argue for specific recommendations on what should or should not be included in the new course. Your paper will be distributed to the other members of the committee, and you will be asked to speak in support of your ideas at the committee's next meeting, which is open to the public.

Sequence Two: Music and Culture

1. Judith Williamson describes the walkman as "a vivid symbol of our time." She uses a particular vocabulary to describe the opposition between the "individual" and the "communal" and the problem of modern "alienation" versus "shared experience" which she values. Write a paper which describes how her argument depends on these binary oppositions to make specific points. Consider how she weights or favors the values of "privacy" versus the values of "public space." Compare your positive or negative sense of these terms to Williamson's and explain how you agree or differ from her view that our culture is somehow threatened by the walkman.

2. Consider Jerry Adler's essay on "The Rap Attitude" and Barbara Dority's essay on the "The War on Rock and Rap Music." Adler describes how some rap lyrics express opinions that support violence, sexism, and racism while other rap lyrics are not offensive at all and even support positive anti-drug messages. Dority also suggests that rap often contains a political message from the disenfranchised, and that we should be vitally concerned about the censorship of rock and rap music. Where do you stand on these issues? What rights do artists have as far as protest and free expression, even when those expressions may be hurtful or damaging to others? Write a paper which argues your position on the freedom of musical expression versus censorship using examples from your own experience and your reading.

3. Write a music review for the student newspaper about some form of popular music, a musical event, an individual performer, or a band. The review will appear in the upcoming special issue on the value and importance of entertainment and culture for students at your university. You may choose a specific kind of music, a local band, a musician, or a nationally known group that may be playing in town. The paper's editor wants you to write about both the performance and the music itself, but she also wants you to provide some commentary on the kind of music you are reviewing, its history, its cultural contexts, and its reception by differing audiences. Also, she wants information about the musicians involved, if you can obtain it. Ideally, you should go hear a concert in person and interview the musician(s). You might also want to do library research. Write that review.

4. Dority compares rap music to opera and argues that banning song lyrics that refer to adultery, incest, illicit drug or alcohol use, murder, or suicide, would also require banning operas such as *Madame Butterfly*, *Tosca*, *Carmen*, *La Traviata*, all of which contain descriptions or

depictions of many of the same kinds of "offensive behavior." How is this comparison valid or invalid for you? How would you justify or deny different standards for rap which comes out of and speaks to a different cultural background? How can rap music be censored, if opera is not? Write a paper supporting your position with specific examples.

5.   Create an anthology of ten to fifteen of your favorite song lyrics. You can include any lyrics at all—from opera to rock opera, from blues to easy listening. Then write an introduction to your anthology in which you explain your rationale for what you included. What makes these lyrics worth reading as forms of poetry or expressions of political and cultural sentiments? Do not include any of the three lyrics in this section.

Sequence Three: Music, History, and Myth

1.   At the very beginning of his essay on "Swing—From Verb to Noun," Amiri Baraka describes the blues as an "emotional confirmation of, and reaction to, the way in which most Negroes were still forced to exist in the United States." He goes on to call the blues "a psychological correlative" that "obscured" or eclipsed the "most extreme ideas of *assimilation*," forbidding their "abandonment of black culture," which meant that "the middle-class spirit could not take root among most Negroes because they sensed the final fantasy involved." What does Baraka mean here? Why, according to him, couldn't most of these blacks assimilate into the American middle class? What does the "final fantasy involved" refer to? How does the blues come to represent the fate of these people for Baraka? How would you relate your ideas to what Baraka describes later in the essay as *attitude* or *stance* as the result of a certain kind of thinking? Write an essay which explores these issues in your own terms.

2.   To fill out your knowledge of blues and jazz history, go to the library and find books, articles, or stories on famous blues and jazz musicians. Consider such figures as Bessie Smith, Billie Holiday, Sam Price, T-Bone Walker, Jelly Roll Morton, Fats Waller, Count Basie, or perhaps some of the figures mentioned in passing in the Baraka and Bethel essays. Read about their lives and environment and listen to their music. Write an essay on the attitude, stance, or perspectives on living that seem to mark these individuals as creative artists within their own time and place.

3.   Several essays talk about musicians as legendary folk heroes and describe the myths and mythology that surround them. Ray Pratt describes Joe Hill and Woody Guthrie as historical figures that have become myths in our time. Linda Ray Pratt's "Elvis, or the Ironies of a Southern Identity" also describes Elvis in larger-than-life terms, and Susan McClary shows how Madonna makes and breaks her own interpretations of common myths. Consider what you have learned about cultural myths from these and other essays in this volume. Write an essay explaining how you see the myths described here as working or not working for you. What do you think constitutes a myth, a mythology, and mythological figure in each of these cases?

4. What contemporary musicians would you describe as having musical and political influence similar to that of Joe Hill and Woody Guthrie? Describe some ideals, beliefs, or controversies that surround today's popular singers. How do these singers generate a "culture hero" or even "anti-hero" status that may have influence in our society? What specific political, social, or moral influence do these figures have and how have you been influenced in particular?

5. Following the same line of thinking developed for the essays described above, write your own historical account of a popular musician or media personality. Describe the images, beliefs, and other factors that helped this person rise to the status of a popular or mythological figure. Draw on articles, books, reviews, and recorded or public performances to write a critical history of how this particular person emerged on the popular culture scene and became identified with certain cultural values. You might consider personalities such as Marilyn Monroe, the Beatles, Cher, Prince, Michael Jackson, or a popular figure you particularly admire or wonder about.

Sequence Four: Music and Gender

1. Marion Meade's "The Degradation of Women" is a powerful indictment of rock music's treatment of women. Since the writing of this essay in 1971, how have things changed for the better or gotten worse? Write your own essay that picks up where Meade left off, providing an account of how you think rock music has treated women in more recent years. Use specific examples to support your arguments.

2. Use your own personal experience with music to write an essay that accounts for Sheryl Garratt's descriptions of the complexities with which girls and women respond to male rock stars and female musicians. How is your experience similar to or different from Garratt's? Has rock music allowed you to engage positively in a social and imaginative life?

3. Watch one of Madonna's music videos and following Susan McClary's lead, write a description in essay form of how Madonna manipulates images, music, and cultural themes to produce certain responses that shock or anger people. Or perhaps you see her retelling an old story or myth in a new way. Be prepared to bring your video into class, show selections of it, and explain your analysis to the rest of the class.

4. You are Madonna. You have just read what Robert Palmer says about the message in rock lyrics and what Susan McClary says about your music and your importance in modern culture. At the same time you have been asked to write a piece for *Music Now*, a monthly magazine that has just begun to compete with *Rolling Stone*. You can say whatever you like about what other people have written and said about you, but you have been asked to talk specifically about the message in your song lyrics. People want to know what your real attitude is in these songs and who the real Madonna is . . . if there is one.

5. You are the poetry editor for a book entitled *The American Book of Modern Poetry*. An assistant editor has submitted three song lyrics for the book, and they are the exact ones offered here by Ochs, Springsteen, and Tracy Chapman. Your responsibility is to decide if they are poetry and worthy of inclusion in *The American Book of Modern Poetry*. Write an analysis, which must include a final judgment. You can take into account any criteria that you think are relevant such as cultural significance, poetic structure, metaphor, style, form, rhyme. In what ways are these song lyrics expressions of poetry? Show whether they retain their power and significance once they are divorced from the music.

3
CRIME AND PUNISHMENT

Almost all of us have a strong interest in crime and punishment. American movies and television abound with kind-hearted criminals, stalwart police officers struggling to maintain justice, superheroes fighting fierce villains, evil henchmen, despicable hitmen, inspirational law enforcement officers. Many people line up hours before court convenes so that they may sit in the back of the courtroom and observe the trial of a mass murderer or celebrity felon. It is as if it is possible to catch a glimpse of something forbidden or mysterious just on the other side of the glass; criminality and its attendant consequences lurk at the edges of our minds as that most unthinkable of possibilities.

This section of *Speculations*, however, moves past a prurient interest to a consideration of crime and punishment within the larger context of social, racial, and economic issues. It addresses a series of questions: What factors encourage a person to break the law? Who within our society becomes labeled a criminal? What is the relationship between law and justice? What kind of careful, inductive thought process leads a police officer through a thicket of confusing possibilities toward the actual perpetrator? What happens to convicted felons once they enter our prison system? What forms of punishment are appropriate—or inappropriate?

These questions and others are considered by writers familiar with crime and punishment. They offer a variety of perspectives which may lead to a great deal of additional reading, researching, analyzing, and speculating.

There is one master text that lies behind this entire section. It is Michel Foucault's brilliant study *Discipline and Punish*. In *Discipline and Punish*, Foucault traces the extraordinary changes that have occurred over the past three hundred years in the ways society conceives of errant behavior and appropriate punishment. For Foucault, the history of discipline and punish is a history of the distribution—and redistribution—of power in society; the ways we punish, for example, have a great deal to do with the ways we define the power of the state in relation to individual autonomy. Anyone interested in reading a challenging and disturbing inquiry into the nature of our prisons and their perverse advocacy of discipline and rehabilitation is urged to read Foucault. The section that follows, although much less theoretical than Foucault's analysis, will provide a starting point for discussions about crime and punishment in contemporary society.

The Criminal Type
JESSICA MITFORD

Jessica Mitford has dedicated much of her professional life to exposing the hypocrisy, venality, and soft underbelly of various American fads and institutions. Her targets include the funeral business (*The American Way of Death*), the American prison system (*Kind and Unusual Punishment: The Prison Business*), and a variety of other subjects including television executives, a "fat farm" for wealthy women, and the Famous Writers School. A collection of her articles can be found in *Poison Penmanship: The Gentle Art of Muckraking*, which has been celebrated as "a virtual textbook on investigative reporting."

Mitford was born in England in 1917 but has spent most of her life in the United States. Daughter of a baron and baroness, she found herself the odd woman out politically compared to her sisters. Although her sympathies leaned toward the liberal left (she ran away to Loyalist Spain during the Spanish Civil War and married a communist sympathizer who also happened to be her cousin and Winston Churchill's nephew), two of her sisters were arch-rightists, and they both were on a first-name basis with Adolph Hitler and other German and British fascists. Her first husband was killed in action during World War II; a few years later she married an American labor lawyer and moved to a racially integrated neighborhood in Oakland, California.

Mitford is best known for her witty and brilliant exposé of the practices of funeral directors, their glorification of dying, and their interest in persuading bereaved families to spend thousands of dollars on exorbitantly outfitted caskets.

Her other work, however, has also hit its target. As *Esquire* put it:

> Her legwork is tireless, her strategies simple but ingenious. . . . Behind these exposés of venal doings, we sense a woman who is jocular, common-sensical, forthright, self-reliant, amused, stout-hearted, opinionated, and utterly intoxicated with the chase.

The excerpt from *Kind and Unusual Punishment* featured here reveals that same sense of character; in it, Mitford examines the ways society perceives and misperceives criminal behavior.

Time was when most crimes were laid at the door of the Devil. The English indictment used in the last century took note of Old Nick's complicity by accusing the defendant not only of breaking the law but of "being prompted and instigated by the Devil," and the Supreme Court of North Carolina declared in 1862: "To know the right and still the wrong pursue proceeds from a perverse will brought about by the seductions of the Evil One."

With the advent of the new science of criminology toward the end of the nineteenth century, the Devil (possibly to his chagrin) was deposed as primary cause of crime by the hand of an Italian criminologist, one of the first of that calling, Cesare Lombroso. Criminals, Lombroso found, are born that way and bear physical stigmata to show it (which presumably saddles God with the responsibility, since He created them). They are "not a variation from a norm but practically a special species, a subspecies, having distinct physical and mental characteristics. In general all criminals have long, large, projecting ears, abundant hair, thin beard, prominent frontal sinuses, protruding chin, large cheekbones." Furthermore, his studies, consisting of exhaustive examination of live prisoners and the skulls of dead ones, enabled him to classify born criminals according to their offense: "Thieves have mobile hands and face; small, mobile, restless, frequently oblique eyes; thick and closely set eyebrows; flat or twisted nose; thin beard; hair frequently thin." Rapists may be distinguished by "brilliant eyes, delicate faces" and murderers by "cold, glassy eyes; nose always large and frequently aquiline; jaws strong; cheekbones large; hair curly, dark and abundant." Which caused a contemporary French savant to remark that Lombroso's portraits were very similar to the photographs of his friends.

A skeptical Englishman named Charles Goring, physician of His Majesty's Prisons, decided to check up on Lombroso's findings. Around the turn of the century he made a detailed study of the physical characteristics of 3,000 prisoners—but took the precaution of comparing these with a group of English university students, impartially applying his handy measuring tape to noses, ears, eyebrows, chins of convicts and scholars alike over a twelve-year period. His conclusion: "In the present investigation we have exhaustively compared with regard to many physical characteristics different kinds of criminals with each other and criminals as a class with the general population. From these comparisons no evidence has emerged of the existence of a physical criminal type."

As the twentieth century progressed, efforts to pinpoint the criminal type followed the gyrations of scientific fashions of the day with bewildering results. Studies published in the thirties by Gustav Aschaffenburg, a distinguished German criminologist, show that the pyknic type (which means stout, squat, with large abdomen) is more prevalent among occasional offenders, while the asthenic type (of slender build and slight muscular development) is more often found among habitual criminals. In the forties came the gland men, Professor William H. Sheldon of Harvard and his colleagues, who divided the human race into three: endomorphs, soft, round, comfort-loving people; ectomorphs, fragile fellows who complain a lot and shrink from crowds; mesomorphs, muscular types with large trunks who walk assertively, talk noisily, and behave aggressively. Watch out for those.

Yet no sooner were these elaborate findings by top people published than equally illustrious voices were heard in rebuttal. Thus Professor M. F. Ashley Montagu, a noted anthropologist: "I should venture the opinion that not one of the reports on the alleged relationship between glandular dysfunctions and criminality has been carried out in a scientific manner, and that all such reports are glaring examples of the fallacy of *false cause* . . . to resort to that system for an explanation of criminality is merely to attempt to explain the known by the unknown."

Practitioners of the emerging disciplines of psychology and psychiatry turned their attention early on to a study of the causes of criminality. Dr. Henry Goddard, Princeton psychologist, opined in 1920 that "criminals, misdemeanants, delinquents, and other antisocial groups" are in nearly all cases persons of low mentality: "It is no longer to be denied that the greatest single cause of delinquency and crime is low-grade mentality, much of it within the limits of feeblemindedness." But hard on his heels came the eminent professor Edwin H. Sutherland of Chicago, who in 1934 declared that the test results "are much more likely to reflect the methods of the testers than the intelligence of the criminals" and that "distribution of intelligence scores of delinquents is very similar to the distribution of intelligence scores of the general population. . . . Therefore, this analysis shows that the relationship between crime and feeblemindedness is, in general, comparatively slight." In *New Horizons in Criminology*, Harry E. Barnes and Negley K. Teeters go further: "Studies made by clinical psychologists of prison populations demonstrate that those behind bars compare favorably with the general population in intelligence. Since we seldom arrest and convict criminals except the poor, inept, and friendless, we can know very little of the intelligence of the bulk of the criminal world. It is quite possible that it is, by and large, superior."

Coexistent with these theories of the criminal type was one that declares the lawbreaker to be a deviant personality, mentally ill, of which more later.

It may be conjectured that prison people were not entirely pleased by the early explanations of criminality; perhaps they welcomed the rebuttals, for if the malfeasant is that way because of the shape of his ears, or because of malfunctioning glands, or because he is dimwitted—none of which he can help—why punish? In this context, George Bernard Shaw points out, "As the obvious conclusion was that criminals were not morally responsible for their actions, and therefore should not be punished for them, the prison authorities saw their occupation threatened, and denied that there was any criminal type. The criminal type was off." The perverse old soul added that he knows what the criminal type is—it is manufactured in prison by the prison system: "If you keep one [man] in penal servitude and another in the House of Lords for ten years, the one will show the stigmata of a typical convict, and the other of a typical peer." Eugene V. Debs expressed the same thought: "I have heard people refer to the 'criminal countenance.' I never saw one. Any man or woman looks like a criminal behind bars."

Skull shape, glands, IQ, and deviant personality aside, to get a more pragmatic view of the criminal type one merely has to look at the composition of the prison population. Today the prisons are filled with the young, the poor white, the black, the Chicano, the Puerto Rican. Yesterday they were filled with the young, the poor native American, the Irish or Italian immigrant.

Discussing the importance of identifying the dangerous classes of 1870, a speaker at the American Prison Congress said: "The quality of being that constitutes a criminal cannot be clearly known, until observed as belonging to the class from which criminals come. . . . A true prison system should take cognizance of criminal classes as such." His examination of 15 prison populations showed that 53,101 were born in foreign countries, 47,957 were native-born, and of these, "full 50 percent were born of foreign parents, making over 76 percent of the whole number whose tastes and habits were those of such foreigners as emigrate to this country."

At the same meeting, J. B. Bittinger of Pennsylvania described the tastes and habits of these dissolute aliens: "First comes *rum,* to keep up spirits and energy for night work; then three fourths of their salaries are spent in *theaters* and *bar-rooms* . . . many go to *low concert saloons* only to kill time . . . they play *billiards* for *drinks,* go to the *opera,* to the *theater, oyster suppers* and *worse* . . . they have their peculiar literature: dime novels, sporting papers, illustrated papers, obscene prints and photographs." Commenting on the large numbers of foreign-born in prison, he added: "The figures here are so startling in their disproportions as to foster, and apparently justify, a strong prejudice against our foreign population."

The criminal type of yesteryear was further elaborated on in 1907 by J. E. Brown, in an article entitled "The Increase of Crime in the United States": "In the poorer quarters of our great cities may be found huddled together the Italian bandit and the bloodthirsty Spaniard, the bad man from Sicily, the Hungarian, Croatian and the Pole, the Chinaman and the Negro, the Cockney Englishman, the Russian and the Jew, with all the centuries of hereditary hate back of them."

In 1970 Edward G. Banfield, chairman of President Nixon's task force on the Model Cities Program, updated these descriptions of the lower-class slum-dweller in his book *The Unheavenly City: The Nature*

and Future of the Urban Crisis, an influential book that is required reading in innumerable college courses. Since it is reportedly also recommended reading in the White House, presumably in reflects the
Administration's conception of the criminal classes as they exist today.

"A slum is not simply a district of low-quality housing," says Mr.
Banfield. "Rather it is one in which the style of life is squalid and
vicious." The lower-class individual is "incapable of conceptualizing
the future or of controlling his impulses and is therefore obliged to live
from moment to moment . . . impulse governs his behavior . . . he is
therefore radically improvident; whatever he cannot consume immediately he considers valueless. His bodily needs (especially for sex)
and his taste for 'action' take precedence over everything else—and
certainly over any work routine." Furthermore he "has a feeble, atten-
uated sense of self. . . .

"The lower-class individual lives in the slum and sees little or no
reason to complain. He does not care how dirty and dilapidated his
housing is either inside or out, nor does he mind the inadequacy of
such public facilities as schools, parks, and libraries; indeed, where
such things exist, he destroys them by acts of vandalism if he can.
Features that make the slum repellent to others actually please him."

Most studies of the causes of crime in this decade, whether contained in sociological texts, high-level governmental commission reports, or best-selling books like Ramsey Clark's *Crime in America,*
lament the disproportionately high arrest rate for blacks and poor
people and assert with wearying monotony that criminality is a product of slums and poverty. Mr. Clark invites the reader to mark on his
city map the areas where health and education are poorest, where
unemployment and poverty are highest, where blacks are concentrated—and he will find these areas also have the highest crime rate.

Hence the myth that the poor, the young, the black, the Chicano
are indeed the criminal type of today is perpetuated, whereas in fact
crimes are committed, although not necessarily punished, at all levels
of society.

There is evidence that a high proportion of people in all walks of
life have at some time or other committed what are conventionally
called "serious crimes." A study of 1,700 New Yorkers weighted toward the upper income brackets, who had never been arrested for
anything, and who were guaranteed anonymity, revealed that 91 percent had committed at least one felony or serious misdemeanor. The
mean number of offenses per person was 18. Sixty-four percent of the
men and 27 percent of the women had committed at least one felony,
for which they could have been sent to the state penitentiary. Thirteen
percent of the men admitted to grand larceny, 26 percent to stealing
cars, and 17 percent to burglary.

If crimes are committed by people of all classes, why the near-universal equation of criminal type and slum-dweller, why the vastly unequal representation of poor, black, brown in the nation's jails and prisons? When the "Italian bandit, bloodthirsty Spaniard, bad man from Sicily," and the rest of them climbed their way out of the slums and moved to the suburbs, they ceased to figure as an important factor in crime statistics. Yet as succeeding waves of immigrants, and later blacks, moved into the same slum area the rates of reported crime and delinquency remained high there.

No doubt despair and terrible conditions in the slums give rise to one sort of crime, the only kind available to the very poor: theft, robbery, purse-snatching; whereas crimes committed by the former slum-dweller have moved up the scale with his standard of living to those less likely to be detected and punished: embezzlement, sale of fraudulent stock, price-fixing. After all, the bank president is not likely to become a bank robber; nor does the bank robber have the opportunity to embezzle depositors' funds.

Professor Theodore Sarbin suggests the further explanation that police are conditioned to perceive some classes of persons (formerly immigrants, now blacks and browns) as being actually or potentially "dangerous," and go about their work accordingly: "The belief that some classes of persons were 'dangerous' guided the search for suspects. . . . Laws are broken by many citizens for many reasons: those suspects who fit the concurrent social type of the criminal are most likely to become objects of police suspicion and of judicial decision-making." The President's Crime Commission comments on the same phenomenon: "A policeman in attempting to solve crimes must employ, in the absence of concrete evidence, circumstantial indicators to link specific crimes with specific people. Thus policemen may stop Negro and Mexican youths in white neighborhoods, may suspect juveniles who act in what the policemen consider an impudent or overly casual manner, and may be influenced by such factors as unusual hair styles or clothes uncommon to the wearer's group or area . . . those who act frightened, penitent, and respectful are more likely to be released, while those who assert their autonomy and act indifferent or resistant run a substantially greater risk of being frisked, interrogated, or even taken into custody."

An experiment conducted in the fall of 1970 by a sociology class at the University of California at Los Angeles bears out these observations. The class undertook to study the differential application of police definitions of criminality by varying one aspect of the "identity" of the prospective criminal subject. They selected a dozen students, black, Chicano, and white, who had blameless driving records free of any moving violations, and asked them to drive to and from school as they normally did, with the addition of a "circumstantial indicator" in the shape of a phosphorescent bumper sticker reading "Black Panther Party." In the first 17 days of the study these students amassed 30 driving citations—failure to signal, improper lane changes, and the like. Two students had to withdraw from the experiment after two days because their licenses were suspended; and the project soon had to be abandoned because the $1,000 appropriation for the experiment had been used up in paying bails and fines of the participants.

The President's Crime Commission Report notes that "the criminal justice process may be viewed as a large-scale screening system. At each stage it tries to sort out the better risks to return to the general population," but the report does not elaborate on *how* these better risks are sorted. Professor Sarbin suggests an answer: "To put the conclusion bluntly, membership in the class 'lawbreakers' is *not* distributed according to economic or social status, but membership in the class 'criminals' *is* distributed according to social or economic status. . . . To account for the disproportionate number of lower class and black prisoners, I propose that the agents of law enforcement and justice engage in decision-making against a backcloth of belief that people can be readily classified into two types, criminal and noncriminal."

This point is underlined by Professor Donald Taft: "Negroes are more likely to be suspected of crime than are whites. They are also more likely to be arrested. If the perpetrator of a crime is known to be a Negro the police may arrest all Negroes who were near the scene—a procedure they would rarely dare to follow with whites. After arrest, Negroes are less likely to secure bail, and so are more liable to be counted in jail statistics. They are more liable than whites to be indicted and less likely to have their cases *nol prossed* or otherwise dismissed. If tried, Negroes are more likely to be convicted. If convicted, they are less likely to be given probation. For this reason they are more likely to be included in the count of prisoners. Negroes are also more liable than whites to be kept in prison for the full terms of their commitments and correspondingly less likely to be paroled."

As anyone versed in the ways of the criminal justice system will tell you, the screening process begins with the policeman on the beat: the young car thief from a "nice home" will be returned to his family with a warning. If he repeats the offense or gets into more serious trouble, the parents may be called in for a conference with the prosecuting authorities. The well-to-do family has a dozen options: they can send their young delinquent to a boarding school, or to stay with relatives in another part of the country, they can hire the professional services of a psychiatrist or counselor—and the authorities will support them in these efforts. The Juvenile Court judge can see at a glance that this boy does not belong in the toils of the criminal justice system, that given a little tolerance and helpful guidance there is every chance he will straighten out by the time he reaches college age.

For the identical crime the ghetto boy will be arrested, imprisoned in the juvenile detention home, and set on the downward path that ends in the penitentiary. The screening process does not end with arrest, it obtains at every stage of the criminal justice system.

To cite one example that any observer of the crime scene—and particularly the black observer—will doubtless be able to match from his own experience: a few years ago a local newspaper reported horrendous goings-on of high school seniors in Piedmont, a wealthy enclave in Alameda County, California, populated by executives, businessmen, rich politicians. The students had gone on a general rampage that included arson, vandalism, breaking and entering, assault, car theft, rape. Following a conference among parents, their lawyers, and prosecuting authorities, it was decided that no formal action should be taken against the miscreants; they were all released to the custody of their families, who promised to subject them to appropriate discipline. In the very same week, a lawyer of my acquaintance told me with tight-lipped fury of the case of a nine-year-old black ghetto dweller in the same county, arrested for stealing a nickel from a white classmate, charged with "extortion and robbery," hauled off to juvenile hall, and, despite the urgent pleas of his distraught mother, there imprisoned for six weeks to wait for his court hearing.

Thus it seems safe to assert that there is indeed a criminal type—but he is not a biological, anatomical, phrenological, or anthropological type; rather, he is a social creation, etched by the dominant class and ethnic prejudices of a given society.

The day may not be far off when the horny-handed policeman on the beat may expect an assist in criminal-type-spotting from practitioners of a new witchcraft: behavior prediction. In 1970, Dr. Arnold Hutschnecker, President Nixon's physician, proposed mass psychological testing of six- to eight-year-old children to determine which were criminally inclined, and the establishment of special camps to house those found to have "violent tendencies." Just where the candidates for the mass testing and the special camps would be sought out was made clear when Dr. Hutschnecker let slip the fact he was proposing this program as an alternative to slum reconstruction. It would be, he said, "a direct, immediate, effective way of attacking the problem at its very origin, by focusing on the criminal mind of the child."

The behavior-predictors would catch the violence-prone *before* he springs, would confine him, possibly treat him, but in any event would certainly not let him out to consummate the hideous deeds of which he is so demonstrably capable. Their recurring refrain: "If only the clearly discernible defects in Oswald's psychological makeup had been detected in his childhood—had he been turned over to us, who have the resources to diagnose such deviant personalities—we would have tried to help him. If we decided he was beyond help, we would have locked him up forever and a major tragedy of this generation could have been averted." They refer, of course, to Lee Harvey Oswald, who allegedly gunned down President Kennedy, not to Russell G. Oswald, the New York Commissioner of Corrections who ordered the troops into Attica, as a result of which 43 perished by gunfire.

SPECULATIONS

1. Early in this chapter, Jessica Mitford summarizes Cesare Lombroso's study of the physical characteristics of various kinds of criminals. Although she dismisses his findings, do you find Lombroso's conclusions persuasive? Do you believe in a "criminal type"? If so, how would you describe the criminal?

2. Mitford's view is that:

> Today the prisons are filled with the young, the poor white, the black, the Chicano, the Puerto Rican. Yesterday they were filled with the young, the poor native American, the Irish or Italian immigrant.

Compare the prison population with society's attitudes toward various socio-economic and ethnic populations.

3. In the opening section of this chapter, Mitford follows a particular rhetorical pattern. How would you describe it? Do you find it effective as a way of presenting the various controversies that have swirled around "the criminal type" during the past several centuries?

4. Have you ever been surprised that someone you thought was a sincere and honest person turned out to be a liar, cheat, or criminal? Conversely, did you view someone as a criminal type who turned out to be a decent, helpful, ethical person? What led you to those false impressions? Would you respond differently now that you are older and wiser? How much difference did certain factors make, such as setting, appearance, clothing, your own fears, the person's demeanor?

5. Mitford wrote *Kind and Unusual Punishment* in the early 1970s. Do you think her analysis of "the criminal type" is dated and invalid? Have the past twenty years seen progress in the ways that the police and society view the criminal? Is her account of class and criminality still relevant?

6. Mitford's tone in this chapter strongly suggests her own attitude toward the various positions that experts hold in regard to criminals and criminality. Describe that tone in relation to: Lombroso, Aschaffenburg, Sheldon, Montagu, and Goddard. What specific words and phrases reveal Mitford's attitude toward the experts she is citing?

Letter from Birmingham Jail

MARTIN LUTHER KING, JR.

Martin Luther King, Jr., winner of the Nobel Peace Prize and a major contributor to the cause of civil rights, race relations, and social justice in this century, was one of the finest orators this country has ever known. King was for many years the conscience of racist America, the president of the Southern Christian Leadership Conference from its inception in 1957 until his death by assassination in 1968.

Born into the black middle class in Atlanta in 1929, King was the son of a minister and a schoolteacher. Although he lived a fairly comfortable life, he suffered many of the same racist indignities as poorer blacks, something that caused him great anger and grief. According to Stephen Oates, King

> had to attend separate, inferior schools, which he sailed through with a modicum of effort, skipping grades as he went. He found out that he—a preacher's boy—could not sit at lunch counters in Atlanta's downtown stores. He had to drink from a "colored" water fountain, relieve himself in a rancid "colored" restroom, and ride a rickety "colored" elevator. If he rode a city bus, he had to sit in the back as though he were contaminated. If he wanted to see a movie in a downtown theater, he had to enter through a side door and sit in the "colored section in the balcony." He discovered that whites referred to blacks as "boys" and "girls" regardless of age . . . and that he resided in "nigger town."

For King, as for virtually all black Americans, there were two worlds—one desirable and white, the other undesirable and black.

King excelled in school and college, earning a B.A. from Morehouse College. He was one of six black students at Crozer Theological Seminar in Pennsylvania where he was awarded a divinity degree. In 1955 he received a PhD. in theology from Boston University, the same year that Rosa Parks refused to give up her seat to a white person on a public bus in Montgomery, Alabama. King returned to the South and ultimately succeeded both his grandfather and his father as pastor of the Ebenezer Baptist Church in Atlanta. But his most significant contribution was dedicated and fearless leadership of the civil rights movement with persistent emphasis on nonviolent civil disobedience. King was reviled in the press, considered a national menace by the FBI, beaten, threatened, imprisoned, and ultimately murdered.

The "Letter from Birmingham Jail" emerged from King's organization of a mass protest on behalf of fair hiring practices in Birmingham, Alabama. Defying a court order barring massive public demonstrations, King was arrested in April, 1963 and jailed. During his confinement, he wrote the now famous Letter which is addressed to the white religious leaders of Birmingham—Catholic, Protestant, and Jewish—who faulted him for his "unwise and untimely" protest.

For more information on the Birmingham boycott, see King's book about the civil rights movement, *Why We Can't Wait* (1964), or consult the excellent biography by Lerone Bennett, Jr. (see his essay in Chapter 1, "Growing Up,"), *What Manner of Man* (1964). Additional reading is helpful, particularly to understand the eloquence, vision, and rhetorical power of King's language which characterize the "Letter."

My Dear Fellow Clergymen:

While confined here in the Birmingham city jail, I came across your recent statement calling my present activities "unwise and untimely." Seldom do I pause to answer criticism of my work and ideas. If I sought to answer all the criticisms that cross my desk, my secretaries would have little time for anything other than such correspondence in the course of the day, and I would have no time for constructive work. But since I feel that you are men of genuine good will and that your criticisms are sincerely set forth, I want to try to answer your statement in what I hope will be patient and reasonable terms.

I think I should indicate why I am here in Birmingham, since you have been influenced by the view which argues against "outsiders coming in." I have the honor of serving as president of the Southern Christian Leadership Conference, an organization operating in every southern state, with headquarters in Atlanta, Georgia. We have some eighty-five affiliated organizations across the South, and one of them is the Alabama Christian Movement for Human Rights. Frequently we share staff, educational, and financial resources with our affiliates. Several months ago the affiliate here in Birmingham asked us to be on call to engage in a nonviolent direct-action program if such were deemed necessary. We readily consented, and when the hour came, we lived up to our promise. So I, along with several members of my staff, am here because I was invited here. I am here because I have organizational ties here.

But more basically, I am in Birmingham because injustice is here. Just as the prophets of the eighth century B.C. left their villages and carried their "thus saith the Lord" far beyond the boundaries of their home towns, and just as the Apostle Paul left his village of Tarsus and carried the gospel of Jesus Christ to the far corners of the Greco-Roman world, so am I compelled to carry the gospel of freedom beyond my own home town. Like Paul, I must constantly respond to the Macedonian call for aid.

Moreover, I am cognizant of the interrelatedness of all communities and states. I cannot sit idly by in Atlanta and not be concerned about what happens in Birmingham. Injustice anywhere is a threat to justice everywhere. We are caught in an inescapable network of mutuality, tied in a single garment of destiny. Whatever affects one directly, affects all indirectly. Never again can we afford to live with the narrow, provincial "outside agitator" idea. Anyone who lives inside the United States can never be considered an outsider anywhere within its bounds.

You deplore the demonstrations taking place in Birmingham. But your statement, I am sorry to say, fails to express a similar concern for the conditions that brought about the demonstrations. I am sure that none of you would want to rest content with the superficial kind of social analysis that deals merely with effects and does not grapple with underlying causes. It is unfortunate that demonstrations are taking place in Birmingham, but it is even more unfortunate that the city's white power structure left the Negro community with no alternative.

In any nonviolent campaign there are four basic steps: collection of the facts to determine whether injustices exist; negotiation; self-purification; and direct action. We have gone through all these steps in Birmingham. There can be no gainsaying the fact that racial injustice engulfs this community. Birmingham is probably the most thoroughly segregated city in the United States. Its ugly record of brutality is widely known. Negroes have experienced grossly unjust treatment in the courts. There have been more unsolved bombings of Negro homes and churches in Birmingham than in any other city in the nation. These are the hard, brutal facts of the case. On the basis of these conditions, Negro leaders sought to negotiate with the city fathers. But the latter consistently refused to engage in good-faith negotiation.

Then, last September, came the opportunity to talk with leaders of Birmingham's economic community. In the course of the negotiations, certain promises were made by the merchants—for example, to remove the stores' humiliating racial signs. On the basis of these promises, the Reverend Fred Shuttlesworth and the leaders of the Alabama Christian Movement for Human Rights agreed to a moratorium on all demonstrations. As the weeks and months went by, we realized that we were the victims of a broken promise. A few signs, briefly removed, returned; the others remained.

As in so many past experiences, our hopes had been blasted, and the shadow of deep disappointment settled upon us. We had no alternative except to prepare for direct action, whereby we would present our very bodies as a means of laying our case before the conscience of the local and the national community. Mindful of the difficulties involved, we decided to undertake a process of self-purification. We began a series of workshops on nonviolence, and we repeatedly asked ourselves: "Are you able to accept blows without retaliating?" "Are you able to endure the ordeal of jail?" We decided to schedule our direct-action program for the Easter season, realizing that except for Christmas, this is the main shopping period of the year. Knowing that a strong economic-withdrawal program would be the by-product of direct action, we felt that this would be the best time to bring pressure to bear on the merchants for the needed change.

Then it occurred to us that Birmingham's mayoral election was coming up in March, and we speedily decided to postpone action until after election day. When we discovered that the Commissioner of Public Safety, Eugene "Bull" Connor, had piled up enough votes to be in the run-off, we decided again to postpone action until the day after the run-off so that the demonstrations could not be used to cloud the issues. Like many others, we wanted to see Mr. Connor defeated, and to this end we endured postponement after postponement. Having aided in this community need, we felt that our direct-action program could be delayed no longer.

You may well ask, "Why direct action? Why sit-ins, marches, and so forth? Isn't negotiation a better path?" You are quite right in calling for negotiation. Indeed, this is the very purpose of direct action. Nonviolent direct action seeks to create such a crisis and foster such a tension that a community which has constantly refused to negotiate is forced to confront the issue. It seeks so to dramatize the issue that it can no longer be ignored. My citing the creation of tension as part of the work of the nonviolent-resister may sound rather shocking. But I must confess that I am not afraid of the word "tension." I have earnestly opposed violent tension, but there is a type of constructive, nonviolent tension which is necessary for growth. Just as Socrates felt that it was necessary to create a tension in the mind so that individuals could rise from the bondage of myths and half-truths to the unfettered realm of creative analysis and objective appraisal, so must we see the need for nonviolent gadflies to create the kind of tension in society that will help men rise from the dark depths of prejudice and racism to the majestic heights of understanding and brotherhood.

The purpose of our direct-action program is to create a situation so crisis-packed that it will inevitably open the door to negotiation. I therefore concur with you in your call for negotiation. Too long has our beloved Southland been bogged down in a tragic effort to live in monologue rather than dialogue.

One of the basic points in your statement is that the action that I and my associates have taken in Birmingham is untimely. Some have asked: "Why didn't you give the new city administration time to act?" The only answer that I can give to this query is that the new Birmingham administration must be prodded about as much as the outgoing one, before it will act. We are sadly mistaken if we feel that the election of Albert Boutwell as mayor will bring the millennium to Birmingham. While Mr. Boutwell is a much more gentle person than Mr. Connor, they are both segregationists, dedicated to maintenance of the status quo. I have hoped that Mr. Boutwell will be reasonable enough to see the futility of massive resistance to desegregation. But he will not see this without pressure from devotees of civil rights. My friends, I must say to you that we have not made a single gain in civil rights without determined legal and nonviolent pressure. Lamentably, it is an historical fact that privileged groups seldom give up their privileges voluntarily. Individuals may see the moral light and voluntarily give up their unjust posture; but, as Reinhold Niebuhr has reminded us, groups tend to be more immoral than individuals.

We know through painful experience that freedom is never voluntarily given by the oppressor; it must be demanded by the oppressed. Frankly, I have yet to engage in a direct-action campaign that was "well timed" in the view of those who have not suffered unduly from the disease of segregation. For years now I have heard the word "Wait!" It rings in the ear of every Negro with piercing familiarity. This "Wait" has almost always meant "Never." We must come to see, with one of our distinguished jurists, that "justice too long delayed is justice denied."

We have waited for more than 340 years for our constitutional and God-given rights. The nations of Asia and Africa are moving with jetlike speed toward gaining political independence, but we still creep at horse-and-buggy pace toward gaining a cup of coffee at a lunch counter. Perhaps it is easy for those who have never felt the stinging darts of segregation to say, "Wait." But when you have seen vicious mobs lynch your mothers and fathers at will and drown your sisters and brothers at whim; when you have seen hate-filled policemen curse, kick, and even kill your black brothers and sisters; when you see the vast majority of your twenty million Negro brothers smothering in an airtight cage of poverty in the midst of an affluent society; when you suddenly find your tongue twisted and your speech stammering as you seek to explain to your six-year-old daughter why she can't go to the public amusement park that has just been advertised on television, and see tears welling up in her eyes when she is told that Funtown is closed to colored children, and see ominous clouds of inferiority beginning to form in her little mental sky, and see her beginning to distort her personality by developing an unconscious bitterness toward white people; when you have to concoct an answer for a five-year-old son who is asking "Daddy, why do white people treat colored people so mean?"; when you take a cross-country drive and find it necessary to sleep night after night in the uncomfortable corners of your automobile because no motel will accept you; when you are humiliated day in and day out by nagging signs reading "white" and "colored"; when your first name becomes "nigger," your middle name becomes "boy" (however old you are) and your last name becomes "John," and your wife and mother are never given the respected title "Mrs."; when you are harried by day and haunted by night by the fact that you are a Negro, living constantly at tiptoe stance, never quite knowing what to expect next, and are plagued with inner fears and outer resentments; when you are forever fighting a degenerating sense of "nobodiness"—then you will understand why we find it difficult to wait. There comes a time when the cup of endurance runs over, and men are no longer willing to be plunged into the abyss of despair. I hope, sirs, you can understand our legitimate and unavoidable impatience.

You express a great deal of anxiety over our willingness to break laws. This is certainly a legitimate concern. Since we so diligently urge people to obey the Supreme Court's decision of 1954 outlawing segregation in the public schools, at first glance it may seem rather paradoxical for us consciously to break laws. One may well ask: "How can you advocate breaking some laws and obeying others?" The answer lies in the fact that here are two types of laws: just and unjust. I would be the first to advocate obeying just laws. One has not only a legal but a moral responsibility to obey just laws. Conversely, one has a moral responsibility to disobey unjust laws. I would agree with St. Augustine that "an unjust law is no law at all."

Now, what is the difference between the two? How does one determine whether a law is just or unjust? A just law is a man-made code that squares with the moral law or the law of God. An unjust law is a code that is out of harmony with the moral law. To put it in the terms of St. Thomas Aquinas: An unjust law is a human law that is not rooted in eternal law and natural law. Any law that uplifts human personality is just. Any law that degrades human personality is unjust. All segregation statutes are unjust because segregation distorts the soul and damages the personality. It gives the segregator a false sense of superiority and the segregated a false sense of inferiority. Segregation, to use the terminology of the Jewish philosopher Martin Buber, substitutes "I–it" relationship for an "I–thou" relationship and ends up relegating persons to the status of things. Hence segregation is not only politically, economically, and sociologically unsound, it is morally wrong and sinful. Paul Tillich has said that sin is separation. Is not segregation an existential expression of man's tragic separation, his awful estrangement, his terrible sinfulness? Thus it is that I can urge men to obey the 1954 decision of the Supreme Court, for it is morally right; and I can urge them to disobey segregation ordinances, for they are morally wrong.

Let us consider a more concrete example of just and unjust laws. An unjust law is a code that a numerical or power majority group compels a minority group to obey but does not make binding on itself.

This is *difference* made legal. By the same token, a just law is a code that a majority compels a minority to follow and that it is willing to follow itself. This is *sameness* made legal.

Let me give another explanation. A law is unjust if it is inflicted on a minority that, as a result of being denied the right to vote, had no part in enacting or devising the law. Who can say that the legislature of Alabama which set up that state's segregation laws was democratically elected? Throughout Alabama all sorts of devious methods are used to prevent Negroes from becoming registered voters, and there are some counties in which, even though Negroes constitute a majority of the population, not a single Negro is registered. Can any law enacted under such circumstances be considered democratically structured?

Sometimes a law is just on its face and unjust in its application. For instance, I have been arrested on a charge of parading without a permit. Now, there is nothing wrong in having an ordinance which requires a permit for a parade. But such an ordinance becomes unjust when it is used to maintain segregation and to deny citizens the First-Amendment privilege of peaceful assembly and protest.

I hope you are able to see the distinction I am trying to point out. In no sense do I advocate evading or defying the law, as would the rabid segregationist. That would lead to anarchy. One who breaks an unjust law must do so openly, lovingly, and with a willingness to accept the penalty. I submit that an individual who breaks a law that conscience tells him is unjust, and who willingly accepts the penalty of imprisonment in order to arouse the conscience of the community over its injustice, is in reality expressing the highest respect for law.

Of course, there is nothing new about this kind of civil disobedience. It was evidenced sublimely in the refusal of Shadrach, Meshach, and Abednego to obey the laws of Nebuchadnezzar, on the ground that a higher moral law was at stake. It was practiced superbly by the early Christians, who were willing to face hungry lions and the excruciating pain of chopping blocks rather than submit to certain unjust laws of the Roman Empire. To a degree, academic freedom is a reality today because Socrates practiced civil disobedience. In our own nation, the Boston Tea Party represented a massive act of civil disobedience.

We should never forget that everything Adolf Hitler did in Germany was "legal" and everything the Hungarian freedom fighters did in Hungary was "illegal." It was "illegal" to aid and comfort a Jew in Hitler's Germany. Even so, I am sure that, had I lived in Germany at the time, I would have aided and comforted my Jewish brothers. If today I lived in a Communist country where certain principles dear

to the Christian faith are suppressed, I would openly advocate diso-
beying that country's anti-religious laws.

I must make two honest confessions to you, my Christian and
Jewish brothers. First, I must confess that over the past few years I
have been gravely disappointed with the white moderate. I have almost reached the regrettable conclusion that the Negro's great stum-
bling block in his stride toward freedom is not the White Citizen's
Counciler or the Ku Klux Klanner, but the white moderate, who is
more devoted to "order" than to justice; who prefers a negative peace
which is the absence of tension to a positive peace which is the presence of justice; who constantly says, "I agree with you in the goal you
seek, but I cannot agree with your methods of direct action"; who
paternalistically believes he can set the timetable for another man's
freedom; who lives by a mythical concept of time and who constantly
advises the Negro to wait for a "more convenient season." Shallow
understanding from people of good will is more frustrating than absolute misunderstanding from people of ill will. Lukewarm acceptance
is much more bewildering than outright rejection.

I had hoped that the white moderate would understand that law
and order exist for the purpose of establishing justice and that when
they fail in this purpose they become the dangerously structured dams
that block the flow of social progress. I had hoped that the white
moderate would understand that the present tension in the South is
a necessary phase of the transition from an obnoxious negative peace,
in which the Negro passively accepted his unjust plight, to a substantive and positive peace, in which all men will respect the dignity and
worth of human personality. Actually, we who engage in nonviolent
direct action are not the creators of tension. We merely bring to the
surface the hidden tension that is already alive. We bring it out in the
open, where it can be seen and dealt with. Like a boil that can never
be cured so long as it is covered up but must be opened with all its
ugliness to the natural medicines of air and light, injustice must be
exposed, with all the tension its exposure creates, to the light of
human conscience and the air of national opinion, before it can be
cured.

In your statement you assert that our actions, even though peaceful, must be condemned because they precipitate violence. But is this
a logical assertion? Isn't this like condemning a robbed man because
his possession of money precipitated the evil act of robbery? Isn't
this like condemning Socrates because his unswerving commitment
to truth and his philosophical inquiries precipitated the act by the
misguided populace in which they made him drink hemlock? Isn't
this like condemning Jesus because his unique God-consciousness
and never-ceasing devotion to God's will precipitated the evil act of

crucifixion? We must come to see that, as the federal courts have consistently affirmed, it is wrong to urge an individual to cease his efforts to gain his basic constitutional rights because the quest may precipitate violence. Society must protect the robbed and punish the robber.

I had also hoped that the white moderate would reject the myth concerning time in relation to the struggle for freedom. I have just received a letter from a white brother in Texas. He writes: "All Christians know that the colored people will receive equal rights eventually, but it is possible that you are in too great a religious hurry. It has taken Christianity almost two thousand years to accomplish what it has. The teachings of Christ take time to come to earth." Such an attitude stems from a tragic misconception of time, from the strangely irrational notion that there is something in the very flow of time that will inevitably cure all ills. Actually, time itself is neutral; it can be used either destructively or constructively. More and more I feel that the people of ill will have used time much more effectively than have the people of good will. We will have to repent in this generation not merely for the hateful words and actions of the bad people, but for the appalling silence of the good people. Human progress never rolls in on wheels of inevitability; it comes through the tireless efforts of men willing to be co-workers with God, and without this hard work, time itself becomes an ally of the forces of social stagnation. We must use time creatively, in the knowledge that the time is always ripe to do right. Now is the time to make real the promise of democracy and transform our pending national elegy into a creative psalm of brotherhood. Now is the time to lift our national policy from the quicksand of racial injustice to the solid rock of human dignity.

You speak of our activity in Birmingham as extreme. At first I was rather disappointed that fellow clergymen would see my nonviolent efforts as those of an extremist. I began thinking about the fact that I stand in the middle of two opposing forces in the Negro community. One is a force of complacency, made up in part of Negroes who, as a result of long years of oppression, are so drained of self-respect and a sense of "somebodiness" that they have adjusted to segregation; and in part of a few middle-class Negroes who, because of a degree of academic and economic security and because in some ways they profit by segregation, have become insensitive to the problems of the masses. The other force is one of bitterness and hatred, and it comes perilously close to advocating violence. It is expressed in the various black nationalist groups that are springing up across the nation, the largest and best-known being Elijah Muhammad's Muslim movement. Nourished by the Negro's frustration over the continued existence of racial discrimination, this movement is made up of people who have lost faith in America, who have absolutely repudiated Christianity, and who have concluded that the white man is an incorrigible "devil."

I have tried to stand between these two forces, saying that we need emulate neither the "do-nothingism" of the complacent nor the hated and despair of the black nationalist. For there is the more excellent way of love and nonviolent protest. I am grateful to God that, through the influence of the Negro church, the way of nonviolence became an integral part of our struggle.

If this philosophy had not emerged, by now many streets of the South would, I am convinced, be flowing with blood. And I am further convinced that if our white brothers dismiss as "rabblerousers" and "outside agitators" those of us who employ nonviolent direct action, and if they refuse to support our nonviolent efforts, millions of Negroes will, out of frustration and despair, seek solace and security in Black-nationalist ideologies—a development that would inevitably lead to a frightening racial nightmare.

Oppressed people cannot remain oppressed forever. The yearning for freedom eventually manifests itself, and that is what has happened to the American Negro. Something within has reminded him of his birthright of freedom, and something without has reminded him that it can be gained. Consciously or unconsciously, he has been caught up by the *Zeitgeist*, and with his black brothers of Africa and his brown and yellow brothers of Asia, South America, and the Caribbean, the United States Negro is moving with a sense of great urgency toward the promised land of racial justice. If one recognizes this vital urge that has engulfed the Negro community, one should readily understand why public demonstrations are taking place. The Negro has many pent-up resentments and latent frustrations, and he must release them. So let him march; let him make prayer pilgrimages to the city hall; let him go on freedom rides—and try to understand why he must do so. If his repressed emotions are not released in nonviolent ways, they will seek expression through violence; this is not a threat but a fact of history. So I have not said to my people, "Get rid of your discontent." Rather, I have tried to say that this normal and healthy discontent can be channeled into the creative outlet of nonviolent direct action. And now this approach is being termed extremist.

But though I was initially disappointed at being categorized as an extremist, as I continued to think about the matter I gradually gained a measure of satisfaction from the label. Was not Jesus an extremist for love: "Love your enemies, bless them that curse you, do good to them that hate you, and pray for them which despitefully use you, and persecute you." Was not Amos an extremist for justice: "Let justice roll down like waters and righteousness like an everflowing stream." Was not Paul an extremist for the Christian gospel: "I bear in my body the marks of the Lord Jesus." Was not Martin Luther an extremist: "Here I stand; I cannot do otherwise, so help me God." And John Bunyan: "I will stay in jail to the end of my days before I make a butchery of my conscience." And Abraham Lincoln: "This nation cannot survive half slave and half free." And Thomas Jefferson: "We hold these truths to be self-evident, that all men are created equal. . . ." So the question is not whether we will be extremists, but what kind of extremists we will be. Will we be extremists for hate or for love? Will we be extremists for the preservation of injustice or for the extension of justice? In that dramatic scene on Calvary's hill three men were crucified. We must never forget that all three were crucified for the same crime—the crime of extremism. Two were extremists for immorality, and thus fell below their environment. The other, Jesus Christ, was an extremist for love, truth, and goodness, and thereby rose above his environment. Perhaps the South, the nation, and the world are in dire need of creative extremists.

I had hoped that the white moderate would see this need. Perhaps I was too optimistic; perhaps I expected too much. I suppose I should have realized that few members of the oppressor race can understand the deep groans and passionate yearnings of the oppressed race, and still fewer have the vision to see that injustice must be rooted out by strong, persistent, and determined action. I am thankful, however, that some of our white brothers in the South have grasped the meaning of this social revolution and committed themselves to it. They are still all too few in quantity, but they are big in quality. Some—such as Ralph McGill, Lillian Smith, Harry Golden, James McBridge Dabbs, Anne Braden, and Sarah Patton Boyle—have written about our struggle in eloquent and prophetic terms. Others have marched with us down nameless streets of the South. They have languished in filthy, roach-infested jails, suffering the abuse and brutality of policemen who view them as "dirty nigger-lovers." Unlike so many of their moderate brothers and sisters, they have recognized the urgency of the moment and sensed the need for powerful "action" antidotes to combat the disease of segregation.

Let me take note of my other major disappointment. I have been so greatly disappointed with the white church and its leadership. Of course, there are some notable exceptions. I am not unmindful of the fact that each of you has taken some significant stands on this issue. I commend you, Reverend Stallings, for your Christian stand on this past Sunday, in welcoming Negroes to your worship service on a nonsegregated basis. I commend the Catholic leaders of this state for integrating Spring Hill College several years ago.

But despite these notable exceptions, I must honestly reiterate that I have been disappointed with the church. I do not say this as one of those negative critics who can always find something wrong with the church. I say this as a minister of the gospel, who loves the church; who was nurtured in its bosom; who has been sustained by its spiritual blessings and who will remain true to it as long as the cord of life shall lengthen.

When I was suddenly catapulted into the leadership of the bus protest in Montgomery, Alabama, a few years ago, I felt we would be supported by the white church. I felt that the white ministers, priests, and rabbis of the South would be among our strongest allies. Instead, some have been outright opponents, refusing to understand the freedom movement and misrepresenting its leaders; all too many others have been more cautious than courageous and have remained silent behind the anesthetizing security of stained glass windows.

In spite of my shattered dreams, I came to Birmingham with the hope that the white religious leadership of this community would see the justice of our cause and, with deep moral concern, would serve as the channel through which our just grievances could reach the power structure. I had hoped that each of you would understand. But again I have been disappointed.

I have heard numerous southern religious leaders admonish their worshipers to comply with a desegregation decision because it is the law, but I have longed to hear white ministers declare: "Follow this decree because integration is morally right and because the Negro is your brother." In the midst of blatant injustices inflicted upon the Negro, I have watched white churchmen stand on the sideline and mouth pious irrelevancies and sanctimonious trivialities. In the midst of a mighty struggle to rid our nation of racial and economic injustice I have heard many ministers say: "Those are social issues, with which the gospel has no real concern." And I have watched many churches commit themselves to a completely otherworldly religion which makes a strange, un-Biblical distinction between body and soul, between the sacred and the secular.

I have traveled the length and breadth of Alabama, Mississippi, and all the other southern states. On sweltering summer days and crisp autumn mornings I have looked at the South's beautiful churches with their lofty spires pointing heavenward. I have beheld the impressive outlines of her massive religious-education buildings. Over and over I have found myself asking: "What kind of people worship here? Who is their God? Where were their voices when the lips of Governor Barnett dripped with words of interposition and nullification? Where were they when Governor Wallace gave a clarion call for defiance and hatred? Where were their voices of support when bruised and weary

Negro men and women decided to rise from the dark dungeons of complacency to the bright hills of creative protest?"

Yes, these questions are still in my mind. In deep disappointment I have wept over the laxity of the church. But be assured that my tears have been tears of love. There can be no deep disappointment where there is not deep love. Yes, I love the church. How could I do otherwise? I am in the rather unique position of being the son, the grandson, and the great-grandson of preachers. Yes, I see the church as the body of Christ. But, oh! How we have blemished and scarred that body through social neglect and through fear of being nonconformists.

There was a time when the church was very powerful—in the time when the early Christians rejoiced at being deemed worthy to suffer for what they believed. In those days the church was not merely a thermometer that recorded the ideas and principles of popular opinion; it was a thermostat that transformed the mores of society. Whenever the early Christians entered a town, the people in power became disturbed and immediately sought to convict the Christians for being "disturbers of the peace" and "outside agitators." But the Christians pressed on, in the conviction that they were "a colony of heaven," called to obey God rather than man. Small in number, they were big in commitment. They were too God-intoxicated to be "astronomically intimidated." By their effort and example they brought an end to such ancient evils as infanticide and gladiatorial contests.

Things are different now. So often the contemporary church is a weak, ineffectual voice with an uncertain sound. So often it is an archdefender of the status quo. Far from being disturbed by the presence of the church, the power structure of the average community is consoled by the church's silent—and often even vocal—sanction of things as they are.

But the judgment of God is upon the church as never before. If today's church does not recapture the sacrificial spirit of the early church, it will lose its authenticity, forfeit the loyalty of millions, and be dismissed as an irrelevant social club with no meaning for the twentieth century. Every day I meet young people whose disappointment with the church has turned into outright disgust.

Perhaps I have once again been too optimistic. Is organized religion too inextricably bound to the status quo to save our nation and the world? Perhaps I must turn my faith to the inner spiritual church, the church within the church, as the true *ekklesia*[1] and the hope of the world. But again I am thankful to God that some noble souls from the

---

[1] A Greek word for the early Christian church. [Eds.]

ranks of organized religion have broken loose from the paralyzing chains of conformity and joined us as active partners in the struggle for freedom. They have left their secure congregations and walked the streets of Albany, Georgia, with us. They have gone down the highways of the South on tortuous rides for freedom. Yes, they have gone to jail with us. Some have been dismissed from their churches, have lost the support of their bishops and fellow ministers. But they have acted in the faith that right defeated is stronger than evil triumphant. Their witness has been the spiritual salt that has preserved the true meaning of the gospel in these troubled times. They have carved a tunnel of hope through the dark mountain of disappointment.

I hope the church as a whole will meet the challenge of this decisive hour. But even if the church does not come to the aid of justice, I have no despair about the future. I have no fear about the outcome of our struggle in Birmingham, even if our motives are at present misunderstood. We will reach the goal of freedom in Birmingham and all over the nation, because the goal of America is freedom. Abused and scorned though we may be, our destiny is tied up with America's destiny. Before the pilgrims landed at Plymouth, we were here. Before the pen of Jefferson etched the majestic words of the Declaration of Independence across the pages of history, we were here. For more than two centuries our forebears labored in this country without wages; they made cotton king; they built the homes of their masters while suffering gross injustice and shameful humiliation—and yet out of a bottomless vitality they continued to thrive and develop. If the inexpressible cruelties of slavery could not stop us, the opposition we now face will surely fail. We will win our freedom because the sacred heritage of our nation and the eternal will of God are embodied in our echoing demands.

Before closing I feel impelled to mention one other point in your statement that has troubled me profoundly. You warmly commended the Birmingham police force for keeping "order" and "preventing violence." I doubt that you would have so warmly commended the police force if you have seen its dogs sinking their teeth into unarmed, nonviolent Negroes. I doubt that you would so quickly commend the policemen if you were to observe their ugly and inhumane treatment of Negroes here in the city jail; if you were to watch them push and curse old Negro women and young Negro girls; if you were to see them slap and kick old Negro men and young boys; if you were to observe them, as they did on two occasions, refuse to give us food because we wanted to sing our grace together. I cannot join you in your praise of the Birmingham police department.

It is true that the police have exercised a degree of discipline in handling the demonstrators. In this sense they have conducted themselves rather "nonviolently" in public. But for what purpose? To preserve the evil system of segregation. Over the past few years I have consistently preached that nonviolence demands that the means we use must be as pure as the ends we seek. I have tried to make clear that it is wrong to use immoral means to attain moral ends. But now I must affirm that it is just as wrong, or perhaps even more so, to use moral means to preserve immoral ends. Perhaps Mr. Connor and his policemen have been rather nonviolent in public, as was Chief Pritchett in Albany, Georgia, but they have used the moral means of nonviolence to maintain the immoral end of racial injustice. As T. S. Eliot has said, "The last temptation is the greatest treason: To do the right deed for the wrong reason."

I wish you had commended the Negro sit-inners and demonstrators of Birmingham for their sublime courage, their willingness to suffer, and their amazing discipline in the midst of great provocation. One day the South will recognize its real heroes. They will be the James Merediths, with the noble sense of purpose that enables them to face jeering and hostile mobs, and with the agonizing loneliness that characterizes the life of the pioneer. They will be old, oppressed, battered Negro women, symbolized in a seventy-two-year-old woman in Montgomery, Alabama, who rose up with a sense of dignity and with her people decided not to ride segregated buses, and who responded with ungrammatical profundity to one who inquired about her weariness: "My feets is tired, but my soul is at rest." They will be the young high school and college students, the young ministers of the gospel and a host of their elders, courageously and nonviolently sitting in at lunch counters and willingly going to jail for conscience' sake. One day the South will know that when these disinherited children of God sat down at lunch counters, they were in reality standing up for what is best in the American dream and for the most sacred values in our Judaeo-Christian heritage, thereby bringing our nation back to those great wells of democracy which were dug deep by the founding fathers in their formulation of the Constitution and the Declaration of Independence.

Never before have I written so long a letter. I'm afraid it is much too long to take your precious time. I can assume you that it would have been much shorter if I had been writing from a comfortable desk, but what else can one do when he is alone in a narrow jail cell, other than write long letters, think long thoughts, and pray long prayers?

If I have said anything in this letter that overstates the truth and indicates an unreasonable impatience, I beg you to forgive me. If I have said anything that understates the truth and indicates my having a patience that allows me to settle for anything less than brotherhood, I beg God to forgive me.

I hope this letter finds you strong in the faith. I also hope that circumstances will soon make it possible for me to meet each of you, not as an integrationist or a civil-rights leader but as a fellow clergyman and a Christian brother. Let us all hope that the dark clouds of racial prejudice will soon pass away and the deep fog of misunderstanding will be lifted from our fear-drenched communities, and in some not too distant tomorrow the radiant stars of love and brotherhood will shine over our great nation with all their scintillating beauty.

Yours for the cause of Peace and Brotherhood,
MARTIN LUTHER KING, JR.

SPECULATIONS

1.   In this famous letter, King is writing to fellow clergymen who have criticized his actions as president of the Southern Christian Leadership Conference. How do you think his professional relationship with them influenced the writing of this letter? What features does this letter have that indicate that it is a correspondence from one clergyman to another?

2.   "Letter from Birmingham Jail" is very long. Why do you think King wrote such a long letter? Would it have been more effective if he had written a more conventional letter of two to three pages? Is this really a letter—and if not, why does King choose to call it one?

3.   Summarize three of King's arguments justifying his actions in Birmingham. How are the three arguments you chose persuasive? Hod do you respond to them on a personal level?

4.   King cites a great many thinkers and writers in the Letter. St. Augustine, Paul Tillich, the Bible, John Bunyan, T. S. Eliot, and Socrates are some of the famous individuals to whom King refers. Why does he do so? How do you think King's fellow clergymen and other readers are likely to respond to these citations?

5.   King's rich style owes a great deal to both the Bible and to a poetic use of parallel phrasing. Select a short section that you find particularly eloquent, powerful, and stylistically effective. Analyze what King is doing as a stylist to make this passage memorable for you.

6.   Have you ever written a letter in which you tried to argue a case, make a sustained plea about something that mattered to you? What kinds of arguments, devices, strategies did you use to make your letter succeed? How successful were you? What would you do differently—if anything—were you to write that letter now?

Crime and Criminals: Address to the Prisoners in the Cook County Jail

CLARENCE DARROW

Clarence Darrow is the real-life hero of "Inherit the Wind," a famous play and movie based on the Scopes trial. In this compelling courtroom drama, Darrow defends the right to teach evolution in the Tennessee schools—and although he loses the jury verdict, he succeeds in a greater objective: to ridicule similar discriminatory legislation out of existence in other states. The play is more fact than fiction; Darrow established his reputation as a champion of reason, social justice, and the poor.

Born in Ohio in 1857 to an intellectual and puritanical mother and a free-thinking father, Darrow was self-educated. He attended one year of law school but received most of his law education by reading and working for an attorney. He became a well-paid railroad lawyer, but he viewed his own cases unsympathetically, siding more with "the little guy" than with railroads and corporations. Ultimately, he achieved national fame for defending criminals and murders, including Nathan Leopold and Richard Loeb in the 1920s.

A large and imposing speaker, Darrow knew how to dominate a courtroom. His intellectual and political ideas were well known by many Americans through the end of the last century and the first few decades of this one. His legal writings—forceful, humane, and written with remarkable clarity—express his judicial philosophy: Poverty is the cause of crime, human beings are often condemned by the law for unconventional behavior rather than for doing evil, and capital punishment is nothing more than "organized, legalized murder." Those views are evident in this address, which offers an analysis that runs counter to a great deal of thinking about crime and punishment in America in the 1990s.

If I looked at jails and crimes and prisoners in the way the ordinary person does, I should not speak on this subject to you. The reason I talk to you on the question of crime, its cause and cure, is that I really do not in the least believe in crime. There is no such thing as a crime as the word is generally understood. I do not believe there is any sort of distinction between the real moral conditions of the people in and out of jail. One is just as good as the other. The people here can no more help being here than the people outside can avoid being outside. I do not believe that people are in jail because they deserve to be. They are in jail simply because they cannot avoid it on account of circumstances which are entirely beyond their control and for which they are in no way responsible.

I suppose a great many people on the outside would say I was doing you harm if they should hear what I say to you this afternoon, but you cannot be hurt a great deal anyway, so it will not matter.

Good people outside would say that I was really teaching you things that were calculated to injure society, but it's worthwhile now and then to hear something different from what you ordinarily get from preachers and the like. These will tell you that you should be good and then you will get rich and be happy. Of course we know that people do not get rich by being good, and that is the reason why so many of you people try to get rich some other way, only you do not understand how to do it quite as well as the fellow outside.

There are people who think that everything in this world is an accident. But really there is no such thing as an accident. A great many folks admit that many of the people in jail ought to be there, and many who are outside ought to be in. I think none of them ought to be here. There ought to be no jails; and if it were not for the fact that the people on the outside are so grasping and heartless in their dealings with the people on the inside, there would be no such institution as jails.

I do not want you to believe that I think all you people here are angels. I do not think that. You are people of all kinds, all of you doing the best you can—and that is evidently not very well. You are people of all kinds and conditions and under all circumstances. In one sense everybody is equally good and equally bad. We all do the best we can under the circumstances. But as to the exact things for which you are sent here, some of you are guilty and did the particular act because you needed the money. Some of you did it because you are in the habit of doing it, and some of you because you are born to it, and it comes to be as natural as it does, for instance, for me to be good.

Most of you probably have nothing against me, and most of you would treat me the same as any other person would, probably better than some of the people on the outside would treat me, because you think I believe in you and they know I do not believe in them. While you would not have the least thing against me in the world, you might pick my pockets. I do not think all of you would, but I think some of you would. You would not have anything against me, but that's your profession, a few of you. Some of the rest of you, if my doors were unlocked, might come in if you saw anything you wanted—not out of any malice to me, but because that is your trade. There is no doubt there are quite a number of people in this jail who would pick my pockets. And still I know this—that when I get outside pretty nearly everybody picks my pocket. There may be some of you who would hold up a man on the street, if you did not happen to have something else to do, and needed the money; but when I want to light my house or my office the gas company holds me up. They charge me one dollar for something that is worth twenty-five cents. Still all these people are good people; they are pillars of society and support the churches, and they are respectable.

When I ride on the streetcars I am held up—I pay five cents for a ride that is worth two and a half cents, simply because a body of men have bribed the city council and the legislature, so that all the rest of us have to pay tribute to them.

If I do not want to fall into the clutches of the gas trust and choose to burn oil instead of gas, then good Mr. Rockefeller holds me up, and he uses a certain portion of his money to build universities and support churches which are engaged in telling us how to be good.

Some of you are here for obtaining property under false pretenses—yet I pick up a great Sunday paper and read the advertisements of a merchant prince—"Shirtwaists for 39 cents, marked down from $3.00."

When I read the advertisements in the paper I see they are all lies. When I want to get out and find a place to stand anywhere on the face of the earth, I find that it has all been taken up long ago before I came here, and before you came here, and somebody says, "Get off, swim into the lake, fly into the air; go anywhere, but get off." That is because these people have the police and they have the jails and the judges and the lawyers and the soldiers and all the rest of them to take care of the earth and drive everybody off that comes in their way.

A great many people will tell you that all this is true, but that it does not excuse you. These facts do not excuse some fellow who reaches into my pocket and takes out a five-dollar bill. The fact that the gas company bribes the members of the legislature from year to year, and fixes the law, so that all you people are compelled to be "fleeced" whenever you deal with them; the fact that the streetcar companies and the gas companies have control of the streets; and the fact that the landlords own all the earth—this, they say, has nothing to do with you.

Let us see whether there is any connection between the crimes of the respectable classes and your presence in the jail. Many of you people are in jail because you have really committed burglary; many of you, because you have stolen something. In the meaning of the law, you have taken some other person's property. Some of you have entered a store and carried off a pair of shoes because you did not have the price. Possibly some of you have committed murder. I cannot tell what all of you did. There are a great many people here who have done some of these things who really do not know themselves why they did them. I think I know why you did them—every one of you; you did these things because you were bound to do them. It looked to you at the time as if you had a chance to do them or not, as you saw fit; but still, after all, you had no choice. There may be people here who had some money in their pockets and who still went out and got some more money in a way society forbids. Now, you may not yourselves see exactly why it was you did this thing, but if you look at the question deeply enough and carefully enough you will see that there were circumstances that drove you to do exactly the thing which you did. You could not help it any more than we outside can help taking the positions that we take. The reformers who tell you to be good and you will be happy, and the people on the outside who have property to protect—they think that the only way to do it is by building jails and locking you up in cells on weekdays and praying for you Sundays.

I think that all of this has nothing whatever to do with right conduct. I think it is very easily seen what has to do with right conduct. Some so-called criminals—and I will use this word because it is handy, it means nothing to me—I speak of the criminals who get caught as distinguished from the criminals who catch them—some of these so-called criminals are in jail for their first offenses, but nine tenths of you are in jail because you did not have a good lawyer and, of course, you did not have a good lawyer because you did not have enough money to pay a good lawyer. There is no very great danger of a rich man going to jail.

Some of you may be here for the first time. If we would open the doors and let you out, and leave the laws as they are today, some of you would be back tomorrow. This is about as good a place as you can get anyway. There are many people here who are so in the habit of coming that they would not know where else to go. There are people who are born with the tendency to break into jail every chance they get, and they cannot avoid it. You cannot figure out your life and see why it was, but still there is a reason for it; and if we were all wise and knew all the facts, we could figure it out.

In the first place, there are a good many more people who go to jail in the wintertime than in summer. Why is this? Is it because people are more wicked in winter? No, it is because the coal trust begins to get in its grip in the winter. A few gentlemen take possession of the coal, and unless the people will pay seven or eight dollars a ton for something that is worth three dollars, they will have to freeze. Then there is nothing to do but to break into jail, and so there are many more in jail in the winter than in summer. It costs more for gas in the winter because the nights are longer, and people go to jail to save gas bills. The jails are electric-lighted. You may not know it, but these economic laws are working all the time, whether we know it or do not know it.

There are more people who go to jail in hard times than in good times—few people, comparatively, go to jail except when they are hard up. They go to jail because they have no other place to go. They may not know why, but it is true all the same. People are not more wicked in hard times. That is not the reason. The fact is true all over the world that in hard times more people go to jail than in good times, and in winter more people go to jail than in summer. Of course it is pretty hard times for people who go to jail at any time. The people who go to jail are almost always poor people—people who have no other place to live, first and last. When times are hard, then you find large numbers of people who go to jail who would not otherwise be in jail.

Long ago, Mr. Buckle, who was a great philosopher and historian, collected facts, and he showed that the number of people who are arrested increased just as the price of food increased. When they put up the price of gas ten cents a thousand, I do not know who will go to jail, but I do know that a certain number of people will go. When the meat combine raises the price of beef, I do not know who is going to jail, but I know that a large number of people are bound to go. Whenever the Standard Oil Company raises the price of oil, I know that a certain number of girls who are seamstresses, and who work night after night long hours for somebody else, will be compelled to go out on the streets and ply another trade, and I know that Mr. Rockefeller and his associates are responsible and not the poor girls in the jails.

First and last, people are sent to jail because they are poor. Sometimes, as I say, you may not need money at the particular time, but you wish to have thrifty forehanded habits, and do not always wait until you are in absolute want. Some of you people are perhaps plying the trade, the profession, which is called burglary. No man in his right senses will go into a strange house in the dead of night and prowl around with a dark lantern through unfamiliar rooms and take chances of his life, if he has plenty of the good things of the world in his own home. You would not take any such chances as that. If a man had clothes in his clothes-press and beefsteak in his pantry and money in the bank, he would not navigate around nights in houses where he knows nothing about the premises whatever. It always requires experience and education for this profession, and people who fit themselves for it are no more to blame than I am for being a lawyer. A man would not hold up another man on the street if he had plenty of money in his own pocket. He might do it if he had one dollar or two dollars, but he wouldn't if he had as much money as Mr. Rockefeller has. Mr. Rockefeller has a great deal better hold-up game than that.

The more that is taken from the poor by the rich, who have the chance to take it, the more poor people there are who are compelled to resort to these means for a livelihood. They may not understand it, they may not think so at once, but after all they are driven into that line of employment.

There is a bill before the legislature of this state to punish kidnaping children with death. We have wise members of the legislature. They know the gas trust when they see it and they always see it—they can furnish light enough to be seen; and this legislature thinks it is going to stop kidnaping children by making a law punishing kidnapers of children with death. I don't believe in kidnaping children, but the legislature is all wrong. Kidnaping children is not a crime, it is a profession. It has been developed with the times. It has been developed with our modern industrial conditions. There are many ways of making money—many new ways that our ancestors knew nothing about. Our ancestors knew nothing about a billion-dollar trust; and here comes some poor fellow who has no other trade and he discovers the profession of kidnaping children.

This crime is born, not because people are bad; people don't kidnap other people's children because they want the children or because they are devilish, but because they see a chance to get some money out of it. You cannot cure this crime by passing a law punishing by death kidnapers of children. There is one way to cure it. There is one way to cure all these offenses, and that is to give the people a chance to live. There is no other way, and there never was any other way since the world began; and the world is so blind and stupid that it will not see. If every man and woman and child in the world had a chance to make a decent, fair, honest living, there would be no jails and no lawyers and no courts. There might be some persons here or there with some peculiar formation of their brain, like Rockefeller, who would do these things simply to be doing them; but they would be very, very few, and those should be sent to a hospital and treated, and not sent to jail; and they would entirely disappear in the second generation, or at least in the third generation.

I am not talking pure theory. I will just give you two or three illustrations.

The English people once punished criminals by sending them away. They would load them on a ship and export them to Australia. England was owned by lords and nobles and rich people. They owned the whole earth over there, and the other people had to stay in the streets. They could not get a decent living. They used to take their criminals and send them to Australia—I mean the class of criminals who got caught. When these criminals got over there, and nobody else had come, they had the whole continent to run over, and so they could raise sheep and furnish their own meat, which is easier than stealing it. These criminals then became decent, respectable people because they had a chance to live. They did not commit any crimes. They were just like the English people who sent them there, only better. And in the second generation the descendants of those criminals were as good and respectable a class of people as there were on the face of the earth, and then they began building churches and jails themselves.

A portion of this country was settled in the same way, landing prisoners down on the southern coast; but when they got here and had a whole continent to run over and plenty of chances to make a living, they became respectable citizens, making their own living just like any other citizen in the world. But finally the descendants of the English aristocracy who sent the people over to Australia found out they were getting rich, and so they went over to get possession of the earth as they always do, and they organized land syndicates and got control of the land and ores, and then they had just as many criminals in Australia as they did in England. It was not because the world had grown bad; it was because the earth had been taken away from the people.

Some of you people have lived in the country. It's prettier than it is here. And if you have ever lived on a farm you understand that if you put a lot of cattle in a field, when the pasture is short they will jump over the fence; but put them in a good field where there is plenty of pasture, and they will be law-abiding cattle to the end of time. The human animal is just like the rest of the animals, only a little more so. The same thing that governs in the one governs in the other.

Everybody makes his living along the lines of least resistance. A wise man who comes into a country early sees a great undeveloped land. For instance, our rich men twenty-five years ago saw that Chicago was small and knew a lot of people would come here and settle, and they readily saw that if they had all the land around here it would be worth a good deal, so they grabbed the land. You cannot be a landlord because somebody has got it all. You must find some other calling. In England and Ireland and Scotland less than five percent own all the land there is, and the people are bound to stay there on any kind of terms the landlords give. They must live the best they can, so they develop all these various professions—burglary, picking pockets and the like.

Again, people find all sorts of ways of getting rich. These are diseases like everything else. You look at people getting rich, organizing trusts and making a million dollars, and somebody gets the disease and he starts out. He catches it just as a man catches the mumps or the measles; he is not to blame, it is in the air. You will find men speculating beyond their means, because the mania of money-getting is taking possession of them. It is simply a disease—nothing more, nothing less. You cannot avoid catching it; but the fellows who have control of the earth have the advantage of you. See what the law is: when these men get control of things, they make the laws. They do not make the laws to protect anybody; courts are not instruments of justice. When your case gets into court it will make little difference whether you are guilty or innocent, but it's better you have a smart lawyer. And you cannot have a smart lawyer unless you have money. First and last it's a question of money. Those men who own the earth make the laws to protect what they have. They fix up a sort of fence or pen around what they have, and they fix the law so the fellow on the outside cannot get in. The laws are really organized for the protection of the men who rule the world. They were never organized or enforced to do justice. We have no system for doing justice, not the slightest in the world.

Let me illustrate: Take the poorest person in this room. If the community had provided a system of doing justice, the poorest person in this room would have as good a lawyer as the richest, would he not? When you went into court you would have just as long a trial and just as fair a trial as the richest person in Chicago. Your case would not be tried in fifteen or twenty minutes, whereas it would take fifteen days to get through with a rich man's case.

Then if you were rich and were beaten, your case would be taken to the Appellate Court. A poor man cannot take his case to the Appellate Court; he has not the price. And then to the Supreme Court. And if he were beaten there he might perhaps go to the United States Supreme Court. And he might die of old age before he got into jail. If you are poor, it's a quick job. You are almost known to be guilty, else you would not be there. Why should anyone be in the criminal court if he were not guilty? He would not be there if he could be anywhere else. The officials have no time to look after all these cases. The people who are on the outside, who are running banks and building churches and making jails, they have no time to examine 600 or 700 prisoners each year to see whether they are guilty or innocent. If the courts were organized to promote justice, the people would elect somebody to defend all these criminals, somebody as smart as the prosecutor—and given him as many detectives and as many assistants to help, and pay as much money to defend you as to prosecute you. We have a very able man for state's attorney, and he has many assistants, detectives and policemen without end, and judges to hear the cases—everything handy.

Most all of our criminal code consists in offenses against property. People are sent to jail because they have committed a crime against property. It is of very little consequence whether one hundred people more or less go to jail who ought not to go—you must protect property, because in this world property is of more importance than anything else.

How is it done? These people who have property fix it so they can protect what they have. When somebody commits a crime it does not follow that he has done something that is morally wrong. The man on the outside who has committed no crime may have done something. For instance: to take all the coal in the United States and raise the price two dollars or three dollars when there is no need of it, and thus kill thousands of babies and send thousands of people to the poorhouse and tens of thousands to jail, as is done every year in the United States—this is a greater crime than all the people in our jails ever committed; but the law does not punish it. Why? Because the fellows who control the earth make the laws. If you and I had the making of the laws, the first thing we would do would be to punish the fellow who gets control of the earth. Nature put this coal in the ground for me as well as for them and nature made the prairies up here to raise wheat for me as well as for them, and then the great railroad companies came along and fenced it up.

Most all of the crimes for which we are punished are property crimes. There are a few personal crimes, like murder—but they are very few. The crimes committed are mostly those against property. If this punishment is right the criminals must have a lot of property. How much money is there in this crowd? And yet you are all here for crimes against property. The people up and down the Lake Shore have not committed crime; still they have so much property they don't know what to do with it. It is perfectly plain why these people have not committed crimes against property; they make the laws and therefore do not need to break them. And in order for you to get some property you are obliged to break the rules of the game. I don't know but what some of you may have had a very nice chance to get rich by carrying a hod for one dollar a day, twelve hours. Instead of taking that nice, easy profession, you are a burglar. If you had been given a chance to be a banker you would rather follow that. Some of you may have had a chance to work as a switchman on a railroad where you know, according to statistics, that you cannot live and keep all your limbs more than seven years, and you can get fifty dollars or seventy-five dollars a month for taking your lives in your hands; and instead of taking that lucrative position you chose to be a sneak thief, or something like that. Some of you made that sort of choice. I don't know which I would take if I was reduced to this choice. I have an easier choice.

I will guarantee to take from this jail, or any jail in the world, five hundred men who have been the worst criminals and law-breakers who ever got into jail, and I will go down to our lowest streets and take five hundred of the most abandoned prostitutes, and go out somewhere where there is plenty of land, and will give them a chance to make a living, and they will be as good people as the average in the community.

There is a remedy for the sort of condition we see here. The world never finds it out, or when it does find it out it does not enforce it. You may pass a law punishing every person with death for burglary, and it will make no difference. Men will commit it just the same. In England there was a time when one hundred different offenses were punishable with death, and it made no difference. The English people strangely found out that so fast as they repealed the severe penalties and so fast as they did away with punishing men by death, crime decreased instead of increased; that the smaller the penalty the fewer the crimes.

Hanging men in our county jails does not prevent murder. It makes murderers.

And this has been the history of the world. It's easy to see how to do away with what we call crime. It is not to easy to do it. I will tell you how to do it. It can be done by giving the people a chance to live—by destroying special privileges. So long as big criminals can get the coal fields, so long as the big criminals have control of the city council and get the public streets for streetcars and gas rights—this is bound to send thousands of poor people to jail. So long as men are allowed to monopolize all the earth, and compel others to live on such terms as these men see fit to make, then you are bound to get into jail.

The only way in the world to abolish crime and criminals is to abolish the big ones and the little ones together. Make fair conditions of life. Give men a chance to live. Abolish the right of private owner-ship of land, abolish monopoly, make the world partners in produc-tion, partners in the good things of life. Nobody would steal if he could get something of his own some easier way. Nobody will commit burglary when he has a house full. No girl will go out on the streets when she has a comfortable place at home. The man who owns a sweatshop or a department store may not be to blame himself for the condition of his girls, but when he pays them five dollars, three dol-lars, and two dollars a week, I wonder where he thinks they will get the rest of their money to live. The only way to cure these conditions is by equality. There should be no jails. They do not accomplish what they pretend to accomplish. If you would wipe them out there would be no more criminals than now. They terrorize nobody. They are a blot upon any civilization, and a jail is an evidence of the lack of charity of the people on the outside who make the jails and fill them with the victims of their greed.

SPECULATIONS

1.   Assess the rhetorical dimension of this speech—that is, a famous lawyer delivering a talk to the inmates of the Cook County Jail. Was Darrow serious? Was he trying to be outrageous just to shock the authorities? Was it appropriate for Darrow to give such a speech?

2.   Darrow attempts to collapse the distinction between those in jail and those out of jail, ultimately claiming that they are all criminals. How does he make this argument? Are you convinced?

3.   Darrow states that "If the community had provided a system of doing justice, the poorest person in this room would have as good a lawyer as the richest, would he not?" Does Darrow's criticism have merit? Should the criminal justice system be "dollar neutral"?

4.   Darrow considers the different legal treatments accorded the rich as opposed to the poor. But what differences in treatment do we see also between the young and the old? Given your own experience, do young people get better or worse treatment from authorities than older people? You might want to consider this question in light of some specific incident in your own life—say, being falsely accused of cheating, shoplifting, lying, or the like.

5.   Do you agree with Darrow that if he took five hundred male criminals and five hundred "of the most abandoned prostitutes" and gave them land and "a chance to make a living," that they would be "as good people as the average in the community"? Discuss, if you wish, the example of settlement in Australia to support your argument.

Hustler

MALCOLM X

In a sense, Malcolm X was born into a life of violence, disruption, and despair—and it took him most of his life and a trip to Mecca to discover the possibilities of hope and brotherhood. Tragically, for Malcolm X, his followers, and America, the great black leader was never able to translate his vision into political and social gains: He was assassinated in 1965 by three men—reputedly followers of the rival black leader, Elijah Muhammad of the Black Muslims—as he addressed a group of supporters in a Harlem ballroom.

Malcolm X was born in Omaha in 1925, one of eight children of Reverend Earl Little, a Baptist minister, and Louise Little. His father was a physically powerful man who could behead chickens or rabbits "with one twist of his big black hands." Earl Little preached a form of black nationalism, was driven out of Nebraska by the Ku Klux Klan, and settled in Lansing, Michigan. There too he was called an "uppity nigger" and his home was torched by a band of white supremists; after one of many frequent battles with his wife, Earl Little stalked out of the house and was later found mutilated and murdered. Malcolm Little was six. His mother, forced to accept welfare and do odd jobs within the same society that had murdered her husband, succumbed to mental illness; the children were sent to a succession of foster homes. In spite of this difficult life, Malcolm Little succeeded in school and aspired to become a lawyer. His high school English teacher, however, told him it was just a pipe dream and that he should be "realistic about being a nigger."

Malcolm X quit school and turned to serious criminal activities. "Hustler," a chapter from his *Autobiography*, recounts part of this experience. Malcolm Little was eventually caught, convicted, and imprisoned. He educated himself in the prison library and became a follower of Elijah Muhammad, who urged his followers to renounce white America in favor of an autonomous black society. Malcolm became a convert and changed his name to Malcolm X.

Upon release from prison in 1952, Malcolm X assumed an increasingly powerful and influential ministerial role within the Black Muslim movement. He grew disillusioned with Elijah Muhammad, who became jealous of his greatest disciple. Concerned that he would be assassinated, Malcolm X left America and toured Mecca, birthplace of the Muslim prophet Mohammed, thereupon renaming himself El-Hajj Mahlik El-Shabazz and rededicating himself to promote harmony among all blacks throughout the world. Within a year he was dead on a Harlem stage.

Malcolm X was also a man, a husband, and a father; he and his wife Betty Shabazz married in 1958 and had six daughters. According to George Metcalf:

> During brief visits home, Malcolm never lost a chance to romp with his children, and filled the free time with voracious reading. Betty marveled at his concentration. He picked up the classics, anthropology, African history, delved into the origins of religion and would tackle anything by or about black people. His capacity for speed reading was now so acute he could devour a difficult book "in three hours and easier ones in one to two hours.

A reading of the entire *Autobiography* (and other published work) reveals Malcolm X's genius, erudition, and vision. This selection offers a more particular view of the whys and wherefores of criminal life for a black man as well as his observations about the class response to crime and punishment.

I can't remember all the hustles I had during the next two years in Harlem, after the abrupt end of my riding the trains and peddling reefers to the touring bands.

Negro railroad men waited for their trains in their big locker room on the lower level of Grand Central Station. Big blackjack and poker games went on in there around the clock. Sometimes five hundred dollars would be on the table. One day, in a blackjack game, an old cook who was dealing the cards tried to be slick, and I had to drop my pistol in his face.

The next time I went into one of those games, intuition told me to stick my gun under my belt right down the middle of my back.

Sure enough, someone had squealed. Two big, beefy-faced Irish cops cam in. They frisked me—and they missed my gun where they hadn't expected one.

The cops told me never again to be caught in Grand Central Station unless I had a ticket to ride somewhere. And I knew that by the next day, every railroad's personnel office would have a blackball on me, so I never tried to get another railroad job.

There I was back in Harlem's streets among all the rest of the hustlers. I couldn't sell reefers; the dope squad detectives were too familiar with me. I was a true hustler—uneducated, unskilled at anything honorable, and I considered myself nervy and cunning enough to live by my wits, exploiting any prey that presented itself. I would risk just about anything.

Right now, in every big city ghetto, tens of thousands of yesterday's and today's school drop-outs are keeping body and soul together by some form of hustling in the same way I did. And they inevitably move into more and more, worse and worse, illegality and immorality. Full-time hustlers never can relax to appraise what they are doing and where they are bound. As is the case in any jungle, the hustler's every waking hour is lived with both the practical and the subconscious knowledge that if he ever relaxes, if he ever slows down, the other hungry, restless foxes, ferrets, wolves, and vultures out there with him won't hesitate to make him their prey.

During the next six to eight months, I pulled my first robberies and stick-ups. Only small ones. Always in other, nearby cities. And I got away. As the pros did, I too would key myself to pull these jobs by my first use of hard dope. I began with Sammy's recommendation—sniffing cocaine.

Normally now, for street wear, I might call it, I carried a hardly noticeable little flat, blue-steel .25 automatic. But for working, I carried a .32, a .38 or a .45. I saw how when the eyes stared at the big black hole, the faces fell slack and the mouths sagged open. And when I spoke, the people seemed to hear as though they were far away, and they would do whatever I asked.

Between jobs, staying high on narcotics kept me from getting nervous. Still, upon sudden impulses, just to play safe, I would abruptly move from one to another fifteen- to twenty-dollars-a-week room, always in my favorite 147th–150th Street area, just flanking Sugar Hill.

Once on a job with Sammy, we had a pretty close call. Someone must have seen us. We were making our getaway, running, when we heard the sirens. Instantly, we slowed to walking. As a police car screeched to a stop, we stepped out into the street, meeting it, hailing it to ask for directions. They must have thought we were about to give them some information. They just cursed us and raced on. Again, it didn't cross the white men's minds that a trick like that might be pulled on them by Negroes.

The suits that I wore, the finest, I bought hot for about thirty-five to fifty dollars. I made it my rule never to go after more than I needed to live on. Any experienced hustler will tell you that getting greedy is the quickest road to prison. I kept "cased" in my head vulnerable places and situations and I would perform the next job only when my bankroll in my pocket began to get too low.

Some weeks, I bet large amounts on the numbers. I still played with the same runner with whom I'd started in Small's Paradise. Playing my hunches, many a day I'd have up to forty dollars on two numbers, hoping for that fabulous six hundred-to-one payoff. But I never did hit a big number full force. There's no telling what I would have done if ever I'd landed $10,000 or $12,000 at one time. Of course, once in a while I'd hit a small combination figure. Sometimes, flush like that, I'd telephone Sophia to come over from Boston for a couple of days.

I went to the movies a lot again. And I never missed my musician friends whenever they were playing, either in Harlem, downtown at the big theaters, or on 52nd Street.

Reginald and I got very close the next time his ship came back into New York. We discussed our family, and what a shame it was that our book-loving oldest brother Wilfred had never had the chance to go to some of those big universities where he would have gone far. And we exchanged thoughts we had never shared with anyone.

Reginald, in his quite way, was a mad fan of musicians and music. When his ship sailed one morning without him, a principal reason was that I had thoroughly exposed him to the exciting musical world. We had wild times backstage with the musicians when they were playing the Roxy, or the Paramount. After selling reefers with the bands as they traveled, I was known to almost every popular Negro musician around New York in 1944–1945.

Reginald and I went the Savoy Ballroom, the Apollo Theater, the Braddock Hotel bar, the nightclubs and speak-easies, wherever Negroes played music. The great Lady Day, Billie Holiday, hugged him and called him "baby brother." Reginald shared tens of thousands of Negroes' feelings that the living end of the big bands was Lionel Hampton's. I was very close to many of the men in Hamp's band; I introduced Reginald to them, and also to Hamp himself, and Hamp's wife and business manager, Gladys Hampton. One of this world's sweetest people is Hamp. Anyone who knows him will tell you that he'd often do the most generous things for people he barely knew. As much money as Hamp has made, and still makes, he would be broke today if his money and his business weren't handled by Gladys, who is one of the brainiest women I ever met. The Apollo Theater's owner, Frank Schiffman, could tell you. He generally signed bands to play for a set weekly amount, but I know that once during those days Gladys Hampton instead arranged a deal for Hamp's band to play for a cut of the gate. Then the usual number of shows was doubled up—if I'm not mistaken, eight shows a day, instead of the usual four—and Hamp's pulling power cleaned up. Gladys Hampton used to talk to me a lot, and she tried to give me good advice: "Calm down, Red." Gladys saw how wild I was. She saw me headed toward a bad end.

One of the things I liked about Reginald was that when I left him to go away "working," Reginald asked me no questions. After he came to Harlem, I went on more jobs than usual. I guess that what influenced me to get my first actual apartment was not my wanting Reginald to be knocking around Harlem without anywhere to call "home." That first apartment was three rooms, for a hundred dollars a month, I think, in the front basement of a house on 147th Street between Convent and St. Nicholas Avenues. Living in the rear basement apartment, right behind Reginald and me, was one of Harlem's most successful narcotics dealers.

With the apartment as our headquarters, I gradually got Reginald introduced around to Creole Bill's, and other Harlem after-hours spots. About two o'clock every morning, as the downtown white nightclubs closed, Reginald and I would stand around in front of this or that Harlem after-hours place, and I'd school him to what was happening.

Especially after the nightclubs downtown closed, the taxis and black limousines would be driving uptown, bringing those white people who never could get enough of Negro *soul*. The places popular with these whites ranged all the way from the big locally famous ones such as Jimmy's Chicken Shack, and Dickie Wells', to the little here-tonight-gone-tomorrow-night private clubs, so-called, where a dollar was collected at the door for "membership."

Inside every after-hours spot, the smoke would hurt your eyes. Four white people to every Negro would be in there drinking whisky from coffee cups and eating fried chicken. The generally flush-faced white men and their makeup-masked, glittery-eyed women would be pounding each other's backs and uproariously laughing and applauding the music. A lot of whites, drunk, would go staggering up to Negroes, the waiters, the owners, or Negroes at tables, wringing their hands, even trying to hug them, "You're just as good as I am—I want you to know that!" The most famous places drew both Negro and white celebrities who enjoyed each other. A jam-packed four-thirty A.M. crowd at Jimmie's Chicken Shack or Dickie Wells' might have such jam-session entertainment as Hazel Scott playing the piano for Billie Holiday singing the blues. Jimmy's Chicken Shack, incidentally, was where once, later on, I worked briefly as a waiter. That's where Redd Foxx was the dishwasher who kept the kitchen crew in stitches.

After a while, my brother Reginald had to have a hustle, and I gave much thought to what would be, for him, a good, safe hustle. After he'd learned his own way around, it would be up to him to take risks for himself—if he wanted to make more and quicker money.

The hustle I got Reginald into really was very simple. It utilized the psychology of the ghetto jungle. Downtown, he paid the two dollars, or whatever it was, for a regular city peddler's license. Then I took him to a manufacturers' outlet where we bought a supply of cheap imperfect "seconds"—shirts, underwear, cheap rings, watches, all kinds of quick-sale items.

Watching me work this hustle back in Harlem, Reginald quickly caught on to how to go into barbershops, beauty parlors, and bars acting very nervous as he let the customers peep into his small valise of "loot." With so many thieves around anxious to get rid of stolen good-quality merchandise cheaply, many Harlemites, purely because of this conditioning, jumped to pay hot prices for inferior goods whose sale was perfectly legitimate. It never took long to get rid of a valiseful for at least twice what it had cost. And if any cop stopped Reginald, he had in his pocket both the peddler's license and the manufacturers' outlet bills of sale. Reginald only had to be certain that none of the customers to whom he sold ever saw that he was legitimate.

I assumed that Reginald, like most of the Negroes I knew, would go for a white woman. I'd point out Negro-happy white women to him, and explain that a Negro with any brains could wrap these women around his fingers. But I have to say this for Reginald: he never liked white women. I remember the one time he met Sophia; he was so cool it upset Sophia, and it tickled me.

Reginald got himself a black woman. I'd guess she was pushing thirty; an "old settler," as we called them back in those days. She was a waitress in an exclusive restaurant downtown. She lavished on Reginald everything she had, she was so happy to get a young man. I mean she bought his clothes, cooked and washed for him, and everything, as though he were a baby.

That was just another example of why my respect for my younger brother kept increasing. Reginald showed, in often surprising ways, more sense than a lot of working hustlers twice his age. Reginald then was only sixteen, but, a six-footer, he looked and acted much older than his years.

All through the war, the Harlem racial picture never was too bright. Tension built to a pretty high pitch. Old-timers told me that

Harlem had never been the same since the 1935 riot, when millions of dollars worth of damage was done by thousands of Negroes, infuriated chiefly by the white merchants in Harlem refusing to hire a Negro even as their stores raked in Harlem's money.

During World War II, Mayor LaGuardia officially closed the Savoy Ballroom. Harlem said the real reason was to stop Negroes from dancing with white women. Harlem said that no one dragged the white women in there. Adam Clayton Powell made it a big fight. He had successfully fought Consolidated Edison and the New York Telephone Company until they had hired Negroes. Then he had helped to battle the U.S. Navy and the U.S. Army about their segregating of uniformed Negroes. But Powell couldn't win this battle. City Hall kept the Savoy closed for a long time. It was just another one of the "liberal North" actions that didn't help Harlem to love the white man any.

Finally, rumor flashed that in the Braddock Hotel, white cops had shot a Negro soldier. I was walking down St. Nicholas Avenue; I saw all of these Negroes hollering and running north from 125th Street. Some of them were loaded down with armfuls of stuff. I remember it was the band-leader Fletcher Henderson's nephew "Shorty" Henderson who told me what had happened. Negroes were smashing store windows, and taking everything they could grab and carry—furniture, food, jewelry, clothes, whisky. Within an hour, every New York City cop seemed to be in Harlem. Mayor LaGuardia and the NAACP's then Secretary, the famed late Walter White, were in a red firecar, riding around pleading over a loudspeaker to all of those shouting, milling, angry Negroes to please go home and stay inside.

Just recently I ran into Shorty Henderson on Seventh Avenue. We were laughing about a fellow whom the riot had left with the nickname of "Left Feet." In a scramble in a women's shoe store, somehow he'd grabbed five shoes, all of them for left feet! And we laughed about the scared little Chinese whose restaurant didn't have a hand laid on it, because rioters just about convulsed laughing when they saw the sign the Chinese had hastily stuck on his front door: "Me Colored Too."

After the riot, things go very tight in Harlem. It was terrible for the night-life people, and for those hustlers whose main income had been the white man's money. The 1935 riot had left only a relative trickle of the money which had poured into Harlem during the 1920s. And now this new riot ended even that trickle.

Today the white people who visit Harlem, and this mostly on weekend nights, are hardly more than a few dozen who do the twist, the frug, the Watusi, and all the rest of the current dance crazes in Small's Paradise, owned now by the great basketball champion "Wilt the Stilt" Chamberlain, who draws crowds with his big, clean, All-

American-athlete image. Most white people today are physically afraid to come to Harlem—and it's for good reasons, too. Even for Negroes, Harlem night life is about finished. Most of the Negroes who have money to spend are spending it downtown somewhere in this hypocritical "integration," in places where previously the police would have been called to haul off any Negro insane enough to try and get in. The already Croesus-rich white man can't get another skyscraper hotel finished and opened before all these integration-mad Negroes, who themselves don't own a tool shed, are booking the swanky new hotel for "cotillions" and "conventions." Those rich whites could afford it when they used to throw away their money in Harlem. But Negroes can't afford to be taking their money downtown to the white man.

Sammy and I, on a robbery job, got a bad scare, a very close call.

Things had grown so tight in Harlem that some hustlers had been forced to go to work. Even some prostitutes had gotten jobs as domestics, and cleaning office buildings at night. The pimping was so poor, Sammy had gone on the job with me. We had selected one of those situations considered "impossible." But wherever people think that, the guards will unconsciously grow gradually more relaxed, until sometimes those can be the easiest jobs of all.

But right in the middle of the act, we had some bad luck. A bullet grazed Sammy. We just barely escaped.

Sammy fortunately wasn't really hurt. We split up, which was always wise to do.

Just before daybreak, I went to Sammy's apartment. His newest woman, one of those beautiful but hot-headed Spanish Negroes, was in there crying and carrying on over Sammy. She went for me, screaming and clawing; she knew I'd been in on it with him. I fended her off. Not able to figure out why Sammy didn't shut her up, I did . . . and from the corner of my eye, I saw Sammy going for his gun.

Sammy's reaction that way to my hitting his woman—close as he and I were—was the only weak spot I'd ever glimpsed. The woman screamed and dove for him. She knew as I did that when your best friend draws a gun on you, he usually has lost all control of his emotions, and he intends to shoot. She distracted Sammy long enough for me to bolt through the door. Sammy chased me, about a block.

We soon made up—on the surface. But things never are fully right again with anyone you have seen trying to kill you.

Intuition told us that we had better lay low for a good while. The worst thing was that we'd been seen. The police in that nearby town had surely circulated our general descriptions.

I just couldn't forget that incident over Sammy's woman. I came to rely more and more upon my brother Reginald as the only one in my world I could completely trust.

Reginald was lazy, I'd discovered that. He had quit his hustle altogether. But I didn't mind that, really, because one could be as lazy as he wanted, if he would only use his head, as Reginald was doing. He had left my apartment by now. He was living off his "old settler" woman—when he was in town. I had also taught Reginald how he could work for a little while for a railroad, then use his identification card to travel for nothing—and Reginald loved to travel. Several times, he had gone visiting all around, among our brothers and sisters. They had now begun to scatter to different cities. In Boston, Reginald was closer to our sister Mary than to Ella, who had been my favorite. Both Reginald and Mary were quiet types, and Ella and I were extroverts. And Shorty in Boston had given my brother a royal time.

Because of my reputation, it was easy for me to get into the numbers racket. That was probably Harlem's only hustle which hadn't slumped in business. In return for a favor to some white mobster, my new boss and his wife had just been given a six-months numbers banking privilege for the Bronx railroad area called Motthaven Yards. The white mobsters had the numbers racket split into specific areas. A designated area would be assigned to someone for a specified period of time. My boss's wife had been Dutch Schultz's secretary in the 1930s, during the time when Schultz had strong-armed his way into control of the Harlem numbers business.

My job now was to ride a bus across the George Washington Bridge where a fellow was waiting for me to hand him a bag of numbers betting slips. We never spoke. I'd cross the street and catch the next bus back to Harlem. I never knew who that fellow was. I never knew who picked up the betting money for the slips that I handled. You didn't ask questions in the rackets.

My boss's wife and Gladys Hampton were the only two women I ever met in Harlem whose business ability I really respected. My boss's wife, when she had the time and the inclination to talk, would tell me many interesting things. She would talk to me about the Dutch Schultz days—about deals that she had known, about graft paid to officials—rookie cops and shyster lawyers right on up into the top levels of police and politics. She knew from personal experience how crime existed only to the degree that the law cooperated with it. She showed me how, in the country's entire social, political and economic structure, the criminal, the law, and the politicians were actually inseparable partners.

It was at this time that I changed from my old numbers man, the one I'd used since I first worked in Small's Paradise. He hated to lose a heavy player, but he readily understood why I would now want to play with a runner of my own outfit. That was how I began placing my bets with West Indian Archie. I've mentioned him before—one of Harlem's really *bad* Negroes; one of those former Dutch Schultz strong-arm men around Harlem.

West Indian Archie had finished time in Sing Sing not long before I came to Harlem. But my boss's wife had hired him not just because she knew him from the old days. West Indian Archie had the kind of photographic memory that put him among the elite of numbers runners. He never wrote down your number; even in the case of combination plays, he would just nod. He was able to file all the numbers in his head, and write them down for the banker only when he turned in his money. This made him the ideal runner because cops could never catch him with any betting slips.

I've often reflected upon such black veteran numbers men as West Indian Archie. If they had lived in another kind of society, their exceptional mathematical talents might have been better used. But they were black.

Anyway, it was status just to be known as a client of West Indian Archie's, because he handled only sizable bettors. He also required integrity and sound credit: it wasn't necessary that you pay as you played; you could pay West Indian Archie by the week. He always carried a couple of thousand dollars on him, his own money. If a client came up to him and said he'd hit for some moderate amount, say a fifty-cent or one dollar combination, West Indian Archie would peel of the three or six hundred dollars, and later get his money back from the banker.

Every weekend, I'd pay my bill—anywhere from fifty to even one hundred dollars, if I had really plunged on some hunch. And when, once or twice, I did hit, always just some combination, as I've described, West Indian Archie paid me off from his own roll.

The six months finally ended for my boss and his wife. They had done well. Their runners got nice tips, and promptly were snatched by other bankers. I continued working for my boss and his wife in a gambling house they opened.

A Harlem madam I'd come to know—through having done a friend of hers a favor—introduced me to a special facet of the Harlem night world, something which the riot had only interrupted. It was the world where, behind locked doors, Negroes catered to monied white people's weird sexual tastes.

The whites I'd known loved to rub shoulders publicly with black folks in the after-hours clubs and speakeasies. These, on the other hand, were whites who did not want it known that they had been anywhere near Harlem. The riot had made these exclusive white customers nervous. Their slipping into and about Harlem hadn't been so noticeable when other whites were also around. But now they would be conspicuous; they also feared the recently aroused anger of Harlem Negroes. So the madam was safeguarding her growing operation by offering me a steerer's job.

During the war, it was extremely difficult to get a telephone. One day the madam told me to stay at my apartment the next morning. She talked to somebody. I don't know who it was, but before the next noon, I dialed the madam from my own telephone—unlisted.

This madam was a specialist in her field. If her own girls could not—or would not—accommodate a customer, she would send me to another place, usually an apartment somewhere else in Harlem, where the requested "specialty" was done.

My post for picking up the customers was right outside the Astor Hotel, that always-busy northwest corner of 45th Street and Broadway. Watching the moving traffic, I was soon able to spot the taxi, car, or limousine—even before it slowed down—with the anxious white faces peering out for the tall, reddish-brown-complexioned Negro wearing a dark suit, or raincoat, with a white flower in his lapel.

If they were in a private car, unless it was chauffeured I would take the wheel and drive where we were going. But if they were in a taxi, I would always tell the cabbie, "The Apollo Theater in Harlem, please," since among New York City taxis a certain percentage are driven by cops. We would get another cab—driven by a black man—and I'd give him the right address.

As soon as I got that party settled, I'd telephone the madam. She would generally have me rush by taxi right back downtown to be on the 45th Street and Broadway corner at a specified time. Appointments were strictly punctual; rarely was I on the corner as much as five minutes. And I knew how to keep moving about so as not to attract the attention of any vice squad plainclothes men or uniformed cops.

With tips, which were often heavy, sometimes I would make over a hundred dollars a night steering up to ten customers in a party—to see anything, to do anything, to have anything done to them, that they wanted. I hardly ever knew the identities of my customers, but the few I did recognize, or whose names I happened to hear, remind me now of the Profumo case in England. The English are not far ahead of rich and influential Americans when it comes to seeking rarities and oddities.

Rich men, middle-aged and beyond, men well past their prime:

these weren't college boys, these were their Ivy League fathers. Even grandfathers, I guess. Society leaders. Big politicians. Tycoons. Important friends from out of town. City government big shots. All kinds of professional people. Star performing artists. Theatrical and Hollywood celebrities. And, of course, racketeers.

Harlem was their sin-den, their fleshpot. They stole off among taboo black people, and took off whatever antiseptic important, dignified masks they wore in their white world. These were men who could afford to spend large amounts of money for two, three, or four hours indulging their strange appetites.

But in this black-white nether world, nobody judged the customers. Anything they could name, anything they could imagine, anything they could describe, they could do, or could have done to them, just as long as they paid.

In the Profumo case in England, Christine Keeler's friend testified that some of her customers wanted to be whipped. One of my main steers to one specialty address away from the madam's house was the apartment of a big, coal-black girl, strong as an ox, with muscles like a dockworker's. A funny thing, it generally was the oldest of these white men—in their sixties, I know, some maybe in their seventies—they couldn't seem to recover quickly enough from their last whipping so they could have me meet them again at 45th and Broadway to take them back to that apartment, to cringe on their knees and beg and cry out for mercy under that black girl's whip. Some of them would pay me extra to come and watch them being beaten. That girl greased her big Amazon body all over to look shinier and blacker. She used small, plaited whips, she would draw blood, and she was making herself a small fortune off those old white men.

I wouldn't tell all the things I've seen. I used to wonder, later on, when I was in prison, what a psychiatrist would make of it all. And so many of these men held responsible positions; they exercised guidance, influence, and authority over others.

In prison later, I'd think, too, about another thing. Just about all of those whites specifically expressed as their preference black, *black*, "the blacker the better!" The madam, having long since learned this, had in her house nothing but the blackest accommodating women she could find.

In all of my time in Harlem, I never saw a white prostitute touched by a white man. White girls were in some of the various Harlem specialty places. They would participate in customers' most frequent exhibition requests—a sleek, black Negro male having a white woman. Was this the white man wanting to witness his deepest sexual fear? A few times, I even had parties that included white women whom the men had brought with them to watch this. I never steered any white women other than in these instances, brought by their own men, or who had been put into contact with me by a white Lesbian whom I knew, who was another variety of specialty madam.

This Lesbian, a beautiful white woman, had a male Negro stable. Her vocabulary was all profanity. She supplied Negro males, on order, to well-to-do white women.

I'd seen this Lesbian and her blonde girl friend around Harlem, drinking and talking at bars, always with young Negroes. No one who didn't know would ever guess that the Lesbian was recruiting. But one night I gave her and her girl friend some reefers which they said were the best they'd ever smoked. They lived in a hotel downtown, and after that, now and then, they would call me, and I would bring them some reefers, and we'd talk.

She told me how she had accidentally gotten started in her specialty. As a Harlem habitué, she had known Harlem Negroes who liked white women. Her role developed from a pattern of talk she often heard from bored, well-to-do white women where she worked, in an East Side beauty salon. Hearing the women complain about sexually inadequate mates, she would tell what she'd "heard" about Negro men. Observing how excited some of the women seemed to become, she finally arranged some dates with some of the Harlem Negroes she knew at her own apartment.

Eventually, she rented three midtown apartments where a woman customer could meet a Negro by appointment. Her customers recommended her service to their friends. She quit the beauty salon, set up a messenger service as an operating front, and ran all of her business by telephone.

She had also noticed the color preference. I never could substitute in an emergency, she would tell me with a laugh, because I was too light. She told me that nearly every white woman in her clientele would specify "a black one"; sometimes they would say "a *real* one," meaning black, no brown Negroes, no red Negroes.

The Lesbian thought up her messenger service idea because some of her trade wanted the Negroes to come to their homes, at times carefully arranged by telephone. These women lived in neighborhoods of swank brownstones and exclusive apartment houses, with doormen dressed like admirals. But white society never thinks about challenging any Negro in a servant role. Doormen would telephone up and hear "Oh, yes, send him right up, James"; service elevators would speed those neatly dressed Negro messenger boys right up—so that they could "deliver" what had been ordered by some of the most privileged white women in Manhattan.

The irony is that those white women had no more respect for those Negroes than white men have had for the Negro women they have been "using" since slavery times. And, in turn, Negroes have no respect for the whites they get into bed with. I know the way I felt about Sophia, who still came to New York whenever I called her.

The West Indian boyfriend of the Profumo scandal's Christine Keeler, Lucky Gordon, and his friends must have felt the same way. After England's leaders had been with those white girls, those girls, for their satisfaction, went to Negroes, to smoke reefers and make fun of some of England's greatest peers as cuckolds and fools. I don't doubt that Lucky Gordon knows the identity of "the man in the mask" and much more. If Gordon told everything those white girls told him, he would give England a new scandal.

It's no different from what happens in some of America's topmost white circles. Twenty years ago, I saw them nightly, with my own eyes. I heard them with my own ears.

The hypocritical white man will talk about Negro's "low morals." But who has the world's lowest morals if not whites? And not only that, but the "upper-class" whites! Recently, details were published about a group of suburban New York City white housewives and mothers operating as a professional call-girl ring. In some cases, these wives were out prostituting with the agreement, even the cooperation of husbands, some of whom even waited at home, attending the children. And the customers—to quote a major New York City morning newspaper: "Some 16 ledgers and books with names of 200 Johns, many important social, financial and political figures, were seized in the raid Friday night."

I have also read recently about groups of young white couples who get together, the husbands throw their house keys into a hat, then, blindfolded, the husbands draw out a key and spend the night with the wife that the house key matches. I have never heard of anything like that being done by Negroes, even Negroes who live in the worst ghettoes and alleys and gutters.

Early one morning in Harlem, a tall, light Negro wearing a hat and with a woman's stocking drawn down over his face held up a Negro bartender and manager who were counting up the night's receipts. Like most bars in Harlem, Negroes fronted, and a Jew really owned the place. To get a license, one had to know somebody in the State Liquor Authority, and Jews working with Jews seemed to have the best S.L.A. contacts. The black manager hired some Negro hoodlums to go hunting for the hold-up man. And the man's description caused them to include me among their suspects. About daybreak that same morning, they kicked in the door of my apartment.

I told them I didn't know a thing about it, that I hadn't had a thing to do with whatever they were talking about. I told them I had been out on my hustle, steering, until maybe four in the morning, and then I had come straight to my apartment and gone to bed.

The strong-arm thugs were bluffing. They were trying to flush out the man who had done it. They still had other suspects to check out—that's all that saved me.

I put on my clothes and took a taxi and I woke up two people, the madam, then Sammy. I had some money, but the madam gave me some more, and I told Sammy I was going to see my brother Philbert in Michigan. I gave Sammy the address, so that he could let me know when things got straightened out.

This was the trip to Michigan in the wintertime when I put congolene on my head, then discovered that the bathroom sink's pipes were frozen. To keep the lye from burning up my scalp, I had to stick my head in the stool and flush and flush to rinse out the stuff.

A week passed in frigid Michigan before Sammy's telegram came. Another red Negro had confessed, which enabled me to live in Harlem again.

But I didn't go back into steering. I can't remember why I didn't. I imagine I must have felt like staying away from hustling for a while, going to some of the clubs at night, and narcotizing with my friends. Anyway, I just never went back to the madam's job.

It was at about this time, too, I remember, that I began to be sick. I had colds all the time. It got to be a steady irritation, always sniffling and wiping my nose, all day, all night. I stayed so high that I was in a dream world. Now, sometimes, I smoked opium with some white friends, actors who lived downtown. And I smoked more reefers than ever before. I didn't smoke the usual wooden-match-sized sticks of marijuana. I was so far gone by now that I smoked it almost by the ounce.

After awhile, I worked downtown for a Jew. He liked me because of something I had managed to do for him. He bought rundown restaurants and bars. Hymie was his name. He would remodel these places, then stage a big, gala reopening, with banners and a spotlight outside. The jam-packed, busy place with the big "Under New Management" sign in the window would attract speculators, usually other Jews who were around looking for something to invest money in. Sometimes even in the week of the new opening, Hymie would resell at a good profit.

Hymie really liked me, and I liked him. He loved to talk. I loved to listen. Half his talk was about Jews and Negroes. Jews who had anglicized their names were Hymie's favorite hate. Spitting and curling his mouth in scorn, he would reel off names of people he said had done this. Some of them were famous names whom most people never thought of as Jews.

"Red, I'm a Jew and you're black," he would say. "These Gentiles don't like either one of us. If the Jew wasn't smarter than the Gentile, he'd get treated worse than your people."

Hymie paid me good money while I was with him, sometimes two hundred and three hundred dollars a week. I would have done anything for Hymie. I did do all kinds of things. But my main job was transporting bootleg liquor that Hymie supplied, usually to those spruced-up bars which he had sold to someone.

Another fellow and I would drive out to Long Island where a big bootleg whisky outfit operated. We'd take with us cartons of empty bonded whisky bottles that were saved illegally by bars we supplied. We would buy five-gallon containers of bootleg, funnel it into the bottles, then deliver, according to Hymie's instructions, this or that many crates back to the bars.

Many people claiming they drank only such-and-such a brand couldn't tell their only brand from pure week-old Long Island bootleg. Most ordinary whisky drinkers are "brand" chumps like this. On the side, with Hymie's approval, I was myself at that time supplying some lesser quantities of bootleg to reputable Harlem bars, as well as to some of the few speakeasies still in Harlem.

But one weekend on Long Island, something happened involving the State Liquor Authority. One of New York State's biggest recent scandals has been the exposure of wholesale S.L.A. graft and corruption. In the bootleg racket I was involved in, someone high up must have been taken for a real pile. A rumor about some "inside" tipster spread among Hymie and the others. One day Hymie didn't show up where he had told me to meet him. I never heard from him again . . . but I did hear that he was put in the ocean, and I knew he couldn't swim.

Up in the Bronx, a Negro held up some Italian racketeers in a floating crap game. I heard about it on the wire. Whoever did it, aside from being a fool, was said to be a "tall, light-skinned" Negro, masked with a woman's stocking. It has always made me wonder if that bar stickup had really been solved, or if the wrong man had confessed under beatings. But, anyway, the past suspicion of me helped to revive suspicion of me again.

Up in Fat Man's Bar on the hill overlooking the Polo Grounds, I had just gone into a telephone booth. Everyone in the bar—all over Harlem, in fact—was drinking up, excited about the news that Branch Rickey, the Brooklyn Dodgers' owner, had just signed Jackie Robinson to play in major league baseball, with the Dodgers' farm team in Montreal—which would place the time in the fall of 1945.

Earlier in the afternoon, I had collected from West Indian Archie for a fifty-cent combination bet; he had paid me three hundred dollars right out of his pocket. I was telephoning Jean Parks. Jean was one of the most beautiful women who ever lived in Harlem. She once sang with Sarah Vaughan in the Bluebonnets, a quartet that sang with Earl Hines. For a long time, Jean and I had enjoyed a standing, friendly deal that we'd go out and celebrate when either of us hit the numbers. Since my last hit, Jean had treated me twice, and we laughed on the phone, glad that now I'd treat her to a night out. We arranged to go to a 52nd Street night club to hear Billie Holiday, who had been on the road and was just back in New York.

As I hung up, I spotted the two lean, tough-looking *paisanos* gazing in at me cooped in the booth.

I didn't need any intuition. And I had no gun. A cigarette case was the only thing in my pocket. I started easing my hand down into my pocket, to try bluffing . . . and one of them snatched open the door. They were dark-olive, swarthy-featured Italians. I had my hand down into my pocket.

"Come on outside, we'll hold court," one said.

At that moment, a cop walked through the front door. The two thugs slipped out. I never in my life have been so glad to see a cop.

I was still shaking when I got to the apartment of my friend, Sammy the Pimp. He told me that not long before, West Indian Archie had been there looking for me.

Sometimes, recalling all of this, I don't know, to tell the truth, how I am alive to tell it today. They say God takes care of fools and babies. I've so often thought that Allah was watching over me. Through all of this time in my life, I really *was* dead—mentally dead. I just didn't know that I was.

Anyway, to kill time, Sammy and I sniffed some of his cocaine, until the time came to pick up Jean Parks, to go down and hear Lady Day. Sammy's having told me about West Indian Archie looking for me didn't mean a thing . . . not right then.

SPECULATIONS

1. In this chapter, Malcolm X aptly describes the life of the hustler. How would you characterize that life? What are its values? What are the central principles by which Malcolm X lived during this time?

2. The white/black racial tensions that ripple throughout this chapter are still prevalent in America. What is Malcolm X's attitudes toward whites as revealed by this chapter? Upon what facts, prejudices, assumptions are these attitudes based?

3. The *Autobiography* is not written by Malcolm X; it is a series of oral interviews that Malcolm X did with the late Alex Haley, author of *Roots*. Do you think this chapter has an oral quality to it? How so? How would you describe the organization of this chapter? Would you describe the overall structure as more characteristic of a written or an oral discourse?

4. Early in this chapter, Malcolm X says:

> Full-time hustlers never can relax to appraise what they are doing and where they are bound. As is the case in any jungle, the hustler's every waking hour is lived with both the practical and the subconscious knowledge that if he ever relaxes, if he ever slows down, the other hungry, restless foxes, ferrets, wolves, and vultures out there with him won't hesitate to make him their prey.

Is this true of Malcolm X's own experience as revealed by this chapter? What allows him to survive the "hustler business?" How appropriate is this Darwinian metaphor to any business or professional person in America?

5. There is an edge of anger throughout much of the *Autobiography*, and certainly one can feel that edge of anger in this chapter. Can you locate specific instances where you feel Malcolm X's anger—at whites, at police, at the value system of 1960s America? How do you respond to Malcolm X's anger and his charges about racist individuals and a racist society? Is Malcolm X himself vulnerable to the same charges, at least as represented in this one chapter? Do you feel at least some of the same anger?

6. Throughout this chapter, Malcolm X refers to people specifically by name—and often those names are of famous Harlem personalities. How does this recitation of names affect you? Does it make this account more or less pleasureful to read? Does it add or detract from Malcolm X's authority or veracity? Do you recognize any of the names, especially those from the Harlem music scene? Why do you think Malcolm X includes those in particular?

Home: The Street Is a Route to Peril

NATHAN McCALL

Nathan McCall is a reporter for the *Washington Post*, but he hasn't always been so securely a part of "the establishment." McCall almost wound up as a statistic in some crime report like many of his high school friends.

Currently on professional leave, McCall is writing an autobiography. Tentatively entitled *It Makes Me Want To Holler*, a line derived from a Marvin Gaye song, the book is under contract and has been optioned to be made into a movie by the director of *Boyz 'n the 'Hood*.

The movie and the book are scheduled to come out in the fall of 1993. McCall stated in a recent interview:

> In this book, I want to talk about the urban scene today, what shaped my views and led me into the streets. I really loved school, but I wanted to be part of that exciting life of the streets—the violence, crime, gangs. Other factors, however, also led me and my friends to make the decisions we did as we got older. For example, we saw our fathers working hard in the white mainstream, but what they were doing and how that was affecting them did not make that mainstream appealing. In fact, by the time I was 18 I was afraid to go out into the white world, because I felt there was no way to win out there; no matter how hard you worked the odds were stacked against you. Like so many kids today who take up guns and sell drugs even when they know what the outcome might be—I figured I had better odds on the street; at least the playing field was level and the rules didn't change.

McCall lived that life, and almost paid for it with his life. He graduated from high school in 1973 and attended Norfolk State University. Immediately after his freshman year he was arrested for attempted murder and placed on probation. A few months later, he was arrested for armed robbery, convicted, and sentenced to twelve years at Southampton Correctional Center in Capron, Virginia. Paroled after three years, he received a tuition scholarship in journalism back at Norfolk State. After graduating, McCall worked as a journalist for several newspapers, including the *Washington Post* where his self-chosen beat is the Department of Corrections.

> One of the reasons I am writing this book is that I discovered that the human spirit is indomitable. With that knowledge, I feel I can do anything. I think about the many times that life could have ended for me, and about the many people who could have made it if they had discovered the truth. That's part of the message—that we all have these possibilities.

This essay inscribes another truth as well—namely, that the limited possibilities available to many of today's youth may well lead them toward a life of crime and punishment.

Two Christmases ago, I went home to Portsmouth, Va., and some of the boys from my old days on the block—Tony, Nutbrain and Roger—dropped by to check me out.

We caught up on the years, and their stories revealed that not much with the old gang had changed: One had just gotten out of jail, he said, "for doing a rain dance" on his estranged girlfriend. Another had lost his house and family to a cocaine habit.

We learned that another old friend was back in town and decided to pay him a surprise visit. We crammed into my car, then stopped and bought a bottle of cheap wine—just like the old days. I slid Marvin Gaye's classic "What's Going On?" into the cassette player and, while cruising along, it struck me: It really was like old times—them passing the wine bottle, Roger and Nutbrain arguing and elbowing each other in the back seat, and everybody trading insults left and right.

When our friend answered the door, he seemed surprised but not glad to see us. Within minutes, we knew the reason for his nervousness. There was a knock, followed by whispers and a stealthy entry of a scraggly-bearded man and a disheveled woman. Clearly, the three of them were about to do some drugs, just like old times.

What was different was that we left. And though I made a point of not being judgmental, I wondered, like Marvin Gaye had nearly two decades earlier, what is going on?

Lately, with the mounting toll of homicides, drug abuse and prison stints threatening to decimate a generation of young black men, I'm still wondering—not as an outsider, but as one who came perilously close to becoming a fatal statistic.

Every day in the District of Columbia, I read dismal accounts of blacks murdered over trivial things—drugs, a coat, a pair of sneakers, pocket change. The people in those stories are faceless to me.

But in my hometown, 200 miles south, the names conjure images of real people who lived down the street or around the corner.

Trips to my old neighborhood, a large, black community called Cavalier Manor, bring a distressingly close-up view of black America's running tragedy.

Most of the guys I hung out with are either in prison, dead, drug zombies or nickel-and-dime street hustlers; Kenny Banks got 19 years for dealing drugs. Baby Joe just finished a 15-year bit for a murder beef. Charlie Gregg was in drug rehabilitation. Bubba Majette was murdered.

Many of my former running pals are insane—literally. I'm talking overcoats in August and voices in their heads.

Of the 10 families on my street that had young males in their households, four—including my own—have had one or more siblings serve time. One of my best buddies, Shane, was recently sent to prison. He shot a man several times, execution-style. He got life.

Often when I go home, I prepare with a pep talk to myself and a pledge to focus on the positive—time spent with family and old friends who are doing well and opportunities to lend a compassionate ear to those not so well off.

I know I will see former buddies. Some are old hoods, hanging on the same corners where I left them 15 years ago. I see in them how far I've come. I'm not sure what they see in me. In exchanges that are sometimes awkward, they recount their hard knocks. I say little about my establishment job or the new life I've found.

What should I say? Get a job? Go to college? Adopt my middle-class success strategies?

The fact is, I know what they've been through. And I understand what they face. I took the plunge myself, several times.

Before I was 20, I'd seen people shot and was shot at myself. When I was 19, in a running rivalry with some other thugs, I shot a man in the chest at point-blank range. He survived, and the following year he shot and killed a man and went to prison.

Many people are puzzled about the culture of violence pervading black communities. Some wonder if there is something innately wrong with black males. And when all else fails, they reach for the easy responses: "Broken homes?" "Misplaced values?" "Impoverished backgrounds?"

I can answer with certainty only about myself. My background and those of my running partners don't fit the conventional theories, and the problems among us are more complex than something we can throw jobs, social programs or more policeman at.

Portsmouth, a Navy town of nearly 103,000, is not the blighted big city that D.C. is. And Cavalier Manor is no ghetto. In fact, my old neighborhood is middle class by black standards and has long symbolized the quest for black upward mobility in Portsmouth. There are sprawling homes, manicured lawns and two-car garages.

Shane and I and the others in our loosely knit gang started out like most other kids. Ebullient and naive, we played sandlot football, mowed neighbors' lawns for spending change, went to the movies and attended church.

Yet somewhere between adolescence and adulthood, something changed. Our optimism faded. Our hearts hardened, and many of us went on to share the same fates as the so-called disadvantaged.

Life in a Hostile World

A psychologist friend once explained that our fates are linked partly to how we perceive our choices in life. Looking back, the reality may well have been that possibilities for us were abundant. But in Cavalier Manor, we perceived our choices as being severely limited.

Nobody flatly said that. But in various ways, inside our community and out, it was communicated early and often that as black men in a hostile world our options would be few.

The perception was powerfully reinforced by what we saw in our families, where we had inherited a legacy of limited choices. My stepfather left school after the 10th grade, and my mother, who dropped out after 11 years, did only slightly better. They all managed to exceed the accomplishments of their forebears, but the lagged behind their white contemporaries.

What is not so easy for outsiders to grasp is why we did not follow our parents' lead and try to seize what we could with what we had. For us, somehow, growing up in the '70s, it was different. Our parents tried to insulate us from the full brunt of racism, but they could not counteract the flood of racial messages, subtle and blatant, filtering into our psyches—messages that artists like Richard Wright, James Baldwin and Ralph Ellison have documented, ones you never get accustomed to: the look in white storekeepers' eyes when you enter; the "click" of door locks when you walk past whites sitting in their cars.

Our parents, we believed, had learned to swallow pride for survival's sake. We came to regard the establishment as the ubiquitous, all powerful "white man" who controlled our parents' lives and, we believed, determined our fates as well.

I think once we resigned ourselves to that notion, we became a lost and angry lot.

Role Models Who Didn't Stand Up

For instance, the concept of education as a passport to a better life was vague to us. That's why it was so easy for my buddies to drop out in our sophomore year.

Still, there were plenty of role models in the neighborhood who were not our parents—teachers, postal workers and a smattering of professionals. But even those we respected seemed unable to articulate, or expose us to choices they had not experienced themselves.

Besides, they were unappealing to us as heroes. They couldn't stand up to the white man.

Instead, we revered the guys on the streets, the thugs who were brazen and belligerent.

Our defiance may have stemmed partly from youthful rebellion, but it came mostly from rage at a world we sensed did not welcome us. And we knew there were countless others out there just like us, armed and on edge. Often all it took was an accidental brush against a coat sleeve or a misunderstood look to trigger a brawl or a shooting.

When your life in your own mind has no value, it becomes frighteningly easy to try to take another's life.

In Portsmouth, black males are assumed to have three post-high-school options: the naval shipyard, the military or college. All of us knew that working in the system carried a price: humiliation on some level. Among us was the lingering fear that the racially integrated work world, with its relentless psychological assaults, was in some ways more perilous than life in the rough-and-tumble streets.

Even among those of us who opted for college, there was the feeling that it was a place to stall. "We didn't know what to do or what we could do," Calvin Roberts, an old school and friend told me recently.

Urban Capitalism

Perhaps for the first time in this nation's history, blacks began searching on a large scale for alternatives, and one option, of course, was the drug trade, the urban answer to capitalism.

Contrary to some assumptions, there is no lack of work ethic in the drug trade. My best friend in school parlayed $20 into a successful drug operation.

My friend didn't get caught, but others who were selling drugs, burglarizing and robbing did. I was one of them.

Seven months after being placed on probation for shooting a man, my journey ended: Nutbrain, Charlie Gregg and myself were caught after holding up a McDonald's. I was the gunman in the late-night robbery, and I came so frighteningly close to pulling the trigger when the store manager tried to flee that my fingers moistened.

We actually got away with the money—about $2,000, I think—and were driving down the highway when several police cruisers surrounded us. I remember staring out the window of the police car and thinking that my life, at age 20, was over.

I also felt relieved, as if I had been saved from something worse. I truly had expected a more tragic fate: to go down in a shootout with police like Prairie Dog, a cross-town hood; to be caught by surprise, like Charles Lee, a neighborhood kid who was shot to death while burglarizing a home.

The Advice of Malcolm X

Prison was my wake-up call. For nearly three years, I was forced to nurture my spirit and ponder all that had gone on before. A job in the prison library exposed me to a world of black literature that helped me understand who I was, and why prison had become—literally—a rite of passage for so many of us. I sobbed when I read Richard Wright's "Native Son" because it captured all those conflicting feelings—Bigger Thomas's restless anger, hopelessness, his tough facade among blacks and his morbid fear of whites—that I had often sensed in myself, but was unable to express.

Malcolm X's autobiography helped me understand the devastating effects of self-hatred and introduced me to a universal principle: that if you change your self-perception, you can change your behavior. I concluded that if Malcolm X, who also went to prison, could pull his life out of the toilet, then maybe I could too.

I have come to believe two things that might seem contradictory: that some of our worst childhood fears were true—the establishment is teeming with racism. Yet, I also believe whites are as befuddled about race as we are, and they're as scared of us as we are of them. Many of them are seeking solutions, just like us.

Whenever people ask, "What is wrong with black men?" it makes me want to lash out. I am reminded of something once said by Malcolm X: "I have no mercy or compassion in me for a society that will crush people and then penalize them for not being able to stand up under the weight."

Sometimes I wonder how I endured when so many others were crushed.

Nutbrain, a mastermind in the ways of the streets, had the kind of raw intellect that probably could not be gauged in achievement tests. Shane, who often breezed effortlessly through tests in school, could have done anything he wanted with his life had he known what to do.

Now he has no choices.

A New Generation in Peril

For those who'd like answers, I have no pithy social formulas to end black-on-black violence. But I do know that I see a younger, meaner generation out there now—more lost and alienated than we were—and placing even less value on life. We were at least touched by role models; this new bunch is totally estranged from the black mainstream. Crack has taken the drug game to a more lethal level and given young blacks far more economic incentive to opt for the streets.

I've come to fear that of the many things a black man can die from, the first may be rage—his own or someone else's.

It makes me wanna holler, and throw up both my hands.

SPECULATIONS

1. This essay first appeared in *The Washington Post*. To whom do you think it is addressed? How does McCall try to make his audience pay attention to his message? Does he succeed?

2. Why does McCall delay offering his personal history until near the end of this essay? How does he prepare the reader for the revelations of his own past? Is his confession powerful? Is it persuasive? What point is he trying to make by telling readers about his own experiences?

3. McCall writes:

> Our parents, we believed, had learned to swallow pride for survival's sake. We came to regard the establishment as the ubiquitous, all powerful "white man" who controlled our parents' lives and, we believed, determined our fates as well.
>
> I think once we resigned ourselves to that notion, we became a lost and angry lot.

What does McCall mean by saying that the "establishment" was "ubiquitous," and that his life and the lives of all the black men and women in Cavalier Manor were controlled by the "white man"? In what specific ways did he feel a loss of power and control? Why didn't he think of education as a "passport to a better life"?

4.   How would you compare your own experiences growing up in your own neighborhood to that of Nathan McCall? Did your neighborhood life offer you inspiration, support, and comfort—or did it make you feel bitter and frustrated? What are the differences between the images of "success" that you perceived while growing up as opposed to McCall's?

5.   McCall describes a paradox:

> I have come to believe two things that might seem contradictory: that some of our worst childhood fears were true—the establishment is teeming with racism. Yet, I also believe whites are as befuddled about race as we are, and they're as scared of us as we are of them. Many of them are seeking solutions, just like us.

How can McCall hold these two contradictory views? How does his essay reflect both perspectives and broaden the reader's view?

6.   What does McCall mean when he says that "of the many things a black man can die from, the first may be rage—his own or someone else's"? How specifically do black men die from rage, especially their own rage?

Effort at Speech

WILLIAM MEREDITH

A distinguished poet and professor of English at Connecticut College, William Meredith is a librettist, an editor of the poems of Percy Bysshe Shelley (*Shelley: Poems*), and a translator of Guillaume Apollinaire (*Alcools: Poems*). His own volumes of poetry include *Love Letter from an Impossible Land* (1944), *Earth Walk* (1970), and *The Cheer* (1980).

Like many poets, Meredith works slowly; he writes approximately six poems a year. Says Meredith in *Corgi Modern Poets in Focus 2*: "Chiefly I think my poverty of output stems from the conviction that an unnecessary poem is an offense to the art." For Meredith, a poem becomes necessary when it attempts to think through a problem or something that Meredith does not understand. "Maybe," says Meredith, "that is the likeliest prescription for a work of art: a puzzle about which one has a glimmering."

Meredith was born in New York City in 1919 and earned a B.A. from Princeton University. A former Air Force pilot in the Korean War, Meredith rose to the rank of lieutenant commander and was awarded two air medals. He is also the recipient of numerous literary awards including Ford Foundation and Guggenheim fellowships.

Meredith writes often about his experience and has been praised often for his eloquence and "conservative sense of people and place." Many of those qualities are apparent in this poem about a crime—and its consequence for the victim.

For Muriel Rukeyser

Climbing the stairway gray with urban midnight,
Cheerful, venial, ruminating pleasure,
Darkness takes me, an arm around my throat and
    Give me your wallet.

Fearing cowardice more than other terrors,
Angry I wrestle with my unseen partner,
Caught in a ritual not of our own making,
    panting like spaniels.

Bold with adrenalin, mindless, shaking,
God damn it, no! I rasp at him behind me,
Wrenching the leather wallet from his grasp. It
    breaks like a wishbone,

So that departing (routed by my shouting,
Not by my strength or inadvertent courage)
Half of the papers lending me a name are
    gone with him nameless.

Only now turning, I see a tall boy running,
Fifteen, sixteen, dressed thinly for the weather.
Reaching the streetlight he turns a brown face briefly
    phrased like a question.

I like a questioner watch him turn the corner
Taking the answer with him, or his half of it.
Loneliness, not a sensible emotion,
    breathes hard on the stairway.

Walking homeward I fraternize with shadows,
Zig-zagging with them where they flee the streetlights,
Asking for trouble, asking for the message
    trouble had sent me.

All fall down has been scribbled on the street in
Garbage and excrement: so much for the vision
Others taunt me with, my untimely humor,
    so much for cheerfulness.

Next time don't wrangle, give the boy the money,
Call across chasms what the world you know is.
Luckless and lied to, how can a child master
                              human decorum?

Next time a switch-blade, somewhere he is thinking,
I should have killed him and took the lousy wallet.
Reading my cards he feels a surge of anger
                    blind as my shame.

Error from Babel mutters in the places,
Cities apart, where now we word our failures:
Hatred and guilt have left us without language
                    who might have held discourse.

SPECULATIONS

1.   In describing the struggle with his assailant, Meredith uses the phrase
"panting like spaniels." Why do you think he uses this comic phrase to describe this serious and potentially deadly encounter?

2.   Meredith presents two separate monologues toward the end of the poem.
How do these monologues prepare us for the final verse of the poem? What
are the implications of that final verse given what precedes it?

Senseless Crimes

RICK TELANDER

Having worked as a gravedigger, a farmer, a merchant seaman, an
insurance salesman, a rock and roll guitarist (for the Del-Crusta-
ceans), and a dog breeder, Rick Telander has now settled firmly upon
the career of writer. A frequent contributor to *Sports Illustrated*, the
now defunct *Sport*, and other magazines, he is also the author of
Heaven is a Playground (1976), *Joe Namath and the Other Guys* (1976),
and *The Hundred Yard Lie: College Football and What We Can Do to Stop
It* (1989). An ex-professional football player, Telander says he began
writing

> . . . after my leg was crushed in a pileup while playing for the Kansas
> City Chiefs. While recovering for 6 months in the hospital I wrote a five
> hundred-page autobiography (unpublished). . . . Encouraged by the re-
> sponse from those who read the book, I wrote several short stories, an-
> other novel and a rock opera (music included). None of these ever
> appeared in print but, undaunted, I continued my career in earnest. After
> two short articles appeared in *Dog World* magazine I finally published in
> *Sports Illustrated*. Today, after some success, I write at least ten hours every
> day.

His writing history is typical; most professional writers spend years learning their craft without a word getting published.

Telander was born in 1948 in Peoria, Illinois. His father was an oilman, his mother a poet. Telander has a B.A. from Northwestern University in Illinois, and currently makes Chicago his home.

In "Senseless Crimes," Telander combines his understanding of sports and his interest in social justice. His essay delineates that blurred line between healthy admiration for sports and sports heroes and an unprincipled dedication toward, at best, amoral commercialism.

Is it the shoes? . . .
Money, it's gotta
be the shoes!
            MARS BLACKMON, TO MICHAEL JORDAN, IN A NIKE COMMERCIAL

For 15-year-old Michael Eugene Thomas, it definitely was the shoes. A ninth-grader at Meade Senior High School in Anne Arundel County, Md., Thomas was found strangled on May 2, 1989. Charged with first-degree murder was James David Martin, 17, a basketball buddy who allegedly took Thomas's two-week-old Air Jordan basketball shoes and left Thomas's barefoot body in the woods near school.

Thomas loved Michael Jordan, as well as the shoes Jordan endorses, and he cleaned his own pair each evening. He kept the cardboard shoe box with Jordan's silhouette on it in a place of honor in his room. Inside the box was the sales ticket for the shoes. It showed he paid $115.50, the price of a product touched by deity.

"We told him not to wear the shoes to school," said Michael's grandmother, Birdie Thomas. "We said somebody might like them, and he said, 'Granny, before I let anyone take those shoes, they'll have to kill me.'"

Michael Jordan sits in the locked press room before a workout at the Chicago Bulls' practice facility in suburban Deerfield, Ill. He is wearing his practice uniform and a pair of black Air Jordans similar to the ones young Thomas wore, except that these have Jordan's number, 23, stitched on the sides. On the shoelaces Jordan wears plastic toggles to prevent the shoes from loosening if the laces should come untied. Two toggles come in each box of Air Jordans, and if kids knew that Jordan actually wears them, they would never step out the door without their own toggles securely in place. The door is locked to keep out the horde of fans, journalists and favor seekers who dog Jordan wherever he goes. Jordan needs a quiet moment. He is reading an account of Thomas's death that a reporter has shown him.

For just an instant it looks as though Jordan might cry. He has so carefully nurtured his image as the all-American role model that he refuses to go anywhere, get into any situation, that might detract from that image. He moves swiftly and smoothly from the court to home to charity events to the golf course, all in an aura of untarnished integrity. "I can't believe it," Jordan says in a low voice. "Choked to death. By his friend." He sighs deeply. Sweat trickles down one temple.

He asks if there have been other such crimes. Yes, he is told. Plenty, unfortunately. Not only for Air Jordans, but also for other brands of athletic shoes, as well as for jackets and caps bearing sports insignia—apparel that Jordan and other athlete endorsers have encouraged American youth to buy.

The killings aren't new. In 1983, 14-year-old Dewitt Duckett was shot to death in the hallway of Harlem Park Junior High in Baltimore by someone who apparently wanted Duckett's silky blue Georgetown jacket. In 1985, 13-year-old Shawn Jones was shot in Detroit after five youths took his Fila sneakers. But lately the pace of the carnage has quickened. In January 1988, an unidentified 14-year-old Houston boy, a star athlete in various sports, allegedly stabbed and killed 22-year-old Eric Allen with a butcher knife after the two argued over a pair of tennis shoes in the home the youths shared with their mothers. Seven months later a gunman in Atlanta allegedly robbed an unnamed 17-year-old of his Mercedes-Benz hat and Avia hightops after shooting to death the boy's 25-year-old friend, Carl Middlebrooks, as Middlebrooks pedaled away on his bike. Last November, Raheem Wells, the quarterback for Detroit Kettering High, was murdered, allegedly by six teenagers who swiped his Nike sneakers. A month later, 17-year-old Tyrone Brown of Hapeville, Ga., was fatally shot in the head, allegedly by two acquaintances who robbed him of money, cocaine and his sneakers. In Baltimore last summer 18-year-old Ronnell Ridgeway was robbed of his $40 sweatpants and then shot and killed. In March, Chris Demby, a 10th-grader at Franklin Learning Center in West Philadelphia, was shot and killed for his new Nikes.

In April 1989, 16-year-old Johnny Bates was shot to death in Houston by 17-year-old Demetrick Walker after Johnny refused to turn over his Air Jordan hightops. In March, Demetrick was sentenced to life in prison. Said prosecutor Mark Vinson, "It's bad when we create an image of luxury about athletic gear that it forces people to kill over it."

Jordan shakes his head.

"I thought I'd be helping out others and everything would be positive," he says. "I though people would try to emulate the good things I do, they'd try to achieve, to be better. Nothing bad. I never thought because of my endorsement of a shoe, or any product, that people would harm each other. Everyone likes to be admired, but when it comes to kids actually killing each other"—he pauses—"then you have to reevaluate things."

We certainly do. In a country that has long been hung up on style over substance, flash over depth, the athletic shoe and sportswear industries (a projected $5.5 billion in domestic sales of name-brand shoes in 1990; more than $2 billion in sweatpants, sweatshirts and warmup suits) suddenly have come to represent the pinnacle of consumer exploitation. In recent months the industries, which include heavyweights Nike and Reebok as well as smaller players Adidas, Asics, British Knights, Brooks, Converse, Ellesse, Etonic, Fila, L.A. Gear, New Balance, Pony, Puma, Starter and numerous other makers of sports shoes, caps and jackets, have been accused of creating a fantasy-fueled market for luxury items in the economically blasted inner cities and willingly tapping into the flow of drug and gang money. This has led to a frightening outbreak of crimes among poor black kids trying to make their mark by "busting fresh," or dressing at the height of fashion.

In some cities muggings for sportswear are commonplace—Atlanta police, for instance, estimate they have handled more than 50 such robberies in the last four months. Yet it is not only the number of violent acts but also the seeming triviality of the booty that has stunned the public. In February, 19-year-old Calvin Wash was about to cross Central Park Avenue on Chicago's West Side when, according to police, two youths drove up in a van and demanded that he give them the Cincinnati Bengal jacket he was wearing. When Wash resisted, one of the youths is alleged to have fatally shot him in the back—through the A in BENGALS.

Chicago police sergeant Michael Chasen, who works in the violent crimes division in Area Four, which covers four of Chicago's 25 police districts, says his districts have about 50 reported incidents involving jackets and about a dozen involving gym shoes each month. "When you really think about the crime itself—taking someone's clothes off their body—you can't get much more basic," he says.

But, of course, these assailants aren't simply taking clothes from their victims. They're taking status. Something is very wrong with a society that has created an underclass that is slipping into economic and moral oblivion, an underclass in which pieces of rubber and plastic held together by shoelaces are sometimes worth more than a human life. The shoe companies have played a direct role in this. With their million-dollar advertising campaigns, superstar spokesmen and over-designed, high-priced products aimed at impressionable young people, they are creating status from thin air to feed those who are starving for self-esteem. "No one person is responsible for this type of violence," says Patricia Graham, principal of Chicago's Simeon

High, one of the city's perennial basketball powers. "It's a combination of circumstances. It's about values and training. Society's values are out of sync, which is why these things have become important."

"The classic explanation in sociology is that these people are driven by peer pressure," says Mervin Daniel, a sociology professor at Morgan State. "What is advertised on TV and whatever your peers are doing, you do it too." Most assuredly, the shoe industry relies heavily on advertising; it spends more than $200 million annually to promote and advertise its products, churning out a blizzard of images and words that make its shoes seem preternaturally hip, cool and necessary. Nike alone will spend $60 million in 1990 on TV and print ads that have built such slogans as "Bo knows," and "Just do it," and "Do you know? Do you know? Do you know?" into mantras of consumerism.

What is baffling, however, is the strength of certain sporting products as icons for drug dealers and gangs. In Boston the Greenwood Street gang wears Green Bay Packers garb, the Vamp Hill Kings wear Los Angeles Kings and Raider gear, and the Castlegate gang wears Cincinnati Reds clothes. "The Intervale gang uses all Adidas stuff exclusively—hats, jackets, sweatpants, shoes," says Bill Stewart III, the probation officer at the Dorchester District Court in Boston, one of the busiest criminal courts in the nation. "They even have an Adidas handshake, copying the three stripes on the product. They extend three fingers when they shake hands."

Stewart knows how certain young drug dealers feverishly load up on the latest models of sneakers, tossing out any old ones that are scuffed or even slightly worn and replacing them with new pairs. "I was in a kid's apartment recently and there were about 50 pairs of brand-new sneakers, all top-of-the-line stuff—Adidas, Reebok and so forth," he says. "I asked the kid's mother how he came into all this stuff. She said she didn't know."

The use of Major League Baseball hats by gangs has prompted some high schools around the nation to ban them from school grounds, and expensive gold chains, major league or major college team jackets and other ostentatious, potentially troublesome items have also been prohibited. "When I look around sometimes, I think I'm in spring training in Florida," says Stewart.

When informed that baseball caps are being used by gangs as part of their uniforms, Major League Baseball public relations director Richard Levin seemed shocked. "I'm not aware of it at all, nor would I understand why," he said. "Obviously, we don't support it in any way."

Could any respectable U.S. corporation support the use of its products in this way? Absolutely not, said most shoe company executives contacted for this article. You better believe it, said a number of sports apparel retailers, as well as some of the more candid shoe execs.

Among the retailers is Wally Grigo, the owner of three sportswear shops in and near New Haven, Conn. Last August, Grigo put a sign in the front window of his inner city store that reads, IF YOU DEAL DRUGS, WE DON'T WANT YOUR BUSINESS. SPEND YOUR MONEY SOMEWHERE ELSE. "Unfortunately, it'll probably have to stay up forever," says Grigo. "I was doing, I'd say $2,000 a week in drug money sales that disappeared after the sign went up. Our industry is sick, addicted to drug money. We're going through the first phase of addiction, which is total denial."

Before he put up the sign, Grigo had been told by sales reps from two sportswear companies that he should "hook up" the local drug dealers to expose the companies' new products to the neighborhood clientele. After the sign went up, Grigo says, the rep from the smaller company returned and said, "Wally, we're thinking about giving you the line. But, you know, I can't do anything until you cut out the crap and take that sign out of your window. The bulk of our business is done with drug dealers. Wake up!"

Grigo was also stunned that he thought of wearing a wire to record the rep making similar statements. He didn't do so, though, figuring the company's officials would dismiss any evidence by saying the rep was a loose cannon. But Grigo says the companies know what's going on, because the reps are "in the trenches, and they go back and report."

Grigo doesn't want to publicly state the names of the suppliers, for economic reasons. "I'm not afraid of the drug dealers," he says. "But the shoe companies could put me out of business anytime, just by canceling my credit."

One obvious question: How does Grigo, or anyone, know when a drug dealer and not a law-abiding citizen is making a buy? "Hey, spend 10 minutes in any city store," says Grigo. "When an 18-year-old kid pulls up in a BMW, walks down the aisle saying, 'I want this, this, this and this,' then peels off 50's from a stack of bills three inches thick, maybe doesn't even wait for change, then comes back a couple weeks later and does the same thing, hey . . . you know what I'm saying?"

And what about all those good guys advertising the shoes? What about Nike's Jordan and Spike Lee, the gifted film-maker and actor who portrays Mars Blackmon, the hero-worshipping nerd in the company's Air Jordan ads? Are they and other pitchmen at fault, too?

"Maybe the problem is those guys don't know what's going on," says Grigo. "There are stores doing $5,000 to $10,000 a week in drug money, all over. Drug money is part of the economic landscape these days. Even if the companies don't consciously go after the money, they're still getting it. Hey, all inner-city kids aren't drug dealers. Most of them are good, honest kids. Drug dealers are a very small percent. But the drug dealers, man, they set fashion trends."

Liz Dolan, director of public relations for Nike, hits the ceiling when she hears such talk. "Our commercials are about sport, they're not about fashion," she says.

But the industry's own figures make that assertion extremely questionable. At least 80% of the athletic shoes sold in the U.S. are not used for their avowed purpose—that is, playing sports.

Dolan sighs. She says that all of Nike's athlete-endorsers are quality citizens as well as superjocks. "We're not putting Leon Spinks in the commercials," she says. Then she says that the people who raise the alarm that Nike, as well as other sports apparel companies, is exploiting the poor and creating crime just to make money, are bizarre and openly racist. "What's baffling to us is how easily people accept the assumption that black youth is an unruly mob that will do anything to get its hands on what it wants," she says, excitedly. "They'll say, 'Show a black kid something he wants, and he'll kill for it.' I think it's racist hysteria, just like the Charles Stuart case in Boston or the way the Bush campaign used Willie Horton."

Lee also says he has heard such panic before. "Everybody says last summer that my movie *Do the Right Thing* was going to cause 30 million black people to riot," he says angrily. "But I haven't heard of one garbage can being thrown through a pizzeria window, have you? I want to work with Nike to address the special problems of inner-city black youths, but the problem is not shoes."

Lee is particularly irate because he has been singled out by *New York Post* sports columnist Phil Mushnick as being untrue to the very people Lee champions in his films. In Mushnick's April 6 [1990] column headlined, SHADDUP, I'M SELLIN' OUT . . . SHADDUP, he sharply criticized Lee for leading the hype. The caption under four photos—one of Lee; the others of soaring pairs of Air Jordans—said, "While Spike Lee watches Michael Jordan (or at least his shoes) dunk all over the world, parents around the country are watching their kids get mugged, or even killed, over the same sneakers Lee and Jordan are promoting." In his column Mushnick said, "It's murder, gentlemen. No rhyme, no reason, just murder. For sneakers. For jackets. Get it, Spike? Murder."

Lee wrote a response in *The National*, the daily sports newspaper, in which he angrily accused Mushnick of "thinly veiled racism" for going after him and other high-profile black endorsers and not white endorsers like Larry Bird or Joe Montana. Lee also questioned Mushnick's sudden "great outpouring of concern for Afro-American youths." Lee wrote, "The Nike commercials Michael Jordan and I do have never gotten anyone killed. . . . The deal is this: Let's try to effectively deal with the conditions that make a kid put so much importance on a pair of sneakers, a jacket and gold. These kids feel they have no options, no opportunities."

Certainly Lee is right about that. Elijah Anderson, a University of Pennsylvania sociologist who specializes in ethnography, the study of individual cultures, links the scourge of apparel-related crimes among young black males to "inequality in race and class. The uneducated, inner-city kids don't have a sense of opportunity. They feel the system is closed off to them. And yet they're bombarded with the same cultural apparatus that the white middle class is. They don't have the means to attain the things offered, and yet they have the same desire. So they value these 'emblems,' these symbols of supposed success. The gold, the shoes, the drug dealer's outfit—those things all belie the real situation, but it's a symbolic display that seems to say that things are all right.

"Advertising fans this whole process by presenting the images that appeal to the kids, and the shoe companies capitalize on the situation, because it exists. Are the companies abdicating responsibility by doing this? That's a hard one to speak to. This is, after all, a free market."

But what about social responsibility? One particularly important issue is the high price of the shoes—many companies have models retailing for considerably more than $100, with the Reebok Pump leading the parade at $170. There is also the specific targeting of young black males as buyers, through the use of seductive, macho-loaded sales pitches presented by black stars.

"You can quibble about our tactics, but we don't stand for the drug trade," says Dolan. She points out that Nike's fall promotion campaign will include $5 million worth of "strictly pro-education, stay-in-school" public service commercials that will "not run late at night, but on the same major sporting events as the prime-time ads." Nike is not alone in playing the good corporate citizen. Reebok recently gave $750,000 to fund Project Teamwork, a program designed to combat racism that is administered by the Center for the Study of Sport in Society at Northeastern University.

Nevertheless, certain products wind up having dubious associations—some products more than others. John Hazard, the head buyer for the chain of City Sports stores in Boston, says, "We used to have brawls in here, robberies, a tremendous amount of stealing. But we cut back on 90 percent of it by getting rid of certain products. We don't carry Adidas, Fila, British Knights. Those things bring in the gangs.

"There's a store not far away that carries all that stuff. They have after-hours sales to show the new lines to big drug dealers. They even have guys on beepers, to let them know when the latest shoes have come in. It would be nothing for those guys to buy 20, 30 pair of shoes to give to their 12-year-old runners."

He thinks for a moment. "I don't know if you can really blame the shoe companies for what happens. Not long ago there was a murder, a gang deal, here in Boston. The cops had the murderer, and they were walking him somewhere. It was on TV. The murderer was bent over at first, and then the cops stood him up, and—I couldn't believe it—all of a sudden you could see he was wearing a City Sports T-shirt. There's no way you can control what people wear."

John Donahoe, manager of a Foot Locker in Chicago's Loop, agrees. "Right now, this is the hottest thing we've got," he says, holding up a simple, ugly, blue nylon running shoe. Behind him are shelves filled with more than 100 different model or color variations. "Nike Cortez: $39," he says. "Been around for 20 years. Why is it hot now?" He shrugs, "I don't know."

Assistant manager, James Crowder chimes in helpfully. "It's not the price, or who's endorsing it. It's just . . . what's happening."

Keeping up with what's happening has shoe manufacturers scrambling these days. "It used to be you could have a product out and fiddle with it for years, to get it just right," says Roger Morningstar, the assistant vice-president of promotions at Converse. "Now, if you don't come out with two or three new models every month, you're dead."

At home I go to my closet and pull out my own meager assortment of sports shoes—nine pairs, all told. A pair of ancient turf football shoes; some nubbed softball shoes; a pair of old running shoes; a pair of original, hideous red-and-black Air Jordans, kept for historical reasons; a pair of Avia volleyball shoes, worn-out, though they were never used for their intended purpose; two pairs of low-cut tennis shoes (or are they walking shoes?); a pair of Nike cross-training shoes (though I don't cross-train or even know what is means) in bad shape; a pair of sweat-stained, yet still awe-inspiring hightop basketball Reebok Pumps, a Christmas gift from my sister and brother-in-law. I pick these up. They are happening.

There are three colors on them, and the words REEBOK BASKETBALL are stitched in the tongue, right below the wondrous pump itself, colored orange and pebbled to resemble a basketball. On the bottom of the shoes are three colors of textured rubber. And there is an indented section in the heel with clear plastic laid over four orange tubes, and embossed with the words REEBOK ENERGY RETURN SYSTEM. On the back of the hightops there is the orange release valve that, when touched, decompresses the whole shebang.

The shoes haven't changed my hoops game at all, thought they are comfortable, unless I pump them up too much and my toes slowly go numb. While I could never bring myself to pay for a pair out of my own pocket, I will admit that when I opened the shoe box on Christmas Day, I was thrilled by the sheer techno-glitz of the things. It was identical to the way felt when, at the age of eight, I received a Robert-the-Robot.

But can promoting athletic shoes possibly be wrong in a capitalist society? Reebok chairman Paul Fireman was recently quoted as describing the Pump as "a product that's aspirational to a young person"—that is, something to be desired. He added, if prospective buyers couldn't afford the shoes, "that's the place for a kid to get a job after school." What, indeed, is the point of ads if not to inform the public of products that it may or may not need, but that it may wish to buy? Should we demand that the sports shoe industry be held to a higher standard than, say, the junk food industry? The advertising community itself thought so highly of Nike's "Bo knows" spot with Bo Jackson and Bo Diddley that *Advertising Age* named Jackson its Star Presenter of 1989.

What are we looking for here, anyway?

"Responsibility," says Grigo, the New Haven store owner. "Have Spike Lee and Michael Jordan look at the camera and say, 'Drug dealers, don't you dare wear my shoes!' Put antidrug labels on the box. I already do at my stores."

"Everybody wants to do everything," says Nike's Dolan. "It's naïve to think an antidrug message on the shoe box is going to change anyone's behavior. Our theme is 'Just do it!' because we want people playing sports, because they'll need more shoes. The healthier people are, the more shoes we'll sell."

Trouble is, young black males—a significant portion of the market—are not healthy right now. In fact, 23% of black males between the ages of 20 and 29 are under the supervision of the criminal justice system—incarcerated, paroled or on probation. According to a 1989 study in the *Journal of the American Medical Association,* a black male is six times more likely to be a homicide victim than a white male. Writes *Washington Post* columnist William Raspberry: "The inability of so many young black men to see themselves as providers, or even as necessary to their families, may be one explanation for their irresponsible behavior." Marc Mauer, of the Sentencing Project, a non-profit group concerned with disparities in the administration of criminal justice, says, "We now risk the possibility of writing off an entire generation of black men."

Obviously we are talking about something bigger than shoes here. Jordan sits up straight in his chair. It's time for practice to start. "I'd rather eliminate the product [the shoes] than know drug dealers are providing the funds that pay me," he says.

Of course drug money is, to a troubling extent, supporting the product, as well as other brands of sneakers and sports apparel. And kids are being killed for them. So what should the shoe companies, the schools, the advertising industry, the endorsers, the media, parents—all of us—do about it?

Do you know? Do you know? Do you know?

SPECULATIONS

1. Telander considers that kids who kill kids over sports clothes are engaging in "senseless" acts. Are these killings really senseless? In what ways can you explain the motives of kids who kill for shoes or jackets?

2. Like many essayists, Telander opens with an anecdote—a short, narrative that pinpoints the central theme. Why do you think he chose to write about the murder of Michael Thomas? Why do you think he described the scene with Michael Jordan in the locker room, a scene he alternates with other accounts of clothes killings?

3. Telander writes:

> Something is very wrong with a society that has created an underclass that is slipping to economic and moral oblivion, an underclass in which pieces of rubber and plastic held together by shoelaces are sometimes worth more than a human life.

What are the causes for such an attitude among poor youths? What kinds of values does the street represent?

4. Telander's method of reporting of these "senseless" crimes is to give one point of view, then its counterpoint. For example, he gives us the account of Grigo, the New Haven shoe store owner; then the shoe salesman; then the Nike director of public relations; then Spike Lee responding to Phil Mushnick; etc. Is this form of presentation effective? Who is right? Who is responsible?

5. What is your attitude toward clothing and personal possessions? Are there things you want so bad that you have—however briefly—contemplated doing almost anything to get them? If you lacked the money to buy something you really wanted or needed, would you under some circumstances steal to get it? If not, what would prevent you from engaging in an "immoral" act?

Date Rape: The Story of an Epidemic and Those Who Deny It

ELLEN SWEET

Very little is known about Ellen Sweet except that she published "Date Rape: The Story of an Epidemic and Those Who Deny It" in the October 1985 issue of *Ms.* magazine as part of the "campus times" feature. According to the byline of that article, Ellen Sweet was the *Ms.* editor who coordinated the *Ms.* Magazine Campus Project on Sexual Assault.

The project to which Sweet refers was a groundbreaking study on date rape (or "campus rape" or "acquaintance rape") researched by Dr. Mary Koss of Kent State University in Ohio. Koss's study consists of a careful compilation of data which paints a frightening picture about the incidence of date rape on college campuses. This report became the foundation of a book entitled *I Never Called It Rape: The* Ms. *Report on Recognizing, Fighting, and Surviving Date and Acquaintance Rape* (1986) by Robin Warshaw. Ellen Sweet served as a consulting editor on that project, which describes case studies of acquaintance rape along with a barrage of stunning statistics, such as:

> Of 3,187 female college students questioned:

15.3% had been raped.
11.8% were victims of attempted rape.
11.2% had experienced sexual coercion.
14.5% had been touched sexually against their will.
42% of the rape victims told no one about their assaults.
55% of the men who raped said they had sex again with their victims.
41% of the raped women said they expect to be raped again.

Such statistics—and the case studies that go along with them—suggest the widespread nature of this particular kind of violent crime—and the social and cultural confusion that often clouds the issue, excusing the perpetrator and blaming the victim. These are the kinds of issues that Sweet analyzes in the following essay.

It was the beginning of spring break when I was a junior. I was in good spirits and had been out to dinner with an old friend. We returned to his college (dorm). There were some seniors on the ground floor, drinking beer, playing bridge. I'm an avid player, so we joined them, joked around a lot. One of them, John, wasn't playing, but he was interested in the game. I found him attractive. We talked, and it turned out we had a mutual friend, shared experiences. It was getting late, and my friend had gone to bed, so John offered to see me safely home. We took our time, sat outside talking for a while. Then he said we could get inside one of the most beautiful campus buildings, which was usually locked at night. I went with him. Once we were inside, he kissed me. I didn't resist, I was excited. He kissed me again. But when he tried for more, I said no. He just grew completely silent. I couldn't get him to talk to me any more. He pinned me down and ripped off my pants. I couldn't believe it was happening to me. . .

Let's call this Yale graduate Judy. Her experience and her disbelief, as she describes them, are not unique. Gretchen, another student victim of date rape (or acquaintance rape, as it is also called), had known for five years the man who invited her to an isolated vacation cabin and then raped her. "I considered him my best friend," she says on a Stanford University videotape used in discussions of the problem. "I couldn't believe it. *I couldn't believe it was actually happening to me.*"

Such denial, the inability to believe that someone they know could have raped them, is a common reaction of victims of date rape, say psychologists and counselors who have researched the topic and treated these women. In fact, so much silence surrounds this kind of crime that many women are not even aware that they have been raped. In one study, Mary P. Koss, a psychology professor at Kent State University, Ohio, asked female students if they had had sexual intercourse against their will through use of or threat of force (the minimal legal definition of rape). Of those who answered yes, only 57 percent went on to identify their experience as rape. Koss also identified the other group (43 percent) as those who hadn't even acknowledged the rape to themselves.

"I can't believe it's happening on our campus," is usually the initial response to reports such as Koss's. She also found that one in eight women students had been raped, and another one in four were victims of attempted rape. Since only 4 percent of all those reported the attack, Koss concluded that "at least ten times more rapes occur among college students than are reflected in official crime statistics." (Rape is recognized to be the most underreported of all crimes, and date rape is among the least reported, least believed, and most difficult to prosecute, second only to spouse rape.)

Working independently of Koss, researchers at Auburn University, Alabama, and more recently, University of South Dakota and St. Cloud State University, Minnesota, all have found that 1 in 5 women students were raped by men they knew.

Koss also found a core group of highly sexually aggressive men (4.3 percent) who use physical force to compel women to have intercourse but who are unlikely to see their act as rape. These "hidden rapists" have "oversubscribed" to traditional male roles, she says. They believe that aggression is normal and that women don't really mean it when they say no to sexual advances. Such men answer "True" to statements like "most women are sly and manipulating when they want to attract a man," "a woman will only respect a man who will lay down the law to her," and "a man's got to show the woman who's boss right from the start or he'll end up hen-pecked."

In Koss's current study, one respondent who answered yes to a question about obtaining intercourse through physical force, wrote in the comment, "I didn't rape the chick, she was enjoying it and responding," and later, "I feel that sex is a very pleasant way to relieve stress. Especially when there are no strings attached."

"He acted like he had a right, like he *didn't believe me*," says a coed from Auburn University on a videotaped dramatization of date rape experiences. And several weeks later, when she confronts him, saying he forced her, he says no, she wanted it. "You raped me," she finally tells him. And the picture freezes on his look of incredulity.

Barry Burkhart, a professor of psychology at Auburn, who has also studied sexual aggression among college men, found that 10 percent had used physical force to have intercourse with a woman against her will, and a large majority admitted to various other kinds of aggression. "These are ordinary males operating in an ordinary social context," he says. "So what we conclude is that there's something wrong with that social context."

The something wrong is that our culture fosters a "rape supportive belief system," according to social psychologist Martha Burt. She thinks that "there's a large category of 'real' rapes, and a much smaller category of what our culture is willing to call a 'real' rape. The question is, how does the culture manage to write off all those other rapes?" The way it's done, says Burt, currently director of the Social Services Research Center at the Urban Institute in Washington, D.C., is by believing in a series of myths about rape, including:

> It didn't really happen (the woman was lying);
> Women like rape (so there's no such thing as rape);
> Yes, it happened, but no harm was done (she wasn't a virgin; she wasn't white);
> Women provoke it (men can't control themselves);
> Women deserve it anyway.

It's easy to write off date rapes with such myths, coupled with what Burt calls our culture's "adversarial sexual beliefs": the gamesmanship theory that everybody is out for what they can get, and that all sexual relationships are basically exploitive and predatory. In fact, most victims of date rape initially blame themselves for what happened, and almost none report it to campus authorities. And most academic institutions prefer to keep it that way, judging from the lack of surveys on date rape—all of which makes one wonder if they don't actually blame the victim, too.

As long as such attacks continue to be a "hidden" campus phenomenon, unreported and unacknowledged by many college administrators, law enforcement personnel, and students, the problem will persist. Of course, the term has become much better known in the three years since *Ms.* reported on the prevalence of experiences such as Judy's and Gretchen's. (See "Date Rape: A Campus Epidemic?" September, 1982.) It has been the subject of talk shows such as "The Donahue Show" and TV dramas ("Cagney and Lacey"). But for most people it remains a contradiction in terms. "Everybody has a stake in denying that it's happening so often," says Martha Burt. "For women, it's self-protective. . . if only bad girls get raped, then I'm personally safe. For men, it's the denial that 'nice' people like them do it."

The fault has not entirely been that of the institutions. "Ten years ago, we were telling women to look over your shoulder when you go out at night and lock your doors," says Py Bateman, director of a nationally known rape education program in Seattle, Alternatives to Fear. The prevailing myth was that most rapes were committed by strangers in dark alleys.

"If you have to think that sixty to eighty percent of rape is by people you know—that's hard to deal with," says Sylvia Callaway, who directed the Austin, Texas, Rape Crisis Center for more than eight years before leaving last July. "No rape center in a university community would be surprised that the university is not willing to deal with the problem."

Statistics alone will not solve the problem of date rape, but they could help bring it out into the open. Which is why *Ms.* undertook the first nationwide survey on college campuses. The *Ms.* Magazine Campus Project on Sexual Assault, directed by Mary P. Koss at Kent State and funded by the National Center for the Prevention and Control of Rape, reached more than 7,000 students at a nationally representative sample of 35 schools, to find out how often, under what circumstances, and with what aftereffects a wide range of sexual assaults, including date rape, took place.

Preliminary results are now ready, and the information is no surprise. (See page 342.) Participating schools were promised anonymity, but each will receive the results applying to its student body. Our hope is that the reaction of "we can't believe it's happening on our campus" will be followed by "what can we do about it—now."

Just how entrenched is denial of this problem today? One gauge might be the difficulty our own researchers had in persuading schools to let us on campus. For every college that approved our study, two others rejected it. Their reasons (in writing and in telephone conversations) were themselves instructive: "we don't want to get involved," "limited foreseeable benefit," "too volatile a topic," "have not had any problems in this area," "worried about publicity," "can't allow surveys in classroom," "just can't invest the time now," "would be overintrusive," "don't want to be left holding the bag if something goes wrong."

Several schools rejected the study on the basis that filling out the questionnaire might upset some students, and that we were not providing adequate follow-up counseling. (Researchers stayed on campus for at least a day after the distribution of the questionnaire, gave the students listings of counselors or rape crisis centers to consult if anything upset them, and offered to meet with school personnel to brief them.) But isn't it less upsetting for a student to recognize and admit that she has been the victim of an acquaintance rape than to have buried the trauma of that rape deep inside herself?

"It's a Catch-22 situation. You want a survey to publicize a problem that has tremendous psychological implications. And the school says, 'Don't do it, because it will get people psychologically upset'," admits John Jung, who heads the human subjects review committee at California State University/Long Beach (a school that declined our study).

One wonders just who are the "people" who will get most psychologically upset: the students, or their parents who pay for their educations, or the administrators who are concerned about the school's image. "There may have been an episode here," said John Hose, executive assistant to the president of Brandeis University, "but there is no cause célèbre surrounding the issue. In such cases, the reaction of Student Affairs is to encourage the student to be in touch with her parents and to take legal action."

"Student Affairs" at Brandeis is headed by Rodger Crafts, who moved to this post about a year ago from the University of Rhode Island. "I don't think we have a significant problem here because we have a sophisticated and intelligent group of students," said Dean Crafts. As for the University of Rhode Island, more students there are "first generation college attenders," as he put it, and therefore have "less respect" for other people. Vandalism and physical harm are more likely to occur with "lower educational levels." Respect for other people goes along with "intelligence level."

Back at the University of Rhode Island, the counseling center is sponsoring a 12-week support and therapy group this fall for male students who are coercive and abusive in their relationships with women. Even though Nancy Carlson, director of Counseling and Career Services, is enthusiastic about such programs and workshops she notes, "the awareness about date rape has been a long time coming."

Another school where administrators were the last to confront the challenge to their school's self-image is Yale. Last year, two student publications reported instances of date rape on campus that surprised students, faculty, and administration. "There are no full statistics available on rape between the students at Yale anywhere. . . . There is no mention of rape in the 1983-1984 Undergraduate Regulations. There is no procedure for a victim to file a formal complaint of rape with the university. But there is rape between students at Yale," wrote Sarah Oates in the *Yale Daily News*. Partly in response to such charges, current Yale undergraduate regulations now list "sexual harassment" under "offenses that are subject to disciplinary action"—but still no mention of rape.

Yale students brave enough to bring a charge of sexual harassment may go before the Yale College Executive Committee, a specially convened group of faculty, administrators, and students that can impose a series of penalties, graduated in severity, culminating in expulsion. All its hearings and decisions are kept secret (but can in theory be subpoenaed in a court of law). But Michael McBride, current chair of the committee, told me that cases of date rape have come up during the past year, leading in one instance to a student being asked to "resign" from the university, and in another, the conclusion that there was not "sufficient evidence." (In Judy's case, described at the beginning of this article, the senior she charged was penalized by being denied the privilege of graduating with his class. But she claims that after he demanded that the case be reconsidered, he was fully exonerated.) Said McBride, "What surprised me the most was how complicated these cases are. It's only one person's word against another's. It's amazing how different their perceptions can be."

Judy chose to take her case before the Executive Committee rather than report it to the local police, because she felt she would have complete confidentiality and quick action. Actually, there were many delays. And then, because the man she accused hired a lawyer, she was forced to hire one too. As a result, the meeting felt very much like a jury trial to her, complete with cross-examinations that challenged her truthfulness and raised excruciatingly embarrassing questions.

Judy's lawyer felt that such painful questions were necessary. But it seems as if the lesson feminists in the sixties and seventies worked so hard and successfully to make understood—not to blame the victim for stranger rape—is one that will have to be learned all over again in the case of acquaintance rape. Only this time, the woman who reports the rape suffers a triple victimization. Not only is she attacked and then not believed, but she carries the added burden of losing faith in her own judgment and trust in other people.

In a recently published study of jurors in rape trials, University of Illinois sociologist Barbara Reskin found that jurors were less likely to convict a man if the victim knew him. "Consent is the preferred rape defense and gets the highest acquittal rates," Reskin observes. "In a date rape situation, I would think the jury would assume that the woman had already accepted his invitation in a romantic sense. It would be a matter of how *much* did she consent to."

Personal characteristics also influence jurors, Reskin says. Those she studied couldn't imagine that certain men would commit rape: if they were attractive, had access to sexual partners such as a girlfriend or a wife. More often than not, they'd say, "But he doesn't look like a rapist." Reskin imagines that this pattern would be "magnified in date rape, because these are men who could get a date, they're not complete losers."

It may turn out that solutions to the problem will turn up at places with a less genteel image to protect. Jan Strout, director of Montana State, Women's Resource Center, wonders if schools such as hers, which recognize that they are dealing with a more conservative student body and a "macho cowboy image," aren't more willing to take the first step toward acknowledging the problem. A group called Students Against Sexual Assault was formed there two-and-a-half years ago after several students who were raped or resisted an attempted rape "went public." With men and women sharing leadership, this group is cosponsored by the Women's Resource Center and the student government.

Admitting to the problem isn't easy even when data is available, as doctoral student Genny Sandberg found at University of South Dakota. Last spring, she announced the results of a dating survey she coauthored with psychologists Tom Jackson and Patricia Petretic-Jackson. The most shocking statistic: 20 percent of the students (most from rural backgrounds and living in a rural campus setting) had been raped in a dating situation. The state board of regents couldn't believe it. "I just think that that's absolutely ridiculous," former regent Michael Rost said, according to the Brookings *Daily Register*, "I can't believe we would allow that to occur. If it is true, it's a very serious problem." Regent William Srstka agreed, "If this is true it's absolutely intolerable."

Following testimony by one of the researchers, the board changed its tune. Members are now discussing how to begin a statewide education and prevention program.

An inspiring example of how an administration can be led to new levels of consciousness took place at the University of Michigan earlier this year. Spurred by an article in *Metropolitan Detroit* magazine, a group of students staged a sit-in at the office of a university vice-president and who had been quoted as saying that "Rape is a red flag word. . . . [The university] wants to present an image that is receptive and palatable to the potential student cohort," and also that "Rape is an issue like Alzheimer's disease or mental retardation [which] impacts on a small but sizable part of the population. . . . Perhaps it has to become a crisis that is commonly shared in order to get things done."

The students who spent the entire day in Vice President Henry Johnson's office claimed that rape had already become a crisis on their campus. They presented a list of 12 demands, ranging from a rape crisis center on campus to better lighting and installation of outdoor emergency phones. By the end of the day, Johnson had started to change his mind. Although he insisted that he had been misquoted and quoted out of context in the press, he told me that "I did not realize [before that] acquaintance rape was so much of a problem, that it was the most prevalent type of rape. There is a heightened awareness now on this campus. Whether we as a faculty and administration are as sensitive as we should be is another issue—and that will take some time."

In the meantime, members of the Michigan Student Assembly Women's Issues Committee (one of the groups active in organizing the protest) took their demands before the school's board of regents. The result: a $75,000 program for rape prevention and education on campus, directly reporting to Johnson's office. "We'll now be in a position to document the problem and to be proactive," says Johnson. Jennifer Faigel, an organizer of the protest, acknowledges a change in the administration's awareness but says the students themselves, disappointed in the amount of funding promised for the program, have already formed a group (Students Organized Against Rape) to develop programs in the dorms.

In just the three years since *Ms.* first reported on date rape, several new campus organizations have sprung up and other ongoing programs have surfaced.

But the real measure of a school's commitment to dealing with this problem is the range of services it provides, says Mary Harvey, who did a nationwide study of exemplary rape programs for the National Center for the Prevention and Control of Rape. "It should have preventive services, crisis intervention, possibilities for long-term treatment, advocacy, and women's studies programs that educate about violence. The quality of a university's services to rape victims can be measured by the degree to which these other things are in place."

Minimally, rape counselors and educators feel, students need to be exposed to information about date rape as soon as they enter college. Studies show that the group most vulnerable to acquaintance rape are college freshmen, followed by high school seniors. In Koss's original survey, for example, the average age of the victim was 18.

"I'd like a program where no first-year students could finish their starting week at college without being informed about the problem of acquaintance rape," says Andrea Parrot, a lecturer in human service studies at Cornell University, who is developing a program to train students and dorm resident advisers as date rape awareness counselors. Parrot and others admit that this would be a bare minimum. Handing out a brochure to read, even conducting a workshop on the subject during the busy orientation week and counting on students voluntarily attending, needs to be followed up with sessions in dormitories or other living units. These are the most common settings for date rapes, according to a study by Parrot and Robin Lynk.

So how do we go about changing attitudes? And how do we do it without "setting student against student?" asks Gretchen Mieszkowski, chair of the Sexual Assault Prevention Committee at the University of Houston/Clear Lake. Chiefly a commuter campus, with a majority of married women students, Clear Lake nevertheless had 17 acquaintance rapes reported to the local crisis hot line last year. "We had always focused on traditional solutions like lighting and escort services at night," Mieszkowski says. "But changing lighting in the parking lot is easy; it's only money."

Many who have studied the problem of rape education believe it has to begin with college-age women and men talking to each other more frankly about their beliefs and expectations about sex. Py Bateman of Alternatives to Fear thinks it has to start earlier, among teenagers, by developing rudimentary dating skills at the lower end of the sexual activity scale. "We need to learn more about holding hands than about sexual intercourse."

Bateman continues: "We've got to work on both sides. Boys don't know what they want any more than girls do. The way our sexual interaction is set up is that boys are supposed to push. Their peers tell them that scoring is what counts. They're as divorced from intimacy as girls."

Gail Abarbanel of the Rape Treatment Center at Santa Monica Hospital agrees. Her Center conducts educational programs for schools in Los Angeles County. In a recent survey of more than 5,000 teenagers, she found a high degree of misconception and lack of information about rape: "Most boys say yes to the question, 'If a girl goes back to a guy's house when she knows no one is home, is she consenting to sex?' And most boys believe that girls don't mean no when they say it."

Women clearly need to get more convincing, and men clearly need to believe them more. But until that ideal time, Montana State's Jan

Strout warns, "Because men have been socialized to hear yes when women say no, we have to scream it."

Results of Ms. Study

One quarter of women in college today have been the victims of rape or attempted rape, and almost 90 percent of them knew their assailants. These are two of the more startling statistics to emerge from the *Ms.* Magazine Campus Project on Sexual Assault, the most far-reaching study to date on patterns of sexual aggression at America's institutions of higher learning. Funded by a grant from the National Center for the Prevention and Control of Rape, and under the direction of Kent State University psychologist Mary P. Koss, the survey reached more than 7,000 students at 35 schools. Preliminary results of the three-year study show:

- Fifty-two percent of all the women surveyed have experienced some form of sexual victimization.

- One in every eight women were the victims of rape, according to the prevailing legal definition.

- One in every 12 men admitted to having fulfilled the prevailing definition of rape or attempted rape, yet virtually none of those men identified themselves as rapists.

- Of the women who were raped, almost three quarters did not identify their experience as rape.

- Forty-seven percent of the rapes were by first or casual dates, or by romantic acquaintances.

- Three quarters of the women raped were between ages 15 and 21; the average age at the time of the rape was 18.

- More than 80 percent of the rapes occurred off-campus, with more than 50 percent on the man's turf: home, car, or other.

- More than one third of the women raped did not discuss their experience with anyone; more than 90 percent did not tell the police.

The full report will be ready later this year. It will include valuable information on the aftermath of date rape, sex-role expectations that may foster such rapes, and details about the circumstances of date rape—all of which will help in developing preventive and educational programs.

SPECULATIONS

1. Ellen Sweet emphasizes statements of denial and disbelief—"I couldn't believe that it was happening to me" or "date rape is not a significant problem on this campus." Why does she do this? What is her point?

2. What is the legal definition of rape? Is that definition meaningful and appropriate?
3. Ellen Sweet says that "most victims of date rape initially blame themselves for what happened, and almost none report it to campus authorities." Why do you think that is the case? Is it still the case now, more than seven years after Sweet published this essay in *Ms.*?
4. What cultural myths perpetuate the tendency toward date rape among American men? Can you come up with additional myths in addition to those cited by Sweet?
5. Have you ever been in a situation where someone you knew used force to make you do something that you did not want to do? How did you feel? What effects did being victimized by violence—even minor violence—have on you?
6. Do you agree with Jan Strout that "because men have been socialized to hear yes when women say no, we have to scream it." What evidence do you see, either supporting or contradicting Strout's assertion, in television shows, movies, music lyrics?

Murder, Inc.

ROBERT SHERRILL

A journalist and editor, author of nine books and hundreds of articles, a self-styled "independent radical," Robert Sherrill has consistently published on politically controversial subjects. Like Jessica Mitford, his work might best be categorized as exposé and critique. A list of his publications includes *Military Justice Is to Justice as Military Music is to Music* (1970), a vivid account of the abuses in the military justice system, *The Saturday Night Special, and Other Guns with which Americans Won the West, Protected Bootleg Franchises, Slew Wildlife, Robbed Countless Banks, Shot Husbands Purposely and by Mistake, and Killed Presidents: Together with the Debate over Continuing Same* (1978), a denunciation of America's love affair with small weaponry, and *The Oil Follies of 1970-1980: How the Petroleum Industry Stole the Show (And Much More Besides)* (1983), a scorching indictment of the petroleum business.

A native of Georgia, Sherrill, who was born in Frogtown in 1925, calls Washington, D.C., his current home—and it provides a source for much of his material. He has held a variety of newspaper jobs and is currently contributing editor to the *Nation*.

Sherrill has been consistently praised for his readable and vivid reportorial style, his "unfailing literary skill." *The Saturday Night Special*, for example, was praised in the *New York Times Book Review* as "an unnerving work by one of the most sensitive writers in America today. . . . As literature or journalism, *The Saturday Night Special* is relentless and irresistible." Equally relentless is "Murder, Inc.", an indictment of corporate America's culpability.

There are something over fifteen hundred men and women on the death rows of America. Given the social context in which they operated, one might reasonably assume that they were sentenced to be executed not because they are murderers but because they were inefficient. Using guns and knives and the usual footpad paraphernalia, they dispatched only a few more than their own number. Had they used asbestos, mislabeled pharmaceutical drugs and devices, defective autos, and illegally used and illegally disposed chemicals, they could have killed, crippled, and tortured many thousands of people. And they could have done it without very much fuss.

Corporate criminals, as we all know, live charmed lives. Not until 1978 had a corporation ever been indicted for murder (Ford Motor Company, which was acquitted), and not until 1985 had corporate executives ever been brought to trial for murder because of the lethal mischief done by their company.

The executives who made history last year were the president, plant manager, and plant foreman of Film Recovery Systems Corporation, a ratty little silver-rendering operation in Elm Grove Village outside Chicago. The silver was recovered by cooking used X-ray films in vats of boiling cyanide. Film Recovery hired mostly illegal immigrants, who were afraid to protest working conditions so foul that they made employees vomit and faint. The illegals were preferred also because they couldn't read much English and would not be spooked by the written warnings on the drums of cyanide. To make doubly sure that fright wouldn't drive workers away, management had the skull-and-cross-bones signs scraped off the drums. Although the antidote for cyanide poisoning is cheap and easy to obtain, Film Recovery Systems didn't keep any on hand.

So it came to pass that Stefan Golab, a sixty-one-year-old illegal immigrant from Poland, took too hefty a lungful of cyanide fumes and died. Charged with murder on the grounds that they had created such unsafe working conditions as to bring about "a strong probability of death and great bodily harm," the three officials were convicted and sentenced to twenty-five years in prison.

Will executives at other villainous corporations be similarly charged and convicted? Don't bet on it. In this instance the law was applied so properly, so rightly, so common-sensically that one would be foolish to expect such usage to appear again soon. It was a sort of Halley's Comet of Justice.

The idea of treating corporate murderers as just plain murderers strikes many people as excessive. Some lawyers who cautiously approved the conviction in principle said they were afraid it would confuse people generally because a bald murder charge is usually associated with a bullet in the gut or an ice pick in the neck, and nice people would have a hard time adapting the charge to the way things are sometimes accomplished in the front office. Speaking for this timid viewpoint, Alan Dershowitz, Harvard's celebrated criminal law specialist, said he thought the Film Recovery case showed we need a new category of crime. "We should have one that specifically reflects our condemnation of this sort of behavior," he said, "without necessarily assimilating it into the most heinous forms of murder"—as if the St. Valentine's Day massacre were any more heinous than Bhopal.

During the trial, the Illinois prosecutor accused the defendants of "callousness, disregard of human lives, and exposing people to dangerous products all for the sake of profits." No wonder the verdict has been so modestly praised. If that's enough to rate a murder charge, our whole commercial system is at risk. If it were to become the rule, we could look forward to a lineup of accused corporate executives extending out the courthouse and around the block several times. Since there is no statute of limitations on murder, prosecutors would be obliged to charge those executives at Firestone who, a few years back, allegedly killed and injured no telling how many people by flooding the market with ten million tires they knew to be defective; and the executives at Ford who sent the Pinto into circulation knowing its gas tank was so poorly designed that a rear-end collision could turn the car into a fire trap (several dozen men, women, and children were burned alive). From the pharmaceutical fraternity would come such as D. William Shedden, former vice-president and chief medical officer for Eli Lilly Research Laboratories, who recently pleaded guilty to fifteen criminal counts relating to the marketing of Oraflex, an arthritis drug that the Food and Drug Administration says has been "possibly" linked to forty-nine deaths in the United States and several hundred abroad, not to mention the hundreds who have suffered nonfatal liver and kidney failure. Seems as how the folks at Lilly, when they sought approval from the FDA, forgot to mention that the drug was already known to have killed at least twenty-eight people in Europe. (Shedden was fined $15,000; Lilly, which earned $3.1 billion in 1984, was fined $25,000.) And let's be sure to save an early murder indictment for those three sly dogs at SmithKline Beckman Corporation who whizzed their product, Selacryn, through the FDA without mentioning that it had caused severe liver damage in some patients in France. False labels were used to peddle it in this country, where it has been linked to thirty-six deaths and five hundred cases of liver and kidney damage.

Now comes a ripple of books that, were there any justice, would put a dozen or so hangdog executives in the dock. Three of the books made particularly persuasive cases. Paul Brodeur's *Outrageous Miscon-*

duct: *The Asbestos Industry on Trial* (Pantheon) is an account of how the largest manufacturer of asbestos products, Manville Corporation (previously known as Johns-Manville Corporation), and other asbestos companies committed over the years what one plaintiff's attorney called "the greatest mass murder in history," which is possibly true if one means industrial mass murder, not political. People who regularly inhale asbestos fibers are likely to die, or at least be crippled, from the lung disease called asbestosis or the even worse (at least it sounds worse) mesothelioma. It sometimes takes twenty or thirty years for asbestosis to appear, so a measure of the slaughter from it is somewhat vague. But the best experts in the field, which means Dr. Irving J. Selikoff and his staff at the Mount Sinai Hospital in New York City, estimate that aside from the many thousands who have died from asbestos diseases in the past, there will be between eight and ten thousand deaths from asbestos-related cancer each year for the next twenty years. These deaths are not accidental. Manville et al. knew exactly what they were doing. Brodeur's book is mainly an account of how the asbestos companies, though they claimed to be ignorant of the deadly quality of their product until a study by Dr. Selikoff was released in 1964, had for forty years known about, and had suppressed or disregarded, hundreds of studies that clearly showed what asbestos was doing to the people who inhaled it. Did the companies even care what was happening? Typically, at a Manville asbestos mine in Canada, company doctors found that of seven hundred and eight workers, only four—who had worked there less than four years—had normal lungs. Those who were dying of asbestosis were not told of their ailment.

The other two books, Susan Perry and Jim Dawson's *Nightmare: Women and the Dalkon Shield* (Macmillan) and Morton Mintz's *At Any Cost: Corporate Greed, Women, and the Dalkon Shield* (Pantheon), remind me of what Dr. Jules Amthor said to my favorite detective: "I'm in a very sensitive profession, Mr. Marlowe. I'm a quack." The murderous quackery of the Dalkon Shield, an intrauterine device, was committed by A. H. Robins, a company that should have stuck to making Chap Stick and Sergeant's Flea & Tick Collars, and left birth-control gadgets to those who knew how to make them properly. These two books should convince anyone, I think, that compared to the fellows at A. H. Robins, the Film Recovery executives were pikers when it came to showing disregard for human lives for the sake of profits. Profits were plentiful, that's for sure. A. H. Robins sold more than 4.5 million Dalkon Shields worldwide (2.8 million in the United States) for $4.35 each; not bad for a device that cost only twenty-five cents to produce. The death count among women who wore the shield still isn't complete; the last I heard it was twenty. But wearers of the shield also have reported stillbirths, babies with major congenital defects, punctured uteri, forced hysterectomies, sterilization from infection, and various tortures and illnesses by the thousands—some generous portion, we may presume, of the 9,230 lawsuits that A. H. Robins has settled out of court. And as both books make clear, the company launched the Dalkon Shield fully aware of the shield's dangers, sold it with false advertising, kept on selling it for several years after the company knew what its consumers were going through, and pulled a complicated cover-up of guilt.

Dershowitz is right in one respect: corporate murderers are not like your typical killer on death row. Corporate murderers do not set out to kill. There's no profit in that. They are simply willing to accept a certain amount of death and physical torment among their workers and customers as a sometimes necessary byproduct of the free enterprise system. Mintz has uncovered a dandy quote from history to illustrate this attitude. When it was suggested to Alfred P. Sloan, Jr., president of General Motors circa 1930, that he should have safety glass installed in Chevrolets, he refused with the explanation, "Accidents or no accidents, my concern in this matter is a matter of profit and loss."

The Sloan spirit is everywhere. Brodeur quotes from a deposition of Charles H. Roemer, once a prominent New Jersey attorney who handled legal matters for the Union Asbestos and Rubber Company. Roemer reveals that around 1942, when Union Asbestos discovered a lot of its workers coming down with asbestos disease, he and some of Union Asbestos's top officials went to Johns-Manville and asked Vandiver Brown, Manville's attorney, and Lewis Brown, president of Manville, if their physical examination program had turned up similar results. According to Roemer, Vandiver Brown said, in effect, Sure, our X-rays show many of our workers have that disease, but we don't tell them they are sick because if we did, they would stop working and sue us. Roemer recalled asking, "Mr. Brown, do you mean to tell me you would let them work until they dropped dead?" and Brown answering, "Yes, we save a lot of money that way."

Saving money, along with making money, was obviously the paramount objective of A. H. Robins, too. This was evident from the beginning, when Robins officials learned—*six months before marketing the device nationally*—that the Dalkon Shield multifilament tail had a wicking tendency and could carry potentially deadly bacteria into the uterus. Did the company hold up marketing the shield until it could be further tested and made safe? No, no. That would have meant a delay, for one thing, in recovering the $750,000 they had paid the shield's inventors. Though Robins knew it was putting its customers in great jeopardy, it hustled the shield onto the market with promotional claims that it was "safe" and "superior" to all other intrauterine devices; and never, during the four years the shield was on the market, did A. H. Robins conduct wicking studies of the string. The shield's promotional literature, by the way, was a classic example of phony drugstore hype. A. H. Robins claimed the shield kept the pregnancy rate at 1.1 percent; the company was well aware that the shield allowed at least a 5 percent pregnancy rate, one of the most slipshod in the birth-control business. A. H. Robins also advertised that the device could be easily inserted in "even the most sensitive woman," although in fact many doctors, before inserting the shield, had to give patients an anesthetic, and many women were in pain for months.

Not long after the shield went on the market, Wayne Crowder, one of the few heroes in this sorry tale, a quality-control engineer at Chap Stick, which manufactured many of the shields for its parent firm, rejected 10,000 of them because he was convinced the strings could wick bacteria. His boss overruled him with the remark, "Your conscience doesn't pay your salary." Crowder also suggested a method for stopping the wicking, but his technique was rejected because it would have cost an extra five cents per device. Crowder kept on complaining (he would ultimately be fired as an irritant) and he finally stirred Daniel French, president of Chap Stick, to convey Crowder's criticisms to the home office. French was told to mind his own business and not worry about the safety of the shield, which prompted him to go into the corporate softshoe routine he knew would please. He wrote A. H. Robins: "It is not the intention of Chap Stick Company to attempt any unauthorized improvements in the Dalkon Shield. My only interest in the Dalkon Shield is to produce it at the lowest possible price, and therefore, increase Robins's gross profit level."

Of course, when thousands of women begin dying, screaming, cursing, and suing, it gets a little difficult to pretend that all is well with one's product, but for more than a decade A. H. Robins did its best, never recalling the gadget, never sending a warning to doctors about possible deadly side effects, and continuing to the last—continuing right up to the present even after losing hundreds of millions of dollars in lawsuits—to argue that the shield is just hunkydory. The A. H. Robins school spirit was beautifully capsulated by one of its officials who told the *National Observer*, "But after all, we are in business to sell the thing, to make a profit. I don't mean we're trying to go out and sell products that are going to be dangerous, fatal, or what have you. But you don't pull all the bad things in big headlines."

Where is the corporate executive who will not savor the easy insouciance of "or what have you"?

One of the more fascinating characteristics of corporate murderers is the way these fellows cover up their dirty work. They are really quite bold and successful in their deviousness. When one considers how many top officials there are at places like Manville and Robins, and when one assumes (obviously naïvely) among the lot of them surely there must be at least one or two with a functioning conscience, the completeness of their cover-ups is indeed impressive. Which isn't to say that their techniques are very sophisticated. They simply lie, or hide or burn the incriminating material. When the litigation flood began to break over Manville Corporation in the late 1960s, the asbestos gang began thwarting their victims' attorneys by claiming certain Manville executives couldn't give depositions because they were dead (when they were very much alive), by refusing to produce documents ordered by the court, and by denying that certain documents existed when in fact they did. A. H. Robins was just as expert at that sort of thing. According to Mintz, "Thousands of documents sought by lawyers for victims of the Dalkon Shield sank from sight in suspicious circumstances. A few were hidden for a decade in a home basement in Tulsa, Oklahoma. Other records were destroyed, some admittedly in a city dump in Columbus, Indiana, and some allegedly in an A. H. Robins furnace. And despite court orders, the company did not produce truckloads of documents for judicial rulings on whether the women's lawyers could see the papers."

A. H. Robins's most notorious effort at a cover-up ultimately failed, thanks to one Roger Tuttle, a classic example of what can happen when the worm turns.

Tuttle was an attorney for A. H. Robins in the early 1970s. He says that immediately after the company lost its first Dalkon Shield lawsuit, his superiors ordered him (they deny it) to search through the company's files and burn every document that he thought might be used against A. H. Robins in future lawsuits—documents that, in Tuttle's words, indicated "knowledge and complicity, if any, of top officials in what at that stage of the game appeared to be a grim situation." Unfortunately for the company, Tuttle did not fully obey orders. He took possession of some of the juiciest documents and kept them. Just why he rebelled isn't clear. Perhaps it was because Tuttle, a plain little guy who admits he isn't the smartest attorney in the world, was tired of having his employers push him around, which they often did. He says he did it because he was ashamed that "I personally lacked the courage" to challenge the order and "I wanted some sop for my own conscience as an attorney." Whatever his motivation, Tuttle sat on the purloined files for nearly ten years. He moved on to other jobs, finally winding up, a born-again Christian, on the Oral Roberts University law faculty. Watching the Dalkon Shields trials from afar, troubled by the plaintiffs' inability to cope with A. H. Robins's cover-up, Tuttle finally decided to step forward and provide the material their attorneys needed for the big breakthrough.

A lucky windfall like that is the only way victims can overcome the tremendous imbalance in legal firepower. In the way they muster defense, corporate murderers bear no resemblance to the broken-down, half-nuts, penniless drifters on death row, dozens of whom have no attorney at all. Corporate killers are like the Mafia in the way they come to court with a phalanx of attorneys. They are fronted by the best, or at least the best known. Griffin Bell, President Carter's Attorney General, has been one of A. H. Robins's attorneys.

There are two other significant differences between corporate killers and the habitués of death rows. In the first place, the latter generally did not murder as part of doing business, except for the relatively few who killed coincidental to a holdup. They did not murder to protect their rackets or territory, as the Mafia does, and they did not murder to exploit a patent or to increase production of sales, as corporate murderers do. One judge accused A. H. Robins officials of taking "the bottom line as your guiding beacon and the low road as your route." Killing for the bottom line has probably not sent a single murderer to death row anywhere. In the second place, most of the men and women on death row were lonely murderers. No part of society supported what they did. But just as the Mafia can commit murder with impunity only because it has the cooperation of police and prosecutors, so too corporate murderers benefit from the collusion of respectable professions, particularly doctors (who, for a price, keep quiet), and insurance companies (who, to help Manville, did not reveal what their actuarial tables told about the risks to asbestos workers; and, for Robins, worked actively backstage to conceal the Dalkon Shield's menace to public health), and government agencies who are supposed to protect public health but look the other way.

It was an old, and in its way valid, excuse that Film Recovery's officials gave the court: "We are just operating like other plants, and none of the government health and safety inspectors who dropped around—neither the Elm Grove Village Public Health Department nor the Environmental Protection Agency—told us we shouldn't be letting our workers stick their heads in vats of boiling cyanide." They were probably telling the truth. That's the way health and safety regulators have usually operated.

Brodeur tells us that a veritable parade of government inspectors marched through the Pittsburgh Corning asbestos plant in Tyler, Texas, over a period of six and a half years without warning the workers that the asbestos dust levels were more than twenty times the maximum recommended for health safety. One Department of Labor official later admitted he had not worn a respirator when inspecting the plant because he did not want to excite the workers into asking questions about their health. Though the Public Health Service several times measured the fallout of asbestos dust, never did it warn the workers that the stuff was eating up their lungs. Finally things got so bad at Tyler that federal inspectors, forced to bring charges against the owners for appalling infractions of health standards, recommended that they be fined $210. Today the men and women who worked in that plant (since closed) are dying of lung cancer at a rate five times greater than the national average.

The most impressive bureaucratic collusion A. H. Robins received was, not surprisingly, from the Food and Drug Administration. When trial attorneys brought evidence that the Dalkon Shield's rotting tail strings were endangering thousands of women and asked FDA officials to remove the device from the market, the agency did nothing. When the National Women's Health Network petitioned the FDA for a recall—paid for by Robins—that would remove the shield from all women then wearing it, the FDA did nothing. For a full decade it pretended to be helpless.

There is one more significant difference between the people on death row and the corporate murderers: the former sometimes say they are sorry; the latter never do. Midway through 1985, Texas executed Charles Milton, thirty-four, because when he stuck up a liquor store the owner and his wife wrestled Milton for the gun, it went off, and the woman died. Shortly before the state killed him with poison, Milton said, "I am sorry Mrs. Denton was killed in the struggle over the gun." There. He said it. It wasn't much, but he said it. And that's more than the folks at Manville have ever said about the thousands of people they killed with asbestos. When it comes to feeling no remorse, A. H. Robins doesn't take a back seat to anybody. In a famous courtroom confrontation between Federal Judge Miles W. Lord and three A. H. Robins officials, including company president E. Claiborne Robins, Jr., Judge Lord asked them to read silently to themselves a long reprimand of their actions. The most scathing passage, quoted both by Mintz and by Perry and Dawson was this:

> Today as you sit here attempting once to more to extricate yourselves from the legal consequences of your acts, none of you has faced up to the fact that more than 9,000 women [the figure two years ago (in 1984)] have made claims that they gave up part of their womanhood so that your company might prosper. It is alleged that others gave their lives so you might so prosper. And there stand behind them legions more who have been injured but who had not sought relief in the courts of this land. . . .
>
> If one poor young man were by some act of his—without authority

or consent—to inflict such damage upon one woman, he would be jailed for a good portion of the rest of his life. And yet your company, without warning to women, invaded their bodies by the millions and caused them injuries by the thousands. And when the time came for these women to make their claims against your company, you attacked their characters. You inquired into their sexual practices and into the identity of their sex partners. You exposed these women—and ruined families and reputations and careers—in order to intimidate those who would raise their voices against you. You introduced issues that had no relationship whatsoever to the fact that you planted in the bodies of these women instruments of death, of mutilation, of disease.

Judge Lord admitted that he did not have the power to make them recall the shield but he begged them to do it on their own: "You've got lives out there, people, women, wives, moms, and some who will never be moms. . . . You are the corporate conscience. Please, in the name of humanity, lift your eyes above the bottom line."

It was a pretty stirring piece of writing (later, when Judge Lord go so pissed off he read it aloud, they say half the courtroom was in tears), and the judge asked them if it had had any impact on them.

Looking sulky, they just stared at him and said nothing.

A few weeks later, at A. H. Robins's annual meeting, E. Claiborne Robins, Jr., dismissed Lord's speech as a "poisonous attack." The company did not recall the shield for another eight months.

Giving deposition for 1984, Ernest L. Bender, Jr., senior vice-president for corporate planning and development, was asked if he had ever heard an officer or employee say he or she was "sorry or remorseful about any infection that's been suffered by any Dalkon Shield wearer." He answered, "I've never heard anyone make such remarks because I've never heard anyone that said the Dalkon Shield was the cause."

What punishment is fitting for these fellows?

If they are murderers, why not the death sentence? Polls show that eighty-four percent of Americans favor the death penalty, but half think the penalty is unfairly applied. Let's restore their faith by applying justice equally and poetically. In Georgia recently it took the state two 2,080 volts spaced over nineteen minutes to kill a black man who murdered during a burglary. How fitting it would be to use the same sort of defective electric chair to execute, for example, auto manufacturers and tire manufacturers who knowingly kill people with defective merchandise. In Texas recently it took the state executioners forty minutes to administer the lethal poison to a drifter who had killed a woman. Could anything be more appropriate than to tie down drug and device manufacturers who have killed many women and let slow-witted executioners poke around their bodies for an hour or so, looking for just the right blood vessel to transport the poison? At a recent Mississippi execution, the prisoner's protracted gasping for breath became such an ugly spectacle that prison authorities, in a strange burst of decorum, ordered witnesses out of the death chamber. That sort of execution for Manville executives who specialized in spreading long-term asphyxiation over thousands of lives would certainly be appropriate.

But these things will never happen. For all our popular declarations of democracy, most Americans are such forelock-tugging toadies that they would be horrified to see, say, Henry Ford II occupying the same electric chair that cooked black, penniless Alpha Otis Stephens.

Nor will we incarcerate many corporate murderers. Though some of us with a mean streak may enjoy fantasizing the reception that our fat-assed corporate killers would get from some of their cellmates in America's more interesting prisons—I like to think of the pious chaps from A. H. Robins spending time in Tennessee's notorious Brushy Mountain Prison—that is not going to happen very often either, the precedent of Film Recovery to the contrary notwithstanding. The Film Recovery trio had the misfortune of working for a crappy little corporation that has since gone defunct. Judges will not be so stern with killers from giant corporations.

So long as we have any army of crassly aggressive plaintiff attorneys to rely on, however, there is always the hope that we can smite the corporations and the men who run them with a punishment they probably fear worse than death or loss of freedom: to wit, massive loss of profits. Pamela C. Van Duyn, whose use of the Dalkon Shield at the age of twenty-six destroyed one Fallopian tube and critically damaged the other (her childbearing chances are virtually nil), says: "As far as I'm concerned, the last dime that is in Claiborne Robins's pocket ought to be paid over to all the people that have suffered." Author Brodeur dreams of an even broader financial punishment for the industry he hates:

> When I was a young man, out of college in 1953, I went into the Army Counterintelligence Corps and went to Germany, where I saw one of the death camps, Dachau. And I saw what the occupational army had done to Dachau. They had razed it, left the chimneys standing, and the barbed wire as a monument—quite the same way the Romans left Carthage. What I would do with some of these companies that are nothing more or less than killing grounds would be to sell their assets totally, reimburse the victims, and leave the walls as a reminder—just the way Dachau was—that a law-abiding and decent society will not tolerate this kind of conduct.

He added, "I know perfectly well that this is not going to happen in the private enterprise system."

How right he is. The laws, the court system, federal and state legislatures, most of the press, the unions—most of the establishment is opposed to applying the final financial solution to killer corporations.

As it became evident that juries were inclined to agree with Mrs. Van Duyn's proposal to wring plenty of money from A. H. Robins, the corporation in 1985 sought protection under Chapter 11 of the Federal Bankruptcy Code. It was a sleazy legal trick they had picked up from Manville Corporation, which had declared bankruptcy in August 1982. Although both corporations had lost hundreds of millions in court fights, neither was actually in financial trouble. Indeed, at the time it copped out under Chapter 11, Manville was the nation's 181st largest corporation and had assets of more than $2 billion. Bankruptcy was a transparent ploy—or, as plaintiff attorneys put it, a fraudulent abuse and perversion of the bankruptcy laws—but with the connivance of the federal courts it is a ploy that has worked. Not a penny has been paid to the victims of either corporation since they declared bankruptcy, and the 16,500 pending lawsuits against Manville and the 5,000 lawsuits pending against A. H. Robins (those figures are climbing every day) have been frozen.

Meanwhile, companies are not even mildly chastised. Quite the contrary. Most major newspapers have said nothing about Manville's malevolent cover-up but have clucked sympathetically over its courtroom defeats. The *New York Times* editorially seemed to deplore the financial problems of the asbestos industry almost as much as it deplored the industry's massacre of workers: "Asbestos is a tragedy, most of all for the victims and their families but also for the companies, which are being made to pay the price for decisions made long ago." Senator Gary Hart, whose home state, Colorado, is corporate headquarters for Manville, pitched in with legislation that would lift financial penalty from the asbestos companies and dump it on the taxpayers. And in Richmond, Virginia, corporate headquarters for the makers of Dalkon Shield, civic leaders threw a banquet for E. Claiborne Robins, Sr. The president of the University of Virginia assured Robins that "Your example will cast its shadow into eternity, as the sands of time carry the indelible footprint of your good works. We applaud you for always exhibiting a steadfast and devoted concern for your fellow man. Truly, the Lord has chosen you as one of His most essential instruments."

After similar encomiums from other community leaders, the top man behind the marketing of the Dalkon Shield was given the Great American Tradition Award.

SPECULATIONS

1.   Regarding the 1,500 men and women on death row in America, Sherrill says, "Given the social context in which they operated, one might reasonably assume that they were sentenced to be executed not because they are murderers but because they were inefficient." In what ways, if any, is he right? In what ways, if any, is he wrong?

2.   How would you describe Sherrill's tone? Can you locate specific diction and phrasing that contribute to the tone of this essay? Is the tone effective in persuading you that Sherrill is justified in making his argument about corporate killers?

3.   Why does Sherrill entitle his essay "Murder, Inc."? What is the literary reference of this title--and why is it significant?

4.   Have you ever been cheated by or injured by a company? What happened? How did it make you feel? What was your response?

5.   Sherrill focuses particularly on three instances of corporate greed and criminality: Film Recovery Systems Corporation, A. II. Robins, and Manville Corporation. Much of his evidence comes from books published recently on the latter two corporations. Is Sherrill's strategy here a good one? What was his purpose, do you think, in focusing on a few corporations? Do you find his account persuasive, or do you think Sherrill has basically done a hatchet job on these corporations?

Jim Chee Pays a Visit

TONY HILLERMAN

From cub reporter for the *Borger News Herald* (Texas) in 1948 to one of the top mystery novelists in America, Tony Hillerman has been a writer for all of his professional life. He has written nonfiction and edited anthologies (*The Best of the West* [1991]), but he is best known for his taut and suspenseful fiction. His novels are set in the dry desert country of the Southwest, and his heroes are Navajo policemen: Lieutenant Joe Leaphorn and Sergeant Jim Chee, both of the Navajo Tribal Police. The books in which they appear carry titles that reflect the rich Navajo culture which they depict: *The Blessing Way* (1970), *Listening Woman* (1977), *The Dark Wind* (1981), *Skinwalkers* (1986), and many more.

Hillerman has lived in the Southwest all his life; he lives now in Albuquerque, New Mexico. A graduate of the University of Oklahoma and the University of New Mexico, Hillerman has not only been a reporter and editor for various southwestern newspapers, he has also served as assistant to the president of the University of New Mexico as well as chair of the school's department of journalism. Hillerman served in the U.S. Army during World War II, for which he received the Silver Star, the Bronze Star, and the Purple Heart.

In 1974, Hillerman was awarded the Edgar Allen Poe Award, by the Mystery Writers of America for *Dance Hall of the Dead* (1973). Hillerman told *Publishers Weekly*, "It's always troubled me . . . that the American people are so ignorant of these rich Indian cultures. For me, studying them has been absolutely fascinating, and I think it's important to show how aspects of ancient Indian ways are still very much alive and are highly germane even to our ways."

The selection that follows comes late in the novel *The Dark Wind* and illustrates some essential principles of discovery and intuition that are celebrated in mystery novels. It also offers an example of the ways an individual from one culture (Navajo) negotiates with someone from another (Hopi).

Sergeant Jim Chee is searching for clues to a mysterious plane crash which seems tied up with murder, narcotics, and the mysterious disappearance of two aluminum suitcases filled with money. Chee is convinced that a Hopi sorcerer, Taylor Sawkatewa, witnessed the event, for Sawkatewa had repeatedly sabotaged a nearby windmill which he felt was violating a sacred Hopi rite. As this chapter opens, we find Chee waiting for another policeman (a Hopi named Cowboy) to drive him to see Sawkatewa.

Cowboy had arranged to meet him at the junction of Arizona Highway 87 and Navajo Route 3. "We're going to have to go to Pi-utki," Cowboy had told him. "That's where he lives. But I don't want to have you floundering around up there by yourself, getting lost. So meet me, and I'll take you up."

"About when?"

"About seven," Cowboy said.

So Chee had arrived about seven. Five minutes before, to be exact. He stood beside his pickup truck, stretching his muscles. The early evening sun lit the slopes of Second Mesa behind him, making a glittering reflection off the hot asphalt of Navajo 3 where it zigzagged upward. Just to the north, the cliff of First Mesa was dappled with shadow. Chee himself stood in the shadow. A cloud which had been building slowly all afternoon over the San Francisco Peaks had broken free of the mountain's updrafts and was drifting eastward. It was still at least twenty miles to the west, but its crest had built high enough now to block out the slanting light of sun. The heat of the day had produced other such thunderheads. Three, in an irregular row, were sailing across the Painted Desert between Chee and Winslow. One, Chee noticed with pleasure, was actually dragging a small tail of rain across Tovar Mesa. But none of the smaller clouds promised much. With sundown they would quickly evaporate in the arid sky. The cloud spawned by the San Francisco Peaks was another matter. It was huge, its top pushed up into the stratospheric cold by its internal winds, and its lower levels blue-black with the promise of rain. As Chee appraised it, he heard the mutter of thunder. The clouds would be visible for a hundred miles in every direction, from Navajo Mountain across the Utah border, as far east as the Chuska Range in New Mexico. One cloud wouldn't break a drought, but it takes one cloud to start the process. For a thousand Navajo sheepmen across this immense dry tableland the cloud meant hope that rain, running arroyos, and new grass would again be part of the *hozro* of their lives. To the Hopis, rain would mean more than that. It would mean the endorsement of the supernatural. The Hopis had called for the clouds, and the clouds had come. It would mean that after a year of blighted dust, things were right again between the Peaceful People of the Hopi Mesas and their kachina spirits.

Chee leaned against the truck, enjoying the cool, damp breeze which the cloud was now producing, enjoying the contrast between the dappled browns and tans of the First Mesa cliffs and the dark-blue sky over them. Above him the rim of the cliff was not cliff at all, but the stone walls of the houses of Walpi. From here it was hard to believe that. The tiny windows seemed to be holes in the living rock of the mesa.

Chee glanced at his watch. Cowboy was late. He retrieved his notebook from the front seat, and turned to a clean page. Across the top he wrote: "Questions and Answers." Then he wrote: "Where is J. Musket? Did Musket kill John Doe? Witch? Crazy? Tied up with the narcotics heist?" He drew a line down the center of the page, separating the Answers section. Here he wrote: "Evidence he was away from work day Doe killed. Musket connected with narcotics. Likely came to Burnt Water to set up delivery. How else? Would have known the country well enough to hide the GMC." Chee studied the entries. He tapped a front tooth with the butt of the ballpoint pen. He wrote under Questions: "Why the burglary? To provide a logical reason for disappearing from the trading post?" Chee frowned at that, and wrote: "What happened to the stolen jewelry?" He drew a line under that all the way across the page. Under it he wrote:

"Who is John Doe? Somebody from the narcotics business? Working with Musket? Did Musket kill him because Doe smelled the double cross? Did Musket make it look like a witch killing to confuse things?" No answers here. Just questions. He drew another horizontal line and wrote under it:

"Where's Palanzer's body? Why hide it in the GMC? To confuse those looking for dope? Why take it out of the GMC? Because someone knew I'd found it? Who knew? The man who walked up the arroyo in the dark? Musket? Dashee?" He stared at the name, feeling disloyal. But Dashee knew. He'd told Dashee where to find the truck. And Dashee could have been at the windmill site when the crash happened. He wondered if he could learn where Dashee had been the night John Doe's body had been hidden. And then he shook his head and drew a line through "Dashee," and then another line. Under that he wrote a single word: "Witch."

Under that he wrote: "Any reason to connect witch killing with dope?" He stared at the question, worrying his lower lip between his teeth. Then he wrote: "Coincidence of time and place." He paused a moment, then jotted beside it: "Doe died July 10, West died July 6." He was still thinking about that when Dashee drove up.

"Right on the money," Cowboy said.

"You're late," Chee said.

"Operating on Navajo time," Cowboy said. "Seven means sometime tonight. Let's take my car."

Chee got in.

"You ever been to Piutki?"

"I don't think so," Chee said. "Where is it?"

"Up on First Mesa," Cowboy said. "Back behind Hano on the ridge." Cowboy was driving more sedately than usual. He rolled the patrol car down Navajo Route 3 and did a left turn onto the narrower asphalt which made the steep, winding climb up the face of the mesa. His face was still, thoughtful.

Worried, Chee thought. We're getting involved in something religious.

"There's not much left of Piutki," Cowboy said. "It's pretty well abandoned. Used to be the village of the Fog Clan with some Bow Clan, and the Fog Clan is just about extinct. Not many Bow left either."

Fog Clan touched a memory. Chee tried to recall what he'd learned about Hopi ethnology in his anthro classes at the University of New Mexico, and what he'd read since, and what he'd picked up from gossip. The Fog Clan had brought to the Hopis the gift of sorcery. That had been its ceremonial contribution to Hopi society. And of course, the sorcerers were the *powaqas*, the "two-hearts," the Hopi culture's peculiar version of what witches were like. There was something about the Bow Clan, too. What? Chee's reliable memory served up the answer. He'd read it in some treatise on Hopi clan history. When the Bow Clan had completed its great migrations and arrived at the Hopi Mesas, it had accumulated such a reputation for creating trouble that the Bear Clan elders had repeatedly refused its request for lands and a village home. And after it had finally been allowed to join the other clans, the Bows had been involved in the single bloody incident in the history of the Peaceful People. When the Arrowshaft Clan at Awatovi had allowed Spanish priests to move into the village, the Bows had suggested a punitive attack. The Arrowshaft males had been slaughtered in their kivas, and the women and children had been scattered among the other villages. The Arrowshaft clan had not survived.

"This man we're going to see," Chee said. "What's his clan?"

Cowboy eyed him. "Why you ask that?"

"You said it was the Fog Clan village. I heard somewhere that the Fog Clan had died out."

"More or less," Cowboy said. "But the Hopis use a sort of linked clan system, and the Fog is linked to the Cloud Clan and the Water Clan and . . . " Cowboy let it trail away. He shifted into second gear for the steep climb along the mesa cliff.

The road reached the saddle of the narrow ridge. It climbed straight ahead of Walpi. Cowboy jerked the patrol car into the narrow turn up the other side of the saddle toward Sichomovi and Hano. The rear wheels skidded. Cowboy muttered something under his breath.

Chee had been watching him. "Had a bad day?"

Cowboy said nothing. Clearly Cowboy had had a bad day.

"What's bothering you?" Chee asked.

Cowboy laughed. But he didn't sound amused. "Nothing," he said.

"You'd just as soon not be doing this?"

Cowboy shrugged.

The patrol car edged past the ancient stone walls of Sichomovi . . . or was it Hano now? Chee wasn't sure yet where one of the villages ended and the other began. It seemed inconceivable to Chee that the Hopis had chosen to live like this—collecting right on top of each other in these tight little towns without privacy or breathing room. His own people had done exactly the opposite. Laws of nature, he thought. Hopis collect, Navajos scatter. But what was bothering Cowboy? He thought about it.

"Who is this guy we're going to see?"

"His name is Taylor Sawkatewa," Cowboy said. "And I think we're wasting our time."

"Don't think he'll tell us anything?"

"Why should he?" Cowboy said. The tone was curt, and Cowboy seemed to realize it. When he continued, there was a hint of apology in his tone. "He's about a million years old. More traditional than the worst traditional. On top of that, I hear he's sort of crazy."

And, Chee thought, you hear he's a *powaqa*. And that's what's making you a little edgy. Chee thought about what he'd heard about *powaqas*. It made him a little edgy, too.

"Not much use appealing to his duty as a law-abiding citizen, I guess," Chee said.

Cowboy laughed. "I don't think so. Be like trying to explain to a

Brahma bull why he should hold still while you're putting a surcingle around him."

They were clear of Hano now, jolting down a stony track which followed the mesa rim. The cloud loomed in the southwest. The sun on the horizon lit the underface of its great anvil top a glittering white, but at its lower level its color varied. A thousand gradations of gray from almost white to almost black, and—from the dying sun—shades of rose and pink and red. To Cowboy Dashee's people such a cloud would have sacred symbolism. To Chee's people, it was simply beautiful, and thus valuable just for itself.

"Another thing," Cowboy said. "Old Sawkatewa don't speak English. That's what they tell me anyway. So I'll have to interpret."

"Anything else I need to know about him?"

Cowboy shrugged.

"You didn't tell me what his clan is."

Cowboy slowed the patrol car, eased it past a jagged rock and over a rut. "He's Fog," he said.

"So the Fog Clan isn't extinct?"

"Really it is," Cowboy said. "Hardly any left. All their ceremonial duties—what's left—they're owned by the Water Clan now, or Cloud Clan. It was that way even when I was a boy. Long before that, I guess. My daddy said the last time the Ya Ya Society did anything was when he was a little boy—and I don't think that was a full ceremony. Walpi kicked them out a long time ago."

"Kicked them out?"

"The Ya Ya Society," Cowboy said. He didn't offer to expand. From what Chee could remember hearing about the society, it controlled initiation into the various levels of sorcery. In other words, it was a sensitive subject and Cowboy didn't want to talk about it to a non-Hopi.

"Why did they kick 'em out?" Chee asked.

"Caused trouble," Cowboy said

"Isn't that the society that used to initiate people who wanted to become two-hearts?"

"Yeah," Cowboy said.

"I remember somebody telling me something about it," Chee said. "Somebody told me the deal where they saw a pine tree trunk on the ground and the sorcerer caused it to move up and down in the air."

Cowboy said nothing.

"That's right?" Chee asked. "A lot of magic at a Ya Ya ceremony."

"But if you have power, and you use it for the wrong reasons, then you lose the power," Cowboy said. "That's what we're told."

"This man we're going to see," Chee said. "He was a member of the Ya Ya Society. That right?"

Cowboy eased the patrol car over another rough spot. The sun was down now, the horizon a streak of fire. The cloud was closer and beginning to drop a screen of rain. It evaporated at least a thousand feet above ground level, but it provided a translucent screen which filtered the reddish light.

"I heard he was a member of the Ya Ya," Cowboy said. "You can hear just about anything."

The village of Piutki had never had the size or importance of such places as Oraibi, or Walpi, or even Shongopovi. At its peak it had housed only part of the small Bow Clan, and the even smaller Fog Clan. That peak had passed long ago, probably in the eighteenth or nineteenth century. Now many of its houses had been abandoned. Their roofs had fallen in and their walls had been quarried for stone to maintain houses still occupied. The great cloud now dominated the sky, and illuminated the old place with a red twilight. The breeze followed the patrol car with outriders of dust. Cowboy flicked on the headlights.

"Place looks empty," Chee said.

"It almost is," Cowboy agreed.

The plaza was small, houses on two sides of it in ruins. Chee noticed that the kiva, too, was in disrepair. The steps that led to its roof were rotted and broken, and the ladder that should have protruded from its rooftop entrance was missing. It was a small kiva, and low, its walls rising only some five feet above the dusty plaza earth. It seemed as dead as the men who had built it so long ago.

"Well," Cowboy said. "Here we are." He stopped the car beside the kiva. Beyond it, one of the houses that still walled two sides of the plaza was occupied. The breeze blew smoke from its chimney toward them, and a small pile of coal stood beside its doorway. The door opened. A boy—perhaps ten or twelve—looked out at them. The boy was an albino.

Cowboy left the car unlocked and walked through the blowing dust without waiting for Chee. He spoke to the boy at the door in Hopi, listened to his answer, thought about it, and spoke again. The boy disappeared inside.

"He said Sawkatewa is working. He'd tell him he had visitors," Cowboy said.

Chee nodded. He heard a thumping of thunder and glanced up at the cloud. Only its upper levels were red with sunset now. Below that, its color shaded from blue to almost black. While he looked at it, the black flashed with yellow, and flashed again. Internal lightning was illuminating it. They waited. Dust eddied in the plaza. The air was much cooler now. It smelled of rain. The sound of thunder reached them. This time it boomed, and boomed again.

The boy reappeared. He looked at Chee through thick-lensed glasses and then at Cowboy, and spoke in Hopi.

"In we go," Cowboy said.

Taylor Sawkatewa was sitting on a small metal chair, winding yarn onto a spindle. He was looking at them, his bright black eyes curious. But his hands never stopped their quick, agile work. He spoke to Cowboy, and motioned toward a green plastic sofa which stood against the entrance wall, and then he examined Chee. He smiled and nodded.

"He says sit down," Cowboy said.

They sat on the green plastic. It was a small room, a little off square, the walls flaking whitewash. A kerosene lamp, its glass chimney sooty, cast a wavering yellow light.

Sawkatewa spoke to both of them, smiling at Chee again. Chee smiled back.

Then Cowboy spoke at length. The old man listened. His hands worked steadily, moving the gray-white wool from a skein in a cardboard beer carton beside his chair onto the long wooden spindle. His eyes left Cowboy and settled on Chee's face. He was a very old man, far beyond the point where curiosity can be interpreted as rudeness. Navajos, too, sometimes live to be very old and Chee's Slow Talking Dinee had its share of them.

Cowboy completed his statement, paused, added a brief postscript, then turned to Chee.

"I told him I would now tell you what I'd told him," Cowboy said. "And what I told him was who you are and that we are here because we are trying to find out something about the plane crash out in Wepo Wash."

"I think you should tell him what happened in a lot of detail," Chee said. "Tell him that two men were killed in the airplane, and that two other men have been killed because of what the airplane carried. And tell him that it would help us a lot if someone had been there and had seen what happened and could tell us what we saw." Chee kept his eyes on Sawkatewa as he said this. The old man was listening intently, smiling slightly. He understands a little English, Chee decided. Maybe he understands more than a little.

Cowboy spoke in Hopi. Sawkatewa listened. He had the round head and the broad fine nose of many Hopis, and a long jaw, made longer by his toothlessness. His cheeks and his chin wrinkled around his sunken mouth, but his skin, like his eyes, looked ageless and his hair, cut in the bangs of the traditional Hopi male, was still mostly black. While he listened, his fingers worked the yarn, limber as eels.

Cowboy finished his translation. The old man waited a polite mo-ment, and then he spoke to Cowboy in rapid Hopi, finished speaking, and laughed.

Cowboy made a gesture of denial. Sawkatewa spoke again, laughed again. Cowboy responded at length in Hopi. Then he looked at Chee.

"He says you must think that he is old and foolish. He says that he has heard that somebody is breaking the windmill out there and that we are looking for the one who broke it to put him in jail. He says that you wish to trick him into saying that he was by the windmill on that night."

"What did you tell him?" Chee asked.

"I denied it."

"But how?" Chee asked. "Tell me everything you told him."

Cowboy frowned. "I told him we didn't think he broke the wind-mill. I said we thought some Navajos broke it because they were angry at having to leave Hopi land."

"Please tell Taylor Sawkatewa that we wish to withdraw that de-nial," Chee said, looking directly into Sawkatewa's eyes as he said it. "Tell him that we do not deny that we think he might be the man who broke the windmill."

"Man," Cowboy said. "You're crazy. What are you driving at?"

"Tell him," Chee said.

Cowboy shrugged. He spoke to Sawkatewa in Hopi. Sawkatewa looked surprised, and interested. For the first time his fingers left off their nimble work. Sawkatewa folded his hands in his lap. He turned and spoke into the darkness of the adjoining room, where the albino boy was standing.

"What did he say?" Chee asked.

"He told the boy to make us some coffee," Cowboy said.

"Now tell him that I am studying to be a *yataalii* among my people and that I study under an old man, a man who like himself is a hosteen much respected by his people. Tell him that this old uncle of mine has taught me respect for the power of the Hopis and for all that they have been taught by their Holy People about bringing the rain and keeping the world from being destroyed. Tell him that when I was a child I would come with my uncle to First Mesa so that our prayers could be joined with those of the Hopis at the ceremonials. Tell him that."

Cowboy put it into Hopi. Sawkatewa listened, his eyes shifting from Cowboy to Chee. He sat motionless. Then he nodded.

"Tell him that my uncle taught me that in many ways the Dinee and the Hopi are very, very different. We are taught by our Holy People, by Changing Woman, and by the Talking God how we must live and the things we must do to keep ourselves in beauty with the world around us. But we were not taught how to call the rain clouds. We cannot draw the blessing of water out of the sky as the Hopis have been taught to do. We do not have this great power that the Hopis were given and we respect the Hopis for it and honor them."

Cowboy repeated it. The sound of thunder came through the roof, close now. A sharp, cracking explosion followed by rumbling echoes. Good timing, Chee thought. The old man nodded again.

"My uncle told me that the Hopis have power because they were taught a way to do things, but they will lose that power if they do them wrong." Chee continued: "That is why we say we do not know whether a Hopi or a Navajo is breaking the windmill. A Navajo might do it because he was angry." Chee paused, raised a hand slightly, palm forward, making sure that the old man noticed the emphasis. "But a Hopi might do it because that windmill is *kahopi*." It was one of perhaps a dozen Hopi words Chee had picked up so far. It meant something like "anti-Hopi," or the reverse-positive of Hopi values.

Cowboy translated. This time Sawkatewa responded at some length, his eyes shifting from Cowboy to Chee and back again.

"What are you leading up to with all this?" Cowboy asked. "You think this old man sabotaged the windmill?"

"What'd he say?" Chee asked.

"He said that the Hopis are a prayerful people. He said many of them have gone the wrong way, and follow the ways the white men teach, and try to let the Tribal Council run things instead of the way we were taught when we emerged from the underworld. But he said that the prayers are working again tonight. He said the cloud will bring water blessings to the Hopis tonight."

"Tell him I said that we Navajos share in this blessing, and are thankful."

Cowboy repeated it. The boy came in and put a white coffee mug on the floor beside the old man. He handed Cowboy a Styrofoam cup and Chee a Ronald McDonald softdrink glass. The light of the kerosene lamp gave his waxy white skin a yellow cast and reflected off the thick lenses of his wire-rimmed glasses. He disappeared through the doorway without speaking.

The old man was speaking again.

Cowboy looked into his cup, cleared his throat. "He said that even if he had been there, he was told that the plane crashed at night. He asks how could anyone see anything?"

"Maybe he couldn't," Chee said.

"But you think he was there?"

"I know he was there," Chee said. "I'd bet my life on it."

Cowboy looked at Chee, waiting. The boy returned with a steaming aluminum pan. He poured coffee from it into the old man's mug, and Cowboy's Styrofoam cup, and Chee's McDonald's glass.

"Tell him," Chee said, looking directly at Sawkatewa, "that my uncle taught me that certain things are forbidden. He taught me that the Navajos and Hopis agree on certain things and that one of those is that we must respect our mother earth. Like the Hopis, we have places which bring us blessings and are sacred. Places where we collect the things we need for our medicine bundles."

Chee turned to Cowboy. "Tell him that. Then I will go on."

Cowboy translated. The old man sipped his coffee, listening. Chee sipped his. It was instant coffee, boiled in water which tasted a little of gypsum and a little of rust from the barrel in which it was stored. Cowboy finished. Again there was a rumble of thunder and suddenly the pounding of hail on the roof over their heads. The old man smiled. The albino, leaning in the doorway now, smiled too. The hail converted itself quickly into rain—heavy, hard-falling drops, but not quite as noisy. Chee raised his voice slightly. "There is a place near the windmill where the earth has blessed the Hopis with water. And the Hopis have repaid the blessing by giving the spirit of the earth there *pahos*. That has been done for a long, long time. But then people did a *kahopi* thing. They drilled a well in the earth and drained away the water from the sacred place. And the spirit of the spring stopped providing water. And then he refused the offering of the *pahos*. When it was offered, the spirit knocked it down. Now, we Navajo, too, are peaceful people. Not as peaceful as the Hopis, perhaps, but peaceful. But even so, my uncle taught me that we must protect our sacred places. If this had been a shrine of the Navajos, if this had been a shrine left for me to protect, then I would protect it." Chee nodded. Cowboy translated. Sawkatewa sipped his coffee again.

"There are higher laws than the white man's law," Chee said.

Sawkatewa nodded, without waiting for Cowboy to translate. He spoke to the boy, who disappeared into the darkness and returned in a moment with three cigarets. He handed one to each of them, took the chimney off the lamp and passed it around to give each of them a light from the wick. Sawkatewa inhaled hugely and let a plume of smoke emerge from the corner of his mouth. Chee puffed lightly. He didn't want a cigaret. The dampness of the rain had flooded into the room, filling it with the smell of water, the ozone of the lightning, the aroma of dampened dust, sage, and the thousand other desert things which release perfume when raindrops strike them. But this smoke had ceremonial meaning somehow. Chee would not alienate the old man. He would smoke skunk cabbage rather than break this mood.

Finally Sawkatewa stood up. He put the cigaret aside. He held his hands before him, palms down, about waist level, and he began speaking. He spoke for almost five minutes.

"I won't translate all of it now," Cowboy said. "He went all the way back to the time when the Hopi emerged into this world through the *sipapuni* and found that Masaw had been appointed guardian of this world. And he tells how Masaw let each of the kinds of peoples pick their way of life, and how the Navajo picked the long ear of soft corn for the easy life and the Hopi picked the short, hard ear so that they would always have hard times but would always endure. And then he tells about how Masaw formed each of the clans, and how the Water Clan was formed, and how the Fog Clan split off from the Water, and all that. I'm not going to translate all that. His point is—"

"If you don't translate for about three or four minutes, he's going to know your cheating," Chee said. "Go ahead and translate. What's the rush?"

So Cowboy translated. Chee heard of the migrations to the end of the continent in the west, and the end of the continent to the east, and the frozen door of the earth to the north, and the other end of the earth to the south. He told how the Fog Clan had left its footprints in the form of abandoned stone villages and cliff dwellings in all directions, and how it had come to make its alliance with the animal people, and how the animal people had joined the clan, and taught them the ceremony to perform so that people could keep their animal hearts as well as their human hearts and change back and forth by passing through the magic hoop. He told how the Fog Clan had finally completed its great cycle of migrations and come to Oraibi and asked the Bear Clan for a village site, and land to grow its corn, and hunting grounds where it could collect the eagles it needed for its ceremonies. He told how the *kikmongwi* at Oraibi had at first refused, but had agreed when the clan had offered to add its Ya Ya ceremonial to the religion of the Hopis. Cowboy stopped finally, and sipped the last of his coffee.

"I'm getting hoarse," he said. "And that's about it anyway. At the end he said, yes, there are higher laws than the white man's. He said the law of the white man is of no concern to a Hopi. He said for a Hopi, or a Navajo, to involve himself in the affairs of white men is not good. He said that even if he did not believe this, it was dark when the plane crashed. He said he cannot see in the dark."

"Did he say exactly that? That he can't see in the dark?"

Cowboy looked surprised. "Well," he said. "Let's see. He said why do you think he could see in the dark?"

Chee thought about it. The gusting wind drove the rain against the windowpane and whined around the roof corners.

"Tell him that what he says is good. It is not good for a Navajo or a Hopi to involve himself in white affairs. But tell him that this time there is no choice for us. Navajos and Hopis have been involved. You and I. And tell him that if he will tell us what he saw, we will tell him something that will be useful for keeping the shrine."

"We will?" Cowboy said. "What?"

"Go ahead and translate," Chee said. "And also say this. Say I think he can see in the dark because my uncle taught me that it is one of the gifts you receive when you step through the hoop of the Ya Ya. Like the animals, your eyes know no darkness."

Cowboy looked doubtful. "I'm not sure I want to tell him that."

"Tell him," Chee said.

Cowboy translated. Chee noticed the albino listening at the doorway. The albino looked nervous. But Sawkatewa smiled.

He spoke.

"He says what can you tell him? He's calling your bluff."

He'd won! Chee felt exultance. There'd been no bargaining now. The agreement had been reached.

"Tell him I said that I know it is very hard to break the windmill. The first time was easy. The bolts come loose and the windmill is pulled over and it takes a long time to undo the damage. The second time it was easy again. An iron bar stuck into the gearbox. The third time it was not so bad. The pump rod is bent and it destroys itself. But now the bolts cannot be removed, and the gearbox is protected, and soon the pump rod will be protected, too. Next time it will be very hard to damage the windmill. Ask him if that is not true."

Cowboy translated. Taylor Sawkatewa simply stared at Chee, waiting.

"If I were the guardian of the shrine," Chee said, "or if I owed a favor to the guardian of the shrine, as I will when he tells me what he saw when the plane crashed, I would buy a sack of cement. I would haul the sack of cement to the windmill and I would leave it there along with a sack full of sand and a tub full of water and a little plastic funnel. If I was the man who owed the favor, I would leave all that there and drive away. And if I was the guardian of the shrine, I would mix up the cement and sand and water into a paste a little thinner than the dough one makes for *piki* bread and I would pour a little through the funnel down into the windmill shaft, and I would then wait a few minutes for it to dry, and then I would pour a little more, and I would do that until all the cement was in the well, and the well was sealed up solid as a rock."

Cowboy's face was incredulous. "I'm not going to tell him that," he said.

"Why not?" Chee asked.

Sawkatewa said something in Hopi. Cowboy responded tersely.

"He got some of it," Cowboy said. "Why not? Because, God damn it, just think about it a minute."

"Who's going to know but us?" Chee asked. "You like that windmill?"

Cowboy shrugged.

"Then tell him."

Cowboy translated. Sawkatewa listened intently, his eyes on Chee.

Then he spoke three words.

"He wants to know when."

"Tell him I want to buy the cement away from the reservation—maybe in Cameron or Flagstaff. Tell him it will be at the windmill two nights from now."

Cowboy told him. The old man's hands rediscovered the wool and the spindle in the beer carton and resumed their work. Cowboy and Chee waited. The old man didn't speak until he had filled the spindle. Then he spoke for a long time.

"He said it is true he can see pretty good in the dark, but not as good as when he was a boy. He said he heard someone driving up Wepo Wash and he went down there to see what was happening. When he got there a man was putting out a row of lanterns on the sand, with another man holding a gun on him. When this was finished, the man who had put out the lanterns sat beside the car and the other man stood there, still pointing the gun." Cowboy stopped abruptly, asked a question, and got an answer.

"It was a little gun, he says. A pistol. In a little while an airplane came over very low to the ground and the man on the ground got up and flashed a flashlight off and on. Little later, the plane came back again. Fellow flashes his light again, and then—just after the airplane crashes—the man with the pistol shoots the man with the flashlight. The airplane hit the rock. The man with the gun takes the flashlight and looks around the airplane some. Then he goes and collects all the lanterns and puts them in the car, except for one. That one he leaves on the rock so he can see something. Then he starts taking things out of the airplane. Then he puts the body of the man he shot up against the rock and gets into the car and drives away. Then Sawkatewa says he went to the plane to see, and he hears you running up, so he goes away."

"What did the man unload out of the airplane?"

Cowboy relayed the question. Sawkatewa made a shape with his hands, perhaps thirty inches long, perhaps eighteen inches high, and provided a description in Hopi with a few English words thrown in. Chee recognized "aluminum" and "suitcase."

"He said there were two things that looked like aluminum suitcases. About so"—Cowboy demonstrated an aluminum suitcase with his hands—"by so."

"He didn't say what he did with them," Chee said. "Put them in the car, I guess."

Cowboy asked.

Sawkatewa shook his head. Spoke. Cowboy looked surprised.

"He said he didn't think he put them in the car."

"Didn't put the suitcases in the car? What the hell did he do with them?"

Sawkatewa spoke again without awaiting a translation.

"He said he disappeared in the dark with them. Just gone a little while. Off in the darkness where he couldn't see anything."

"How long is a little while? "Three minutes? Five? It couldn't have been very long. I got there about twenty minutes after the plane hit."

Cowboy relayed the question. Sawkatewa shrugged. Thought. Said something.

"About as long as it takes to boil an egg hard. That's what he says."

"What did the man look like?"

Sawkatewa had not been close enough to see him well in the bad light. He saw only shape and movement.

Outside, the rain had gone now. Drifted off to the east. They could hear it muttering its threats and promises back over Black Mesa. But the village stones dripped with water, and muddy rivulets ran here and there over the stone track, and the rocks reflected wet in the headlights of Cowboy's car. Maybe a quarter inch, Chee thought. A heavy shower, but not a real rain. Enough to dampen the dust, and wash things off, and help a little. Most important, there had to be a first rain before the rainy season could get going.

"You think he knows what he's talking about?" Cowboy asked. "You think that guy didn't load the dope into the car?"

"I think he told us what he saw," Chee said.

"Doesn't make sense," Cowboy said. He pulled the patrol car out of a skid on the slick track. "You really going to haul that cement out there for him to plug up the well?"

"I refuse to answer on grounds that it might tend to incriminate me," Chee said.

"Hell," Cowboy said. "That won't do me any good. You got me in so deep now, I'm just going to pretend I never heard any of that."

"I'll pretend, too," Chee said.

"If he didn't haul those suitcases off in that car, how the devil did he haul them out?"

"I don't know," Chee said. "Maybe he didn't."

SPECULATIONS

1.   Although the selection begins in the middle of the mystery novel, you can understand why and what Jim Chee is doing. How would you characterize Jim Chee's method of solving a murder? What reasons can you think of for his list-making as he waits for Cowboy Dashee? What does it allow him to do?

2.   Dashee Cowboy is a Hopi Indian, and Taylor Sawkatewa is also Hopi. Why is Cowboy so reluctant to bring Jim Chee, a Navajo, to interview Sawkatewa? What is he afraid of?

3.   Why does Hillerman emphasize the setting so much—the dryness, the sky, the desert landscape, the road to Piutki? What is the significance of the young boy being an albino? Of Sawkatewa winding yarn onto a spindle? Of sharing coffee in three very different containers? Of smoking cigarettes? Of the brief rainstorm?

4.   What is it that finally gets Sawkatewa to talk about what he saw in Wepo Wash? Is it what Jim Chee says, what he does, who he is? How does Jim Chee, a Navajo policeman who is also studying ancient, religious Navajo traditions, persuade a Hopi sorcerer to provide essential information?

5.   Jim Chee agrees to commit a crime in order to solve a crime. What is his justification? Why do Jim Chee and Sawkatewa agree that Hopi or Navajo law takes precedence over white man's law?

The Brother

JOHN EDGAR WIDEMAN

John Edgar Wideman has been called "the black Faulkner, the soft-cover Shakespeare." Aside from extraordinary literary talent as revealed in novels, short stories, and nonfiction, the phrase has its root in Wideman's penchant to publish his works in paperback. His reasons as explained in a *New York Times* interview: "I spend an enormous amount of time and energy writing and I want to write good books, but I also want people to read them." Thus it was his hope that by publishing in paperback he would discover a wider readership, particularly among "the people and the world I was writing about. A $15.95 novel had nothing to do with that world."

That world is Homewood, Wideman's boyhood home. A black ghetto in Pittsburgh, Homewood has been the setting for three works of fiction: *Damballah* (1981), *Hiding Place* (1981), and *Sent for You Yesterday* (1983). His powerful memoir, *Brothers and Keepers* (from which the following excerpt is drawn), also draws upon his early family life there—and especially the life of his younger brother, Robby, who ends up living a street life of crime and—ultimately—punishment. Although Wideman wasn't born in Homewood (he was born in Washington, D.C., in 1941), he spent his formative years there. He earned a B.A. from the University of Pennsylvania, a B.Phil. from Oxford, and began writing early, winning a creative writing prize while still an undergraduate. His novel *Sent for You Yesterday* won the coveted P.E.N./Faulkner Award in 1984, the only major literary award in America which is judged, administered, and largely funded by writers.

In *Brothers and Keepers,* Wideman struggles to explain how he and his brother could be products of the same environment. Wideman attended Oxford as a Rhodes scholar, became a college basketball star, earned a fellowship to the University of Iowa Writers Workshop, and is currently a professor of English at the University of Wyoming; his younger brother by ten years, on the other hand, became a thief, a drug user, a reputed danger to society. In 1976, Robby was sentenced to life in prison for taking part in a fencing operation in which a man was murdered.

But *Brothers and Keepers* is more than an attempt at explanation; it is also a confession, an open-ended speculation, an act of trust, a search backward for one's brother. It possesses a kind of Cain and Abel mythic quality, which is emphasized in part by the fictional techniques Wideman uses to give a voice to Robert. Wideman also hoped that this joint effort with his brother would lead to a pardon; because of the nature of his sentence, Robby cannot be paroled. Since being in prison, Robby has earned an associate's degree in engineering technology; the graduation speech he gave on that occasion can be found at the end of *Brothers and Keepers.* So far, there has been no indication that Robert Wideman will be paroled.

The business of making a book together was new for both of us. Difficult. Awkward. Another book could be constructed about a writer who goes to a prison to interview his brother but comes away with his own story. The conversations with his brother would provide a stage for dramatizing the writer's tortured relationship to other people, himself, his craft. The writer's motives, the issue of exploitation, the inevitable conflict between his role as detached observer and his responsibility as a brother would be at the center of such a book. When I stopped hearing Robby and listened to myself listening, that kind of book shouldered its way into my consciousness. I didn't like the feeling. That book compromised the intimacy I wanted to achieve with my brother. It was as obtrusive as the Wearever pen in my hand, the little yellow sheets of Yard Count paper begged from the pad of the guard in charge of overseeing the visiting lounge. The borrowed pen and paper (I was not permitted into the lounge with my own) were necessary props. I couldn't rely on memory to get my brother's story down and the keepers had refused my request to use a tape recorder, so there I was. Jimmy Olson, cub reporter, poised on the edge of my seat, pen and paper at ready, asking to be treated as a brother.

We were both rookies. Neither of us had learned very much about sharing our feelings with other family members. At home it had been assumed that each family member possessed deep, powerful feelings and that very little or nothing at all needed to be said about these feelings because we all were stuck with them and talk wouldn't change them. Your particular feelings were a private matter and family was a protective fence around everybody's privacy. Inside the perimeter of the fence each family member resided in his or her own quarters. What transpired in each dwelling was mainly the business of its inhabitant as long as nothing generated within an individual unit threatened the peace or safety of the whole. None of us knew how traditional West African families were organized or what values the circular shape of their villages embodied, but the living arrangements we had worked out among ourselves resembled the ancient African patterns. You were granted emotional privacy, independence, and space to commune with your feelings. You were encouraged to deal with as much as you could on your own, yet you never felt alone. The high wall of the family, the collective, communal reality of other souls, other huts like yours eliminated some of the dread, the isolation experienced when you turned inside and tried to make sense out of the chaos of your individual feelings. No matter how grown you thought you were or how far you believed you'd strayed, you knew you could cry *Mama* in the depths of the night and somebody would tend to you. Arms would wrap round you, a soft soothing voice lend its support. If not a flesh-and-blood mother then a mother in the form of song or story or a surrogate, Aunt Geral, Aunt Martha, drawn from the network of family numbers.

Privacy was a bridge between you and the rest of the family. But you had to learn to control the traffic. You had to keep it uncluttered, resist the temptation to cry wolf. Privacy in our family was a birthright, a union card granted with family membership. The card said you're one of us but also certified your separateness, your obligation to keep much of what defined your separateness to yourself.

An almost aesthetic consideration's involved. Okay, let's live together. Let's each build a hut and for security we'll arrange the individual dwellings in a circle and then build an outer ring to enclose the whole village. Now your hut is your own business, but let's in general agree on certain outward forms. Since we all benefit from the larger pattern, let's compromise, conform to some degree on the materials, the shape of each unit. Because symmetry and harmony please the eye. Let's adopt a style, one that won't crimp anybody's individuality, one that will buttress and enhance each member's image of what a living place should be.

So Robby and I faced each other in the prison visiting lounge as familiar strangers, linked by blood and time. But how do you begin talking about blood, about time? He's been inside his privacy and I've been inside mine, and neither of us in thirty-odd years had felt the need to exchange more than social calls. We shared the common history, values, and style developed within the tall stockade of family, and that was enough to make us care about each other, enough to insure a profound depth of mutual regard, but the feelings were undifferentiated. They'd seldom been tested specifically, concretely. His privacy and mine had been exclusive, sanctioned by family traditions. Don't get too close. Don't ask too many questions or give too many answers. Don't pry. Don't let what's inside slop out on the people around you.

The stories I'd sent to Robby were an attempt to reveal what I thought about certain matters crucial to us both. Our shared roots and destinies. I wanted him to know what I'd been thinking and how that thinking was drawing me closer to him. I was banging on the door of his privacy. I believed I'd shed some of my own.

We were ready to talk. It was easy to begin. Impossible. We were neophytes, rookies. I was a double rookie. A beginner at this kind of intimacy, a beginner at trying to record it. My double awkwardness kept getting in the way. I'd hidden the borrowed pen by dropping my hand below the level of the table where we sat. Now when in hell would be the right moment to raise it? To use it? I had to depend on my brother's instincts, his generosity. I had to listen, listen.

Luckily there was catching up to do. He asked me about my kids, about his son, Omar, about the new niece and nephews he'd never seen. That helped. Reminded us we were brothers. We got on with it. Conditions in the prisons. Robby's state of mind. The atmosphere behind the prison walls had been particularly tense for over a year. A group of new, younger guards had instituted a get-tough policy. More strip searchers, cell shakedowns, strict enforcement of penny-ante rules and regulations. Grown men treated like children by other grown men. Inmates yanked out of line and punished because a button is undone or hair uncombed. What politicians demanded in the free world was being acted out inside the prison. A crusade, a war on crime waged by a gang of gung-ho guards against men who were already certified casualties, prisoners of war. The walking wounded being beaten and shot up again because they're easy targets. Robby's closest friends, including Cecil and Mike, are in the hole. Others who were considered potential troublemakers had been transferred to harsher prisons. Robby was warned by a guard. We ain't caught you in the shit yet, but we will. We know what you're thinking and we'll catch you in it. Or put you in it. Got your buddies and we'll get you.

The previous summer, 1980, a prisoner, Leon Patterson, had been asphyxiated in his cell. He was an asthma sufferer, a convicted murderer who depended on medication to survive the most severe attacks of his illness. On a hot August afternoon when the pollution index had reached its highest count of the summer, Patterson was locked in his cell in a cellblock without windows and little air. At four o'clock, two hours after he'd been confined to the range, he began to call for help. Other prisoners raised the traditional distress signal, rattling tin cups against the bars of their cells. Patterson's cries for help became screams, and his fellow inmates beat on the bars and shouted with him. Over an hour passed before any guards arrived. They carted away Patterson's limp body. He never revived and was pronounced dead at 10:45 that evening. His death epitomized the polarization in the prison. Patterson was seen as one more victim of the guards' inhumanity. A series of incidents followed in the ensuing year, hunger strikes, melees between guards and prisoners, culminating in a near massacre when the dog days of August hung once more over the prison.

One of the favorite tactics of the militant guards was grabbing a man from the line as the prisoners moved single-file through an archway dividing the recreation yard from the main cell blocks. No reason was given or needed. It was a simple show of force, a reminder of the guards' absolute power, their right to treat the inmates any way they chose, and do it with impunity. A sit-down strike in the prison auditorium followed one of the more violent attacks on an inmate. The prisoner who had resisted an arbitrary seizure and strip search was smacked in the face. He punched back and the guards jumped him, knocked him to the ground with their fists and sticks. The incident took place in plain view of over a hundred prisoners and it was the last straw. The victim had been provoked, assaulted, and surely would be punished for attempting to protect himself, for doing what any man would and should do in similar circumstances. The prisoner would suffer again. In addition to the physical beating they'd administered, the guards would attack the man's record. He'd be written up. A kangaroo court would take away his *good time,* thereby lengthening the period he'd have to wait before becoming eligible for probation or parole. Finally, on the basis of the guards' testimony he'd probably get a sixty-day sojourn in the hole. The prisoners realized it was time to take a stand. What had happened to one could happen to any of them. They rushed into the auditorium and locked themselves in. The prisoners held out till armed state troopers and prison guards in riot gear surrounded the building. Given the mood of that past year and the unmistakable threat in the new warden's voice as he repeated through a loudspeaker his refusal to meet with the prisoners and discuss their grievances, everybody inside the building knew that the authorities meant business, that the forces of law and order would love nothing better than an excuse to turn the auditorium into a shooting gallery. The strike was broken. The men filed out. A point was

driven home again. Prisoners have no rights the keepers are bound
to respect.

That was how the summer had gone. Summer was bad enough
in the penitentiary in the best of times. Warm weather stirred the
prisoners' blood. The siren call of the streets intensified. Circus time.
The street blooming again after the long, cold winter. People outdoors. On their stoops. On the corners. In bright summer clothes or
hardly any clothes at all. The free-world sounds and sights more real
as the weather heats up. Confinement a torture. Each cell a hotbox.
The keepers take advantage of every excuse to keep you out of the
yard, to deprive you of the simple pleasure of a breeze, the blue sky.
Why? So that the pleasant weather can be used as a tool, a boon to be
withheld. So punishment has a sharper edge. By a perverse turn of
the screw something good becomes something bad. Summer a bitch
at best, but this past summer as the young turks among the guards
ran roughshod over the prisoners, the prison had come close to blowing, to exploding like a piece of rotten fruit in the sun. And if the lid
blew, my brother knew he'd be one of the first to die. During any
large-scale uprising, in the first violent, chaotic seconds no board of
injury would ever be able to reconstruct, scores would be settled. A
bullet in the back of the brain would get rid of troublemakers, remove
potential leaders, uncontrollable prisoners the guards hated and
feared. You were supremely eligible for a bullet if the guards couldn't
press your button. If they hadn't learned how to manipulate you, if
you couldn't be bought or sold, if you weren't into drug and sex
games, if you weren't cowed or depraved, then you were a threat.

Robby understood that he was sentenced to die. That all sentences
were death sentences. If he didn't buckle under, the guards would do
everything in their power to kill him. If he succumbed to the pressure
to surrender dignity, self-respect, control over his own mind and
body, then he'd become a beast, and what was good in him would
die. The death sentence was unambiguous. The question for him became: How long could he survive in spite of the death sentence? Nothing he did would guarantee his safety. A disturbance in a cell block
halfway across the prison could provide an excuse for shooting him
and dumping him with the other victims. Anytime he was ordered to
go with guards out of sight of other prisoners, his escorts could claim
he attacked them, or attempted to escape. Since the flimsiest pretext
would make murdering him acceptable, he had no means of protecting himself. Yet to maintain sanity, to minimize their opportunities to
destroy him, he had to be constantly vigilant. He had to discipline
himself to avoid confrontations, he had to weigh in terms of life and
death every decision he made; he had to listen and obey his keepers'
orders, but he also had to determine in certain threatening situations

whether it was better to say no and keep himself out of a trap or take his chances that this particular summons was not the one inviting him to his doom. Of course to say no perpetuated his reputation as one who couldn't be controlled, a bad guy, a guy you never turn you back on, one of the prisoners out to get the guards. That rap made you more dangerous in the keepers' eyes and therefore increased the likelihood they'd be frightened into striking first. Saying no put you in no less jeopardy than going along with the program. Because the program was contrived to kill you. Directly or indirectly, you knew where you were headed. What you didn't know was the schedule. Tomorrow. Next week. A month. A minute. When would one of them get itchy, get beyond waiting a second longer? Would there be a plan, a contrived incident, a conspiracy they'd talk about and set up as they drank coffee in the guards' room or would it be the hair-trigger impulse of one of them who held a grudge, harbored an antipathy so elemental, so irrational that it could express itself only in a burst of pure, unrestrained violence?

If you're Robby and have the will to survive, these are the possibilities you must constantly entertain. Vigilance is the price of survival. Beneath the vigilance, however, is a gnawing awareness boiling in the pit of your stomach. You can be as vigilant as you're able, you can keep fighting the good fight to survive, and still your fate is out of your hands. If they decide to come for you in the morning, that's it. Your ass is grass and those minutes, and hours, days and years you painfully stitched together to put off the final reckoning won't matter at all. So the choice, difficult beyond words, to say yes or say no is made in light of the knowledge that in the end neither your yes nor your no matters. Your life is not in your hands.

The events, the atmosphere of the summer had brought home to Robby the futility of resistance. Power was absurdly apportioned all on one side. To pretend you could control your own destiny was a joke. You learned to laugh at your puniness, as you laughed at the stink of your farts lighting up your cell. Like you laughed at the seriousness of the masturbation ritual that romanticized, cloaked in darkness and secrecy, the simple, hungry shaking of your penis in your fist. You had no choice, but you always had to decide to go on or stop. It had been a stuttering, stop, start, maybe, fuck it, bitch of a summer, and now, for better or worse, we were starting up something else. Robby backtracks his story from Garth to another beginning, the house on Copeland Street in Shadyside where we lived when he was born.

I know that had something to do with it. Living in Shadyside with only white people around. You remember how it was. Except for us and them couple other families it was a all-white neighborhood. I got a thing about black. See, black was like the forbidden fruit. Even when we went to Freed's in Homewood, Geraldine and them never let me go no farther than the end of the block. All them times I stayed over there I didn't go past Mr. Conrad's house by the vacant lot or the other corner where Billy Shields and them stayed. Started to wondering what was so different about a black neighborhood. I was just a little kid and I was curious. I really wanted to know why they didn't want me finding out what was over there. Be playing with the kids next door to Freed, you know, Sonny and Gumpy and them, but all the time I'm wondering what's round the corner, what's up the street. Didn't care if it was *bad* or good or dangerous or what, I had to find out. If it's something bad I figured they would have told me, tried to scare me off. But nobody said nothing except, No. Don't you go no farther than the corner. Then back home in Shadyside nothing but white people so I couldn't ask nobody what was special about black. Black was a mystery and in my mind I decided I'd find out what it was all about. Didn't care if it killed me. I was going to find out.

One time, it was later, I was close to starting high school, I overheard Mommy and Geraldine and Sissy talking in Freed's kitchen. They was talking about us moving from Shadyside back to Homewood. The biggest thing they was worried about was me. How would it be for me being in Homewood and going to Westinghouse? I could tell they was scared. Specially Mom. You know how she is. She didn't want to move. Homewood scared her. Not so much the place but how I'd act if I got out there in the middle of it. She already knew I was wild, hard to handle. There'd be too much mess for me to get into in Homewood. She could see trouble coming.

And she was right. Me and trouble hooked up. See, it was a question of being somebody. Being my own person. Like youns had sports and good grades sewed up. Wasn't nothing I could do in school or sports that youns hadn't done already. People said, Here comes another Wideman. He's gon be a good student like his brothers and sister. That's the way it was spozed to be. I was another Wideman, the last one, the baby, and everybody knew how I was spozed to act. But something inside me said no. Didn't want to be like the rest of youns. Me, I had to be a rebel. Had to get out from under youns' good grades and do. Way back then I decided I wanted to be a star. I wanted to make it big. My way. I wanted the glamour. I wanted to sit high up.

Figured out school and sports wasn't the way. I got to thinking my brothers and sister was squares. Loved youall but wasn't no room left for me. Had to figure out a new territory. I had to be a rebel.

Along about junior high I discovered Garfield. I started hanging out up on Garfield Hill. You know, partying and stuff in Garfield cause that's where the niggers was. Garfield was black, and I finally found what I'd been looking for. That place they was trying to hide from me. It was heaven. You know. Hanging out with the fellows. Drinking wine and trying anything else we could get our hands on. And the ladies. Always a party on the weekends. Had me plenty sweet little soft-leg Garfield ladies. Niggers run my butt off the hill more than a couple times behind messing with somebody's piece but I'd be back next weekend. Cause I'd found heaven. Looking back now, wasn't much to Garfield. Just a rinky-dink ghetto up on a hill, but it was the street. I'd found my place.

Having a little bit of a taste behind me I couldn't wait to get to Homewood. In a way I got mad with Mommy and the rest of them. Seemed to me like they was trying to hold me back from a good time. Seemed like they just didn't want me to have no fun. That's when I decided I'd go on about my own business. Do it my way. Cause I wasn't getting no slack at home. They still expected me to be like my sister and brothers. They didn't know I thought youns was squares. Yeah. I knew I was hipper and groovier than youns ever thought of being. Streetwise, into something. Had my own territory and I was bad. I was a rebel. Wasn't following in nobody's footsteps but my own. And I was a hip cookie, you better believe it. Wasn't a hipper thing out there than your brother, Rob. I couldn't wait for them to turn me loose in Homewood.

Me being the youngest and all, the baby in the family, people always said, ain't he cute. That Robby gon be a ladykiller. Been hearing that mess since day one so ain't no surprise I started to believing it. Youns had me pegged as a lady's man so that's what I was. The girls be talking the same trash everybody else did. Ain't he cute. Be petting me and spoiling me like I'm still the baby of the family and I sure ain't gon tell them stop. Thought I was cute as the girls be telling me. Thought sure enough, I'm gon be a star. I loved to get up and show my behind. Must have been good at it too cause the teacher used to call me up in front of the class to perform. The kids'd get real quiet. That's probably why the teacher got me up. Keep the class quiet while she nods off. Cause they'd listen to me. Sure nuff pay attention.

Performing always come natural to me. Wasn't nervous or nothing. Just get up and do my thing. They liked for me to do impressions. I could mimic anybody. You remember how I'd do that silly stuff around the house. Anybody I'd see on TV or hear on a record I could mimic to a T. Bob Hope, Nixon, Smokey Robinson, Ed Sullivan. White or black. I could talk just like them or sing a song just like they did. The class yell out a famous name and I'd do the one they wanted to hear. If things had gone another way I've always believed I could have made it big in show business. If you could keep them little frisky kids in Liberty School quiet you could handle any audience. Always could sing and do impressions. You remember Mom asking me to do them for you when you came home from college.

I still be performing. Read poetry in the hole. The other fellows get real quiet and listen. Sing down in there too. Nothing else to do, so we entertain each other. They always asking me to sing or read. "Hey, Wideman. C'mon man and do something." Then it gets quiet while they waiting for me to start. Quiet and it's already dark. You in your own cell and can't see nobody else. Barely enough light to read by. The other fellows can hear you but it's just you and them walls so it feels like being alone much as it feels like you're singing or reading to somebody else.

Yeah. I read my own poems sometimes. Other times I just start in on whatever book I happen to be reading. One the books you sent me, maybe. Fellows like my poems. They say I write about the things they be thinking. Say it's like listening to their own self thinking. That's cause we all down there together. What else you gonna do but think of the people on the outside. Your woman. Your kids or folks, if you got any. Just the same old sad shit we all be thinking all the time. That's what I write and the fellows like to hear it.

Funny how things go around like that. Go round and round and keep coming back to the same place. Teacher used to get me up to pacify the class and I'm doing the same thing in prison. You said your teachers called on you to tell stories, didn't they? Yeah. It's funny how much we're alike. In spite of everything I always believed that. Inside. The feeling side. I always believed we was the most alike out of all the kids. I see stuff in your books. The kinds of things I be thinking or feeling.

Your teachers got you up, too. To tell stories. That's funny ain't it.

I listen to my brother Robby. He unravels my voice. I sit with him in the darkness of the Behavioral Adjustment Unit. My imagination creates something like a giant seashell, enfolding, enclosing us. Its inner surface is velvet-soft and black. A curving mirror doubling the darkness. Poems are Jean Toomer's petals of dusk, petals of dawn. I want to stop. Savor the sweet, solitary pleasure, the time stolen from time in the hole. But the image I'm creating is a trick of the glass. The mirror that would swallow Robby and then chime to me: You're the fairest of them all. The voice I hear issues from a crack in the glass. I'm two or three steps ahead of my brother, making fiction out of his words. Somebody needs to snatch me by the neck and say, Stop. Stop and listen, listen to him.

The Behavioral Adjustment Unit is, as one guard put it, "a maximum-security prison within a maximum-security prison." The "Restricted Housing Unit" or "hole" or "Home Block" is a squat, two-story cement building containing thirty-five six-by-eight-foot cells. The governor of Pennsylvania closed the area in 1972 because of "inhumane conditions," but within a year the hole was reopened. For at least twenty-three hours a day the prisoners are confined to their cells. An hour of outdoor exercise is permitted only on days the guards choose to supervise it. Two meals are served three hours apart, then nothing except coffee and bread for the next twenty-one. The regulation that limits the time an inmate can serve in the BAU for a single offense is routinely sidestepped by the keepers. "Administrative custody" is a provision allowing officials to cage men in the BAU indefinitely. Hunger strikes are one means the prisoners have employed to protest the harsh conditions of the penal unit. Hearings prompted by the strikes have produced no major changes in the way the hole operates. Law, due process, the rights of the prisoners are irrelevant to the functioning of this prison within a prison. Robby was sentenced to six months in the BAU because a guard suspected he was involved in an attempted escape. The fact that a hearing, held six months later, established Robby's innocence, was small consolation since he'd already served his time in the hole.

Robby tells me about the other side of being the youngest: Okay, you're everybody's pet and that's boss, but on the other hand you sometimes feel you're the least important. Always last. Always bringing up the rear. You learn to do stuff on your own because the older kids are always busy, off doing their things, and you're too young, left behind because you don't fit, or just because they forget you're back here, at the end, bringing up the rear. But when orders are given out, you sure get your share. "John's coming home this weekend. Clean up your room." Robby remembers being forced to get a haircut on the occasion of one of my visits. Honor thy brother. Get your hair cut, your room rid up, and put on clean clothes. He'll be here with his family and I don't want the house looking like a pigpen.

I have to laugh at the image of myself as somebody to get a haircut for. Robby must have been fit to be tied.

Yeah, I was hot. I mean, you was doing well and all that, but shit, you were my brother. And it was my head. What's my head got to do with you? But you know how Mommy is. Ain't no talking to her when her mind gets set. Anything I tried to say was "talking *back*," so I just went ahead to the man and got my ears lowered.

I was trying to be a rebel but back then the most important thing still was what the grown-ups thought about me. How they felt meant everything. Everything. Me and Tish and Dave were the ones at home then. You was gone and Gene was gone so it was the three of us fighting for attention. And we fought. Every crumb, everytime something got cut up or parceled out or it was Christmas or Easter, we so busy checking out what the other one got wasn't hardly no time to enjoy our own. Like a dogfight or cat fight all the time. And being the youngest I'm steady losing ground most of the time. Seemed like to me, Tish and Dave the ones everybody talked about. Seemed like my time would never come. That ain't the way it really was, I know. I had my share cause I was the baby and ain't he cute and lots of times I know I got away with outrageous stuff or got my way cause I could play that baby mess to the hilt. Still it seemed like Dave and Tish was the ones really mattered. Mommy and Daddy and Sis and Geral and Big Otie and Ernie always slipping some change in their pockets or taking them to the store or letting them stay over all night in Homewood. I was a jealous little rascal. Sometimes I thought everybody thought I was just a spoiled brat. I'd say damn all youall. I'd think, Go on and love those square turkeys, but one day I'll be the one coming back with a suitcase full of money and a Cadillac. Go on and love them good grades. Robby gon do it his own way.

See, in my mind I was Superfly. I'd drive up slow to the curb. My hog be half a block long and these fine foxes in the back. Everybody looking when I ease out the door clean and mean. Got a check in my pocket to give to Mom. Buy her a new house with everything in it new. Pay her back for the hard times. I could see that happening as real as I can see your face right now. Wasn't no way it wasn't gon happen. Rob was gon make it big. I'd be at the door, smiling with the check in my hand and Mommy'd be so happy she'd be crying.

Well, it's a different story ain't it. Turned out different from how I used to think it would. The worst thing I did, the thing I feel most guilty behind is stealing Mom's life. It's like I stole her youth. Can't nothing change that. I can't give back what's gone. Robbing white people didn't cause me to lose no sleep back then. Couldn't feel but so bad about that. How you gon feel sorry when society's so corrupt, when everybody got their hand out or got their hand in somebody else's pocket and ain't no rules nobody listens to if they can get away with breaking them? How you gon apply the rules? It was dog eat dog out there, so how was I spozed to feel sorry if I was doing what everybody else doing. I just got caught is all. I'm sorry about that, and damned sorry that guy Stavros got killed, but as far as what I did, as far as robbing white people, ain't no way I was gon torture myself over that one.

I tried to write Mom a letter. Not too long ago. Should say I did write the letter and put it in a envelope and sent it cause that's what

I did, but I be crying so much trying to write it I don't know what wound up in that letter. I wanted Mom to know I knew what I'd done. In a way I wanted to say I was sorry for spoiling her life. After all she did for me I turned around and made her life miserable. That's the wrongest thing I've done and I wanted to say I was sorry but I kept seeing her face while I was writing the letter. I'd see her face and it would get older while I was looking. She'd get this old woman's face all lined and wrinkled and tired about the eyes. Wasn't nothing I could do but watch. Cause I'd done it and knew I done it and all the letters in the world ain't gon change her face. I sit and think about stuff like that all the time. It's better now. I think about other things too. You know like trying to figure what's really right and wrong, but there be days the guilt don't never go away.

I'm the one made her tired, John. And that's my greatest sorrow. All the love that's in me she created. Then I went and let her down.

When you in prison you got plenty of time to think, that's for damned sure. Too much time. I've gone over and over my life. Every moment. Every little thing again and again. I lay down on my bed and watch it happening over and over. Like a movie. I get it all broke down in pieces then I break up the pieces then I take the pieces of the pieces and run them through my hands so I remember every word a person said to me or what I said to them and I weigh the words till I think I know what each and every one meant. Then I try to put it back together. Try to understand where I been. Why I did what I did. You got time for that in here. Time's all you got in here.

Going over and over things sometimes you can make sense. You know. Like the chinky-chinky Chinaman sittin' on the fence. You put it together and you think, yes. That's why I did thus and so. Yeah. That's why I lost that job or lost that woman or broke that one's heart. You stop thinking in terms of something being good or being evil, you just try to say this happened because that happened because something else came first. You can spend days trying to figure out just one little thing you did. People out there in the world walk around in a daze cause they ain't got time to think. When I was out there, I wasn't no different. Had this Superfly thing and that was the whole bit. Nobody could tell me nothing.

Seems like I should start the story back in Shadyside. In the house on Copeland Street. Nothing but white kids around. Them little white kids had everything, too. That's what I thought, anyway. Nice houses, nice clothes. They could buy pop and comic books and candy when they wanted to. We wasn't that bad off, but compared to what them little white kids had I always felt like I didn't have nothing. It made me kinda quiet and shy around them. Me knowing all the time I wanted what they had. Wanted it bad. There was them white kids with everything and there was the black world Mommy and them was holding back from me. No place to turn, in a way. I guess you could say I was stuck in the middle. Couldn't have what the white kids in Shadyside had, and I wasn't allowed to look around the corner for something else. So I'd start the story with Shadyside, the house on Copeland.

SPECULATIONS

1.   In *"The Brother,"* Wideman struggles to think through a seeming contradiction: How could he be a successful, educated writer and his youngest brother end up in prison for murder? How does the style and structure of this excerpt reflect Wideman's purpose?

2.   Wideman describes conditions inside the prison:

> Grown men treated like children by other grown men. Inmates yanked out of line and punished because a button is undone or hair uncombed. What politicians demanded in the free world was being acted out inside the prison. A crusade, a war on crime waged by a gang of gung-ho guards against men who were already certified casualties, prisoners of war.

Assess this description—and the one that follows—as accurate versions. What purposes, if any, does such a regimen serve?

3.   If an immediate member of your family was convicted of a serious crime, how do you think you would respond? What would be the differences between that person and yourself? What would happen to your relationship to that person as a member of your family?

4.   If Robby is speaking in certain sections in this excerpt, why aren't those sections in quotation marks? How can you tell Robby's voice from Wideman's? What is the purpose of alternating voices?

5.   How does Robby explain his own rebellious behavior? Who or what was he rebelling against? Assess his feeling that he was "stuck in the middle. Couldn't have what the white kids in Shadyside had, and I wasn't allowed to look around the corner for something else."

Notes from the Country Club
KIMBERLY WOZENCRAFT

"I have no misgivings about why I went to prison," Kimberly Wozencraft writes in this essay. "I deserved it. I was a cop, I got strung out on cocaine, I violated the rights of a pornographer. My own drug use as an undercover narcotics agent was a significant factor in my crime. But I did it and I deserved to be punished."

Such candor is typical of Wozencraft whose novel, *Rush* (1991), has been made into a film that brings viewers inside the world of America's addicts.

Kimberly Wozencraft was born in Dallas, Texas, in 1954, and dropped out of college to join the police force. She began her work as a narcotics agent and, as she confesses, became an addict and ultimately a felon. She was convicted in 1981 of violating the rights of an accused child pornographer and served eighteen months in the Federal Correctional Institute in Lexington, Kentucky. "Notes from the Country Club" is drawn largely from that experience.

Since her release, she has lived in New York City. She earned a Master of Fine Arts degree from Columbia University, and has published essays, poems, and stories in many literary magazines including *Northwest Review* and *Quarto*. Her work has been very well received. A critic commenting recently on *Rush* in the *National Review* wrote:

> Miss Wozencraft also has down cold something normal people don't often consider: that an addict's life is boring. Addicts are boring, drugs become boring, everything that isn't drugs even more boring. To convey this numbing triviality without exemplifying it is no mean feat. In this regard, it may help to read *Rush* as both Miss Wozencraft's agent and I first read it: with a case of flu. The enforced immobility of illness and the narrowed mental horizons of addiction make a good fit.

That same sense of enforced immobility and enforced meaninglessness is carefully etched by Wozencraft in the following essay, which offers an insider's view of punishment—and complements the selection by Jessica Mitford that began this section.

They had the Haitians up the hill, in the "camp" section where they used to keep the minimum security cases. The authorities were concerned that some of the Haitians might be diseased, so they kept them isolated from the main coed prison population by lodging them in the big square brick building surrounded by eight-foot chain-link with concertina wire on top. We were not yet familiar with the acronym AIDS.

One or two of the Haitians had drums, and in the evenings when the rest of us were in the Big Yard, the drum rhythms carried over the bluegrass to where we were playing gin or tennis or softball or just hanging out waiting for dark. When they really got going some of them would dance and sing. Their music was rhythmic and beautiful, and it made me think of freedom.

There were Cubans loose in the population, spattering their guttural Spanish in streams around the rectangular courtyard, called Central Park, at the center of the prison compound. These were Castro's Boat People, guilty of no crime in this country, but requiring sponsors before they could walk the streets as free people.

Walking around the perimeter of Central Park was like taking a trip in microcosm across the United States. Moving leftward from the main entrance, strolling along under the archway that covers the wide sidewalk, you passed the doorway to the Women's Unit, where I lived, and it was how I imagined Harlem to be. There was a white face here and there, but by far most of them were black. Ghetto blasters thunked out rhythms in the sticky evening air, and folks leaned against the window sills, smoking, drinking Cokes, slinking and nodding. Every once in a while a joint was passed around, and always there was somebody pinning, checking for hacks on patrol.

Past Women's Unit was the metal door to the Big Yard, the main recreation area of three or four acres, two sides blocked by the building, two sides fenced in the usual way—chain-link and concertina wire.

Past the Big Yard you entered the Blue Ridge Mountains, a sloping grassy area on the edge of Central Park, where the locals, people from Kentucky, Tennessee, and the surrounding environs, sat around playing guitars and singing, and every once in a while passing around a quart of hooch. They make it from grapefruit juice and a bit of yeast smuggled out of the kitchen. Some of the inmates who worked in Cable would bring out pieces of a black foam rubber substance and wrap it around empty Cremora jars to make thermos jugs of sorts. They would mix the grapefruit juice and yeast in the containers and stash them in some out-of-the-way spot for a few weeks until presto! you had hooch, bitter and tart and sweet all at once, only mildly alcoholic, but entirely suitable for evening cocktails in Central Park.

Next, at the corner, was the Commissary, a tiny store tucked inside the entrance to Veritas, the second women's unit. It wasn't much more than a few shelves behind a wall of Plexiglas, with a constant line of inmates spilling out of the doorway. They sold packaged chips, cookies, pens and writing paper, toiletries, some fresh fruit, and the ever-popular ice cream, sold only in pints. You had to eat the entire pint as soon as you bought it, or else watch it melt, because there weren't any refrigerators. Inmates were assigned one shopping night per week, allowed to buy no more than seventy-five dollars' worth of goods per month, and were permitted to pick up a ten-dollar roll of quarters if they had enough money in their prison account. Quarters were the basic spending unit in the prison; possession of paper money was a shippable offense. There were vending machines stocked with junk food and soda, and they were supposedly what the quarters were to be used for. But we gambled, we bought salami or fried chicken sneaked out by the food service workers, and of course people sold booze and drugs. The beggars stood just outside the Commissary door. Mostly they were Cubans, saying "Oyez! Mira! Mira! Hey, Poppy, one quarter for me. One cigarette for me, Poppy?"

There was one Cuban whom I was specially fond of. His name was Shorty. The name said it, he was only about five-two, and he looked just like Mick Jagger. I met him in Segregation, an isolated section of tiny cells where prisoners were locked up for having violated some institutional rule or another. They tossed me in there the day I arrived; again the authorities were concerned, supposedly for my safety. I was a police woman before I became a convict, and they weren't too sure that the other inmates would like that. Shorty saved me a lot of grief when I went into Seg. It didn't matter if you were male or female there, you got stripped and handed a tee shirt, a pair of boxer shorts and a set of Peter Pans—green canvas shoes with thin rubber soles designed to prevent you from running away. As if you could get past three steel doors and a couple of hacks just to start with. When I was marched down the hall between the cells the guys started whistling and hooting and they didn't shut up even after I was locked down. They kept right on screaming until finally I yelled out, "Yo no comprendo!" and then they all moaned and said, "Another . . . Cuban," and finally got quiet. Shorty was directly across from me, I could see his eyes through the rectangular slot in my cell door. He rattled off a paragraph or two of Spanish, all of which was lost on me, and I said quietly, "Yo no comprendo bien español. Yo soy de Texas, yo hablo inglés?" I could tell he was smiling by the squint of his eyes, and he just said, "Bueno." When the hacks came around to take us out for our mandatory hour of recreation, which consisted of standing around in the Rec area while two guys shot a game of pool on the balcony above the gym, Shorty slipped his hand into mine and smiled up at me until the hack told him to cut it out. He knew enough English to tell the others in Seg that I was not really Spanish, but he kept quiet about it, and they left me alone.

Beyond the Commissary, near the door to the dining hall, was East St. Louis. The prison had a big portable stereo system which they rolled out a few times a week so that an inmate could play at being a disc jockey. They had a good-sized collection of albums and there was usually some decent jazz blasting out of there. Sometimes people danced, unless there were uptight hacks on duty to tell them not to.

California was next. It was a laid back kind of corner near the doors to two of the men's units. People stood around and smoked hash or grass or did whatever drugs happened to be available and there was sometimes a sort of slow-motion game of handball going on. If you wanted drugs, this was the place to come.

If you kept walking, you would arrive at the Power Station, the other southern corner where the politicos-gone-wrong congregated. It might seem odd at first to see these middle-aged government mavens standing around in their Lacoste sport shirts and Sans-a-belt slacks, smoking pipes or cigars and waving their arms to emphasize some point or other. They kept pretty much to themselves and ate together at the big round tables in the cafeteria, sipping cherry Kool-Aid and pretending it was Cabernet Sauvignon.

That's something else you had to deal with—the food. It was worse than elementary school steam table fare. By the time they finished cooking it, it was tasteless, colorless, and nutritionless. The first meal I took in the dining room was lunch. As I walked toward the entry, a tubby fellow was walking out, staggering really, rolling his eyes as though he were dizzy. He stopped and leaned over, and I heard someone yell, "Watch out, he's gonna puke!" I ducked inside so as to miss the spectacle. They were serving some rubbery, faint pink slabs that were supposed to be ham, but I didn't even bother to taste mine. I just slapped at it a few times to watch the fork bounce off and then ate my potatoes and went back to the unit.

Shortly after that I claimed that I was Jewish, having gotten the word from a friendly New York lawyer who was in for faking some of his clients' immigration papers. The kosher line was the only way to get a decent meal in there. In fact, for a long time they had a Jewish baker from Philadelphia locked up, and he made some truly delicious cream puffs for dessert. They sold for seventy-five cents on the black market, but once I had established myself in the Jewish community I got them as part of my regular fare. They fed us a great deal of peanut butter on the kosher line; every time the "goyim" got meat, we got peanut butter, but that was all right with me. Eventually I was asked to light the candles at the Friday evening services, since none of the real Jewish women bothered to attend. I have to admit that most of the members of our little prison congregation were genuine *alter kokers*, but some of them were amusing. And I enjoyed learning first hand about Judaism. The services were usually very quiet, and the music, the ancient intoning songs, fortified me against the screeching, pop-rock vocal assaults that were a constant in the Women's Unit. I learned to think of myself as the *shabot shiksa*, and before my time was up, even the rabbi seemed to accept me.

I suppose it was quite natural that the Italians assembled just "down the street" from the offending ex-senators, judges, and power brokers. Just to the left of the main entrance. The first night I made the tour, a guy came out of the shadows near the building and whispered to me, "What do you need, sweetheart? What do you want, I can get it. My friend Ahmad over there, he's very rich, and he wants to buy you things. What'll it be, you want some smoke, a few ludes, vodka, cigarettes, maybe some kosher salami fresh from the kitchen? What would you like?" I just stared at him. The only thing I wanted at that moment was out, and even Ahmad's millions, if they existed at all, couldn't do that. The truth is, every guy I met in there claimed to be wealthy, to have been locked up for some major financial crime. Had I taken all of them up on their offers of limousines to pick me up at the front gate when I was released and take me to the airport for a ride home in a private Lear jet, I would have needed my own personal cop out front just to direct traffic.

Ahmad's Italian promoter eventually got popped for zinging the cooking teacher one afternoon on the counter in the home economics classroom, right next to the new Cuisinart. The assistant warden walked in on the young lovebirds, and before the week was up, even the Cubans were walking around singing about it. They had a whole song down, to the tune of "Borracho Me Acosté a Noche."

At the end of the tour, you would find the jaded New Yorkers, sitting at a picnic table or two in the middle of the park, playing gin or poker and bragging about their days on Madison Avenue and Wall Street, lamenting the scarcity of good deli, even on the kosher line, and planning where they would take their first real meal upon release.

If you think federal correctional institutions are about the business of rehabilitation, drop by for an orientation session one day. There at the front of the classroom, confronting rows of mostly black faces, will be the warden, or the assistant warden, or the prison shrink, pacing back and forth in front of the blackboard and asking the class, "Why do you think you're here?" This gets a general grumble, a few short, choked laughs. Some well-meaning soul always says it—rehabilitation.

"Nonsense!" the lecturer will say. "There are several reasons for locking people up. Number one is incapacitation. If you're in here, you can't be out there doing crime. Secondly, there is deterrence. Other people who are thinking about doing crime see that we lock people up for it and maybe they think twice. But the real reason you are here is to be punished. Plain and simple. You done wrong, now you got to pay for it. Rehabilitation ain't even part of the picture. So don't be looking to us to rehabilitate you. Only person can rehabilitate you is you. If you feel like it, go for it, but leave us out. We don't want to play that game."

So that's it. You're there to do time. I have no misgivings about why I went to prison. I deserved it. I was a cop, I got strung out on cocaine, I violated the rights of a pornographer. My own drug use as an undercover narcotics agent was a significant factor in my crime. But I did it and I deserved to be punished. Most of the people I met in Lexington, though, were in for drugs, and the majority of them hadn't done anything more than sell an ounce of cocaine or a pound of pot to some apostle of the law.

It seems lately that almost every time I look at the *New York Times* op-ed page, there is something about the drug problem. I have arrested people for drugs, and I have had a drug problem myself. I have seen how at least one federal correctional institution functions. It does not appear that the practice of locking people up for possession or distribution of an insignificant quantity of a controlled substance makes any difference at all in the amount of drug use that occurs in the United States. The drug laws are merely another convenient source of political rhetoric for aspiring officeholders. Politicians know that an antidrug stance is an easy way to get votes from parents who are terrified that their children might wind up as addicts. I do not advocate drug use. Yet, having seen the criminal justice system from several angles, as a police officer, a court bailiff, a defendant, and a prisoner, I am convinced that prison is not the answer to the drug problem, or for that matter to many other white-collar crimes. If the taxpayers knew how their dollars were being spent inside some prisons, they might actually scream out loud.

There were roughly 1,800 men and women locked up in Lex, at a ratio of approximately three men to every woman, and it did get warm in the summertime. To keep us tranquil they devised some rather peculiar little amusements. One evening I heard a commotion on the steps at the edge of Central Park and looked over to see a rec specialist with three big cardboard boxes set up on the plaza, marked 1, 2, and 3. There were a couple of hundred inmates sitting at the bottom of the steps. Dennis, the rec specialist, was conducting his own version of the television game show "Let's Make a Deal!" Under one of the boxes was a case of soda, under another was a racquetball glove, and under a third was a fly swatter. The captive contestant picked door number 2, which turned out to contain the fly swatter, to my way of thinking the best prize there. Fly swatters were virtually impossible to get through approved channels, and therefore cost as much as two packs of cigarettes on the black market.

Then there was the Annual Fashion Show, where ten or twenty

inmates had special packages of clothing sent in, only for the one evening, and modeled them on stage while the baddest drag queen in the compound moderated and everyone else ooohed and aahhed. They looked good up there on stage in Christian Dior and Ralph Lauren instead of the usual fatigue pants and white tee shirts. And if such activities did little to prepare inmates for a productive return to society, well, at least they contributed to the fantasyland aura that made Lexington such an unusual place.

I worked in Landscape, exiting the rear gate of the compound each weekday morning at about nine after getting a half-hearted frisk from one of the hacks on duty. I would climb on my tractor to drive to the staff apartment complex and pull weeds or mow the lawn. Landscape had its prerogatives. We raided the gardens regularly and at least got to taste fresh vegetables from time to time. I had never eaten raw corn before, but it could not have tasted better. We also brought in a goodly supply of real vodka, and a bit of hash now and then, for parties in our rooms after lights out. One guy strapped a six-pack of Budweiser to his arms with masking tape and then put on his prison-issue Army field jacket. When he got to the rear gate, he raised his arms straight out at shoulder level, per instructions, and the hack patted down his torso and legs, never bothering to check his arms. The inmate had been counting on that. He smiled at the hack and walked back to his room, a six-pack richer.

I was fortunate to be working Landscape at the same time as Horace, a fellow who had actually lived in the city of Lexington before he was locked up. His friends made regular deliveries of assorted contraband, which they would stash near a huge elm tree near the outer stone fence of the reservation. Horace would drive his tractor over, make the pickup, and the rest of us would carry it, concealed, through the back gate when we went back inside for lunch or at the end of the day. "Contraband" included everything from drugs to blue eye shadow. The assistant warden believed that female inmates should wear no cosmetics other than what she herself used—a bit of mascara and a light shade of lipstick. I have never been a plaything of Fashion, but I did what I could to help the other women prisoners in their never-ending quest for that Cover Girl look.

You could depend on the fact that most of the hacks would rather have been somewhere else, and most of them really didn't care *what* the inmates did, as long as it didn't cause any commotion. Of course, there were a few you had to look out for. The captain in charge of security was one of them. We tried a little experiment once, after having observed that any time he saw someone laughing, he took immediate steps to make the inmate and everyone around him acutely miserable. Whenever we saw him in the area, we immediately assumed expressions of intense unhappiness, even of despair. Seeing no chance to make anyone more miserable than they already appeared to be, the captain left us alone.

Almost all of the female hacks, and a good number of the males, had outrageously large derrières, a condition we inmates referred to as "the federal ass." This condition may have resulted from the fact that most of them appeared, as one inmate succinctly described it, simply to be "putting in their forty a week to stay on the government teat." Employment was not an easy thing to find in Kentucky.

Despite the fact that Lexington is known as a "country club" prison, I must admit that I counted days. From the first moment that I was in, I kept track of how many more times I would have to watch the sun sink behind eight feet of chain-link, of how many more days I would have to spend eating, working, playing and sleeping according to the dictates of a "higher authority." I don't think I can claim that I was rehabilitated. If anything I underwent a process of dehabilitation. What I learned was what Jessica Mitford tried to tell people many years ago in her book *Kind and Usual Punishment*. Prison is a business, no different from manufacturing tires or selling real estate. It keeps people employed and it provides cheap labor for NASA, the U.S. Postal Service, and other governmental or quasi-governmental agencies. For a short time, before I was employed in Landscape, I worked as a finisher of canvas mailbags, lacing white ropes through metal eyelets around the top of the bags and attaching clamps to the ropes. I made one dollar and fourteen cents for every one hundred that I did. If I worked very hard, I could do almost two hundred a day.

It's not about justice. If you think it's about justice, look at the newspapers and notice who walks. Not the little guys, the guys doing a tiny bit of dealing, or sniggling a little on their income tax, or the woman who pulls a stunt with welfare checks because her husband has skipped out and she has no other way to feed her kids. I do not say that these things are right. But the process of selective prosecution, the "making" of cases by D.A.s and police departments, and the presence of some largely unenforceable statutes currently on the books (it is the reality of "compliance": no law can be forced on a public which chooses to ignore it, hence, selective prosecution) make for a criminal justice system which cannot realistically function in a fair and equitable manner. Criminal justice—I cannot decide if it is the ultimate oxymoron or a truly accurate description of the law enforcement process in America.

In my police undercover capacity, I have sat across the table from an armed robber who said, "My philosophy of life is slit thy neighbor's throat and pimp his kids." I believe that the human animals who maim and kill people should be dealt with, as they say, swiftly and surely. But this business of locking people up, at enormous cost, for minor, nonviolent offenses does not truly or effectively serve the interest of the people. It serves only to promote the wasteful aspects of the federal prison system, a system that gulps down tax dollars and spews up "Let's Make a Deal!"

I think about Lexington almost daily. I will be walking up Broadway to shop for groceries, or maybe riding my bike in the original Central Park and suddenly I'm wondering who's in there now, at this very moment, and for what inane violations, and what they are doing. Is it chow time, is the Big Yard open, is some inmate on stage in the auditorium singing "As Time Goes By" in a talent show? It is not a fond reminiscence, or a desire to be back in the Land of No Decisions. It is an awareness of the waste. The waste of tax dollars, yes, but taxpayers are used to that. It is the unnecessary trashing of lives that leaves me uneasy. The splitting of families, the enforced monotony, the programs which purport to prepare an inmate for re-entry into society but which actually succeed only in occupying a few more hours of the inmate's time behind the walls. The nonviolent offenders, such as small-time drug dealers and the economically deprived who were driven to crime out of desperation, could remain in society under less costly supervision, still undergoing "punishment" for their crime, but at least contributing to rather than draining the resources of society.

Horace, who was not a subtle sort of fellow, had some tee shirts made up. They were delivered by our usual supplier out in Landscape, and we wore them back in over our regular clothes. The hacks tilted their heads when they noticed, but said nothing. On the front of each shirt was an outline of the state of Kentucky, and above the northwest corner of the state were the words "Visit Beautiful Kentucky!" Inside the state boundary were:

- Free Accommodations
- Complimentary Meals
- Management Holds Calls
- Recreational Exercise

In small letters just outside the southwest corner of the state was: "Length of Stay Requirement." And in big letters across the bottom:

Take Time to Do Time
F.C.I. Lexington

I gave mine away on the day I finished my sentence. It is a time-honored tradition to leave some of your belongings to friends who have to stay behind when you are released. But you must never leave shoes. Legend has it that if you do, you will come back to wear them again.

SPECULATIONS

1.   A common technique for opening a narrative is to begin *in medias res*, which is Latin for "in the middle of things." How does Wozencraft use that strategy here? Why do you think she starts the reader off right in the middle of things?

2.   Wozencraft describes everyday life inside the prison. How would you describe the life and culture of the Federal Correctional Institute at Lexington, Kentucky? What are its rewards and punishments? How does the illegal "contraband" affect the prisoner's life?

3.   Wozencraft chooses to use quite a bit of prison slang in writing this essay. Select three to five words or phrases that you think contribute to the meaning and intent of "Notes from the Country Club." Define them, using everyday English, and discuss why and how they add to your enjoyment and understanding of the selection.

4.   Wozencraft admits that she is in prison because she has violated a law. What laws have you ever wanted to violate? Any that might have caused you to be arrested and possibly imprisoned? How did the fear of consequences inhibit you? What laws do you think are worth breaking, even if the consequences are severe?

5.   At various points in this essay, Wozencraft says:

> If the taxpayers knew how their dollars were being spent inside some prisons, they might actually scream out loud.

> Prison is a business, no different from manufacturing tires or selling real estate.

> . . . the process of selective prosecution, the "making" of cases by D.A.s and police departments, and the presence of some largely unenforceable statutes currently on the books . . . make for a criminal justice system which cannot realistically function in a fair and equitable manner.

How does her essay support these assertions? How do you assess those claims? In what ways is Wozencraft a credible spokesperson for these views? In what ways is she not?

The Colonel

CAROLYN FORCHÉ

Encouraged by her mother, Carolyn Forché (pronounced For·*shay*) began writing poetry at the age of nine. She has never stopped. "I used writing as an escape," she told Jonathan Cott, "Writing and daydreaming. . . . I told myself narratives, and I made a parallel life to my own. . . . I suspected, when I was young, that this was madness, but I couldn't give it up." That "madness" led Forché to write poems and essays and to be hailed as one of America's most accomplished young poets—and "one of the best poets writing anywhere in the world today."

Forché has published two volumes of poetry, *Gathering the Tribes* (1976) and *The Country Between Us* (1981). In addition, she edited a volume entitled *Women and War in El Salvador* (1980), translated the work of Claribel Alegria, and published nonfiction including *El Salvador: The Work of Thirty Photographers* (1983). Her political commitment to justice is a strong one; Joyce Carol Oates has said that Forché's poetry fuses the "political" with the "personal," placing her in the esteemed company of poets like Pablo Neruda and Denise Levertov.

Born in Detroit in 1950, Forché lives in Greenwich Village in New York City. With a B.A. from Michigan State and an M.F.A. from Bowling Green, Forché has been a visiting writer at San Diego State University, Vassar, New York University, and the University of Minnesota, and the recipient of the Yale Series of Younger Poets award, a Guggenheim fellowship, and the Lamont Selection from the Academy of American Poets. In "The Colonel," we see her now-famous encounter with a Salvadoran colonel who pursues a ruthless agenda of corporal punishment for unknown crimes "against the state."

What you have heard is true. I was in his house. His wife carried a tray of coffee and sugar. His daughter filed her nails, his son went out for the night. There were daily papers, pet dogs, a pistol on the cushion beside him. The moon swung bare on its black cord over the house. On the television was a cop show. It was in English. Broken bottles were embedded in the walls around the house to scoop the kneecaps from a man's legs or cut his hands to lace. On the windows there were gratings like those in liquor stores. We had dinner, rack of lamb, good wine, a gold bell was on the table for calling the maid. The maid brought green mangoes, salt, a type of bread. I was asked how I enjoyed the country. There was a brief commercial in Spanish. His wife took everything away. There was some talk then of how difficult it had become to govern. The parrot said hello on the terrace. The colonel told it to shut up, and pushed himself from the table. My friend said to me with his eyes: say nothing. The colonel returned with a sack used to bring groceries home. He spilled many human ears on the table. They were like dried peach halves. There is no other way to say this. He took one of them in his hands, shook it in our faces, dropped it into a water glass. It came alive there. I am tired of fooling around he said. As for the rights of anyone, tell your people they can go fuck themselves. He swept the ears to the floor with his arm and held the last of his wine in the air. Something for your poetry, no? he said. Some of the ears on the floor caught this scrap of his voice. Some of the ears on the floor were pressed to the ground.

SPECULATIONS

1.   Carolyn Forché's Colonel offers us a different alternative to punishment, one that was prevalent for much of recorded human history. What point do you think she wants to make? What kind of mentality does this punishment represent? Is it an effective deterrent?

2.   Forché is a poet. How is "The Colonel" a poem? Or is it? If you were the author, how would you present the information in this selection?

ASSIGNMENT SEQUENCES

Sequence One: Defining Crime

1.   Crime and the rise of crime are talked about a lot in contemporary American society. In an essay that draws specifically on selections by Darrow, Sherrill, and Wozencraft, define and discuss the concept of crime. What is crime, both in general and specifically? How do we sort out crimes from pranks, jokes, and offensive behavior of a more benign sort? If you were attempting to define the concept of crime according to a social and legal code of conduct, what would you want to say? If you were attempting to define it from a cultural, economic, or political point of view, how would your definition differ?

2.   Defining a criminal is easier than defining crime; a criminal, after all, is someone who commits a crime. In an analytic and descriptive essay, tell what and who a criminal is. Show different kinds, types, and degrees of criminals. In thinking of the word "criminal," how do you define gender, class, race, economic station, setting? What does a criminal look like? How does a criminal act? What kinds of character traits does a criminal possess? How does a criminal relate to other people in society? Offer your own view, based on your direct or indirect experience with criminals. To support your argument, include relevant arguments from selections by Mitford, Telander, and McCall.

3.   As a follow-up, discuss why you created that particular definition of a "criminal." To what extent is your account based on personal experience? To what extent is it based on books, newspaper accounts, television news shows, television crime shows, movies, conversations with friends and family? Basically what you are being asked to do here is consider how your views and attitudes about who and what a criminal is have been shaped by the culture of images and values that surrounds you.

4.   In "The Criminal Type," Jessica Mitford writes:

> No doubt despair and terrible conditions in the slums give rise to one sort of crime, the only kind available to the very poor: theft, robbery, purse-snatching; whereas crimes committed by the former slum-dweller have moved up the scale with his standard of living to those less likely to be detected and punished: embezzlement, sale of fraudulent stock, price-fixing. After all, the bank president is not likely to become a bank robber; nor does the bank robber have the opportunity to embezzle depositors' funds.

In an investigative report, contrast recent cases of typical crimes committed by the poor with typical crimes committed by the affluent. To find the information, you will need to check recent newspapers, factual databases, perhaps even make some phone calls to courthouses. Offer your findings in a report that analyzes the crimes and punishments—and makes recommendations for the future.

5. Imagine that you are asked either to prosecute or to defend a youth accused of killing for clothes, the kind of "senseless" crime that Rick Telander and Nathan McCall analyze in their two essays. Write the specific argument that you would make to the jury. Whether the defendant actually committed the killing is not the issue: Eyewitnesses and the defendant do not deny the crime. Your job as either prosecutor or defense lawyer is to make the best case, provide the most compelling argument for or against the defendant. You can do some research on how these kinds of summations are put together by observing actual court sessions (on TV or in person) or finding appropriate research materials in the library.

Sequence Two: Criminal Justice

1. Kimberly Wozencraft speculates as to what prison is all about—the purposes it serves within society, its ostensible goal of rehabilitation, its philosophy of punishment, its usefulness as a place of quarantine. In an essay that takes into account Wozencraft's perspective, as well as others in this section, develop your own philosophy about appropriate consequences to the criminal. Think of specific crimes: burglary, robbery, rape, extortion, theft, assault, child abuse, neglect, fraud, white-collar crime, etc. Elaborate on prison as the appropriate response to these various crimes. Consider the treatment of one class of criminal over another. What are alternatives to prison? What is meant by *rehabilitate*? As you work on this essay, you might want to do additional research, including interviews with appropriate individuals in your community.

2. Consider that a new country is just now being settled called "Newland." People are coming to Newland from all over the United States because they have heard that life there promises to be good. The originators of that country are very optimistic, but they are also realists. They know that any country inevitably is going to need laws and must find ways to persuade people to live together in harmony. They have hired a group of founding mothers and fathers who will create a constitution and laws, and they are looking for people to serve as judges and law enforcers. You are to create for them an effective, thoughtful, state-of-the-art criminal justice system, beginning with the concept of the prison. Based on the reading you have done in this book—and any additional reading or research that you undertake—offer the founders of Newland a proposal about criminality and prisons. In your proposal, consider what (and whom) prisons are for, what they should look like, what kinds of activities should go on in them, etc. You might even want to consider whether society can survive without prisons. As you write, draw specifically on the essays by Wideman and Wozencraft.

3.   In *"The Brother,"* Robby says:

> Robbing white people didn't cause me to lose no sleep back then. Couldn't feel but so bad about that. How you gon feel sorry when society's so corrupt, when everybody got their hand out or got their hand in somebody else's pocket and ain't no rules nobody listens to if they can get away with breaking them? How you gon apply the rules? It was dog eat dog out there, so how was I spozed to feel sorry if I was doing what everybody else doing. I just got caught is all. I'm sorry about that, and damned sorry that guy Stavros got killed, but as far as what I did, as far as robbing white people, ain't no way I was gon torture myself over that one.

In a letter drawing upon what you have read—and any other relevant readings and experience you have had—write a letter to Robby in which you respond to his point of view. What kind of moral alternative can you offer? What kind of moral code of conduct do you advocate? What kinds of personal and society responsibilities does Robby have? How can those best be articulated so that Robby would be willing to enter into a dialogue with you about them?

4.   Jim Chee has gotten himself into trouble: He was spotted by another member of the Navajo Tribal Police dropping off concrete supplies at the site of the windmill. Now that the concrete has been set and poured by person or persons unknown, Chee has been brought up on charges as an accessory to vandalism and a public nuisance. Your job as a member of the Grand Jury is to decide if Chee should be prosecuted, knowing what you know from reading the chapter from *The Dark Wind*. Argue your case.

5.   Martin Luther King, Jr., focuses considerable attention on the differences between just and unjust laws, in part resting his justification for engaging in civil disobedience on God's law and natural law. Assess his argument. Discuss whether you agree with King that "an individual who breaks a law that conscience tells him is unjust, and who willingly accepts the penalty of imprisonment in order to arouse the conscience of the community over its injustice, is in reality expressing the highest respect for law."

Sequence Three: Presumed Innocent

1. Here are five different situations in which at least one victim ends up dead:

  a. A young woman kills a rival in a fit of jealous rage in the victim's apartment after a loud, verbal confrontation.
  b. A young man, driving home after spending two hours in a tavern, kills an elderly woman in a car accident; evaluated on the scene, the young man tests above the blood alcohol limit.
  c. A doctor helps a terminally ill patient who wants to die kill himself.
  d. The owner of an apartment building refuses to correct safety violations or to install smoke alarms; an electrical fire results, killing a family of seven.
  e. The president of a corporation knowingly markets a product that is unsafe; fourteen individuals die.

  In an essay that analyzes these five cases and which draws upon the readings you have done in this section, relate your views about these crimes and what kinds of punishments you think fit the crime.

2. Assume that you are Tony Hillerman, the author of *The Dark Wind*. You have just written the chapter in which Jim Chee visits Taylor Sawkatewa. As part of his investigation into the plane crash and murder, Jim Chee decides to visit your campus to talk with a student, staff member, or professor whom he thinks can help solve this perplexing case. Write the next chapter of *The Dark Wind*. As closely as possible, work to maintain Jim Chee's character and method of operation. Try also to maintain Hillerman's style.

3. In his address to the prisoners in the Cook County Jail, Clarence Darrow analyzes the proposed Illinois law (1902) which would make kidnapping a crime punishable by death. He thinks the proposed legislation is "all wrong" because

> You cannot cure this crime by passing a law punishing by death kidnappers of children. There is one way to cure it. There is one way to cure all these offenses, and that is to give the people a chance to live. . . . If every man and woman and child in the world had a chance to make a decent, fair, honest living, there would be no jails and no lawyers and no courts.

What is your opinion? Do you believe that criminal laws are effective deterrents? How does Darrow develop his case? Do you find his argument inadequate? Basing your argument on selections by Rick Telander, Robert Sherrill, and John Edgar Wideman, analyze Darrow's position. You might want to look at some of the essays in the "Work and Wealth" section as well.

4.   Martin Luther King, Jr., has just been tried for refusing to respond to the orders of the police in Birmingham, Alabama. You are a member of the jury. Based on "Letter from Birmingham Jail," offer an account of the debate that ensued in the jury room. What arguments would jurors have to consider as they decide whether to find Reverend King "guilty" or "not guilty." That he violated the law is not the issue—or is it? As you write up your account of the jurors' deliberations, remember that jurors have considerable latitude in deciding cases and can consider motive and extenuating circumstances. As a juror, you are also aware that the entire nation is watching this case in Birmingham; you want Birmingham to present a positive image as a city that is law-abiding, humane, and responsible. Most important, you want the interests of law and justice to be served

5.   You are a resident of south Los Angeles in spring of 1992—poor, sharing an apartment with two friends, and working at a job that pays $130 a week. The jury in Simi Valley has just found the Los Angeles police officers innocent in the beating of Rodney King, and you hear lots of commotion out in the streets. You go outside, watch the riot progress, and see the looting. You now have a decision to make: do you join the looting or go back to your apartment? What do you decide? What principles inform that decision? Does the context—the King verdict, the socio-economic conditions in south Los Angeles—influence your decision? Write a thoughtful analysis concerning why you would or would not engage in the looting.

Sequence Four: Dating and Date Rape

1.   In late 1991 and early 1992, a lot of attention was focused on the issue of rape because of the trials of two notable figures: William Kennedy Smith and Michael Tyson. Smith was acquitted while Tyson was convicted. Employing your research skills, look up some magazine and newspaper accounts of one of these trials. In an essay, analyze at least three different accounts of one trial. What position did the writer of each article take? Evaluate whether the reporting was fair. What differences and similarities do you find—and how can you explain those differences?

2.   Formulate a set of guidelines that you think should be distributed to all college students concerning dating and sexual conduct. In your guidelines, offer a specific section on acquaintance rape and the ways you think it can be avoided.

3.   Clarence Darrow does not consider the crime of date rape. Assume for this assignment that you are Clarence Darrow and that *Ms.* magazine has asked you to do a follow-up article to Ellen Sweet's essay. Write that essay.

4.   Taking into account the selections by Wideman, McCall, and Wozencraft, what punishment do you consider appropriate for a man convicted of date rape? What punishment is appropriate for a repeat offender? In an essay that offers a logical and persuasive position, offer your view. You may want also to consider what penalty should be levied against an individual who falsely charges that a rape has occurred.

4

SELF AND SOCIETY

American society is beginning to tear at the edges. Through the media we hear about an increase in the number of hate crimes, about crosses burnt on the front lawns of black families, about swastikas smeared on synagogues. Television news reports on youth gangs who engage in gay bashing while skinheads attack Asians, blacks, or newly arrived residents. As problems mount—AIDS, family poverty, unemployment—many people find it increasingly acceptable to vent frustrations on certain groups or individuals—often black, gay, Asian, Native American—whose culture differs from their own.

This section, Self and Society, addresses the issue of societal hatred by highlighting the problems and possibilities for solution that exist within American society. This section also acknowledges the resiliency of American life, the general willingness of most Americans to accept difference without emphasizing it. To that end, we have included several birth/rebirth narratives to introduce the section, some of which offer a more hopeful interpretation than others. The next group of readings relate to specific groups within our culture, especially blacks and Hispanics—the two largest ethnic groups in America. It is impossible to consider multicultural America in all its complexity; such an agenda would require several volumes. These selections represent a microcosm, underlining a cross-section of American writing that is rooted, provocative, and powerful.

In his 1978 book entitled *Orientalism*, the intellectual critic Edward Said describes the ways that people create a "type" for those whom they consider to be different, exotic, or strange. After a brief encounter, for example, a Northerner and a Southerner might exaggerate certain aspects of the other's appearance, character, or habits so as to reinforce their differences. Edward Said describes this process as "orientalizing the other," making individuals into peculiar and outlandish figures whom we then find easy to dismiss, despise, or treat in some subhuman way. "An Oriental man," Said states, "was first an Oriental and only second a man." If we take this concept of "the Oriental" and make it into a metaphor describing any person or group that we see as different or strange, we begin to see the problem. As with any society struggling to resolve complex problems, it is easy to search for scapegoats. Yet often scapegoats tend to be the minority groups within society whom we orientalize.

To some, there is only one viable solution: find a way to make the strange familiar. These selections speak to the problems—and the solutions—that society needs if it is to continue to function.

Other Lives

GRETEL EHRLICH

"I wasn't lost, I just didn't know where I was for a few weeks," is the way Gretel Ehrlich describes herself when she moved to Wyoming in 1976. When friends in New York and California accused her of "hiding out," she began to realize that "what appeared to them as a landscape of lunar desolation and intellectual backwardness was luxurious to me. For the first time I was able to take up residence on earth with no alibis, no self-promoting schemes." Sixteen years later, Ehrlich still lives in remote and rugged northwestern Wyoming on a sheep ranch with her husband, whom she met at a John Wayne film festival.

Ehrlich was born in California in 1946 and educated at Bennington College, the UCLA Film School, and the New School for Social Research. She worked as a filmmaker for the Public Broadcasting System, which brought her to Wyoming. Through her own dedication and love of reading, she found a way to translate visual images into verbal ones. Her published poetry and prose, which include *The Solace of Open Spaces, Heart Mountain,* and a collection of essays on nature tentatively entitled *Islands, Universe, and Home,* reveal a writer who is, according to Annie Dillard, "vivid, tough, and funny—exuberant and powerful."

Ehrlich admits that she started to write as a way of coming to terms with the death of the man she loved. She has also said that she doesn't think

> everybody has to have a tragedy in their life in order to create art. That is a terrible American myth. . . . Writing is an ongoing process of exposing yourself to the world and what goes on around you, whether it involves pain or joy or curiosity, whatever. I try to be a sponge to it without being self-destructive.

When asked what advice she would give to beginning writers, Ehrlich responded:

> They need to know that nothing is too ordinary to write about, and that writing wildly is perfectly acceptable . . . I mean writing without a plan and all out of order. You have to love something to write about it. That's the best that anyone can do is write from the heart.

A dedicated journal writer, Ehrlich stated:

> I put my heart into whatever I write in the journal. I don't put something in which isn't provocative to me. . . . That's what I've always been interested in: an expression that has meaning to it.

The ground had just thawed when I drove to Wyoming in 1976. It was night. All I could see of the state was white peaks, black sky, and the zigzag promenade of rabbits unwinding in front of the car. It's said that sudden warmth drives frost deeper into the ground before it loses its grip, as if to drive home one last tentstake of numbness before the protective canvas unfolds. That's what happened to me that year: things seemed better than they were, then took a declivitous slide before they improved.

I arrived in the town of Lovell in the early morning hours and took a room in a pink motel called the Western. The kitchenette came equipped with a coffeepot and a frying pan; there was an antiquated black phone by the bed, and the proprietor, who was asthmatic, listened in on all my calls.

I was there for Public Broadcasting to film four old sheepherders on the Big Horn Mountains from June through September. I had come alone because my partner in the project—also the man I loved—had just been told he was dying. He was not quite thirty.

After a month of ranch work and long hours spent at each sheep camp, John, the sheep foreman, invited me to use the spare bedroom in his trailerhouse. "Catty corner" to the bar and the Mormon church (as he described it), the trailer was set at an angle to the main and only paved street in a town so bland it might have been tipped on its side and all the life drained from it. The interior was extraordinary: crushed red velvet loveseats, gold lamps hung from what looked like anchor chain, a pink kitchen with blue rugs, an empty bookshelf, a statute of Adonis on an end table.

The grandson of the original Mormom rancher who used the homestead laws to amass 200,000 acres of land, John is tall and long-legged with a homely-handsome face. His high cheekbones give him a startled look and he has a bachelor's hotheaded fussiness. "You wanted to come to an outfit where things was done ass-backwards, and you've come to the right place," he said. On the way to sheep camp a coyote crossed the road in front of us. "God, I don't want to shoot that dirty little sonofabitch," he said. He stopped the truck, rummaging in back of the seat for his rifle while the coyote disappeared from sight. We drove on. "Hell, I don't carry any shells anyway," he confessed a few moments later. He had once kept a pet coyote tied up in his back yard, but when he came home from school one day, the animal was gone. "Your grandfather just didn't think it looked right having a predator staked out front," his grandmother explained.

That night one of the would-be "stars" of the film stumbled into John's trailer at two in the morning drunk and on a binge. "Wake up, Hollywood," he yelled into John's bedroom, then ran outside to where his horse was tied to the door handle of a car and threw up. "Don't you get sick in there or I'll take you so far out in them hills you'll never find your way back," John said in his mock-stern voice. The more brusque he sounded, the more affectionate the message he was sending. At three-thirty the coffeepot started perking, waking us by four.

In June my crew—Joan and Nick—and I moved to John's cabin on top of the Big Horns which served as summer headquarters for the ranch. Filming began. Every two or three days I'd drive down the mountain to phone David. His voice was raspy, but his mind was bright. He said, "All this to become a ghost." There was no aspect of dying we hadn't talked about, and now our conversations often came to a halt. Thought I was content just to hear him breathing, the silences were sometimes queasy, at others, purely ironic—an emotional iron ore flecked with rust.

Born in Swansea, Wales, David had a Welshman's hard-drinking indignation, but his brilliant sardonic asides were cooled and keenly balanced by a roll-with-the-punches good-naturedness. His dark hair curled away from a sharp down-curved nose and twinkling black eyes. A minister's son, he raged against false piousness and gentility, accepting a scholarship at Harvard only to play hockey with the French-Canadian toughs, though he read literature on the side. Once in a New York hotel room he asked me to stand naked next to him in front of a mirror. "Look at how different we are," he said as if our rushing, mutual love had hatched out of antithesis. Except for our looks, quite the opposite was true. Having corresponded long before we met, we already knew how alike we were in all ways but one: I was healthy and he was dying.

Earlier in the spring we had holed up in a windowless cabin in a forest of birch, larch, and beech. We ate raw vegetables and drank Guiness Stout. He fed a loaf of stale bread we had found to the "pinto" mouse that crawled into our sleeping bags. Night after night we listened to my one tape of Beethoven's late quartets. Finally the batteries wore down. David slept little and when he did drift off, searing pain awakened him. I'd massage his back and legs until morning came, continuing on into the day until my hands moved on their own and I'd lose track of where on his body they were.

Because dying prunes so much away—everything extraneous, everything that has not been squeezed into paradox—we'd often lie on the floor wordlessly, holding hands, looking at the spectacle of the other, then break into uproarious laughter that convulsed into tears. There is no joke as big as death, we agreed.

By the time David joined me in Wyoming we had stopped talking about marriage. The doctor's prognosis had vacillated: first there was hope of remission; now he said David's chances of making it were "pie in the sky." His stay was brief. "All this space reminds me of possibility, of the life you and I could have had together," he said. His pain worsened and after ten days he wanted to go home and see his children.

We stopped for a beer on the way to the airport. It was the Fourth of July. Kids were setting off firecrackers in a grainfield next to the highway. "I'm not sure what we're celebrating," David said as we held each other in the motel room, rented for an hour, while bottle rockets and "black cats" exploded in the air over us.

The film became an absurd chore. During the next month of phone calls David's voice grew thinner. The elegant, ironic torque decelerated, then dropped away. At the same time the Wyoming sky changed. Its ebullient blue depths contracted and the white bedsheets of autumn clouds pulled it flat. After fits and starts the filming came to an end. It was late September. The last night at summer headquarters I dreamed a fierce windstorm felled two trees. Three ravens circled them; they cawed and cawed.

There was, in fact, a storm: two forty-foot pines in front of John's cabin snapped in half. Attached to them was the crossbar where, for years, he had butchered mutton ewes for food. That was the day the ranch's retired foreman came to stay at the cabin. His usually well-behaved dog acted strangely: he clawed at the picture window and whined but refused to go outside. That night I slept in town. There was a phone call in the morning: Keith had been found dead on the cabin floor. When I woke John to tell him the news he was silent for a moment, then said, "The dog knew."

I made a reservation to fly east the next day. David had been experiencing massive pain and in delirium had called out for me. Another dream crowded in: There was a ferry pulling two plywood platforms. I stood on one, my mother on another. We moved toward a small island. David's young son stood on the shore holding a message. When I debarked to read it, the paper shook so violently I could decipher nothing.

In the morning I packed and was in the bathtub when David's mother called: David was dead.

I stayed in Wyoming and went to Keith's funeral instead of David's. Keith's wife, supported on either side by her children, slumped into the shape of an "S" and could not stop the flow of tears. I was dry-eyed for a while. David's presence—his "ghost"—appeared everywhere, mischievous and glinting. It felt scandalous to be alive, obscene to experience pleasure or pain. Then a wheel of emptiness turned inside me and churned there for a long time.

The tears came and lasted for two years. I traveled. One childhood friend was indulgent enough to let me stay in his Sante Fe house and lie on top of his bed while he slept under the covers. To be alone in a room at night was anathema. Windows flew open and voices yelled, "Wake up!" I'd call John at the ranch. "You still driftin'?" he'd ask.

After many months he said, "One place is as good as another, you might as well come home."

When I pulled up to the trailerhouse—after a nonstop, seventeen-hour stint of driving—John was packing groceries to go to sheep camp. "You might as well come along," he said, trying to sound nonchalant. "I don't know why, but these guys have been worrying about you."

In the next weeks a handful of women befriended me. One of the myths about the West is its portrayal as "a boy's world," but the women I met—descendants of outlaws, homesteaders, ranchers, and Mormon pioneers—were as tough and capable as the men were soft-hearted. BobbyJo, juggling five young children and a temperamental husband, called. "Come on over and cry in my kitchen," she said until I laughed. Dorothy, a cowgirl in her forties whose parents' homestead was an overnight depot for stolen horses coming down the outlaw trail, showed up at John's one night: "Let's go honky-tonky-ing," she yelled through the window, but because she didn't drink and there was no place to dance, we'd go for a ride instead. "Most people don't know what it is to grow up lonely. The only friends I had growing up were desperados and the army guys going by on the train," she said. We ran our horses across the foothills of the Wild Horse Range. A stud bunch (a stallion and mares) lunged up out of a dry wash as we passed by. We came across the carcass of a horse. Its stiff hid was draped over the bones. I wanted to cut it away and wear it around my shoulders. This was how I could wear death and still be alive. "If they ever operate on our hearts they'll need a gallon of glue," Dorothy said as we rode away.

When I visited her house, two goats, a milk cow, a steer, geese, and two dogs chained to a tree greeted me. In the kitchen a Shetland pony warmed himself by the cookstove. Dorothy appeared holding a magpie. "It's for you," she said. "You can teach these guys to talk; then you won't be lonely." She told me about another Wyoming ranch woman who, having survived her husband, brought her saddle horse into the living room on winter nights for company; she suggested I do the same.

Summer brought no rain and one hailstorm. In half an hour a friend's hundred acres of alfalfa were a field of sticks. That's how I felt—stiff, weightless, exposed. I drove to town with the rancher. He ate a whole bag of sunflower seeds, laughing nervously about his loss, and the floor of his pickup looked like a parrot's cage.

By Labor Day the gray, clayish ground had cracked. Between clumps of sagebrush it looked smooth and pale as a mask. John, two rancher friends, and I went "on a party." To "go on a party" means being carbound for a couple of days and part of the fun was feeling their legs next to mine and being destinationless. We went to a bar just over the Montana line called Snuff's. Dust from the calcium plant across the road washed everything pink. I danced in the parking lot with Rex and Chuck while John danced inside with the wallflowers—three obese young women in sundresses. Later we drove on a back road to Red Lodge, Luther, and Roscoe, handing out beers along the way to cowboys who were gathering cattle.

At one bar a woman bent a cowboy backward over the fender of a pickup and kissed him. When she finally let him go he dropped, mocking unconsciousness. We drove home. I woke from a toxic snooze on someone's front lawn. The truck we had driven was parked in the middle of a cornfield. The horn was blaring. When I woke up again, it was gone.

My life felt flat, then euphoric, then flat again. These fluctuations gained momentum like a paddlewheel: I was dry and airy, then immersed again. Was it a lie to be here? Was I an impostor? My city friends called and asked when I was going to stop hiding. Wyoming hospitality was an extravagant blend of dry humor and benign neglect. But I wavered. One morning a couple in a car from New York drove by. "Ah . . ." they must have thought, "a real cowgirl." As the car slowed to go through town I found myself trotting behind it. I wanted to pound on the windows and explain that I knew every subway stop on the Seventh Avenue IRT. They speeded up and drove on. I laughed at myself, then went inside and wrote to a friend: "True solace is finding none, which is to say, it is everywhere."

After a good many tequilas-and-something (that was one of the odd liberties of the state: you could buy a mixed drink in a "go-cup" from the drive-up window of any bar), I decided to winter alone in a one-room log cabin on the North Fork of the Shoshone River. I was betting against masochism in thinking that solitude might work as an antidote to solitude.

Nineteen seventy-eight turned out to be the third worst Wyoming winter on record. After an extreme of sixty below zero, the thermometer rose to ten below and the air felt balmy. One cowboy lit a fire under his pickup to thaw out the antifreeze, then drove over the Continental Divide wrapped in horse blankets because his heater fan had snapped and he had 120 horses to feed in the valley below.

Another friend's transmission froze while he was in a bar. The only gear that worked was reverse so he drove the eight miles home backward through two towns and up the hill past the hospital, waving at astonished onlookers all the way. When his wife accused him of drunkenness he said, "I just got tired of looking at things the same old way."

It was hard to know who suffered more—the livestock or the ranchers who fed and cared for them. One rancher's herd of Angus cattle started aborting spontaneously. He performed an autopsy on one of the cows. "She was just jelly inside. Everything in her had been plumb used up," he said.

Days when the temperature never rose above zero my log cabin felt like a forest pulled around me. Outside, hard windpacked snow-drifts grew, flanking the cabin like monstrous shoulder pads. Rusty, the dog John and I quarreled over and whose custody I won, was my only companion. I played Scrabble with him every night and he won.

Ellen Cotton, who ranches alone northeast of the Big Horns, called me late one night: "I just don't think I can get this feeding done by myself. This snow is so darned deep and this old team of mime won't stand still for me when I get down to open the gates. Could you come over and help?" The next morning, after a passing rancher towed my pickup three miles down the highway to get it started, I drove across the Basin, trying one unplowed road after another. No route would take me to Ellen's. Defeated, I returned to my solitary roost.

I had once asked Ellen how she withstood the frustrations of ranching alone. Because she is the granddaughter of Ralph Waldo Emerson, I imagined she possessed unusual reserves of hardiness. But she protested. "I don't do a very good job of it," she said modestly. "I get in these hoarding moods and get mad at myself for all the stupid things I do. Then I pick up this old kaleidoscope and give it a whirl. See, it's impossible to keep just one thing in view. It gives way to other things and they're all beautiful."

Winter scarified me. Under each cheekbone I thought I could feel claw marks and scar tissue. What can seem like a hard-shell veneer on the people here is really a necessary spirited resilience. One woman who ran a ranch by herself had trouble with a neighbor who let his cattle in on her pastures. She rode out one morning to confront him. When he laughed, she shot the hat off his head. He promptly gathered his steers and departed. "When you want that hat back, it'll be hanging over my mantel," she yelled as he loped away. When he suffered a stroke a few months later, she nursed him, though his hat still hangs over the fireplace today.

Living well here has always been the art of making do in emotional as well as material ways. Traditionally, at least, ranch life has gone against materialism and has stood for the small achievements of the human conjoined with the animal, and the simpler pleasures—like listening to the radio at night or picking out constellations. The tough-ness I was learning was not a martyred doggedness, a dumb heroism, but the art of accommodation. I thought: to be tough is to be fragile; to be tender is to be truly fierce.

In June I moved again—all the way across the Basin to a rambling house near a town of fifty, "including the dead ones." Though the rightness of anything had long since vanished, I had a chemical reaction to this old-fashioned ranching community. I was loved, hated, flirted with, tolerated. I fitted in. The post office, miniature-sized and adorned with deer antlers, provided a hitchrail out front. I rode my horse there every day. Mail was handed out in person by a postmaster who had a haggard, beaten look. He once stood in the middle of the road, trying to shoot a crop duster's plane out of the sky.

Across the street a gorgeous, ramshackle stone building housed the general store where the selection of undusted canned goods was spotty, and peeling green paint fell on customers like snow. The entire north end was a majestic mullioned window comparable to any in a Parisian atelier.[1] A big copper-colored dog named Bum ruled the roost, and the proprietors, oddly mismatched, were generous and convivial. They were native anarchists, showing no interest in false appearances, orderliness, or the art of making money.

Above town on a sage-covered bench I was told a hermit lived in the low-slung house that faced the mountains. He was a painter but kept his windows covered with army blankets, afraid not of seeing but of being seen. I visited him one day. The stench inside the house was of billy goats, dead mice, and unaired emotions. He sat on the floor with his head in his hands, but his lilting, ethereal voice lightened the squalor of the rooms. His bed was a narrow plank blanketed with torn overcoats; hanging from the ceiling by a piece of barbed wire were a baseball bat and a paintbrush—icons, perhaps, of the battle he had taken up with the problems of imagination and survival.

I met Reyna and Pete, who lived in a tree-shrouded house next to the tiny cemetery. They had come north from Arizona to find ranch jobs. As soon as they moved in, a transformation took place: Reyna painted the mailbox purple, hung a canary cage from the eaves, and festooned dead tree branches with garlands of plastic flowers. Small, big-breasted, and vivacious, she told me she came from a poor family and went to work when she was twelve. "I've been everything," she said. "I've slept on the dirt floors and also in the best houses. I've eaten just beans and the best steaks. That's how I am. I know what the world is made of, and I still love all of it." She met Pete when he was working horses at a racetrack. He had a gnarled, intense hand-

---

[1] Studio or workshop. [Eds.]

someness and attributed his vigor to the potion of powdered rattlesnake skin he ate every day.

After the first cold spell hit, Reyna and Pete decided to go south
for the winter. She gave a party and invited the ranchers she had
worked for. After they ate she played a pretaped farewell speech
because she was afraid she would cry if she had to face them. "God
almighty, there wasn't a dry eye in the place. I didn't know some of
those old buzzards knew how to cry," one guest said. A box of Kleen-
ex made its way ceremoniously around the room. After Pete and
Reyna moved out, the owners of the house inexplicably cut all the
trees down. That's how the community felt without them.

Radiating up and down the small valley were the third- and
fourth-generation family ranches. When Mary Francis—"Mike"—
asked me to go cowboying with her, nothing could have stopped
me. Thus began an apprenticeship that continues to this day. Now
in her sixties, she had grown up on one of the big cattle ranches near
Kaycee. "When I told my father I wanted to ride with the men, he
said, 'Okay, but you damned well better make a good hand of yourself.'" She rode and roped, doctored and held night herd, gathered,
and branded, and rode with the steers on the train to market. "That really
caused a stir," she told me. "When one of those green-eyed wives
asked about my sleeping arrangements, I told her I'd slept with all
the men but I liked the horse wrangler best."

Tall, fastidious, an elegant dresser, there's nothing mannish about
her. "I guess they didn't mind having a woman cowboy with them—it
was kind of unusual at the time—but they damned near burst their
bladders until they figured out they could hang back and I wouldn't
turn to watch them."

When Mike taught me to rope I practiced all winter inside my
house, where no one could see me. After I made my "debut" she was
insulted if I declined any invitation to rope and gave praises when I
did, no matter how many calves I missed. That's how her seamless
loyalty worked: once she had taken me on as a friend, there was no
turning back.

Two other women in the valley cowboyed: Laura, who had
herded sheep for John, then moved to Shell, and Mary, who ranched
right alongside her husband, Stan. At branding, spring roundup, and
fall gathering, the four of us rode together and worked as a team.

During calving, the camaraderie grew even thicker. One night I
helped Laura, Mary, and Stan perform a Caesarean. After the epidural
I held the flashlight while Stan shaved the cow's side, then cut
through seven layers of skin. "Why don't they put zippers on these
sonsofbitches?" he asked as the calf bobbed up in a pool of liquid,
then disappeared again. Holding the flank apart, we went elbow-deep

in blood to pull the calf out, our hands grappling for a leg. "Okay, one, two, three—pull!" We yanked the calf straight up, then swung violently to the side and the calf came free. Breathing began. "Looks like a damned yearling," Stan said. Mary peered into the cow's gaping side. "I think I lost my wedding ring in there," she said. Stan groaned. "These cows sure are getting expensive." Laura rubbed the calf's back with straw while Stan sewed up the cow. Both patients lived.

Walking to the ranch house from the shed, we saw the Northern Lights. They looked like talcum powder fallen from a woman's face. Rouge and blue eyeshadow streaked the spires of white light which exploded, then pulsated, shaking the colors down—like lives—until they faded from sight.

During one of those early weeks in Shell a young rancher rode into my yard looking for stray cows. This wasn't an unusual occurrence, but something about him startled me. His wide blue eyes sagged at the far corners as if pulled from innocence into irony. His mouth hung open a little bit. Always, he had a canny, astonished look quickly obliterated by a white-fence–tooth-flash smile. We discussed the missing cattle and he left.

Another day we passed each other on the road and talked. That was the day I saw a grasshopper chase a chipmunk in circles. Later in the week, at six in the morning, there was a knock on the door. I let him in. We talked at the kitchen table. When he stood up to leave he embraced me ardently, then apologized, stepped backward out the door, vaulted the fence, and sprinted up the hill to the pickup he had left idling.

He stopped by often after that, at odd times of the day. Every time before he arrived, I'd start trembling—a signal that he was in the vicinity. The same ritual ensued each time: fragmented conversation, awkward mutual clasping, troubled departures. Sometimes there were other visitors at the house but the chemical razzle-dazzle between us was trance-like and nothing interrupted our meetings.

In September we rode the mountain to check cows, fishing with a flyrod from horseback the creeks we crossed. All summer there had been the silent, whimsical archery of seeds: timothy and fescue, cottonwood puffs, the dilapidated, shingled houses of pine cones letting go of their seeds. Now his full weight on me was ursine, brooding, tender. Sexual passion became the thread between having been born and dying. For the first time the concussive pain I had been living with began to ebb. One never gets over a death, but the pain was mixed now with tonic undulations.

The next morning, at the spot where I had seen the grasshopper and chipmunk, I found the note my friend had scrawled in red dust: "Hello!" it read, as if greeting me after a long trip away from home.

SPECULATIONS

1.   What is the significance of the title, "Other Lives"? Who are the "others" and how do their lives affect Ehrlich's?

2.   How would you characterize the imagery in Ehrlich's writing? How does Ehrlich make use of the natural world, the weather, and the landscape of Wyoming to express her theme? Cite at least two specific examples to illustrate your response.

3.   At one point, Ehrlich describes her search for solace as "toughness" and an "art of accommodation" in which "to be tough is to be fragile; to be tender is to be truly fierce." What does she mean by this seeming paradox? What examples does she provide to explain this mixture of opposites in her self and other individuals she meets in Wyoming?

4.   Have you ever felt a similar sense of renewal during your own travels? If so, explain how and why this happened. What is it about traveling to a new place that often makes one feel like a different person? If you have ever experienced such a change, was it temporary or permanent? Explain.

5.   In what ways do Erlich's descriptions of men and women sometimes cross over sexual barriers or even erase gender boundaries? Identify specific examples of women and men described in this narrative who show qualities normally associated with the opposite sex, or who reflect an androgynous view. How are these descriptions effective or appropriate?

6.   This essay is about healing, but Ehrlich does not explicitly summarize how she recovers from the death of the man she loved. How is Ehrlich healed? What makes that healing possible?

Imelda

RICHARD SELZER

A practicing surgeon for over twenty-five years, Richard Selzer began writing when he was in his forties. His first published story retold the Biblical story of Jonah and the whale. "Who better to describe the interior of a whale than a surgeon," Selzer has said playfully. Perhaps more importantly, the Jonah story is one of spiritual death and rebirth, a process Selzer himself experienced as he moved from the vocation of surgery to writing stories and essays.

Born in 1928 in Troy, New York, Selzer is a graduate of Union College where he earned a B.S. After receiving his M.D. from Albany Medical College, Selzer was a clinical professor of surgery at Yale Medical School until 1985. With Bernie Siegel, author of *Love, Medicine and Miracles*, he also maintained a private practice. "Whenever I look out upon an audience," Selzer will say, "I see row upon row of gall bladders and appendixes—former patients all."

In his writing, Selzer combines the clinical eye of the doctor with the intense emotions of the patient. His work includes *Mortal Lessons* (1977), *Confessions of a Knife* (1979), *Letters to a Young Doctor* (1982), and *Imagine a Woman* (1991).

When Selzer's days were filled with patients and surgery, he would force himself awake and write between 1:00 and 3:00 in the morning, then return to bed until 6:00 to start work at his practice. He still works twelve-hour days, but now they are devoted to reading and writing.

Selzer briefly offered advice to writers based on his own composing process: "Get it all said as fast as possible," he said.

> Sometimes those are the best moments, the moments of inspiration, when the idea comes and you can hardly write it down fast enough. Even if you've written the sentences all wrong—and don't have a subject or predicate or they're just lousy—you've got it done and that's your first draft. Now that's a body of work, no matter how awful it is. Then begins the tinkering. I take it apart, word by word. I rearrange the words, change a phrase, polish it, kick out a certain sentence, add something new. That's the craft of it—the tinkering, and it can be endless. Very neurotic writers never finish—they just keep going over it, afraid to let it go. I myself am not so compulsive. In the end, I abandon it in despair. I go on to the next one.

Selzer has been described as a religious writer, as someone in love with death and the grotesque. He refers to literary influences, such as Charles Lamb, Sir Thomas Browne, Patrick White, Gaston Bachelard, and the French symbolist poets. He tries to capture the joys and agonies in every particular incident. "I write so that the reader will taste my voice at the back of his throat."

I heard the other day that Hugh Franciscus had died. I knew him once. He was the Chief of Plastic Surgery when I was a medical student at Albany Medical College. Dr. Franciscus was the archetype of the professor of surgery—tall, vigorous, muscular, as precise in his technique as he was impeccable in his dress. Each day a clean lab coat monkishly starched, that sort of thing. I doubt that he ever read books. One book only, that of the human body, took the place of all others. He never raised his eyes from it. He read it like a printed page as though he knew that in the calligraphy there just beneath the skin were all the secrets of the world. Long before it became visible to anyone else, he could detect the first sign of granulation at the base of a wound, the first blue line of new epithelium at the periphery that would tell him that a wound would heal, or the barest hint of necrosis that presaged failure. This gave him the appearance of a prophet. "This skin graft will take," he would say, and you must believe beyond all cyanosis, exudation and inflammation that it would.

He had enemies, of course, who said he was arrogant, that he exalted activity for its own sake. Perhaps. But perhaps it was no more than the honesty of one who knows his own worth. Just look at a scalpel, after all. What a feeling of sovereignty, megalomania even, when you know that it is you and you alone who will make certain use of it. It was said, too, that he was a ladies' man. I don't know about that. It was all rumor. Besides, I think he had other things in mind than mere living. Hugh Franciscus was a zealous hunter. Every fall during the season he drove upstate to hunt deer. There was a glass-front case in his office where he showed his guns. How could he shoot a deer? we asked. But he knew better. To us medical students he was someone heroic, someone made up of several gods, beheld at a distance, and always from a lesser height. If he had grown accustomed to his miracles, we had not. He had no close friends on the staff. There was something a little sad in that. As though once long ago he had been flayed by friendship and now the slightest breeze would hurt. Confidences resulted in dishonor. Perhaps the person in whom one confided would scorn him, betray. Even though he spent his days among those less fortunate, weaker than he—the sick, after all—Franciscus seemed aware of an air of personal harshness in his environment to which he reacted by keeping his own counsel, by a certain remoteness. It was what gave him the appearance of being haughty. With the patients he was forthright. All the facts laid out, every question anticipated and answered with specific information. He delivered good news and bad with the same dispassion.

I was a third-year student, just turned onto the wards for the first time, and clerking on Surgery. Everything—the operating room, the morgue, the emergency room, the patients, professors, even the nurses—was terrifying. One picked one's way among the mines and booby traps of the hospital, hoping only to avoid the hemorrhage and perforation of disgrace. The opportunity for humiliation was everywhere.

It all began on Ward Rounds. Dr. Franciscus was demonstrating a cross-leg flap graft he had constructed to cover a large fleshy defect in the leg of a merchant seaman who had injured himself in a fall. The man was from Spain and spoke no English. There had been a comminuted fracture of the femur, much soft tissue damage, necrosis. After weeks of debridement and dressings, the wound had been made ready for grafting. Now the patient was in his fifth postoperative day. What we saw was a thick web of pale blue flesh arising from the man's left thigh, and which had been sutured to the open wound on the right thigh. When the surgeon pressed the pedicle with his finger, it blanched; when he let up, there was a slow return of the violaceous color.

"The circulation is good," Franciscus announced. "It will get better." In several weeks, we were told, he would divide the tube of flesh at its site of origin, and tailor it to fit the defect to which, by then, it would have grown more solidly. All at once, the webbed man in the bed reached out, and gripping Franciscus by the arm, began to speak rapidly, pointing to his groin and hip. Franciscus stepped back at once to disengage his arm from the patient's grasp.

"Anyone here know Spanish? I didn't get a word of that."

"The cast is digging into him up above," I said. "The edges of the plaster are rough. When he moves, they hurt."

Without acknowledging my assistance, Dr. Franciscus took a plaster shears from the dressing cart and with several large snips cut away the rough edges of the cast.

"*Gracias, gracias.*" The man in the bed smiled. But Franciscus had already moved on to the next bed. He seemed to me a man of immense strength and ability, yet without affection for the patients. He did not want to be touched by them. It was less kindness that he showed them than a reassurance that he would never give up, that he would bend every effort. If anyone could, he would solve the problems of their flesh.

Ward Rounds had disbanded and I was halfway down the corridor when I heard Dr. Franciscus's voice behind me.

"You speak Spanish." It seemed a command.

"I lived in Spain for two years," I told him.

"I'm taking a surgical team to Honduras next week to operate on the natives down there. I do it every year for three weeks, somewhere. This year, Honduras. I can arrange the time away from your duties here if you'd like to come along. You will act as interpreter. I'll show you how to use the clinical camera. What you'd see would make it worthwhile."

So it was that, a week later, the envy of my classmates, I joined the mobile surgical unit—surgeons, anesthetists, nurses and equipment—aboard a Military Air Transport plane to spend three weeks performing plastic surgery on people who had been previously selected by an advance team. Honduras. I don't suppose I shall ever see it again. Nor do I especially want to. From the plane it seemed a country made of clay—burnt umber, raw sienna, dry. It had a dead-weight quality, as though the ground had no buoyancy, no air sacs through which a breeze might wander. Our destination was Comayagua, a town in the Central Highlands. The town itself was situated on the edge of one of the flatlands that were linked in a network between the granite mountains. Above, all was brown, with only an occasional Spanish cedar tree; below, patches of luxuriant tropical growth. It was a day's bus ride from the airport. For hours, the town kept appearing and disappearing with the convolutions of the road. At last, there it lay before us, panting and exhausted at the bottom of the mountain.

That was all I was to see of the countryside. From then on, there was only the derelict hospital of Comayagua, with the smell of spoiling bananas and the accumulated odors of everyone who had been sick there for the last hundred years. Of the two, I much preferred the frank smell of the sick. The heat of the place was incendiary. So hot that, as we stepped from the bus, our own words did not carry through the air, but hung limply at our lips and chins. Just in front of the hospital was a thirsty courtyard where mobs of waiting people squatted or lay in the meager shade, and where, on dry days, a fine dust rose through which untethered goats shouldered. Against the walls of this courtyard, gaunt, dejected men stood, their faces, like their country, preternaturally solemn, leaden. Here no one looked up at the sky. Every head was bent beneath a wide-brimmed straw hat. In the days that followed, from the doorway of the dispensary, I would watch the brown mountains sliding about, drinking the hospital into their shadow as the afternoon grew later and later, flattening us by their very altitude.

The people were mestizos, of mixed Spanish and Indian blood. They had flat, broad, dumb museum feet. At first they seemed to me indistinguishable the one from the other, without animation. All the vitality, the hidden sexuality, was in their black hair. Soon I was to know them by the fissures with which each face was graven. But, even so, compared to us, they were masked, shut away. My job was to follow Dr. Franciscus around, photograph the patients before and after surgery, interpret and generally act as aide-de-camp. It was exhilarating. Within days I had decided that I was not just useful, but essential. Despite that we spent all day in each other's company, there were no overtures of friendship from Dr. Franciscus. He knew my place, and I knew it, too. In the afternoon he examined the patients scheduled for the next day's surgery. I would call out a name from the doorway to the examining room. In the courtyard someone would rise. I would usher the patient in, and nudge him to the examining table where Franciscus stood, always, I thought, on the verge of irritability. I would read aloud the case history, then wait while he carried out his examination. While I took the "before" photographs, Dr. Franciscus would dictate into a tape recorder:

"Ulcerating basal cell carcinoma of the right orbit—six by eight centimeters—involving the right eye and extending into the floor of the orbit. Operative plan: wide excision with enucleation of the eye. Later, bone and skin grafting." The next morning we would be in the operating room where the procedure would be carried out.

We were more than two weeks into our tour of duty—a few days to go—when it happened. Earlier in the day I had caught sight of her through the window of the dispensary. A thin, dark Indian girl about fourteen years old. A figurine, orange-brown, terra-cotta, and still attached to the unshaped clay from which she had been carved. An older, sun-weathered woman stood behind and somewhat to the left of the girl. The mother was short and dumpy. She wore a broad-brimmed hat with a high crown, and a shapeless dress like a cassock. The girl had long, loose black hair. There were tiny gold hoops in her ears. The dress she wore could have been her mother's. Far too big, it hung from her thin shoulders at some risk of slipping down her arms. Even with her in it, the dress was empty, something hanging on the back of a door. Her breasts made only the smallest imprint in the cloth, her hips none at all. All the while, she pressed to her mouth a filthy, pink, balled-up rag as though to stanch a flow or buttress against pain. I knew that what she had come to show us, what we were there to see, was hidden beneath that pink cloth. As I watched, the woman handed down to her a gourd from which the girl drank, lapping like a dog. She was the last patient of the day. They had been waiting in the courtyard for hours.

"Imelda Valdez," I called out. Slowly she rose to her feet, the cloth never leaving her mouth, and followed her mother to the examining-room door. I shooed them in.

"You sit up there on the table," I told her. "Mother, you stand over there, please." I read from the chart:

"This is a fourteen-year-old girl with a complete, unilateral, left-sided cleft lip and cleft palate. No other diseases or congenital defects. Laboratory tests, chest X-ray—negative."

"Tell her to take the rag away," said Dr. Franciscus. I did, and the girl shrank back, pressing the cloth all the more firmly.

"Listen, this is silly," said Franciscus. "Tell her I've got to see it. Either she behaves, or send her away."

"Please give me the cloth," I said to the girl as gently as possible. She did not. She could not. Just then, Franciscus reached up and, taking the hand that held the rag, pulled it away with a hard jerk. For an instant the girl's head followed the cloth as it left her face, one arm still upflung against showing. Against all hope, she would hide herself. A moment later, she relaxed and sat still. She seemed to me then like an animal that looks outward at the infinite, at death, without fear, with recognition only.

Set as it was in the center of the girl's face, the defect was utterly hideous—a nude rubbery insect that had fastened there. The upper lip was widely split all the way to the nose. One white tooth perched upon the protruding upper jaw projecting through the hole. Some of the bone seemed to have been gnawed away as well. Above the thing, clear almond eyes and long black hair reflected the light. Below, a slender neck where the pulse trilled visibly. Under our gaze the girl's eyes fell to her lap where her hands lay palms upward, half open. She was a beautiful bird with a crushed beak. And tense with the expectation of more shame.

"Open your mouth," said the surgeon. I translated. She did so, and the surgeon tipped back her head to see inside.

"The palate, too. Complete," he said. There was a long silence. At last he spoke.

"What is your name?" The margins of the wound melted until she herself was being sucked into it.

"Imelda." The syllables leaked through the hole with a slosh and a whistle.

"Tomorrow," said the surgeon, "I will fix your lip. *Mañana.*"

It seemed to me that Hugh Franciscus, in spite of his years of experience, in spite of all the dreadful things he had seen, must have been awed by the sight of this girl. I could see it flit across his face for an instant. Perhaps it was her small act of concealment, that he had had to demand that she show him the lip, that he had had to force her to show it to him. Perhaps it was her resistance that intensified the disfigurement. Had she brought her mouth to him willingly, without shame, she would have been for him neither more nor less than any other patient.

He measured the defect with calipers, studied it from different angles, turning her head with a finger at her chin.

"How can it ever be put back together?" I asked.

"Take her picture," he said. And to her, "Look straight ahead." Through the eye of the camera she seemed more pitiful than ever, her humiliation more complete.

"Wait!" The surgeon stopped me. I lowered the camera. A strand of her hair had fallen across her face and found it way to her mouth, becoming stuck there by saliva. He removed the hair and secured it behind her ear.

"Go ahead," he ordered. There was the click of the camera. The girl winced.

"Take three more, just in case."

When the girl and her mother had left, he took paper and pen and with a few lines drew a remarkable likeness of the girl's face.

"Look," he said. "If this dot is A, and this one B, this, C, and this, D, the incisions are made A to B, then C to D. CD must equal AB. It is all equilateral triangles." All well and good, but then came X and Y and rotation flaps and the rest.

"Do you see?" he asked.

"It is confusing," I told him.

"It is simply a matter of dropping the upper lip into a normal position, then crossing the gap with two triangular flaps. It is geometry," he said.

"Yes," I said. "Geometry." And relinquished all hope of becoming a plastic surgeon.

In the operating room the next morning the anesthesia had already been administered when we arrived from Ward Rounds. The tube emerging from the girl's mouth was pressed against her lower lip to be kept out of the field of surgery. Already, a nurse was scrubbing the face which swam in a reddish-brown lather. The tiny gold earring were included in the scrub. Now and then, one of them gave a brave flash. The face was washed for the last time, and dried. Green towels were placed over the face to hide everything but the mouth and nose. The drapes were applied.

"Calipers!" The surgeon measured, locating the peak of the distorted Cupid's bow.

"Marking pen!" He placed the first blue dot at the apex of the bow. The nasal sills were dotted; next, the inferior philtral dimple, the vermilion line. The A flap and the B flap were outlined. On he worked, peppering the lip and nose, making sense of chaos, realizing the lip that lay waiting in that deep essential pink, that only he could see. The last dot and line were placed. He was ready.

"Scalpel!" He held the knife above the girl's mouth.

"O.K. to go ahead?" he asked the anesthetist.

"Yes."

He lowered the knife.

"No! Wait!" The anesthetist's voice was tense, staccato. "Hold it!"

The surgeon's hand was motionless.

"What's the matter?"

"Something's wrong. I'm not sure. God, she's hot as a pistol. Blood pressure is way up. Pulse one eighty. Get a rectal temperature." A nurse fumbled beneath the drapes. We waited. The nurse retrieved the thermometer.

"One hundred seven . . . no . . . eight." There was disbelief in her voice.

"Malignant hyperthermia," said the anesthetist. "Ice! Ice! Get lots of ice!" I raced out the door, accosted the first nurse I saw.

"Ice!" I shouted. "Hielo!"[1] Quickly! Hielo!" The woman's expression was blank. I ran to another. "Hielo! Hielo! For the love of God, ice."

---

[1] Ice. [Eds.]

"*Hielo?*" She shrugged. "*Nada.*"[2] I ran back to the operating room.

"There isn't any ice." I reported. Dr. Franciscus had ripped off his rubber gloves and was feeling the skin of the girl's abdomen. Above the mask his eyes were the eyes of a horse in battle.

"The EKG is wild. . ."

"I can't get a pulse. . ."

"What the hell. . ."

The surgeon reached for the girl's groin. No femoral pulse.

"EKG flat. My God! She's dead!"

"She can't be."

"She is."

The surgeon's fingers pressed the groin where there was no pulse to be felt, only his own pulse hammering at the girl's flesh to be let in.

It was noon, four hours later, when we left the operating room. It was a day so hot and humid I felt steamed open like an envelope. The woman was sitting on a bench in the courtyard in her dress like a cassock. In one hand she held the piece of cloth the girl had used to conceal her mouth. As we watched, she folded it once neatly, and then again, smoothing it, cleaning the cloth which might have been the head of the girl in her lap that she stroked and consoled.

"I'll do the talking here, " he said. He would tell her himself, in whatever Spanish he could find. Only if she did not understand was I to speak for him. I watched him brace himself, set his shoulders. How could he tell her? I wondered. What? But I knew he would tell her everything, exactly as it had happened. As much for himself as for her, he needed to explain. But suppose she screamed, fell to the ground, attacked him, even? All that hope of love . . . gone. Even in his discomfort I knew that he was teaching me. The way to do it was professionally. Now he was standing above her. When the woman saw that he did not speak, she lifted her eyes and saw what he held crammed in his mouth to tell her. She knew, and rose to her feet.

"*Señora*," he began, "I am sorry." All at once he seemed to me shorter than he was, scarcely taller than she. There was a place at the crown of his head where the hair had grown thin. His lips were stones. He could hardly move them. The voice dry, dusty.

"No one could have known. Some bad reaction to the medicine for sleeping. It poisoned her. High fever. She did not wake up." The last, a whisper. The woman studied his lips as though she were deaf. He tried, but could not control a twitching at the corner of his mouth.

---

[2] Nothing. [Eds.]

He raised a thumb and forefinger to press something back into his eyes.

"*Muerte*,"[3] the woman announced to herself. Her eyes were human, deadly.

"*Sí, muerte.*" At that moment he was like someone cast, still alive, as an effigy for his own tomb. He closed his eyes. Nor did he open them until he felt the touch of the woman's hand on his arm, a touch from which he did not withdraw. Then he looked and saw the grief corroding her face, breaking it down, melting the features so that eyes, nose, mouth ran together in a distortion, like the girl's. For a long time they stood in silence. It seemed to me that minutes passed. At last her face cleared, the features rearranged themselves. She spoke, the words coming slowly to make certain that he understood her. She would go home now. The next day her sons would come for the girl, to take her home for burial. The doctor must not be sad. God has decided. And she was happy now that the harelip had been fixed so that her daughter might go to Heaven without it. Her bare feet retreating were the felted pads of a great bereft animal.

The next morning I did not go to the wards, but stood at the gate leading from the courtyard to the road outside. Two young men in striped ponchos lifted the girl's body wrapped in a straw mat onto the back of a wooden cart. A donkey waited. I had been drawn to this place as one is drawn, inexplicably, to certain scenes of desolation—executions, battlefields. All at once, the woman looked up and saw me. She had taken off her hat. The heavy-hanging coil of her hair made her head seem larger, darker, noble. I pressed some money into her hand.

"For flowers," I said. "A priest." Her cheeks shook as though minutes ago a stone had been dropped into her navel and the ripples were just now reaching her head. I regretted having come to that place.

"*Sí, sí,*" The woman said. Her own face was stitched with flies. "The doctor is one of the angels. He has finished the work of God. My daughter is beautiful."

What could she mean! The lip had not been fixed. The girl had died before he would have done it.

"Only a fine line that God will erase in time," she said.

I reached into the cart and lifted a corner of the mat in which the girl had been rolled. Where the cleft had been there was now a fresh line of tiny sutures. The Cupid's bow was delicately shaped, the vermilion border aligned. The flattened nostril had now the same

---

[3] Dead. [Eds.]

rounded shape as the other one. I let the mat fall over the face of the dead girl, but not before I had seen the touching place where the finest black hairs sprang from the temple.

"*Adiós, adiós. . . .*" And the cart creaked away to the sound of hooves, a tinkling bell.

There are events in a doctor's life that seem to mark the boundary between youth and age, seeing and perceiving. Like certain dreams, they illuminate a whole lifetime of past behavior. After such an event, a doctor is not the same as he was before. It had seemed to me then to have been the act of someone demented, or at least insanely arrogant. An attempt to reorder events. Her death had come to him out of order. It should have come after the lip had been repaired, not before. He could have told the mother that, no, the lip had not been fixed. But he did not. He said nothing. It had been an act of omission, one of those strange lapses to which all of us are subject and which we live to regret. It must have been then, at that moment, that the knowledge of what he would do appeared to him. The words of the mother had not consoled him; they had hunted him down. He had not done it for her. The dire necessity was his. He would not accept that Imelda had died before he could repair her lip. People who do such things break free from society. They follow their own lonely path. They have a secret which they can never reveal. I must never let on that I knew.

How often I have imagined it. Ten o'clock at night. The hospital of Comayagua is all but dark. Here and there lanterns tilt and skitter up and down the corridors. One of these lamps breaks free from the others and descends the stone steps to the underground room that is the morgue of the hospital. This room wears the expression as if it had waited all night for someone to come. No silence so deep as this place with its cargo of newly dead. Only the slow drip of water over stone. The door closes gassily and clicks shut. The lock is turned. There are four tables, each with a body encased in a paper shroud. There is no mistaking her. She is the smallest. The surgeon takes a knife from his pocket and slits open the paper shroud, that part in which the girl's head is enclosed. The wound seems to be living on long after she has died. Waves of heat emanate from it, blurring his vision. All at once, he turns to peer over his shoulder. He sees nothing, only a wooden crucifix on the wall.

He removes a package of instruments from a satchel and arranges them on a tray. Scalpel, scissors, forceps, needle holder. Sutures and gauze sponges are produced. Stealthy, hunched, engaged, he begins. The dots of blue dye are still there upon her mouth. He raises the scalpel, pauses. A second glance into the darkness. From the wall a small lizard watches and accepts. The first cut is made. A sluggish flow of dark blood appears. He wipes it away with a sponge. No new blood comes to take its place. Again and again he cuts, connecting each of the blue dots until the whole of the zigzag slice is made, first on one side of the cleft, then on the other. Now the edges of the cleft are lined with fresh tissue. He sets down the scalpel and takes up scissors and forceps, undermining the little flaps until each triangle is attached only at one side. He rotates each flap into its new position. He must be certain that they can be swung without tension. They can. He is ready to suture. He fits the tiny curved needle into the jaws of the needle holder. Each suture is placed precisely the same number of millimeters from the cut edge, and the same distance apart. He ties each knot down until the edges are apposed. Not too tightly. These are the most meticulous sutures of his life. He cuts each thread close to the knot. It goes well. The vermilion border with its white skin roll is exactly aligned. One more stitch and the Cupid's bow appears as if by magic. The man's face shines with moisture. Now the nostril is incised around the margin, released, and sutured into a round shape to match its mate. He wipes the blood from the face of the girl with gauze the he has dipped in water. Crumbs of light are scattered on the girl's face. The shroud is folded once more about her. The instruments are handed into the satchel. In a moment the morgue is dark and a lone lantern ascends the stairs and is extinguished.

Six weeks later I was in the darkened amphitheater of the Medical School. Tiers of seats rose in a semicircle above the small stage where Hugh Franciscus stood presenting the case material he had encountered in Honduras. It was the highlight of the year. The hall was filled. The night before he had arranged the slides in the order in which they were to be shown. I was at the controls of the slide projector.

"Next slide!" he would order from time to time in that military voice which had called forth blind obedience from generations of medical students, interns, residents and patients.

"This is a fifty-seven-year-old man with a severe burn contracture of the neck. You will notice the rigid webbing that has fused the chin to the presternal tissues. No motion of the head on the torso is possible. . . . Next slide!"

"Click," went the projector.

"Here he is after the excision of the scar tissue and with the head in full extension for the first time. The defect was then covered. . . . Next slide!"

"Click."

". . . with full-thickness drums of skin taken from the abdomen with the Padgett dermatome. Next slide!"

"Click."

And suddenly there she was, extracted from the shadows, suspended above and beyond all of us like a resurrection. There was the oval face, the long black hair unbraided, the tiny gold hoops in her ears. And that luminous gnawed mouth. The whole of her life seemed to have been summed up in this photograph. A long silence followed that was the surgeon's alone to break. Almost at once, like the anesthetist in the operating room in Comayagua, I knew that something was wrong. It was not that the man would not speak as that he could not. The audience of doctors, nurses and students seemed to have been infected by the black, limitless silence. My own pulse doubled. It was hard to breathe. Why did he not call out for the next slide? Why did he not save himself? Why had he not removed this slide from the ones to be shown? All at once I knew that he had used his camera on her again. I could see the long black shadows of her hair flowing into the darker shadows of the morgue. The sudden blinding flash . . . The next slide would be the one taken in the morgue. He would be exposed.

In the dim light reflected from the slide, I saw him gazing up at her, seeing not the colored photograph, I thought, but the negative of it where the ghost of the girl was. For me, the amphitheater had become Honduras. I saw again that courtyard littered with patients. I could see the dust in the beam of light from the projector. It was then that I knew that she was his measure of perfection and pain—the one lost, the other gained. He, too, had heard the click of the camera, had seen her wince and felt his mercy enlarge. At last he spoke.

"Imelda." It was the one word he had heard her say. At the sound of his voice I removed the next slide from the projector. "Click" . . . and she was gone. "Click" again, and in her place the man with the orbital cancer. For a long moment Franciscus looked up in my direction, on his face an expression that I have given up trying to interpret. Gratitude? Sorrow? It made me think of the gaze of the girl when at last she understood that she must hand over to him the evidence of her body.

"This is a sixty-two-year-old man with a basal cell carcinoma of the temple eroding into the bony orbit . . ." he began as though nothing had happened.

At the end of the hour, even before the lights went on, there was loud applause. I hurried to find him among the departing crowd. I could not. Some weeks went by before I caught sight of him. He seemed vaguely convalescent, as though a fever had taken its toll before burning out.

Hugh Franciscus continued to teach for fifteen years, although he operated a good deal less, then gave it up entirely. It was as though he had grown tired of blood, of always having to be involved with blood, of having to draw it, spill it, wipe it away, stanch it. He was a quieter, softer man, I heard, the ferocity diminished. There were no more expeditions to Honduras or anywhere else.

I, too, have not been entirely free of her. Now and then, in the years that have passed, I see that donkey-cart cortège, or his face bent over hers in the morgue. I would like to have told him what I now know, that his unrealistic act was one of goodness, one of those small, persevering acts done, perhaps, to ward off madness. Like lighting a lamp, boiling water for tea, washing a shirt. But, of course, it's too late now.

SPECULATIONS

1. According to the description of the doctor, Hugh Franciscus, at the beginning of the essay, what kind of a manner does he have? When relating how he will repair Imelda's disfigurement, Dr. Franciscus says, "It is geometry." Why does Selzer dwell on this point? What does it tell you about Dr. Franciscus?

2. This essay is filled with complex terms: necrosis, granulated, violaceous, ulcerating basal cell carcinoma. Why does Selzer use these technical terms? What do they contribute to the essay?

3. Does Dr. Franciscus fit your impression of doctors? What has your experience taught you about medical practitioners and their qualities in general? What has your experience taught you about what it means to be a patient?

4. Near the end of the essay, Selzer conjectures the details of Imelda's operation. Why does he speculate on what happened to such a degree? What is the author trying to create? What does this scene add to the essay?

5. Why does Dr. Franciscus repair Imelda's lip? What does this act reveal about him?

6. Why does the narrator remove the slide from the presentation? What does this act reveal about him—and his relationship to Dr. Franciscus? What does Selzer mean by asking, "Why did he not save himself?" Save himself from what, from whom?

No Name Woman

MAXINE HONG KINGSTON

One of a writer's roles, according to Maxine Hong Kingston, is to be an avenger of wrongs. In the "White Tigers" section of *Woman Warrior* she writes, "The idioms for revenge are 'report a crime' and 'report to five families.' The reporting is the vengeance—not the beheading, not the gutting, but the words. And I have so many words." Her book *China Men*, for example, chronicles the discriminatory laws regarding Chinese immigration and reaffirms the accomplishments of the generations of Chinese-Americans whose hard labor helped build this country. When Jane Kramer interviewed her in 1976 for a *New York Times Book Review*, she said, "What I am doing in this book is claiming America."

Born in Stockton, California, in 1940 to Chinese immigrants, Maxine Hong Kingston grew up listening to her mother's "talk-stories" of Chinese myths, legends, and family history. Her family ran the New Port Laundry, where many immigrants from her parents' Cantonese village met to speak Say Yup and tell stories. These tales, told in the singsong cadence of Say Yup, became the basis for her autobiographical works: *The Woman Warrior*, which won the 1976 National Book Critics Circle Award; *China Men*; and *Tripmaster Monkey*. She views her narratives about the coming of the Chinese to America and their contribution to the growth of the country as thematically linked to other American writers, notably William Carlos Williams.

In a 1976 *People* magazine interview, Kingston described how the cadence of the "talk-story" imbued her writing with poetic force and originality: "I wanted to get a Chinese rhythm in my voice. I tried to make [*The Woman Warrior*] typical of Chinese-American speech, rich with images." In a 1980 interview with Peter Grier of the *Christian Science Monitor*, she explained, "Each story changes from day to day, in the telling. The listener changes and the speaker changes and the situation changes. I want to capture that changeable quality in writing."

The selection that follows is the opening chapter of *The Woman Warrior*.

"You must not tell anyone," my mother said, "what I am about to tell you. In China your father had a sister who killed herself. She jumped into the family well. We say that your father has all brothers because it is as if she had never been born.

"In 1924 just a few days after our village celebrated seventeen hurry-up weddings—to make sure that every young man who went 'out on the road' would responsibly come home—your father and his brothers and your grandfather and his brothers and your aunt's new husband sailed for America, the Gold Mountain. It was your grandfather's last trip. Those lucky enough to get contracts waved good-bye from the decks. They fed and guarded the stowaways and helped them off in Cuba, New York, Bali, Hawaii. 'We'll meet in California next year,' they said. All of them sent money home.

"I remember looking at your aunt one day when she and I were dressing; I had not noticed before that she had such a protruding melon of a stomach. But I did not think, 'She's pregnant,' until she began to look like other pregnant women, her shirt pulling and the white tops of black pants showing. She could not have been pregnant, you see, because her husband had been gone for years. No one said anything. We did not discuss it. In early summer she was ready to have the child, long after the time when it could have been possible.

"The village had also been counting. On the night the baby was to be born the villagers raided our house. Some were crying. Like a great saw, teeth strung with lights, files of people walked zigzag across our land, tearing the rice. Their lanterns doubled in the disturbed black water, which drained away through the broken bunds. As the villagers closed in, we could see that some of them, probably men and women we knew well, wore white masks. The people with long hair hung it over their faces. Women with short hair made it stand up on end. Some had tied white bands around their foreheads, arms, and legs.

"At first they threw mud and rocks at the house. Then they threw eggs and began slaughtering our stock. We could hear the animals scream their deaths—the roosters, the pigs, a last great roar from the ox. Familiar wild heads flared in our night windows; the villagers encircled us. Some of the faces stopped to peer at us, their eyes rushing like searchlights. The hands flattened against the panes, framed heads, and left red prints.

"The villagers broke in the front and the back doors at the same time, even though we had not locked the doors against them. Their knives dripped with the blood of our animals. They smeared blood on the doors and walls. One woman swung a chicken, whose throat she had slit, splattering blood in red arcs about her. We stood together in the middle of our house, in the family hall with the pictures and tables of the ancestors around us, and looked straight ahead.

"At that time the house had only two wings. When the men came back, we would build two more to enclose our courtyard and a third one to begin a second courtyard. The villagers pushed through both wings, even your grandparents' rooms, to find your aunt's, which was also mine until the men returned. From this room a new wing for one of the younger families would grow. They ripped up her clothes and shoes and broke her combs, grinding them underfoot. They tore her work from the loom. They scattered the cooking fire and rolled the new weaving in it. We could hear them in the kitchen breaking our bowls and banging the pots. They overturned the great waist-high earthenware jugs; duck eggs, pickled fruits, vegetables burst out and mixed in acrid torrents. The old woman from the next field swept a broom through the air and loosed the spirits-of-the-broom over our heads. 'Pig.' 'Ghost.' 'Pig,' they sobbed and scolded while they ruined our house.

"When they left, they took sugar and oranges to bless themselves. They cut pieces from the dead animals. Some of them took bowls that were not broken and clothes that were not torn. Afterward we swept up the rice and sewed it back up into sacks. But the smells from the spilled preserves lasted. Your aunt gave birth in the pigsty that night.

The next morning when I went for the water, I found her and the baby plugging up the family well.

"Don't let your father know that I told you. He denies her. Now that you have started to menstruate, what happened to her could happen to you. Don't humiliate us. You wouldn't like to be forgotten as if you had never been born. The villagers are watchful."

Whenever she had to warn us about life, my mother told stories that ran like this one, a story to grow up on. She tested our strength to establish realities. Those in the emigrant generations who could not reassert brute survival died young and far from home. Those of us in the first American generations have had to figure out how the invisible world the emigrants built around our childhoods fits in solid America.

The emigrants confused the gods by diverting their curses, misleading them with crooked streets and false names. They must try to confuse their offspring as well, who, I suppose, threaten them in similar ways—always trying to get things straight, always trying to name the unspeakable. The Chinese I know hide their names; sojourners take new names when their lives change and guard their real names with silence.

Chinese-Americans, when you try to understand what things in you are Chinese, how do you separate what is peculiar to childhood, to poverty, insanities, one family, your mother who marked your growing with stories, from what is Chinese? What is Chinese tradition and what is the movies?

If I want to learn what clothes my aunt wore, whether flashy or ordinary, I would have to begin, "Remember Father's drowned-in-the-well sister?" I cannot ask that. My mother has told me once and for all the useful parts. She will add nothing unless powered by Necessity, a riverbank that guides her life. She plants vegetable gardens rather than lawns; she carries the odd-shaped tomatoes home from the fields and eats food left for the gods.

Whenever we did frivolous things, we used up energy; we flew high kites. We children came up off the ground over the melting cones our parents brought home from work and the American movie on New Year's Day—*Oh, You Beautiful Doll* with Betty Grable one year, and *She Wore a Yellow Ribbon* with John Wayne another year. After the one carnival ride each, we paid in guilt; our tired father counted his change on the dark walk home.

Adultery is extravagance. Could people who hatch their own chicks and eat the embryos and the heads for delicacies and boil the feet in vinegar for party food, leaving only the gravel, eating even the gizzard lining—could such people engender a prodigal aunt? To be a woman, to have a daughter in starvation time was a waste enough. My aunt could not have been the lone romantic who gave up everything for sex. Women in the old China did not choose. Some man had commanded her to lie with him and be his secret evil. I wonder whether he masked himself when he joined the raid on her family.

Perhaps she had encountered him in the fields or on the mountain where the daughters-in-law collected fuel. Or perhaps he first noticed her in the marketplace. He was not a stranger because the village housed no strangers. She had to have dealings with him other than sex. Perhaps he worked an adjoining field, or he sold her the cloth for the dress she sewed and wore. His demand must have surprised, then terrified her. She obeyed him; she always did as she was told.

When the family found a young man in the next village to be her husband, she had stood tractably beside the best rooster, his proxy, and promised before they met that she would be his forever. She was lucky that he was her age and she would be the first wife, an advantage secure now. The night she first saw him, he had sex with her. Then he left for America. She had almost forgotten what he looked like. When she tried to envision him, she only saw the black and white face in the group photograph the men had had taken before leaving.

The other man was not, after all, much different from her husband. They both gave orders: she followed. "If you tell your family, I'll beat you. I'll kill you. Be here again next week." No one talked sex, ever. And she might have separated the rapes from the rest of living if only she did not have to buy her oil from him or gather wood in the same forest. I want her fear to have lasted just as long as rape lasted so that the fear could have been contained. No drawn-out fear. But women at sex hazarded birth and hence lifetimes. The fear did not stop but permeated everywhere. She told the man, "I think I'm pregnant." He organized the raid against her.

On nights when my mother and father talked about their life back home, sometimes they mentioned an "outcast table" whose business they still seem to be settling, their voices tight. In a commensal tradition, where food is precious, the powerful older people made wrong-doers eat alone. Instead of letting them start separate new lives like the Japanese, who could become samurais and geishas, the Chinese family, faces averted but eyes glowering sideways, hung on to the offenders and fed them leftovers. My aunt must have lived in the same house as my parents and eaten at an outcast table. My mother spoke about the raid as if she had seen it, when she and my aunt, a daughter-in-law to a different household, should not have been living together at all. Daughters-in-law lived with their husbands' parents, not their own; a synonym for marriage in Chinese is "taking a daughter-in-law." Her husband's parents could have sold her, mortgaged her, stoned her. But they had sent her back to her own mother and father, a mysterious act hinting at disgraces not told me. Perhaps they had thrown her out to deflect the avengers.

She was the only daughter; her four brothers went with her father, husband, and uncles "out on the road" and for some years became western men. When the goods were divided among the family, three of the brothers took land, and the youngest, my father, chose an education. After my grandparents gave their daughter away to her husband's family, they had dispensed all the adventure and all the property. They expected her alone to keep the traditional ways, which her brothers, now among the barbarians, could fumble without detection. The heavy, deep-rooted women were to maintain the past against the flood, safe for returning. But the rare urge west had fixed upon our family, and so my aunt crossed boundaries not delineated in space.

The work of preservation demands that the feelings playing about in one's guts not be turned into action. Just watch their passing like cherry blossoms. But perhaps my aunt, my forerunner, caught in a slow life, let dreams grow and fade and after some months or years went toward what persisted. Fear at the enormities of the forbidden kept her desires delicate, wire and bone. She looked at a man because she liked the way the hair was tucked behind his ears, or she liked the question-mark line of a long torso curving at the shoulder and straight at the hip. For warm eyes or a soft voice or a slow walk—that's all—a few hairs, a line, a brightness, a sound, a pace, she gave up family. She offered us up for a charm that vanished with tiredness, a pigtail that didn't toss when the wind died. Why, the wrong lighting could erase the dearest thing about him.

It could very well have been, however, that my aunt did not take subtle enjoyment of her friend, but, a wild woman, kept rollicking company. Imagining her free with sex doesn't fit, though. I don't know any women like that, or men either. Unless I see her life branching into mine, she gives me no ancestral help.

To sustain her being in love, she often worked at herself in the mirror, guessing at the colors and shapes that would interest him, changing them frequently in order to hit on the right combination. She wanted him to look back.

On a farm near the sea, a woman who tended her appearance reaped a reputation for eccentricity. All the married women blunt-cut their hair in flaps about their ears or pulled it back in tight buns. No nonsense. Neither style blew easily into heart-catching tangles. And at their weddings they displayed themselves in their long hair for the last time. "It brushed the backs of my knees," my mother tells me. "It was braided, and even so, it brushed the backs of my knees."

At the mirror my aunt combed individuality into her bob. A bun could have been contrived to escape into black streamers blowing in the wind or in quiet wisps about her face, but only the older women in our picture album wear buns. She brushed her hair back from her forehead, tucking the flaps behind her ears. She looped a piece of thread, knotted into a circle between her index fingers and thumbs, and ran the double strand across her forehead. When she closed her fingers as if she were making a pair of shadow geese bite, the string twisted together catching the little hairs. Then she pulled the thread away from her skin, ripping the hairs out neatly, her eyes watering from the needles of pain. Opening her fingers, she cleaned the thread, then rolled it along her hairline and the tops of her eyebrows. My mother did the same to me and my sisters and herself. I used to believe that the expression "caught by the short hairs" meant a captive held with a depilatory string. It especially hurt at the temples, but my mother said we were lucky we didn't have to have our feet bound when we were seven. Sisters used to sit on their beds and cry together, she said, as their mothers or their slave removed the bandages for a few minutes each night and let the blood gush back into their veins. I hope that the man my aunt loved appreciated a smooth brow, that he wasn't just a tits-and-ass man.

Once my aunt found a freckle on her chin, at a spot that the almanac said predestined her for unhappiness. She dug it out with a hot needle and washed the wound with peroxide.

More attention to her looks than these pullings of hairs and pickings at spots would have caused gossip among the villagers. They owned work clothes and good clothes, and they wore good clothes for feasting the new seasons. But since a woman combing her hair hexes beginnings, my aunt rarely found an occasion to look her best. Women looked like great sea snails—the corded word, babies, and laundry they carried were the whorls on their backs. The Chinese did not admire a bent back; goddesses and warriors stood straight. Still there must have been a marvelous freeing of beauty when a worker laid down her burden and stretched and arched.

Such commonplace loveliness, however, was not enough for my aunt. She dreamed of a lover for the fifteen days of New Year's, the time for families to exchange visits, money, and food. She plied her secret comb. And sure enough she cursed the year, the family, the village, and herself.

Even as her hair lured her imminent lover, many other men looked at her. Uncles, cousins, nephews, brothers would have looked, too, had they been home between journeys. Perhaps they had already been restraining their curiosity, and they left, fearful that their glances, like a field of nesting birds, might be startled and caught.

Poverty hurt, and that was their first reason for leaving. But another, final reason for leaving the crowded house was the never-said.

She may have been unusually beloved, the precious only daughter, spoiled and mirror gazing because of the affection the family lavished on her. When her husband left, they welcomed the chance to take her back from the in-laws; she could live like the little daughter for just a while longer. There are stories that my grandfather was different from other people, "crazy ever since the little Jap bayoneted him in the head." He used to put his naked penis on the dinner table, laughing. And one day he brought home a baby girl, wrapped up inside his brown western-style greatcoat. He had traded one of his sons, probably my father, the youngest, for her. My grandmother made him trade back. When he finally got a daughter of his own, he doted on her. They must have all loved her, except perhaps my father, the only brother who never went back to China, having once been traded for a girl.

Brothers and sisters, newly men and women, had to efface their sexual color and present plain miens. Disturbing hair and eyes, a smile like no other, threatened the ideal of five generations living under one roof. To focus blurs, people shouted face to face and yelled from room to room. The immigrants I know have loud voices, unmodulated to American tones even after years away from the village where they called their friendships out across the fields. I have not been able to stop my mother's screams in public libraries or over telephones. Walking erect (knees straight, toes pointed forward, not pigeon-toed, which is Chinese-feminine) and speaking in an inaudible voice, I have tried to turn myself American-feminine. Chinese communication was loud, public. Only sick people had to whisper. But at the dinner table, where the family members came nearest one another, no one could talk, not the outcasts nor any eaters. Every word that falls from the mouth is a coin lost. Silently they gave and accepted food with both hands. A preoccupied child who took his bowl with one hand got a sideways glare. A complete moment of total attention is due everyone alike. Children and lovers have no singularity here, but my aunt used a secret voice, a separate attentiveness.

She kept the man's name to herself throughout her labor and dying; she did not accuse him that he be punished with her. To save her inseminator's name she gave silent birth.

He may have been somebody in her own household, but intercourse with a man outside the family would have been no less abhorrent. All the village were kinsmen, and the titles shouted in loud country voices never let kinship be forgotten. Any man within visiting distance would have been neutralized as a lover—"brother," "younger brother," "older brother"—one hundred and fifteen relationship titles. Parents researched birth charts probably not so much to assure good fortune as to circumvent incest in a population that has but one hundred surnames. Everybody has eight million relatives. How useless then sexual mannerisms, how dangerous.

As if it came from an atavism deeper than fear, I used to add "brother" silently to boys' names. It hexed the boys, who would or would not ask me to dance and made them less scary and as familiar and deserving of benevolence as girls.

But, of course, I hexed myself also—no dates. I should have stood up, both arms waving, and shouted out across libraries, "Hey, you! Love me back." I had no idea, though, how to make attraction selective, how to control its direction and magnitude. If I made myself American-pretty so that the five or six Chinese boys in the class fell in love with me, everyone else—the Caucasian, Negro, and Japanese boys—would too. Sisterliness, dignified and honorable, made much more sense.

Attraction eludes control so stubbornly that whole societies designed to organize relationships among people cannot keep order, not even when they bind people to one another from childhood and raise them together. Among the very poor and the wealthy, brothers married their adopted sisters, like doves. Our family allowed some romance, paying adult brides' prices and providing dowries so that their sons and daughters could marry strangers. Marriage promises to turn strangers into friendly relatives—a nation of siblings.

In the village structure, spirits shimmered among the live creatures, balanced and held in equilibrium by time and land. But one human being flaring up into violence could open up a black hole, a maelstrom that pulled in the sky. The frightened villagers, who depended on one another to maintain the real, went to my aunt to show her a personal, physical representation of the break she had made in the "roundness." Misallying couples snapped off the future, which was to be embodied in true offspring. The villagers punished her for acting as if she could have a private life, secret and apart from them.

If my aunt had betrayed the family at a time of large grain yields and peace, when many boys were born, and wings were being built on many houses, perhaps she might have escaped such severe punishment. But the men—hungry, greedy, tired of planting in dry soil—and had been forced to leave the village in order to send food-money home. There were ghost plagues, bandit plagues, wars with the Japanese, floods. My Chinese brother and sister had died of an unknown sickness. Adultery, perhaps only a mistake during good times, became a crime when the village needed food.

The round moon cakes and round doorways, the round tables of graduated size that fit one roundness inside another, round windows and rice bowls—these talismans had lost their power to warn this family of the law: a family must be whole, faithfully keeping the descent line by having sons to feed the old and the dead, who in turn look after the family. The villagers came to show my aunt and her lover-in-hiding a broken house. The villagers were speeding up the circling of events because she was too shortsighted to see that her infidelity had already harmed the village, that waves of consequences would return unpredictably, sometimes in disguise, as now, to hurt her. This roundness had to be made coin-sized so that she would see its circumference: punish her at the birth of her baby. Awaken her to the inexorable. People who refused fatalism because they could invent small resources insisted on culpability. Deny accidents and wrest fault from the stars.

After the villagers left, their lanterns now scattering in various directions toward home, the family broke their silence and cursed her. "Aiaa, we're going to die. Death is coming. Death is coming. Look what you've done. You've killed us. Ghost! Dead ghost! Ghost! You've never been born." She ran out into the fields, far enough from the house so that she could no longer hear their voices, and pressed herself against the earth, her own land no more. When she felt the birth coming, she thought that she had been hurt. Her body seized together. "They've hurt me too much," she thought. "This is gall, and it will kill me." With forehead and knees against the earth, her body convulsed and then relaxed. She turned on her back, lay on the ground. The black well of sky and stars went out and out and out forever; her body and her complexity seemed to disappear. She was one of the stars, a bright dot in blackness, without home, without a companion, in eternal cold and silence. An agoraphobia rose in her, speeding higher and higher, bigger and bigger; she would not be able to contain it; there would be no end to fear.

Flayed, unprotected against space, she felt pain return, focusing her body. This pain chilled her—a cold, steady kind of surface pain. Inside, spasmodically, the other pain, the pain of the child, heated her. For hours she lay on the ground, alternately body and space. Sometimes a vision of normal comfort obliterated reality: she saw the family in the evening gambling at the dinner table, the young people massaging their elders' backs. She saw them congratulating one another, high joy on the mornings the rice shoots came up. When these pictures burst, the stars drew yet further apart. Black space opened.

She got to her feet to fight better and remembered that old-fashioned women gave birth in their pigsties to fool the jealous, pain-dealing gods, who do not snatch piglets. Before the next spasms could stop her, she ran to the pigsty, each step a rushing out into emptiness.

She climbed over the fence and knelt in the dirt. It was good to have a fence enclosing her, a tribal person alone.

Laboring, this woman who had carried her child as a foreign growth that sickened her every day, expelled it at last. She reached down to touch the hot, wet, moving mass, surely smaller than anything human, and could feel that it was human after all—fingers, toes, nails, nose. She pulled it up on to her belly, and it lay curled there, butt in the air, feet precisely tucked one under the other. She opened her loose shirt and buttoned the child inside. After resting, it squirmed and thrashed and she pushed it up to her breast. It turned its head this way and that until it found her nipple. There, it made little snuffling noises. She clenched her teeth at its preciousness, lovely as a young calf, a piglet, a little dog.

She may have gone to the pigsty as a last act of responsibility: she would protect this child as she had protected its father. It would look after her soul, leaving supplies on her grave. But how would this tiny child without family find her grave when there would be no marker for her anywhere, neither in the earth nor the family hall? No one would give her a family hall name. She had taken the child with her into the wastes. At its birth the two of them had felt the same raw pain of separation, a wound that only the family pressing tight could close. A child with no descent line would not soften her life but only trail after her, ghost-like, begging her to give it purpose. At dawn the villagers on their way to the fields would stand around the fence and look.

Full of milk, the little ghost slept. When it awoke, she hardened her breasts against the milk that crying loosens. Toward morning she picked up the baby and walked to the well.

Carrying the baby to the well shows loving. Otherwise abandon it. Turn its face into the mud. Mothers who love their children take them along. It was probably a girl; there is some hope of forgiveness for boys.

"Don't tell anyone you had an aunt. Your father does not want to hear her name. She has never been born." I have believed that sex was unspeakable and words so strong and fathers so frail that "aunt" would do my father mysterious harm. I have thought that my family, having settled among immigrants who had also been their neighbors in the ancestral land, needed to clean their name, and a wrong word would incite the kinspeople even here. But there is more to this silence: they want me to participate in her punishment. And I have.

In the twenty years since I heard this story I have not asked for details nor said my aunt's name; I do not know it. People who can comfort the dead can also chase after them to hurt them further—a reverse ancestor worship. The real punishment was not the raid swiftly inflicted by the villagers, but the family's deliberately forgetting her. Her betrayal so maddened them, they saw to it that she would suffer forever, even after death. Always hungry, always needing, she would have to beg food from other ghosts, snatch and steal it from those whose living descendants give them gifts. She would have to fight the ghosts massed at crossroads for the buns a few thoughtful citizens leave to decoy her away from village and home so that the ancestral spirits could feast unharassed. At peace, they could act like gods, not ghosts, their descent lines providing them with paper suits and dresses, spirit money, paper houses, paper automobiles, chicken, meat, and rice into eternity—essences delivered up in smoke and flames, steam and incense rising from each rice bowl. In an attempt to make the Chinese care for people outside the family, Chairman Mao encourages us now to give our paper replicas to the spirits of outstanding soldiers and workers, no matter whose ancestors they may be. My aunt remains forever hungry. Goods are not distributed evenly among the dead.

My aunt haunts me—her ghost drawn to me because now, after fifty years of neglect, I alone devote pages of paper to her, though not origamied into houses and clothes. I do not think she always means me well. I am telling on her, and she was a spite suicide, drowning herself in the drinking water. The Chinese are always very frightened of the drowned one, whose weeping ghost, wet hair hanging and skin bloated, waits silently by the water to pull down a substitute.

SPECULATIONS

1. What is the significance of the title, "No Name Woman"? Compare what it would mean to be a person without a name in Chinese society to what it would mean to be a person without a name in the United States. Use examples from this excerpt of how the Chinese treat their names.

2. Kingston uses the "talk-story" method of retelling in different ways to describe who her aunt was and what she was like. What is significant about this method of storytelling? Compared to traditional storytelling, how does the talk-story develop a picture of the aunt? Kingston? Chinese values?

3. After looking closely at Kingston's descriptions of her aunt, her mother, and other women, how would you describe women's position in Chinese society? How is the "place" of women bound up in silence and having no name?

4. Why do you think the villagers' collective punishment of the aunt and her family was so extreme? What rationale do you think the villagers might offer for inflicting this punishment? What does Kingston mean when she says the villagers wanted to show the aunt "a personal, physical representation of the break she had made in the 'roundness'" of their society?

5. Have you ever condemned the "immoral" behavior of another person—someone you really did not know? How did your response affect you, affect the other person, affect (if at all) the community in which you lived? Were you influenced by the responses of others around you? In retrospect, do you feel any differently? Explain.

6. How do you interpret the opening paragraph in which Kingston reports her mother's admonition, "You must not tell anyone what I am about to tell you"? What is the rhetorical effect of Kingston telling what her mother said and then telling us the story that her mother demanded that she never tell?

Three Generations of Native American Women's Birth Experience

JOY HARJO

A Native American writer of mixed Cherokee, Creek, and white descent, Joy Harjo is best known as a poet. Her first three books of published poetry—*The Last Song* (1975), *What Moon Drove Me to This?* (1980), and *She Had Some Horses* (1983)—express Harjo's sense of the circular processes of life. In a personal interview with Marylin Kallet, Harjo explained:

> I write poetry because it is a way to travel to internal landscapes/starscapes which also become the external. It helps in traveling between many worlds and helps in speaking them. Lately I am sensing the transformative use of poetry. Words are not just words but sounds, which are voices, which are connected, growing to others. The world is not static, but shifts, changes.

For Harjo, poetry is a way of being and becoming in the world.

Born 1951 in Tulsa, Oklahoma, Joy Harjo earned a B.A. from the University of New Mexico in 1976 and an M.F.A. from the University of Iowa in 1978—while raising two children as a single mother. In 1978 she obtained a grant from the National Endowment for the Arts and continued her work of fostering and retaining Indian culture. As she explains in her essay, "My work in this life has to do with reclaiming the memory stolen from our peoples when we were dispossessed from our lands east of the Mississippi."

In addition to teaching and writing poetry, Harjo has written several screenplays, including *Origin of Apache Crown Dance* and *The Beginning*. A writer and consultant for the National Indian Youth Council and the Native American Broadcasting Consortium, she is the producer of *The Beginning* and a professor of creative writing at the University of New Mexico.

It was still dark when I awakened in the stuffed back room of my mother-in-law's small rented house with what felt like hard cramps. At 17 years of age I had read everything I could from the Tahlequah

Public Library about pregnancy and giving birth. But nothing prepared me for what was coming. I awakened my child's father and then ironed him a shirt before we walked the four blocks to the Indian hospital because we had no car and no money for a taxi. He had been working with another Cherokee artist silk-screening signs for specials at the supermarket and making $5 a day, and had to leave me alone at the hospital because he had to go to work. We didn't awaken his mother. She had to get up soon enough to fix breakfast for her daughter and granddaughter before leaving for her job at the nursing home. I knew my life was balanced at the edge of great, precarious change and I felt alone and cheated. Where was the circle of women to acknowledge and honor this birth?

It was still dark as we walked through the cold morning, under oaks that symbolized the stubbornness and endurance of the Cherokee people who had made Tahlequah their capital in the new lands. I looked for handholds in the misty gray sky, for a voice announcing this impending miracle. I wanted to change everything; I wanted to go back to a place before childhood, before our tribe's removal to Oklahoma. What kind of life was I bringing this child into? I was a poor, mixed-blood woman heavy with a child who would suffer the struggle of poverty, the legacy of loss. For the second time in my life I felt the sharp tug of my own birth cord, still connected to my mother. I believe it never pulls away, until death, and even then it becomes a streak in the sky symbolizing that most important warrior road. In my teens I had fought my mother's weaknesses with all my might, and here I was at 17, becoming as my mother, who was in Tulsa, cooking breakfasts and preparing for the lunch shift at a factory cafeteria as I walked to the hospital to give birth. I should be with her; instead, I was far from her house, in the house of a mother-in-law who later would try to use witchcraft to destroy me.

After my son's father left me I was prepped for birth. This meant my pubic area was shaved completely and then I endured the humiliation of an enema, all at the hands of strangers. I was left alone in a room painted government green. An overwhelming antiseptic smell emphasized the sterility of the hospital, a hospital built because of the U.S. government's treaty and responsibility to provide health care to Indian people.

I intellectually understood the stages of labor, the place of transition, of birth—but it was difficult to bear the actuality of it, and to bear it alone. Yet in some ways I wasn't alone, for history surrounded me. It is with the birth of children that history is given form and voice. Birth is one of the most sacred acts we take part in and witness in our lives. But sacredness seemed to be far from my lonely labor room in the Indian hospital. I heard a woman screaming in the next room with her pain, and I wanted to comfort her. The nurse used her as a bad example to the rest of us who were struggling to keep our suffering silent.

The doctor was a military man who had signed on this watch not for the love of healing or out of awe at the miracle of birth, but to fulfill a contract for medical school payments. I was another statistic to him; he touched me as if he were moving equipment from one place to another. During my last visit I was given the option of being sterilized. He explained to me that the moment of birth was the best time to do it. I was handed the form but chose not to sign it, and am amazed now that I didn't think too much of it at the time. Later I would learn that many Indian women who weren't fluent in English signed, thinking it was a form giving consent for the doctor to deliver their babies. Others were sterilized without even the formality of signing. My light skin had probably saved me from such a fate. It wouldn't be the first time in my life.

When my son was finally born I had been deadened with a needle in my spine. He was shown to me—the incredible miracle nothing prepared me for—then taken from me in the name of medical progress. I fell asleep with the weight of chemicals and awoke yearning for the child I had suffered for, had anticipated in the months proceeding from this unexpected genesis when I was still 16 and a student at Indian school. I was not allowed to sit up or walk because of the possibility of paralysis (one of the drug's side effects), and when I finally got to hold him, the nurse stood guard as if I would hurt him. I felt enmeshed in a system in which the wisdom that had carried my people from generation to generation was ignored. In that place I felt ashamed I was an Indian woman. But I was also proud of what my body had accomplished despite the rape by the bureaucracy's machinery, and I got us out of there as soon as possible. My son would flourish on beans and fry bread, and on the dreams and stories we fed him.

My daughter was born four years later, while I was an art student at the University of New Mexico. Since my son's birth I had waitressed, cleaned hospital rooms, filled cars with gas (while wearing a miniskirt), worked as a nursing assistant, and led dance classes at a health spa. I knew I didn't want to cook and waitress all my life, as my mother had done. I had watched the varicose veins grow branches on her legs, and as they grew, her zest for dancing and sports dissolved into utter tiredness. She had been born with a caul over her face, the sign of a gifted visionary.

My earliest memories are of my mother writing songs on an ancient Underwood typewriter after she had washed and waxed the kitchen floor on her hands and knees. She too had wanted something different for her life. She had left an impoverished existence at age 17, bound for the big city of Tulsa. She was shamed in a time in which to be even part Indian was to be an outcast in the great U.S. system. Half her relatives were Cherokee full-bloods from near Jay, Oklahoma, who for the most part had nothing to do with white people. The other half were musically inclined "white trash" addicted to country-western music and Holy Roller fervor. She thought she could disappear in the city; no one would know her family, where she came from. She had dreams of singing and had once been offered a job singing on the radio but turned it down because she was shy. Later one of her songs would be stolen before she could copyright it and would make someone else rich. She would quit writing songs. She and my father would divorce and she would be forced to work for money to feed and clothe four children, all born within two years of each other.

As a child growing up in Oklahoma, I liked to be told the story of my birth. I would beg for it while my mother cleaned and ironed. "You almost killed me," she would say. "We almost died." That I could kill my mother filled me with remorse and shame. And I imagined the push-pull of my life, which is a legacy I deal with even now when I am twice as old as my mother was at my birth. I loved to hear the story of my warrior fight for my breath. The way it was told, it had been my decision to live. When I got older, I realized we were both nearly casualties of the system, the same system flourishing in the Indian hospital where later my son Phil would be born.

My parents felt lucky to have insurance, to be able to have their children in the hospital. My father came from a fairly prominent Muscogee Creek family. *His* mother was a full-blood who in the early 1920s got her degree in art. She was a painter. She gave birth to him in a private hospital in Oklahoma City; at least that's what I think he told me before he died at age 53. It was something of which they were proud.

This experience was much different from my mother's own birth. She and five of her six brothers were born at home, with no medical assistance. The only time a doctor was called was when someone was dying. When she was born her mother named her Wynema, a Cherokee name my mother says means beautiful woman, and Jewell, for a can of shortening stored in the room where she was born.

I wanted something different for my life, for my son, and for my daughter, who later was born in a university hospital in Albuquerque. It was a bright summer morning when she was ready to begin her journey. I still had no car, but I had enough money saved for a taxi for a ride to the hospital. She was born "naturally," without drugs. I could look out of the hospital window while I was in labor at the bluest sky in the world. I had support. Her father was present in the delivery room—though after her birth he disappeared on a drinking binge. I understood his despair, but did not agree with the painful means to describe it. A few days later Rainy Dawn was presented to the sun at her father's pueblo and given a name so that she will always be recognized as a part of the people, as a child of the sun.

That's not to say that my experience in the hospital reached perfection. The clang of metal against metal in the delivery room had the effect of a turning fork reverberating fear in my pelvis. After giving birth I held my daughter, but they took her from me for "processing." I refused to lie down to be wheeled to my room after giving birth: I wanted to walk out of there to find my daughter. We reached a compromise and I rode in a wheelchair. When we reached the room I stood up and walked to the nursery and demanded my daughter. I knew she needed me. That began my war with the nursery staff, who deemed me unknowledgeable because I was Indian and poor. Once again I felt the brushfire of shame, but I'd learned to put it out much more quickly, and I demanded early release so I could take care of my baby without the judgment of strangers.

I wanted something different for Rainy, and as she grew up I worked hard to prove that I could make "something" of my life. I obtained two degrees as a single mother. I wrote poetry, screenplays, became a professor, and tried to live a life that would be a positive influence for both of my children. My work in this life has to do with reclaiming the memory stolen from our peoples when we were dispossessed from our lands east of the Mississippi; it has to do with restoring us. I am proud of our history, a history so powerful that it both destroyed my father and guarded him. It's a history that claims my mother as she lives not far from the place her mother was born, names her as she cooks in the cafeteria of a small college in Oklahoma.

When my daughter told me she was pregnant, I wasn't surprised. I had known it before she did, or at least before she would admit it to me. I felt despair, as if nothing had changed or ever would. She had run away from Indian school with her boyfriend and they had been living in the streets of Gallup, a border town notorious for the suicides and deaths of Indian peoples. I brought her and her boyfriend with me because it was the only way I could bring her home. At age 16, she was fighting me just as I had so fiercely fought my mother. She was making the same mistakes. I felt as if everything I had accomplished had been in vain. Yet I felt strangely empowered, too, at this repetition of history, this continuance, by a new possibility of life and love, and I steadfastly stood by my daughter.

I had a university job, so I had insurance that covered my daughter. She saw an obstetrician in town who was reputed to be one of the best. She had the choice of a birthing room. She had the finest care.

Despite this, I once again battled with a system in which physicians are taught the art of healing by dissecting cadavers. My daughter went into labor a month early. We both knew intuitively the baby was ready, but how to explain that to a system in which numbers and statistics provide the base of understanding? My daughter would have her labor interrupted: her blood pressure would rise because of the drug given to her to stop the labor. She would be given an unneeded amniocentesis and would have her labor induced—after having it artifically stopped! I was warned that if I took her out of the hospital so her labor could occur naturally my insurance would cover nothing.

My daughter's induced labor was unnatural and difficult, monitored by machines, not by touch. I was shocked. I felt as if I'd come full circle, as if I were watching my mother's labor and the struggle of my own birth. But I was there in the hospital room with her, as neither my mother had been for me, nor her mother for her. My daughter and I went through the labor and birth together.

And when Krista Rae was born she was born to her family. Her father was there for her, as were both her grandmothers and my friend who had flown in to be with us. Her paternal great-grandparents and aunts and uncles had also arrived from the Navajo Reservation to honor her. Something *had* changed.

Four days later, I took my granddaughter to the Saguaro forest before dawn and gave her the name I had dreamed for her just before her birth. Her name looks like clouds of mist settling around a sacred mountain as it begins to speak. A female ancestor approaches on a horse. We are all together.

SPECULATIONS

1. In the opening paragraph of this essay, Harjo describes her life when she gave birth to her first child. How would you describe the life that she—and her immediate family—are living? Why do you think Harjo supplies all these details about her husband, her mother-in-law, the library, her husband's job?

2. Why do you think Harjo chose to write about giving birth in the first place? What larger point(s) do you think she is trying to make about Native American values? About values of the general culture?

3. What differences does Harjo describe between Native American traditions of birthing and standard hospital procedure? Which ways appear more satisfactory in providing women the help they need to give birth?

4. Harjo states that her husband was present for the birth of her daughter but then "disappeared on a drinking binge. I understood his despair. . . ." What do you think she means? What do you think caused his despair?

5. This essay does not proceed in a predictable way—some readers might say that it moves almost haphazardly from one subtopic to another. Explain whether you agree or disagree. How does Harjo organize this essay? What would the effect be if it moved in a more linear fashion—from Harjo's mother, to Harjo, to Harjo's daughter?

6.   Harjo weaves the histories of her mother, herself, her daughter, and her granddaughter's birth together. What do these stories tell you about the history and status of Native Americans in this country? What particular conclusions do you draw from the final two paragraphs of the essay which describe the birth of Krista Rae?

Indian Camp

ERNEST HEMINGWAY

Ernest Hemingway's fiction often merges with his own experience; both express toughness, endurance, stoicism—an ability to suffer pain as part of the human condition. During his lifetime, Hemingway was lionized by the press; he was associated with wartime heroism, bullfights, drinking, carousing, and the creation of an American literary style. As critic John Aldridge put it:

> He was Hemingway of the rugged outdoor grin and the hairy chest posing beside a marlin he had just landed or a lion he had just shot; he was Tarzan Hemingway, crouching in the African bush with elephant gun at ready, Bwana Hemingway commanding his native bearers in terse Swahili; he was War Correspondent Hemingway writing a play in the Hotel Florida in Madrid while thirty Fascist shells crashed through the roof; later on he was Task Force Hemingway swathed in ammunition belts and defending his post single-handed against fierce German attacks.

He represented a certain American ideal, and his best writing captured those same qualities of understated gutsiness in the face of overwhelming odds.

Born in Oak Park, Illinois, in 1899, Hemingway's first job was writing for the *Kansas City Star*. In World War I in Italy, he drove an ambulance for the Red Cross and worked as a war correspondent for several newspapers. His fiction drew attention early; his most notable novels include *The Sun Also Rises*, *A Farewell to Arms*, *For Whom the Bell Tolls*, and *The Old Man and The Sea*, which won the 1953 Pulitzer Prize. Many of his short stories are regarded as classics and are frequently anthologized. He received the Nobel Prize for Literature in 1954. Married four times, Hemingway survived two plane crashes and other close calls with death. He often boasted of his ability to endure, but during his last few years critics attacked his self-parodic style. Unable to write—to rediscover himself through his art—Ernest Hemingway committed suicide in 1961.

Hemingway's desire to write honestly and truthfully is reflected in his terse, economical prose. It is a pared-down style characterized by short and simple sentences full of repetition, parallelism, fragments, a purged diction that is concrete and realistic. "The writer's job is to tell the truth," Hemingway once said. "Do not worry. . . . All you have to do is write one true sentence. Write the truest sentence you know." This selection illustrates many "Hemingway-esque" qualities and offers a complementary view to the Native American birthing experience described by Joy Harjo.

At the lake shore there was another rowboat drawn up. The two Indians stood waiting.

Nick and his father got in the stern of the boat and the Indians shoved it off and one of them got in to row. Uncle George sat in the stern of the camp rowboat. The young Indian shoved the camp boat off and got in to row Uncle George.

The two boats started off in the dark. Nick heard the oarlocks of the other boat quite a way ahead of them in the mist. The Indians rowed with quick choppy strokes. Nick lay back with his father's arm around him. It was cold on the water. The Indian who was rowing them was working very hard, but the other boat moved further ahead in the mist all the time.

"Where are we going, Dad?" Nick asked.

"Over to the Indian camp. There is an Indian lady very sick."

"Oh," said Nick.

Across the bay they found the other boat beached. Uncle George was smoking a cigar in the dark. The young Indian pulled the boat way up on the beach. Uncle George gave both the Indians cigars.

They walked up from the beach through a meadow that was soaking wet with dew, following the young Indian who carried a lantern. Then they went into the woods and followed a trail that led to the logging road that ran back into the hills. It was much lighter on the logging road as the timber was cut away on both sides. The young Indian stopped and blew out his lantern and they all walked on along the road.

They came around a bend and a dog came out barking. Ahead were the lights of the shanties where the Indian bark-peelers lived. More dogs rushed out at them. The two Indians sent them back to the shanties. In the shanty nearest the road there was a light in the window. An old woman stood in the doorway holding a lamp.

Inside on a wooden bunk lay a young Indian woman. She had been trying to have her baby for two days. All the old women in the camp had been helping her. The men had moved off up the road to sit in the dark and smoke out of range of the noise she made. She screamed just as Nick and the two Indians followed his father and Uncle George into the shanty. She lay in the lower bunk, very big under a quilt. Her head was turned to one side. In the upper bunk was her husband. He had cut his foot very badly with an ax three days before. He was smoking a pipe. The room smelled very bad.

Nick's father ordered some water to be put on the stove, and while it was heating he spoke to Nick.

"This lady is going to have a baby, Nick," he said.

"I know," said Nick.

"You don't know," said his father. "Listen to me. What she is going through is called being in labor. The baby wants to be born and she wants it to be born. All her muscles are trying to get the baby born. That is what is happening when she screams."

"I see," Nick said.

Just then the woman cried out.

"Oh, Daddy, can't you give her something to make her stop screaming?" asked Nick.

"No. I haven't any anesthetic," his father said. "But her screams are not important. I don't hear them because they are not important."

The husband in the upper bunk rolled over against the wall.

The woman in the kitchen motioned to the doctor that the water was hot. Nick's father went into the kitchen and poured about half of the water out of the big kettle into a basin. Into the water left in the kettle he put several things he unwrapped from a handkerchief.

"Those must boil," he said, and began to scrub his hands in the basin of hot water with a cake of soap he had brought from the camp. Nick watched his father's hands scrubbing each other with the soap. While his father washed his hands very carefully and thoroughly, he talked.

"You see, Nick, babies are supposed to be born head first but sometimes they're not. When they're not they make a lot of trouble for everybody. Maybe I'll have to operate on this lady. We'll know in a little while."

When he was satisfied with his hands he went in and went to work.

"Pull back that quilt, will you, George?" he said. "I'd rather not touch it."

Later when he started to operate Uncle George and three Indian men held the woman still. She bit Uncle George on the arm and Uncle George said, "Damn squaw bitch!" and the young Indian who had rowed Uncle George over laughed at him. Nick held the basin for his father. It all took a long time.

His father picked the baby up and slapped it to make it breathe and handed it to the old woman.

"See, it's a boy, Nick," he said. "How do you like being an intern?"

Nick said, "All right." He was looking away so as not to see what his father was doing.

"There. That gets it," said his father and put something into the basin.

Nick didn't look at it.

"Now," his father said, "there's some stitches to put in. You can watch this or not, Nick, just as you like. I'm going to sew up the incision I made."

Nick did not watch. His curiosity had been gone for a long time.

His father finished and stood up. Uncle George and the three Indian men stood up. Nick put the basin out in the kitchen.

Uncle George looked at his arm. The young Indian smiled reminiscently.

"I'll put some peroxide on that, George," the doctor said.

He bent over the Indian woman. She was quiet now and her eyes were closed. She looked very pale. She did not know what had become of the baby or anything.

"I'll be back in the morning," the doctor said, standing up. "The nurse should be here from St. Ignace by noon and she'll bring everything we need."

He was feeling exalted and talkative as football players are in the dressing room after a game.

"That's one for the medical journal, George," he said. "Doing a Caesarean with a jack-knife and sewing it up with nine-foot, tapered gut leaders."

Uncle George was standing against the wall, looking at his arm.

"Oh, you're a great man, all right," he said.

"Ought to have a look at the proud father. They're usually the worst sufferers in these little affairs," the doctor said. "I must say he took it all pretty quietly."

He pulled back the blanket from the Indian's head. His hand came away wet. He mounted on the edge of the lower bunk with the lamp in one hand and looked in. The Indian lay with his face toward the wall. His throat had been cut from ear to ear. The blood had flowed down into a pool where his body sagged the bunk. His head rested on his left arm. The open razor lay, edge up, in the blankets.

"Take Nick out of the shanty, George," the doctor said.

There was no need of that. Nick, standing in the door of the kitchen, had a good view of the upper bunk when his father, the lamp in one hand, tipped the Indian's head back.

It was just beginning to be daylight when they walked along the logging road back toward the lake.

"I'm terribly sorry I brought you along, Nickie," said his father, all his post-operative exhilaration gone. "It was an awful mess to put you through."

"Do ladies always have such a hard time having babies?" Nick asked.

"No, that was very, very exceptional."

"Why did he kill himself, Daddy?"

"I don't know, Nick. He couldn't stand things, I guess."
"Do many men kill themselves, Daddy?"
"Not very many, Nick."
"Do many women?"
"Hardly ever."
"Don't they ever?"
"Oh, yes. They do sometimes."
"Daddy?"
"Yes."
"Where did Uncle George go?"
"He'll turn up all right."
"Is dying hard, Daddy?"
"No, I think it's pretty easy, Nick. It all depends."

They were seated in the boat, Nick in the stern, his father rowing. The sun was coming up over the hills. A bass jumped, making a circle in the water. Nick trailed his hand in the water. It felt warm in the sharp chill of the morning.

In the early morning on the lake sitting in the stern of the boat with his father rowing, he felt quite sure that he would never die.

SPECULATIONS

1.   How would you describe Hemingway's style in this story in terms of sentence structure, paragraphing, description, and tone? How does it contrast with the subject matter? Explain your response to the style as fully as you can.

2.   Hemingway carefully chooses to name certain characters in the story and to leave others unnamed. What conclusions do you draw from his choices? Why, for example, do you think Nick's father is not named?

3.   Toward the beginning of the story, Nick and his father have the following exchange:

> "Oh, Daddy, can't you give her something to make her stop scream-ing?" asked Nick.
> "No. I haven't any anesthetic," his father said. "But her screams are not important. I don't hear them because they are not important."

How do you interpret this passage? Comment on the objective manner of Nick's father. If he listened to her screams, would he have to alter the way he practices medicine?

4.   What is the relationship between the Indians and the whites in this story? What does the incident of Uncle George's being bitten tell us about this rela-tionship? When Uncle George looks at his arm after the birth, why does Hemingway write, "The young Indian smiled reminiscently"?

5.   In what ways does Hemingway prepare us for the suicide of the father? In a rereading, analyze those few but significant passages which describe the father and his actions.

6.   Doctors sometimes have to cause pain in order to heal. Describe a painful treatment by a doctor you may have endured in order to improve your physical health. What was your response to the doctor? How was what happened to you similar to or different from what Hemingway describes in "Indian Camp"?

A Modern Story

ROGER WILKINS

In his 1982 autobiography, *A Man's Life*, Roger Wilkins tells about a young, black adolescent who tries to gain acceptance in a predominantly white setting; who cannot connect easily to his black peers; who accepts a position as an international law attorney for the government and then for the Ford Foundation. Even with success, he still finds himself in crisis. He became "an ersatz white man. . . . I had no aspirations that would have seemed foreign to my white contemporaries," he wrote. Gradually, the contrast between his culturally elite friends and the poor blacks he saw around him caused Wilkins to abandon the white establishment and become an advocate for all black people. James Baldwin calls *A Man's Life* "so unprecedented a performance . . . that I consider it to be indispensable reading."

Born in 1932, the son of college-educated, middle-class, black parents (his uncle was NAACP director Roy Wilkins), Wilkins lived in Kansas City, Missouri, and New York City until the age of eleven, when his widowed mother remarried and moved to Grand Rapids, Michigan, an all-white suburb. There Wilkins felt the painful rift between himself and his schoolmates: "With my friends in the North, race was never mentioned. Ever. I carried my race around with me like an open basket of rotten eggs."

After earning a B.A. and a law degree from the University of Michigan, Wilkins started off as a welfare worker in Cleveland and after a long period was placed on the editorial board of top newspapers and magazines including the *Washington Post* (1972–74), the *New York Times* (1974–77), and *The Nation* (1979–present).

Roger Wilkins modestly confessed that he had fallen short of his "youthful dream of becoming a true professional writer. . . . Rather, the sentences, the paragraphs, and even the book have been forged as weapons and hurled into the struggle for justice, which has been my real lifelong occupation." Posterity may not judge Wilkins so harshly. He was nominated for a Pulitzer Prize for his editorials on the Watergate scandal, and he is a frequent contributor to *Esquire*, *Foreign Policy*, *Fortune*, *Mother Jones*, the *Nation*, the *New Yorker*, and the *Village Voice*. This selection, published in the October, 1991, issue of *Mother Jones*, begins by responding to President Bush's 1990 speech at the University of Michigan which alluded to the "Political Correctness" or "PC" debate concerning academic freedom and the teaching of diverse political perspectives in the university.

When President Bush went to Ann Arbor last May [1990] to warn graduating seniors about the great PC threat, I took it as a personal insult. This year I am celebrating two anniversaries of my graduation from the University of Michigan—the thirty-fifth anniversary of my graduation from the Law School and the thirty-eighth of my graduation from the College of Literature, Science, and the Arts. Bush was littering *my* place with his political cynicism.

The president informed the graduates and their families that free speech was endangered by PC. I find that weird, since I had never even heard of PC last September when the academic year began. But by the time the president made his ghastly commencement speech, the idea of PC oppression was a prairie fire being driven across the nation by gales of hot air. The whole thing was brought into focus for me when I debated Dinesh D'Souza on *Face the Nation*. It was bemusing to listen to the former editor of the *Dartmouth Review* posing as a champion of civility on campus. I was even more bemused when I realized that D'Souza wasn't even born when I was at Michigan, a time when narrow white male hegemony had a far tighter grip on academe.

Now, don't get me wrong here. I love the University of Michigan and I had a swell time there. But I love it warts and all, the way black soldiers and sailors who fought bravely for their segregated country in the segregated armed forces loved America.

Michigan wasn't entirely civil to blacks when I went there, and incivility and insensitivity started right at the top with the regents and went on down to the lowest instructional level. The university was a white place when I arrived as a seventeen-year-old freshman in the fall of 1949. Despite the fact that most of the black students were from Michigan and our parents were taxpayers, we were made to feel like partially welcome guests, grudgingly accepted. Nobody took to the campus radio and told racist jokes or put threatening racist notes around the campus as has been done in Ann Arbor in recent years. That behavior, designed to slam blacks back into their "place," wasn't necessary. We *were* in our place, and there was precious little we could do about it.

What place was that? Our place then can be illustrated by the fact that I remember being assigned no book by a black writer in all the years I attended Michigan. I remember no blacks in any instructional capacity whatsoever. I do remember a white teaching fellow suggesting that elevator operator might be an occupation for which I was suited.

I do not remember the subject of Africa ever being raised seriously in a classroom, nor any course offering that touched on the contributions of slaves to the nation or the slaves' struggles and their descendants' struggles for decency. Needless to say, in my seven years at Michigan, I received no instruction of any kind that suggested that anybody black, Negro, or colored had contributed anything of value to this country.

I never found material about such subjects, and there was no adult on the campus who showed the least inclination to give me assistance in that direction. I did have a faculty adviser who was relentlessly rude to me in our one meeting during my freshman year. As I was leaving, but not yet out of earshot, I heard him—speaking to a third party—refer to me as a nigger.

The texture of campus life wasn't wonderful either. My girlfriend, Eve, was not permitted to try on clothes, as the white girls were, when she shopped on State Street. When I got to Michigan, no black had ever played on the basketball team. During my early college years, blacks were not served at the campus drinking hangout, the Pretzel Bell, where it was traditional to celebrate one's twenty-first birthday with friends and a free pitcher of beer. In my seven years on the Michigan campus, I never attended one party at a white fraternity or sorority. We blacks created our own rich, segregated social lives.

The student government was decent. It did try to have discriminatory clauses removed from sorority and fraternity charters, but the regents and the administration always rebuffed those efforts. It was most important, we were admonished by higher authorities, to protect the property rights of these organizations.

Michigan wasn't a uniformly racist place, and far better than most campuses at that time. There were good white people there, both teachers and students. I still have close and wonderful white friends from those days, and a couple of white adults did nurture me in very constructive ways. Moreover, some blacks were able to gain prominence in campus life. A black had been president of the LS&A class of 1949, just before I arrived. A black All-American football player, Lowell Perry, was probably the most popular man on campus our senior year. And I was president of our class.

Nevertheless, in its policies and practices, Michigan taught one overwhelming racial lesson: blacks were peripheral to the life of the nation, and their capacities to contribute were limited at best. That was a heavy burden for our young black souls to bear, and I'm sure it did some of us permanent damage.

But the white kids were at least as severely damaged. They were learning the same lessons about the capacities and human worth of people of color. Michigan wasn't unique. That was the traditional way for whites to be trained nationwide. Some people wondered why, in the next decade, the country's "best and brightest" couldn't accurately assess the political and fighting abilities of the Vietnamese enemy. I was never puzzled because I had seen how they had been educated.

The great American struggle of the last half of the twentieth century has been to throw off the self-satisfied hegemony of narrowness and ignorance that has crippled our nation for so long. Change is rarely smooth or free of rancor. Some stridency and moral rigidity can be expected from those long denied their voices, but those excesses can soon be corrected by the ordinary processes of rational discussion and debate.

There are cynical excesses in this situation, however, which arise exactly where you would expect—in the bastions of unchallenged privilege. Though it is quite disgusting for the president to cry, "Political extremists roam the land, abusing the privileges of free speech, setting citizens against one another on the basis of their class or race," this is not surprising coming from a member of the former, exclusionary and secret Yale society, Skull and Bones. What is startling about the president's utterance is that it so aptly describes Bush's own manipulation, of Willie Horton and quotas, in the nation's political dialogue.

For all its prominence in the recent drama of racial turmoil on U.S. campuses, Michigan is a far better place now than it was when I went there in the 1950s. This is largely attributable to the efforts made to diversify the student body, the faculty, and the curriculum—those efforts now labeled "PC oppression" by the snooty ol' boys who long so for the good ol' days.

SPECULATIONS

1. In one or two paragraphs, describe blacks' "place" at the University of Michigan in Ann Arbor when Wilkins was a student in the early 1950s.
2. Why do you think the regents and administration at the university rejected the student government attempt to remove discriminatory clauses from fraternity and sorority charters? Assume in your answer that they were not just being small-minded bigots.
3. Wilkins describes learning several lessons at Michigan about how white America viewed blacks, but he adds that white kids were also "severely damaged" by these lessons. What does he mean by this? Why for example does he say that Americans, especially whites, were incapable of accurately assessing the powerful fighting abilities of the Vietnamese?
4. Explain why you think Wilkins feels that Bush's statements about "political extremists" and their threat to free speech are "quite disgusting" and "startling." How does Wilkins's article use specific examples and an example of his own experience to prepare us for his rejection of Bush's statements?
5. Have you ever been treated unfairly because of qualities related to your

5. Have you ever been treated unfairly because of qualities related to your race, religion, gender, or physical attributes? What happened? What was your response? What did the incident teach you about yourself and others?
6. How does Wilkins balance positive and negative views of the University of Michigan in this piece? How does this view of the University affect the way we, as readers, perceive his authority and credibility?

How It Feels to Be Colored Me

ZORA NEALE HURSTON

Alice Walker once said that if she had only ten books to take to a desert island, two of them would be by Zora Neale Hurston: *Mules and Men* (1935) and *Their Eyes Were Watching God* (1937). For Walker, Hurston writes with

> a sense of black people as complete, complex, *undiminished* human beings, a sense that is lacking in so much black writing and literature. . . . Zora Neale Hurston was never afraid to let her characters be themselves, funny talk and all. She was incapable of being embarrassed by anything black people did, and so was able to write about everything with freedom and fluency.

Hurston's novel of a young black woman growing up through the social relationships of marriage and community—*Their Eyes Were Watching God*—has become a standard text in many literature courses.

Hurston was born in Florida in the first incorporated all-black town in America. Both parents instilled in her a sense of pride and possibility. Hurston attended Howard University and graduated from Barnard, working under Franz Boas, the founder of scientific anthropology. Hurston learned anthropology, says Walker, so she could study "the ways of her own people, and what ancient rituals, customs, and beliefs had made them unique." Her collection of folklore and voodoo traditions reflected the vitality of black culture in the Caribbean and North America.

Hurston's writing shows black life existing within a positive, spirited, life-loving community. From 1930 through 1960, Hurston was the most prolific black woman writer in America. She wrote nine books including an autobiography, *Dust Tracks on a Road*, which won the Anisfield-Wolf Award for its contribution to better race relations, and the play *Mule Bone: A Comedy of Negro Life in Three Acts*.

Hurston influenced many major black American writers including Toni Morrison, Ralph Ellison, and Toni Cade Bambara. Her fiction and essays spurred controversy for blacks because she insisted on individual autonomy rather than assimilation, a quality evident in "How It Feels to Be Colored Me."

Hurston's political opinions also caused friction. She claimed that "the Jim Crow system works." She was "flamboyant yet vulnerable, self-centered yet kind, a Republican conservative and an early black nationalist."

> In 1948, she was falsely accused of performing an immoral act with
> a ten-year-old child. She stopped speaking to her friends and ceased
> to publish. She died in 1960 and is buried in a pauper's graveyard.

I am colored but I offer nothing in the way of extenuating circumstances except the fact that I am the only Negro in the United States whose grandfather on the mother's side was *not* an Indian chief.

I remember the very day that I became colored. Up to my thirteenth year I lived in the little Negro town of Eatonville, Florida. It is exclusively a colored town. The only white people I knew passed through the town going to or coming from Orlando. The native whites rode dusty horses, the Northern tourists chugged down the sandy village road in automobiles. The town knew the Southerners and never stopped cane chewing when they passed. But the Northerners were something else again. They were peered at cautiously from behind curtains by the timid. The more venturesome would come out on the porch to watch them go past and got just as much pleasure out of the tourists as the tourists got out of the village.

The front porch might seem a daring place for the rest of the town, but it was a gallery seat for me. My favorite place was atop the gatepost. Proscenium box for a born first-nighter. Not only did I enjoy the show, but I didn't mind the actors knowing that I liked it. I usually spoke to them in passing. I'd wave at them and when they returned my salute, I would say something like this: "Howdy-do-well-I-thank-you-where-you-goin'?" Usually automobile or the horse paused at this, and after a queer exchange of compliments, I would probably "go a piece of the way" with them, as we say in farthest Florida. If one of my family happened to come to the front in time to see me, of course negotiations would be rudely broken off. But even so, it is clear that I was the first "welcome-to-our-state" Floridian, and I hope the Miami Chamber of Commerce will please take notice.

During this period, white people differed from colored to me only in that they rode through town and never lived there. They liked to hear me "speak pieces" and sing and wanted to see me dance the parse-me-la, and gave me generously of their small silver for doing these things, which seemed strange to me for I wanted to do them so much that I needed bribing to stop. Only they didn't know it. The colored people gave no dimes. They deplored any joyful tendencies in me, but I was their Zora nevertheless. I belonged to them, to the nearby hotels, to the country—everybody's Zora.

But changes came in the family when I was thirteen, and I was sent to school in Jacksonville. I left Eatonville, the town of the oleanders, as Zora. When I disembarked from the river-boat at Jacksonville, she was no more. It seemed that I had suffered a sea change. I was not Zora of Orange County any more, I was now a little colored girl.

I found it out in certain ways. In my heart as well as in the mirror, I became a fast brown—warranted not to rub nor run.

But I am not tragically colored. There is no great sorrow dammed up in my soul, nor lurking behind my eyes. I do not mind at all. I do not belong to the sobbing school of Negrohood who hold that nature somehow has given them a lowdown dirty deal and whose feelings are all hurt about it. Even in the helter-skelter skirmish that is my life, I have seen that the world is to the strong regardless of a little pigmentation more or less. No, I do not weep at the world—I am too busy sharpening my oyster knife.

Someone is always at my elbow reminding me that I am the granddaughter of slaves. It fails to register depression with me. Slavery is sixty years in the past. The operation was successful and the patient is doing well, thank you. The terrible struggle that made me an American out of a potential slave said "On the line!" The Reconstruction said "Get set!"; and the generation before said "Go!" I am off to a flying start and I must not halt in the stretch to look behind and weep. Slavery is the price I paid for civilization, and the choice was not with me. It is a bully adventure and worth all that I have paid through my ancestors for it. No one on earth ever had a greater chance for glory. The world to be won and nothing to be lost. It is thrilling to think—to know that for any act of mine, I shall get twice as much praise or twice as much blame. It is quite exciting to hold the center of the national stage, with the spectators not knowing whether to laugh or to weep.

The position of my white neighbor is much more difficult. No brown specter pulls up a chair beside me when I sit down to eat. No dark ghost thrusts its leg against mine in bed. The game of keeping what one has is never so exciting as the game of getting.

I do not always feel colored. Even now I often achieve the unconscious Zora of Eatonville before the Hegira.[1] I feel most colored when I am thrown against a sharp white background.

For instance at Barnard. "Beside the waters of the Hudson" I feel my race. Among the thousand white persons, I am a dark rock surged upon, and overswept, but through it all, I remain myself. When covered by the waters, I am; and the ebb but reveals me again.

Sometimes it is the other way around. A white person is set down in our midst, but the contrast is just as sharp for me. For instance, when I sit in the drafty basement that is The New World Cabaret with a white person, my color comes. We enter chatting about any little

---

[1] Refers to Mohammad's flight from Mecca in 622 and more generally means an escape from danger. [Eds.]

nothing that we have in common and are seated by the jazz waiters. In the abrupt way that jazz orchestras have, this one plunges into a number. It loses no time in circumlocutions, but gets right down to business. It constricts the thorax and splits the heart with its tempo and narcotic harmonies. This orchestra grows rambunctious, rears on its hind legs and attacks the tonal veil with primitive fury, rending it, clawing it until it breaks through to the jungle beyond. I follow those heathen—follow them exultingly. I dance wildly inside myself; I yell within, I whoop; I shake my assegai[2] above my head, I hurl it true to the mark *yeeeeooww!* I am in the jungle and living in the jungle way. My face is painted red and yellow and my body is painted blue. My pulse is throbbing like a war drum. I want to slaughter some-thing—give paid, give death to what, I do not know. But the piece ends. The men of the orchestra wipe their lips and rest their fingers. I creep back slowly to the veneer we call civilization with the last tone and find the white friend sitting motionless in his seat, smoking calmly.

"Good music they have here," he remarks, drumming the table with his fingertips.

Music. The great blobs of purple and red emotion have not touched him. He has only heard what I felt. He is far away and I see him but dimly across the ocean and the continent that have fallen between us. He is so pale with his whiteness then and I am so colored.

At certain times I have no race, I am *me*. When I set my hat at a certain angle and saunter down Seventh Avenue, Harlem City, feeling as snooty as the lions in front of the Forty Second Street Library, for instance. So far as my feelings are concerned, Peggy Hopkins Joyce on the Boule Mich with her gorgeous raiment, stately carriage, knees knocking together in a most aristocratic manner, has nothing on me. The cosmic Zora emerges. I belong to no race nor time. I am the eternal feminine with its string of beads.

I have no separate feeling about being an American citizen and colored. I am merely a fragment of the Great Soul that surges within the boundaries. My country, right or wrong.

Sometimes, I feel discriminated against, but it does not make me angry. It merely astonishes me. How *can* any deny themselves the pleasure of my company? It's beyond me.

But in the main, I feel like a brown bag of miscellany propped against a wall. Against a wall in company with other bags, white, red and yellow. Pour out the contents, and there is discovered a jumble

---

[2] Hunting spear. [Eds.]

of small things priceless and worthless. A first-water diamond, an empty spool, bits of broken glass, lengths of string, a key to a door long since crumbled away, a rusty knife-blade, old shoes saved for a road that never was and never will be, a nail bent under the weight of things too heavy for any nail, a dried flower or two still a little fragrant. In your hand is the brown bag. On the ground before you is the jumble it held—so much like the jumble in the bags, could they be emptied, that all might be dumped in a single heap and the bags refilled without altering the content of any greatly. A bit of colored glass more or less would not matter. Perhaps that is how the Great Stuffer of Bags filled them in the first place—who knows?

SPECULATIONS

1. Why does Hurston open her essay by claiming that "I am the only Negro in the United States whose grandfather on the mother's side was *not* an Indian chief"? What tone is she using here and how does this set the mood and perspective for the essay as a whole?

2. On what day did Hurston "become colored"? How did this change come about and what differences did it make for her?

3. What does Hurston mean when she refers to the popular expression "The world is my oyster" by saying, "No, I do not weep at the world—I am too busy sharpening my oyster knife"? What other metaphors and playful phrasing does she use in this essay?

4. In this essay, Hurston celebrates a condition that many people (at least during her time) saw as a liability—namely her identity as an African-American woman. If you wanted to celebrate yourself, what would you say? What qualities and features about yourself, your friends, your ambitions, your condition of life would you focus on?

5. If you had to describe Hurston's personality to a friend using three specific examples from this essay, what specific examples would you use?

6. How does the music mentioned in this essay affect Hurston? How does she use language to create the effect music has on her?

Incident

COUNTEE CULLEN

Countee Cullen was one of the leading poets of the Harlem Renaissance, an extraordinary flowering of Afro-American arts in the 1920s. Born in 1903, Cullen was raised in Harlem—the black ghetto of New York City. He distinguished himself as one of few blacks at DeWitt-Clinton High School, the alma mater of Lionel Trilling and James Baldwin; at New York University; at Harvard, where he was elected to Phi Beta Kappa; and at the Sorbonne, where he wrote poetry on a 1928 Guggenheim fellowship. He published nine books of poetry (including *Copper Sun*, *The Black Christ*, and *The Lost Zoo*) and a novel, *One Way to Heaven*. He also wrote extensively for the most important black literary journals of the day: *Opportunity* and the NAACP's journal *Crisis*. His poetry awards and honors include the Witter Bynner Poetry Contest Prizes (1923, 1924, and 1925); *Poetry* magazine's John Reed Memorial Prize (1925); and the Harmon Foundation Literary Award (1927). Friends described him as "a sensitive, gentle man, with a love for fun—a quiet intellectual." He spent the last twelve years of his life teaching French and creative writing at Frederick Douglass Junior High in New York City. He died in 1946.

Once riding in old Baltimore,
 Heart-filled, head-filled with glee,
I saw a Baltimorean
 Keep looking straight at me.

Now I was eight and very small,
 And he was no whit bigger,
And so I smiled, but he poked out
 His tongue, and called me, "Nigger."

I saw the whole of Baltimore
 From May until December;
Of all the things that happened there
 That's all that I remember.

SPECULATIONS

1. In what ways do the age and perspective of the man's memory from childhood contribute to the effect of this poem?
2. The poetic meter in this poem might best be described as iambic tetrameter (four beats) followed by iambic trimeter (three beats), a meter characteristic of nursery rhymes. How does this meter add to the power of the poem?

Just Walk on By: A Black Man Ponders His Power to Alter Public Space

BRENT STAPLES

Brent Staples was born in Chester, Pennsylvania, in 1951. In this selection, he describes Chester as a "small, angry industrial town" that provided an unnerving backdrop of "gang warfare, street knifings, and murders." Familiar with street violence and sensitive to the vulnerability we all sometimes feel in public spaces, Staples describes himself as shy and "one of the good boys" who had only a few fist fights when he was growing up. As an adult he learned to smother his own anger at being taken for a criminal and to whistle cheerful tunes on dark streets so his own large frame would not frighten others passing by.

Staples earned a Ph.D. in psychology from the University of Chicago and is a member of the editorial board of the *New York Times,* where he writes on politics and culture. He has published articles in many magazines and newspapers, and has been a staff reporter for the *Chicago Sun Times.* His memoir *Parallel Time: A Memoir* will be published in 1993.

My first victim was a woman—white, well dressed, probably in her early twenties. I came upon her late one evening on a deserted street in Hyde Park, a relatively affluent neighborhood in an otherwise mean, impoverished section of Chicago. As I swung onto the avenue behind her, there seemed to be a discreet, uninflammatory distance between us. Not so. She cast back a worried glance. To her, the youngish black man—a broad six feet two inches with a beard and billowing hair, both hands shoved into the pockets of a bulky military jacket—seemed menacingly close. After a few more quick glimpses, she picked up her pace and was soon running in earnest. Within seconds she disappeared into a cross street.

That was more than a decade ago. I was twenty-two years old, a graduate student newly arrived at the University of Chicago. It was in the echo of that terrified woman's footfalls that I first began to know the unwieldy inheritance I'd come into—the ability to alter public space in ugly ways. It was clear that she thought herself the quarry of a mugger, a rapist, or worse. Suffering a bout of insomnia, however, I was stalking sleep, not defenseless wayfarers. As a softy who is scarcely able to take a knife to a raw chicken—let alone hold it to a person's throat—I was surprised, embarrassed, and dismayed all at once. Her flight made me feel like an accomplice in tyranny. It also made it clear that I was indistinguishable from the muggers who occasionally seeped into the area from the surrounding ghetto. That first encounter, and those that followed, signified that a vast, unnerving gulf lay between nighttime pedestrians—particularly women—and me. And I soon gathered that being perceived as dangerous is a hazard in itself. I only needed to turn a corner into a dicey situation, or crowd some frightened, armed person in a foyer somewhere, or make an errant move after being pulled over by a policeman. Where fear and weapons meet—and they often do in urban America—there is always the possibility of death.

In that first year, my first away from my hometown, I was to become thoroughly familiar with the language of fear. At dark, shadowy intersections in Chicago, I could cross in front of a car stopped at a traffic light and elicit the *thunk, thunk, thunk, thunk* of the driver—black, white, male, or female—hammering down the door locks. On less traveled streets after dark, I grew accustomed to but never comfortable with people who crossed to the other side of the street rather than pass me. Then there were the standard unpleasantries with police, doormen, bouncers, cab drivers, and others whose business it is to screen out troublesome individuals *before* there is any nastiness.

I moved to New York nearly two years ago and I have remained an avid night walker. In central Manhattan, the near-constant crowd cover minimizes tense one-on-one street encounters. Elsewhere—visiting friends in SoHo, where sidewalks are narrow and tightly spaced buildings shut out the sky—things can get very taut indeed.

Black men have a firm place in New York mugging literature. Norman Podhoretz in his famed (or infamous) 1963 essay, "My Negro Problem—And Ours," recalls growing up in terror of black males; they "were tougher than we were, more ruthless," he writes—and as an adult on the Upper West Side of Manhattan, he continues, he cannot constrain his nervousness when he meets black men on certain streets. Similarly, a decade later, the essayist and novelist Edward Hoagland extols a New York where once "Negro bitterness bore down mainly on other Negroes." Where some see mere panhandlers, Hoagland sees "a mugger who is clearly screwing up his nerve to do more than just *ask* for money." But Hoagland has "the New Yorker's quickhunch posture for broken-field maneuvering," and the bad guy swerves away.

I often witness that "hunch posture," from women after dark on the warrenlike streets of Brooklyn where I live. They seem to set their faces on neutral and, with their purse straps strung across their chests bandolier style, they forge ahead as though bracing themselves against being tackled. I understand, of course, that the danger they perceive is not a hallucination. Women are particularly vulnerable to street violence, and young black males are drastically overrepresented among the perpetrators of that violence. Yet these truths are no solace against the kind of alienation that comes of being ever the suspect, against being set apart, a fearsome entity with whom pedestrians avoid making eye contact.

It is not altogether clear to me how I reached the ripe old age of twenty-two without being conscious of the lethality nighttime pedestrians attributed to me. Perhaps it was because in Chester, Pennsylvania, the small, angry industrial town where I came of age in the 1960s, I was scarcely noticeable against a backdrop of gang warfare, street knifings, and murders. I grew up one of the good boys, had perhaps a half-dozen fist fights. In retrospect, my shyness of combat has clear sources.

Many things go into the making of a young thug. One of those things is the consummation of the male romance with the power to intimidate. An infant discovers that random flailings send the baby bottle flying out of the crib and crashing to the floor. Delighted, the joyful babe repeats those motions again and again, seeking to duplicate the feat. Just so, I recall the points at which some of my boyhood friends were finally seduced by the perception of themselves as tough guys. When a mark cowered and surrendered his money without resistance, myth and reality merged—and paid off. It is, after all, only manly to embrace the power to frighten and intimidate. We, as men, are not supposed to give an inch of our lane on the highway; we are to seize the fighter's edge in work and in play and even in love; we are to be valiant in the face of hostile forces.

Unfortunately, poor and powerless young men seem to take all this nonsense literally. As a boy, I saw countless tough guys locked away; I have since buried several, too. They were babies, really—a teenage cousin, a brother of twenty-two, a childhood friend in his mid-twenties—all gone down in episodes of bravado played out in the streets. I came to doubt the virtues of intimidation early on. I chose, perhaps even unconsciously, to remain a shadow—timid, but a survivor.

The fearsomeness mistakenly attributed to me in public places often has a perilous flavor. The most frightening of these confusions occurred in the late 1970s and early 1980s when I worked as a journalist in Chicago. One day, rushing into the office of a magazine I was writing for with a deadline story in hand, I was mistaken for a burglar. The office manager called security and, with an ad hoc posse, pursued me through the labyrinthine halls, nearly to my editor's door. I had no way of proving who I was. I could only move briskly toward the company of someone who knew me.

Another time I was on assignment for a local paper and killing time before an interview. I entered a jewelry store on the city's affluent Near North Side. The proprietor excused herself and returned with an enormous red Doberman pinscher straining at the end of a leash. She stood, the dog extended toward me, silent to my questions, her eyes bulging nearly out of her head. I took a cursory look around, nodded, and bade her good night. Relatively speaking, however, I never fared as badly as another black male journalist. He went to nearby Waukegan, Illinois, a couple of summers ago to work on a story about a murderer who was born there. Mistaking the reporter for the killer, police hauled him from his car at gunpoint and but for his press credentials would probably have tried to book him. Such episodes are not uncommon. Black men trade tales like this all the time.

In "My Negro Problem—And Ours," Podhoretz writes that the hatred he feels for blacks makes itself known to him through a variety of avenues—one being his discomfort with that "special brand of paranoid touchiness" to which he says blacks are prone. No doubt he is speaking here of black men. In time, I learned to smother the rage I felt at so often being taken for a criminal. Not to do so would surely have led to madness—via that special "paranoid touchiness" that so annoyed Podhoretz at the time he wrote the essay.

I began to take precautions to make myself less threatening. I move about with care, particularly late in the evening. I give a wide berth to nervous people on subway platforms during the wee hours, particularly when I have exchanged business clothes for jeans. If I happen to be entering a building behind some people who appear skittish, I may walk by, letting them clear the lobby before I return, so as not to seem to be following them. I have been calm and extremely congenial on those rare occasions when I've been pulled over by the police.

And on late-evening constitutionals along streets less traveled by, I employ what has proved to be an excellent tension-reducing measure: I whistle melodies from Beethoven and Vivaldi and the more popular classical composers. Even steely New Yorkers hunching toward nighttime destinations seem to relax, and occasionally they even join in the tune. Virtually everybody seems to sense that a mugger wouldn't be warbling bright, sunny selections from Vivaldi's *Four Seasons*. It is my equivalent of the cowbell that hikers wear when they know they are in bear country.

SPECULATIONS

1. "My first victim was a woman—white, well dressed, probably in her early twenties," Staples writes. Why does he choose to open his essay this way?

2. Staples talks about the "male romance with the power to intimidate" as a way of explaining why boys grow up to be young thugs. Describe what alternatives existed to bravado and street death other than "remain a shadow—timid, but a survivor"?

3. Staples describes the fear and intimidation which his presence on dark streets caused in others. How does his recognition of their fear help him understand himself and his relationship to others? What does he learn about himself from the ways others see him?

4. Have you either been the perpetrator or the victim in a situation similar to the ones that Staples describes? What happened? What factors created the fear and intimidation? How could the situation have been prevented? How did the experience change you?

5.   Comparing the first three paragraphs of this essay with the last two paragraphs, describe the changes that take place in Staples's behavior.

Complexion

RICHARD RODRIGUEZ

Alienation—the alienation of self and language, self and family, self and society—is the theme that dominates Richard Rodriguez's work. Rodriguez sees *his* alienation, however, as a necessary precondition to becoming a writer and journalist.

A Mexican-American, Rodriguez was born in 1944 in San Francisco. His choice to master English and abandon Spanish is sensitively chronicled in his autobiography, *Hunger of Memory*, published in 1982. As a self-described "scholarship boy," he earned a B.A. at Stanford University in 1967 and did graduate work at the University of California at Berkeley and at London's Warburg Institute as a Fulbright fellow from 1972–1973. He refused to accept offers to teach at the university level because, as he told *New York Times* critic Le Anne Schreiber, "he could not withstand the irony of being counted a 'minority' when he was, in fact, a fully assimilated member of the majority." Instead, he began writing.

Rodriguez has been criticized for his conservative and unpopular views concerning bilingualism. In a *Publishers Weekly* interview with Suzanne Dalezal, he said that teachers

> have an obligation to teach a public language. Public language isn't just English or Spanish. . . . It is the language of public society. . . . For Appalachian children who speak a fractured English or black children in a ghetto, the problem is the same. . . . My argument has always been that the imperative is to get children away from those languages that increase their sense of alienation from public society.

As Rodriguez explained in an interview with *Contemporary Authors*:

> I see myself straddling two worlds of writing, journalism and literature. . . . It takes me a very long time to write. What I try to do when I write is break down the line separating the prosaic world from the poetic word. I try to write about everyday concerns—an educational issue, say, or the problems of the unemployed—but to write about them as powerfully, as richly, as well as I can.

This excerpt is taken from his autobiography, *Hunger of Memory*.

Visiting the East Coast or the gray capitals of Europe during the long months of winter, I often meet people at deluxe hotels who comment on my complexion. (In such hotels it appears nowadays a mark of leisure and wealth to have a complexion like mine.) Have I been skiing? In the Swiss Alps? Have I just returned from a Caribbean vacation? No. I say no softly but in a firm voice that intends to explain: My complexion is dark. (My skin is brown. More exactly, terra-cotta in sunlight, tawny in shade. I do not redden in sunlight. Instead, my skin becomes progressively dark; the sun singes the flesh.)

When I was a boy the white summer sun of Sacramento would darken me so, my T-shirt would seem bleached against my slender dark arms. My mother would see me come up the front steps. She'd wait for the screen door to slam at my back. "You look like a *negrito*," she'd say, angry, sorry to be angry, frustrated almost to laughing, scorn. "You know how important looks are in this country. With *los gringos* looks are all that they judge on. But you! Look at you! You're so careless!" Then she'd start in all over again. "You won't be satisfied till you end up looking like *los pobres* who work in the fields, *los braceros*."

(*Los braceros:* Those men who work with their *brazos,* their arms; Mexican nationals who were licensed to work for American farmers in the 1950s. They worked very hard for very little money, my father would tell me. And what money they earned they sent back to Mexico to support their families, my mother would add. *Los pobres* —the poor, the pitiful, the powerless ones. But paradoxically also powerful men. They were the men with brown-muscled arms I stared at in awe on Saturday mornings when they showed up downtown like gypsies to shop at Woolworth's or Penney's. On Monday nights they would gather hours early on the steps of the Memorial Auditorium for the wrestling matches. Passing by on my bicycle in summer, I would spy them there, clustered in small groups, talking—frightening and fascinating men—some wearing Texas *sombreros* and T-shirts which shone fluorescent in the twilight. I would sit forward in the back seat of our family's '48 Chevy to see them, working alongside Valley highways: dark men on an even horizon, loading a truck amid rows of straight green. Powerful, powerless men. Their fascinating darkness—like mine—to be feared.)

"You'll end up looking just like them."

Regarding my family, I see faces that do not closely resemble my own. Like some other Mexican families, my family suggests Mexico's confused colonial past. Gathered around a table, we appear to be from separate continents. My father's face recalls faces I have seen in France. His complexion is white—he does not tan; he does not burn. Over the years, his dark wavy hair has grayed handsomely. But with time his face has sagged to a perpetual sigh. My mother, whose surname is inexplicably Irish—Moran—has an olive complexion. People have frequently wondered if, perhaps, she is Italian or Portuguese. And, in fact, she looks as though she could be from southern Europe. My mother's face has not aged as quickly as the rest of her body; it remains smooth and glowing—a cool tan—which her gray hair cleanly accentuates. My older brother has inherited her good looks. When he was a boy people would tell him that he looked like Mario Lanza, and hearing it he would smile with dimpled assurance. He would come home from high school with girl friends who seemed to me glamorous (because they were) blonds. And during those years I envied him his skin that burned red and peeled like the skin of the *gringos*. His complexion never darkened like mine. My youngest sister is exotically pale, almost ashen. She is delicately featured, Near Eastern, people have said. Only my older sister has a complexion as dark as mine, though her facial features are much less harshly defined than my own. To many people meeting her, she seems (they say) Polynesian. I am the only one in the family whose face is severely cut to the line of ancient Indian ancestors. My face is mournfully long, in the classical Indian manner; my profile suggests one of those beaknosed Mayan sculptures—the eaglelike face upturned, openmouthed, against the deserted, primitive sky.

"We are Mexicans," my mother and father would say, and taught their four children to say whenever we (often) were asked about our ancestry. My mother and father scorned those "white" Mexican-Americans who tried to pass themselves off as Spanish. My parents would never have thought of denying their ancestry. I never denied it: My ancestry is Mexican, I told strangers mechanically. But I never forgot that only my older sister's complexion was as dark as mine.

My older sister never spoke to me about her complexion when she was a girl. But I guessed that she found her dark skin a burden. I knew that she suffered for being a "nigger." As she came home from grammar school, little boys came up behind her and pushed her down to the sidewalk. In high school, she struggled in the adolescent competition for boyfriends in a world of football games and proms, a world where her looks were plainly uncommon. In college, she was afraid and scornful when dark-skinned foreign students from countries like Turkey and India found her attractive. She revealed her fear of dark skin to me only in adulthood when, regarding her own three children, she quietly admitted relief that they were all light.

That is the kind of remark women in my family have often made before. As a boy, I'd stay in the kitchen (never seeming to attract any notice), listening while my aunts spoke of their pleasure at having light children. (The men, some of whom were dark-skinned from years of working out of doors, would be in another part of the house.) It was the woman's spoken concern: the fear of having a dark-skinned son or daughter. Remedies were exchanged. One aunt prescribed to her sisters the elixir of large doses of castor oil during the last weeks of pregnancy. (The remedy risked an abortion.) Children born dark grew up to have their faces treated regularly with a mixture of egg white and lemon juice concentrate. (In my case, the solution never would take.) One Mexican-American friend of my mother's, who regarded it a special blessing that she had a measure of English blood, spoke disparagingly of her husband, a construction worker, for being so dark. "He doesn't take care of himself," she complained. But the remark, I noticed, annoyed my mother, who sat tracing an invisible design with her finger on the tablecloth.

There was affection too and a kind of humor about these matters. With daring tenderness, one of my uncles would refer to his wife as *mi negra*. An aunt regularly called her dark child *mi feito* (my little ugly one), her smile only partially hidden as she bent down to dig her mouth under his ticklish chin. And at times relatives spoke scornfully of pale, white skin. A *gringo*'s skin resembled *masa*—baker's dough—someone remarked. Everyone laughed. Voices chuckled over the fact that the *gringos* spent so many hours in summer sunning themselves. ("They need to get sun because they look like *los muertos*.")[1]

I heard the laughing but remembered what the women had said, with unsmiling voices, concerning dark skin. Nothing I heard outside the house, regarding my skin, was so impressive to me.

In public I occasionally heard racial slurs. Complete strangers would yell out at me. A teenager drove past, shouting, "Hey, Greaser! Hey, Pancho!" Over his shoulder I saw the giggling face of his girl friend. A boy pedaled by and announced matter-of-factly, "I pee on dirty Mexicans." Such remarks would be said so casually that I wouldn't quickly realize that they were being addressed to me. When I did, I would be paralyzed with embarrassment, unable to return the insult. (Those times I happened to be with white grammar school friends, *they* shouted back. Imbued with the mysterious kindness of children, my friends would never ask later why I hadn't yelled out in my own defense.)

In all, there could not have been more than a dozen incidents of name-calling. That there were so few suggests that I was not a primary victim of racial abuse. But that, even today, I can clearly remember particular incidents is proof of their impact. Because of such incidents, I listened when my parents remarked that Mexicans were often mistreated in California border towns. And in Texas. I listened carefully when I heard that two of my cousins had been refused admittance to

---

[1] Dead people. [Eds.]

an "all-white" swimming pool. And that an uncle had been told by some man to go back to Africa. I followed the progress of the southern black civil rights movement, which was gaining prominent notice in Sacramento's afternoon newspaper. But what most intrigued me was the connection between dark skin and poverty. Because I heard my mother speak so often about the relegation of dark people to menial labor, I considered the great victims of racism to be those who were poor and forced to do menial work. People like the farmworkers whose skin was dark from the sun.

After meeting a black grammar school friend of my sister's, I re-member thinking that she wasn't really "black." What interested me was the fact that she wasn't poor. (Her well-dressed parents would come by after work to pick her up in a shiny green Oldsmobile.) By contrast, the garbage men who appeared every Friday morning seemed to me unmistakably black. (I didn't bother to ask my parents why Sacramento garbage men always were black. I thought I knew.) One morning I was in the backyard when a man opened the gate. He was an ugly, square-faced black man with popping red eyes, a pail slung over his shoulder. As he approached, I stood up. And in a voice that seemed to me very weak, I piped, "Hi." But the man paid me no heed. He strode past to the can by the garage. In a single broad movement, he overturned its contents into his larger pail. Our can came crashing down as he turned and left me watching, in awe.

"*Pobres negros,*" my mother remarked when she'd notice a head-line in the paper about a civil rights demonstration in the South. "How the *gringos* mistreat them." In the same tone of voice she'd tell me about the mistreatment her brother endured years before. (After my grandfather's death, my grandmother had come to America with her son and five daughters.) "My sisters, we were still all just teenagers. And since *mi pápa* was dead, my brother had to be the head of the family. He had to support us, to find work. But what skills did he have! Twenty years old. *Pobre.* He was tall; like your grandfather. And strong. He did construction work. 'Construction!' The *gringos* kept him digging all day, doing the dirtiest jobs. And they would pay him next to nothing. Sometimes they promised him one salary and paid him less when he finished. But what could he do? Report them? We weren't citizens then. He didn't even know English. And he was dark. What chances could he have? As soon as we sisters got older, he went right back to Mexico. He hated this country. He looked so tired when he left. Already with a hunchback. Still in his twenties. But old-look-ing. No life for him here. *Pobre.*"

Dark skin was for my mother the most important symbol of a life of oppressive labor and poverty. But both my parents recognized other symbols as well.

My father noticed the feel of every hand he shook. (He'd smile sometimes—marvel more than scorn—remembering a man he'd met who had soft, uncalloused hands.)

My mother would grab a towel in the kitchen and rub my oily face sore when I came in from playing outside. "Clean the *graza* off of your face!" (*Greaser!*)

Symbols: When my older sister, then in high school, asked my mother if she could do light housework in the afternoons for a rich lady we knew, my mother was frightened by the idea. For several weeks she troubled over it before granting conditional permission: "Just remember, you're not a maid. I don't want you wearing a uniform." My father echoed the same warning. Walking with him past a hotel, I watched as he stared at a doorman dressed like a Beefeater. "How can anyone let himself be dressed up like that? Like a clown. Don't you ever get a job where you have to put on a uniform." In summertime neighbors would ask me if I wanted to earn extra money by mowing their lawns. Again and again my mother worried: "Why did they ask *you*? Can't you find anything better?" Inevitably, she'd relent. She knew I needed the money. But I was instructed to work after dinner. ("When the sun's not so hot.") Even then, I'd have to wear a hat. *Un sombrero de* baseball.

(*Sombrero*. Watching gray cowboy movies, I'd brood over the meaning of the broad-rimmed hat—that troubling symbol—which comically distinguished a Mexican cowboy from real cowboys.)

From my father came no warnings concerning the sun. His fear was of dark factory jobs. He remembered too well his first jobs when he came to this country, not intending to stay, just to earn money enough to sail on to Australia. (In Mexico he had heard too many stories of discrimination in *los Estados Unidos*. So it was Australia, that distant island-continent, that loomed in his imagination as his "America.") The work my father found in San Francisco was work for the unskilled. A factory job. Then a cannery job. (He'd remember the noise and the heat.) Then a job at a warehouse. (He'd remember the dark stench of old urine.) At one place there were fistfights; at another a supervisor who hated Chinese and Mexicans. Nowhere a union.

His memory of himself in those years is held by those jobs. Never making money enough for passage to Australia; slowly giving up the plan of returning to school to resume his third-grade education—to become an engineer. My memory of him in those years, however, is lifted from photographs in the family album which show him on his honeymoon with my mother—the woman who had convinced him to stay in America. I have studied their photographs often, seeking to find in those figures some clear resemblance to the man and the woman I've known as my parents. But the youthful faces in the photos remain, behind dark glasses, shadowy figures anticipating my mother and father.

They are pictured on the grounds of the Coronado Hotel near San Diego, standing in the pale light of a winter afternoon. She is wearing slacks. Her hair falls seductively over one side of her face. He appears wearing a double-breasted suit, an unneeded raincoat draped over his arm. Another shows them standing together, solemnly staring ahead. Their shoulders barely are touching. There is to their pose an aristocratic formality, an elegant Latin hauteur.

The man in those pictures is the same man who was fascinated by Italian grand opera. I have never known just what my father saw in the spectacle, but he has told me that he would take my mother to the Opera House every Friday night—if he had money enough for orchestra seats. ("Why go to sit in the balcony?") On Sundays he'd don Italian silk scarves and a camel's hair coat to take his new wife to the polo matches in Golden Gate Park. But one weekend my father stopped going to the opera and polo matches. He would blame the change in his life on one job—a warehouse job, working for a large corporation which today advertises its products with the smiling faces of children. "They made me an old man before my time," he'd say to me many years later. Afterward, jobs got easier and cleaner. Eventually, in middle age, he got a job making false teeth. But his youth was spent at the warehouse. "Everything changed," his wife remembers. The dapper young man in the old photographs yielded to the man I saw after dinner: haggard, asleep on the sofa. During "The Ed Sullivan Show" on Sunday nights, when Roberta Peters or Licia Albanese would appear on the tiny blue screen, his head would jerk up alert. He'd sit forward while the notes of Puccini sounded before him. ("Un bel dí.")

By the time they had a family, my parents no longer dressed in very fine clothes. Those symbols of great wealth and the reality of their lives too noisily clashed. No longer did they try to fit themselves, like paper-doll figures, behind trappings so foreign to their actual lives. My father no longer wore silk scarves or expensive wool suits. He sold his tuxedo to a second-hand store for five dollars. My mother sold her rabbit fur coat to the wife of a Spanish radio station disc jockey. ("It looks better on you than it does on me," she kept telling the lady until the sale was completed.) I was six years old at the time, but I recall watching the transaction with complete understanding. The woman I knew as my mother was already physically unlike the woman in her honeymoon photos. My mother's hair was short. Her shoulders were thick from carrying children. Her fingers were swollen red, roughened by housecleaning. Already my mother would admit to foreseeing herself in her own mother, a woman grown old, bald and bowlegged, after a hard lifetime of working.

In their manner, both my parents continued to respect the symbols of what they considered to be upper-class life. Very early, they taught me the *propria* way of eating *como los ricos*. And I was carefully taught elaborate formulas of polite greeting and parting. The dark little boy would be invited by classmates to the rich houses on Forty-fourth and Forty-fifth streets. "How do you do?" or "I am very pleased to meet you," I would say, bowing slightly to the amused mothers of classmates. "Thank you very much for the dinner; it was very delicious."

I made an impression. I intended to make an impression, to be invited back. (I soon realized that the trick was to get the mother or father to notice me.) From those early days began my association with rich people, my fascination with their secret. My mother worried. She warned me not to come home expecting to have the things my friends possessed. But she needn't have said anything. When I went to the big houses, I remembered that I was, at best, a visitor to the world I saw there. For that reason, I was an especially watchful guest. I was my parents' child. Things most middle-class children wouldn't trouble to notice, I studied. Remembered to see: the starched black and white uniform worn by the maid who opened the door; the Mexican gardeners—their complexions as dark as my own. (One gardener's face, glassed by sweat, looked up to see me going inside.)

"Take Richard upstairs and show him your electric train," the mother said. But it was really the vast polished dining room table I'd come to appraise. Those nights when I was invited to stay for dinner, I'd notice that my friend's mother rang a small silver bell to tell the black woman when to bring in the food. The father, at his end of the table, ate while wearing his tie. When I was not required to speak, I'd skate the icy cut of crystal with my eye; my gaze would follow the golden threads etched onto the rim of china. With my mother's eyes I'd see my hostess's manicured nails and judge them to be marks of her leisure. Later, when my schoolmate's father would bid me goodnight, I would feel his soft fingers and palm when we shook hands. And turning to leave, I'd see my dark self, lit by chandelier light, in a tall hallway mirror.

Complexion. My first conscious experience of sexual excitement concerns my complexion. One summer weekend, when I was around seven years old, I was at a public swimming pool with the whole family. I remember sitting on the damp pavement next to the pool and seeing my mother, in the spectators' bleachers, holding my younger sister on her lap. My mother, I noticed, was watching my father as he stood on a diving board, waving to her. I watched her wave back. Then saw her radiant, bashful, astonishing smile. In that second I sensed that my mother and father had a relationship I knew nothing about. A nervous excitement encircled my stomach as I saw my mother's eyes follow my father's figure curving into the water. A second or two later, he emerged. I heard him call out. Smiling, his voice sounded, buoyant, calling me to swim to him. But turning to see him, I caught my mother's eye. I heard her shout over to me, In Spanish she called through the crowd: "Put a towel on over your shoulders." In public, she didn't want to say why. I knew.

That incident anticipates the shame and sexual inferiority I was to feel in later years because of my dark complexion. I was to grow up an ugly child. Or one who thought himself ugly. (*Feo.*) One night when I was eleven or twelve years old, I locked myself in the bathroom and carefully regarded my reflection in the mirror over the sink. Without any pleasure I studied my skin. I turned on the faucet. (In my mind I heard the swirling voices of aunts, and even my mother's voice, whispering, whispering incessantly about lemon juice solutions and dark, *feo* children.) With a bar of soap, I fashioned a thick ball of lather. I began soaping my arms. I took my father's straight razor out of the medicine cabinet. Slowly, with steady deliberateness, I put the blade against my flesh, pressed it as close as I could without cutting, and moved it up and down across my skin to see if I could get out, somehow lessen, the dark. All I succeeded in doing, however, was in shaving my arms bare of their hair. For as I noted with disappointment, the dark would not come out. It remained. Trapped. Deep in the cells of my skin.

Throughout adolescence, I felt myself mysteriously marked. Nothing else about my appearance would concern me so much as the fact that my complexion was dark. My mother would say how sorry she was that there was not money enough to get braces to straighten my teeth. But I never bothered about my teeth. In three-way mirrors at department stores, I'd see my profile dramatically defined by a long nose, but it was really only the color of my skin that caught my attention.

I wasn't afraid that I would become a menial laborer because of my skin. Nor did my complexion make me feel especially vulnerable to racial abuse. (I didn't really consider my dark skin to be a racial characteristic. I would have been only too happy to look as Mexican as my light-skinned older brother.) Simply, I judged myself ugly. And, since the women in my family had been the ones who discussed it in such worried tones, I felt my dark skin made me unattractive to women.

Thirteen years old. Fourteen. In a grammar school art class, when the assignment was to draw a self-portrait, I tried and I tried but could not bring myself to shade in the face on the paper to anything like my actual tone. With disgust then I would come face to face with myself in mirrors. With disappointment I located myself in class photographs—my dark face undefined by the camera which had clearly described the white faces of classmates. Or I'd see my dark wrist against my long-sleeved white shirt.

I grew divorced from my body. Insecure, overweight, listless. On hot summer days when my rubber-soled shoes soaked up the heat from the sidewalk, I kept my head down. Or walked in the shade. My mother didn't need anymore to tell me to watch out for the sun. I denied myself a sensational life. The normal, extraordinary, animal excitement of feeling my body alive—riding shirtless on a bicycle in the warm wind created by furious self-propelled motion—the sensations that first had excited in me a sense of my maleness, I denied. I was too ashamed of my body. I wanted to forget that I had a body because I had a brown body. I was grateful that none of my classmates ever mentioned the fact.

I continued to see the *braceros,* those men I resembled in one way and, in another way, didn't resemble at all. On the watery horizon of a Valley afternoon, I'd see them. And though I feared looking like them, it was with silent envy that I regarded them still. I envied them their physical lives, their freedom to violate the taboo of the sun. Closer to home I would notice the shirtless construction workers, the roofers, the sweating men tarring the street in front of the house. And I'd see the Mexican gardeners. I was unwilling to admit the attraction of their lives. I tried to deny it by looking away. But what was denied became strongly desired.

In high school physical education classes, I withdrew, in the regular company of five or six classmates, to a distant corner of a football field where we smoked and talked. Our company was composed of bodies too short or too tall, all graceless and all—except mine—pale. Our conversation was usually witty. (In fact we were intelligent.) If we referred to the athletic contests around us, it was with sarcasm. With savage scorn I'd refer to the "animals" playing football or baseball. It would have been important for me to have joined them. Or for me to have taken off my shirt, to have let the sun burn on my skin, and to have run barefoot on the warm wet grass. It would have been very important. Too important. It would have been too telling a gesture—to admit the desire for sensation, the body, my body.

Fifteen, sixteen. I was a teenager shy in the presence of girls.

Never dated. Barely could talk to a girl without stammering. In high school I went to several dances, but I never managed to ask a girl to dance. So I stopped going. I cannot remember high school years now with the parade of typical images: bright drive-ins or gliding blue shadows of a Junior Prom. At home most weekend nights, I would pass evenings reading. Like those hidden, precocious adolescents who have no real-life sexual experiences, I read a great deal of romantic fiction. "You won't find it in your books," my brother would playfully taunt me as he prepared to go to a party by freezing the crest of the wave in his hair with sticky pomade. Through my reading, however, I developed a fabulous and sophisticated sexual imagination. At seventeen, I may not have known how to engage a girl in small talk, but I had read *Lady Chatterley's Lover*.

It annoyed me to bear my father's teasing: that I would never know what "real work" is; that my hands were so soft. I think I knew it was his way of admitting pleasure and pride in my academic success. But I didn't smile. My mother said she was glad her children were getting their educations and would not be pushed around like *los pobres*. I heard the remark ironically as a reminder of my separation from *los braceros*. At such times I suspected that education was making me effeminate. The odd thing, however, was that I did not judge my classmates so harshly. Nor did I consider my male teachers in high school effeminate. It was only myself I judged against some shadowy, mythical Mexican laborer—dark like me, yet very different.

Language was crucial. I knew that I had violated the ideal of the *macho* by becoming such a dedicated student of language and literature. *Machismo* was a word never exactly defined by the persons who used it. (It was best described in the "proper" behavior of men.) Women at home, nevertheless, would repeat the old Mexican dictum that a man should be *feo, fuerte, y formal*. "The three F's," my mother called them, smiling slyly. *Feo* I took to mean not literally ugly so much as ruggedly handsome. (When my mother and her sisters spent a loud, laughing afternoon determining ideal male good looks, they finally settled on the actor Gilbert Roland, who was neither too pretty nor ugly but had looks "like a man.") *Fuerte*, "strong," seemed to mean not physical strength as much as inner strength, character. A dependable man is *fuerte*. *Fuerte* for that reason was a characteristic subsumed by the last of the three qualities, and the one I most often considered—*formal*. To be *formal* is to be steady. A man of responsibility, a good provider. Someone *formal* is also constant. A person to be relied upon in adversity. A sober man, a man of high seriousness.

I learned a great deal about being *formal* just by listening to the way my father and other male relatives of his generation spoke. A man was not silent necessarily. Nor was he limited in the tones he could sound. For example, he could tell a long, involved, humorous story and laugh at his own humor with high-pitched giggling. But a man was not talkative the way a woman could be. It was permitted a woman to be gossipy and chatty. (When one heard many voices in a room, it was usually women who were talking.) Men spoke much less rapidly. And often men spoke in monologues. (When one voice sounded in a crowded room, it was most often a man's voice one heard.) More important than any of this was the fact that a man never verbally revealed his emotions. Men did not speak about their unease in moments of crisis or danger. It was the woman who worried aloud when her husband got laid off from work. At times of illness or death in the family, a man was usually quiet, even silent. Women spoke up to voice prayers. In distress, women always sounded quick ejaculations to God or the Virgin; women prayed in clearly audible voices at a wake held in a funeral parlor. And on the subject of love, a woman was verbally expansive. She spoke of her yearning and delight. A married man, if he spoke publicly about love, usually did so with playful, mischievous irony. Younger, unmarried men more often were quiet. (The *macho* is a silent suitor. *Formal.*)

At home I was quiet, so perhaps I seemed *formal* to my relations and other Spanish-speaking visitors to the house. But outside the house—my God!—I talked. Particularly in class or alone with my teachers, I chattered. (Talking seemed to make teachers think I was bright.) I often was proud of my way with words. Though, on other occasions, for example, when I would hear my mother busily speaking to women, it would occur to me that my attachment to words made me like her. Her son. Not *formal* like my father. At such times I even suspected that my nostalgia for sounds—the noisy, intimate Spanish sounds of my past—was nothing more than effeminate yearning.

High school English teachers encouraged me to describe very personal feelings in words. Poems and short stories I wrote, expressing sorrow and loneliness, were awarded high grades. In my bedroom were books by poets and novelists—books that I loved—in which male writers published feelings the men in my family never revealed or acknowledged in words. And it seemed to me that there was something unmanly about my attachment to literature. Even today, when so much about the myth of the *macho* no longer concerns me, I cannot altogether evade such notions. Writing these pages, admitting my embarrassment or my guilt, admitting my sexual anxieties and my physical insecurity, I have not been able to forget that I am not being *formal.*

So be it.

I went to college at Stanford, attracted partly by its academic reputation, partly because it was the school rich people went to. I found myself on a campus with golden children of western America's upper middle class. Many were students both ambitious for academic success *and* accustomed to leisured life in the sun. In the afternoon, they lay spread out, sunbathing in front of the library, reading Swift or Engels or Beckett. Others went by in convertibles, off to play tennis or ride horses or sail. Beach boys dressed in tank-tops and shorts were my classmates in undergraduate seminars. Tall tan girls wearing white strapless dresses sat directly in front of me in lecture rooms. I'd study them, their physical confidence. I was still recognizably kin to the boy I had been. Less tortured perhaps. But still kin. At Stanford, it's true, I began to have something like a conventional sexual life. I don't think, however, that I really believed that the women I knew found me physically appealing. I continued to stay out of the sun. I didn't linger in mirrors. And I was the student at Stanford who remembered to notice the Mexican-American janitors and gardeners working on campus.

It was at Stanford, one day near the end of my senior year, that a friend told me about a summer construction job he knew was available. I was quickly alert. Desire uncoiled within me. My friend said that he knew I had been looking for summer employment. He knew I needed some money. Almost apologetically he explained: It was something I probably wouldn't be interested in, but a friend of his, a contractor, needed someone for the summer to do menial jobs. There would be lots of shoveling and raking and sweeping. Nothing too hard. But nothing more interesting either. Still, the pay would be good. Did I want it? Or did I know someone who did?

I did. Yes, I said, surprised to hear myself say it.

In the weeks following, friends cautioned that I had no idea how hard physical labor really is. ("You only *think* you know what it is like to shovel for eight hours straight.") Their objections seemed to me challenges. They resolved the issue. I became happy with my plan. I decided, however, not to tell my parents. I wouldn't tell my mother because I could guess her worried reaction. I would tell my father only after the summer was over, when I could announce that, after all, I did know what "real work" is like.

The day I met the contractor (a Princeton graduate, it turned out), he asked me whether I had done any physical labor before. "In high school, during the summer," I lied. And although he seemed to regard me with skepticism, he decided to give me a try. Several days later, expectant, I arrived at my first construction site. I would take off my shirt to the sun. And at last grasp desired sensation. No longer afraid.

At last become like a *bracero*. "We need those tree stumps out of here by tomorrow," the contractor said. I started to work.

I labored with excitement that first morning—and all the days after. The work was harder than I could have expected. But it was never as tedious as my friends had warned me it would be. There was too much physical pleasure in the labor. Especially early in the day, I would be most alert to the sensations of movement and straining. Beginning around seven each morning (when the air was still damp but the scent of weeds and dry earth anticipated the heat of the sun), I would feel my body resist the first thrusts of the shovel. My arms, tightened by sleep, would gradually loosen; after only several minutes, sweat would gather in beads on my forehead and then—a short while later—I would feel my chest silky with sweat in the breeze. I would return to my work. A nervous spark of pain would fly up my arm and settle to burn like an ember in the thick of my shoulder. An hour, two passed. Three. My whole body would assume regular movements; my shoveling would be described by identical, even movements. Even later in the day, my enthusiasm for primitive sensation would survive the heat and the dust and the insects pricking my back. I would strain wildly for sensation as the day came to a close. At three-thirty, quitting time, I would stand upright and slowly let my head fall back, luxuriating in the feeling of tightness relieved.

Some of the men working nearby would watch me and laugh. Two or three of the older men took the trouble to teach me the right way to use a pick, the correct way to shovel. "You're doing it wrong, too fucking hard," one man scolded. Then proceeded to show me—what persons who work with their bodies all their lives quickly learn—the most economical way to use one's body in labor.

"Don't make your back do so much work," he instructed. I stood impatiently listening, half listening, vaguely watching, then noticed his work-thickened fingers clutching the shovel. I was annoyed. I wanted to tell him that I enjoyed shoveling the wrong way. And I didn't want to learn the right way. I wasn't afraid of back pain. I liked the way my body felt sore at the end of the day.

I was about to, but, as it turned out, I didn't say a thing. Rather it was at that moment I realized that I was fooling myself if I expected a few weeks of labor to gain me admission to the world of the laborer. I would not learn in three months what my father had meant by "real work." I was not bound to this job; I could imagine its rapid conclusion. For me the sensations of exertion and fatigue could be savored. For my father or uncle, working at comparable jobs when they were my age, such sensations were to be feared. Fatigue took a different toll on their bodies—and minds.

It was, I know, a simple insight. But it was with this realization that I took my first step that summer toward realizing something even more important about the "worker." In the company of carpenters, electricians, plumbers, and painters at lunch, I would often sit quietly, observant. I was not shy in such company. I felt easy, pleased by the knowledge that I was casually accepted, my presence taken for granted by men (exotics) who worked with their hands. Some days the younger men would talk and talk about sex, and they would howl at women who drove by in cars. Other days the talk at lunchtime was subdued; men gathered in separate groups. It depended on who was around. There were rough, good-natured workers. Others were quiet. The more I remember that summer, the more I realize that there was no single *type* of worker. I am embarrassed to say I had not expected such diversity. I certainly had not expected to meet, for example, a plumber who was an abstract painter in his off hours and admired the work of Mark Rothko. Nor did I expect to meet so many workers with college diplomas. (They were the ones who were not surprised that I intended to enter graduate school in the fall.) I suppose what I really want to say here is painfully obvious, but I must say it nevertheless: The men of that summer were middle-class Americans. They certainly didn't constitute an oppressed society. Carefully completing their work sheets; talking about the fortunes of local football teams; planning Las Vegas vacations; comparing the gas mileage of various makes of campers—they were not *los pobres* my mother had spoken about.

On two occasions, the contractor hired a group of Mexican aliens. They were employed to cut down some trees and haul off debris. In all, there were six men of varying age. The youngest in his late twenties; the oldest (his father?) perhaps sixty years old. They came and they left in a single old truck. Anonymous men. They were never introduced to the other men at the site. Immediately upon their arrival, they would follow the contractor's directions, start working—rarely resting—seemingly driven by a fatalistic sense that work which had to be done was best done as quickly as possible.

I watched them sometimes. Perhaps they watched me. The only time I saw them pay me much notice was one day at lunchtime when I was laughing with the other men. The Mexicans sat apart when they ate, just as they worked by themselves. Quiet. I rarely heard them say much to each other. All I could hear were their voices calling out sharply to one another, giving directions. Otherwise, when they stood briefly resting, they talked among themselves in voices too hard to overhear.

The contractor knew enough Spanish, and the Mexicans—or at least the oldest of them, their spokesman—seemed to know enough English to communicate. But because I was around, the contractor decided one day to make me his translator. (He assumed I could speak

Spanish.) I did what I was told. Shyly I went over to tell the Mexicans that the *patrón* wanted them to do something else before they left for the day. As I started to speak, I was afraid with my old fear that I would be unable to pronounce the Spanish words. But it was a simple instruction I had to convey. I could say it in phrases.

The dark sweating faces turned toward me as I spoke. They stopped their work to hear me. Each nodded in response. I stood there. I wanted to say something more. But what could I say in Spanish, even if I could have pronounced the words right? Perhaps I just wanted to engage them in small talk, to be assured of their confidence, our familiarity. I thought for a moment to ask them where in Mexico they were from. Something like that. And maybe I wanted to tell them (a lie, if need be) that my parents were from the same part of Mexico.

I stood there.

Their faces watched me. The eyes of the man directly in front of me moved slowly over my shoulder, and I turned to follow his glance toward *el patrón* some distance away. For a moment I felt swept up by that glance into the Mexicans' company. But then I heard one of them returning to work. And then the others went back to work. I left them without saying anything more.

When they had finished, the contractor went over to pay them in cash. (He later told me that he paid them collectively "for the job," though he wouldn't tell me their wages. He said something quickly about the good rate of exchange "in their own country.") I can still hear the loudly confident voice he used with the Mexicans. It was the sound of the *gringo* I had heard as a very young boy. And I can still hear the quiet, indistinct sounds of the Mexican, the oldest, who replied. At hearing that voice I was sad for the Mexicans. Depressed by their vulnerability. Angry at myself. The adventure of the summer seemed suddenly ludicrous. I would not shorten the distance I felt from *los pobres* with a few weeks of physical labor. I would not become like them. They were different from me.

After that summer, a great deal—and not very much really—changed in my life. The curse of physical shame was broken by the sun; I was no longer ashamed of my body. No longer would I deny myself the pleasing sensations of my maleness. During those years when middle-class black Americans began to assert with pride, "Black is beautiful," I was able to regard my complexion without shame. I am today darker than I ever was as a boy. I have taken up the middle-class sport of long-distance running. Nearly every day now I run ten or fifteen miles, barely clothed, my skin exposed to the California winter rain and wind or the summer sun of late afternoon. The torso, the soccer player's calves and thighs, the arms of the twenty-year-old I never was, I possess now in my thirties. I study the youthful parody shape in the mirror: the stomach lipped tight by muscle; the shoulders rounded by chin-ups; the arms veined strong. This man. A man. I meet him. He laughs to see me, what I have become.

The dandy. I wear double-breasted Italian suits and custom-made English shoes. I resemble no one so much as my father—the man pictured in those honeymoon photos. At that point in life when he abandoned the dandy's posture, I assume it. At the point when my parents would not consider going on vacation, I register at the Hotel Carlyle in New York and the Plaza Athenée in Paris. I am as taken by the symbols of leisure and wealth as they were. For my parents, however, those symbols became taunts, reminders of all they could not achieve in one lifetime. For me those same symbols are reassuring reminders of public success. I tempt vulgarity to be reassured. I am filled with the gaudy delight, the monstrous grace of the nouveau riche.

In recent years I have had occasion to lecture in ghetto high schools. There I see students of remarkable style and physical grace. (One can see more dandies in such schools than one ever will find in middle-class high schools.) There is not the look of casual assurance I saw students at Stanford display. Ghetto girls mimic high-fashion models. Their dresses are of bold, forceful color; their figures elegant, long; the stance theatrical. Boys wear shirts that grip at their overdeveloped muscular bodies. (Against a powerless future, they engage images of strength.) Bad nutrition does not yet tell. Great disappointment, fatal to youth, awaits them still. For the moment, movements in school hallways are dancelike, a procession of postures in a sexual masque. Watching them, I feel a kind of envy. I wonder how different my adolescence would have been had I been free. . . . But no, it is my parents I see—their optimism during those years when they were entertained by Italian grand opera.

The registration clerk in London wonders if I have just been to Switzerland. And the man who carries my luggage in New York guesses the Caribbean. My complexion becomes a mark of my leisure. Yet no one would regard my complexion the same way if I entered such hotels through the service entrance. That is only to say that my complexion assumes its significance from the context of my life. My skin, in itself, means nothing. I stress the point because I know there are people who would label me "disadvantaged" because of my color. They make the same mistake I made as a boy, when I thought a disadvantaged life was circumscribed by particular occupations. That summer I worked in the sun may have made me physically indistinguishable from the Mexicans working nearby. (My skin was actually darker because, unlike them, I worked without wearing a shirt. By late August my hands were probably as tough as theirs.) But I was not one of *los pobres*. What made me different from them was an attitude of *mind*, my imagination of myself.

I do not blame my mother for warning me away from the sun when I was young. In a world where her brother had become an old man in his twenties because he was dark, my complexion was something to worry about. "Don't run in the sun," she warns me today. I run. In the end, my father was right—though perhaps he did not know how right or why—to say that I would never know what real work is. I will never know what he felt at his last factory job. If tomorrow I worked at some kind of factory, it would go differently for me. My long education would favor me. I could act as a public person—able to defend my interests, to unionize, to petition, to speak up—to challenge and demand. (I will never know what real work is.) I will never know what the Mexicans knew, gathering their shovels and ladders and saws.

Their silence stays with me now. The wages those Mexicans received for their labor were only a measure of their disadvantaged condition. Their silence is more telling. They lack a public identity. They remain profoundly alien. Persons apart. People lacking a union obviously, people without grounds. They depend upon the relative good will or fairness of their employers each day. For such people, lacking a better alternative, it is not such an unreasonable risk.

Their silence stays with me. I have taken these many words to describe its impact. Only: the quiet. Something uncanny about it. Its compliance. Vulnerability. Pathos. As I heard their truck rumbling away, I shuddered, my face mirrored with sweat. I had finally come face to face with *los pobres*.

SPECULATIONS

1.   Rodriguez describes how he was intrigued by "the connection between dark skin and poverty." How does he describe this connection and what notable examples does he use to describe it? What examples of your own can you think of?

2.   Rodriguez's mother warns his sister against wearing a maid's uniform, and his father reacts negatively when he sees a doorman in uniform, saying "Don't you ever get a job where you have to put on a uniform." What does the uniform symbolize? What other symbols related to "lightness" and "darkness" of skin are his parents concerned about?

3.   Rodriguez went to the rich houses of his wealthy classmates. He writes:

> I made an impression. I intended to make an impression, to be invited back. (I soon realized that the trick was to get the mother or father to notice me.) From those early days began my association with rich people, my fascination with their secret.

How would you describe Rodriguez's motivation? What does he want? What is his own attitude toward this desire as revealed in the tone of this writing?

4. Have you ever felt like an alien, that is, so out of place that you felt you had no way to talk with others around you? Describe the situation and where it occurred—at a party, in a store, in a foreign country. Explain how it came about and what you felt and experienced as an "alien."

5. Rodriguez's experience as a construction worker had a major impact on him. What does the experience teach him about himself, about the other workers, the contractor, the Mexican aliens?

6. Toward the end of the excerpt, Rodriguez describes himself as a "dandy," as someone who tempts "vulgarity to be reassured," as successful, leisured, yet distanced from himself, even a bit cynical about his own pretensions. He contrasts himself with the Mexican laborers who are lacking "a public identity," silent, and "profoundly alien." Evaluate Rodriguez's attitude toward his accomplishments. How does he see himself in comparison to the Mexicans? How do you sort out Rodriguez's point of view?

Black Women and Men: Partnership in the 1990s

bell hooks (GLORIA WATKINS)

bell hooks is the pen name of Gloria Watkins, a teacher at Oberlin College and a regular contributor to *Zeta* magazine. In her work (*Ain't I A Woman: Black Women and Feminism, Feminist Theory: From Margin to Center, Talking Back: Thinking Feminist, Thinking Black,* and *Yearning: Race, Gender, and Cultural Politics*), hooks reinterprets the feminist movement from the perspective of black women. Using the metaphor of marginality, which she describes as being "part of the whole but outside the main body," hooks questions whether traditional feminism, which "emerges from privileged women who live at the center," addresses the needs of working-class, poor, and minority women.

Hooks grew up in the 1950s in a small Kentucky town whose railroad tracks symbolized the marginality of the black townspeople's lives. In the preface to *Feminist Theory: From Margin to Center* (1984), she describes how blacks could cross the tracks to work, but only in service jobs. They could not live there.

> Living as we did—on the edge—we developed a particular way of seeing reality. We looked both from the outside in and from the inside out. We focused our attention on the center as well as on the margin. We understood both. This mode of seeing reminded us of the existence of a whole universe, a main body made up of both margin and center. Our survival depended on an ongoing public awareness of the separation between margin and center and an ongoing private acknowledgment that we were a necessary, vital part of that whole.

This dual perspective gives hooks a "willingness to explore all possibilities." She remains convinced that feminism "must become a mass based political movement if it is to have a revolutionary, transformative impact on society. . . . As we educate one another to acquire critical consciousness, we have the chance to see how important airing diverse perspectives can be for any progressive political struggle that is serious about transformation." Precisely that kind of open discussion characterizes this dialogue between hooks and noted black scholar and intellectual Cornel West at Yale University in the late 1980s.

CORNEL WEST

Cornel West was born in Tulsa, Oklahoma, in 1953. He received his undergraduate degree in 1973 from Harvard, and an M.A. and Ph.D. from Yale. Since 1977, he has taught and worked as an educator and professor of philosophy at the Union Theological Seminary and Yale School of Divinity. He has published three scholarly books which provide important new perspectives on the history of philosophical thinking: *Post-Analytic Philosophy*, edited with John Rajehman, in 1985; *The American Evasion of Philosophy: A Genealogy of Pragmatism* in 1989; and *The Ethical Dimensions of Marxism* in 1991.

b.h.: I requested that Charles sing "Precious Lord" because the conditions that led Thomas Dorsey to write this song always make me think about gender issues, issues of black masculinity. Mr. Dorsey wrote this song after his wife died in childbirth. That experience caused him to have a crisis of faith. He did not think he would be able to go on living without her. That sense of unbearable crisis truly expresses the contemporary dilemma of faith. Mr. Dorsey talked about the way he tried to cope with this "crisis of faith." He prayed and prayed for a healing and received the words to this song. This song has helped so many folk when they are feeling low, feeling as if they can't go on. It was my grandmother's favorite song. I remember how we sang it at her funeral. She died when she was almost ninety. And I am moved now as I was then by the knowledge that we can take our pain, work with it, recycle it, and transform it so that it becomes a source of power.

Let me introduce to you my "brother," my comrade Cornel West.

C.W.: First I need to just acknowledge the fact that we as black people have come together to reflect on our past, present, and objective future. That, in and of itself, is a sign of hope. I'd like to thank the Yale African-American Cultural Center for bringing us together. bell and I thought it would be best to present in dialogical form a series of reflections on the crisis of black males and females. There is a state of siege raging now in black communities across this nation linked not only to drug addiction but also to consolidation of corporate power as we know it, and redistribution of wealth from the bottom to the top, coupled with the ways with which a culture and society centered on the market, preoccupied with consumption, erode structures of feeling, community, tradition. Reclaiming our heritage and sense of history are prerequisites to any serious talk about black freedom and black liberation in the twenty-first century. We want to try to create that kind of community here today, a community that we hope will be a place to promote understanding. Critical understanding is a prerequisite for any serious talk about coming together, sharing, participating, creating bonds of solidarity so that black people and other progressive people can continue to hold up the blood-stained banners that were raised when that song was sung in the civil rights movement. It was one of Dr. Martin Luther King's favorite songs, reaffirming his own struggle and that of many others who have tried to link some sense of faith, religious faith, political faith, to the struggle for freedom. We thought it would be best to have a dialogue to put forth analysis and provide a sense of what form a praxis would take. That praxis will be necessary for us to talk seriously about black power, black liberation in the twenty-first century.

b.h.: Let us say a little bit about ourselves. Both Cornel and I come to you as individuals who believe in God. That belief informs our message.

C.W.: One of the reasons we believe in God is due to the long tradition of religious faith in the black community. I think, that as a people who have had to deal with the absurdity of being black in America, for many of us it is a question of God and sanity, or God and suicide. And if you are serious about black struggle you know that in many instances you will be stepping out on nothing, hoping to land on something. That is the history of black folks in the past and present, and it continually concerns those of us who are willing to speak out with boldness and a sense of the importance of history and struggle. You speak knowing that you won't be able to do that for too long because America is such a violent culture. Given those conditions you have to ask yourself what links to a tradition will sustain you given the absurdity and insanity we are bombarded with daily. And so the belief in God itself is not to be understood in a noncontextual manner. It is understood in relation to a particular context, to specific circumstances.

b.h.: We also come to you as two progressive black people on the left.

C.W.: Very much so.

b.h.: I will read a few paragraphs to provide a critical framework for our discussion of black power, just in case some of you may not know what black power means. We are gathered to speak with one another about black power in the twenty-first century. In James Boggs's essay, "Black Power: A Scientific Concept Whose Time Has Come," first published in 1968, he called attention to the radical political significance of the black power movement, asserting: "Today the concept of black power expresses the revolutionary social force which must not only struggle against the capitalist but against the workers and all who benefit by and support the system which has oppressed us." We speak of black power in this very different context to remember, reclaim, re-vision, and renew. We remember first that the historical struggle for black liberation was forged by black women and men who were concerned about the collective welfare of black people. Renewing our commitment to this collective struggle should provide a grounding for new direction in contemporary political practice. We speak today of political partnership between black men and women. The late James Baldwin wrote in his autobiographical preface to *Notes of a Native Son:* "I think that the past is all that makes the present coherent and further that the past will remain horrible for as long as we refuse to accept it honestly." Accepting the challenge of this prophetic statement as we look at our contemporary past as black people, the space between the sixties and the nineties, we see a weakening of political solidarity between black men and women. It is crucial for the future black liberation struggle that we remain ever mindful that ours is a shared struggle, that we are each other's faith.

C.W.: I think we can even begin by talking about the kind of existentialist chaos that exists in our own lives and our inability to overcome the sense of alienation and frustration we experience when we try to create bonds of intimacy and solidarity with one another. Now part of this frustration is to be understood again in relation to structures and institutions. In the way in which our culture of consumption has promoted an addiction to stimulation—one that puts a premium on bottled commodified stimulation. The market does this in order to convince us that our consumption keeps oiling the economy in order for it to reproduce itself. But the effect of this addiction to stimulation is an undermining, a waning of our ability for qualitatively rich relationships. It's no accident that crack is the postmodern drug, that it is the highest form of addiction known to humankind, that it provides a feeling ten times more pleasurable than orgasm.

b.h.: Addiction is not about relatedness, about relationships. So it comes as no surprise that as addiction becomes more pervasive in black life it undermines our capacity to experience community. Just recently, I was telling someone that I would like to buy a little house next door to my parents' house. This house used to be Mr. Johnson's house but he recently passed away. And they could not understand why I would want to live near my parents. My explanation that my parents were aging did not satisfy. Their inability to understand or appreciate the value of sharing family life inter-generationally was a sign to me of the crisis facing our communities. It's as though as black people we have lost our understanding of the importance of mutual inter-dependency, of communal living. That we no longer recognize as valuable the notion that we collectively shape the terms of our survival is a sign of crisis.

C.W.: And when there is crisis in those communities and institutions that have played a fundamental role in transmitting to younger generations our values and sensibility, our ways of life and our ways of struggle, we find ourselves distanced, not simply from our predecessors but from the critical project of black liberation. And so more and more we seem to have young black people who are very difficult to understand, because it seems as though they live in two very different worlds. We don't really understand their music. Black adults may not be listening to NWA (Niggers With Attitude) straight out of Compton, California. They may not understand why they are doing what Stetsasonic is doing, what Public Enemy is all about, because young people have been fundamentally shaped by the brutal side of American society. Their sense of reality is shaped on the one hand by a sense of coldness and callousness, and on the other hand by a sense of passion for justice, contradictory impulses which surface simultaneously. Mothers may find it difficult to understand their children. Grandparents may find it difficult to understand us—and it's this slow breakage that has to be restored.

b.h.: That sense of breakage, or rupture, is often tragically expressed in gender relations. When I told folks that Cornel West and I were talking about partnership between black women and men, they thought I meant romantic relationships. I replied that it was important for us to examine the multi-relationships between black women and men, how we deal with fathers, with brothers, with sons. We are talking about all our relationships across gender because it is not just the heterosexual love relationships between black women and men that are in trouble. Many of us can't communicate with parents, siblings, etc. I've talked with many of you and asked, "What is it you feel should be addressed?" And many of you responded that you wanted us to talk about black men and how they need to "get it together."

Let's talk about why we see the struggle to assert agency—that is, the ability to act in one's best interest—as a male thing. I mean, black men are not the only ones among us who need to "get it together." And if black men collectively refuse to educate themselves for critical consciousness, to acquire the means to be self-determined, should our communities suffer, or should we not recognize that both black women and men must struggle for self-actualization, must learn to "get it together"? Since the culture we live in continues to equate blackness with maleness, black awareness of the extent to which our survival depends on mutual partnership between women and men is undermined. In renewed black liberation struggle, we recognize the position of black men and women, the tremendous role black women played in every freedom struggle.

Certainly Septima Clark's book *Ready from Within* is necessary reading for those of us who want to understand the historical development of sexual politics in black liberation struggle. Clark describes her father's insistence that she not fully engage herself in civil rights struggle because of her gender. Later, she found the source of her defiance in religion. It was the belief in spiritual community, that no difference must be made between the role of women and that of men, that enabled her to be "ready within." To Septima Clark, the call to participate in black liberation struggle was a call from God. Remembering and recovering the stories of how black women learned to assert historical agency in the struggle for self-determination in the context of community and collectivity is important for those of us who struggle to promote black liberation, a movement that has at its core a commitment to free our communities of sexist domination, exploitation, and oppression. We need to develop a political terminology that will enable black folks to talk deeply about what we mean when we urge black women and men to "get it together."

C.W.: I think again that we have to keep in mind the larger context of American society, which has historically expressed contempt for black men and black women. The very notion that black people are human beings is a new notion in Western civilization and is still not widely accepted in practice. And one of the consequences of this pernicious idea is that it is very difficult for black men and women to remain attuned to each other's humanity, so when bell talks about black women's agency and some of the problems black men have when asked to acknowledge black women's humanity, it must be remembered that this refusal to acknowledge one another's humanity is a reflection of the way we are seen and treated in the larger society. And it's certainly not true that white folks have a monopoly on human relationships. When we talk about a crisis in Western civilization, black people are a part of that civilization even though we have been beneath it, our backs serving as a foundation for the building of that civilization, and we have to understand how it affects us so that we may remain attuned to each other's humanity, so that the partnership that bell talks about can take on real substance and content. I think partnerships between black men and black women can be made when we learn how to be supportive and think in terms of critical affirmation.

b.h.: Certainly black people have not talked enough about the importance of constructing patterns of interaction that strengthen our capacity to be affirming.

C.W.: We need to affirm one another, support one another, help, enable, equip, and empower one another to deal with the present crisis, but it can't be uncritical, because if it's uncritical then we are again refusing to acknowledge other people's humanity. If we are serious about acknowledging and affirming other people's humanity then we are committed to trusting and believing that they are forever in process. Growth, development, maturation happens in stages. People grow, develop, and mature along the lines in which they are taught. Disenabling critique and contemptuous feedback hinders.

b.h.: We need to examine the function of critique in traditional black communities. Often it does not serve as a constructive force. Like we have that popular slang word "dissin'" and we know that "dissin'" refers to a kind of disenabling contempt—when we "read" each other in ways that are so painful, so cruel, that the person can't get up from where you have knocked them down. Other destructive forces in our lives are envy and jealously. These undermine our efforts to work for a collective good. Let me give a minor example. When I came in this morning I saw Cornel's latest book on the table. I immediately wondered why my book was not there and caught myself worrying about whether he was receiving some gesture of respect or recognition denied me. When he heard me say "Where's my book?" he pointed to another table.

Often when people are suffering a legacy of deprivation, there is a sense that there are never any goodies to go around, so that we must viciously compete with one another. Again this spirit of competition creates conflict and divisiveness. In a larger social context, competition between black women and men has surfaced around the issue of whether black female writers are receiving more attention than black male writers. Rarely does anyone point to the reality that only a small minority of black women writers are receiving public accolades. Yet the myth that black women who succeed are taking something away from black men continues to permeate black psyches and inform how we as black women and men respond to one another. Since capitalism is rooted in unequal distribution of resources, it is not surprising that we as black women and men find ourselves in situations of competition and conflict.

C.W.: I think part of the problem is deep down in our psyche we recognize that we live in such a conservative society, a society of business elites, a society in which corporate power influences are assuring that a certain group of people do get up higher.

b.h.: Right, including some of you in this room.

C.W.: And this is true not only between male and female relations but also black and brown relations and black and Korean, and black and Asian relations. We are struggling over crumbs because we know that the bigger part of lower corporate America is already received. One half of one percent of America owns twenty-two percent of the wealth, one percent owns thirty-two percent, and the bottom forty-five percent of the population has twenty percent of the wealth. So, you end up with this kind of crabs-in-the-barrel mentality. When you see someone moving up you immediately think they'll get a bigger cut in big-loaf corporate America and you think that's something real because we're still shaped by the corporate ideology of the larger context.

b.h.: Here at Yale many of us are getting a slice of that mini-loaf and yet are despairing. It was discouraging when I came here to teach and found in many black people a quality of despair which is not unlike that we know is felt in "crack neighborhoods." I wanted to understand the connection between underclass black despair and that of black people here who have immediate and/or potential access to so much material privilege. This despair mirrors the spiritual crisis that is happening in our culture as a whole. Nihilism is everywhere. Some of this despair is rooted in a deep sense of loss. Many black folks who have made it or are making it undergo an identity crisis. This is especially true for individual black people working to assimilate into the "mainstream." Suddenly, they may feel panicked, alarmed by the knowledge that they do not understand their history, that life is without purpose and meaning. These feelings of alienation and estrangement create suffering. The suffering many black people experience today is linked to the suffering of the past, to "historical memory." Attempts by black people to understand that suffering, to come to terms with it, are the conditions which enable a work like Toni Morrison's *Beloved* to receive so much attention. To look back, not just to describe slavery but to try and reconstruct a psycho-social history of its impact has only recently been fully understood as a necessary stage in the process of collective black self recovery.

C.W.: The spiritual crisis that has happened, especially among the well-to-do blacks, has taken the form of the quest for therapeutic release. So that you can get very thin, flat, and uni-dimensional forms of spirituality that are simply an attempt to sustain the well-to-do black folks as they engage in their consumerism and privatism. The kind of spirituality we're talking about is not the kind that remains superficial just physically but serves as an opium to help you justify and rationalize your own cynicism vis-à-vis the disadvantaged folk in our community. We could talk about churches and their present role in the crisis of America, religious faith as the American way of life, the gospel of health and wealth, helping the bruised psyches of the black middle class make it through America. That's not the form of spirituality that we're talking about. We're talking about something deeper—you used to call it conversion—so that notions of service and risk and sacrifice once again become fundamental. It's very important, for example, that those of you who remember the days in which black colleges were hegemonic among the black elite remember them critically but also acknowledge that there was something positive going on there. What was going on was that you were told every Sunday, with the important business of chapel, that you had to give service to the race. Now it may have been a petty bourgeois form, but it created a moment of accountability, and with the erosion of the service ethic the very possibility of putting the needs of others alongside of one's own diminishes. In this syndrome, me-ness, selfishness, and egocentricity become more and more prominent, creating a spiritual crisis where you need more psychic opium to get you over.

b.h.: We have experienced such a change in that communal ethic of service that was so necessary for survival in traditional black communities. That ethic of service has been altered by shifting class relations. And even those black folks who have little or no class mobility may buy into a bourgeois class sensibility; TV shows like "Dallas" and "Dynasty" teach ruling class ways of thinking and being to underclass poor people. A certain kind of bourgeois individualism of the mind prevails. It does not correspond to actual class reality or circumstances of deprivation. We need to remember the many economic structures and class politics that have led to a shift of priorities for "privileged" blacks. Many privileged black folks obsessed with living out a bourgeois dream of liberal individualistic success no longer feel as though they have any accountability in relation to the black poor and underclass.

C.W.: We're not talking about the narrow sense of guilt privileged black people can feel, because guilt usually paralyzes action. What we're talking about is how one uses one's time and energy. We're talking about the ways in which the black middle class, which is relatively privileged vis-à-vis the black working class, working poor, and underclass, needs to acknowledge that along with that privilege goes responsibility. Somewhere I read that for those to whom much is given, much is required. And the question becomes, "How do we exercise that responsibility given our privilege?" I don't think it's a credible notion to believe the black middle class will give up on its material toys. No, the black middle class will act like any other middle class in the human condition; it will attempt to maintain its privilege. There is something seductive about comfort and convenience. The black middle class will not return to the ghetto, especially given the territorial struggles going on with gangs and so forth. Yet, how can we use what power we do have to be sure more resources are available to those who are disadvantaged? So the question becomes "How do we use our responsibility and privilege?" Because, after all, black privilege is a result of black struggle.

I think the point to make here is that there is a new day in black America. It is the best of times and the worst of times in black America. Political consciousness is escalating in black America, among black students, among black workers, organized black workers and trade unions, increasingly we are seeing black leaders with vision. The black church is on the move, black popular music, political themes and motifs are on the move. So don't think in our critique we somehow ask you to succumb to a paralyzing pessimism. There are grounds for hope and when that corner is turned, and we don't know what particular catalytic event will serve as the take-off for it (just like we didn't know December 1955 would be the take-off), but when it occurs we have got to be ready. The privileged black folks can play a rather crucial role if we have a service ethic, if we want to get on board, if we want to be part of the progressive, prophetic bandwagon. And that is the question we will have to ask ourselves and each other.

b.h.: We also need to remember that there is a joy in struggle. Recently, I was speaking on a panel at a conference with another black woman from a privileged background. She mocked the notion of struggle. When she expressed, "I'm just tired of hearing about the importance of struggle; it doesn't interest me," the audience clapped. She saw struggle solely in negative terms, a perspective which led me to question whether she had ever taken part in any organized resistance movement. For if you have, you know that there is joy in struggle. Those of us who are old enough to remember segregated schools, the kind of political effort and sacrifice folks were making to ensure we would have full access to educational opportunities, surely remember the sense of fulfillment when goals that we struggled for were achieved. When we sang together "We shall overcome" there was a sense of victory, a sense of power that comes when we strive to be self-determining. When Malcolm X spoke about his journey to Mecca, the awareness he achieved, he gives expression to that joy that comes from struggling to grow. When Martin Luther King talked about having been to the mountain top, he was sharing with us that he arrived at a peak of critical awareness, and it gave him great joy. In our liberatory pedagogy we must teach young black folks to understand that struggle is process, that one moves from circumstances of difficulty and pain to awareness, joy, fulfillment. That the struggle to be critically conscious can be that movement which takes you to another level, that lifts you up, that makes you feel better. You feel good, you feel your life has meaning and purpose.

C.W.: A rich life is fundamentally a life of serving others, a life of trying to leave the world a little better than you found it. That rich life comes into being in human relationships. This is true at the personal level. Those of you who have been in love know what I am talking about. It is also true at the organizational and communal level. It's difficult to find joy by yourself even if you have all the right toys. It's difficult. Just ask somebody who has got a lot of material possessions but doesn't have anybody to share them with. Now that's at the personal level. There is a political version of this. It has to do with what you see when you get up in the morning and look in the mirror and ask yourself whether you are simply wasting time on the planet or spending time in an enriching manner. We are talking fundamentally about the meaning of life and the place of struggle. bell talks about the significance of struggle and service. For those of us who are Christians there are certain theological foundations on which our commitment to serve is based. Christian life is understood to be a life of service. Even so, Christians have no monopoly on the joys that come from service and those of you who are part of secular culture can also enjoy this sense of enrichment. Islamic brothers and sisters share in a religious practice which also places emphasis on the importance of service. When we speak of commitment to a life of service we must also talk about the fact that such a commitment goes against the grain, especially the foundations of our society. To talk this way about service and struggle we must also talk about strategies that will enable us to sustain this sensibility, this commitment.

b.h.: When we talk about that which will sustain and nurture our spiritual growth as a people, we must once again talk about the importance of community. For one of the most vital ways we sustain ourselves is by building communities of resistance, places where we know we are not alone. In *Prophetic Fragments*, Cornel began his essay on Martin Luther King by quoting the lines of the spiritual, "He promised never to leave me, never to leave me alone." In black spiritual tradition the promise that we will not be alone cannot be heard as an affirmation of passivity. It does not mean we can sit around and wait for God to take care of business. We are not alone when we build community together. Certainly there is a great feeling of community in this room today. And yet when I was here at Yale I felt that my labor was not appreciated. It was not clear that my work was having meaningful impact. Yet I feel that impact today. When I walked into the room a black woman sister let me know how much my teaching and writing had helped her. There's more of the critical affirmation Cornel spoke of. That critical affirmation says, "Sister, what you're doing is uplifting me in some way." Often folks think that those folks who are spreading the message are so "together" that we do not need affirmation, critical dialogue about the impact of all that we teach and write about and how we live in the world.

C.W.: It is important to note the degree to which black people in particular, and progressive people in general, are alienated and estranged from communities that would sustain and support us. We are often homeless. Our struggles against a sense of nothingness and attempts to reduce us to nothing are ongoing. We confront regularly the question: "Where can I find a sense of home?" That sense of home can only be found in our construction of those communities of resistance bell talks about and the solidarity we can experience within them. Renewal comes through participating in community. That is the reason so many folks continue to go to church. In religious experience they find a sense of renewal, a sense of home. In community one can feel that we are moving forward, that struggle can be sustained. As we go forward as black progressives, we must remember that community is not about homogeneity. Homogeneity is dogmatic imposition, pushing your way of life, your way of doing things onto somebody else. That is not what we mean by community. Dogmatic insistence that everybody think and act alike causes rifts among us, destroying the possibility of community. That sense of home that we are talking about and searching for is a place where we can find compassion, recognition of difference, of the importance of diversity, of our individual uniqueness.

b.h.: When we evoke a sense of home as a place where we can renew ourselves, where we can know love and the sweet communion of shared spirit, I think it's important for us to remember that this location of well-being cannot exist in a context of sexist domination, in a setting where children are the objects of parental domination and abuse. On a fundamental level, when we talk about home, we must speak about the need to transform the African-American home, so that there, in that domestic space, we can experience the renewal of political commitment to the black liberation struggle. So that there in that domestic space we learn to serve and honor one another. If we look again at the civil rights, at the black power movement, folks organized so much in homes. They were the places where folks got together to educate themselves for critical consciousness. That sense of community, cultivated and developed in the home, extended outward into a larger more public context. As we talk about black power in the twenty-first century, about political partnership between black women and men, we must talk about transforming our notions of how and why we bond. In *Beloved*, Toni Morrison offers a paradigm for relationships between black men and women. Sixo describes his love for Thirty-Mile Woman, declaring, "She is a friend of mind. She gather me, man. The pieces I am, she gather them and give them back to me in all the right order. It's good, you know, when you got a woman who is a friend of your mind." In this passage Morrison evokes a notion of bonding that may be rooted in passion, desire, even romantic love, but the point of connection between black women and men is that space of recognition and understanding, where we know one another so well, our histories, that we can take the bits and pieces, the fragments of who we are, and put them back together, remember them. It is this joy of intellectual bonding, of working together to create liberatory theory and analysis that black women and men can give one another, that Cornel and I give to each other. We are friends of one another's mind. We find a home with one another. It is that joy in community we celebrate and share with you this morning.

SPECULATIONS

1. How do bell hooks and Cornel West use the term "critical" in this essay? What are the different ways they use the term? For example, they talk about establishing a "critical framework" at the beginning, and later they say that affirming another's humanity "can't be uncritical" and that we need to struggle for "critical consciousness." What is so important about the notion of being critical here?
2. What does the slang term "dissin'" mean and how do bell hooks and Cornel West use it as a negative example of a certain attitude and kind of thinking?
3. What are the two kinds of religion that bell hooks and Cornel West talk about and how are they different?

4.   What is the tone of this dialogue? How does the tone, mood, and presentation of the information affect you as a reader? How would you describe the manner in which these two people are trying to appeal to their audience and what sense of authority and feeling are they communicating to their audience?
5.   Describe how community is defined and presented in this dialogue and compare it to your own sense and experience of community.

The Welder

CHERRÍE MORAGA

Cherríe Moraga is a writer who describes herself as "a very tired Chicana/half-breed/feminist/lesbian/writer/teacher/talker/waitress. And I am not alone in this. I am the first in my family to ever be published in a book. Of this, I am proud for all of us." Poet, playwright, and editor, Moraga is the co-founder of *Kitchen Table/Women of Color Press*, a New York press devoted to publishing the works of minority women.

This Bridge Called My Back: Writings by Radical Women of Color, winner of the 1986 American Book Award from the Before Columbus Foundation, is Moraga's best known work. This collection of poetry, fiction, and essays by women of color emphasizes the differences as well as similarities between feminists of different cultures, recognizing difference builds a "mutual respect far firmer than bland generalizations of sisterhood."

A native of Whittier, California, Moraga was born in 1952 and earned a B.A. and M.A. from San Francisco State. Moraga considers herself to be a woman-centered feminist rather than a separatist. Her first collection of poems, *Loving in the War Years: Lo Que Nunca Paso Por Sus Labios*, includes the essay "A Long Line of Vendidas," which critiques stereotypes of Chicano gender and sexuality. Both heterosexual and homosexual Chicanas, she says, must resist the cultural tendency to put men's needs ahead of their own.

The poem "The Welder" anchors itself in the power of the individual to heal society of its hatred and divisions—even if that healing is costly.

I am a welder.
Not an alchemist.
I am interested in the blend
of common elements to make
a common thing.

No magic here.
Only the heat of my desire to fuse
what I already know
exists. Is possible.

We plead to each other,
we all come from the same rock
we all come from the same rock
ignoring the fact that we bend
at different temperatures
that each of us is malleable
up to a point.

Yes, fusion *is* possible
but only if things get hot enough—
all else is temporary adhesion,
patching up.

It is the intimacy of steel melting
into steel, the fire of our individual
passion to take hold of ourselves
that makes sculpture of our lives,
builds buildings.

And I am not talking about skyscrapers,
merely structures that can support us
without fear
of trembling.

For too long a time
the heat of my heavy hands
has been smoldering
in the pockets of other
people's business—
they need oxygen to make fire.

I am now
coming up for air.
Yes, I *am*
picking up the torch.

I am the welder.
I understand the capacity of heat
to change the shape of things.
I am suited to work
within the realm of sparks
out of control.

I am the welder.
I am taking the power
into my own hands.

SPECULATIONS

1.   What does the image of "The Welder" represent in this poem? Is the metaphor appropriate? What does Moraga mean when she writes: "I am a welder/Not an alchemist."?
2.   What tension does Moraga exploit between society and the individual members of society? What do you think she means by:

> For too long a time
> the heat of my heavy hands
> has been smoldering
> in the pockets of other
> people's business—
> they need oxygen to make fire.

ASSIGNMENT SEQUENCES

Sequence One: Self, Others, and Personal Development

1. Gretel Ehrlich, Richard Selzer, Countee Cullen, Richard Rodriguez, and other authors in this section learn a great deal about themselves and their own identity through their relationships with others. Choose a specific incident in your life in which an encounter with one or more individuals left a lasting impression on you. It may be a very brief encounter in a few words, such as the poem "Incident" by Countee Cullen. Or it may be a more extended encounter such as the summer job experience Rodriguez describes near the end of his essay, "Complexion." Describe this experience and explore its meaning, especially your relationship with those who differ substantially from you. You might want to include observations about what you knew before and after the incident and about what you know now that helps you understand the incident more fully.

2. Imagine that you are Maxine Hong Kingston's aunt, the "No Name Woman." You know that you are going to jump into the well, killing yourself and your child. Before you do, however, you decide you must write a letter to your descendants, explaining how you feel and what you think about the events that have transpired. Write the letter. You may be angry, defiant, woeful, disturbed, or contrite. You may analyze the situation, focusing on the psychology and motivations behind the culture that condemned you. You may try to understand and forgive those who have wronged you. You may ask for forgiveness and understanding. You may explain what really happened—the true story that nobody in the village (except perhaps your lover) knows. Choose your story and stick to it, remembering that someday, others may need to know what you thought and felt in those last moments.

3. Using Maxine Hong Kingston's method of "talk-story," rewrite the essay you completed in assignment 1. Remember that the "talk-story" technique emphasizes oral storytelling with multiple accounts of the same experience, even contradictory versions of one event. You may want to put yourself in the position of some other person that you described or imagine yourself as a kind of outside narrator so you can offer variations of what happened or might have happened, what others might have thought or done. Your primary purpose is to create meaningful and provocative versions and interpretations.

4. According to Richard Selzer's essay, Hugh Franciscus is a man of science. He believes in the benefits of surgery and might be said to occupy a firm place at the center of a geometry of values which empha-sizes objectivity, reason, and the empirical. The story Selzer tells might best be described as one in which Dr. Franciscus suffers a break-down in logic. He loses something, but he also gains something.

In an essay, reflect on the influence of Imelda in the life and career of Dr. Franciscus. What does Imelda represent? Why does Dr. Fran-ciscus operate on her? If you choose, you may write this assignment as a letter from Dr. Franciscus to Richard Selzer, a letter that Selzer finds on Franciscus's desk just after his death.

5.   During adolescence, it is easy to feel pressures to conform to socie-tal norms. Richard Rodriguez's parents, for example, thrust their son toward a genteel, middle-class life of material and intellectual success; Maxine Hong Kingston's aunt, on the other hand, is ultimately crushed by the pressures of family and village. Other times the pres-sure can come from peers as we see in selections by Brent Staples and Roger Wilkins (or elsewhere in this book in essays by Nathan McCall, Donna Gaines, and Elizabeth Marek). At one time or another, every-one has felt like an outcast, isolated from family and community. In an essay, analyze a specific time when you (or someone close to you) experienced this sense of coming into conflict with the norms and pressures of society. What is at stake in such a struggle? How can such struggles be avoided—or at least mediated so they end in growth rather than frustration? As you write, draw upon several of the ac-counts in *Speculations* to support and expand your essay.

Sequence Two: Home

1.   A place called home is familiar to almost everyone. Sometimes it is a specific house, a neighborhood, a community. Sometimes it is the home of a relative, a loving grandparent, as we see in the bell hooks essay. Sometimes it is a landscape, such as Gretel Ehrlich's Wyoming.

In an essay that is both descriptive and analytical, offer your own version of home. Writing this essay may entail some research in the library or through interviews. Or it may simply emerge out of your memory. Anchor this home to a particular place. In your essay, ex-plain the qualities that make this place home to you.

2.   In another essay entitled "Homeplace," bell hooks writes:

> In our young minds houses belonged to women, were their special domain, not as property, but as places where all that truly mattered in life took place—the warmth and comfort of shelter, the feeding of our bodies, the nurturing of our souls. There we learned dignity, integrity of being; there we learned to have faith. The folks who

made this life possible, who were our primary guides and teachers, were black women.

Write a profile of a person who made home possible for you. It might be a parent, a neighbor, a friend. It might be a minister, a teacher, a store-owner. In your essay, analyze the person's qualities without idealizing them. Remember that no person is perfect; one of the strategies of a successful profile is to reveal all the facets of a person in order to make that individual a real human being.

3.   For some, public space is home. Some people are more comfortable in shopping malls than at home. An institution, such as a school or a hospital, can be a place of pleasant socialization and comfort, or of isolation and embarrassment. Choose a specific public place that you know well. Visit this place and observe what goes on for at least an hour. You might choose a hospital, the public library, a bus station, or a city street. You may visit this place more often, taking notes and speculating on what you observe about the physical locale and how people act in it. Write an essay that considers this public space in relation to the values of home that you developed in your previous essays. Consider what Staples says in his essay about how people can be vulnerable in public spaces and how some people alter public space.

4.   bell hooks and Cornel West describe a special sense of community as a "place where we can find compassion, recognition of difference, of the importance of diversity, of our individual uniqueness." Consider what they mean by this and their other descriptions of community. Consider what they mean when they describe the connection that must take place between people in order for this "space of understanding and recognition to take place." Using the issues of connecting with others brought up in this essay and other essays from this selection, write an essay about what a sense of community means to you, how you would define community, and which institutions and places help you to discover a "space of understanding and recognition" with others.

5.   Zora Neale Hurston claims, "I do not weep at the world—I am too busy sharpening my oyster knife," implying that if the world presents itself as closed tight to her she sets about finding ways to pry it open. She also writes that "the game of keeping is never so exciting as the game of getting."

In an essay, assess Hurston's exuberant attitude. Do you believe that a person can open closed spaces in society? Are Hurston's claims naïve and overly optimistic, or do they represent our one great possibility for creating change? In your essay, make use of relevant facts, stories, and ideas that you find in Hurston's own essay, from other reading selections in *Speculations,* and from your own experience.

6.   You have been asked to deliver a major speech at the University of Michigan at Ann Arbor, where Roger Wilkins went to school. Your speech is to be given to Undergraduates and is sponsored by a student action group called the Committee for the Improvement of Community and Student Participation on Campus. The president of this campus group explains that the members will have all read the article by Roger Wilkins and what they want to hear is your reaction to the Wilkins essay along with a subtext: namely, how a campus can become a home to students from varying ethnic, racial, and cultural backgrounds. In your speech, you can draw up experiences from your own campus as well as on any other reading or research you have done.

Sequence Three: Birth, Death, and Transformation

1.   Gretel Ehrlich's "Other Lives" deals with the death of her lover. At one point she says:

> because dying prunes so much away—everything extraneous, everything that has not been squeezed into paradox—we'd often lie on the floor wordlessly, holding hands, looking at the spectacle of the other, then break into uproarious laughter that convulsed into tears. There is no joke as big as death, we agreed.

Later, after David's death, she sees the carcass of a horse with its "stiff hide draped over the bones," and realizes "This was how I could wear death and still be alive." Ultimately, of course, she does in a sense "wear death" and eventually overcomes it, partly through friendships and new relationships.

Imagine that you are Gretel Ehrlich, living in Wyoming, recovering from David's death. It is close to autumn. One day while riding you discover "Hello!" scrawled in red dust. You decide to write a letter to the rancher to explain your feelings, your thoughts about the past and the future, and about relationships and possibilities. In the letter, try to remain true to Ehrlich's style and philosophy of life as expressed in "Other Lives."

2.   In the essay "Three Generations of Native American Women's Birth Experience," Joy Harjo describes how she felt on the way to deliver her first baby: "I knew my life was at the edge of great, precarious change and I felt alone and cheated. Where was the circle of women to acknowledge and honor this birth?" Write an essay which explores how Harjo works to rediscover her connection with her mother and daughter and how she finds a renewed sense of self in her relationship to her Native American culture. To help develop your essay, you may draw on your own history of growth and change to illuminate how you understand Harjo's experience of birth, renewal, and reconnection with family and cultural heritage.

3. You are the editor of a book entitled *Women, Birth, and Societal Values.* The argument of the book is that the values and attitudes that society has toward women and children are reflected in the ways that women are treated when they are giving birth. You have three possible selections in front of you: Kingston's "No Name Woman," Harjo's "Three Generations," and Hemingway's "Indian Camp." Unfortunately, your publisher insists that you only have room for one of these selections in the book. Which selection would you choose—and why? Write a rationale that will make your case.

4. Hemingway's story and Harjo's essay both describe the birth experience of Native American women attended by white doctors. Selzer's narrative similarly describes an American doctor's experience with mestizos (people of mixed Spanish and Indian blood) in Honduras. Like Hemingway, Selzer describes how a tragic and sudden death brings an individual to a moment of self-scrutiny and transformation. Consider how these birth and death experiences show two cultures in conflict. With these narratives in mind, go to the library and do some research on Native American stories, customs, and myths. You might also, if possible, go to a Native American Studies department to interview a professor about Native American culture. Write an essay that explores this theme of conflict and tension between two cultures as revealed in the narrative that you select.

5. Several essays in Self and Society suggest that society is changed when we transform ourselves first. Hurston insists that by changing her attitude and thinking, by maintaining a positive identity, she can transform the world. bell hooks and Cornel West urge others to change their thinking and thus transform their community. Write an essay using at least two selections from Self and Society or from another section of *Speculations* to argue how transformation of an individual can transform society; or you may choose to argue that individuals cannot change unless society changes at the same time. Cite specific examples from the essays that you choose and from your personal experience.

6. For this assignment, work with a peer collaborator or partner in your class. Using bell hooks's and Cornel West's dialogue as a model, you and your collaborator must write a dialogue about "Birth, Death, and Transformation within American Society." You will need to focus on some specific theme or issue: a problem discussed recently on television or in the newspaper, a subject that has been plaguing you lately about campus politics, and so on. If you wish, take an idea from the readings in this book. Your audience will include students and peers from your local community. You and your collaborator should be prepared to read your dialogue aloud in class.

Sequence Four: Self and Other

1. For this assignment, work with a partner in your class. Interview each other and then write biographies or profiles of one another. Ask your partner about the community values, cultural background, and school experiences that shaped his or her sense of belonging to social groups outside of his or her immediate family. Include any significant events, activities, or life changes that this person experienced. Write your profiles and exchange them with each other. Respond in writing, adding information, making suggestions, and commenting on ways that you think will improve the profile and make it more accurate or meaningful. Then, incorporating your partner's comments and suggestions, rewrite the profile.

2. Although Brent Staples may alter his space in more dramatic ways than most people, all of us have some impact on people around us. In an essay, speculate on what kind of power you possess to alter public space and the people in it. Assess how you alter it in different ways at different times. Examine whether you wish to alter it in ways other than you actually do. Use a public space that is not limited to your immediate environment.

3. Near the end of "Imelda," Richard Selzer describes how after showing the first slide of Imelda with her cleft palate, Dr. Franciscus hesitates, and Selzer removes the next slide from the projector so the audience will not see Imelda in the morgue with her palate fixed. Imagine yourself in Selzer's place, and in an analytical and speculative essay explain why you would or would not have acted the same way as Selzer did. Why did Selzer do this? What relationship between the doctor, this particular patient, and this professional audience causes Selzer to remove the slide? What does Selzer's action tell you about the doctor? About Selzer? About the practice of surgery? About relationships between doctors and patients? Consider these questions and your ideas in your essay.

4. Richard Rodriguez has frequently been attacked by members of the American Hispanic community for his views, for being against bilingualism and advocating that all children in this country should learn English (as opposed to learning both English and Spanish). He has been criticized for abandoning Hispanic culture and the Hispanic community. During a television interview with Bill Moyers, the following exchange occurred:

> RODRIGUEZ: You can be born again in this country. You can become a new man. You can even change your name. You can dye your hair. You can go to Muscle Beach and get a new body. . . . People always accuse me of having lost my culture, as though it was a little suitcase that I left in some train station back there. And I suppose I have, in the sense that I'm not my father. But that's inevitable I think. I belong to a different time. I belong to your culture.
> MOYERS: What do you mean "my culture"?
> RODRIGUEZ: That is to say, I'm an American. You know, I'm not a Mexican. I think of myself now as having been converted to America, and in that sense, I'm not a missionary from Mexico. . . . The pity of America I think is always that we don't understand just how enormously seductive we are to the world. . . . [America] is a culture. It is an idea. It is an advertisement. It's a lipstick. It's a Coke bottle.

Having read "Complexion" and other essays in this book by authors from a variety of cultural backgrounds, respond to Rodriguez and his critics in an essay that considers the relationship of self to American culture—and to other individuals within that culture. How should one maintain oneself in American culture? What is American culture anyway?

5. As a follow-up to assignment 4, focus specifically on the issue of race. Rodriguez's essay describes how his dark skin created a constant awareness of himself as different from white society. Zora Neale Hurston also describes feeling different as follows: "Among the thousand white persons, I am a dark rock surged upon, and overswept." She also describes how "Sometimes it is the other way around. A white person is set down in our midst, but the contrast is just as sharp for me." Using these authors' observations and examples from other essays in this section (and other sections), write an essay which discusses your understanding of racial difference in our society and how it creates a sense of otherness. Identify what is learned from that otherness—as made evident in a specific situation comedy on television: you might write about "The Cosby Show" or "In Living Color" or "All in the Family." Consider the roles that race and racial difference play in the ways that people are represented and the ways that self and society are represented.

6.   As a follow-up to assignment 5, imagine that you are a television producer who wants to create a television show on some issue of "self" and "other." You decide that the selections in this book offer more than enough possibilities. Choose one and offer a rationale for why you have chosen it and a brief description of what the show would be like, who would star in it, its setting, message, appeal, and so on. Write so as to persuade a television network to put your show on prime time.

Sequence Five: Self and Gender Differences

1.   What difference does gender make? In an essay, explore the different cultural expectations our society has for boys as opposed to girls. You might want to focus on kids' toys, or on kids' television programs, or on kids' clothing. Describe what differences exist, and how these differences affect you. What sexist or gender differences are important? Express your point of view; you will need to do some research to make this essay meaningful.

2.   Imagine that you are the doctor who just returned from the experience at Indian Camp that Hemingway writes about. Write a reflective essay on what you learned from that experience about Native Americans, about women and men, and about birth and death.

3.   Occasionally, writers disguise their identity. A number of years ago, John Howard Griffin, a white man, tinted his skin a dark-brown color to experience life as an African-American. He described this experience in *Black Like Me*. A young woman dressed up as a man for a week in New York City and described it in "My Life as a Man" (the *Village Voice*). For the purpose of this essay, imagine life as a member of the opposite sex. The title is "What My Life Would Be Like if I Were a _____ ." Write an essay grounded in an understanding of what it means to be a man or a woman in our society with specific references to a male or female point of view. Your essay may be humorous or serious. This is an opportunity to be someone else and to contend with everyday problems and conflicts that may now pass unnoticed.

4.   In "Other Lives," Gretel Ehrlich describes men and women whose identities are composed of both masculine and feminine qualities. Write an essay that discusses the ways that Ehrlich's descriptions of men and women sometimes cross over sexual barriers or even erase gender boundaries. Identify specific qualities of the women and men described in this narrative. Explain how these descriptions seem odd, familiar, likable, unlikable, or special in some way. If possible, read another essay from Ehrlich's *Solace of Open Spaces* entitled "About Men."

5.   Rodriguez discusses in detail three words that define the "proper" attributes of a man in Mexican culture. They are *feo* (rugged handsomeness), *fuerte* (inner strength and character), and *formal* (being responsible, sober, and a good provider). Write an essay in which you identify three or more terms in American culture that typically define what it means to be a man or to be a woman. Give a full explanation as to why these terms are essential to your definition of what it means to be a woman or a man.

6.   As a follow-up to assignments 3, 4, and 5, write an essay which analyzes and responds to bell hooks's and Cornel West's portrayal of the partnership between men and women. Consider carefully their argument that men's and women's critical awareness of each other must develop in order to transform the community they live in. What kinds of changes would you advocate? How would you make those changes? How can men and women overcome gender differences to solve problems like racism, pollution, homelessness, and so on? In your essay, focus on a specific set of problems or individuals.

5

WORK AND WEALTH

Work and Wealth is placed last in this book because working and acquiring some degree of wealth are two major concerns for students leaving the academic world to earn a living. Over the past thirty years, higher education has leaned toward vocational-technical curricula, as suggested by schools of nursing, engineering, business, and health. Many requirements have all but disappeared (foreign language, physical education, and literature, to name three), and have been replaced by preprofessional courses and intensive concentration in a single area of expertise. For many students, college is a means to an end—and that end is largely bound up in finding a job and making enough money to afford a house and some comforts.

The intent of this section is to raise an awareness about the nature of work and wealth in America, to compel some hard thinking about the choices that are available and the direction in which the country is heading. A brief statistical overview of the ownership of America is sobering. Cornel West (Self and Society section) reports on the distribution of wealth: "One half of one percent of America owns twenty-two percent of the wealth, one percent owns thirty-two percent, and the bottom forty-five percent of the population has twenty percent of the wealth."

Doug Henwood, in the *Nation* (September 9, 1991), informs us that worker productivity has stopped growing, that any recent increase in growth was due to harder work and longer hours, both of which contributed to a rise in the occupational injury rate of 35 percent over the last six years. Between 1969 and 1989, writes Henwood, the American work force added 138 hours a year of paid employment, yet the number of unemployed or underemployed workers has more than doubled in that same period of time.

What are some of the effects of America's problems with work and wealth? According to a feature in *Mother Jones* (May/June, 1991):

Families headed by women comprised 23% of all poor families in 1959; by 1988 that number had increased to 53%. Children in single-parent families are 5 times more likely to be poor as children born to married couples.

For young minority men and women, the jobless rate is close to 30%.

Federally funded job-training programs have been cut by 69% since 1981.

Nearly one out of two black children is defined as poor by federal poverty standards.

Fewer than half of U.S. 17-year-olds in high school have the reading, math, and science skills they need to perform entry-level jobs.

It is clear that the country needs to redefine the ways work and wealth are conceived if the majority of American citizens are to be genuine beneficiaries of the wealthiest country on earth. The editors feel that if democratic principles are to be preserved, meaningful work and material comfort—good jobs, food, education, health care, retirement—must be attainable for all American citizens. The selections in this section contribute to a dialogue about how this goal may be realized.

Economy and Pleasure

WENDELL BERRY

Wendell Berry is a poet, novelist, and essayist whose work reflects a concern with the preservation of the land. Born in 1934 in Henry County, Kentucky, Berry earned a B.A. and M.A. from the University of Kentucky, where he teaches English. He farms his own land, using traditional farming methods. According to Roland Sawyer, Berry "left his native hills and valleys for a time but returned in the conviction that in the surroundings to which a man is closest, which he loves and understands best, he makes his greatest contribution to his fellow men." But Berry is not simply a regionalist; his work is rooted in the land and in the values of older America.

Berry has published more than ten books of poetry, including *November Twenty-six Ninteen Hundred Sixty-Three*, *The Broken Ground*, and *A Place on Earth*, which includes the poem "Six Poems," the winner of the Bess Hokin Prize in 1967. He has published many collections of essays, including *A Continuous Harmony: Essays Cultural and Agricultural* and *The Unforseen Wilderness: An Essay on Kentucky's Red River Gorge*, which he wrote with Ralph Eugene Meatyard. His poems and essays have also appeared in many journals, such as the *Nation*, *New World Writing*, *New Directions Annual*, *Prairie Schooner*, *Contact*, *Chelsea Review*, and the *Quarterly Review of Literature*. In 1971, Berry won the National Institute of Arts and Letters literary award. Published in *Harper's*, this essay was delivered as a sermon to the congregation at New York City's Cathedral of St. John the Divine in 1987.

To those who still uphold the traditions of religious and political thought that influenced the shaping of our society and the founding of our government, it is astonishing, and of course discouraging, to see economics now elevated to the position of ultimate justifier and explainer of all the affairs of our daily life, and competition enshrined as the sovereign principle and ideal of economics.

As thousands of small farms and small local businesses of all kinds falter and fail under the effects of adverse economic policies or live under the threat of what we complacently call "scientific progress," the economist sits in the calm of professorial tenure and government subsidy, commenting and explaining for the illumination of the press and the general public. If those who fail happen to be fellow humans, neighbors, children of God, and citizens of the republic, all that is outside the purview of the economist. As the farmers go under, as communities lose their economic supports, as all of rural America sits as if condemned in the shadow of the "free market" and "revolutionary science," the economist announces pontifically to the press that "there will be some winners and some losers"—as if that might justify and clarify everything, or anything. The sciences, one gathers, mindlessly serve economics, and the humanities defer abjectly to the sciences. All assume, apparently, that we are in the grip of the determination of economic laws that are the laws of the universe. The newspapers quote the economists as the ultimate authorities. We read their pronouncements, knowing that the last word has been said.

"Science," President Reagan says, "tells us that the breakthroughs in superconductivity bring us to the threshold of a new age." He is speaking to "a federal conference on the commercial applications of the new technology," and we know that by "science" he means scientists in the pay of corporations. "It is our task at this conference," he says, "to herald in that new age with a rush." A part of his program to accomplish this task is a proposal to "relax" the antitrust laws.[1] Thus even the national executive and our legal system itself must now defer to the demands of "the economy." Whatever "new age" is at hand at the moment must be heralded in "with a rush" because of the profits available to those who will rush it in.

It seems that we have been reduced almost to a state of absolute economics, in which people and all other creatures and things may be considered purely as economic "units," or integers of production, and in which a human being may be dealt with, as John Ruskin put it, "merely as a covetous machine."[2] And the voices bitterest to hear are those saying that all this destructive work of mindless genius, money, and power is regrettable but cannot be helped.

Perhaps it cannot. Surely we would be fools if, having understood the logic of this terrible process, we assumed that it might not go on in its glutton's optimism until it achieves the catastrophe that is its logical end. But let us suppose that a remedy is possible. If so, perhaps the best beginning would be in understanding the falseness and silliness of the economic ideal of competition, which is destructive both of nature and of human nature because it is untrue to both.

The ideal of competition always implies, and in fact requires, that any community must be divided into a class of winners and a class of losers. This division is radically different from other social divisions: that of the more able and the less able, or that of the richer and the poorer, or even that of the rulers and the ruled. These latter divisions have existed throughout history and at times, at least, have been ameliorated by social and religious ideals that instructed the strong to help the weak. As a purely economic ideal, competition does not contain or imply any such instructions. In fact, the defenders of the ideal of competition have never known what to do with or for the losers. The

---

[1] "Reagan calls for effort to find commercial uses for superconductors," *Louisville Courier-Journal*, July 29, 1987, p. A3.
[2] John Ruskin, *Unto This Last* (Lincoln: University of Nebraska Press, 1967), p. 11.

losers simply accumulate in human dumps, like stores of industrial waste, until they gain enough misery and strength to overpower the winners. The idea that the displaced and dispossessed "should seek retraining and get into another line of work" is, of course, utterly cynical; it is only the hand-washing practiced by officials and experts.[3] A loser, by definition, is somebody whom nobody knows what to do with. There is no limit to the damage and the suffering implicit in this willingness that losers should exist as a normal economic cost.

The danger of the ideal of competition is that it neither proposes nor implies any limits. It proposes simply to lower costs at any cost, and to raise profits at any cost. It does not hesitate at the destruction of the life of a family or the life of a community. It pits neighbor against neighbor as readily as it pits buyer against seller. Every transaction is *meant* to involve a winner and a loser. And for this reason the human economy is pitted without limit against nature. For in the unlimited competition of neighbor and neighbor, buyer and seller, all available means must be used; none may be spared.

I will be told that indeed there are limits to economic competitiveness as now practiced—that, for instance, one is not allowed to kill one's competitor. But, leaving aside the issue of whether or not murder would be acceptable as an economic means if the stakes were high enough, it is a fact that the destruction of life is a part of the daily business of economic competitions as now practiced. If one person is willing to take another's property or to accept another's ruin as a normal result of economic enterprise, then he is willing to destroy that other person's life as it is and as it desires to be. That this person's biological existence has been spared seems merely incidental; it was spared because it was not worth anything. That this person is now "free" to "seek retraining and get into another line of work" signifies only that his life as it was has been destroyed.

But there is another implication in the limitlessness of the ideal of competition that is politically even more ominous: namely, that unlimited economic competitiveness proposes an unlimited concentration of economic power. Economic anarchy, like any other free-for-all, tends inevitably toward dominance by the strongest. If it is normal for economic activity to divide the community into a class of winners and a class of losers, then the inescapable implication is that the class of winners will become ever smaller, the class of losers ever larger. And that, obviously, is now happening; the usable property of our country, once divided somewhat democratically, is owned by fewer and fewer people every year. That the president of the republic can,

---

[3] Reed Karaim, "Loss of million farms in 14 years projected," *Des Moines Register*, March 18, 1986, p. 1A.

without fear, propose the "relaxation" of antitrust laws in order to "rush" the advent of a commercial "new age" suggests not merely that we are "rushing" toward plutocracy, but that this is now a permissible goal for the would-be winning class for which Mr. Reagan speaks and acts, and a burden acceptable to nearly everybody else.

Nowhere, I believe, has this grossly oversimplified version of economics made itself more at home than in the land-grant universities. The colleges of agriculture, for example, having presided over the now nearly completed destruction of their constituency—the farm people and the farm communities—are now scrambling to ally themselves more firmly than ever, not with "the rural home and rural life"[4] that were, and are, their trust, but with the technocratic aims and corporate interests that are destroying the rural home and rural life. This, of course, is only a new intensification of an old alliance. The revolution that began with machines and chemicals proposes now to continue with automation, computers, and biotechnology. That this has been and is a revolution is undeniable. It has not been merely a "scientific revolution," as its proponents sometimes like to call it, but also an economic one, involving great and profound changes in property ownership and the distribution of real wealth. It has done by insidious tendency what the communist revolutions have done by fiat: it has dispossessed the people and usurped the power and integrity of community life.

This work has been done, and is still being done, under the heading of altruism; its aims, as its proponents never tire of repeating, are to "serve agriculture" and to "feed the world." These aims, as stated, are irreproachable; as pursued, they raise a number of doubts. Agriculture, it turns out, is to be served strictly according to the rules of competitive economics. The aim is "to make farmers more competitive" and "to make American agriculture more competitive." Against whom, we must ask, are our farmers and our agriculture to be made more competitive? And we must answer, because we know: Against other farmers, at home and abroad. Now, if the colleges of agriculture "serve agriculture" by helping farmers to compete against one another, what do they propose to do to help the farmers who have been out-competed? Well, those people are not farmers anymore, and therefore are of no concern to the academic servants of agriculture. Besides, they are the beneficiaries of the inestimable liberty to "seek retraining and get into another line of work."

And so the colleges of agriculture, entrusted though they are to serve the rural home and rural life, give themselves over to a hysterical

---

[4] This is the language of the Hatch Act, *United States Code*, Section 361b.

rhetoric of "change," "the future," "the frontiers of modern science," "competition," "the competitive edge," "the cutting edge," "early adoption," and the like, as if there is nothing worth learning from the past and nothing worth preserving in the present. The idea of the teacher and scholar as one called upon to preserve and pass on a common cultural and natural birthright has been almost entirely replaced by the idea of the teacher and scholar as a developer of "human capital" and a bestower of economic advantage. The ambition is to make the university an "economic resource" in a competition for wealth and power that is local, national, and global. Of course, all this works directly against the rural home and rural life, because it works directly against community.

There is no denying that competitiveness is a part of the life both of an individual and of a community, or that, within limits, it is a useful and necessary part. But it is equally obvious that no individual can lead a good or a satisfying life under the rule of competition, and that no community can succeed except by limiting somehow the competitiveness of its members. One cannot maintain one's "competitive edge" if one helps other people. The advantage of "early adoption" would disappear—it would not be thought of—in a community that put a proper value on mutual help. Such advantages would not be thought of by people intent on loving their neighbors as themselves. And it is impossible to imagine that there can be any reconciliation between local and national competitiveness and global altruism. The ambition to "feed the world" or "feed the hungry," rising as it does out of the death struggle of farmer with farmer, proposes not the filling of stomachs, but the engorgement of "the bottom line." The strangest of all the doctrines of the cult of competition, in which admittedly there must be losers as well as winners, is that the result of competition is inevitably good for everybody, that altruistic ends may be met by a system without altruistic motives or altruistic means.

In agriculture, competitiveness has been based throughout the industrial era on constantly accelerating technological change—the very *principle* of agricultural competitiveness is ever-accelerating change—and this has encouraged an ever-accelerating dependency on purchased products, products purchased ever farther from home. Community, however, aspires toward stability. It strives to balance change with constancy. That is why community life places such high value on neighborly love, marital fidelity, local loyalty, the integrity and continuity of family life, respect for the old, and instruction of the young. And a vital community draws its life, so far as possible, from local sources. It prefers to solve its problems, for example, by non-monetary exchanges of help, not by buying things. A community cannot survive under the rule of competition.

But the land-grant universities, in espousing the economic determinism of the industrialists, have caught themselves in a logical absurdity that they may finally discover to be dangerous to themselves. If competitiveness is the economic norm, and the "competitive edge" the only recognized social goal, then how can these institutions justify public support? Why, in other words, should the public be willing to permit a corporation to profit privately from research that has been subsidized publicly? Why should not the industries be required to afford their own research, and why should not the laws of competition and the free market—if indeed they perform as advertised—enable industries to do their own research a great deal more cheaply than the universities can do it?

The question that we finally come to is a practical one, though it is not one that is entirely answerable by empirical methods: Can a university, or a nation, *afford* this exclusive rule of competition, this purely economic economy? The great fault of this approach to things is that it is so drastically reductive; it does not permit us to live and work as human beings, as the best of our inheritance defines us. Rats and roaches live by competition under the law of supply and demand; it is the privilege of human beings to live under the laws of justice and mercy. It is impossible not to notice how little the proponents of the ideal of competition have to say about honesty, which is the fundamental economic virtue, and how *very* little they have to say about community, compassion, and mutual help.

But what the ideal of competition most flagrantly and disastrously excludes is affection. The affections, John Ruskin said, are "an anomalous force, rendering every one of the ordinary political economist's calculations nugatory; while, even if he desired to introduce this new element into his estimates, he has no power of dealing with it; for the affections only become a true motive power when they ignore every other motive power and condition of political economy."[5] Thus, if we are sane, we do not dismiss or abandon our infant children or our aged parents because they are too young or too old to work. For human beings, affection is the ultimate motive, because the force that powers us, as Ruskin also said, is not "steam, magnetism, or gravitation," but "a Soul."

I would like now to attempt to talk about economy from the standpoint of affection—or, as I am going to call it, pleasure, advancing just a little beyond Ruskin's term, for pleasure is, so to speak, affection in action. There are obvious risks in approaching an economic prob-

---

[5] Ruskin, *Unto This Last*, p. 16.

lem by a way that is frankly emotional—to talk, for example, about the pleasures of nature and the pleasures of work. But these risks seem to me worth taking, for what I am trying to deal with here is the grief that we increasingly suffer as a result of the loss of those pleasures.

It is necessary, at the outset, to make a distinction between pleasure that is true or legitimate and pleasure that is not. We know that a pleasure can be as heavily debited as an economy. Some people undoubtedly thought it pleasant, for example, to have the most onerous tasks of their economy performed by black slaves. But this proved to be a pleasure that was temporary and dangerous. It lived by an enormous indebtedness that was inescapably to be paid not in money, but in misery, waste, and death. The pleasures of fossil fuel combustion and nuclear "security" are, as we are beginning to see, similarly debited to the future. These pleasures are in every way analogous to the self-indulgent pleasures of individuals. They are pleasures that we are allowed to have merely to the extent that we can ignore or defer the logical consequences.

That there is pleasure in competition is not to be doubted. We know from childhood that winning is fun. But we probably begin to grow up when we begin to sympathize with the loser—that is, when we begin to understand that competition involves costs as well as benefits. Sometimes perhaps, as in the most innocent games, the benefits are all to the winner and the costs all to the loser. But when the competition is more serious, when the stakes are higher and greater power is used, then we know that the winner shares in the cost, sometimes disastrously. In war, for example, even the winner is a loser. And this is equally true of our present economy; in unlimited economic competition, the winners are losers; that they may appear to be winners is owing only to their temporary ability to charge their costs to other people or to nature.

But a victory over community or nature can be won only at everybody's cost. For example, we now have in the United States many landscapes that have been defeated—temporarily or permanently—by strip mining, by clear-cutting, by poisoning, by bad farming, or by various styles of "development" that have subjugated their sites entirely to human purposes. These landscapes have been defeated for the benefit of what are assumed to be victorious landscapes: the suburban housing developments and the places of amusement (the park systems, the recreational wildernesses) of the winners—so far—in the economy. But these victorious landscapes and their human inhabitants are already paying the costs of their defeat of other landscapes: in air and water pollution, overcrowding, inflated prices, and various diseases of body and mind. Eventually, the cost will be paid in scarcity or want of necessary goods.

Is it possible to look beyond this all-consuming "rush" of winning and losing to the possibility of countrysides, a nation of countrysides, in which use is not synonymous with defeat? It is. But in order to do so we must consider our pleasures. Since we all know, from our own and our nation's experience, of some pleasures that are canceled by their costs, and of some that result in unredeemable losses and miseries, it is natural to wonder if there may not be such phenomena as *net* pleasures, pleasures that are free or without a permanent cost. And we know that there are. These are the pleasures that we take in our own lives, our own wakefulness in this world, and in the company of other people and other creatures—pleasures innate in the Creation and in our own good work. It is in these pleasures that we possess the likeness to God that is spoken of in Genesis.

"This curious world we inhabit is more wonderful than convenient; more beautiful than it is useful; it is more to be admired and enjoyed than used."[6] Henry David Thoreau said that to his graduating class at Harvard in 1837. We may assume that to most of them it sounded odd, as to most of the Harvard graduating class of 1987 it undoubtedly still would. But perhaps we will be encouraged to take him seriously, if we recognize that this idea is not something that Thoreau made up out of thin air. When he uttered it, he may very well have been remembering Revelation 4:11: "Thou art worthy, O Lord, to receive glory and honour and power; for thou hast created all things, and for thy pleasure they are and were created." That God created "all things" is in itself an uncomfortable thought, for in our workaday world we can hardly avoid preferring some things above others, and this makes it hard to imagine *not* doing so. That God created all things for His pleasure, and that they continue to exist because they please Him, is formidable doctrine indeed, as far as possible both from the "anthropocentric" utilitarianism that some environmentalist critics claim to find in the Bible and from the grouchy spirituality of many Christians.

It would be foolish, probably, to suggest that God's pleasure in all things can be fully understood or appreciated by mere humans. The passage suggests, however, that our truest and profoundest religious experience may be the simple, unasking pleasure in the existence of other creatures that *is* possible to humans. It suggests that God's pleasure in all things must be respected by us in our use of things, and even in our displeasure in some things. It suggests too that we

---

[6] *Familiar Letters of Henry David Thoreau*, ed. F. B. Sanborn (Boston and New York: Houghton Mifflin, 1894), p. 9.

have an obligation to preserve God's pleasure in all things, and surely this means not only that we must not misuse or abuse anything, but also that there must be some things and some places that by common agreement we do not use at all, but leave wild. This bountiful and lovely thought that all creatures are pleasing to God—and potentially pleasing, therefore, to us—is unthinkable from the point of view of an economy divorced from pleasure, such as the one we have now, which completely discounts the capacity of people to be affectionate toward what they do and what they use and where they live and the other people and creatures with whom they live.

It may be argued that our whole society is more devoted to pleasure than any whole society ever was in the past, that we support in fact a great variety of pleasure industries and that these are thriving as never before. But that would seem only to prove my point. That there can be pleasure industries at all, exploiting our apparently limitless inability to be pleased, can only mean that our economy is divorced from pleasure and that pleasure is gone from our workplaces and our dwelling places. Our workplaces are more and more exclusively given over to production, and our dwelling places to consumption. And this accounts for the accelerating division of our country into defeated landscapes and victorious (but threatened) landscapes.

More and more, we take for granted that work must be destitute of pleasure. More and more, we assume that if we want to be pleased we must wait until evening, or the weekend, or vacation, or retirement. More and more, our farms and forests resemble our factories and offices, which in turn more and more resemble prisons—why else should we be so eager to escape them? We recognize defeated landscapes by the absence of pleasure from them. We are defeated at work because our work gives us no pleasure. We are defeated at home because we have no pleasant work there. We turn to the pleasure industries for relief from our defeat, and are again defeated, for the pleasure industries can thrive and grow only upon our dissatisfaction with them.

Where is our comfort but in the free, uninvolved, finally mysterious beauty and grace of this world that we did not make, that has no price? Where is our sanity but there? Where is our pleasure but in working and resting kindly in the presence of this world?

And in the right sort of economy, our pleasure would not be merely an addition or by-product or reward; it would be both an empowerment of our work and its indispensable measure. Pleasure, Ananda Coomaraswamy said, *perfects* work. In order to have leisure and pleasure, we have mechanized and automated and computerized our work. But what does this do but divide us ever more from our work and our products—and, in the process, from one another and the world? What have farmers done when they have mechanized and computerized their farms? They have removed themselves and their pleasure from their work.

I was fortunate, late in his life, to know Henry Besuden of Clark County, Kentucky, the premier Southdown sheep breeder and one of the great farmers of his time. He told me once that his first morning duty in the spring and early summer was to saddle his horse and ride across his pastures to see the condition of the grass when it was freshest from the moisture and coolness of the night. What he wanted to see in his pastures at that time of year, when his spring lambs would be fattening, was what he called "bloom"—by which he meant not flowers, but a certain visible delectability. He recognized it, of course, by his delight in it. He was one of the best of the traditional livestockmen—the husbander or husband of his animals. As such, he was not interested in "statistical indicators" of his flock's "productivity." He wanted his sheep to be pleased. If they were pleased with their pasture, they would eat eagerly, drink well, rest, and grow. He knew their pleasure by his own.

The nearly intolerable irony in our dissatisfaction is that we have removed pleasure from our work in order to remove "drudgery" from our lives. If I could pick any rule of industrial economics to receive a thorough re-examination by our people, it would be the one that says that all hard physical work is "drudgery" and not worth doing. There are of course many questions surrounding this issue: What is the work? In whose interest is it done? Where and in what circumstances is it done? How well and to what result is it done? In whose company is it done? How long does it last? And so forth. But this issue is personal and so needs to be re-examined by everybody. The argument, if it is that, can proceed only by personal testimony.

I can say, for example, that the tobacco harvest in my own home country involves the hardest work that I have done in any quantity. In most of the years of my life, from early boyhood until now, I have taken part in the tobacco cutting. This work usually occurs at some time between the last part of August and the first part of October. Usually the weather is hot; usually we are in a hurry. The work is extremely demanding, and often, because of the weather, it has the character of an emergency. Because all of the work still must be done by hand, this event has maintained much of its old character; it is very much the sort of thing the agriculture experts have had in mind when they have talked about freeing people from drudgery.

That the tobacco cutting *can* be drudgery is obvious. If there is too much of it, if it goes on too long, if one has no interest in it, if one cannot reconcile oneself to the misery involved in it, if one does not like or enjoy the company of one's fellow workers, then drudgery would be the proper name for it.

But for me, and I think for most of the men and women who have been my companions in this work, it has not been drudgery. None of us would say that we take pleasure in all of it all of the time, but we do take pleasure in it, and sometimes the pleasure can be intense and clear. Many of my dearest memories come from these times of hardest work.

The tobacco cutting is the most protracted social occasion of our year. Neighbors work together; they are together all day every day for weeks. The quiet of the work is not much interrupted by machine noises, and so there is much talk. There is the talk involved in the management of the work. There is incessant speculation about the weather. There is much laughter; because of the unrelenting difficulty of the work, everything funny or amusing is relished. And there are memories.

The crew to which I belong is the product of kinships and friendships going far back; my own earliest associations with it occurred nearly forty years ago. And so as we work we have before us not only the present crop and the present fields, but other crops and other fields that are remembered. The tobacco cutting is a sort of ritual of remembrance. Old stories are re-told; the dead and the absent are remembered. Some of the best talk I have ever listened to I have heard during these times, and I am especially moved to think of the care that is sometimes taken to speak well—that is, to speak fittingly—of the dead and the absent. The conversation, one feels, is ancient. Such talk in barns and at row ends must go back without interruption to the first farmers. How long it may continue is now an uneasy question; not much longer perhaps, but we do not know. We only know that while it lasts it can carry us deeply into our shared life and the happiness of farming.

On many days we have had somebody's child or somebody's children with us, playing in the barn or around the patch while we worked, and these have been our best days. One of the most regrettable things about the industrialization of work is the segregation of children. As industrial work excludes the dead by social mobility and technological change, it excludes children by haste and danger. The small scale and the handwork of our tobacco cutting permit margins both temporal and spatial that accommodate the play of children. The children play at the grownups' work, as well as at their own play. In their play the children learn to work; they learn to know their elders and their country. And the presence of playing children means invariably that the grown-ups play too from time to time.

(I am perforce aware of the problems and the controversies about tobacco. I have spoken of the tobacco harvest here simply because it is the only remaining farm job in my part of the country that still involves a traditional neighborliness.)

Ultimately, in the argument about work and how it should be done, one has only one's pleasure to offer. It is possible, as I have learned again and again, to be in one's place, in such company, wild or domestic, and with such pleasure, that one cannot think of another place that one would prefer to be—or of another place at all. One does not miss or regret the past, or fear or long for the future. Being there is simply all, and is enough. Such times give one the chief standard and the chief reason for one's work.

Last December, when my granddaughter, Katie, had just turned five, she stayed with me one day while the rest of the family was away from home. In the afternoon we hitched a team of horses to the wagon and hauled a load of dirt for the barn floor. It was a cold day, but the sun was shining; we hauled our load of dirt over the tree-lined gravel lane beside the creek—a way well known to her mother and to my mother when they were children. As we went along, Katie drove the team for the first time in her life. She did very well, and she was proud of herself. She said that her mother would be proud of her, and I said that I was proud of her.

We completed our trip to the barn, unloaded our load of dirt, smoothed it over the barn floor, and wetted it down. By the time we started back up the creek road the sun had gone over the hill and the air had turned bitter. Katie sat close to me in the wagon, and we did not say anything for a long time. I did not say anything because I was afraid that Katie was not saying anything because she was cold and tired and miserable and perhaps homesick; it was impossible to hurry much, and I was unsure how I would comfort her.

But then, after a while, she said, "Wendell, isn't it fun?"

SPECULATIONS

1.   What is Berry's main argument about the relationship between work and pleasure in this article? Explain why you agree or disagree with this argument.

2.   Why does Berry say that it is "discouraging to see economics now elevated to the position of ultimate justifier and explainer of all the affairs of our daily life"? Explain what he means by this and why he sees it as destructive of certain values.

3.   What do you think Berry means by "pleasure industries"? How and why does he distinguish pleasures that are "true and legitimate" from pleasures that are "temporary and dangerous?" Give specific examples from this article and from your own notion of pleasure to support your explanation.

4. Based on Berry's concept of "work's pleasure," describe your own experiences of work and explain how those experiences either fulfill or contradict Berry's ideal.

5. Berry's essay was delivered as a sermon. What stories, words, and values does Berry use that should appeal to this particular audience?

Greenmarket

JOHN MCPHEE

"I write about what interests me at the moment" is how John McPhee chooses a subject. His interests are diverse. McPhee has written about everything from the Swiss military to the history, growth cycle, and processing of oranges. Although part of the appeal of McPhee's writing is its offbeat subject matter, his writing style is what transfixes his readers. *Time* magazine called *The Survival of the Bark Canoe* "part shop manual, part history, and part unforgettable character sketch." Many critics consider him the finest writer of journalistic nonfiction in America.

A staff writer for the *New Yorker*, McPhee's work has been collected into twenty-one books. The *New York Times Book Review* described McPhee's prose style as:

> Elegant without being elaborate, casual but never flippant, the prose always serves the material at hand, and combined with an obsession for detail . . . it enables [the author] to translate for the layman the mysteries that preoccupy professionals, be they athletes or engineers. He can reveal character in the description of a basketball toss, discover literary metaphors in the movement of subatomic particles.

In the *John McPhee Reader*, William Howarth outlines the steps of McPhee's composing process. McPhee starts by interviewing people related to the subject. As he asks questions, he tries to be as blank and ignorant as possible, in order to get "a solid, knotty answer." He then transcribes his interview notes and uses library research to fill in any gaps. He works through the notes until an organization discovers itself which he then arranges accordingly, and writes his way through the book, usually toward a last line that he has chosen at an early stage of the writing.

Born in Princeton, New Jersey, in 1931, McPhee earned a B.A. at Princeton University. He is a fellow in the Geological Society of America and has written two books on geology: *Basin and Range* (1981) and *In Suspect Terrain* (1983). Recipient of many literary awards, he won the the the award in literature from the American Academy and Institute of Arts and Letters in 1977 and the 1982 Woodrow Wilson Award from Princeton University.

In response to criticism about not writing about personal subjects, McPhee says:

> There are limitations everywhere you look. Critics may think I should be doing things on a grander scale and maybe I should be writing theological novels in Urdu. But fundamentally, I'm a working journalist and I've got to go out and work.

The following selection represents less than half of the original essay; it also has two internal cuts made with John McPhee's kind permission. The cuts are indicated by an ellipsis and three stars.

You people come into the market—the Greenmarket, in the open air under the downpouring sun—and you slit the tomatoes with your fingernails. With your thumbs, you excavate the cheese. You choose your stringbeans one at a time. You pulp the nectarines and rape the sweet corn. You are something wonderful, you are—people of the city—and we, who are almost without exception strangers here, are as absorbed with you as you seem to be with the numbers on our hanging scales.

"Does every sink grow on your farm?"

"Yes, ma'am."

"It's marvellous. Absolutely every sink?"

"Some things we get from neighbors up the road."

"You don't have no avocados, do you?"

"Avocados don't grow in New York State."

"Butter beans?"

"They're a Southern crop."

"Who baked this bread?"

"My mother. A dollar twenty-five for the cinnamon. Ninety-five cents for the rye."

"I can't eat rye bread anymore. I like it very much, but it gives me a headache."

Short, born abroad, and with dark hair and quick eyes, the woman who likes rye bread comes regularly to the Brooklyn Greenmarket, at Flatbush and Atlantic. I have seen her as well at the Fifty-ninth Street Greenmarket, in Manhattan. There is abundant evidence that she likes to eat. She must have endured some spectacular hangovers from all that rye.

Farm goods are sold off trucks, vans, and pickups that come into town in the dark of the morning. The site shifts with the day of the week: Tuesdays, black Harlem; Wednesdays, Brooklyn; Fridays, Amsterdam at 102nd. There are two on Saturdays—the one at Fifty-ninth Street and Second Avenue, the other in Union Square. Certain farms are represented everywhere, others at just one or two of the markets, which have been primed by foundation funds and developed under the eye of the city. If they are something good for the urban milieu—tumbling horns of fresh plenty at the people's feet—they are an even better deal for the farmers, whose disappearance from the metropolitan borders may be slowed a bit by the many thousands of city people who flow through streets and vacant lots and crowd up six deep at the trucks to admire the peppers, fight over the corn, and gratefully fill our money aprons with fresh green city lettuce.

"How much are the tomatoes?"

"Three pounds for a dollar."

"Peaches?"

"Three pounds for a dollar twenty-five."

"Are they freestones?"

"No charge for the pits."

"How much are the tomatoes?"

"Three pounds for a dollar. It says so there on the sign."

"Venver the eggs laid?"

"Yesterday."

"Kon you eat dum raw?"

We look up from the cartons, the cashbox, the scales, to see who will eat the eggs raw. She is a good-looking big-framed young blonde.

"You bet. You can eat them raw."

"How much are the apples?"

"Three pounds for a dollar."

Three pounds, as we weigh them out, are anywhere from forty-eight to fifty-two ounces. Rich Hodgson says not to charge for an extra quarter pound. He is from Hodgson Farms, of Newburgh, New York, and I (who come from western New Jersey) have been working for him off and on for three months, summer and fall. I thought at first that I would last only a week, but there is a mesmerism in the selling, in the coins and the bills, the all-day touching of hands. I am often in charge of the peppers, and, like everyone else behind the tables by our truck, I can look at a plastic sack of them now and tell its weight.

"How much these weigh? Have I got three pounds?"

"That's maybe two and a quarter pounds you've got there."

"Weigh them, please."

"There it is. Two and a quarter pounds."

"*Very* good."

"Fantastic! Fantastic! You see that? You see that? He knew exactly how much it weighed."

I scuff a boot, take a break for a shiver in the bones. There are unsuspected heights in this game, moments that go right off the scale.

This is the Brooklyn market, in appearance the most cornucopian of all. The trucks are drawn up in a close but ample square and spill into its center the colors of the country. Greengage plums. Ruby Red onions. Yellow crookneck squash. Sweet white Spanish onions. Starking Delicious plums.

Fall pippins ("Green as grass and curl your teeth"). McIntoshes,

Cortlands, Paulareds. ("Paulareds are new and are lovely apples. I'll bet they'll be in the stores in the next few years.")

Pinkish-yellow Gravensteins. Gold Star cantaloupes. Patty Pan squash.

Burpless cucumbers.

Cranberry beans.

Silver Queen corn. Sweet Sue bicolor corn, with its concise tight kernels, its well-filled tips and butts. Boston salad lettuce. Parris Island romaine lettuce. Ithaca iceberg crunchy pale lettuce. Orange tomatoes.

Cherry Bell tomatoes.

Moreton Hybrid, Jet Star, Setmore, Supersonic, Roma, Saladette tomatoes.

Campbell 38s.

Campbell 1327s.

Big Boy, Big Girl, Redpak, Ramapo, Rutgers London-broil thick-slice tomatoes.

Clean-shouldered, supple-globed Fantastic tomatoes. Celery (Imperial 44).

Hot Portugal peppers. Four-lobed Lady Bell glossy green peppers. Aconcagua frying peppers.

Parsley, carrots, collard greens.

Stuttgarter onions, mustard greens.

Dandelions.

The people, in their throngs, are the most varied we see—or that anyone is likely to see in one place west of Suez. This intersection is the hub if not the heart of Brooklyn, where numerous streets converge, and where Fourth Avenue comes plowing into the Flatbush-Atlantic plane. It is also a nexus of the race. "Weigh these, please." "Will you please weigh these?" Greeks. Italians. Russians. Finns. Haitians. Puerto Ricans. Nubians. Muslim women in veils of shocking pink. Sunnis in total black. Women in hiking shorts, with babies in their backpacks. Young Connecticut-looking pants-suit women. Their hair hangs long and as soft as cornsilk. There are country Jamaicans, in loose dresses, bandannas tight around their heads. "Fifty cents? Yes, dahling. Come on a sweetheart, mon." There are Jews by the minyan, Jews of all persuasions—white-bearded, black-bearded, split-bearded Jews. Down off Park Slope and Cobble Hill come the neo-bohemians, out of the money and into the arts. "Will you weigh this tomato, please?" And meantime let us discuss theatre, books, environmental impacts. Maybe half the crowd are men—men in cool Haspel cords and regimental ties, men in lipstick, men with blue eyelids. Corporate-echelon pinstripe men. Their silvered hair is perfect in coif; it appears to have been audited. Easygoing old neighborhood men with their shirts hanging open in the summer heat are walking galleries of abdominal and thoracic scars—Brooklyn Jewish Hospital's bastings and tackings. . . .

* * *

On a sidewalk around the corner, people with a Coleman stove under a fifty-five-gallon drum are making sauce with our tomatoes. Tall black man in a business suit now picks up a slim hot pepper. Apparently he thinks it sweet, because he takes most of it with a single bite and chews it with anticipant relish. Three . . . two . . . one. The small red grenade explodes on his tongue. His eyeballs seem to smoke. By the fistful, he grabs cool stringbeans and stuffs them into his mouth.

I forget to give change to a middle-aged woman with bitter eyes. I charged her forty-five cents for a pound and a third of apples and she gave me half a dollar. Now she is demanding her nickel, and her eyes are narrower than the sides of dimes. She is a round-shouldered person, beaky and short—short-changed. In her stare at me, there is an entire judiciary system—accusation, trial, and conviction. "You give me my nickel, mister."

"I'm sorry. I forgot. Here is your nickel."

She does not believe my mistake a mistake. She walks away in a white huff. Now she stops, turns, glowers. She moves on. Twice more, as she departs from the market, she stops, turns, and stares angrily back. I watch her all the way to the curb. She waves at the traffic and gets into a cab.

A coin will sink faster through bell peppers than it will through water. When people lose their money they go after it like splashing bears. Peppers everywhere. Peppers two deep over the apples, three deep over the plums. Peppers all over the ground. Sooner or later, the people who finger the eggs will spill and break the eggs, and the surface they walk on becomes a gray-and-yellow slurry of parking-lot gravel and egg—a Brooklyn omelette. Woman spills a dozen now. Her purse is hanging open and a falling egg plops in. Eleven smash on the ground. She makes no offer to pay. Hodgson, who is young and whimsical, grins and shrugs. He is not upset. He is authentically amused. Always, without a sign of stress, he accepts such losses. The customer fingers another dozen eggs, and asks if we are sure they are good.

I err again, making change—count our four ones, and then a five, "and ten makes twenty."

The customer says, "I gave you a ten-dollar bill, not a twenty."

I look at her softly, and say to her, "Thanks very much. You're very nice."

"What do you mean I'm very nice? I gave you a ten-dollar bill. Why does that make me very nice?"

"I meant to say I'm glad you noticed. I'm really glad you noticed."

"How much are the tomatoes?"

"Weigh these, please."

"Three pounds for a dollar."

"How much the corn?"

"Ten cents an ear. Twelve for a dollar."

"Everything is so superior. I'd forgotten what tomatoes taste like."

"Will you weigh these, please?"

"The prices are so ridiculously cheap."

"How can you charge so little?"

"In nine years in the city, I've never seen food like this."

"How much are these?"

"Fifty-five cents."

"Wow! What a rip-off!"

"Three pounds for a dollar is too much for tomatoes. You know that, don't you? I don't care how good they are."

"How much are these?"

"A dollar-ten."

"A dollar-*ten*?"

"Three eggplants. Three and a half pounds. Three pounds for a dollar. You can have them for a dollar-ten."

"Keep them."

"In the supermarket, the vegetables are unspeakable."

"They are brought in from California."

"You can't see what you are getting."

"When the frost has come and you are gone, what will we do without you?"

Around the market square, some of the trucks have stickers on them: "NO FARMERS, NO FOOD." Alvina Frey is here, and Ronald Binaghi, from farms in Bergen County, New Jersey. John Labanowski and his uncle Andy Labanowski are from the black-dirt country, the mucklands, of Orange County, New York. Bob Engle and Kim Kent tend orchards in the Hudson Valley. Bill Merriman, the honey man, is from Canaan, Connecticut; Joan Benack and Ursula Plock, the bakers, from Milan, New York. Ed and Judy Dart grow "organic" on Long Island, Richard Finch in Frenchtown, New Jersey. John Henry. Vincent Neglia. Ilija Sekulovski. Don Keller. Cleather Slade completes the ring. Slade is young, tall, paunchy, silent, and black. His wife, Dorothy, sells with him. She has a nicely lighted smile that suggests repose. Their family farmland is in Red Springs, North Carolina, but the Slades are mainly from Brooklyn. They make occasional trips South for field peas, collards, okra, yams, and for the reddest watermelons north of Chichicastenango.

Jeffrey Mack works for Hodgson part time. He has never seen a farm. He says he has never been out of the city. He lives five blocks away. He is eight years old, black. He has a taut, hard body, and glittering eyes, a round face. He piles up empty cartons for us and sometimes weighs tomatoes. On his better days he is some help.

"Jeffrey, that's enough raisin bread."

"Jeffrey, how many times do I have to tell you: get yourself out of the way."

"What are you doing here, Jeffrey? You ought to be in school."

He is not often pensive, but he is pensive for a moment now. "If you had a kid would you put him up for adoption?" he asks.

"What is that supposed to mean, Jeffrey? Why are you asking me that?"

"My mother says she's going to put me up for adoption."

With two, three, and four people working every truck, the farmers can occasionally take breaks, walk around—eat each other's apples, nectarines, and pears. Toward the end of the day, when their displays have been bought low and the crowd is becoming thin, they move around even more, and talk in small groups.

"What always surprises me is how many people are really nice here in the city."

"I was born in New York. My roots are here, you know. I'd throw away a bad cantaloupe, anything, so the people would come back."

"We have to leave them touch tomatoes, but when they do my guts go up and down. They paw them until if you stuck a pin in them they'd explode."

"They handle the fruit as if they were getting out all their aggressions. They press on the melons until their thumbs push through. I don't know why they have to handle the fruit like that. They're brutal on the fruit."

"They inspect each egg, wiggle it, make sure it's not stuck in the carton. You'd think they were buying diamonds."

"They're bag crazy. They need a bag for everything, sometimes two."

"They're nervous. So nervous."

"Today I had my third request from someone who wanted to come stay on the farm, who was looking for peace and quiet for a couple of days. He said he had found Jesus. It was unreal."

"I had two Jews in yarmulkes fighting over a head of lettuce. One called the other a kike."

"I've had people buy peppers from me and take them to another truck to check on the weight."

"Yeah, and meanwhile they put thirteen ears of corn in a bag, hand it to you, and say it's a dozen. I let them go. I only get after them when they have sixteen."

"They think we're hicks. 'Yeah,' I say. 'We're hicks and you're hookers. You're muggers and you breathe dirty air.'"

"I hardly smoke in the city. Down home I can smoke a whole pack of cigarettes and still have energy all night. You couldn't pay me to live here. I can't breathe."

If the farmers have a lot to say about their clients, they have even more to say about each other. Friendly from the skin out, they are deep competitors, and one thing that they are (in a sense) competing for is their right to be a part of the market. A high percentage of them seems to feel that a high percentage of the others should be shut down and sent away.

The Greenmarket was started in 1976. Farmers were recruited. Word got around. A wash of applicants developed. There was no practical or absolute way to check out certain facts about them—nor is there yet. For example, if some of the goods on a truck were not grown by the farmer selling them, who did grow them, and when, and where? The Greenmarket quickly showed itself to be a prime outlet for the retailing of farm produce. On a good day, one truck with an eighteen-foot box could gross several thousand dollars. So every imaginable kind of seller became attracted. The ever-present problem was that anyone in jeans with a rustic address painted on his truck could load up at Hunts Point, the city's wholesale fruit-and-vegetable center, and head out at 5 A.M. for the Greenmarket—a charter purpose of which was to help the regional farmer, not the fast-moving speculator, survive. Authentic farmers, moreover, could bring a little from home and a lot from Hunts Point. Wholesale goods, having been grown on big mass-production acreages (and often shipped in underripe from distant states), could be bought at Hunts Point and retailed—in some instances—at lower prices than the custom-grown produce of a small Eastern farm. Prices, however, were an incidental issue. The customers, the people of the city, believed—and were encouraged to believe—that when they walked into a Greenmarket they were surrounded by true farmers who had grown the produce they displayed and were offering it fresh from the farm. That was the purpose and promise of the Greenmarket—if not the whole idea, an unarguably large part of it—and in the instances where wholesale, long-distance, gassed-out goods were being presented (as some inevitably were) the principle was being subverted. In fact, the term Greenmarket had been coined—and registered in Albany—to set apart these markets in the public mind from certain "farmers' markets" around the city that are annually operated by Hunts Point hicks.

"Are you a farmer, or are you buying from an auction?" was a challenge the farmers began to fling around. Few were neighbors at home—in positions to know about each other. They lived fifty, a hundred, a hundred and fifty miles apart, and came to the city to compete as strangers. They competed in sales, and they competed in slander. They still do. To a remarkable—and generally inaccurate—extent, they regard one another as phonies.

"He doesn't even know what shoe-peg corn is."

"Never trust a farmer who doesn't know shoe-peg corn."

"What exactly is shoe-peg corn?"

"Look at *him*. He has clean fingernails."

"I happen to know he has them manicured."

"I bust my hump seven days a week all summer long and I don't like to see people bring to market things they don't grow."

"Only farmers who are not farmers can ruin this market."

"These hustlers are going to work us off the block."

"There's farmers selling stuff they don't know what it is."

"What exactly is shoe-peg corn?"

"I like coming here. It gets me out of Vineland. Of course, you pick your ass off the night before."

"Look at Don Keller's hands. You can see the farm dirt in them."

"His nails. They'll never be clean."

"Rich Hodgson. See him over there? He has the cleanest fingernails in New York State."

"That Hodgson, he's nice enough, but he doesn't know what a weed looks like. I'll tell you this: he's never even *seen* a weed."

Around the buildings of Hodgson Farms are some of the tallest volunteers in New York, topheavy plants that sway overhead—the Eastern rampant weed. With everybody working ninety hours a week, there is not much time for cosmetics. For the most part, the buildings are chicken houses. Rich's father, Dick Hodgson, went into the egg business in 1946 and now has forty thousand hens. When someone in the city cooks a Hodgson egg, it has quite recently emerged from a chicken in a tilted cage, rolled onto a conveyor, and gone out past a candler and through a grader and into a waiting truck. A possible way to taste a fresher egg would be to boil the chicken with the egg still in it.

Dick Hodgson—prematurely white-haired, drivingly busy—is an agrarian paterfamilias whose eighty-two-year-old mother-in-law grades tomatoes for him. His wife, Frances, is his secretary and book-keeper. He branched into truck farming some years ago specifically to keep his daughter, Judy, close to home. Judy runs the Hodgsons' roadside stand, in Plattekill, and her husband, Jan Krol, is the family's vegetable grower, the field boss—more than a hundred acres now under cultivation. Rich, meanwhile, went off to college and studied horticulture, with special emphasis on the fate of tropical houseplants. To attract him home, his father constructed a greenhouse, where Rich now grows wandering Jews, spider plants, impatiens, coleus, asparagus ferns—and he takes them with him to Harlem and wherever else he is allowed to sell them. Rich, who likes the crowds and the stir of the city, is the farm's marketer. . . .

* * *

Rich is in his mid-twenties, has a tumbling shag of bright-red hair, a beard that comes and goes. When it is gone, as now, in the high season of 1977, he retains not only a mustache but also a pair of frontburns: a couple of pelts that descend from either end of the mustache and pass quite close to his mouth on their way to his chin. He is about six feet tall and wears glasses. Their frames are pale blue. His energy is of the steady kind, and he works hard all day with an easygoing imperturbability—always bemused; always a controlled, sly smile. Rarely, he looks tired. On market days, he gets up at four, is on the Thruway by five, is setting up tables and opening cartons at seven, has a working breakfast around nine (Egg McMuffin), and, with only a short break, sells on his feet until six or seven, when he packs up to drive home, take a shower, drop into bed, and rise again at four. His companion, Melissa Mousseau, shares his schedule and sells beside him. There is no market on Mondays, so Rich works a fourteen-hour day at home. He packs cartons at the farm—cartons of cauliflowers, cartons of tomatoes—and meanders around the county collecting a load for Harlem. The truck is, say, the six-ton International with the Fruehauf fourteen-foot box—"HODGSON FARMS, NEWBURGH, N.Y., SINCE 1946." Corn goes in the nose—corn in dilapidating lath-and-wire crates that are strewn beside the fields where Jan has been bossing the pickers. The pickers are Newburgh high-school students. The fields, for the most part, are rented from the State of New York. A few years ago, the state bought Stewart Air Force Base, outside Newburgh, with intent to lengthen the main runway and create an immense international freightport, an all-cargo jetport. The state also bought extensive farms lying off the west end of the base. Scarcely were the farmers packed up and on the road to Tampa Bay when bulldozers flattened their ancestral homes and dump trucks took off with the debris. The big freightport is still in the future, and meanwhile the milieu of the vanished farms is ghostly with upgrowing fields and clusters of shade trees around patches of smoothed ground where families centered their lives. The Hodgsons came upon this scene as farmers moving in an unusual direction. With the number of farms and farmers in steady decline in most places on the urban fringe, the Hodgsons were looking for land on which to expand. For the time being, rented land will do, but they hope that profits will be sufficient to enable them before long to buy a farm or two—to acquire land that would otherwise, in all likelihood, be industrially or residentially developed. The Greenmarket is the outlet—the sole outlet—that has encouraged their ambition. In the penumbral world of the airport land, there are occasional breaks in the sumac where long clean lines of Hodgson peppers reach to distant hedgerows, Hodgson canta-loupes, Hodgson cucumbers, Hodgson broccoli, collards, eggplants, Hodgson tomatoes, cabbages, corn—part vegetable patch, part disen-franchised farm, and a tractor, a sprayer, and a spreader housed not in sheds and barns but under big dusty maples. The family business is integrated by the spreader, which fertilizes the Greenmarket vegeta-bles with the manure of the forty thousand chickens.

Corn in the nose, Rich drives to the icehouse, where he operates a machine that grinds up a three-hundred-pound block and sprays granulated snow all over the corn. Corn snow. He stops, too, at local orchards for apples, Seckel pears, nectarines, peaches, and plums. The Greenmarket allows farmers to amplify their offerings by bringing the produce of neighbors. A neighbor is not a wholesale market but another farmer, whose farm is reasonably near—a rule easier made than enforced. The Hodgsons pick things up—bread included—from several other farms in the county, but two-thirds to three-quarters of any day's load for the city consists of goods they grow themselves.

In the cooler of E. Borchert & Sons, the opiate aroma of peaches is overwhelming, unquenched by the refrigerant air. When the door opens, it frames, in summer heat, hazy orchards on ground that falls away to rise again in far perspective, orchards everywhere we can see. While loading half-bushel boxes onto the truck, we stop to eat a couple of peaches and half a dozen blue free plums. Not the least of the pleasures of working with Hodgson is the bounty of provender at hand, enough to have made the most sybaritic Roman prop himself up on one elbow. I eat, most days, something like a dozen plums, four apples, seven pears, six peaches, ten nectarines, six tomatoes, and a green pepper.

Eating his peach, Rich says, "The people down there in the city can't imagine this. They don't believe that peaches come from New-burgh, New York. They say that peaches come only from Georgia. People in the city have no concept of what our farming is like. They have no idea what a tomato plant looks like, or how a tomato is picked. They can't envision a place with forty thousand chickens. They have no concept how sweet corn grows. And the people around here have a false concept of the city. Before we went down there the first time, people up here said, 'You're out of your mind. You're going to get robbed. You're going to get stabbed.' But I just don't have any fears there. People in black Harlem are just as nice as people anywhere. City people generally are a lot calmer than I expected. I thought they would be loud, pushy, aggressive, and mean. But eighty per cent of them are nice and calm. Blacks and whites get along much better there then they do in Newburgh. Newburgh Free Academy, where I went to high school, was twenty-five per cent black. We had riots every year and lots of tension. Cars were set on fire. Actually, I prefer Harlem to most of the other markets. Harlem people are not so fussy. They don't manhandle the fruit. And they buy in quantity. They'll buy two dozen ears of corn, six pounds of tomatoes, and three dozen eggs. At Fifty-ninth Street, someone will buy one ear of corn for ten cents and want it in a bag. The reason we're down there is the money, of course. But the one-to-one contact with the people is really good—especially when they come back the next week and say, 'Those peaches were really delicious.'"

In the moonless night, with the air too heavy for much sleep anyway, we are up and on the road, four abreast: Anders Thueson, Rich Hodgson, David Hemingway . . . A door handle is cracking my fifth right rib. Melissa Mousseau is not with us today, and for Hemingway it is the first time selling. He is a Newburgh teen-ager in sneakers and a red football shirt lettered "OKLAHOMA." Hemingway is marking time. He has mentioned January half a dozen ways since we started out, in a tone that reveres the word—January, an arriving milestone in his life, with a college out there waiting for him, and, by implication, the approach of stardom. Hemingway can high-jump seven feet. He remarks that the Greenmarket will require endurance and will therefore help build his stamina for January. He is black, and says he is eager to see Harlem, to be "constantly working with different people—that's a trip in the head by itself."

When the truck lurches onto the Thruway and begins the long rollout to the city, Hodgson falls asleep. Anders Thueson is driving. He is an athlete, too, with the sort of legs that make football coaches whistle softly. Thueson has small, fine features, light-blue eyes, and short-cropped hair, Scandinavian yellow. He is our corn specialist, by predilection—would apparently prefer to count ears than to compute prices from weights. When he arrives in Harlem he will touch his toes and do deep knee bends to warm himself up for the corn.

Dawn is ruddy over Tappan Zee, the far end of the great bridge indistinct in mist. Don Keller, coming from Middletown, broke down on the bridge not long ago, rebuilt his starter at the toll-booth apron, and rolled into market at noon. Days later, Jim Kent's truck was to-talled on the way to Greenmarket—Hudson Valley grapes, apples, peaches, and corn all over the road. Gradually now, Irvington and Dobbs Ferry come into view across the water—big square houses of the riverbank, molars, packed in cloud. In towns like that, where somnolence is the main resource, this is the summit of the business day. Hodgson wakes up for the toll. For five minutes he talks sports and vegetable prices, and again he dozes away. On his lap is a carton of double-yolk eggs. His hands protect them. The fingernails are clean. Hodgson obviously sees no need to dress like Piers Plowman. He wears a yellow chemise Lacoste. The eggs are for Derryck Brooks-Smith, a Brooklyn schoolteacher, who is a regular Hodgson city employee. Brooks-Smith is by appearances our best athlete. He runs long distances and lifts significant weights. He and Thueson have repeatedly tried to see who can be the first to throw an egg over an eight-story building on Amsterdam Avenue. To date their record of failure is one hundred per cent—although each has succeeded with a peach.

We arrive at six-fifteen, to find Van Houten, Slade, and Keller already setting up—in fact, already selling. People are awake, and much around, and Dorothy Slade is weighing yams, three pounds for a dollar. Meanwhile, it is extremely difficult to erect display tables, open boxes, and pile up peppers and tomatoes when the crowd helps take off the lids. They grab the contents.

"Weigh these, please."

"May I have a plastic bag?"

"Wait—while I get the scales off the truck." The sun has yet to show above the brownstones.

This is the corner of 137th Street and Adam Clayton Powell Jr. Boulevard, known elsewhere in the city as Seventh Avenue. The entire name—Adam Clayton Powell Jr. Boulevard—is spelled out on the street sign, which, as a result, has a tip-to-tip span so wide it seems prepared to fly. The big thoroughfare itself is of extraordinary width, and islanded, like parts of Broadway and Park Avenue. A few steps north of us are the Harlem Performance Center and the Egbe Omo Nago African Music Center, and just east along 137th Street from our trucks is the Mother A.M.E. Zion Church. For the Tuesday Greenmarket, the street has been barricaded and cars sent out, an exception being an old Plymouth without tires that rests on flaking steel. On the front wall of the church is a decorous advertisement: "Marion A. Daniels & Sons, Funeral Directors." The block has four young sycamores, and contiguous buildings in every sort of shape from the neat and trim to broken-windowed houses with basements that are open like caves. On 137th Street beyond Adam Clayton Powell are two particularly handsome facing rows of brownstones, their cornices convex and dentilled, their entrances engrandeured with high, ceremonious flights of stairs. Beyond them, our view west is abruptly shut off by the City College cliffs in St. Nicholas Park—the natural wall of Harlem.

The farm trucks are parked on the sidewalks. Displays are in the street. Broad-canopied green, orange, purple, and red umbrellas shield produce from the sun. We have an awning, bolted to the truck. Anders Thueson, with a Magic Marker, is writing our prices on brown paper bags, taping them up as signs. "Is plums spelled with a 'b'?" he asks.

Hemingway tells him no.

A tall, slim woman in a straw hat says to me, "I come down here and get broke every Tuesday. Weigh these eggplants, please."

"There you are. Do you want those in a bag?"

"You gave me good weight. You don't have to give me bags."

Minerva Coleman walks by, complaining. She is short and acidulous, with graying hair and quick, sardonic eyes. She wears bluejeans and a white short-sleeved sweatshirt. She has lived in this block twenty-three years. "You farmers come in too early," she says. "Why do you have to come in so early? I have to get up at four o'clock every Tuesday, and that don't make sense. I don't get paid."

Not by the Greenmarket, at any rate. Minerva works for Harlem Teams for Self-Help, an organization that is something like a Y.M.-Y.W.C.A. It is housed, in fact, in a former Y, the entrance to which is behind our truck. Minerva is Director of Economic Development. As such, she brought the Greenmarket to 137th Street—petitioned the city for it, arranged with the precinct to close off the street. While her assistants sell Harlem Teams for Self-Help shopping bags (fifteen cents), Minerva talks tomatoes with the farmers, and monitors the passing crowd. As the neighborhood kleptos come around the corner, she is quick to point them out. When a middle-aged man in a business suit appears on the scene wearing a sandwich board, she reads the message—"HARLEM TEAM FOR DESTROYING BLACK BUSINESS"—and at once goes out of her tree. "What do you mean, 'destroying black business'? Who is destroying black business? *What* is destroying black business? Get your ass off this block. Can't you see this market is good for everybody? The quality and the price against the quality and the price at the supermarket—there's no comparison."

Exit sandwich board.

"How much are the apples?"

"Three pounds for a dollar, madam."

"Are they sweet?"

"You can eat them straight or bake them in a pie."

"Give me six pounds of apples, six pounds of tomatoes, and three dozen extra-large eggs. Here the boxes from the eggs I bought last week."

Mary Hill, Lenox Avenue. Florrie Thomas, Grand Concourse. Leroy Price, Bradhurst Avenue. Les Boyd, the Polo Grounds. Ylonia Phillips, 159th Street. Selma Williamson, 141st Street. Hattie Mack, Lenox Avenue. Ten in the morning and the crowd is thick. The sun is high and hot. People are drinking from fireplugs. A white cop goes by, the radio on his buttock small and volcanic, erupting: ". . . beating her for two hours." In the upstairs windows of the houses across the street, women sit quietly smoking.

"Are these peppers hot?"

"Those little ones? Yeah. They're hot as hell."

"How do you know how hot hell is? How do you know?"

The speaker is male and middle-aged, wears a jacket and tie, and is small, compact, peppery. He continues, "How do you know how hot hell is? You been over there? I don't think you know how hot hell is."

"Fifty cents, please."

The hundreds of people add up into thousands, and more are turning the corner—every face among them black. Rarely, a white one will come along, an oddity, a floating moon. Just as a bearded person becomes unaware of his beard and feels that he looks like everyone else, you can forget for a time that your own face is white. There are no reminders from the crowd.

Middle-aged man with a woman in blue. She reaches for the roll of thin plastic bags, tugs one off, and tries to open it. The sides are stuck together and resist coming apart. She looks up helplessly, looks at me. Like everyone else on this side of the tables, I am an expert at opening plastic bags.

"These bags are terrible," I tell her, rubbing one between my thumb and fingers. When it comes open, I hand it to her.

"Why, thank you," she says. "You're nice to do that for me. I guess that is the privilege of a lady."

Her husband looks me over, and explains to her, "He's from the old school." There is pause, some handling of fruit. Then he adds, "But the old schools are closing these days."

"They're demolished," she says. "The building's gone."

They fill their sack with peppers (Lady Bell).

The older the men are here, the more likely it is that they are wearing suits and ties. Gray fedoras. Long cigars. The younger they are, the more likely it is that they are carrying shoulder-strapped Panasonics, turned on, turned up—blaring. Fortunately, the market seems to attract a high proportion of venerable people, dressed as if for church, exchanging news and some opinion.

Among our customers are young women in laboratory smocks with small gold rings in the sides of their noses—swinging from a pierced nostril. They work in Harlem Hospital, at the end of the block, on Lenox Avenue.

Fat man stops to assess the peppers. His T-shirt says, "I SURVIVED THE BERMUDA TRIANGLE." Little boy about a foot high. His T-shirt says, "MAN'S BEST FRIEND."

Our cabbages are in full original leaf, untrimmed, each one so broad and beautiful it appears to be a carnation from the lapel of the Jolly Green Giant. They do not fit well in collapsible shopping carts, so people often ask me to strip away the wrapper leaves. I do so, and sell the cabbage, and go back to weighing peppers, making change, more peppers, more change. Now comes a twenty-dollar bill. When I go into my money apron for some ones, a five, a ten, all I come up with is cabbage.

I prefer selling peppers. When you stay in one position long enough, a proprietary sense develops—as with Thueson and the corn. Hodgson, the true proprietor, seems to enjoy selling any-thing—houseplants and stringbeans, squash and pears. Derryck Brooks-Smith likes eggs and tomatoes. Hemingway is an apple man. Or seems to be. It is early to tell. He is five hours into his first day, and I ask how he is getting along. Hemingway says, "These women in Harlem are driving me nuts, but the Jews in Brooklyn will be worse." Across his dark face flies a quick, sarcastic smile. "How *you* doing?" he asks me.

"Fine. I am a pepper seller who long ago missed his calling."

"You like peppers?"

"I have come to crave them. When I go home, I take a sackful with me, and slice them, and fill a big iron skillet to the gun-wales—and when they're done I eat them all myself."

"Cool."

"These tomatoes come from a remote corner of Afghanistan," Derryck Brooks-Smith is saying to some hapless client. "They will send you into ecstasy." She is young and appears to believe him, but she may be in ecstasy already. Brooks-Smith is a physical masterpiece. He wears running shorts. Under a blue T-shirt, his breasts bulge. His calves and thighs are ribbed with muscle. His biceps are smooth brown loaves. His hair is short and for the most part black, here and there brindled with gray. His face is fine-featured, smile disarming. He continues about the tomatoes: "The smaller ones are from Hunza, a little country in the Himalayas. The people of Hunza attribute their longevity to these tomatoes. Yes, three pounds for a dollar. They also attribute their longevity to yogurt and a friendly family. I like your dress. It fits you well."

Brooks-Smith teaches at John Marshall Intermediate School, in Brooklyn. "A nice white name in a black neighborhood," he once remarked. He was referring to the name of the school, but he could as well have meant his own. He was born in the British West Indies. His family moved to New York in 1950, when he was ten. He has a master's degree from City University. "It is exciting for me to be up here in Harlem, among my own people," he has told me over the scale. "Many of them are from the South. They talk about Georgia, about South Carolina. They have a feeling for the farm a lot of people in the city don't have." He quotes Rimbaud to his customers. He fills up the sky for them with the "permanganate sunsets" of Henry Miller. He instructs them in nutrition. He lectures on architecture in a manner that makes them conclude correctly that he is talking about them. They bring him things. Books, mainly. Cards of salutation and fare-well, anticipating his return to the school. "Peace, brother, may you always get back the true kindness you give." The message is hand-written. The card and its envelope are four feet wide. A woman in her eighties who is a Jehovah's Witness hands him a book, her purpose to immortalize his soul. She will miss him. He has always given her a little more than good weight. "I love old people," he says when she departs. "We have a lot to learn from them."

"This is where it is, man. This is where it is!" says a basketball player, shouldering through the crowd toward the eggplants and to-matoes, onions and pears. He is well on his way to three metres in height, and his friend is taller still. They wear red shorts with blue stripes and black-and-white Adidas shoes. The one who knows where it is picks up seven or eight onions, each the size of a baseball, and holds them all in one hand. He palms an eggplant and it disappears. "Man," he goes on, "since these farmers came here I don't hardly eat meat no more."

Now comes a uniformed racing cyclist—All-Sports Day at the Greenmarket. He is slender, trained, more or less thirty, and he seems to be on furlough from the Tour de France. He looks expensive in his yellow racing gloves, his green racing shoes. Partly walking, partly gliding, he straddles his machine. He leans over and carefully chooses peppers, apparently preferring the fire-engine-red ones. Brooks-Smith whispers to me, "That bicycle frame is a Carlton, made in Eng-land. It's worth at least five hundred dollars. They're rare. They're not made much anymore."

"That will be one dollar, please," I say to the cyclist, and he pays me with a food stamp.

Woman says, "What is this stuff on these peaches?"

"It's called fuzz."

"It was on your peaches last week, too."

"We don't take it off. When you buy peaches in the store, the fuzz has been rubbed off."

"Well, I never."

"You never saw peach fuzz before? You're kidding."

"I don't like that fuzz. It makes me itchy. How much are the tomatoes?"

"Three pounds for a dollar."

"Give me three pounds. Tomatoes don't have fuzz."

"I'm a bachelor. Give me a pound of plums." The man is tall, is wearing a brown suit, and appears to be nearing seventy. "They're only for me, I don't need more," he explains. "I'm a bachelor. I don't like the word 'bachelor.' I'm really a widower. A bachelor sounds like a playboy."

"Thirty-five cents, please. Who's next?"

"Will somebody lend me a dollar so I can get some brandy and act like a civilized human for a change?" We see very few drunks. This one wears plaid trousers, a green blazer, an open-collared print shirt. He has not so much as feigned interest in the peppers but is asking directly for money. "This is my birthday," he continues. "Happy birthday, Gus. My mother and father are dead. If they were alive, I'd kick the hell out of them. They got me into this bag. For twenty years, I shined shoes outside the Empire State Building. And now I'm here, a bum. I need to borrow a dollar. Happy birthday, Gus."

SPECULATIONS

1. What purpose does the Greenmarket serve? Why do so many residents of New York City buy food there?

2. Rich Hodgson describes the impression that city people have of the country—and that country people have of the city. What kinds of assumptions lie behind those stereotypic impressions? How does the Greenmarket affect these stereotypes?

3. McPhee's writing has abundant detail, including lists, facts, observations, and descriptions of minute objects and events. Write about two descriptive parts in this essay—and explain how these examples contribute to the essay's overall effect.

4. McPhee describes a testy encounter with a "middle-aged woman with bitter eyes" whom he overcharges one nickel. After she confronts him, he apologizes and describes her response as follows:

> She does not believe my mistake a mistake. She walks away in a white huff. Now she stops, turns, glowers. She moves on. Twice more, as she departs from the market, she stops, turns, and stares angrily back. I watch her all the way to the curb. She waves at the traffic and gets into a cab.

What point do you think McPhee is making? How does all this detail fit together?

5.   A marketplace such as the one McPhee describes represents many kinds of values, all revolving around buying and selling, supply and demand, multiplicity and difference. What evidence do you see that McPhee is aware of these symbolic meanings? Or is he simply describing a New York City marketplace?

McDonald's— We Do It All for You

BARBARA GARSON

Barbara Garson, who characterizes herself as a "socialist agitator and educator," caused a great deal of controversy when her play *MacBird* was produced Off-Broadway in New York in 1967. The play became a hit, was produced over three hundred times, and has been translated into French, Portuguese, and Spanish. *MacBird* is a parody of modern politics and propaganda, converting President Lyndon Johnson and *Macbeth* to its own uses and exposing the absurd pronouncements of extreme left-wing and right-wing politicians as little more than cartoon-like imitations of popular truths. The play demonstrates how pop art and propaganda can be stirred together with hot emotions to satirize the times.

Garson was born in Brooklyn, New York, and attended the University of California. Her children's play "The Dinosaur Door" won an Obie award. In addition to writing four successful plays, her articles have appeared in *Harper's*, the *New York Times*, *Ms.*, *Ramparts*, *Liberation*, *Mother Jones*, *McCall's*, and the *Washington Post*.

Garson demonstrates an ability to create a sense of place and dialogue that shapes an argument and persuades readers. Her book *All the Livelong Day: The Meaning and Demeaning of Routine Work* was described by *Newsweek* as a "loving book" that "celebrates man's vitality and ingenuity." Similarly, this essay from *The Electronic Sweatshop: How Computers Are Transforming the Office of the Future into the Factory of the Past* provides a sense of diverse working people whose insights speak about the struggles in the modern workplace.

Jason Pratt:

"They called us the Green Machine," says Jason Pratt, recently retired McDonald's griddleman, "'cause the crew had green uniforms then. And that's what it is, a machine. You don't have to know how to cook, you don't have to know how to think. There's a procedure for everything and you just follow the procedures."

"Like?" I asked. I was interviewing Jason in the Pizza Hut across from his old McDonald's.

"Like, uh," the wiry teenager searched for a way to describe the all-encompassing procedures. "O.K., we'll start you off on something simple. You're on the ten-in-one grill, ten patties in a pound. Your basic burger. The guy on the bin calls, 'Six hamburgers,' So you lay your six pieces of meat on the grill and set the timer." Before my eyes Jason conjures up the gleaming, mechanized McDonald's kitchen. "Beep-beep, beep-beep, beep-beep. That's the beeper to sear 'em. It goes off in twenty seconds. Sup, sup, sup, sup, sup, sup." He presses each of the six patties down on the sizzling grill with an imaginary silver disk. "Now you turn off the sear beeper, put the buns in the oven, set the oven timer and then the next beeper is to turn the meat. This one goes beep-beep-beep, beep-beep-beep. So you turn your patties and then you drop your re-cons on the meat, t-con, t-con, t-con." Here Jason takes two imaginary handfuls of reconstituted on-ions out of water and sets them out, two blops at a time, on top of the six patties he's arranged in two neat rows on our grill. "Now the bun oven buzzes [there are over a half dozen different timers with distinct beeps and buzzes in a McDonald's kitchen]. "This one turns itself off when you open the oven door so you just take out your crowns, line 'em up and give 'em each a squirt of mustard and a squirt of ketchup." With mustard in his right hand and ketchup in his left, Jason wields the dispensers like a pair of six-shooters up and down the lines of buns. Each dispenser has two triggers. One fires the premeasured squirt for ten-in-ones—the second is set for quarter-pounders.

"Now," says Jason, slowing down, "now you get to put on the pickles. Two if they're regular, three if they're small. That's the crea-tive part. Then the lettuce, then you ask for a cheese count ('cheese on four please'). Finally the last beep goes off and you lay your burger on the crowns."

"On the *crown* of the buns?" I ask, unable to visualize. "On top?"

"Yeah, you dress 'em upside down. Put 'em in the box upside down too. They flip 'em over when they serve 'em."

"Oh, I think I see."

"Then scoop up the heels [the bun bottoms] which are on top of the bun warmer, rake the heels with one hand and push the tray out from underneath and they land (plip) one on each burger, right on top of the re-cons, neat and perfect. [The official time allotted by Ham-burger Central, the McDonald's headquarters in Oak Brook, Ill., is ninety seconds to prepare and serve a burger.] It's like I told you. The procedures makes the burgers. You don't have to know a thing."

McDonald's employs 500,000 teenagers at any one time. Most don't stay long. About 8 million Americans—7 per cent of our labor force—have worked at McDonald's and moved on.[1] Jason is not a typical ex-employee. In fact, Jason is a legend among the teenagers at the three McDonald's outlets in his suburban area. It seems he was so fast at the griddle (or maybe just fast talking) that he'd been taken back three times by two different managers after quitting.

But Jason became a real legend in his last stint at McDonald's. He'd been sent out the back door with the garbage, but instead of coming back in he got into a car with two friends and just drove away. That's the part the local teenagers love to tell. "No fight with the manager or anything . . . just drove away and never came back. . . . I don't think they'd give him a job again."

"I would never go back to McDonald's," says Jason. "Not even as a manager." Jason is enrolled at the local junior college. "I'd like to run a real restaurant someday, but I'm taking data processing to fall back on." He's had many part-time jobs, the highest-paid at a hospital ($4.00 an hour), but that didn't last, and now dishwashing (at the $3.35 minimum). "Same as McDonald's. But I would never go back there. You're a complete robot."

"It seems like you can improvise a little with the onions," I suggested. "They're not premeasured." Indeed, the reconstituted onion shreds grabbed out of a container by the unscientific-looking wet handful struck me as oddly out of character in the McDonald's kitchen.

"There's supposed to be twelve onion bits per patty," Jason informed me. "They spot check."

"Oh come on."

"You think I'm kiddin'. They lift your heels and they say, 'You got too many onions.' It's portion control."

"Is there any freedom anywhere in the process?" I asked.

"Lettuce. They'll leave you alone as long as it's neat."

"So lettuce is freedom; pickles is judgment?"

"Yeah but you don't have time to play around with your pickles. They're never gonna say just six pickles except on the disk. [Each store has video disks to train the crew for each of about twenty work stations, like fries, register, lobby, quarter-pounder grill.] What you'll hear in real life is 'twelve and six on a turn-lay.' The first number is your hamburgers, the second is your Big Macs. On a turn-lay means you lay the first twelve, then you put down the second batch after

---

[1] These statistics come from John F. Love, *McDonald's Behind the Golden Arches* (New York: Bantam, 1986). Additional background information in this chapter comes from Ray Kroc and Robert Anderson, *Grinding It Out* (Chicago: Contemporary Books, 1977), and Max Boas and Steve Chain, *Big Mac* (New York: Dutton, 1976).

you turn the first. So you got twenty-four burgers on the grill, in shifts. It's what they call a production mode. And remember you also got your fillets, your McNuggets. . . ."

"Wait, slow down." By then I was losing track of the patties on our imaginary grill. "I don't understand this turn-lay thing."

"Don't worry, you don't have to understand. You follow the beepers, you follow the buzzers and you turn your meat as fast as you can. It's like I told you, to work at McDonald's you don't need a face, you don't need a brain. You need to have two hands and two legs and move 'em as fast as you can. That's the whole system. I wouldn't go back there again for anything."

June Sanders:

McDonald's french fries are deservedly the pride of their menu: uniformly golden brown all across America and in thirty-one other countries. However, it's difficult to standardize the number of fries per serving. The McDonald's fry scoop, perhaps their greatest technological innovation, helps to control this variable. The unique flat funnel holds the bag open while it aligns a limited number of fries so that they fall into the package with a paradoxically free, overflowing cornucopia look.

Despite the scoop, there's still a spread. The acceptable fry yield is 400 to 420 servings per 100-lb. bag of potatoes. It's one of the few areas of McDonald's cookery in which such a range is possible. The fry yield is therefore one important measure of a manager's efficiency. "Fluffy, not stuffy," they remind the young workers when the fry yield is running low.

No such variation is possible in the browning of the fries. Early in McDonald's history Louis Martino, the husband of the secretary of McDonald's founder Ray Kroc, designed a computer to be submerged in the fry vats. In his autobiography, *Grinding It Out*, Kroc explained the importance of this innovation. "We had a recipe . . . that called for pulling the potatoes out of the oil when they got a certain color and grease bubbles formed in a certain way. It was amazing that we got them as uniform as we did because each kid working the fry vats would have his own interpretation of the proper color and so forth. [The word "kid" was officially replaced by "person" or "crew person" in McDonald's management vocabulary in 1973 in response to union organizing attempts.] Louis's computer took all the guesswork out of it, modifying the frying to suit the balance of water to solids in a given batch of potatoes. He also engineered the dispenser that allowed us to squirt exactly the right amount of catsup and mustard onto our premeasured hamburger patties. . . ."

The fry vat probe is a complex miniature computer. The fry scoop, on the other hand, is as simple and almost as elegant as the wheel. Both eliminate the need for a human being to make "his own interpretation," as Ray Kroc puts it.

Together, these two innovations mean that a new worker can be trained in fifteen minutes and reach maximum efficiency in a half hour. This makes it economically feasible to use a kid for one day and replace him with another kid the next day.

June Sanders worked at McDonald's for one day.

"I needed money, so I went in and the manager told me my hours would be 4 to 10 P.M." This was fine with June, a well-organized black woman in her early twenties who goes to college full time.

"But when I came in the next day the manager said I could work till 10 for that one day. But from then on my hours would be 4 P.M. to 1 A.M. And I really wouldn't get off at 1 because I'd have to stay to clean up after they closed. . . . Yes it was the same manager, a Mr. O'Neil.

"I told him I'd have to check first with my family if I could come home that late. But he told me to put on the uniform and fill out the forms. He would start me out on french fries.

"Then he showed me an orientation film on a TV screen all about fries. . . . No, I still hadn't punched in. This was all in the basement. Then I went upstairs, and *then* I punched in and went to work. . . . No, I was not paid for the training downstairs. Yes, I'm sure."

I asked June if she had had any difficulty with the fries.

"No, it was just like the film. You put the french fries in the grease and you push a button which doesn't go off till the fries are done. Then you take them out and put them in a bin under a light. Then you scoop them into the bags with this thing, this flat, light metal—I can't really describe it—scoop thing that sits right in the package and makes the fries fall in place."

"Did they watch you for a while?" I asked. "Did you need more instruction?"

"Someone leaned over once and showed me how to make sure the fry scooper was set inside the opening of the bag so the fries would fall in right."

"And then?"

"And then, I stood on my feet from twenty after four till the manager took over my station at 10:35 P.M.

"When I left my legs were aching. I knew it wasn't a job for me. But I probably would have tried to last it out—at least more than a day—if it wasn't for the hours. When I got home I talked it over with my mother and my sister and then I phoned and said I couldn't work there. They weren't angry. They just said to bring back the uniform. . . . The people were nice, even the managers. It's just a rushed system."

"June," I said, "does it make any sense to train you and have you work for one day? Why didn't he tell you the real hours in the first place?"

"They take a chance and see if you're desperate. I have my family to stay with. That's why I didn't go back. But if I really needed the money, like if I had a kid and no family, I'd have to make arrangements to work any hours.

"Anyway, they got a full day's work out of me."

Damita:

I waited on line at my neighborhood McDonald's. It was lunch hour and there were four or five customers at each of the five open cash registers. "May I take your order?" a very thin girl said in a flat tone to the man at the head of my line.

"McNuggets, large fries and a Coke," said the man. The cashier punched in the order. "That will be—".

"Big Mac, large fries and a shake," said the next woman on line. The cashier rang it up.

"Two cheeseburgers, large fries and a coffee," said the third customer. The cashier rang it up.

"How much is a large fries?" asked the woman directly in front of me.

The thin cashier twisted her neck around trying to look up at the menu board.

"Sorry," apologized the customer, "I don't have my glasses."

"Large fries is seventy-nine," a round-faced cashier with glasses interjected from the next register.

"Seventy-nine cents," the thin cashier repeated.

"Well how much is a *small* fries?"

As they talked I leaned over the next register. "Say, can I interview you?" I asked the clerk with glasses, whose line was by then empty.

"Huh?"

"I'm writing a story about jobs at fast-food restaurants."

"O.K. I guess so."

"Can I have your phone number?"

"Well . . . I'll meet you when I get off. Should be sometime between 4 and 4:30."

By then it was my turn.

"Just a large fries," I said.

The thin cashier pressed 'lge fries.' In place of numbers, the keys on a McDonald's cash register say "lge fries," "reg fries," "med coke," "big mac," and so on. Some registers have pictures on the key caps.

The next time the price of fries goes up (or down) the change will be entered in the store's central computer. But the thin cashier will continue to press the same button. I wondered how long she'd worked there and how many hundreds of 'lge fries' she'd served without learning the price.

Damita, the cashier with the glasses, came up from the crew room (a room in the basement with lockers, a table and a video player for studying the training disks) at 4:45. She looked older and more serious without her striped uniform.

"Sorry, but they got busy and, you know, here you get off when they let you."

The expandable schedule was her first complaint. "You give them your availability when you sign on. Mine I said 9 to 4. But they scheduled me for 7 o'clock two or three days a week. And I needed the money. So I got to get up 5 in the morning to get here from Queens by 7. And I don't get off till whoever's supposed to get here gets here to take my place. . . . It's hard to study with all the pressures."

Damita had come to the city from a small town outside of Detroit. She lives with her sister in Queens and takes extension courses in psychology at New York University. Depending on the schedule posted each Friday, her McDonald's paycheck for a five-day week has varied from $80 to $114.

"How long have you worked at McDonald's?" I asked.

"Well, see I only know six people in this city, so my manager from Michigan . . . yeah, I worked for McDonald's in high school . . . my manager from Michigan called this guy Brian who's the second assistant manager here. So I didn't have to fill out an application. Well, I mean the first thing I needed was a job," she seemed to apologize, "and I knew I could always work at McDonald's. I always say I'm gonna look for something else, but I don't get out till 4 and that could be 5 or whenever."

The flexible scheduling at McDonald's only seems to work one way. One day Damita had arrived a half hour late because the E train was running on the R track.

"The assistant manager told me not to clock in at all, just to go home. So I said O.K. and I left."

"What did you do the rest of the day?" I asked.

"I went home and studied, and I went to sleep."

"But how did it make you feel?"

"It's like a humiliating feeling 'cause I wasn't given any chance to justify myself. But when I spoke to the Puerto Rican manager he said it was nothing personal against me. Just it was raining that day, and they were really slow and someone who got here on time, it wouldn't be right to send them home."

"Weren't you annoyed to spend four hours traveling and then lose a day's pay?" I suggested.

"I was mad at first that they didn't let me explain. But afterwards I understood and I tried to explain to my sister: 'Time waits for no man.'"

"Since you signed on for 9 to 4," I asked Damita, "and you're going to school, why can't you say, 'Look, I have to study at night, I need regular hours'?"

"Don't work that way. They make up your schedule every week and if you can't work it, you're responsible to replace yourself. If you can't stay they can always get someone else."

"But Damita," I tried to argue with her low estimate of her own worth, "anyone can see right away that your line moves fast, yet you're helpful to people. I mean, you're a valuable employee. And this manager seems to like you."

"Valuable! $3.35 an hour. And I can be replaced by any [pointing across the room] kid off the street." I hadn't noticed. At a small table under the staircase a manager in a light beige shirt was taking an application from a lanky black teenager.

"But you know the register. You know the routine."

"How long you think it takes to learn the six steps? Step 1. Greet the customer, 'Good morning, can I help you?' Step 2. Take his order. Step 3. Repeat the order. They can have someone off the street working my register in five minutes."

"By the way," I asked, "on those cash registers without numbers, how do you change something after you ring it up? I mean if somebody orders a cheeseburger and then they change it to a hamburger, how do you subtract the slice of cheese?"

"I guess that's why you have step 3, repeat the order. One cheeseburger, two Cokes, three . . ."

"Yeah but if you punched a mistake or they don't want it after you get it together?"

"Like if I have a crazy customer, which I do be gettin' 'specially in this city, and they order hamburger, fries and shake, and it's $2.95 and then they just walk away?"

"I once did that here," I said. "About a week ago when I first started my research. All I ordered was some french fries. And I was so busy watching how the computer works that only after she rang it up I discovered that I'd walked out of my house without my wallet. I didn't have a penny. I was so embarrassed."

"Are you that one the other day? Arnetta, this girl next to me, she said, 'Look at that crazy lady going out. She's lookin' and lookin' at everything and then she didn't have no money for a bag of fries.' I saw you leaving, but I guess I didn't recognize you. [I agreed it was probably me.] O.K., so say this crazy lady comes in and orders french fries and leaves. In Michigan I could just zero it out. I'd wait till I start the next order and press zero and large fries. But here you're supposed to call out 'cancel sale' and the manager comes over and does it with his key.

"But I hate to call the manager every time, 'specially if I got a whole line waiting. So I still zero out myself. They can tell I do it by the computer tape, and they tell me not to. Some of them let me, though, because they know I came from another store. But they don't show the girls here how to zero out. Everybody thinks you need the manager's key to do it."

"Maybe they let you because they can tell you're honest," I said. She smiled, pleased, but let it pass. "That's what I mean that you're valuable to them. You know how to use the register. You're good with customers."

"You know there was a man here," Damita said, a little embarrassed about bragging, "when I was transferred off night he asked my manager, 'What happened to that girl from Michigan?'"

"Did your manager tell you that?"

"No, another girl on the night shift told me. The manager said it to her. They don't tell you nothing nice themselves."

"But, see, you are good with people and he appreciates it."

"In my other McDonald's—not the one where they let me zero out but another one I worked in in Michigan—I was almost fired for my attitude. Which was helping customers who had arthritis to open the little packets. And another bad attitude of mine is that you're supposed to suggest to the customer, 'Would you like a drink with that?' or 'Do you want a pie?'—whatever they're pushing. I don't like to do it. And they can look on my tape after my shift and see I didn't push the suggested sell item."

McDonald's computerized cash registers allow managers to determine immediately not only the dollar volume for the store but the amount of each item that was sold at each register for any given period. Two experienced managers, interviewed separately, both insisted that the new electronic cash registers were in fact slower than the old mechanical registers. Clerks who knew the combination—hamburger, fries, Coke: $2.45—could ring up the total immediately, take the cash and give change in one operation. On the new register you have to enter each item and may be slowed down by computer response time. The value of the new registers, or at least their main selling point (McDonald's franchisers can choose from several approved registers), is the increasingly sophisticated tracking systems, which monitor all the activity and report with many different statistical breakdowns.

"Look, there." said Damita as the teenage job applicant left and the manager went behind the counter with the application. "If I was to say I can't come in at 7, they'd cut my hours down to one shift a week, and if I never came back they wouldn't call to find out where I was.

"I worked at a hospital once as an X-ray assistant. There if I didn't come in there were things that had to be done that wouldn't be done. I would call there and say, 'Remember to run the EKGs.' Here, if I called and said, 'I just can't come by 7 no more,' they'd have one of these high schools kids off the street half an hour later. And they'd do my job just as good."

Damita was silent for a while and then she made a difficult plea. "This might sound stupid, I don't know," she said, "but I feel like, I came here to study and advance myself but I'm not excelling myself in any way. I'm twenty years old but—this sounds terrible to say—I'm twenty but I'd rather have a babysitting job. At least I could help a kid and take care. But I only know six people in this city. So I don't even know how I'd find a babysitting job."

"I'll keep my ears open," I said. "I don't know where I'd hear of one but . . . ."

Damita seemed a little relieved. I suppose she realized there wasn't much chance of babysitting full-time, but at least she now knew seven people in the city.

Jon DeAngelo:
Jon DeAngelo, twenty-two, has been a McDonald's manager for three years. He started in the restaurant business at sixteen as a busboy and planned even then to run a restaurant of his own someday. At nineteen, when he was the night manager of a resort kitchen, he was hired away by McOpCo, the McDonald's Operating Company.

Though McDonald's is primarily a franchise system, the company also owns and operates about 30 percent of the stores directly. These McOpCo stores, including some of the busiest units, are managed via a chain of command including regional supervisors, store managers and first and second assistants who can be moved from unit to unit. In addition, there's a network of inspectors from Hamburger Central who make announced and unannounced checks for QSC (quality, service, cleanliness) at both franchise and McOpCo installations.

Jon was hired at $14,000 a year. At the time I spoke with him his annual pay was $21,000—a very good salary at McDonald's. At first he'd been an assistant manager in one of the highest-volume stores in his region. Then he was deliberately transferred to a store with productivity problems.

"I got there and found it was really a great crew. They hated being hassled, but they loved to work. I started them having fun by putting the men on the women's jobs and vice versa. [At most McDonald's the women tend to work on the registers, the men on the grill. But everyone starts at the same pay.] Oh, sure, they hated it at first, the guys that is. But they liked learning all the stations. I also ran a lot of register races."

Since the computer tape in each register indicates sales per hour, per half hour or for any interval requested, the manager can rev the crew up for a real "on your mark, get set, go!" race with a printout ready as they cross the finish line, showing the dollars taken in at each register during the race.

The computer will also print out a breakdown of sales for any particular menu item. The central office can check, therefore, how many Egg McMuffins were sold on Friday from 9 to 9:30 two weeks or two years ago, either in the entire store or at any particular register.

This makes it possible to run a register race limited to Cokes for instance, or Big Macs. Cashiers are instructed to try suggestive selling ("Would you like a drink with that?") at all times. But there are periods when a particular item is being pushed. The manager may then offer a prize for the most danish sold.

A typical prize for either type of cash register race might be a Snoopy mug (if that's the current promotion) or even a $5 cash bonus.

"This crew loved to race as individuals," says Jon of his troubled store, "but even more as a team. They'd love to get on a production mode, like a chicken-pull-drop or a burger-turn-lay and kill themselves for a big rush.

"One Saturday after a rock concert we did a $1,900 hour with ten people on crew. We killed ourselves but when the rush was over everyone said it was the most fun they ever had in a McDonald's."

I asked Jon how managers made up their weekly schedule. How would he decide who and how many to assign?

"It comes out of the computer," Jon explained. "It's a bar graph with the business you're going to do that week already printed in."

"The business you're *going* to do, already printed in?"

"It's based on the last week's sales, like maybe you did a $300 hour on Thursday at 3 P.M. Then it automatically adds a certain percent, say 15 percent, which is the projected annual increase for your particular store. . . . No, the person scheduling doesn't have to do any of this calculation. I just happen to know how it's arrived at. Really, it's simple, it's just a graph with the numbers already in it. $400 hour, $500 hour. According to Hamburger Central you schedule two crew members per $100 hour. So if you're projected for a $600 hour on Friday between 1 and 2, you know you need twelve crew for that lunch hour and the schedule sheet leaves space for their names."

"You mean you just fill in the blanks on the chart?"

"It's pretty automatic except in the case of a special event like the concert. Then you have to guess the dollar volume. Scheduling under could be a problem, but over would be a disaster to your crew labor productivity."

"Crew labor productivity?"

"Everything at McDonald's is based on the numbers. But crew labor productivity is pretty much *the* number a manager is judged by."

"Crew labor productivity? You have to be an economist."

"It's really simple to calculate. You take the total crew labor dollars paid out, divide that into the total food dollars taken in. That gives you your crew labor productivity. The more food you sell and the less people you use to do it, the better your percentage. It's pretty simple."

Apparently, I still looked confused.

"For example, if you take an $800 hour and you run it with ten crew you get a very high crew labor percent."

"That's good?"

"Yes that's good. Then the manager in the next store hears Jon ran a 12 percent labor this week, I'll run a 10 percent labor. Of course you burn people out that way. But . . ."

"But Jon," I asked, "if the number of crew you need is set in advance and printed by the computer, why do so many managers keep changing hours and putting pressure on kids to work more?"

"They advertise McDonald's as a flexible work schedule for high school and college kids," he said, "but the truth is it's a high-pressure job, and we have so much trouble keeping help, especially in fast stores like my first one (it grossed $1.8 million last year), that 50 percent never make it past two weeks. And a lot walk out within two days.

"When I was a first assistant, scheduling and hiring was my responsibility and I had to fill the spots one way or another. There were so many times I covered the shifts myself. Times I worked 100 hours a week. A manager has to fill the spaces on his chart somehow. So if a crew person is manipulable they manipulate him."

"What do you mean?"

"When you first sign on, you give your availability. Let's say a person's schedule is weeknights, 4 to 10. But after a week the manager schedules him as a closer Friday night. He calls in upset, 'Hey, my availability isn't Friday night.' The manager says 'Well the schedule is already done. And you know the rule. If you can't work it's up to you to replace yourself.' At that point the person might quit, or he might not show up or he might have a fight with the manager."

"So he's fired?"

"No. You don't fire. You would only fire for cause like drugs or stealing. But what happens is he signed up for thirty hours a week and suddenly he's only scheduled for four. So either he starts being more available or he quits."

"Aren't you worried that the most qualified people will quit?"

"The only qualification to be able to do the job is to be able physically to do the job. I believe it says that in almost those words in my regional manual. And being there is the main part of being physically able to do the job."

"But what about your great crew at the second store? Don't you want to keep a team together?"

"Let me qualify that qualification. It takes a special kind of person to be able to move before he can think. We find people like that and use them till they quit."

"But as a manager don't you look bad if too many people are quitting?"

"As a manager I am judged by the statistical reports which come off the computer. Which basically means my crew labor productivity. What else can I really distinguish myself by? I could have a good fry yield, a low M&R [Maintenance and Repair budget]. But these are minor."

As it happens, Jon is distinguished among McDonald's managers in his area as an expert on the computerized equipment. Other managers call on him for cash register repairs. "They say, 'Jon, could you look at my register? I just can't afford the M&R this month.' So I come and fix it and they'll buy me a beer."

"So keeping M&R low is a real feather in a manager's cap," I deduced.

"O.K., it's true, you can over spend your M&R budget; you can have a low fry yield; you can run a dirty store; you can be fired for bothering the high school girls. But basically, every Coke spigot is monitored. [At most McDonald's, Coke doesn't flow from taps that turn on and off. Instead the clerk pushes the button "sm," "med" or "lge," which then dispenses the premeasured amount into the appropriate-size cup. This makes the syrup yield fairly consistent.] Every ketchup squirt is measured. My costs for every item are set. So my crew labor productivity is my main flexibility."

I was beginning to understand the pressures toward pettiness. I had by then heard many complaints about slight pilferage of time. For instance, as a safety measure no one was allowed to stay in a store alone. There was a common complaint that a closer would be clocked out when he finished cleaning the store for the night, even though he might be required to wait around unpaid till the manager finished his own nightly statistical reports. At other times kids clocked out and then waited hours (unpaid) for a crew chief training course (unpaid).

Overtime is an absolute taboo at McDonald's. Managers practice every kind of scheduling gymnastic to see that no one works over forty hours a week. If a crew member approaching forty hours is needed to close the store, he or she might be asked to check out for a long lunch. I had heard of a couple of occasions when, in desperation, a manager scheduled someone to stay an hour or two over forty hours. Instead of paying time-and-a-half, he compensated at straight time listing the extra hours as miscellaneous and paying through a fund reserved for things like register race bonuses. All of this of course to make his statistics look good.

"There must be some other way to raise your productivity," I suggested, "besides squeezing it out of the kids."

"I try to make it fun," Jon pleaded earnestly. "I know that people like to work on my shifts. I have the highest crew labor productivity in the area. But I get that from burning people out. Look, you can't squeeze a McDonald's hamburger any flatter. If you want to improve your productivity there is nothing for a manager to squeeze but the crew."

"But if it's crew dollars paid out divided by food dollars taken in, maybe you can bring in more dollars instead of using less crew."

"O.K., let me tell you about sausage sandwiches."

"Sausage sandwiches?" (Sounded awful.)

"My crew was crazy about sausage sandwiches. [Crew members are entitled to one meal a day at reduced prices. The meals are deducted from wages through a computerized link to the time clocks.] They made it from a buttered English muffin, a slice of sausage and a slice of cheese. I understand this had actually been a menu item in some parts of the country but never here. But the crew would make it for themselves and then all their friends came in and wanted them.

"So, I decided to go ahead and sell it. It costs about 9¢ to make and I sold it for $1.40. It went like hotcakes. My supervisor even liked the idea because it made so much money. You could see the little dollar signs in his eyes when he first came into the store. And he said nothing. So we kept selling it.

"Then someone came from Oak Brook and they made us stop it.

"Just look how ridiculous that is. A slice of sausage is 60¢ as a regular menu item, and an English muffin is 45¢. So if you come in and ask for a sausage and an English muffin I can still sell them to you today for $1.05. But there's no way I can add the slice of cheese and put it in the box and get that $1.40.

"Basically, I can't be any more creative than a crew person. I can't take any more initiative than the person on the register."

"Speaking of cash registers and initiative," I said . . . and told him about Damita. I explained that she was honest, bright and had learned how to zero out at another store. "Do you let cashiers zero out?" I asked.

"I might let her in this case," Jon said. "The store she learned it at was probably a franchise and they were looser. But basically we don't need people like her. Thinking generally slows this operation down.

"When I first came to McDonald's, I said, 'How mechanical! These kids don't even know how to cook.' But the pace is so fast that if they didn't have all the systems, you couldn't handle it. It takes ninety seconds to cook a hamburger. In those seconds you have to toast the bun, dress it, sear it, turn it, take it off the grill and serve it. Meanwhile you've got maybe twenty-four burgers, plus your chicken, your fish. You haven't got time to pick up a rack of fillet and see if it's done. You have to press the timer, drop the fish and know, without looking, that when it buzzes it's done.

"It's the same thing with management. You have to record the money each night before you close and get it to the bank the next day by 11 A.M. So you have to trust the computer to do a lot of the job. These computers also calculate the payrolls, because they're hooked into the time clocks. My payroll is paid out of a bank in Chicago. The computers also tell you how many people you're going to need each hour. It's so fast that the manager hasn't got time to think about it. He has to follow the procedures like the crew. And if he follows the procedures everything is going to come out more or less as it's supposed to. So basically the computer manages the store."

Listening to Jon made me remember what Ray Kroc had written about his own job (head of the corporation) and computers:

> We have a computer in Oak Brook that is designed to make real estate surveys. But those printouts are of no use to me. After we find a promising location, I drive around it in a car, go into the corner saloon and the neighborhood supermarket. I mingle with the people and observe their comings and goings. That tells me what I need to know about how a McDonald's store would do there.[2]

By combining twentieth-century computer technology with nineteenth-century time-and-motion studies, the McDonald's corporation has broken the jobs of griddleman, waitress, cashier and even manager down into small, simple steps. Historically these have been service jobs involving a lot of flexibility and personal flair. But the corporation has systematically extracted the decision-making elements from filling french fry boxes or scheduling staff. They've siphoned the know-how from the employees into the programs. They relentlessly weed out all variables that might make it necessary to make a decision at the store level, whether on pickles or on cleaning procedures.

---

[2] Ray Kroc and Robert Anderson, *Grinding It Out* (Chicago: Contemporary Books, 1977), p. 176.

It's interesting and understandable that Ray Kroc refused to work that way. The real estate computer may be as reliable as the fry vat probe. But as head of the company Kroc didn't have to surrender to it. He'd let the computer juggle all the demographic variables, but in the end Ray Kroc would decide, intuitively, where to put the next store.

Jon DeAngelo would like to work that way, too. So would Jason, June, and Damita. If they had a chance to use some skill or intuition at their own levels, they'd not only feel more alive, they'd also be treated with more consideration. It's job organization, not malice, that allows (almost requires) McDonald's workers to be handled like paper plates. They feel disposable because they are.

I was beginning to wonder why Jon stayed on at McDonald's. He still yearned to open a restaurant. "The one thing I'd take from McDonald's to a French restaurant of my own is the fry vat computer. It really works." He seemed to have both the diligence and the style to run a personalized restaurant. Of course he may not have had the capital.

"So basically I would tell that girl [bringing me back to Damita] to find a different job. She's thinking too much and it slows things down. The way the system is set up, I don't need that in a register person, and they don't need it in me."

"Jon," I said, trying to be tactful, "I don't exactly know why you stay at McDonald's."

"As a matter of fact, I have already turned in my resignation."

"You mean you're not a McDonald's manager any more?" I was dismayed.

"I quit once before and they asked me to stay."

"I have had such a hard time getting a full-fledged manager to talk to me and now I don't know whether you count."

"They haven't actually accepted my resignation yet. You know I heard of this guy in another region who said he was going to leave and they didn't believe him. They just wouldn't accept his resignation. And you know what he did? One day, at noon, he just emptied the store, walked out, and locked the door behind him."

For a second Jon seemed to drift away on that beautiful image. It was like the kids telling me about Jason, the crewman who just walked out the back door.

"You know what that means to close a McDonald's at noon, to do a zero hour at lunch?"

"Jon," I said. "This has been fantastic. You are fantastic. I don't think anyone could explain the computers to me the way you do. But I want to talk to someone who's happy and moving up in the

McDonald's system. Do you think you could introduce me to a manager who . . ."

"You won't be able to."

"How come?"

"First of all, there's the media hotline. If any press comes around or anyone is writing a book I'm supposed to call the regional office immediately and they will provide someone to talk to you. So you can't speak to a real corporation person except by arrangement with the corporation.

"Second, you can't talk to a happy McDonald's manager because 98 percent are miserable.

"Third of all, there is no such thing as a McDonald's manager. The computer manages the store."

SPECULATIONS

1. Why did Jason Pratt become a legend among the teenagers in his neighborhood? How would you describe his values and response to working at McDonald's?

2. What did you learn about McDonald's from this article that you did not know before? What surprised you or was most striking about this description of how McDonald's works?

3. How do you interpret the title of this essay?

4. What is the primary perspective or point of view from which the essay is written? How is this perspective reinforced by McDonald's as an employer?

5. How would you compare the data in this article to your own perspective and experience of McDonald's? Explain how your experience as a customer and as someone familiar with McDonald's advertisements is altered or reinforced by reading this article.

6. Using examples from your own work experience, describe how your values and goals as an employee resemble or differ from the values and goals of one or more of the working people interviewed in this essay.

Disposable Heroes

DONNA GAINES

In the introduction to *Teenage Wasteland: Suburbia's Dead End Kids*, Donna Gaines writes:

> History is always written by those who survive, rarely by those silenced by it. The radical pedagogue Paulo Freire has said about the United States, "This is one of the most alienated of all countries, people know they are exploited and dominated, but they feel incapable of breaking down the dehumanized wall."

In her book, Gaines attempts both to articulate the exploitation and to break down those invisible walls that separate teenager from teenager and teenager from parent.

A journalist and sociologist who writes feature stories for the *Village Voice* and who contributes to a variety of scholarly conferences and journals, Gaines considers herself to be a radical educator who acknowledges and reinforces the alienation Americans sometimes feel from their culture. In *Teenage Wasteland* she writes:

> The radical educator begins by validating the dominated person's local, intuitive knowledge of the world. Likewise, the therapeutic intervention must reinforce this knowledge, acknowledge it, constitute it as a truth. That means—to borrow my neighbor Scott's words—"calling out the bullshit" when and how you see it coming down.
>
> I wanted to do that for every kid who survived "the decade of greed," and for all the ones who didn't.

The selection reprinted here from *Teenage Wasteland* paints a disturbing picture of working life gone awry for teenagers living in the seeming comfort of suburbia.

Almost half of American high school seniors now work. Not in the skilled trades or factory settings of a generation ago, but in service jobs. The jobs are low-paying, demanding little discipline or skill. For most kids, cash is hoarded for partying, and to subsidize teen-status commodity-consumption patterns that many kids adhere to. While adults feel working is good, teaches you a sense of responsibility, even kids who do well in school learn very little about responsibility in most job settings. By the time they are seniors, over two-thirds of America's employed youth will spend fifteen hours or more a week at their workplace. Eighty percent of American kids will have held a job during the school year at some point during their high school careers.

Actually, suburban communities offer the most favorable opportunities for youth employment. In my neighborhood a tour up and down the turnpike in the middle of the afternoon allows me to drop in on people working at the deli, card store, record store, hardware store, several supermarkets. And then there are friends working at restaurants and mall shops, driving taxis. The abuse and boredom suffered in a shit job can be compensated for by sticky fingers—nobody buys records, beer, cigarettes, or car parts anymore. Not when your friends can get them for you free.

Income from these jobs rarely contributes to "the future." Maybe car payments, abortions in extreme cases, apartments, and school. But usually movies, leathers, fast foods, videos, shows, and memorable overnight trips upstate.

Not only does the youth labor force dominate turnpike commerce, but adults rarely enter into things. The boss becomes a little like the narc. At Metal 24, we had a code: the Sun was rising, if the boss, Mr. Sun, was due in; setting, if he was leaving soon and we should hang around and wait so we could watch horror movies or rock videos on the surveillance camera VCR. Eddie's technological prowess came to the fore as soon as the Sun set.

It's fun, but ultimately self-defeating. There is very little opportunity on such jobs for kids to learn anything from adult employers. They are generally supervised by a more experienced peer; they rarely interact with the boss. The virtues of self-management, cooperation, autonomy, initiative, and personal and social responsibility are learned by default, after a blunder. Up to the point of getting fired. This is how the discipline of labor is learned.

Everything Eddie and Cliff have learned at Metal 24 they already knew. Mr. Sun took Eddie under his wing, recognizing that he was smart. He even posted the bail when Eddie was arrested for outstanding warrants. Mr. Sun thinks American kids are fucked up. He's amazed at the lack of discipline, the "laziness." It just doesn't seem worth it to go out of your way for them, since they don't seem to want to help themselves. Mr. Sun is an immigrant from mainland China. He thinks like my father. If you work, you get somewhere. But most kids just don't see it that way.

"No job is worth cutting your hair for. No matter how much money they'll offer." This articulates a tenet of faith that is central to the metal orthodoxy. When Eddie got fired from the convenience store for sneaking free beers to his friends, he was busy looking for a new job. The only criterion he had was not having to cut his hair.

Two weeks after he lost his job, he couldn't pay his rent and he was living on the street. His car had been stolen a few months earlier and he had cut his ties to his family. He had no resources and his only marketable skills were in food preparation and dealing. He had worked in delis and restaurants but that wasn't the kind of work he wanted anymore. Eddie was determined to make it straight. But he would resort to crime—he laughs—rather than cut his hair.

At first I laughed with him but he was serious. "No metalhead would ever cut his hair. First of all, that would be the end of my leather jacket. I mean how could I wear my leathers with a guido haircut? Can you imagine that?" Besides, he's in a band—he'd have to quit! Eddie also knows his girlfriend of two years would break up with him if he ever got a haircut; "she told me so." What could there be left to live for, he asks, if Metallica toured and he had short hair? No way!

For kids tracked into dead-end jobs, cutting your hair is a political issue, a statement even more radical than smoking cigarettes was in the fifties high school. People felt that way in the 1960s and 1970s, and maybe they suffered the ridicule of "straight" society. But in the 1980s the stakes are much higher.

This time it's for real. If you get thrown out on your ass, if you're an outcast, you're *really* out. Eddie says he's a rebel. Undisciplined, messy, and wild, he would rather freeze and starve than give in. This isn't as romantic as it once seemed. Eddie cannot fathom the absurdity of having to cut his hair to "make it" economically. "Can you imagine me cutting my hair to get a job at Burger King?" He probably could walk right into a management position in food preparation. But it just wasn't worth selling yourself for that. It would drive him crazy. He would die, he says.

Still, the kids have tried to carve out some honor, and so alternative "underground" economies have sprung up to tide them over. If small-time dealing and petty crimes were once helpful in the transition from the poverty of adolescence to the self-sufficiency of early adulthood, now they are crucial. So the Italian-American kids in Bensonhurst who can't get coveted jobs in the dying construction industry, or with city sanitation, find small-time careers as local "wiseguys." They spend their time running small scams, regulating turf, and acting as neighborhood border guards. Living off the economic organizations developed by immigrant fathers and grandfathers. Girls work, hoping to marry soon.

In urban settings there are even fewer "youth employment" jobs to go around. One alternative economy that is highly developed among low-income urban youth is the drug industry run by "cocaine kids." Black and Latino street gangs have organized themselves into local drug-dealing cartels. There isn't any better economic opportunity to be had, adult community representatives have lamented.

Meanwhile, suburban white kids are not so organized. They have failed to nurture such flourishing alternatives to blocked mobility. And so they look up to minority kids, city kids, for their superior economic organization on the street.

Where I live, all the white people are ethnic—Greek, Jewish, Italian, Irish—and most are members of the "third-generation nation." Their parents and grandparents got jobs, made connections, and organized opportunities for their sons and daughters to follow. In my neighborhood there are second and third generations of same-trade families: cops, carpenters, bartenders. Kids with families who can set them up with something do well. Everyone else improvises.

I know a guy named Jackie. I met him up at the Pathmark, where he works in the dairy section. He also works as a nonunion bricklayer when he can. We became friends initially because of Jackie's tattoos. He has several dedicated to his favorite band, Metallica. One is a tombstone with a bass slung over it, a testimony to Cliff Burton. Cliff died in a bus accident while Metallica was on tour. Jackie has another one that says "Damage Inc." Jackie is twenty-two. Sometimes I see him at Slayer shows. In the summer he conducts business down at the beach. You can always find him there. It's his "third job."

He describes his customers: "All these people do is hang out. They're all alcoholics. They can't hold jobs. Some of them never worked more than three days here or there, never really worked in their lives. They don't know how to keep from getting fired. I know what to do to keep from getting fired but these people, they get busted, they go into rehab, they come out, and before long they're back, doing more coke. It doesn't take much for it to start again."

Jackie says a lot of kids scam off their parents, deal, fuck up, get busted. That's it. Jackie doesn't know why they're so fucked up. "They just don't give a shit." Partying becomes the main thing, the only thing. Besides that, there is burglary, assault, car theft, criminal mischief (vandalism, trespassing, menacing, disorderly conduct). This is how people express their desire to create, how they use their smarts. Street life in suburbia is disorganized in this way.

In Bergenfield Lenny and Ray were two street innovators I sometimes ran into. They could usually be found hanging around by the archway that leads from the garden apartments to the Foster Village Shopping Center. This was prime, since from here they could easily duck into the complex to conduct business, or to reduce their visibility on the Ave. Ray and Lenny didn't go to school anywhere. They were full-time street soldiers, from a very different crowd than Joe and Randy. Some overlapping friends, maybe even a past party episode, but Ray and Lenny had a different look, musical interests—another scene, basically. They weren't metalheads or thrashers, just your basic American dirts. Ray and Lenny went for the older bands, Cream, the Who, Blind Faith, and of course, Led Zep, now playing a street-side concerto off Lenny's box.

While they wait around for something to come down they usually pass the time hustling people passing by to buy them beers; they're well under twenty-one. Ray's folks let him have a few at home but that's no fun. Lenny lives with his mom and his two uncles. One goes to A.A. and the other was in Vietnam.

At eighteen, Ray knows the score. "I'm old enough to go into the Army, to kill, but not mature enough to drink in a bar!" Ray looks a lot like Robert Plant. He dropped out of Bergenfield High School two months ago. He hated school; they got all this "drug money," so they tried to get him to go in to see one of their "drug counselors." Lenny laughs. "And Ray doesn't even get high!"

Lenny goes by bus, then subway, to Washington Square Park to buy pot. He laughs about the enforcement of New Jersey's drinking age of twenty-one. "I can get any drug I want in five minutes but I can't buy a few beers, pretty stupid, isn't it?"

As usual, there is nothing going on. But Ray has a better attitude these days. He has recently decided to go into the Army. A month from now he is leaving Bergenfield for good. "I can't get a job around here except one that pays $3.50 an hour." And then he'd have to cut his hair, he says, work real shitty hours, give up his free time, and for what? Ray really wants to buy a Harley. His cousin is in the Army, making big money "black market" and living well. "He has a house, a bike, a truck . . . he's doing something besides getting hassled by the cops and sponging off his folks." Ray is ashamed of living this way, but he's glad it's only temporary. I figure he'll be sorry to see the hair go. But no, it won't be so bad, at least he can keep the earring. That's why he went Army. "They'll let you keep your earring." That's what his cousin said.

Both of these guys look imported from the late sixties: the flannel shirts, faded concert T-shirts, ragged-bottom jeans, an earring, and a bandanna. But there's a hard-metal overlay, an assertive edge, little details in their clothing that pin them to the late eighties.

Lenny looks to the economic side of situations. The Army and Navy recruiters want their commission. The school needs to keep enrollment for tax monies. There have been budget cuts in education. The shrinks just take your money. They need kids to justify drug money from the government. So they like to call you down to see "drug counselors" at school. Everything is a scam. At fifteen, Lenny is jaded. Lenny's alienated, populist intellect naturally gravitates to the bottom line. The doctrine behind the veil—adults getting rich off kids, pretending they give a shit. Kids snaking around the rules, and throwing it in their faces. Then there are the police.

As usual, the afternoon is structured around drama after drama. The police car across the parking lot, a guy they owe money to, a relative, some girls, drugs, food. Then the police again. "Yeah, they'll confiscate our beers and drive behind an abandoned building and get wasted themselves!" Lenny and Ray are further convinced that the police are in on burglaries, on the take. And then there are stories of beatings.

I ask about the jocks. "They get pretty wasted too, they're real party animals." Lenny says he doesn't hate jocks, just the inequality of how they are treated. He says, "If you get busted for beer, the cops look the other way because they know the kid from the station bench press, from sports. Me, I'll end up getting nailed." Why give a good kid a record, mess up his chances for the future? Kids like Lenny are somewhat more expendable. Like everyone else, Lenny and Ray speculate about what might have driven their four friends to suicide. "They just couldn't take it anymore." "Take what?" I ask. "This town!"

Lenny and Ray were archetypical teenage toxic waste that people here didn't want to know about. While the bad boys they could label as mentally disabled were safely tucked away in special education, and the less promising students were farmed out to Bergen Vo-Tech, *these* guys were the lumpenscum of the town. They were the reminders of how bad it could be if any footing was lost. Suburbia's white-trash, hard-core losers. Lenny and Ray were everyday eyesores. They were like old bedding that has been discarded but hasn't yet been carted off, just sitting there, for weeks, soiled by rain and then more trash, rotting right in your face. People just wanted them to go away, they didn't care how.

I look at Lenny. On the surface he's a mess. Bad teeth, dirty clothes, just hanging around. But he's curious, articulate, sharp. And at fifteen, he's a de facto high school dropout, waiting to be old enough to sign out legally, waiting another year after that until he can go for his equivalency diploma. He laughs at the hustle he had going at the school. He just comes in and signs his name so the school has him on the books. They'll look the other way while he disappears. A nice symbiotic setup. Kid gets to blow off school while school keeps the statistics nice and puffy. They don't want too many dropouts, Lenny says. They probably figure they're doing him a favor. And he's sure he's getting over.

Lenny wants confirmation—"You went to school," he asks me, "I mean, you understand. . . ." Very little was ever said about what was going on here; it was understood. But sometimes we did get into more formal discussions. I went to school, so Lenny figures I can validate his view of things. So we start talking about the difference between schooling and education. Lenny reads whatever his uncle has around the house. Both guys listen heavily to old Frank Zappa music. "He's cool, he stuck up for us." Lenny was referring to rock censorship debates. Zappa was very strong on kids' knowing their civil rights. He was definitely someone they respected.

Knowledge is power, true, but school had nothing to do with that, did it? Lenny's mother said he might as well drop out because she was tired of the school bugging her. He agreed he should at least get the equivalency, though.

Lenny and Ray did what they could to keep moving forward, but they were somewhat confused about the direction. First step, recoil from the mainstream. Recognize it's them, not you, who's crazy. You drop out and stay out of their sight whenever possible. Finally, you had to develop economic alternatives.

There were few satisfying legitimate avenues open to them: Lenny and Ray acknowledged that they were being manipulated, exploited, and fucked over. They tacitly understood that adults were the perpetrators.

They also understood that they were identified losers. Lenny and Ray were much more alienated than guys like Joe, who were viewed essentially as poseurs. It was too late and they were too hip for all the empty promises. Why hustle for the limited, dreary options open to them? Lenny was a street philosopher of the highest order. In one mid-afternoon dialogue he posited Lenin's rhetorical "What is to be done?" How can people extricate themselves from this shitty little game?

Lenny and Ray were also not racist; they extended their friendship on universal grounds of righteousness. Lenny had friends who played sports, were smart, or nonwhite. And it was no problem to understand how some mainstream kids' hatred of dirts and burnouts paralleled the collective hatred of newly arrived "dotheads" and "gooks."

We are stuck looking for a well-traveled answer, like "brotherhood" or "revolution," or even "looking out for number one." Truth to borrow for the moment. An explanatory scheme to tuck this all away. Something to hold on to beyond goodwill.

So I figure maybe I should give personal advice. Tell Lenny to just hang in for the new situation. Don't get depressed; be patient. The world is changing. Things will come around; they always do. It's the darkness before the dawn. I try to explain their personal hell in terms of ruptures and transformations in monopoly capitalism. History has motion, and lately everybody is reeling.

But it starts to sound really stupid. Imagine, "Well dudes, it's a real bummer, but your class of origin is now obsolete. Too bad. Your country won't be needing your labor anymore. America is a scrap yard of rusty metal. Production is over. Bon voyage, baby." But these guys are way too hip for a Springsteen whine. That's for college kids.

Maybe I could get high-toned and postmodern. "Hey, guys, welcome to the simulacrum. There's nothing to believe in here, but don't worry, Lenny, there never was. It was always . . . pretty vacant. There's nothing to hold on to and there never was.

"Look," I could say, with sincerity, "the world is changing and nobody really understands it. I don't get it. Your parents don't have a clue either. And forget about your teachers. They're doing their best just to keep the lid on. The shrinks and the police are there to scrape you off the walls if needed. We love you, but we mostly hope you'll withdraw, stay numb, and keep out of the way till we figure out what we're doing and where we can fit you in."

Words of encouragement—"So what if it's the end of the world as you know it. You'll find a new place, eventually. Meantime, have you thought about the service sector? I hear they have lovely jobs! Why not put in an application *today*. Meanwhile, even though the world around you is falling to bits gloriously, please say no to drugs and don't forget to use condoms."

I do say that sometimes, when we get confused, we seem to think it's the end of the world. Yet we always seem to survive: the Cuban missile crisis, Great Depression, world wars, industrialization. But it gets hard to say anything, so I just try to make sweet promises to them from the heart that life will go on, no matter how bad it seems. It *has* to.

Hendrix spanks a chord along the watchtower as a beer possibility walks by, ending our conversation.

SPECULATIONS

1.   What is your opinion about Gaines's statement that "even kids who do well in school learn very little about responsibility in most job settings"? Explain your response.

2.   In talking about work, Gaines states that Mr. Sun "thinks like my father. If you work, you get somewhere. But most kids just don't see it that way." Explain whether you view most jobs as "dead ends" or as a means of getting somewhere. Describe where you hope to get to and whether a job will take you there.

3.   Why does Gaines believe that Lenny and Ray will not benefit from her advice to be "patient" and that "things will come around"? What does she mean when she says "these guys are too hip for a Springsteen whine"? If you were in Lenny's or Ray's shoes, how would you respond to Gaines's arguments?

4.   For whom is Gaines writing this essay? What evidence in the text suggests that she may be trying to reach a specific audience? Going back to your own experiences as a teenager, explain why you were or were not a member of the audience Gaines is trying to reach.

5.   Like several other selections in this book, Gaines uses language that some readers might find objectionable. What are some reasons she does this? What effect does this language have in relation to her subject and her readers? What would be lost and what would be gained if she "cleaned it up"?

The Bingo Van

LOUISE ERDRICH

Born in 1954, Louise Erdrich grew up in North Dakota and belongs to the Turtle Mountain band of Chippewa Native Americans. In an interview in *Contemporary Authors*, she describes how her parents sparked her interest in reading and writing when she was a child:

My father used to give me a nickel for every story I wrote, and my mother wove strips of construction paper together and stapled them into book covers. . . . I felt myself to be a published author earning substantial royalties. Mine were wonderful parents.

Drawing upon her Chippewa heritage, Erdrich's writing describes ancestral history, family ties, sexual relationships, and eccentricities of midwestern Native Americans and their conflicts with surrounding white communities. Critics have praised Erdrich for her use of metaphor and for utilizing the stories passed through generations into the daily lives of contemporary Native Americans.

Erdrich received a B.A. from Dartmouth College and an M.A. from Johns Hopkins University. Her first novel, *Love Medicine*, which won the National Book Critics Circle Award in 1984, retells fourteen interconnected stories of several tribe members in the Mountain Chippewa community. Her second book, *The Beet Queen*, focuses on the community outside the reservation, and *Tracks*, Erdrich's third novel, deals with the struggle of Native Americans to reconcile their culture with the encroachments of the white world. "The Bingo Van" first appeared in the *New Yorker* in 1990.

When I walked into bingo that night in early spring, I didn't have a girlfriend, a home or an apartment, a piece of land or a car, and I wasn't tattooed yet, either. Now look at me. I'm walking the reservation road in borrowed pants, toward a place that isn't mine, downhearted because I'm left by a woman. All I have of my temporary riches is this black pony running across the back of my hand—a tattoo I had Lewey's Tattoo Den put there on account of a waking dream. I'm still not paid up. I still owe for the little horse. But if Lewey wants to repossess it, then he'll have to catch me first.

Here's how it is on coming to the bingo hall. It's a long, low quonset barn. Inside, there used to be a pall of smoke, but now the smoke-eater fans in the ceiling take care of that. So upon first entering you can pick out your friends. On that night in early spring, I saw Eber, Clay, and Robert Morrissey sitting about halfway up toward the curtained stage with their grandmother Lulu. By another marriage, she was my grandma, too. She had five tickets spread in front of her. The boys each had only one. When the numbers rolled, she picked up a dabber in each hand. It was the Earlybird game, a one-hundred-dollar prize, and nobody had got too wound up yet or serious.

"Lipsha, go get us a Coke," said Lulu when someone else bingoed. "Yourself, too."

I went to the concession with Eber, who had finished high school with me. Clay and Robert were younger. We got our soft drinks and came back, set them down, pulled up to the table, and laid out a new set of tickets before us. Like I say, my grandmother, she played five at once, which is how you get the big money. In the long run, much more than breaking even, she was one of those rare Chippewas who actually profited by bingo. But, then again, it was her only way of gambling. No pull-tabs, no blackjack, no slot machines for her. She never went into the back room. She banked all the cash she won. I thought I should learn from Lulu Lamartine, whose other grandsons had stiff new boots while mine were worn down into the soft shape of moccasins. I watched her.

Concentration. Before the numbers even started, she set her mouth, snapped her purse shut. She shook her dabbers so that the foam-rubber tips were thoroughly inked. She looked at the time on her watch. The Coke, she took a drink of that, but no more than a sip. She was a narrow-eyed woman with a round jaw, curled hair. Her eyeglasses, blue plastic, hung from her neck by a gleaming chain. She raised the ovals to her eyes as the caller took the stand. She held her dabbers poised while he plucked the ball from the chute. He read it out: B-7. Then she was absorbed, scanning, dabbing, into the game. She didn't mutter. She had no lucky piece to touch in front of her. And afterward, even if she lost a blackout game by one square, she never sighed or complained.

All business, that was Lulu. And all business paid.

I think I would have been all business too, like her, if it hadn't been for what lay behind the stage curtain to be revealed. I didn't know it, but that was what would change the order of my life. Because of the van, I'd have to get stupid first, then wise. You see, I had been floundering since high school, trying to catch my bearings in the world. It all lay ahead of me, spread out in the sun like a giveaway at a naming ceremony. Only thing was, I could not choose a prize. Something always stopped my hand before it reached.

"Lipsha Morrissey, you got to go for a vocation." That's what I told myself, in a state of nervous worry. I was getting by on almost no money, relying on my job as night watchman in a bar. That earned me a place to sleep, twenty dollars per week, and as much beef jerky, Beer Nuts, and spicy sausage sticks as I could eat.

I was now composed of these three false substances. No food in a bar has a shelf life of less than forty months. If you are what you eat, I would live forever, I thought.

And then they pulled aside the curtain, and I saw that I wouldn't live as long as I had coming unless I owned that van. It had every option you could believe—blue plush on the steering wheel, diamond side windows, and complete carpeted interior. The seats were easy chairs, with little headphones, and it was wired all through the walls. You could walk up close during intermission and touch the sides. The paint was cream, except for the design picked out in blue, which was a Sioux Drum border. In the back there was a small refrigerator and a carpeted platform for sleeping. It was a home, a portable den with front-wheel drive. I could see myself in it right off. I could see I *was* it.

On TV, they say you are what you drive. Let's put it this way: I wanted to be that van.

Now, I know that what I felt was a symptom of the national decline. You'll scoff at me, scorn me, say, What right does that waste Lipsha Morrissey, who makes his living guarding beer, have to comment outside of his own tribal boundary? But I was able to investigate the larger picture, thanks to Grandma Lulu, from whom I learned to be one-minded in my pursuit of a material object.

I went night after night to the bingo. Every hour I spent there, I grew more certain I was close. There was only one game per night at which the van was offered, a blackout game, where you had to fill every slot. The more tickets you bought, the more your chances increased. I tried to play five tickets, like Grandma Lulu did, but they cost five bucks each. To get my van, I had to shake hands with greed. I got unprincipled.

You see, my one talent in this life is a healing power I get passed down through the Pillager branch of my background. It's in my hands. I snap my fingers together so hard they almost spark. Then I blank out my mind, and I put on the touch. I had a reputation up to then for curing sore joints and veins. I could relieve ailments caused in an old person by a half century of grinding stoop-over work. I had a power in myself that flowed out, resistless. I had a richness in my dreams and waking thoughts. But I never realized I would have to give up my healing source once I started charging for my service.

You know how it is about charging. People suddenly think you are worth something. Used to be, I'd go anyplace I was called, take any price or take nothing. Once I let it get around that I charged a twenty for my basic work, however, the phone at the bar rang off the hook.

"Where's that medicine boy?" they asked. "Where's Lipsha?"

I took their money. And it's not like beneath the pressure of a twenty I didn't try, for I did try, even harder than before. I skipped my palms together, snapped my fingers, positioned them where the touch inhabiting them should flow. But when it came to blanking out my mind I consistently failed. For each time, in the center of the cloud that came down into my brain, the van was now parked, in perfect focus.

I suppose I longed for it like for a woman, except I wasn't that bad yet, and, anyway, then I did meet a woman, which set me back in my quest.

Instead of going for the van with everything, saving up to buy as many cards as I could play when they got to the special game, for a few nights I went short term, for variety, with U-Pickem cards, the kind where you have to choose the numbers for yourself.

First off, I wrote in the shoe and pants sizes of those Morrissey boys. No luck. So much for them. Next I took my birth date and a double of it—still no go. I wrote down the numbers of my grandma's address and her anniversary dates. Nothing. Then one night I realized if my U-Pickem was going to win it would be more like *revealed*, rather than a forced kind of thing. So I shut my eyes, right there in the middle of the long bingo table, and I let my mind blank out, white and fizzing like the screen of a television, until something formed. The van, as always. But on its tail this time a license plate was officially fixed and numbered. I used that number, wrote it down in the boxes, and then I bingoed.

I got two hundred dollars from that imaginary license. The money was in my pocket when I left. The next morning, I had fifty cents. But it's not like you think with Serena, and I'll explain that. She didn't want something from me; she didn't care if I had money, and she didn't ask for it. She was seventeen and had a two-year-old boy. That tells you about her life. Her last name was American Horse, an old Sioux name she was proud of even though it was strange to Chippewa country. At her older sister's house Serena's little boy blended in with the younger children, and Serena herself was just one of the teen-agers. She was still in high school, a year behind the year she should have been in, and she had ambitions. Her idea was to go into business and sell her clothing designs, of which she had six books.

I don't know how I got a girl so decided in her future to go with me, even that night. Except I told myself, "Lipsha, you're a nice-looking guy. You're a winner." And for the moment I was. I went right up to her at the Coin-Op and said, "Care to dance?," which was a joke—there wasn't any place to dance. Yet she liked me. We had a sandwich and then she wanted to take a drive, so we tagged along with some others in the back of their car. They went straight south, toward Hoopdance, off the reservation, where action was taking place.

"Lipsha," she whispered on the way, "I always liked you from a distance."

"Serena," I said, "I liked you from a distance, too."

So then we moved close together on the car seat. My hand was on my knee, and I thought of a couple of different ways I could gesture, casually pretend to let it fall on hers, how maybe if I talked fast she wouldn't notice, in the heat of the moment, her hand in my hand, us holding hands, our lips drawn to one another. But then I decided to boldly take courage, to take her hand as, at the same time, I looked into her eyes. I did this. In the front, the others talked among themselves. Yet we just sat there. After a while she said, "You want to kiss me?"

But I answered, not planning how the words would come out, "Our first kiss has to be a magic moment only we can share."

Her eyes went wide as a deer's, and her big smile bloomed. Her skin was dark, her long hair a burnt-brown color. She wore no jewelry, no rings, just the clothing she had sewed from her designs—a suit jacket and pair of pants that were the tan of eggshells, with symbols picked out in blue thread on the borders, the cuffs, and the hem. I took her in, admiring, for some time on that drive before I realized that the reason Serena's cute outfit nagged me so was on account of she was dressed up to match my bingo van. I could hardly tell her this surprising coincidence, but it did convince me that the time was perfect, the time was right.

They let us off at a certain place just over the reservation line, and we got out, hardly breaking our gaze from each other. You want to know what this place was? I'll tell you. O.K. So it was a motel—a long, low double row of rooms, painted white on the outside, with brown wooden doors. There was a beautiful sign set up, featuring a lake with some fish jumping out of it. We stood beside the painted water.

"I haven't done this since Jason," she said. That was the name of her two-year-old son. "I have to call up my sister first."

There was a phone near the office, inside a plastic shell. She went over there.

"He's sleeping," she said when she returned.

I went into the office, stood before the metal counter. There was a number floating in my mind.

"Is Room 22 available?" I asked.

I suppose, looking at me, I look too much like an Indian. The owner, a big sandy-haired woman in a shiny black blouse, noticed that. You get so you see it cross their face the way wind blows a disturbance on water. There was a period of contemplation, a struggle in this woman's thinking. Behind her the television whispered. Her mouth opened, but I spoke first.

"This here is Andrew Jackson," I said, tenderizing the bill. "Known for setting up our Southern relatives for the Trail of Tears. And to keep him company we got two Mr. Hamiltons."

The woman turned shrewd, and took the bills.

"No parties." She held out a key attached to a square of orange plastic.

"Just sex." I could not help but reassure her. But that was talk, big talk from a person with hardly any experience and nothing that resembled a birth-control device. I wasn't one of those so-called studs who couldn't open up their wallets without dropping a foil-wrapped square. No, Lipsha Morrissey was deep at heart a romantic, a wild-minded kind of guy, I told myself, a fool with no letup. I went out to Serena, and took her hand in mine. I was shaking inside but my voice was steady and my hands were cool.

"Let's go in." I showed the key. "Let's not think about to-morrow."

"That's how I got Jason," said Serena.

So we stood there.

"I'll go in," she said at last. "Down two blocks, there's an all-night gas station. They sell 'em."

I went. O.K. Life in this day and age might be less romantic in some ways. It seemed so in the hard twenty-four-hour fluorescent light, as I tried to choose what I needed from the rack by the counter. It was quite a display; there were dazzling choices—textures, shapes. I saw I was being watched, and I suddenly grabbed what was near my hand—two boxes, economy size.

"Heavy date?"

I suppose the guy on the late shift was bored, could not resist. His T-shirt said "Big Sky Country." He was grinning in an ugly way. So I answered.

"Not really. Fixing up a bunch of my white buddies from Montana. Trying to keep down the sheep population."

His grin stayed fixed. Maybe he had heard a lot of jokes about Montana blondes, or maybe he was from somewhere else. I looked at the boxes in my hand, put one back.

"Let me help you out," the guy said. "What you need is a bag of these."

He took down a plastic sack of little oblong party balloons, Day-Glo pinks and oranges and blues.

"Too bright," I said. "My girlfriend's a designer. She hates clashing colors." I was breathing hard suddenly, and so was he. Our eyes met and narrowed.

"What does she design?" he said. "Bedsheets?"

"What does yours design?" I said. "Wool sweaters?"

I put money between us. "For your information, my girlfriend's not only beautiful but she and I are the same species."

"Which is?"

"Take the money," I said. "Hand over my change and I'll be out of here. Don't make me do something I'd regret."

"I'd be real threatened." The guy turned from me, ringing up my sale. "I'd be shaking, except I know you Indian guys are chickenshit."

I took my package, took my change.

"Baaaaa," I said, and beat it out of there. It's strange how a bashful kind of person like me gets talkative in some of our less pleasant border-town situations.

I took a roundabout way back to Room 22 and tapped on the door. There was a little window right beside it. Serena peeked through, and let me in.

"Well," I said then, in that awkward interval, "guess we're set."

She took the bag from my hand and didn't say a word, just put it on the little table beside the bed. There were two chairs. Each of us took one. Then we sat down and turned on the television. The romance wasn't in us now for some reason, but there was something invisible that made me hopeful about the room.

It was just a small place, a modest kind of place, clean. You could smell the faint chemical of bug spray the moment you stepped inside. You could look at the television hung on the wall, or examine the picture of golden trees and a waterfall. You could take a shower for a long time in the cement shower stall, standing on your personal shower mat for safety. There was a little tin desk. You could sit down there and write a letter on a sheet of plain paper from the drawer. The lampshade was made of reeds, pressed and laced tight together. The spread on the double mattress was reddish, a rusty cotton material. There was an airconditioner, with a fan we turned on.

"I don't know why we're here," I said at last. "I'm sorry."

Serena took a small brush from her purse.

"Comb my hair?"

I took the brush and sat on the bed, just behind her. I began at the ends, very careful, but there were hardly any tangles to begin with. Her hair was a quiet brown without variation. My hand followed the brush, smoothing after each stroke, until the fall of her hair was a hypnotizing silk. I could lift my hand away from her head and the hair would follow, electric to my touch, in soft strands that hung suspended until I returned to the brushing. She never moved, except to switch off the light and then the television. She sat down again in the total dark and said, "Please, keep on," so I did. The air got thick. Her hair got lighter, full of blue static, charged so that I was held in place by the attraction. A golden spark jumped on the carpet. Serena turned toward me. Her hair floated down around her at that moment like a tent of energy.

Well, the money part is not related to that. I gave it all to Serena, that's true. Her intention was to buy material and put together the creations that she drew in her notebooks. It was fashion with a Chippewa flair, as she explained it, and sure to win prizes at the state home-ec. contest. She promised to pay me interest when she opened her own shop. The next day, after we had parted, after I had checked out the bar I was supposed to night-watch, I went off to the woods to sit and think. Not about the money, which was Serena's—and good luck to her—but about her and me.

She was two years younger than me, yet she had direction and a child, while I was aimless, lost in hyperspace, using up my talent, which was already fading from my hands. I wondered what our future could hold. One thing was sure: I never knew a man to support his family by playing bingo, and the medicine calls for Lipsha were getting fewer by the week, and fewer, as my touch failed to heal people, fled from me, and lay concealed.

I sat on ground where, years ago, my greats and my great-greats, the Pillagers, had walked. The trees around me were the dense birch and oak of old woods. The lake drifted in, gray waves, white foam in a bobbing lace. Thin gulls lined themselves up on a sandbar. The sky went dark. I closed my eyes, and that is when the little black pony galloped into my mind. It sped across the choppy waves like a skipping stone, its mane a banner, its tail a flag, and vanished on the other side of the shore.

It was luck. Serena's animal. American Horse.

"This is the last night I'm going to try for the van," I told myself. I always kept three twenties stuffed inside the edging of my blanket in back of the bar. Once that stash was gone I'd make a real decision. I'd open the yellow pages at random, and where my finger pointed I would take that kind of job.

Of course, I never counted on winning the van.

I was playing for it on the shaded side of a blackout ticket, which is always hard to get. As usual, I sat with Lulu and her boys. Her vigilance helped me. She let me use her extra dabber and she sat and smoked a filter cigarette, observing the quiet frenzy that was taking place around her. Even though that van had sat on the stage for five months, even though nobody had yet won it and everyone said it was a scam, when it came to playing for it most people bought a couple of tickets. That night, I went all out and purchased eight.

A girl read out the numbers from the hopper. Her voice was clear and light on the microphone. I didn't even notice what was happening—Lulu pointed out one place I had missed on the winning ticket. Then I had just two squares left to make a bingo and I suddenly sweated, I broke out into a chill, I went cold and hot at once. After all my pursuit, after all my plans, I was N-6 and G-60. I had narrowed myself, shrunk into the spaces on the ticket. Each time the girl read a number and it wasn't that 6 or 60 I sickened, recovered, forgot to breathe.

She must have read twenty numbers out before N-6. Then, right after that, G-60 rolled off her lips.

I screamed. I am ashamed to say how loud I yelled. That girl came over, got the manager, and then he checked out my numbers slow and careful while everyone hushed.

He didn't say a word. He checked them over twice. Then he pursed his lips together and wished he didn't have to say it.

"It's a bingo," he finally told the crowd.

Noise buzzed to the ceiling—talk of how close some others had come, green talk—and every eye was turned and cast on me, which was uncomfortable. I never was the center of looks before, not Lipsha, who everybody took for granted around here. Not all those looks were for the good, either. Some were plain envious and ready to believe the first bad thing a sour tongue could pin on me. It made sense in a way. Of all those who'd stalked that bingo van over the long months, I was now the only one who had not lost money on the hope.

O.K., so what kind of man does it make Lipsha Morrissey that the keys did not tarnish his hands one slight degree, and that he beat it out that very night in the van, completing only the basic paperwork? I didn't go after Serena, and I can't tell you why. Yet I was hardly ever happier. In that van, I rode high, but that's the thing. Looking down on others, even if it's only from the seat of a van that a person never really earned, does something to the human mentality. It's hard to say. I changed. After just one evening riding the reservation roads, passing with a swish of my tires, I started smiling at the homemade hot rods, at the clunkers below me, at the old-lady cars nosing carefully up and down the gravel hills.

I started saying to myself that I should visit Serena, and a few nights later I finally did go over there. I pulled into her sister's driveway with a flourish I could not help, as the van slipped into a pothole and I roared the engine. For a moment, I sat in the dark, letting my headlamps blaze alongside the door until Serena's brother-in-law leaned out.

"Cut the lights!" he yelled. "We got a sick child."

I rolled down my window, and asked for Serena.

"It's her boy. She's in here with him." He waited. I did, too, in the dark. A dim light was on behind him and I saw some shadows, a small girl in those pajamas with the feet tacked on, someone pacing back and forth.

"You want to come in?" he called.

But here's the gist of it: I just said to tell Serena hi for me, and then I backed out of there, down the drive, and left her to fend for herself. I could have stayed there. I could have drawn my touch back from wherever it had gone to. I could have offered my van to take Jason to the I.H.S. I could have sat there in silence as a dog guards its mate, its own blood. I could have done something different from what I did, which was to hit the road for Hoopdance and look for a better time.

I cruised until I saw where the party house was located that night. I drove the van over the low curb, into the yard, and I parked there. I watched until I recognized a couple of cars and saw the outlines of Indians and mixed, so I knew that walking in would not involve me in what the newspapers term an episode. The door was white, stained and raked by a dog, with a tiny fan-shaped window. I went through and stood inside. There was movement, a kind of low-key swirl of bright hair and dark hair tossing alongside each other. There were about as many Indians as there weren't. This party was what we call around here a Hairy Buffalo, and most people were grouped around a big brown plastic garbage can that served as the punch bowl for the all-purpose stuff, which was anything that anyone brought, dumped in along with pink Hawaiian Punch. I grew up around a lot of the people, and others I knew by sight. Among those last, there was a young familiar-looking guy.

It bothered me. I recognized him, but I didn't know him. I hadn't been to school with him, or played him in any sport, because I did not play sports. I couldn't think where I'd seen him until later, when the heat went up and he took off his bomber jacket. Then "Big Sky Country" showed, plain letters on a bright-blue background.

I edged around the corner of the room, into the hall, and stood there to argue with myself. Would he recognize me, or was I just another face, a customer? He probably wasn't really from Montana, so he might not even have been insulted by our little conversation, or remember it anymore. I reasoned that he had probably picked up the shirt vacationing, though who would want to go across that border, over to where the world got meaner? I told myself that I should calm my nerves, go back into the room, have fun. What kept me from doing that was the sudden thought of Serena, of our night together and what I had bought and used.

Once I remembered, I was lost to the present moment. One part of me caught up with the other. I realized that I had left Serena to face her crisis, alone, while I took off in my brand-new van.

I have a hard time getting drunk. It's just the way I am. I start thinking and forget to fill the cup, or recall something I have got to do, and just end up walking from a party. I have put down a full can of beer before and walked out to weed my grandma's rhubarb patch, or work on a cousin's car. Now I was putting myself in Serena's place, feeling her feelings.

What would he want to do that to me for?

I heard her voice say this out loud, just behind me, where there was nothing but wall. I edged along until I came to a door, and then I went through, into a tiny bedroom full of coats, and so far nobody either making out or unconscious upon the floor. I sat on a pile of parkas and jean jackets in this little room, an alcove in the rising buzz of the party outside. I saw a phone, and I dialed Serena's number. Her sister answered.

"Thanks a lot," she said when I said it was me. "You woke up Jason."

"What's wrong with him?" I asked.

There was a silence, then Serena's voice got on the line. "I'm going to hang up."

"Don't."

"He's crying. His ears hurt so bad he can't stand it."

"I'm coming over there."

"Forget it. Forget you."

She said the money I had loaned her would be in the mail. She reminded me it was a long time since the last time I had called. And then the phone went dead. I held the droning receiver in my hand, and tried to clear my mind. The only thing I saw in it, clear as usual, was the van. I decided this was a sign for me to get in behind the wheel. I should drive straight to Serena's house, put on the touch, help her son out. So I set my drink on the windowsill. Then I slipped out the door and I walked down the porch steps, only to find them waiting.

I guess he had recognized me after all, and I guess he was from Montana. He had friends, too. They stood around the van, and their heads were level with the roof, for they were tall.

"Let's go for a ride," said the one from the all-night gas pump.

He knocked on the window of my van with his knuckles. When I told him no thanks, he started karate-kicking the door. He wore black cowboy boots, pointy-toed, with hard-edged new heels. They left ugly dents every time he landed a blow.

"Thanks anyhow," I repeated. "But the party's not over." I tried to get back into the house, but, like in a bad dream, the door was stuck, or locked. I hollered, pounded, kicked at the very marks that desperate dog had left, but the music rose and nobody heard. So I ended up in the van. They acted very gracious. They urged me to drive. They were so polite that I tried to tell myself they weren't all that bad. And sure enough, after we had drove for a while, these Montana guys said they had chipped in together to buy me a present.

"What is it?" I asked. "Don't keep me in suspense."

"Keep driving," said the pump jockey.

"I don't really go for surprises," I said. "What's your name anyhow?"

"Marty."

"I got a cousin named Marty," I said.

"Forget it."

The guys in the back exchanged a grumbling kind of laughter, a knowing set of groans. Marty grinned, turned toward me from the passenger seat.

"If you really want to know what we're going to give you, I'll tell. It's a map. A map of Montana."

Their laughter got wild and went on for too long.

"I always liked the state," I said in a serious voice.

"No shit," said Marty. "Then I hope you like sitting on it." He signalled where I should turn, and all of a sudden I realized that Lewey's lay ahead. Lewey ran his Tattoo Den from the basement of his house, kept his equipment set up and ready for the weekend.

"Whoa," I said. I stopped the van. "You can't tattoo a person against his will. It's illegal."

"Get your lawyer on it tomorrow." Marty leaned in close for me to see his eyes. I put the van back in gear but just chugged along, desperately thinking. Lewey was a strange kind of guy, an old Dutch sailor who got beached here, about as far as you can get from salt water. I decided that I'd ask Marty, in a polite kind of way, to beat me up instead. If that failed, I would tell him that there were many states I would not mind so much—smaller, rounder ones.

"Are any of you guys from any other state?" I asked, anxious to trade.

"Kansas."

"South Dakota."

It wasn't that I really had a thing against those places, understand; it's just that the straight-edged shape is not a Chippewa preference. You look around you, and everything you see is round, everything in nature. There are no perfect boundaries, no borders. Only human-made things tend toward cubes and squares—the van, for instance. That was an example. Suddenly I realized that I was driving a wheeled version of the state of North Dakota.

"Just beat me up, you guys. Let's get this over with. I'll stop."

But they laughed, and then we were at Lewey's.

The sign on his basement door said "COME IN." I was shoved from behind and strapped together by five pairs of heavy, football-toughened hands. I was the first to see Lewey, I think, the first to notice that he was not just a piece of all the trash and accumulated junk that washed through the concrete-floored cellar but a person, sitting still as any statue, in a corner, on a chair that creaked and sang when he rose and walked over.

He even looked like a statue—not the type you see in history books, I don't mean those, but the kind you see for sale as you drive along the highway. He was a Paul Bunyan, carved with a chain saw. He was rough-looking, finished in big strokes.

"Please," I said, "I don't want . . ."

Marty squeezed me around the throat and tousled up my hair, like friendly.

"He's just got cold feet. Now remember, Lewey, map of Montana, You know where. And put in a lot of detail."

I tried to scream.

"Like I was thinking," Marty went on, "of those maps we did in grade school showing products from each region. Cows' heads, oil wells, those little sheaves of wheat, and so on."

"Tie him up," said Lewey. His voice was thick, with a commanding formal accent. "Then leave."

They did. They took my pants and the keys to the van. I heard the engine roar and die away, and I rolled from side to side in my strict bindings. I felt Lewey's hand on my shoulder.

"Be still." His voice had changed, now that the others were gone, to a low sound that went with his appearance and did not seem at all unkind. I looked up at him. A broke-down God is who he looked like from my worm's-eye view. His beard was pure white, long and patchy, and his big eyes frozen blue. His head was half bald, shining underneath the brilliant fluorescent tubes in the ceiling. You never know where you're going to find your twin in the world, your double. I don't mean in terms of looks—I'm talking about mind-set. You never know where you're going to find the same thoughts in another brain, but when it happens you know it right off, just like the two of you were connected by a small electrical wire that suddenly glows red-hot and sparks. That's what happened when I met Lewey Koep.

"I don't have a pattern for Montana," he told me. He untied my ropes with a few quick jerks, sneering at the clumsiness of the knots. Then he sat in his desk chair again, and watched me get my bearings.

"I don't want anything tattooed on me, Mr. Koep," I said. "It's a kind of revenge plot."

He sat in silence, in a waiting quiet, hands folded and face composed. By now I knew I was safe, but I had nowhere to go, and so I sat down on a pile of magazines. He asked, "What revenge?" and I told him the story, the whole thing right from the beginning, when I walked into the bingo hall. I left out the personal details about Serena and me, but he got the picture. I told him about the van.

"That's an unusual piece of good fortune."

"Have you ever had any? Good fortune?"

"All the time. Those guys paid plenty, for instance, though I suppose they'll want it back. You pick out a design. You can owe me."

He opened a book he had on the table, a notebook with plastic pages that clipped in and out, and handed it over to me. I didn't want a tattoo, but I didn't want to disappoint this man, either. I leafed through the dragons and the hearts, thinking how to refuse, and then suddenly I saw the horse. It was the same picture that had come into my head as I sat in the woods. Now here it was. The pony skimmed, legs outstretched, reaching for the edge of the page. I got a thought in my head, clear and vital, that this little horse would convince Serena I was serious about her.

"This one."

Lewey nodded, and heated his tools.

That's why I got it put on, that little horse, and suffered pain. Now my hand won't let me rest. It throbs and aches as if it was coming alive again after a hard frost had made it numb. I know I'm going somewhere, taking this hand to Serena. Even walking down the road in a pair of big-waisted green pants belonging to Lewey Koep, toward the So Long Bar, where I keep everything I own in life, I'm going forward. My hand is a ball of pins, but when I look down I see the little black horse running hard, fast, and serious.

I'm ready for what will come next. That's why I don't fall on the ground, and I don't yell, when I come across the van in a field. At first, I think it is the dream van, the way I always see it in my vision. Then I look, and it's the real vehicle. Totalled.

My bingo van is smashed on the sides, kicked and scratched, and the insides are scattered. Stereo wires, glass, and ripped pieces of carpet are spread here and there among the new sprouts of wheat. I force open a door that is bent inward. I wedge myself behind the wheel, which is tipped over at a crazy angle, and I look out. The windshield is shattered in a sunlight burst, through which the world is cut to bits.

I've been up all night, and the day stretches long before me, so I decide to sleep where I am. Part of the seat is still wonderfully upholstered, thick and plush, and it reclines now—permanently, but so what? I relax into the small comfort, my body as warm as an animal, my thoughts drifting. I know I'll wake to nothing, but at this moment I feel rich. Sinking away, I feel like everything worth having is within my grasp. All I have to do is put my hand into the emptiness.

SPECULATIONS

1.   What does Lipsha Morrissey mean when he says that the order of his life would change and that "because of the van, I'd have to get stupid first, then wise"?

2.   What circumstances cause Lipsha to lose the one talent he had in this life? Why does he see it as a "symptom of national decline"?

3.   What initiates the conflict between Lipsha and the gas station attendant from Montana? How do you interpret Lipsha's comment: "It's strange how a bashful kind of person like me gets talkative in some of our less pleasant border-town situations"?

4.   Why does Erdrich tell this story from Lipsha's point of view? If you think Erdrich made the right choice, explain why.

5.   Erdrich often makes us feel Lipsha's greatest moments of doubt, humiliation, and good fortune. Describe the points at which you identify with Lipsha's emotional state and use examples from your own life to explain how you are able to identify with his feelings. Or, describe how your experience of such feelings is different.

6.   Why does Lipsha say at the end "at this moment I feel rich"? What has he learned? And what have you learned about him, his life, his values, and his idea of wealth?

Mike LeFevre, Steelworker

STUDS TERKEL

"Next to Richard Nixon, the person whose life has been most dramatically affected by the tape recorder is Studs Terkel," according to a *Time* magazine book review. Terkel's particular genius has been his ability to interview a vast cross section of Americans. He has chronicled Americans talking about how they see themselves and their work in more than seven books.

Studs Terkel was born Louis Terkel in 1912 in New York City, but his roots are in Chicago. He grew up there, earned his law degree from the University of Chicago, worked for years on radio in Chicago, and took his nickname from the fictional Chicago character, Studs Lonigan. An enthusiastic liberal, Terkel credits blacklisting in the 1950s with ending his television career and starting his writing career. He was blacklisted for petitioning for rent control and social security and for petitioning against Jim Crow laws and poll taxes.

His first book was a collection of revealing, first-person narratives about the Depression called *Division Street: America and Hard Times*, which he followed up with *Hard Times: An Oral History of the Great Depression*. His next book, *Working: People Talk about What They Do All Day and How They Feel about What They Do*, is perhaps his best-known work, a compendium of over fifty interviews from Americans in all walks of life. In 1985 he won a Pulitzer Prize for *The Good War: An Oral History of World War II.*

Terkel's interviews are with "real people." "I celebrate the non-celebrated," the author once said. "I've found that average people want to talk about themselves, their hopes, dreams, aspirations, provided they sense that you're interested in what they're saying." In a talk to the Friends of Libraries U.S.A., Terkel said,

> The key ingredient in democracy is not saluting a flag or standing tall. It is the aware citizenry. . . . And behind each informed citizen, there is a book. . . . It may not be a major work, but some piece of reading or some story told by a grandmother or by an old stranger. And that is what enriches the life and gives that person a kind of insight.

It is a two-flat dwelling, somewhere in Cicero, on the outskirts of Chicago. He is thirty-seven. He works in a steel mill. On occasion, his wife Carol works as a waitress in a neighborhood restaurant; otherwise, she is at home, caring for their two small children, a girl and a boy.

At the time of my first visit, a sculpted statuette of Mother and Child was on the floor, head severed from body. He laughed softly as he indicated his three-year-old daughter: "she Doctor Spock'd it."

I'm a dying breed. A laborer. Strictly muscle work . . . pick it up, put it down, pick it up, put it down. We handle between forty and fifty thousand pounds of steel a day. (Laughs.) I know this is hard to believe—from four hundred pounds to three- and four-pound pieces. It's dying.

You can't take pride any more. You remember when a guy could point to a house he built, how many logs he stacked. He built it and he was proud of it. I don't really think I could be proud if a contractor built a home for me. I would be tempted to get in there and kick the carpenter in the ass (laughs), and take the saw away from him. 'Cause I would have to be part of it, you know.

It's hard to take pride in a bridge you're never gonna cross, in a door you're never gonna open. You're mass-producing things and you never see the end result of it. (Muses.) I worked for a trucker one time. And I got this tiny satisfaction when I loaded a truck. At least I could see the truck depart loaded. In a steel mill, forget it. You don't see where nothing goes.

I got chewed out by my foreman once. He said, "Mike, you're a good worker but you have a bad attitude." My attitude is that I don't get excited about my job. I do my work but I don't say whoopee-doo. The day I get excited about my job is the day I got to a head shrinker. How are you gonna get excited about pullin' steel? How are you gonna get excited when you're tired and want to sit down?

It's not just the work. Somebody built the pyramids. Somebody's going to build something. Pyramids, Empire State Building—these things just don't happen. There's hard work behind it. I would like to see a building, say, the Empire State, I would like to see on one side of it a foot-wide strip from top to bottom with the name of every bricklayer, the name of every electrician, with all the names. So when a guy walked by, he could take his son and say, "See, that's me over there on the forty-fifth floor. I put the steel beam in." Picasso can point to a painting. What can I point to? A writer can point to a book. Everybody should have something to point to.

It's the not-recognition by other people. To say a woman is *just* a housewife is degrading, right? Okay. *Just* a housewife. It's also degrading to say *just* a laborer. The difference is that a man goes out and maybe gets smashed.

When I was single, I could quit, just split. I wandered all over the country. You worked just enough to get a poke, money in your pocket. Now I'm married and I got two kids . . . (trails off). I worked on a truck dock one time and I was single. The foreman came over and he grabbed my shoulder, kind of gave me a shove. I punched him and knocked him off the dock. I said, "Leave me alone. I'm doing my work, just stay away from me, just don't give me the with-the-hands business."

Hell, if you whip a damn mule he might kick you. Stay out of my way, that's all. Working is bad enough, don't bug me. I would rather work my ass off for eight hours a day with nobody watching me than five minutes with a guy watching me. Who you gonna sock? You can't sock General Motors, you can't sock anybody in Washington, you can't sock a system.

A mule, an old mule, that's the way I feel. Oh yeah. See. (Shows black and blue marks on arms and legs, burns.) You know what I heard from more than one guy at work? "If my kid wants to work in a factory, I am going to kick the hell out of him." I want my kid to be an effete snob. Yeah, mm-hmm. (Laughs.) I want him to be able to quote Walt Whitman, to be proud of it.

If you can't improve yourself, you improve your posterity. Otherwise life isn't worth nothing. You might as well go back to the cave and stay there. I'm sure the first caveman who went over the hill to see what was on the other side—I don't think he went there wholly out of curiosity. He went there because he wanted to get his son out of the cave. Just the same way I want to send my kid to college.

I work so damn hard and want to come home and sit down and lay around. *But I gotta get it out.* I want to be able to turn around to somebody and say, "Hey, fuck you." You know? (Laughs.) The guy sitting next to me on the bus too. 'Cause all day I wanted to tell my foreman to go fuck himself, but I can't.

So I find a guy in a tavern. To tell him that. And he tells me too. I've been in brawls. He's punching me and I'm punching him, because we actually want to punch somebody else. The most that'll happen is the bartender will bar us from the tavern. But at work, you lose your job.

This one foreman I've got, he's a kid. He's a college graduate. He thinks he's better than everybody else. He was chewing me out and I was saying, "Yeah, yeah, yeah." He said, "What do you mean, yeah, yeah, yeah. Yes, *sir*." I told him, "Who the hell are you, Hitler? What is this '*Yes, sir*' bullshit? I came here to work, I didn't come here to crawl. There's a fuckin' difference." One word led to another and I lost.

I got broke down to a lower grade and lost twenty-five cents an hour, which is a hell of a lot. It amounts to about ten dollars a week. He came over—after breaking me down. The guy comes over and smiles at me. I blew up. He didn't know it, but he was about two seconds and two feet away from a hospital. I said, "Stay the fuck away from me." He was just about to say something and was pointing his finger. I just reached my hand up and just grabbed his finger and I just put it back in his pocket. He walked away. I grabbed his finger because I'm married. If I'd a been single, I'd a grabbed his head. That's the difference.

You're doing this manual labor and you know that technology can do it. (Laughs.) Let's face it, a machine can do the work of a man; otherwise they wouldn't have space probes. Why can we send a rocket ship that's unmanned and yet send a man in a steel mill to do a mule's work?

Automation? Depends how it's applied. It frightens me if it puts me out on the street. It doesn't frighten me if it shortens my work week. You read that little thing: What are you going to do when this computer replaces you? Blow up computers. (Laughs.) Really. Blow up computers. I'll be goddamned if a computer is gonna eat before I do! I want milk for my kids and beer for me. Machines can either liberate man or enslave 'im, because they're pretty neutral. It's man who has the bias to put the thing one place or another.

If I had a twenty-hour workweek, I'd get to know my kids better, my wife better. Some kid invited me to go on a college campus. On a Saturday. It was summertime. Hell, if I had a choice of taking my wife and kids to a picnic or going to a college campus, it's gonna be the picnic. But if I worked a twenty-hour week, I could go do both. Don't you think with that extra twenty hours people could really expand? Who's to say? There are some people in factories just by force of circumstance. I'm just like the colored people. Potential Einsteins don't have to be white. They could be in cotton fields, they could be in factories.

The twenty-hour week is a possibility today. The intellectuals, they always say there are potential Lord Byrons, Walt Whitmans, Roosevelts, Picassos working in construction or steel mills or factories. But I don't think they believe it. I think what they're afraid of is the potential Hitlers and Stalins that are there too. The people in power fear the leisure man. Not just the United States. Russia's the same way.

What do you think would happen in this country if, for one year, they experimented and gave everybody a twenty-hour week? How do they know that the guy who digs Wallace today doesn't try to resurrect Hitler tomorrow? Or the guy who is mildly disturbed at pollution doesn't decide to go to General Motors and shit on the guy's desk? You can become a fanatic if you had the time. The whole thing is time. That is, I think, one reason rich kids tend to be fanatic about politics: They have time. Time, that's the important thing.

It isn't that the average working guy is dumb. He's tired, that's all. I picked up a book on chess one time. That thing laid in the drawer for two or three weeks, you're too tired. During the weekends you want to take your kids out. You don't want to sit there and the kid comes up: "Daddy, can I go to the park?" You got your nose in a book? Forget it.

I know a guy fifty-seven years old. Know what he tells me? "Mike, I'm old and tired *all* the time." The first thing happens at work: When the arms start moving, the brain stops. I punch in about ten minutes to seven in the morning. I say hello to a couple of guys I like, I kid around with them. One guy says good morning to you and you say good morning. To another guy you say fuck you. The guy you say fuck you to is your friend.

I put on my hard hat, change into my safety shoes, put on my safety glasses, go to the bonderizer. It's the thing I work on. They rake the metal, they wash it, they dip it in a paint solution, and we take it off. Put it on, take it off, put it on, take it off, put it on, take it off. . . .

I say hello to everybody but my boss. At seven it starts. My arms get tired about the first half-hour. After that, they don't get tired any more until maybe the last half-hour at the end of the day. I work from seven to three thirty. My arms are tired at seven thirty and they're tired at three o'clock. I hope to God I never get broke in, because I always want my arms to be tired at seven thirty and three o'clock. (Laughs.) 'Cause that's when I know that there's a beginning and there's an end. That I'm not brainwashed. In between, I don't even try to think.

If I were to put you in front of a dock and I pulled up a skid in front of you with fifty hundred-pound sacks of potatoes and there are fifty more skids just like it, and this is what you're gonna do all day, what would you think about—potatoes? Unless a guy's a nut, he never thinks about work or talks about it. Maybe about baseball or about getting drunk the other night or he got laid or he didn't get laid. I'd say one out of a hundred will actually get excited about work.

Why is it that the communists always say they're for the working-man, and as soon as they set up a country, you got guys singing to tractors? They're singing about how they love the factory. That's where I couldn't buy communism. It's the intellectuals' utopia, not mine. I cannot picture myself singing to a tractor, I just can't. (Laughs.) Or singing to steel. (Singsongs.) Oh whoop-dee-doo, I'm at the bonderizer, oh how I love this heavy steel. No thanks. Never happen.

Oh yeah, I daydream. I fantasize about a sexy blonde in Miami who's got my union dues. (Laughs.) I think of the head of the union the way I think of the head of my company. Living it up. I think of February in Miami. Warm weather, a place to lay in. When I hear a college kid say, "I'm oppressed," I don't believe him. You know what I'd like to do for one year? Live like a college kid. Just for one year. I'd love to. Wow! (Whispers.) Wow! Sports car! Marijuana! (Laughs.) Wild, sexy broads. I'd love that, hell yes, I would.

Somebody has to do this work. If my kid ever goes to college, I just want him to have a little respect, to realize that his dad is one of those somebodies. This is why even on—(muses) yeah, I guess, sure—on the black thing. . . . (Sighs heavily.) I can't really hate the colored fella that's working with me all day. The black intellectual I got no respect for. The white intellectual I got no use for. I got no use for the black militant who's gonna scream three hundred years of slavery to me while I'm busting my ass. You know what I mean? (Laughs.) I have one answer for that guy: Go see Rockefeller. See Harriman. Don't bother me. We're in the same cotton field. So just don't bug me. (Laughs.)

After work I usually stop off at a tavern. Cold beer. Cold beer right away. When I was single, I used to go into hillbilly bars, get in a lot of brawls. Just to explode. I got a thing on my arm here (indicates scar). I got slapped with a bicycle chain. Oh, wow! (Softly.) Mmm. I'm getting older. (Laughs.) I don't explode as much. You might say I'm broken in. (Quickly.) No, I'll never be broken in. (Sighs.) When you get a little older, you exchange the words. When you're younger, you exchange the blows.

When I get home, I argue with my wife a little bit. Turn on TV, get mad at the news. (Laughs.) I don't even watch the news that much. I watch Jackie Gleason. I look for any alternative to the ten o'clock news. I don't want to go to bed angry. Don't hit a man with anything heavy at five o'clock. He just can't be bothered. This is his time to relax. The heaviest thing he wants is what his wife has to tell him.

When I come home, know what I do for the first twenty minutes? Fake it. I put on a smile. I got a kid three years old. Sometimes she says, "Daddy, where've you been?" I say, "Work." I could have told her I'd been in Disneyland. What's work to a three-year-old kid? If I feel bad, I can't take it out on the kids. Kids are born innocent of everything but birth. You can't take it out on your wife either. This is why you go to a tavern. You want to release it there rather than do it at home. What does an actor do when he's got a bad movie? I got a bad movie every day.

I don't even need the alarm clock to get up in the morning. I can go out drinking all night, fall asleep at four, and bam! I'm up at six—no matter what I do. (Laughs.) It's a pseudo-death, more or less. Your whole system is paralyzed and you give all the appearance of death. It's an ingrown clock. It's a thing you just get used to. The hours differ. It depends. Sometimes my wife wants to do something crazy like play five hundred rummy or put a puzzle together. It could be midnight, could be ten o'clock, could be nine thirty.

What do you do weekends?

Drink beer, read a book. See that one? *Violence in America.* It's one of them studies from Washington. One of the committees they're always appointing. A thing like that I read on a weekend. But during the weekdays, gee . . . I just thought about it. I don't do that much reading from Monday through Friday. Unless it's a horny book. I'll read it at work and go home and do my homework. (Laughs.) That's what the guys at the plant call it—homework. (Laughs.) Sometimes my wife works on Saturday and I drink beer at the tavern.

I went out drinking with one guy, oh, a long time ago. A college boy. He was working where I work now. Always preaching to me about how you need violence to change the system and all that garbage. We went into a hillbilly joint. Some guy there, I didn't know him from Adam, he said, "You think you're smart," I said, "What's your pleasure?" (Laughs.) He said, "My pleasure's to kick your ass." I told him I really can't be bothered. He said, "What're you, chicken?" I said, "No, I just don't want to be bothered." He came over and said something to me again. I said, "I don't beat women, drunks, or fools. Now leave me alone."

The guy called his brother over. This college boy that was with

me, he came nudging my arm, "Mike, let's get out of here." I said,
"What are you worried about?" (Laughs.) This isn't unusual. People
will bug you. You fend it off as much as you can with your mouth
and when you can't, you punch the guy out.

It was close to closing time and we stayed. We could have left,
but when you go into a place to have a beer and a guy challenges
you—if you expect to go in that place again, you don't leave. If you
have to fight the guy, you fight.

I got just outside the door and one of these guys jumped on me
and grabbed me around the neck. I grabbed his arm and flung him
against the wall. I grabbed him here (indicates throat), and jiggled his
head against the wall quite a few times. He kind of slid down a little
bit. This guy who said he was his brother took a swing at me with a
garrison belt. He just missed and hit the wall. I'm looking around for
my junior Stalin (laughs), who loves violence and everything. He's
gone. Split. (Laughs.) Next day I see him at work. I couldn't get mad
at him, he's a baby.

He saw a book in my back pocket one time and he was amazed.
He walked up to me and he said, "You read?" I said, "What do you
mean, I read?" He said, "All these dummies read the sports pages
around here. What are you doing with a book?" I got pissed off at the
kid right away. I said, "What do you mean, all these dummies? Don't
knock a man who's paying somebody else's way through college."
He was a nineteen-year-old effete snob.

Yet you want your kid to be an effete snob?

Yes. I want my kid to look at me and say, "Dad, you're a nice
guy, but you're a fuckin' dummy." Hell yes, I want my kid to tell me
that he's not gonna be like me. . . .

If I were hiring people to work, I'd try naturally to pay them a
decent wage. I'd try to find out their first names, their last names,
keep the company as small as possible, so I could personalize the
whole thing. All I would ask a man is a handshake, see you in the
morning. No applications, nothing. I wouldn't be interested in the
guy's past. Nobody ever checks the pedigree on a mule, do they? But
they do on a man. Can you picture walking up to a mule and saying,
"I'd like to know who his granddaddy was"?

I'd like to run a combination bookstore and tavern. (Laughs.) I
would like to have a place where college kids came and a steelworker
could sit down and talk. Where a workingman could not be ashamed
of Walt Whitman and where a college professor could not be ashamed
that he painted his house over the weekend.

If a carpenter built a cabin for poets, I think the least the poets owe the carpenter is just three or four one-liners on the wall. A little plaque: Though we labor with our minds, this place we can relax in was built by someone who can work with his hands. And his work is as noble as ours. I think the poet owes something to the guy who builds the cabin for him.

I don't think of Monday. You know what I'm thinking about on Sunday night? Next Sunday. If you work real hard, you think of a perpetual vacation. Not perpetual sleep. . . . What do I think of on a Sunday night? Lord, I wish the fuck I could do something else for a living.

I don't know who the guy is who said there is nothing sweeter than an unfinished symphony. Like an unfinished painting and an unfinished poem. If he creates this thing one day—let's say, Michelangelo's Sistine Chapel. It took him a long time to do this, this beautiful work of art. But what if he had to create this Sistine Chapel a thousand times a year? Don't you think that would even dull Michelangelo's mind? Or if da Vinci had to draw his anatomical charts thirty, forty, fifty, sixty, eighty, ninety, a hundred times a day? Don't you think that would even bore da Vinci?

Way back, you spoke of the guys who built the pyramids, not the pharaohs, the unknown. You put yourself in their category?

Yes. I want my signature on 'em, too. Sometimes, out of pure meanness, when I make something, I put a little dent in it. I like to do something to make it really unique.

SPECULATIONS

1. What shapes Mike LeFevre's attitude toward his work? What does he feel he is missing and how has it created his attitude?

2. How would you describe the problems that haunt LeFevre with regard to automation and the workplace? How would you respond to his question, "Why can we send a rocket ship that's unmanned [into space] and yet send a man in a steel mill to do a mule's work?"

3. Explain why you agree or disagree with LeFevre's assertion that if people had more time "to expand," they would upset the balance of political power because "The people in power fear the leisure man. Not just the United States. Russia's the same way."

4. What speaking style dominates LeFevre's description of work and his relationships at work? How does his way of speaking change when he talks about his family?

5. How would you characterize LeFevre's politics? Use specific examples and statements he makes about political figures and political movements. What motivates his view?

Ella, in a square apron, along Highway 80

JUDY GRAHN

By the time Judy Grahn was twenty-five, she had worked as a waitress, short-order cook, barmaid, and typesetter. Then she became deathly ill and lapsed into a coma; the experience was a turning point. When she recovered, Grahn committed herself to poetry, something she had wanted to do since the age of twelve. Grahn is now a well-known writer, a lesbian feminist who has devoted her professional life to improving public awareness and acceptance of not only gay women but all women struggling to find a place in the world of work and wealth.

Grahn's first collection, *Edward the Dyke and Other Poems*, a satire written in 1965, was turned down unanimously by publishers. Her frustration led her to form the Women's Press Collective in Oakland, California, which Grahn described in *Contemporary Authors*:

> Our press was deliberately located in a public place, in one room of a bookstore. This room had a huge plate-glass wall, and we didn't curtain it. We were a living exhibition for about three years. Women would come and stand at the window and watch us. They would come in and burst into tears, because they had never seen women doing what we were doing. It gave them lots of ideas.

Born in Chicago in 1940, Grahn has been living in San Francisco for twenty years. She helped start the Lesbian Mother's Union and A Woman's Place Bookstore (in Oakland), and has been active in many other political movements.

Grahn's most acclaimed works are *The Work of a Common Woman: The Collected Poetry of Judy Grahn, 1964–1977*, and *Queen of Wands*, an account of Helen of Troy, which won the American Book Award for multicultural merit in 1982. She has, in addition, written *Another Mother Tongue: Gay Words, Gay Worlds* (1984); *The Highest Apple: Sappho and the Lesbian Poetic Tradition* (1985); and *Blood and Bread and Roses* (1986), a work of nonfiction.

She's a copperheaded waitress,
tired and sharp-worded, she hides
her bad brown tooth behind a wicked
smile, and flicks her ass
out of habit, to fend off the pass
that passes for affection.
She keeps her mind the way men
keep a knife—keen to strip the game
down to her size. She has a thin spine,
swallows her eggs cold, and tells lies.
She slaps a wet rag at the truck drivers

if they should complain. She understands
the necessity for pain, turns away
the smaller tips, out of pride, and
keeps a flask under the counter. Once,
she shot a lover who misused her child.
Before she got out of jail, the courts had pounced
and given the child away. Like some isolated lake,
her flat blue eyes take care of their own stark
bottoms. Her hands are nervous, curled, ready
to scrape.
The common woman is as common
as a rattlesnake.

SPECULATIONS

1.   Why is Ella compared to a rattlesnake? What do they have in common?
2.   What is the role of work in this poem? How does it shape Ella and her
responses to the world?

The Wages of the Backlash: The Toll on Working Women

SUSAN FALUDI

In the introduction to *Backlash: The Undeclared War Against American
Women*, Susan Faludi asks the following questions:

> If American women are so equal, why do they represent two-thirds of all
> poor adults? Why are nearly 75 percent of full-time working women mak-
> ing less than $20,000 a year, nearly double the male rate? Why are they
> still far more likely than men to live in poor housing and receive no health
> insurance, and twice as likely to draw no pension? Why does the average
> working woman's salary still lag as far behind the average man's as it did
> twenty years ago? Why does the average female college graduate today
> earn less than a man with no more than a high school diploma (just as
> she did in the '50s)—and why does the average female high school gradu-
> ate today earn less than a male high school dropout? Why do American
> women, in fact, face one of the worst gender-based pay gaps in the devel-
> oped world?

Faludi's book addresses these issues in what she calls the "backlash" effect, which has eroded women's economic position while
trumpeting their supposed equality.
   Faludi, a Pulitzer Prize-winning writer, has been nominated for a
National Book Award. A reporter for the *Wall Street Journal*, America's most prestigious business newspaper, Faludi's essays and arti-

cles have also appeared in *West,* the Sunday magazine of the *San Jose Mercury News.*

Faludi describes herself as a "female writer with strong convictions . . . I write so forcefully because I speak so tentatively." She recalls how as editor of her high school newspaper she would speak out against injustices in print but would seldom speak during class discussions: "We saw what happened to the girls who argued in class. The boys called them 'bitches,' and they sat home Saturday nights. Popular girls raised their voices only at pep squad."

As a popular public speaker because of *Backlash,* Faludi has learned that "the writer asserts herself from behind the veil of the printed page . . . [but] until you translate personal words on a page into public connections with other people, you aren't really part of a political movement. . . ."

The backlash against women's rights would be just one of several powerful forces creating a harsh and painful climate for women at work. Reaganomics, the recession, and the expansion of a minimum-wage service economy also helped, in no small measure, to slow and even undermine women's momentum in the job market.

But the backlash did more than impede women's opportunities for employment, promotions, and better pay. Its spokesmen kept the news of many of these setbacks from women. Not only did the backlash do grievous damage to working women—it did it on the sly. The Reagan administration downplayed or simply shelved reports that revealed the extent of working women's declining status. Corporations claimed women's numbers and promotions were at record highs. And the press didn't seem to mind. As the situation of working women fell into increasing peril in the '80s, the backlash media issued ever more upbeat reports—assuring that women's only problem at work was that they would rather be home.

Many myths about working women's "improving" circumstances made the rounds in the '80s—while some discouraging and *real* trends that working women faced didn't get much press. Here are just a few examples.

The trend story we all read about women's wages:
PAY GAP BETWEEN THE SEXES CLOSING!
The difference between the average man's and woman's paycheck, we learned in 1986, had suddenly narrowed. Women who work full-time were now said to make an unprecedented 70 cents to a man's dollar. Newspaper editorials applauded and advised feminists to retire their "obsolete" buttons protesting female pay of 59 cents to a man's dollar.
The trend story we should have seen:
IT'S BACK! THE '50s PAY GAP

The pay gap did *not* suddenly improve to 70 cents in 1986. Women working full-time made only 64 cents to a man's dollar that year, actually slightly *worse* than the year before—and exactly the same gap that working women had faced in *1955*.

The press got the 70-cent figure from a onetime Census Bureau report that was actually based on data from another year and that departed from the bureau's standard method for computing the gap. This report artificially inflated women's earnings by using weekly instead of the standard yearly wages—thus grossly exaggerating the salary of part-time workers, a predominantly female group, who don't work a full year. Later, the Census Bureau calculated the pay gap for 1986 using its standard formula and came up with 64 cents. This report, however, managed to elude media notice.

By that year, in fact, the pay gap had only "improved" for women by less than five percentage points since 1979. And as much as half of that improvement was due to men's falling wages, not women's improving earnings. Take out men's declining pay as a factor and the gap had closed only three percentage points.

By 1988, women with a college diploma could still wear the famous 59-cent buttons. They were still making 59 cents to their male counterparts' dollar. In fact, the pay gap for them was now a bit worse than five years earlier. Black women, who had made almost no progress in the decade, could wear the 59-cent buttons, too. Older and Hispanic women couldn't—but only because their pay gap was even worse now than 59 cents. Older working women had actually fared better in *1968*, when they had made hourly wages of 61 cents to a man's dollar; by 1986, they were down to 58 cents. And Hispanic women, by 1988, found their wages backsliding; they were now making an abysmal 54 cents to a white man's dollar.

The pay gap was also getting worse in many occupations, from social work to screenwriting to real estate management, as U.S. Labor Department data detail. By 1989, the pay gap for women in all full-time managerial jobs was growing worse again; that year, while the average male manager enjoyed a four-percent income boost, his average female counterpart received none. And the gap was widening most in the very fields where female employment was growing most, a list that includes food preparation and service supervisory jobs, waiting tables, and cleaning services. In public relations, where women doubled their ranks in the decade, the pay gap grew so massively that communications professor Elizabeth Lance Toth, who tracks women's status in this profession, reported, "In a forty-year career, a woman will lose $1 million on gender alone.

The trend story we all read about integrating the workplace:
WOMEN INVADE MAN'S WORLD!

Women, we learned, charged into traditional "male" occupations. A sea of women in their dress-for-success suits and stride-to-work sneakers abandoned the "pink-collar" ghettos and descended on Wall Street, law firms, and corporate suites. Still other women laced up army boots, slapped on hard hats, and barged into the all-male military and blue-collar factories.

The trend story we should have seen:

MORE AND MORE, WOMEN STUCK IN SECRETARIAL POOL

While the level of occupational segregation between the sexes eased by 9 percent in the 1970s—the first time it had improved in the century—that progress stalled in the '80s. The Bureau of Labor Statistics soon began projecting a more sex-segregated work force. This was a bitter financial pill for women: as much as 45 percent of the pay gap is caused by sex segregation in the work force. (By one estimate, for every 10 percent rise in the number of women in an occupation, the annual wage for women drops by roughly $700.) A resegregating work force was one reason why women's wages fell in the '80s; by 1986, more working women would be taking home poverty-level wages than in 1973.

Women were pouring into many low-paid female work ghettos. The already huge proportion of working women holding down menial clerical jobs climbed to nearly 40 percent by the early '80s, higher than it had been in 1970. By the late '80s, the proportion of women consigned to the traditionally female service industries had grown, too. A long list of traditionally "female" jobs became *more* female-dominated, including salesclerking, cleaning services, food preparation, and secretarial, administrative, and reception work. The proportion of bookkeepers who were women, for example, rose from 88 to 93 percent between 1979 and 1986. Black women, especially, were resegregated into such traditional female jobs as nursing, teaching, and secretarial and social work. And the story was the same at the office of the nation's largest employer, the federal government. Between 1976 and 1986, the lowest job rungs in the civil service ladder went from 67 to 71 percent female. (At the same time at the top of the ladder, the proportion of women in senior executive services had not improved since 1979—it was still a paltry 8 percent. And the rate of women appointed to top posts had declined to the point that, by the early '80s, less than 1 percent of the G.S. 13 and 14 grade office holders were women.)

In the few cases where working women did make substantial inroads into male enclaves, they were only admitted by default. As a job-integration study by sociologist Barbara Reskin found, in the dozen occupations where women had made the most progress entering "male " jobs—a list that ranged from typesetting to insurance adjustment to pharmaceuticals—women succeeded only because the pay and status of these jobs had fallen dramatically and men were bailing out. Computerization, for example, had demoted male typesetters to typists; the retail chaining of drugstores had turned independent pharmacists into poorly paid clerks. Other studies of women's "progress" in bank management found that women were largely just inheriting branch-manager jobs that men didn't want anymore because their pay, power, and status had declined dramatically. And still another analysis of occupational shifts concluded that one-third of the growth of female employment in transportation and half of the growth in financial services could be attributed simply to a loss of status in the jobs that women were getting in these two professions.

In many of the higher-paying white-collar occupations, where women's successes have been most heavily publicized, the rate of progress slowed to a trickle or stopped altogether by the end of the decade. The proportion of women in some of the more elite or glamorous fields actually shrank slightly in the last half of the '80s. Professional athletes, screenwriters, commercial voice-overs, producers and orchestra musicians, economists, geologists, biological and life scientists were all a little *less* likely to be female by the late '80s than earlier in the decade.

The breathless reports about droves of female "careerists" crashing the legal, medical, and other elite professions were inflated. Between 1972 and 1988, women increased their share of such professional jobs by only 5 percent. In fact, only 2 percent more of all working women were in professional specialties in 1988 than fifteen years earlier—and that increase had been largely achieved by the early '80s and barely budged since.

Hardly any progress occurred in the upper echelons of corporations. In fact, according to scattered studies, in the top executive suites in many industries, from advertising to retailing, women's already tiny numbers were beginning to fall once more by the end of the decade. The rate of growth in numbers of women appointed to Fortune 1000 boards slacked off by the late '80s, after women's share of the director chairs had reached only 6.8 percent. Even the many reports of the rise of female "entrepreneurs" founding their own companies masked the nickel-and-dime reality: the majority of white female-owned businesses had sales of less than $5,000 a year.

Under Reagan, women's progress in the military soon came under fire. In the mid-'70s, after quota ceilings on female recruits had been lifted and combat classifications rewritten to open more jobs to women, women's ranks in the armed services had soared—by 800 percent by 1980. But shortly after Reagan's election, the new army chief of staff declared, "I have called a pause to further increases in the number of army women"—and by 1982, the army had revised combat classifications to bar women from an additional twenty-three career occupations. All the services reined in their recruitment efforts, subsequently slowing female employment growth in the military throughout the '80s.

The blue-collar working world offered no better news. After 1983, as a Labor Department study quietly reported to no fanfare, women made *no* progress breaking into the blue-collar work force with its better salaries. By 1988, the tiny proportions of women who had squeezed into the trades were shrinking in a long list of job categories from electricians and plumbers to automotive mechanics and machine operators. The already tiny ranks of female carpenters, for example, fell by half, to 0.5 percent, between 1979 and 1986. Higher up the ladder, women's share of construction inspector jobs fell from 7 to 5.4 percent between 1983 and 1988.

Where women did improve their toeholds in blue-collar jobs, the increments were pretty insubstantial. The proportion of women in construction, for example, rose from 1.1 to 1.4 percent between 1978 and 1988. Women made the most progress in the blue-collar professions as motor vehicle operators—more than doubling their numbers between 1972 and 1985—but that was only because women were being hired to drive school buses, typically a part-time job with the worst pay and benefits of any transportation position.

The trend story we all read about equal opportunity:
DISCRIMINATION ON THE JOB: FADING FAST!

Corporations, we read, were now welcoming women. "Virtually all large employers are now on [women's] side," *Working Woman* assured female readers in 1986. Discrimination was dropping, mistreatment of female workers was on the wane—and any reports to the contrary were just "propaganda from self-interested parties," as *Forbes* asserted in 1989—in its story on the "decline" of sexual harassment on the job.

The trend story we should have seen:
NOW MORE THAN EVER! INEQUITY AND INTIMIDATION

Reports of sex discrimination and sexual harassment reached record highs in the decade—by both private and federal employees. Women's sex discrimination complaints to the Equal Employment Opportunity Commission (EEOC) climbed by nearly 25 percent in the Reagan years—and by 40 percent among federally employed women just in the fist half of the '80s. Complaints of exclusion, demotions, and discharges on the basis of sex rose 30 percent. General harassment of women, excluding sexual harassment, more than doubled. And while the EEOC's public relations office issued statements claiming that sexual harassment in corporate America was falling, its own figures showed that annual charges of sexual harassment nearly doubled in the decade.

Throughout much of the '80s, women were also far more likely than men to lose their jobs or get their wages cut—and legal challenges to remedy the imbalance went nowhere in the courts. Press accounts to the contrary, the mass layoffs of the '80s actually took a greater toll on female service workers than male manufacturing workers—the service sector accounted for almost half of the job displacement in the decade, nearly 10 percentage points more than manufacturing. And even among blue-collar workers, women suffered higher unemployment rates than men. In the federal "reductions in force" in the early '80s, too, women who held higher-paid civil-service jobs (G.S. 12 and above) got laid off at more than twice the average rate. Far more working women than men were also forced into the part-time work force and expanding "temp" pools of the '80s, where women faced an extraordinary pay gap of 52 cents to a man's dollar and labored with little to no job security, insurance, benefits, or pension. Even among displaced workers who managed to get rehired, women had it worse. Women in service jobs who were reemployed had to settle for pay reductions of 16 percent, nearly double the reductions borne by their male counterparts.

If we heard less about discrimination in the '80s workplace, that was partly because the federal government had muzzled, or fired, its equal-employment investigators. At the same time that the EEOC's sex discrimination files were overflowing, the Reagan administration was cutting the agency's budget in half and jettisoning its caseload. The year Reagan came into office, the EEOC had twenty-five active class-action cases; a year later, it had none. The agency scaled back the number of suits it pursued by more than 300 percent. A House Education and Labor Committee report found that in the first half of the '80s, the number of discrimination victims receiving compensation fell by two-thirds. By 1987, a General Accounting Office study found that EEOC district offices and state equal-employment agencies were closing 40 to 80 percent of their cases without proper, or any, investigation.

A similar process was taking place in the other federal agencies charged with enforcing equal opportunity for women and minorities. At the Office of Federal Contract Compliance (OFCC), for example, back-pay awards fell from $9.3 million in 1980 to $600,000 in 1983; the number of government contractors that this agency barred from federal work because of discrimination fell from five in the year before Reagan took office to none a year after his inauguration. In fact, in a 1982 study, every OFCC staff member interviewed said that they had never found a company *not* to be in compliance. This wasn't because American corporations had suddenly reformed: the majority of federal contractors polled in the same study said they just felt no pressure to comply with the agency's affirmative action requirements anymore.

An exhaustive study of women's occupational patterns in the '80s would be outside the scope of this *book*. But it is possible to tell the stores of some women in key representative employment areas—from the white-collar media to the pink-collar sales force to the most embattled blue-collar universe. These are women who, one way or another, set themselves against the backlash in the work force and, in the process, ran up against the barriers built by employers, male peers, judges, government officials, and even "feminist" scholars. They had to face ridicule, ostracism, threats and even physical assaults—as they simply tried to make a living.

Diane Joyce: Women in the Blue-Collar World

It would take Diane Joyce nearly ten years of battles to become the first female skilled crafts worker ever in Santa Clara County history. It would take another seven years of court litigation, pursued all the way to the U.S. Supreme Court, before she could actually start work. And then, the real fight would begin.

For blue-collar women, there was no honeymoon period on the job; the backlash began the first day they reported to work—and only intensified as the Reagan economy put more than a million blue-collar men out of work, reduced wages, and spread mounting fear. While the white-collar world seemed capable of absorbing countless lawyers and bankers in the '80s, the trades and crafts had no room for expansion. "Women are far more economically threatening in blue-collar work, because there are a finite number of jobs from which to choose," Mary Ellen Boyd, executive director of Non-Traditional Employment for Women, observes. "An MBA can do anything. But a plumber is only a plumber." While women never represented more than a few percentage points of the blue-collar work force, in this powder-keg situation it only took a few female faces to trigger a violent explosion.

Diane Joyce arrived in California in 1970, a thirty-three-year-old widow with four children, born and raised in Chicago. Her father was a tool-and-die maker, her mother a returned-goods clerk at a Walgreen's warehouse. At eighteen, she married Donald Joyce, a tool-and-die maker's apprentice at her father's plant. Fifteen years later, after working knee-deep in PCBs for years, he died suddenly of a rare form of liver cancer.

After her husband's death, Joyce taught herself to drive, packed her children in a 1966 Chrysler station wagon and headed west to San Jose, California, where a lone relative lived. Joyce was an experienced bookkeeper and she soon found work as a clerk in the county Office of Education, at $506 a month. A year later, she heard that the county's transportation department had a senior account clerk job vacant that paid $50 more a month. She applied in March 1972.

"You know, we wanted a man," the interviewer told her as soon as she walked through the door. But the account clerk jobs had all taken a pay cut recently, and sixteen women and no men had applied for the job. So he sent her on to the second interview. "This guy was a little politer," Joyce recalls. "First, he said, 'Nice day, isn't it?' before he tells me, 'You know, we wanted a man.' I wanted to say, 'Yeah, and where's my man? I am the man in my house.' But I'm sitting there with four kids to feed and all I can see is dollar signs, so I kept my mouth shut."

She got the job. Three months later, Joyce saw a posting for a "road maintenance man." An eighth-grade education and one year's work experience was all that was required, and the pay was $723 a month. Her current job required a high-school education, bookkeeping skills, and four years' experience—and paid $150 less a month. "I saw that flier and I said, 'Oh wow, I can do that.' Everyone in the office laughed. They thought it was a riot. . . . I let it drop."

But later that same year, every county worker got a 2 to 5 percent raise except for the 70 female account clerks. "Oh now, what do you girls need a raise for?" the director of personnel told Joyce and some other women who went before the board of supervisors to object. "All you'd do is spend the money on trips to Europe." Joyce was shocked. "Every account clerk I knew was supporting a family through death or divorce. I'd never seen Mexico, let alone Europe." Joyce decided to apply for the next better-paying "male" job that opened. In the meantime, she became active in the union; a skillful writer and one of the best-educated representatives there, Joyce wound up composing the safety language in the master contract and negotiating what became the most powerful county agreement protecting seniority rights.

In 1974, a road dispatcher retired, and both Joyce and a man named Paul Johnson, a former oil-fields roustabout, applied for the post. The supervisors told Joyce she needed to work on the road crew first and handed back her application. Johnson didn't have any road crew experience either, but his application was accepted. In the end, the job went to another man.

Joyce set out to get road crew experience. As she was filling out her application for the next road crew job that opened, in 1975, her supervisor walked in, asked what she was doing, and turned red. "You're taking a man's job away!" he shouted. Joyce sat silently for a minute, thinking. Then she said, "No, I'm not. Because a man can sit right here where I'm sitting."

In the evenings, she took courses in road maintenance and truck and light equipment operation. She came in third out of 87 applicants on the job test; there were ten openings on the road crew, and she got one of them.

For the next four years, Joyce carried tar pots on her shoulder, pulled trash from the median strip, and maneuvered trucks up the mountains to clear mud slides. "Working outdoors was great," she says. "You know, women pay fifty dollars a month to join a health club, and here I was getting paid to get in shape."

The road men didn't exactly welcome her arrival. When they trained her to drive the bobtail trucks, she says, they kept changing instructions; one gave her driving tips that nearly blew up the engine. Her supervisor wouldn't issue her a pair of coveralls; she had to file a formal grievance to get them. In the yard, the men kept the ladies' room locked, and on the road they wouldn't stop to let her use the bathroom. "You wanted a man's job, you learn to pee like a man," her supervisor told her.

Obscene graffiti about Joyce appeared on the sides of trucks. Men threw darts at union notices she posted on the bulletin board. One day, the stockroom storekeeper, Tony Laramie, who says later he liked to call her "the piglet," called a general meeting in the depot's Ready Room. "I hate the day you came here," Laramie started screaming at Joyce as the other men looked on, many nodding. "We don't want you here. You don't belong here. Why don't you go the hell away?"

Joyce's experience was typical of the forthright and often violent backlash within the blue-collar work force, an assault undisguised by decorous homages to women's "difference." At a construction site in New York, for example, where only a few female hard-hats had found work, the men took a woman's work boots and hacked them into bits. Another woman was injured by a male co-worker; he hit her on the head with a two-by-four. In Santa Clara County, where Joyce worked, the county's equal opportunity office files were stuffed with reports of ostracism, hazing, sexual harassment, threats, verbal and physical abuse "It's pervasive in some of the shops," says John Longabaugh, the county's equal employment officer at the time. "They mess up their tools, leave pornography on their desks. Safety equipment is made difficult to get, or unavailable." A maintenance worker greeted the first women in his department with these words: "I know someone who would break your arm or leg for a price." Another new woman was ordered to clean a transit bus by her supervisor—only to find when she climbed aboard that the men had left a little gift for her: feces smeared across the seats.

In 1980, another dispatcher job opened up. Joyce and Johnson both applied. They both got similarly high scores on the written exam. Joyce now had four years' experience on the road crew; Paul Johnson only had a year and a half. The three interviewers, one of whom later referred to Joyce in court as "rabble-rousing" and "not a lady," gave the job to Johnson. Joyce decided to complain to the county affirmative action office.

The decision fell to James Graebner, the new director of the transportation department, an engineer who believed that it was about time the county hired its first woman for its 238 skilled-crafts jobs. Graebner confronted the roads director, Ron Shields. "What's wrong with the women?" Graebner asked. "I hate her," Shields said, according to other people in the room. "I just said I thought Johnson was more qualified," is how Shields remembers it. "She didn't have the proficiency with heavy equipment." Neither, of course, did Johnson. Not that it was relevant anyway: dispatch is an office job that doesn't require lifting anything heavier than a microphone.

Graebner told Shields he was being overruled; Joyce had the job. Later that day, Joyce recalls, her supervisor called her into the conference room. "Well, you got the job," he told her. "But you're not qualified." Johnson, meanwhile, sat by the phone, dialing up the chain of command. "I felt like tearing something up," he recalls later. He demanded a meeting with the affirmative action office. "The affirmative action man walks in," Johnson says, "and he's this big black guy. He can't tell me anything. He brings in this minority who can barely speak English. . . . I told them, 'You haven't heard the last of me.'" Within days, he had hired a lawyer and set his reverse discrimination suit in motion, contending that the county had given the job to a "less qualified" woman.

In 1987, the Supreme Court ruled against Johnson. The decision was hailed by women's and civil rights groups. But victory in Washington was not the same as triumph in the transportation yard. For Joyce and the road men, the backlash was just warming up. "Something like this is going to hurt me one day," Gerald Pourroy, a foreman in Joyce's office, says of the court's ruling, his voice low and bitter. He stares at the concrete wall above his desk. "I look down the tracks and I see the train coming toward me."

The day after the Supreme Court decision, a woman in the county office sent Joyce a congratulatory bouquet, two dozen carnations. Joyce arranged the flowers in a vase on her desk. The next day they were gone. She found them finally, crushed in a garbage bin. A road foreman told her, "I drop-kicked them across the yard."

Several months after the court's verdict, on a late summer afternoon, the county trucks groan into the depot yard, lifting the dust in slow, tired circles. The men file in, and Joyce takes their keys and signs them out. Four men in one-way sunglasses lean as far as they can over the counter.

"Well, well, well, Diii-ane. How the hell are you?"

"Hey, Diane, how the fuck are you?"

"Oh, don't ask her. She don't know that."

"Yeah, Diane, she don't know nothing."

Diane Joyce continues to smile, thinly, as she collects the keys. Some of the men drift over to the Ready Room. They leaf through dog-eared copies of *Guns* magazine and kick an uncooperative snack vending machine. When asked about Diane Joyce, they respond with put-downs and bitterness.

"She thinks she is high class now that she's got her face on TV," one of the men says. "Like we are dirt or something."

"Now all a girl has got to do is say, Hey, they're discriminating, and she gets a job. You tell me how a man's supposed to get a promotion against something like that."

"She's not qualified for ninety-nine percent of the jobs, I'll tell you that right now. I bet next foreman's job opens up, she'll get it just because she's female. I've been a road maintenance worker sixteen years. Now you tell me what's fair?"

Paul Johnson has since retired to the tiny fishing town of Sequim, Washington. From there, he dispatches an "Open Letter to the White Males of America" to newspaper offices across the country: "Fellow men," he writes, "I believe it is time for us to object to OUR suppression." His wife Betty, Johnson explains, helped compose and typed the letter. Her job at a bank also helped pay the bills—and underwrote much of his reverse discrimination lawsuit.

Women's numbers in the Santa Clara County's skilled-crafts jobs, after the Supreme Court ruling, increased by a paltry two to three a year. By the end of 1988, while the total number of available craft slots had grown from 238 to 468, the number of women rose only to 12. This was not because women had lost interest in these jobs. They were enrolling in union craft apprenticeship programs in the area in record numbers. And a county survey of its own female employees (who were still overwhelmingly relegated to the clerical pool) found that 85 percent of these women were interested in higher-paying "men's" jobs. Moreover, 90 percent of the women surveyed said they believed they knew the reason why they weren't getting these higher-paying positions: discrimination.

Lady Bench-Hands and Gentlemen Testers

The Supreme Court would ultimately undercut Diane Joyce's legal victory, too—only two years after she "won" in Washington. Within ten days in June 1989, the U.S. Supreme Court rolled back two decades of landmark civil rights decisions in four separate rulings. The court opened the way for men to challenge affirmative action suits, set up new barriers that made it far more difficult to demonstrate discrimination in court with statistics, and ruled that an 1866 civil rights statute doesn't protect employees from discrimination that occurs after they are hired.

One of the four cases that summer, *Lorance* v. *AT&T Technologies*, dealt a particularly hard blow to blue-collar women. The court ruled that women at AT&T's electronics plant in Illinois couldn't challenge a 1979 seniority system that union and company officials had openly devised to lock out women. The reason: the women had missed the 180-day federal filing deadline for lodging unfair employment practices. The court made this ruling even though five past court rulings had all allowed employees to file such challenges after the deadline had passed. And ironically enough, that very same day the court ruled that a group of white male firefighters were not too late to file *their* reverse discrimination suit—against a settlement of an affirmative action case filed in 1974.

In the economically depressed town of Montgomery, Illinois, forty miles outside Chicago, nearly all the jobs pay minimum wage—except at the Western Electric plant, where circuit boards are assembled and tested for AT&T. As long as anyone at the plant can remember, the factory had been rigidly divided by sex: the women had virtually all the lowly "bench-hand" jobs (assembling and wiring switching systems by hand) and the men had virtually all the high-paying "testing" jobs (checking the circuit boards). So it had remained until 1976, when three women decided, without so much as a nudge from affirmative action recruiters, to cross the gender line.

Pat Lorance was one of the first to ford the divide. She had been working since adolescence, ever since her father had deserted the family and left her mother with no job and five children to raise. She joined the plant in 1970 as a bench-hand; after nine years she was weary of the tedious work and even wearier of the low pay. When she heard that the local community college was offering courses to qualify as a tester, Lorance decided to give it a try. She brought two women, both bench-hands, with her.

"In the beginning, it was a little intimidating because the teacher, who was from Western Electric, told us, 'You know, women don't usually finish.' But by the fourth course, we won his respect." She eventually completed sixteen courses, including electronic circuitry, computer programming, and "AC/DC fundamentals." To fit it all in, Lorance worked the five A.M.—or sometimes even the three A.M.—shift, studied in the afternoon, and attended class until 9:30 at night.

Officials at Western Electric–AT&T were closely, and uneasily, following the women's efforts. At the time, the EEOC was pursuing its highly visible round of class-action suits against industrial employers, including other divisions of AT&T, and the company's managers knew that if the women at the plant began raising questions publicly about the company's equal employment record, they could well be the next target. In 1976, as employees at the time recall, the personnel office suddenly began calling in some of the female bench-hands, one by one, and offering them a deal. As several women who got the summons remember, a personnel manager informed them that the company had "mistakenly" overlooked them for some job openings. They could now receive a check of several hundred dollars as "compensation"; all they had to do in return was sign a statement promising never to sue the company for discrimination. The women say they were also instructed not to discuss the matter with their co-workers. "Some of the girls wanted to know what the jobs were," recalls one woman, a bench-hand, who, like the others, asked that her name not be used for fear she will lose her job. "Some didn't want to take the money. But it was like, 'Take the money or you are out the door.' I got over $600." (Company officials say they have no record of these sessions in the personnel office. "We have found no facts to support such claims," the company's attorney Charles Jackson says.)

By the fall of 1978, Lorance had all the academic credentials she needed and she applied for the first vacancy in testing. Company officials accepted her for the job—then, a week later, told her the job had been eliminated. Then she heard that the company had hired three men as testers that same week. She protested to the union, and after a struggle, finally became the company's first female tester.

By the end of 1978, about fifteen of the two hundred testers were women. To the men in the shops, that was fifteen too many. "They made these comments about how women were dumb and couldn't do the job," Lorance recalls. "I have a pretty good personality and I just shrugged it off, figured they'd get over it." But as the number of women rose, so did the men's resentment.

Some of the men began sabotaging women's test sets, hooking up the wires the wrong way while the women were on their breaks or spilling ink on their schematic notebooks. They tacked up a series of humiliating posters around the plant. A typical example: a picture of a grotesquely fat woman standing on a table with her nylons down around her calves and money spilling out of her shoes. The men wrote on it: "Yesterday I couldn't spell tester. Today I are a tester."

In 1980, Jan King joined the second round of women to break into the tester ranks. She had worked at the company as a bench-hand since 1966, starting at $1.97 an hour. King desperately needed the extra money: her husband, a violent alcoholic, spent most of the money he earned on drink and gambling, and she had a child to support. "I looked around at the plant one day and I realized I had just accepted what I saw there," she says. "I thought I wasn't any good in math because that's what they said about women. But part of my brain said, Wait a minute, if they can do it, I can. Just because I was brought up to be a certain way, that doesn't mean I have to stay that way."

King had to fight for the job on two fronts, work and home. "My husband said, 'You are not going to go to school for this. It's a waste of time.'" First he threatened her. Then, when she went to class anyway, "he'd do stuff like five minutes before it was time for me to leave, he'd announce that he wasn't going to baby-sit. But I just kept at it because there was this little voice in the back of my mind saying, 'You are going to end up taking care of your daughter by yourself.' I knew if he left, he was the kind of guy who was not going to be paying child support."

The company officials weren't any more helpful. As King recalls, "The whole attitude at the company was, women can't do it. Women can't do math, women can't do electronics." As women began applying to become testers, the company suddenly issued a new set of training and examination requirements. Some of the tactics were peculiar. One of the top managers tried to require that female testers be sent home if they didn't carry see-through purses, a strategy supposedly to discourage thieving.

When some of the men who were testers heard that twelve more female bench-hands had signed up for training at the community college, they decided matters had gone far enough. The younger men were the most upset; because they had the least seniority, they knew that the bench-hand women who had worked at the plant for years would be ahead of them for advancement—and behind them for lay-offs. In the winter of 1978, the men organized a secret union meeting; when Lorance heard about it, she and a female co-workers made a surprise appearance.

"They weren't real happy to see us," she recalls. Lorance sat in the union hall and listened. She discovered they were drafting a new seniority system that would prevent women from counting their years as bench-hands in calculating their length of employment. If approved, it would mean that women would take the brunt of any layoff in the testing department. Lorance and her friend went back and spread the word to the other female testers.

At the union meeting to vote on the new seniority proposal, ninety men gathered on one side of the hall, fifteen women on the other. One man after another stood up to speak on behalf of the proposed seniority plan: "I have a family to feed. Do you know how much a loaf of bread costs now?" Then the women stood up, to say that many of them were divorced mothers with families to feed, too; their ex-husbands weren't paying any child support. "This is a man's job," one of the men yelled. "Yes, but this is a woman's factory," a woman retorted, pointing out that more women than men were on the company payroll; he just didn't notice them because they were tucked away in the lowest-paying jobs.

In the end, the men won the vote; in the testing universe, anyway, they still had numbers on their side. The union officialdom assured Lorance and the other women at the time that the seniority plan would have no effect on downgrades or layoffs, just advancement. Company officials, who had helped design the new seniority system and quickly approved it, made similar promises about layoffs. The women accepted their guarantees—and didn't file suit. As Lorance points out, no one was being laid off in 1978, so "why cause trouble when you don't have to?" None of the women wanted to risk losing the jobs they had fought so hard to get.

Jan King, for one, needed her paycheck more than ever; she was facing even more problems at home. "It was like every step I took toward improving myself, every step forward, he saw it as a rejection of him," she says of her husband. "As long as he could keep me dependent on him, then he could think that I would stay." Her husband turned even more violent; he began dragging her out of bed by the hair, beating and, ultimately, raping her. Whenever she made a move toward divorce, he would threaten murder. "If you leave me, you're dead," he told her. "If I can't have you, no one can."

When the recession hit in 1982, the women discovered that the union and company officials had misled them; the seniority plan *did* apply to layoffs, and the women were the first ones out the door. Eventually, women with nearly twenty years' experience would lose their jobs. Even women who weren't let go were downgraded and shunted back to the bench-hand side of the plant, a demotion that cost some women more than $10,000 in yearly wages.

Lorance was downgraded immediately. She went to a superior she trusted and asked for an explanation. He spoke to his bosses, then came back and told her, "I'm sorry, Patty, but they told me I have to write you up [for a reprimand]." But what, she asked, had she done?

He explained that she had "asked a question." Then he pulled her aside and said he suspected the real reason was they hoped this would discourage her from taking legal action. "Well, you know what that made me do," Lorance says. The next day she pulled out the *Yellow Pages* and started dialing lawyers.

Ultimately, Lorance and three other female testers filed suit against the company. (One of the women later dropped out, after her husband forbade her to pursue the litigation.) Bridget Arimond, a Chicago attorney who specializes in sex discrimination law, took the case, which was promptly derailed in the courts over a technical debate about the filing deadline for unfair employment practices. The company contended that the clock started running in 1978, when the seniority system was first adopted, and their complaints constituted "stale claims." "The ladies hadn't exercised their legal rights at the appropriate time," Charles Jackson, Western Electric's counsel on the case, asserts later. "It was really their fault." The women maintained the clock started when they were fired; how could they have known until then that the policy was unfair? "The irony of it all," Arimond says, "was that the whole fight in court came down to whether women who had no background in the law didn't file on time. Yet, the judge [in the lower court] waited over a year to rule on the motion." That judge: John Nordberg of the Sears case.

Meanwhile, Pat Lorance kept getting laid off and rehired. Finally, on March 31, 1989, she was laid off for good. She had to take a job as a bartender. Two months later, when she turned on the television set one night to watch the news, she learned that she had lost the ruling. "I was very disappointed," she says. "I don't think the court gave it a fair look. None of us were screaming. We just wanted to right a wrong, that's all."

King wasn't surprised by the decision. "You could see, the way the court had been going, we weren't in good water." The ruling was financial disaster for King, who was now a single mother. Her violent husband had been killed in a street brawl in 1983. After his death, she took a leave of absence to pull herself together. While she was away, the company fired her, maintaining she had failed to notify the personnel office at the appropriate time of her return date. Desperate for work to support her two children, King cleaned houses, then took a job as a waitress. She lost all her benefits. "Today I cleaned the venetian blinds at work," she says. "I make $2.01 an hour and that's it, top pay. It's demeaning, degrading. It makes you feel like you are not worthwhile."

As she scrapes gravy from diners' plates, King replays the scenes that led her to this dismal point. "Whenever I'm thinking about it, the feeling I get is of all these barricades, the ones with the yellow lights, and every time you try to take a step, they throw another barricade at you." But in spite of everything, she says—the legal defeat, her late husband's reign of terror, the humiliating descent to dishwasher—she has never regretted her decision to ask for more. "If it gets someone fired up enough to say, 'We've got to turn this thing around,' then its' been worth it," she says.

That same year, back at the "Breakthroughs and Backlash" media conference in California, some of the most influential female journalists and women's rights leaders were busy recoiling from conflict. They were pondering the question of whether women really wanted "male" jobs and "male" power. Jan King, who likes to say, "Just call me one of those women's libbers," would have doubtless found such proceedings strange and depressing—even shameful. She hasn't lost sight of what she and many other economically deprived women want, and she is still willing to rush the backlash barricades to get it. "I don't believe you have to accept things the way they are," she says. "I'll never change my mind about that."

SPECULATIONS

1.   Susan Faludi states that:

> . . . the backlash did more than impede women's opportunities for employment, promotions, and better pay. Its spokesmen kept the news of many of these setbacks from women. Not only did the backlash do grievous damage to working women—it did it on the sly.

Does Faludi offer sufficient evidence to make her case? Cite other evidence that either proves or disproves her statement.
2.   How would you describe Faludi's rhetoric in this essay? That is, what kinds of images, metaphors, diction, use of facts and figures, and data of people's attitudes and sentiments does she use to get her point across?
3.   Respond to the treatment of either Diane Joyce, Pat Lorance, or Jan King by their male co-workers. How is this behavior justified by the men? What is their rationale? What would you have done if you were trying to secure a better job?
4.   In describing the effect of the backlash on working women, Faludi presents several case studies that reveal what happened to specific women in specific jobs and in specific court cases. Is this an effective way of exemplifying her argument? Do you find yourself persuaded by Faludi? Why or why not?
5.   What assumptions about society, work, and money are revealed in Faludi's essay? What basic assumptions does it reveal about women in the workforce, at least as Faludi describes their situation?
6.   Based on your personal experience and insights as a working man or a working woman, give specific examples of how you have witnessed the psychology and mechanisms of the backlash against women's rights operating in the workplace.

George

DUDLEY RANDALL

Interested in poetry all of his life, Dudley Randall, Detroit's poet-laureate, wrote his first poem at the age of four. During his subsequent distinguished career, Randall has written, co-authored, and edited over fifteen books of poetry and criticism. One of Randall's greatest achievements is founding the Broadside Press, which made low-priced books available to small bookstores and established a vehicle for poets of the vernacular to find their own voices. The result was that Randall provided a forum for many black poets who emerged between 1965 to 1977, difficult years for writers in the African-American literary community to find presses to publish their work.

Dudley Randall was born in 1914 in Washington, D.C.; his mother was a teacher and his father a minister in the Congregational Church. Before receiving an M.A. from the University of Michigan, he worked for Ford Motor Company and for the U.S. Post Office. After graduate study at the University of Ghana in 1970, he worked as a librarian at several state university and county libraries, eventually becoming reference librarian and poet-in-residence at the University of Detroit.

Winner of the Tompkins Award, the Kuumba Liberation Award, the Michigan Foundation Arts Award in Literature, and a National Endowment for the Arts fellowship among others, Randall has been widely anthologized. Among his best known volumes of poetry are *Poem Counterpoem* (with Margaret Danner), *Cities Burning*, and *More to Remember: Poems of Four Decades*.

When I was a boy desiring the title of man
And toiling to earn it
In the inferno of the foundry knockout,
I watched and admired you working by my side,
As, goggled, with mask on your mouth and shoulders bright with
   sweat,
You mastered the monstrous, lumpish cylinder blocks,
And when they clotted the line and plunged to the floor
With force enough to tear your foot in two,
You calmly stepped aside.

One day when the line broke down and the blocks reared up
Groaning, grinding, and mounted like an ocean wave
And then rushed thundering down like an avalanche,
And we frantically dodged, then braced our heads together
To form an arch to lift and stack them,
You gave me your highest accolade:
You said: "You not afraid of sweat. You strong as a mule."

Now, here, in the hospital,
In a ward where old men wait to die,
You sit, and watch time go by.
You cannot read the books I bring, not even
Those that are only picture books,
As you sit among the senile wrecks,
The psychopaths, the incontinent.

One day when you fell from your chair and stared at the air
With the look of fright which sight of death inspires,
I lifted you like a cylinder block, and said,
"Don't be afraid
Of a little fall, for you'll be here
A long time yet, because you're strong as a mule."

SPECULATIONS

1.   Explain the connections that take place between the two men in this poem. How are those moments meaningful?
2.   What are the specific images and words related to actual work in this poem? How does that sense of work correspond to the final image?

In the Belly of the Death Ship

B. TRAVEN

The biography of B. Traven is a mystery. Is he Berick Traven Torsvan? Is he Ret Marut? Is his name merely a pseudonym used by Jack London after he faked his own death? Is he an African-American escaping American racism, a leper, or perhaps a political refugee from the Industrial Workers of the World—, a Wobbly (see Phil Ochs and Ray Pratt on the Wobblies in the Music and Morality section)?

Regardless of the mystery that surrounds him, Traven's work has been published in thirty-six languages and in over five hundred editions since 1926. Although he was not popular in America, American readers might recognize the following titles: *The Treasure of the Sierra Madre*, published in 1935 and made into a film in 1947; *The Cotton Pickers*, and *The White Rose*.

When his novel *The Death Ship* went to press in the early 1930s, his German publishers received the following response when they asked for a photograph and brief biography:

> My personal history would not be disappointing to readers, but it is my own affair which I want to keep to myself. . . . I am in fact no way more important than is the typesetter for my books, the man who works the mill . . . no more important than the man who binds my books and the woman who wraps them and the scrubwoman who cleans up the office.

Traven's prose often treats working people, anarchy, and loss of control. His books have recurrent themes: sickness, death, cruelty, hard work for low wages, loneliness, fear, and superstition. In the former Soviet Union, he is regarded as an important American proletarian writer. His is "an anarchist message," wrote a reviewer in the *Times Literary Supplement*; "it is equally committed to opposing capitalism, authority, bureaucracy, the state, the oppressor."

The excerpt below from *The Death Ship* (American edition, 1934) is a grueling description of what it means to be a coal drag in a death ship; that is, a ship that has no registry and will ultimately be sunk (with crew aboard) so that its owners can claim insurance money. The *Yorikke* comes to be a metaphor for working life and its crew represents anonymous working people everywhere. Pippip, the narrator, has found himself essentially shanghaied on board and in this section recounts what it means to work in the bowels of the ship.

Of all the schooling the *Yorikke* had to offer, there was nothing which could yield better results than fishing dropped grate-bars and setting them back into the grate-frame.

Each of the three boilers had three furnaces. Two of these furnaces were side by side, with a space of about two feet between them. The third furnace was squeezed in between these two, but above them. All three furnaces were actually located inside the boiler. The furnaces were not square, but cylindrical. The fuel rested upon a grate. This grate was a heavy iron frame along the length of which were lying nine bars which could be removed from the frame one by one. Each bar was about five feet long, about an inch and a half thick, and four inches wide. In front and at the back the frame had a rim upon which the bars rested. This rim was less than a half-inch deep. Hence the bars rested rather uncertainly. Neither in front nor at the back was there a higher rim against which the bars would have found a brace. It was only this three-eighths of an inch against which the bars could be fixed. Each bar weighed between eighty and a hundred pounds.

The grates were really simple affairs. Only the use of these grates made them such a horror. When the boilers and the grates had been new, which, as I figure, must have been about the time when the good old British Queen married, even then it must already have been quite a job to hold these bars in the frame, or to put them back after they had dropped. In the course of so many thousands of trips the *Yorikke* had accomplished to make money for her owners these rims had burned away.

The slightest disrespect of the fireman toward the grate when knocking off the slags was inevitably punished by a bar dropping into the ash-hole. As soon as this happened the fire had to be left alone, and the combined efforts of the fireman and his drag had to be exerted to set the bar back into its berth.

First thing to do was to fish the bar out of the ash-hole. This was done with the help of a pair of tongs which weighed about forty pounds. These tongs did not work the way the tongs a blacksmith uses work. They were, like all things on the *Yorikke*, the other way round. That is to say, if you pushed the handles together the mouth opened, and vice versa. It would have been too easy for us had it been otherwise.

The bar was red-hot, and the furnace was white-hot. One of us held the bar up with the tongs, the other steered the bar into the furnace and then steered it alongside of those bars still quietly resting in their berth, until the opposite end of the bar reached the rim at the back. There, with the help of the poker from beneath—that is, from the ash-hole—the bar was slowly and carefully moved into the rim at the back. Then we worked to get the bar into the front rim too. One push too much toward the back rim, or one very slight pull too much toward the front rim, and the bar said good-by and dropped off again into the ash-hole. One of us lay flat on the ground to use the poker while the one that held the tongs tried once more to move, with tenderness, the bar back onto the rim. All this was done while the bar was red-hot, and while the open furnace roared into our faces, scorching face, hands, chest.

Now, of course, to set in one bar, hard and cruel as this job could be, was considered merely an interruption of the regular work. The real torture began when, on trying to set in one bar, other bars were stirred and pushed so that they also dropped, until five, six, or even seven bars had dropped into one fire alone. If this happened—and it happened so often that we forgot how often—then the whole fire went out of commission, because all the fuel broke through into the ash-pit. The furnace had to stay open, for otherwise the bars could not be set in it again. So after a while the whole boiler cooled off so much that the two remaining fires could not keep it working at even half its capacity. Consequently the boiler became practically worthless. The more time we had to spend at the bars, the less time we could afford for the two boilers which alone had to furnish the steam necessary to keep the engine running. No wonder these two boilers also began to slack and we had to leave the dropped bars for a long while and bring up the remaining boilers to a point where they were ready to explode any minute. As soon as we had them going far above their power, we again started to work at the dropped bars. Seldom did we get a bar in right at the first attempt. It dropped in again and again, often ten times, until we, finally, had them all in—to last only until they were ready to drop once more during the same hour or the next.

When, after long slaving, the bars were now in again, we had to build up the fires anew. Having accomplished this also, both of us dropped as if we were lifeless into a pile of coal or wherever there was any space free from embers and red-hot cinders. For ten minutes we could not stir a toe. Our hands, our arms, our faces were bleeding. Our skin was scorched; whole patches and strips had been torn off or burned off. We did not feel pain any more, we only felt exhausted beyond description.

Then a glimpse at the steam-gauge whipped us into action. The steam would not stay. The fires had to be stirred, broken up, and filled.

When bars were out I had to assist the fireman. One man alone could not put them back. While I helped the fireman with the bars I could not haul in coal. But whether I could carry in coal or not was of no concern to the fires. They ate and ate, and if they did not get enough to eat, the steam came down. So whatever huge piles had been in the stoke-hold just before the bars began to drop were all gone by now. To drag in the coal needed during one watch took all the hard work the coaler could give. There was hardly a free minute left to step up to the galley and bring below a drink of coffee or cold water to the fireman. The oftener bars dropped, the harder the drag had to work afterwards to pile up coal in the stoke-hold, which always, no matter what happened, had to be a certain load, of which not ten pounds could be cut off. Within four hours the fires of the *Yorikke* swallowed about sixteen hundred well-filled large shovelfuls of fuel. The fuel was in many instances so far away from the boilers that these sixteen hundred shovelfuls had to be thrown in four shifts before they reached the fireman, so that the real hauling for the drag was not sixteen hundred shovels, but sometimes close to seventy hundred shovels. Some of the bunkers were located close to the foc'sle, others close to the stern.

This work, unbelievable any place on earth outside of the *Yorikke*, had to be done by only one man, by the drag. It had to be done by the filthiest and dirtiest member of the crew, by one who had no mattress to sleep on, no pillow to rest his tired head upon, no blanket, no coffee-cup, no fork, no spoon. It had to be done by a man whom the company could not afford to feed properly on account of the competition with other companies. But the company had to stand competition, because it was very patriotic, and every company had to go the limit to keep a good record in shipping in favor of its country. The country had to be first in all things, exportation, importation, production, shipping, railroad mileage. All was done for the good and for the glory and for the greatness of the country. A company cannot take care of two things that are contrary each to the other. If the company wants to beat competition, the drag and the fireman have to pay for it. Some way or other. Both the company and the crew cannot win. One has to be the loser in this battle, as in all other battles. Here on the *Yorikke* the biggest losers were Stanislav and I.

The *Yorikke* has taught me another big thing for which I am grateful. She taught me to see the soul in apparently lifeless objects. Before I shipped on the *Yorikke* I never thought that a thing like a burned match, or a scrap of paper in the mud, or a fallen leaf, or a rusty worthless nail might have a soul. The *Yorikke* taught me otherwise. Since then life for me has become a thousand times richer, even without a motor-car or a radio. No more can I ever feel alone. I feel I am a tiny part of the universe, always surrounded by other tiny parts of the universe; and if one is missing, the universe is not complete—in fact does not exist.

The winch used for heaving ashes had personality, and it had to be treated accordingly. Everything and every part of the *Yorikke* had individuality and soul. The *Yorikke* as a whole had the greatest personality of all of us.

When once on a trip from Santander making for Lisbon we were caught in one of those terrible cross-gales in the Bay of Biscay, the *Yorikke* was thrown about so that we all thought she would never weather it out. When we—my fireman and I—came below to relieve the former watch, and I saw how the pile of fuel was thrown from port side to starboard unceasingly, I had only one thought: what will happen to us or to the *Yorikke* if six bars should drop in one fire. If the steam in such a heavy sea is too low, the ship will easily get out of control, and it may be smashed against cliffs or helplessly driven ashore or upon sandbanks.

Any sailor who is not superstitious—which would be the rarest thing under heaven—would certainly become so after being on the *Yorikke* hardly a week. My fireman was no exception. So that night, when we came below, the fireman knocked his head three times against the boiler-wall, then spat out, and said: "*Yorikke* dear, please, don't drop any bars this night, please, just this night." He said it almost like a prayer. Since the *Yorikke* was not something dead, but a ship with a soul, she understood what Spainy had said. You may believe it or not, but the truth is that for thirty hours, while the heavy weather lasted, not one single bar fell off. When we were near Lisbon and the sea had become fine again, the *Yorikke* joyfully dropped nine bars in our watch, four in fire number two, one in fire six, three in fire seven, and one in fire number nine, just to keep us from getting haughty. We did not mind the nine bars, hard as it always was to bring them in, and Spainy swore only fifteen times, while usually he never ceased to swear, nor did I, for a full hour after the bars were in.

My fireman was relieved at four. My watch did not end until six.

I went to call Stanislav at twenty to five. We had to clear ashes for an hour. I could not get him out of the bunk. He was like a stone. He had already been a good long time on the *Yorikke*. He had still not got used to it. People who do not know what hard work really means and do nothing but just figure out new laws against criminal syndicalism and against communist propaganda usually say, when they see a man at hard work: "Oh, these guys are used to it, they don't feel it at all. They have no refined thinking capacity, as we have. The chain gang means nothing to them; it's just like a vacation."

They use that speech as a dope to calm their consciences, which, underneath, hurt them when they see human beings treated worse than mules. But there is no such thing in the world as getting used to pain and suffering. With that "Oh, they are used to that!" people justify even the beating of defenseless police-prisoners. Better kill them; it is truly more merciful. Stanislav, a very robust fellow, never got used to the dropped bars or to all the rest of the hard work on the *Yorikke*. I never became used to it. And I do not know of anybody that ever became accustomed to it. Whenever a fireman with fairly good papers, or on reaching his country, had a chance, he skipped off; if he could do no better he skipped without waiting for his pay. There is no getting used to pain and suffering. You become only hard-boiled, and you lose a certain capacity to be impressed by feelings. Yet no human being will ever become used to sufferings to such an extent that his heart will cease to cry out that eternal prayer of all human beings: "I hope that my liberator comes!" He is the master of the world, he who can make his coins out of the hope of slaves.

"You don't mean? Is it five already?" asked Stanislav. "I just lay down. It cannot be five." He was still as dirty as when he had left the fire-hold. He had no ambition now to wash up. He was too tired.

"I tell you, Stanislav," I said, "I cannot stand it. We had six bars out in one fire, and two in another. I cannot come at eleven to help you clear the ashes and then start dragging again at twelve. I am going over the railing, I tell you."

Stanislav was sitting on his bunk. His face black. In the thick kerosene smoke of the quarter I could not distinguish his face well. He turned his head to me and he said with a swollen sleepy voice: "Nope, don't you do it, Pippip. Don't leave me. I cannot do your watch also. I will have to make the railing also. No. Hell, I won't. I would rather bury two cans of plum marmalade in the furnaces and let the whole thing go to blazes, so that they could no longer catch lost souls to get their insurance with. I still feel something in my breast here for the poor guys who might come after us. Geecries, that game with the plum marmalade might be a pretty come-off. I have to think it over some time."

Plum marmalade? Poor Stanislav, he was still dreaming. So I thought.

My watch ended at six in the morning with an hour's work clearing ashes with Stanislav. I could not leave any reserve fuel for him. The shovel dropped out of my hands. "It's okay, Pippip, don't mind. We'll get even some day when I am down."

I did not miss mattress, pillow, blanket, soap. I understood now why such things were not supplied on the *Yorikke*. They really were not needed. Covered with soot, dirt, oil, grease, as I was, I fell into my bunk. What meaning inborn cleanliness? All culture and civilization depend on leisure. My pants were torn, burned, and stiff from oily water and soot. My shoes and my shirt looked no better. Now, when we put in the next port and I stand at the railing and look down upon the pier, side by side with my fellow-sailors, I shall not look any longer different from those who I thought were the worst of pirates when first I saw them. I, like the rest, was now clothed in striped garments, in prison clothes, in death-sheets, in which I no longer could escape without falling into the hands of the guards of the world of bureaucrats, who would pinch me and bring me back to where I now properly belonged. I had become part of the *Yorikke*. Where she was, I had to be; where she went, I had to go. There was no longer any escape to the living.

Somebody yelled into my ear: "Breakfast ready." Not even an ambassador's breakfast would get me up and out of my bunk. What was food to me? A saying goes: "I am so tired I can hardly move a finger." He who can say that does not know what it means to be tired. I could not even move an eyelid. My eyelids did not close fully. So tired they were. The daylight could not make my eyelids close. No power was left within me even to desire that the daylight go away and give my eyes a rest.

And at that very instant when I had the feeling: "Why worry about daylight?" the huge iron mouth of a gigantic crane gripped me, then tossed me violently up into the air, high up, where I hung for a second. The man who tended the crane had a quarrel with something or somebody; and, being a bit careless, the brake slipped off his hand and down I fell from a height of five thousand feet, and I dropped squashing upon a pier. A mob gathered around me and cried: "Get up, you, come, come, snap out of it, twenty to eleven, heave ashes."

After I had heaved ashes with Stanislav, there were just about ten minutes left. I had to hurry to the galley to carry dinner for the black gang to the foc'sle. I swallowed a few prunes swimming in the watery starch. I could not eat one bite more. The jaws would not work. Somebody bellowed: "Hey, drag, where is my dinner? Hop at it." It was the donkey-man, who had to be served separately in his own quarter. For the drags were the stewards of the donkey-man, who was their petty officer. He could have done all this alone, because he had practically no work to do. Yet he would have lost his dignity if he had to go to the galley and get his dinner himself. Hardly had I set the dishes on his table when the bell rang and the watch on the bridge sang out the watch-relief. I went below to help the fireman break up the fires and haul in the fuel from the bunkers.

At six in the evening I was relieved. Supper was on the table in the quarters. It had come in at five. It was now cold and everything edible had been picked by the other hungry men. I did not care to see what was left. I was too tired to eat anyway. I did not wash myself. Not for all civilizations present and gone did I care to have a clean face. I fell into my bunk like a log.

That lasted three days and three nights. No other thought entered my mind and my feelings but: "Eleven to six, eleven to six, eleven to six." The whole universe, all religions, all creeds, and my entire consciousness became concentrated in this idea: eleven to six. I had vanished from existence. Two painful yells cut into what had once been my flesh, my brain, my soul, my heart. These yells caused a piercing pain, as the feeling might be when the bared brain is tickled with a needle. The yells came, apparently, always from far away, falling upon me like avalanches of rocks and timber, thundering into my shattered body like the onrush of a hundred express trains gone wild. "Up, twenty to eleven!" was one of the yells. And the other: "Holy sons of fallen saints, three bars have dropped! Turn to it."

When four days and four nights had passed, I felt hungry. I ate heartily. Now I was initiated and a true member of the *Yorikke*. And I began to get accustomed to it. I had lost the last tiny little connection which up to this hour had bound me to the living. I had become so dead that no feeling in mind, soul, or body was left. There were times when I felt that my hands were steam-shovels, that my legs and arms moved on ball-bearings, and that all the insides of my body were but running wheels.

"It is not so bad after all, Stanislav," I said ironically to him when I came below to relieve his watch. "The hash tastes all right. The grandfather is not so bad a cook. If, the hell of it, we could get only more milk. I say, brother, the pile of coal you are leaving me here in reserve isn't very much to brag about. We stoke it off in three fires without even saying so much as pem-pem. Listen, how do you think I can loosen the chief from a good shot of rum? Haven't you got a good tip?"

"Nothing easier than that, Pippip. You are looking sour enough. You will make it. Go right up and tell him your stomach won't hold, you spill it all at the fuel, and if you won't get a stomach-cleaner you cannot stand the watch through. Tell him you are spilling all green. You will get a good full-sized swinger from him. You can ride this same horse twice a week. Only make sure not to come too often. Then he gets wise and he may fill your glass with castor. Being used to good clean drainings, you won't notice it until you have shot it all in. Then it is too late. You cannot spit it into his cabin. You have to finish up and get it all down. It won't do you any good if, after having sipped the castor, you drop six or eight bars in your watch. Believe me, it sure would not be a sweet watch. Keep that prescription for yourself. If you spill it, it will be ineffective. The firemen have got one of their own invention. They don't give it away, those sinners. They often make as many as four, even five shots a week. But they don't know genuine comradeship, those knights in shining armor."

The time came, though slowly, when I began to get my own ideas again, and this was when the two piercing yells ceased to have any corrupt effect upon me. No longer did I stagger about the bucket in a dazed and unconscious state. I began to see and to understand. Rebirth had taken place. I could now, without the slightest feeling of remorse, bark at the second that I would allow him to throw me overboard for bragging if I would not smash his head with a hammer and drill his back with the poker if he ever came into the stoke-hold again when we were on high sea, and bars were out, and the steam was falling to a hundred twenty. I swore to his face that this time he would not get away through the gangway safely like he did the other night. He could not have done it anyhow. Maybe he knew it. We had placed in the gangway a heavy poker, hung up in such manner that when, from a certain spot in the stoke-hold, one of us pulled a string, the poker fell down, making impossible the get-away of anybody in that gangway. Whether he, once trapped, got off with his life or only with a bleeding head and shins depended in the last decision not on what he had said to us but only on how many bars had dropped into the various ash-pits.

There were no regulations and rules for the fire-hold. Articles, of course, were signed when signing on, but the articles were never read to anybody as is required by law. Yet we had proof that people can live without laws and do well. The fire gang had built up among themselves rules which were never mentioned, but, nevertheless, kept religiously. No one was there to command, no one to obey. It was done to keep the engine, and so the ship, going, and at the same time give each member of the fire gang exactly the same amount of work and worry. Since there were nine fires to serve, each fireman left to his relief three fires elegantly cleaned of all slags and cinders.

The first watch cleaned fires number one, four, and seven; second watch fires number two, five, eight; third watch fires number three, six, nine. The relief could depend on these fires being left clean by the former watch. Therefore, no matter how much trouble the new watch had with their bars, they were sure to have at least three fires going at full blast. The relief, furthermore, found a certain amount of fuel ready in front of the fires. The former watch did not leave the stoke-hold until the ash-pits were drawn clear. Without this unwritten agreement in the black gang, work would have been nearly impossible.

Another important agreement was that the outgoing watch did not leave one single bar dropped. All bars were in when the watch was relieved. Sometimes a watch worked half an hour into the new watch just to bring in the bars which had fallen out ten minutes before the relief came.

Now let us have a heavy sea with all the trimmings. Such as we had once when sailing along the Gold Coast of western Africa.

The pleasure began with the heaving of ashes. I released the heavy ash-can from the hooks, and, hot as the can was, I carried it against my chest across the gangway toward the railing. Long before I reached the railing, the *Yorikke* swung out on a swell roller, and I with my hot can rolled some thirty feet toward the bow. I had not yet got up on my feet when the *Yorikke* fell off to the stern, and I, still with my can, had, of course, to follow the command of the *Yorikke*. After two of these rollers there was nothing left in the can, and the first mate cried from the bridge: "Hey, drag, if you want to go overboard it's all right with me. But you'd better leave the ash-can with us, you really won't need it when you go fishing."

In such a heavy sea it is considered a good job if you can get half of the ashes over the rail. The other half is strewn over all the decks. And since they are ashes, it is the job of the drags to clear the decks of this useless cargo.

Below, in the fire-hold, things are just as interesting as they are up on deck. The fireman is about to swing a beautiful shovelful into the furnace when the roller meets him square. He is thrown, and the whole shovelful of coal goes splashing right into the face of the drag. When the roller comes over from astern, the fireman, with his shovel, disappears into a pile of coal, out of which he emerges again when the *Yorikke* falls off from afore.

Jolly dances take place in the bunkers. I have a huge pile of fuel, one hundred and fifty shovels, right near the hatchway to the fire-hold when a breaker throws the *Yorikke* over to port and my pile of coal goes the same way, back to where I had just taken it from. So this swell job has to be repeated. After a while one learns to time the rollers, and as soon as a certain amount of fuel is near the chute, one shovels it down into the stoke-hold so quickly that, before the bucket falls off to the other side, nothing is left that can go with her. A coal-drag has to know how to time the rollers correctly in heavy weather. He must therefore understand the principles of navigation just as well as the skipper does. If he could not time the moves of a ship, he might never get a single shovelful of coal in front of the boilers. But by the time a good coal-drag is through with his studies in navigation, he comes from his watch in a heavy sea brown and blue all over, with bruises and with bleeding knuckles and shins. What a merry adventurous life a sailor has! Just read the sea-stories. They can tell you all about it.

A merry life. Hundreds of *Yorikkes*, hundreds of death ships are sailing the seven seas. All nations have their death ships. Proud companies with fine names and beautiful flags are not ashamed to sail death ships. There have never been so many of them as since the war for liberty and democracy that gave the world passports and immigration restrictions, and that manufactured men without nationalities and without papers by the ten thousand.

A good capitalist system does not know waste. This system cannot allow these tens of thousands of men without papers to roam about the world. Why are insurance premiums paid? For pleasure? Everything must produce its profit. Why not make premiums produce profit?

Why passports? Why immigration restriction? Why not let human beings go where they wish to go, North Pole or South Pole, Russia or Turkey, the States or Bolivia? Human beings must be kept under control. They cannot fly like insects about the world into which they were born without being asked. Human beings must be brought under control, under passports, under finger-print registrations. For what reason? Only to show the omnipotence of the state, and of the holy servant of the state, the bureaucrat. Bureaucracy has come to stay. It has become the great and almighty ruler of the world. It has come to stay to whip human beings into discipline and make them numbers within the state. With foot-printings of babies it has begun; the next stage will be the branding of registration numbers upon the back, properly filed, so that no mistake can be made as to the true nationality of the insect. A wall has made China what she is today. The walls all nations have built up since the war for democracy will have the same effect. Expanding markets and making large profits are a religion. It is the oldest religion perhaps, for it has the best-trained priests, and it has the most beautiful churches; yes, sir.

SPECULATIONS

1. Why does Pippip refer to the *Yorrike* and other ships like it as "death ships"? Support your answer with specific examples and ideas from the text.
2. What is the role that patriotism, capitalism, and competition play in creating the working conditions on the *Yorrike*?
3. What does Pippip mean when he says, "He is maŝter of the world, he who can make his coins out of the hope of slaves"?
4. How does B. Traven use specific images, diction, and descriptions to build an impression of oppression and exhaustion in Pippip's labor? Support your answer with examples from the text.
5. What kind of social bonding takes place among the crew of the *Yorrike* and how does it overcome oppression? Describe your own experience of social bonding with peers in school or the workplace and explain its effect on difficult situations.
6. When and how does a "rebirth" take place for Pippip in this story? How does it change the tone of his narrative and his relationship to the ship and specific crew members?

The Face of Rural Poverty

LEE SMITH

A New York City native who graduated cum laude from Yale University, Lee Smith is head of the Washington bureau and a senior editor of *Fortune* magazine. Smith began his career as an Associated Press reporter and later became an associated editor for *Newsweek*. Smith also worked at *Dun's Review* and *Black Enterprise*, and he has contributed articles to *Columbia Journalism Review*, *More*, *Skeptic*, and *New York Magazine*.

In "The Face of Rural Poverty," Smith turns his attention to the largely invisible plight of poor people living outside of metropolitan areas. The essay first appeared in *Fortune* in 1990.

Let us now praise famous men. More than 50 years ago, *Fortune* commissioned writer James Agee and photographer Walker Evans to memorialize the hardscrabble existences of Alabama tenant farmers; though their research never appeared in the magazine, it resulted in the classic book of that title. Since then, the lot of America's rural poor—men, women, and children—has improved greatly. Today few starve. Almost all have shelter of some sort, and life spans are considerably longer than in grandpa and grandma's day.

Hidden in the hollows of Appalachia, in makeshift villages along the Rio Grande, in shriveled industrial towns in Pennsylvania, on the back roads of Maine, and at the edge of cotton fields in Mississippi, the world that Agee and Evans uncovered endures. What's changed is that, for most Americans, the rural poor are even more remote and invisible than they were in the 1930s.

Now it is the urban poor who are the insistent, troubling presence, never long out of mind. Day begins with fresh reports of the overnight death toll in ghetto drug wars. The homeless in the streets block our path and demand our help.

Yet their country cousins are no better off. The poverty rate in rural counties, those without a town of 50,000, has climbed to 16%, almost as dismal as the inner cities' 18%. And their future is equally bleak. Despite scattered bright patches—rustic counties where tourism is flourishing, the handful of communities that have flowered around transplanted Japanese auto factories—much of the U.S. countryside is quietly and painfully dying.

That wasn't the case in the 1970s, when the long-term migration of jobs from the backwoods to the cities briefly reversed itself as corporations moved electronic assembly, apparel, and other low-tech plants to the sticks to take advantage of cheaper land and labor. For a decade rural manufacturing jobs grew at twice the rate of those in the city. But in the 1980s industry discovered even greater savings in Hong Kong, Mexico, and other foreign lands, and the backwoods boom went bust.

With the world economy becoming ever more global, America's nearly nine million rural poor are stuck on the part turned away from the sun. Any policy to ease their plight must start with a basic principle: People, not places, matter. Compassion does not require that U.S. taxpayers save small towns for their own sakes, despite the sentimental view that such places are reservoirs of virtue. Sometimes they are. They can also be backwaters of misery.

Who are the rural poor? Put aside a misconception. The victims are not those farmers besieged by drought and debt who received so much attention from politicians, rock stars, and the media a few years back. "The world's biggest myth is that there are millions of poor farmers," says Agriculture Department economist Kenneth Deavers. Farm families, who make up only about 10% of the rural population of 23 million, are by and large doing well. Their average income reached an all-time high of $43,323 in 1989, aided by $11 billion in taxpayer subsidies.

The poor are farmhands, who never had any land to mortgage. They are also coal miners, sawmill cutters, foundry men, and Jacks of whatever trades are hiring. Or Janes. Women make up 45% of the rural work force. A "go-getter" in many places refers not to a striver but to a fellow who picks up his wife after her shift.

Walk with us through a few representative towns, for a look at work and life at the bottom.

Belfast, Maine

President Bush's home in Kennebunkport is the Maine that outsiders know—the one where New England patricians summer in rambling, weathered shingle houses. But Maine has the lowest per capita income in the Northeast ($15,092 in 1988, $1,398 below the national average). About 130 miles up the coast from the Bush spread is Belfast, where a typical dwelling is a second-hand mobile home on a bare patch of ground.

Storms from way off shore have battered Belfast, a port town of 6,200, for two decades. During the 1970s rising fuel prices made it too expensive to heat chicken coops through the frigid winters and to import Midwestern feed grain. By the mid-1980s, the town's two big poultry processing plants, which once employed 1,100 people, had both shut down.

One of Belfast's few remaining enterprises is the Stinson Seafood Co., which cans herring pulled from local waters. For a visitor accustomed to entering a suburban plant through a colonnade of comely shrubs and trees that lead to a smart, polished reception lounge, Stinson comes as a shock. Alongside the entrance, an enormous dumpster full of ripening fish heads and tails waits to be carted off for fertilizer. A flock of seagulls almost hides the door.

Inside, several dozen women with kitchen shears, their hands rarely pausing, snip heads and tails off the fish and slap the bodies into cans. Base pay at Stinson is $4 an hour—a tad above minimum wage. An experienced packer raises her wages to $5 or $6 by filling 350 tins or more an hour. If she's lucky enough to clock 40 hours a week for 50 weeks a year, she can gross $12,000—still $600 below the waterline that defines poverty for a family of four.

But at two snips to a fish and four fish to a tin, earning $5 an hour requires some 20,000 scissor squeezes a day, a routine that over time can be crippling. Ruthie Robbins, 58, has been cutting fish for 20 years, makes $6 an hour tops, and suffers from chronic tendinitis. "The doctor could immobilize my arm," she says, "but then I couldn't work." Her arthritic husband earns a few extra dollars repairing lawn mowers.

Stinson's workers don't complain much. A steady job is not easy to find in Belfast. Across from Robbins sits her daughter, Lisa, 19, who smiles but won't take time out to chat. Carrying on family tradition, she trims fish at a furious pace.

Tunica, Mississippi

About 30 miles south of Memphis where the cotton and soybean fields begin their long flat run down the Delta lies Tunica, which has long held the miserable distinction of being the poorest American county in the poorest American state.

More than half of Tunica's 8,100 people live below the poverty line. Two-thirds occupy what is euphemistically called substandard housing. That usually means an unpainted pine shack patched with asphalt tile and protected uncertainly by a rusted tin roof. Front porches rise and fall like waterbeds. Inside, the standard three small rooms may hold a cot, a stick or two of furniture, a hot plate, and a television set. Some dwellings have no running water, so occupants share an outdoor tap and privy with neighbors.

Tunica has one manufacturing plant. Pillowtex, where 300 workers earn $7 an hour on average making pillows and mattress coverings, primarily for Wal-Mart stores. But agriculture is still its mainstay.

Picking cotton is no longer cruel hand labor. It is hard but dignified. Black men pilot 16-foot-tall John Deere pickers that straddle two rows of cotton plants at once. Pay is $4.50 an hour with no fringe benefits, tolerable work if there were only more of it. One man on a machine can clear 400 acres in a week, a job that required 25 people or more a generation ago. At the peak, during the harvest from October through Christmas, Tunica's cotton and soybean industries employ only 1,000.

After that the county lapses into a coma. The pulse beats once a month, during the first week, when the welfare, Social Security, and other transfer payments that sustain half the population arrive.

Tunica's children look as lively as those anywhere. Better nutrition has been one of the true advances in recent decades, so physicians no longer routinely encounter the near starvation common before the 1960s War on Poverty. Give much of the credit to food stamps and to the federal WIC (Women, Infants, and Children) program, which supplies pregnant women and preschool children with fruit juice, cereal, infant formula, and other protein.

But when these youths reach adolescence, their spirits start to die. "Their dreams are so small," says Tunica Chamber of Commerce president Lawrence Johnson. "A 16-year-old told me the other day that no one anywhere lives as well as the Cosbys on TV, not even white folks." Only one in three graduates from high school. Some leave town. Many more turn into the men who pop cans of Budweiser in the late morning and stare blankly from dusty stoops.

Las Milpas, Texas

All the wrecked cars and splintered lumber in North America eventually roll and tumble down to the strip of Texas that lies just above the Rio Grande from Brownsville to El Paso—or so it looks from the highway. Fields of mesquite and acres of vegetables alternate with vast junkyards that advertise: "We repair used tires, starters, wind-shield-wiper motors."

This frugal land is where migrant workers from Mexico spend their winters in hundreds of *colonias*, or unincorporated communities, whose collective population is roughly 140,000. Some are U.S. citizens; others are resident aliens with green cards. The rest have slipped across the border illegally. Whatever their status, they pick the California lettuce, Washington State strawberries, and Illinois broccoli that end up in the nation's refrigerators.

Life in the U.S. doesn't get any more meager than in Las Milpas. With a population of 8,800, it is larger than most other *colonias* but otherwise typical. The better homes of Las Milpas are made of sturdy cinder block, the worst are discarded school buses or huts a notch or two below even Tunica's wretched norm. When migrants return from their trek north, they push their broken '73 Mercuries and '75 Chevrolets into the welding shops for mending. Or junkman Antonio Hernandez buys the heaps for as little as $10 each and resells the serviceable parts for perhaps twice that.

Jesus Villagomez could not afford to fix his truck, so this past summer he had to skip the northern harvests where he might have earned $200 or more a week. Instead he made about $30 a week picking vegetables on local farms. The walls of his home are rigged from odd pieces of plywood; the roof is a composite of broken tin and plastic sheeting held in place by a used tire.

In a space about the size of a secretary's cubicle, Villagomez lives with his wife and five children, ages 4 to 14. The parents sleep on a cot, the children on a mat ripped from the floor of a ruined car, amid a jumble of faded clothes, mud-encrusted boots, kitchen pots—and a small black-and-white TV. Even the poorest hovels of Las Milpas are electrified, as are 99.1% of all U.S. homes. But the crude "cowboy wiring," as it is known locally, that hooks the hut to a power line is a mixed blessing. Homes in the *colonias* burn with distressing frequency.

The Villagomez family shares with neighbors an outdoor water tap and a toilet that empties into an overworked septic tank. Even this far south the temperature in winter frequently falls below freezing, so the family huddles even closer than the hut demands. Can this life be better than the one they left in Mexico? "Yes," says Mrs. Villagomez without hesitation. "At school the children get an education—and also lunch."

The notion persists that even at its worst, rural poverty is preferable to the urban kind. That's doubtful. True, poor families in the country are more likely to have both mother and father in residence (53%, vs. 38% in the cities) and at least one of those parents is more likely to have a job (65%, vs. 54%). There is also far less crime. No drug dealers terrorize Belfast, Tunica, or Las Milpas with nightly turf battles.

But alcohol is abundant, and cocaine use is increasing. Even little Tunica has an intersection known as Crack Corner. And guess what state leads the nation in marijuana production? Missouri, followed by Kentucky. Not all of this crop leaves for the big cities.

Nor is rural life necessarily healthier. Country folk have a slightly lower mortality rate than city dwellers. But they are more likely to suffer from chronic disease and disabilities. That's partly because much of their work is dangerous and also because they are less likely to be covered fully by Medicaid, which is jointly financed by federal and state governments. New York, for example, pays for physical therapy for all patients, Alabama only for some.

On balance, low wages probably stretch further in the country, but not much. The major edge is in housing, which is substantially cheaper, though often shoddier, than city quarters. A shabby three room apartment in Belfast rents for less than $200 a month, compared with $450 in Boston's rundown Roxbury section. Shacks in Tunica go for less than $150 and hovels in Las Milpas for under $100. But even at those prices, three out of four poor rural families spend more than 30% of their income on shelter.

Food, surprisingly, is sometimes more expensive in the country. People without land don't grow their own, and groceries are pricey, driven up by the distance from distribution centers and lack of competition. On average, urban counties have 29 supermarkets each; their rural counterparts only four. A five-pound bag of Pillsbury all-purpose flour was recently selling for $1.39 at a Giant Food market in Washington, D.C., $1.59 at Junior's supermarket in Las Milpas, and $1.79 at the Piggly Wiggly in Tunica.

The sharp run-up in gasoline prices in recent months has been particularly burdensome for low-wage rural workers, who must commute over long distances in older cars that chug-a-lug fuel. At roughly minimum wage, four or five hours of toil a week go just to pay for the daily 50-mile round-trip routine in states like Kentucky, North Carolina, Maine, and, of course, Texas.

But the great—and growing—disadvantage for country folk, even in the many places where the work ethic remains solid, is that opportunity is vanishing. Bad roads have long been a barrier to manufacturers. Now rural telecommunications systems that lag in everything from Touch-Tone dialing to fiber optics are discouraging service companies, which are also shipping overseas low-wage, low-skill jobs, such as key punching. As for rural education systems, "They are mostly abysmal," says Susan Sechler of Washington's Aspen Institute, which studies rural poverty.

Small wonder the brightest and most ambitious youngsters leave. "They see the flour barrel is empty and know it's time to go," says Robert Simmons, 44, who fled Tunica for Memphis, where he sells real estate. "The ones who stay behind are afraid to take a chance." As the local talent pool dries up, outsiders become even more reluctant to locate a new plant in Smallville.

Is there any way to break this vicious cycle? Market forces offer a few glimmers of hope. Las Milpas is likely to benefit from the prospering *maquiladoras* just across the Rio Grande, where U.S. and other foreign companies assemble cars, TV sets, and other goods for the American market. Those plants need warehouses and support facilities on the Texas side.

Recreation and retirement will keep some areas alive. The Ozarks and the Great Smoky Mountains already draw the elderly who are looking for inexpensive and safe quarters surrounded by pleasant scenery. As the population ages, those places could boom. Jobs in construction, resort management, and nursing would multiply.

William Galston, a senior scholar at the University of Maryland's Institute for Philosophy and Public Policy, advises rural America to offer government services at lower cost than the cities. "If I were a small town," says Galston, "I'd look at the controversy about prison overcrowding in the population centers and offer my help."

Still, only a small fraction of the countryside will be required to fill those needs. For the rest, the best thing the government could do would be to persuade residents to migrate not to a troubled megalopolis like New York, but to Columbus, Ohio; Jacksonville, Florida; Austin, Texas; and dozens of other promising smaller cities.

That's not likely to happen. By temperament Americans are reluctant to write off regions as finished. Says Agriculture Department economist Robert Hoppe: "It's antigrowth, defeatist." Legislators are also unenthusiastic about programs that encourage constituents to clear out. A final problem: The less educated people are the more attached they tend to be to a place.

But while government cannot force such folk to move on, it should at least stop giving them incentives to stay where they have no future. In Tunica, for example, Washington and the Mississippi state legislature have spent almost $7 million over the past several years constructing and subsidizing apartments. Humane though it is, this program merely houses people more comfortably in a place that is unlikely to ever generate enough jobs for them.

Instead, new policy initiatives should focus on helping individuals. Some already do, most notably the earned-income tax credit. This tax break is especially beneficial to the rural poor, who are more likely to be working than their city brethren. In the recent budget bill, Congress and the Bush Administration agreed to enrich the credit, so that in 1991 a wage earner who makes as much as $11,250 and has two dependent children will be eligible for a cash payment from the U.S. Treasury of up to $1,235. That's a 30% increase over 1990.

Why not take a similar approach to housing? Rather than build apartments in dead-end towns like Tunica, give people housing vouchers similar to food stamps they could exchange for rent. Recipients would then at least have the choice of using them in places where they might find work.

For all of human history, people have migrated from where opportunity has died to where it is being born. For those unable or unwilling to face such hard economic realities, government can do little more than offer more resources and more encouragement. "This isn't living, it's existing," says PamaLee Ashmore, a 32-year-old food cooperative manager, of her life in Belfast, Maine. She hopes her two children will move on—someday.

SPECULATIONS

1.   According to Lee Smith, what significant differences exist between the "urban poor" and the "rural poor"? Who are the rural poor? If they are not farmers what are their occupations?

2.   Why does Smith refer to James Agee's and Walker Evans's book, *Let Us Now Praise Famous Men*? What is the significance of this reference?

3.   What does Smith mean when he says that "People, not places, matter," and how does this principle shape his ideas for solving the problems of the rural poor?

4.   Smith vividly describes the people and their lifestyles in Belfast, Maine, Tunica, Mississippi, and Las Milpas, Texas. Why do you think he does this? How do these descriptions affect your view about poverty and values, welfare and work?

5.   Explain why you either agree or disagree that government policies and programs should encourage the rural poor to move from economically depressed regions to areas with better opportunities. Is this a good idea?

6.   How would you describe Smith's tone in this essay? How does the tone and his connection to the subject matter and his audience affect you?

Why Women Aren't Getting to the Top

SUSAN FRAKER

In 1984, "Why Women Aren't Getting to the Top" appeared in *Fortune* magazine. It was introduced by the following statement:

> No women are on the fast track to the chief executive's job at any *Fortune* 500 corporation. That's incongruous, given the number of years women have been working in management. The reasons are elusive and tough for management to deal with.

Susan Faludi (see "Backlash: The Toll on Working Women" in this section) and others have written about the problems women face in the workforce—the glass ceiling that prevents women from rising to the higher echelons of the corporate culture. According to a 1990 poll of *Fortune* 1000 companies, eighty percent of corporate executives said that sex discrimination was preventing women from achieving their career goals—but less than one percent agreed that their personnel departments should actively intervene in ending such discrimination. Such polls reinforce Fraker's main argument.

At the time Fraker's essay was published, she was an associate editor at *Fortune*, where she had been since 1983. Before that, she served as a senior editor at *Newsweek*. Fraker is a graduate of Carleton College and holds an M.S. in journalism from Columbia University. In 1973, she was awarded the Pulitzer Traveling Fellowship.

Ten years have passed since U.S. corporations began hiring more than token numbers of women for jobs at the bottom rung of the management ladder. A decade into their careers, how far up have these women climbed? The answer: not as far as their male counterparts. Despite impressive progress at the entry level and in middle management, women are having trouble breaking into senior management. "There is an invisible ceiling for women at that level," says Janet Jones-Parker, executive director of the Association of Executive Search Consultants Inc. "After eight or ten years, they hit a barrier."

The trouble begins at about the $75,000 to $100,000 salary level, and seems to get worse the higher one looks. Only one company on *Fortune*'s list of the 500 largest U.S. industrial corporations has a woman chief executive. That woman, Katharine Graham of the Washington Post Co. (No. 342), readily admits she got the job because her family owns a controlling share of the corporation.

More surprising, given that women have been on the ladder for ten years, is that none currently seems to have a shot at the top rung. Executive recruiters, asked to identify women who might become presidents or chief executives of *Fortune* 500 companies, draw a blank. Even companies that have women in senior management privately concede that these women aren't going to occupy the chairman's office.

Women have only four of the 154 spots this year at the Harvard Business School's Advanced Management Program—a prestigious 13-week conclave to which companies send executives they are grooming for the corridors of power. The numbers aren't much better at comparable programs at Stanford and at Dartmouth's Tuck School. But perhaps the most telling admission of trouble comes from men at the top. "The women aren't making it," confessed the chief executive of a *Fortune* 500 company to a consultant. "Can you help us find out why?"

All explanations are controversial to one faction or another in this highly charged debate. At one extreme, many women—and some men—maintain that women are the victims of blatant sexism. At the other extreme, many men—and a few women—believe women are unsuitable for the highest managerial jobs: they lack the necessary assertiveness, they don't know how to get along in this rarefied world, or they have children and lose interest in—or time for—their careers. Somewhere in between is a surprisingly large group of men and women who see "discrimination" as the major problem, but who often can't define precisely what they mean by the term.

The discrimination they talk about is not the simple-minded sexism of dirty jokes and references to "girls." It is not born of hatred, or indeed of any ill will that the bearer may be conscious of. What they call discrimination consists simply of treating women differently from men. The notion dumbfounds some male managers. You mean to say, they ask, that managerial women don't want to be treated differently from men in any respect, and that by acting otherwise—as I was raised to think only decent and gentlemanly—I'm somehow prejudicing their chances for success? Yes, the women respond.

"Men I talk to would like to see more women in senior management," says Ann Carol Brown, a consultant to several *Fortune* 500 companies. "But they don't recognize the subtle barriers that stand in the way." Brown thinks the biggest hurdle is a matter of comfort, not competence. "At senior management levels, competence is assumed," she says. "What you're looking for is someone who fits, someone who gets along, someone you trust. Now that's subtle stuff. How does a group of men feel that a woman is going to fit? I think it's very hard."

The experience of an executive at a large Northeastern bank illustrates how many managerial women see the problem. Promoted to senior vice president several years ago, she was the first woman named to that position. But she now believes it will be many years before the bank appoints a woman executive vice president. "The men just don't feel comfortable," she says. "They make all sorts of excuses—that I'm not a banker [she worked as a consultant originally], that I don't know the culture. There's a smoke screen four miles thick. I attribute it to being a woman." Similarly, 117 to 300 women executives polled recently by UCLA's Graduate School of Management and Korn/Ferry International, an executive search firm, felt that being a woman was the greatest obstacle to their success.

A common concern among women, particularly in law and investment banking, is that the best assignments go to men. "Some departments—like sales and trading or mergers and acquisitions—are considered more macho, hence more prestigious," says a woman at a New York investment bank. "It's nothing explicit. But if women can't get the assignments that allow them to shine, how can they advance?"

Women also worry that they don't receive the same kind of constructive criticism that men do. While these women probably overestimate the amount of feedback their male colleagues receive, even some men acknowledge widespread male reluctance to criticize a woman. "There are vast numbers of men who can't do it," says Eugene Jennings, professor of business administration at Michigan State University and a consultant to a dozen large companies. A male banking executive agrees: "A male boss will haul a guy aside and just kick ass if the subordinate performs badly in front of a client. But I heard about a woman here who gets nervous and tends to giggle in front of customers. She's unaware of it and her boss hasn't told her. But behind her back he downgrades her for not being smooth with customers."

Sometimes the message that has to be conveyed to a woman manager is much more sensitive. An executive at a large company says he once had to tell a woman that she should either cross her legs or keep her legs together when she sat. The encounter was obviously painful to him. "She listened to me and thanked me and expressed shock at what she was doing," he recalls, with a touch of agony in his voice. "My God, this is something only your mother tells you. I'm a fairly direct person and a great believer in equal opportunity. But it was damn difficult for me to say this to a woman whom I view to be very proper in all other respects."

Research by Anne Harlan, a human resource manager at the Federal Aviation Administration, and Carol Weiss, a managing associate of Charles Hamilton Associates, a Boston consulting firm, suggests that the situation doesn't necessarily improve as the number of women in an organization increases. Their study, conducted at the Wellesley College Center for Research on Women and completed in 1982, challenges the theory advanced by some experts that when a corporation attained a "critical mass" of executive women—defined as somewhere between 30% and 35%—job discrimination would vanish naturally as men and women began to take each other for granted.

Harlan and Weiss observed the effects of different numbers of women in an organization during a three-year study of 100 men and women managers at two Northeastern retailing corporations. While their sample of companies was not large, after their results were published, other companies said they had similar experiences. Harlan and Weiss found that while overt resistance drops quickly after the first few women become managers, it seems to pick up again as the number of women reaches 15%. In one company they studied, only 6% of the managers were women, compared with 19% in the second company. But more women in the second company complained of discrimination, ranging from sexual harassment to inadequate feedback. Could something other than discrimination—very different corporate cultures, say—have accounted for the result? Harlan and Weiss say no, that the two companies were eminently comparable.

Consultants and executives who think discrimination is the problem tend to believe it persists in part because the government has relaxed its commitment to affirmative action, which they define more narrowly than some advocates do. "We're not talking about quotas or preferential treatment," says Margaret Hennig who, along with Anne Jardim, heads the Simmons College Graduate School of Management. "That's stupid management. We just mean the chance to compete equally." Again, a semantic chasm separates women and men. Women like Hennig and Jardim think of affirmative action as a vigorous effort on the part of companies to ensure that women are treated equally and that sexist prejudices aren't permitted to operate. Men think the term means reverse discrimination, giving women preferential treatment.

Legislation such as the Equal Employment Opportunity Act of 1972 prohibits companies from discriminating against women in hiring. The laws worked well—indeed, almost too well. After seven or eight years, says Jennings of Michigan State, the pressure was off and no one pushed hard to see that discrimination was eliminated in selecting people for senior management. Jennings thinks the problem began in the latter days of the Carter administration, when the economy was lagging and companies worried more about making money than about how their women managers were doing. The Reagan administration hasn't made equal opportunity a priority either.

What about the belief that women fall behind not because of discrimination, but because they are cautious, unaggressive, and differently motivated than men—or less motivated? Even some female executives believe that women derail their careers by choosing staff jobs over high-risk, high-reward line positions. One woman, formerly with a large consumer goods company and now president of a market research firm, urges women to worry less about sexism and more about whether the jobs they take are the right route to the top. "I spent five years thinking the only reason I didn't become a corporate officer at my former company was because of my sex," she says. "I finally had to come to grips with the fact that I overemphasized being a woman and underemphasized what I did for a living. I was in a staff function—the company didn't live and die by what I did."

Men and women alike tend to believe that because women are raised differently they must manage differently. Research to support this belief is hard to come by, though. The women retail managers studied by Harlan and Weiss, while never quarterbacks or catchers, had no trouble playing on management teams. Nor did they perform less well on standardized tests measuring qualities like assertiveness and leadership. "Women don't manage differently," Harlan says flatly.

In a much larger study specifically addressing management styles, psychologists Jay Hall and Susan Donnell of Teleometrics International Inc., a management training company, reached the same conclusion. They matched nearly 2,000 men and women managers according to age, rank in their organization, kind of organization, and the number of people they supervised. The psychologists ran tests to assess everything from managerial philosophies to the ability to get along with people, even quizzing subordinates on their views of the boss. Donnell and Hall concluded, "Male and female managers do not differ in the way they manage the organization's technical and human resources."

Data on how women's expectations—and therefore, arguably, their performance—may differ from men's are more confusing. Stanford Professor Myra Strober studied 150 men and 26 women who graduated from the Stanford Business School in 1974. When she and a colleague, Francine Gordon, polled the MBAs shortly before graduation, they discovered that the women had much lower expectations for their peak earnings. The top salary the women expected during their careers was only 60% of the men's. Four years later the ratio had fallen to 40%.

Did this mean that women were less ambitious or were willing to take lower salaries to get management jobs? Strober doesn't think so. She says a major reason for the women's lower salary expectations was that they took jobs in industries that traditionally pay less, but which, the women thought, offered opportunities for advancement. Almost 20% of the women in her sample went into government, compared with 3% of the men. On the other hand, no women went into investment banking or real estate development, which each employed about 6% of the men. Strober points out, however, that investment banking and big-time real estate were all but closed to women in the early 1970s. "One way people decide what their aspirations are," she says, "is to look around and see what seems realistic. If you look at a field and see no women advancing, you may modify your goals."

Some of what Mary Ann Devanna found in her examination of MBAs contradicts Strober's conclusions. Devanna, research coordinator of the Columbia Business School's Center for Research in Career Development, matched 45 men and 45 women who graduated from the Columbia Business School from 1969 to 1972. Each paired man and woman had similar backgrounds, credentials, and marital status. The starting salaries of the women were 98% of the men's. Using data collected in 1980, Devanna found a big difference in the salaries men and women ultimately achieved, though. In manufacturing, the highest paying sector, women earned $41,818 after ten years vs. $59,733 for the men. Women in finance had salaries of $42,867 vs. $46,786 for the men. The gap in the service industries was smallest: $36,666 vs. $38,600. She then tested four hypotheses in seeking to explain the salary differences: (1) that women are less successful because they are motivated differently than men, (2) that motherhood causes women to divert attention from their careers, (3) that women seek jobs in low-paying industries, and (4) that women seek types of jobs—in human resources, say—that pay less.

Devanna found no major differences between the sexes in the importance they attached to the psychic or monetary rewards of work. "The women did not expect to earn less than the men," she says. Nor did she find that motherhood led women to abandon their careers. Although several women took maternity leaves, all returned to work full time within six months. Finally, Devanna found no big differences in the MBAs' choice of industry or function, either when they took their first jobs or ten years later.

Devanna concluded that discrimination, not level of motivation or choice of job, accounted for the pay differences. Could the problem simply have been performance—that the women didn't manage as well as men? Devanna claims that while she couldn't take this variable into account specifically, she controlled for all the variables that should have made for a difference in performance—from family background to grades in business school.

In their discussions with male executives, researchers like Devanna hear a recurrent theme—a conviction that women don't take their careers seriously. Even though most female managers were regarded as extremely competent, the men thought they would eventually leave—either to have children or because the tensions of work became too much. Both are legitimate concerns. A woman on the fast track is under intense pressure. Many corporate types believe that she gets much more scrutiny than a man and must work harder to succeed. The pressures increase geometrically if she has small children at home.

Perhaps as a result, thousands of women have careers rather than husbands and children. In the UCLA-Korn/Ferry study of executive women, 52% had never married, were divorced, or were widowed, and 61% had no children. A similar study of male executives done in 1979 found that only 5% of the men had never married or were divorced and even fewer—3%—had no children.

Statistics on how many women bear children and then leave the corporation are incomplete. Catalyst, a nonprofit organization that encourages the participation of women in business, studied 815 two-career families in 1980. It found that 37% of the new mothers in the study returned to work within two months; 68% were back after 4½ months; 87% in eight months. To a company, of course, an eight-month absence is a long time. Moreover, the 10% or so who never come back—most males are convinced the figure is higher—represent a substantial capital investment lost. It would be naive to think that companies don't crank this into their calculation of how much the women who remain are worth.

Motherhood clearly slows the progress of women who decide to take long maternity leaves or who choose to work part time. But even those committed to working full time on their return believe they are sometimes held back—purposely or inadvertently. "Men make too many assumptions that women with children aren't free to take on time-consuming tasks," says Gene Kofke, director of human resources at AT&T. Karen Gonçalves, 34, quit her job as a consultant when she was denied challenging assignments after the birth of her daughter. "I was told clearly that I couldn't expect to move ahead as fast as I had been," she says. Later, when Gonçalves began working at the consulting firm of Arthur D. Little Inc. in Cambridge, Massachusetts, she intentionally avoided discussions of family and children: "I didn't keep a picture of my daughter in the office, and I would travel anywhere, no matter how hard it was for me."

Sometimes pregnancy is more of an issue for the men who witness it than for the women who go through it. Karol Emmerich, 35, now treasurer of Dayton Hudson Corp., was the first high-level woman at the department-store company to become pregnant. "The men didn't really know what to do," she recalls. "They were worried when I wanted to take three months off. But they wanted to encourage me to come back. So they promoted me to treasurer when I was seven months pregnant. Management got a lot of good feedback." Emmerich's experience would please Simmons Dean Anne Jardim, who worries that most organizations aren't doing enough to keep women who want to have children. "It's mind-boggling," she argues. "Either some of the brightest women in this country aren't going to reproduce or the companies are going to write off women in whom they have a tremendous investment."

To the corporation it may seem wasteful to train a woman and then be unable to promote her because she won't move to take the new job. The Catalyst study found that 40% of the men surveyed had moved for their jobs, vs. only 21% of the women. An argument can be made that an immobile executive is worthless to the corporation—and hence may be paid less.

Where women frequently do go is out of the company and into business for themselves. "When the achievements you want aren't forthcoming, it makes going out on your own easier," says a woman who has set up her own consultancy. "I was told I wouldn't make it into senior management at my bank. Maybe I just didn't have it. But the bank never found any woman who did. They were operating under a consent decree and they brought in a lot of women at the vice president level. Every single one of them left." Karen Gonçalves left Arthur D. Little to do part-time teaching and consulting when she was pregnant with her second child. "I didn't think I would get the professional satisfaction I wanted at ADL," she says.

From 1977 to 1980, according to the Small Business Administration, the number of businesses owned by women increased 33%, compared with an 11% increase for men—though admittedly the women's increase started from a much smaller base. While it's not clear from the numbers that women are entering the entrepreneurial ranks in greater numbers than they are joining corporations, some experts think so. "It's ironic," says Strober of Stanford. "The problem of the 1970s was bringing women into the corporation. The problem of the 1980s is keeping them there."

A few companies, convinced that women face special problems and that it's in the corporation's interest to help overcome them, are working hard at solutions. At Penn Mutual Life Insurance Co. in Philadelphia, where nearly half the managers are women, executives conducted a series of off-site seminars on gender issues and sex-role stereotypes. Dayton Hudson provides support (moral and financial) for a program whereby women in the company trade information on issues like personal financial planning and child care.

What women need most, the experts say, are loud, clear, continuing statements of support from senior management. Women have come a long way at Merck, says B. Lawrence Branch, the company's director of equal employment affairs, because Chairman John J. Horan insisted that their progress be watched. Merck has a program that identifies 10% of its women and 10% of minorities as "most promising." The company prepares a written agenda of what it will take for them to move to the next level. Progress upward may mean changing jobs or switching functions, so Merck circulates their credentials throughout the company. "We have a timetable and we track these women carefully," says Branch. Since 1979 almost 40% of the net growth in Merck's managerial staff has been women.

Sensitive to charges of reverse discrimination, Branch explains that Merck has for years singled out the best employees to make sure they get opportunities to advance. Women, he notes, were consistently underrepresented in that group. In his view the tracking program simply allows women to get into the competition with fast-track men. Others might not be so charitable. Any company that undertakes to do something on behalf of its managerial women leaves itself open to the charge that it too is discriminating—treating women and men differently.

What everyone may be able to agree on is that opening corporations to competition in the executive ranks is clearly good for performance and profits. But how can a company do this? It can try to find productive part-time work for all employees who want to work part time—even managers. It can structure promotions so that fewer careers are derailed by an absence of a few months or the unwillingness to relocate. It can make sure that the right information, particularly on job openings, reaches everyone. Perhaps most importantly, it can reward its managers for developing talent of all sorts and sexes, penalize them if they don't, and vigilantly supervise the process.

SPECULATIONS

1.   What arguments does Susan Fraker provide in response to the title of her essay, "Why Women Aren't Getting to the Top"?

2.   After reading Fraker's essay, how would you define discrimination against women as managers in U.S. corporations? Provide examples of the types of discrimination that support your definition.

3.   Do you think women should be treated differently from men in the workplace? Explain your position and support your argument with specific examples from your own experience and from Fraker's essay.

4.   What do you think Fraker's position is about women and the workplace? Is she sympathetic to one faction more than another? Cite evidence that she is more sympathetic or less sympathetic to the feminist perspective.

5.   Based on Fraker's perspective, do you think corporations should support pregnancy leaves? How do you respond to the view that women's commitment to having children implies that they do not take their careers seriously?

Ben and Jerry's: Sweet Ethics Evince Social Awareness

MAXINE LIPNER

Maxine Lipner is a freelance writer who specializes in business issues. She contributes to publications such as *New York, Entrepreneur,* and *Executive Female.* She is a 1982 graduate of Cornell University with a B.S. degree in communication arts. Her essay first appeared in *Compass Readings.*

At Ben and Jerry's Homemade, Inc., an ice cream empire, headquartered in Waterbury, Vermont, the taste of success is sweet but not just for the usual reasons. Co-founders Ben Cohen and Jerry Greenfield have made it their business to give something back to their employees, their community, and the world at large.

Among their most recent ventures is the Peace Pop, an ice cream bar on a stick with a marketing twist—1 percent of profits is used to build awareness and raise funds for peace.

Other social endeavors include purchasing nuts harvested from the all too quickly disappearing rain forests for Rainforest Crunch ice cream, and buying brownies made by homeless people for flavors like Chocolate Fudge Brownie and Brownie Bars.

"We believe that business can be profitable and improve the quality of life for people at the same time," says Cohen, a jovial-looking entrepreneur, whose tousled, thinning hair and unruly beard harken back to the era when he and his partner came of age—the now much-heralded 60s.

Greenfield, who gives a slightly trimmer, more mainstream appearance with his close-cropped cut and clean-shaven look, concurs. "Business has an opportunity and a responsibility to be more than just a money-making machine," he notes.

The company's offbeat philosophy also extends to employees. While other businesses may have a yawning salary gap between top executives and office workers, not so at Ben and Jerry's. Here, there's a 7-to-1 salary ratio limiting top salaries to seven times that earned by the lowest-paid staff members—the idea being that employees will have more of a sense of working together as a team if they're not competing for wages.

Such concern for employees and social conscience must be good for business; last year alone, the company sold a whopping six million gallons of ice cream and topped $70 million in sales.

Not bad for an operation that started out as nothing more than a homemade ice cream parlor operating out of a renovated Burlington, Vermont, gas station. It all began quite simply.

Two close friends from Merrick, Long Island, who first partnered up in junior high school where they were the "slowest, chubbiest kids" in the class, Cohen and Greenfield had always toyed with the idea of going into business together. In 1977, after Cohen had tried his hand at everything from being a short-order cook to a Pinkerton guard and Greenfield had reconciled himself to the fact that a career in medicine was not to be, both decided the time was right to start their own venture.

Since the two enjoyed eating so much, starting a food business seemed only fitting. Selecting what to make was easier than one would think. "It seemed like the two things that were starting to become popular in the bigger cities were bagels and ice cream," recalls Cohen. When the would-be entrepreneurs discovered just how much it would cost to start a bagel shop, the choice was clear.

They happened on their Vermont location in much the same back-handed way. "We wanted to locate in a warm, rural college town, but what we discovered was that all the warm, rural college towns already had homemade ice cream parlors," remembers Greenfield. Un-daunted, the partners simply changed their plans. "We decided to throw out the criteria of warm and we picked Burlington, Vermont, because they didn't have any ice cream here at all, because it was so cold," he goes on.

The two took $12,000, garnered from their savings as well as a $4,000 bank loan, and bought themselves some secondhand equipment. Then they put an old five-gallon, rock salt, ice cream maker in the window of an abandoned gas station and, with the help of a $5 correspondence course from Penn State University, began churning out their own brand of rich, all-natural ice cream chock full of sweet, crunchy bits of cookies and candies.

In addition to the ice cream, Cohen and Greenfield also initially served food to help make ends meet, particularly during the cold winter months. From the start, each found his own niche. "Ben would cook, I'd make the ice cream, and we'd both scoop," Greenfield re-calls.

They were a hit. Sometimes there would be more people in line for the ice cream than there was ice cream available. But, despite the growing popularity of their product, when the time came to tally up, Cohen and Greenfield found they were having trouble turning a profit. "No matter how much ice cream we sold, we always just broke even and never made any money," Greenfield says. He adds with a laugh, "We couldn't figure it out because our sales kept going up, and it seemed like we ought to start making money, but we weren't."

After pondering the situation for awhile, the two realized what the problem was—they were scooping away their profits with every ultra-packed ice cream cone. "We realized that we had to control the size of the scoops of ice cream we were serving," Greenfield explains.

Another more daunting problem was the seasonal nature of their product. To keep the business alive during the slow winter months, Greenfield held down the fort and Cohen took to the road and began selling their ice cream to some of the local restaurants.

Then one day he came up with a brainstorm: why not put the ice cream in packages and stop at some of the local grocery stores along the way as well? Within three months, over 150 stores in the state were carrying their ice cream.

To help raise local awareness of their product, Cohen and Greenfield sponsored a variety of festivals ranging from Fall Down, an autumn celebration marked by Cohen's appearance as the "noted Indian mystic" Habeeni Ben Coheeni, to an ice cream eating marathon where Vermont schoolchildren had a chance to enjoy the world's largest sundae, made from a whopping nine tons of ice cream.

Word soon got around about the unconventional duo and they found themselves with a loyal local following and mounting sales. Greenfield attributes much of this success to the ripe Vermont market. "I think Vermont is the only state in the country that still doesn't have a Baskin Robbins; it's not really perceived by big companies to be a good ice cream market, so there was a real need here," he observes.

With such success came some unexpected conflicts. By 1982, Greenfield, whose own belief was that business should never be a drag, found that as the company was growing, it was becoming less personal to him.

"We'd started as this homemade ice cream parlor and evolved into a sort of a manufacturing plant," he says woefully. "Where it used to be that we made every batch of ice cream and scooped every cone, now there were people buying our ice cream who had never met Ben or Jerry." Disillusioned by the business, he opted out for a time.

Meanwhile, Cohen found his 60s' value systems at odds with his growing business status. No longer a humble hippie simply cranking out ice cream, suddenly he had turned into that all too familiar symbol of the establishment: a businessman.

After much soul searching, which brought Cohen to the brink of selling the company, a friend pointed out that he could change the business and make it into whatever he wanted it to be. This inspired Cohen to try something new—something he called "caring capitalism."

This meant that instead of pocketing all profits or channeling them back into the business, a portion would go to worthy causes. It also involved finding creative ways to improve the quality of life for employees and the community in which they worked: the state of Vermont.

Accordingly, in 1984, when Cohen needed to raise some money to build a new manufacturing plant, he held a statewide stock offering, the idea being that if the locals were part owners of the business, as it prospered, the community would automatically prosper as well. By the end of the stock offering, 1 out of every 100 Vermont families owned stock in the company.

Informal social gestures and charitable endeavors were all well and good, but Cohen was not satisfied. In 1985, before he held a national stock offering, he set up the Ben and Jerry's Foundation. This organization is dedicated to facilitating social change and charged with finding worthy causes to which 7.5 percent of Ben and Jerry's yearly pretax profits could be donated.

"We wanted to formalize our charitable giving policy and procedures," Cohen explains. "It was at the same time we had our national public offering and we wanted people to understand that when they invested in the business, 7.5 percent of the profits were leaving the company."

Greenfield gravitated back to the company around this time, and found growth was no longer something to be feared—it was a way to ensure that there would be plenty of money for charitable endeavors.

With the company poised for expansion into other markets, Ben and Jerry's began to run into some difficulties with competitors like Steve's Homemade Ice Cream, which, according to Greenfield, launched a look-alike campaign. "When Steve's decided to go national, it put a lot of pressure on us to expand really rapidly because they were essentially copying the flavors we were making and coming up with a package that was flatteringly similar," he says. "We were concerned that if they got into markets before we did, we would be perceived as the imitators, even though it wasn't true."

While rapid expansion helped quell difficulties with Steve's, it led to a distribution dispute with a large, well-known competitor. Claiming that the competitor was keeping Ben and Jerry's out of certain markets, Cohen and Greenfield mounted a national campaign that brought their plight and their ice cream to national attention.

This innovative grass-roots campaign is the stuff that the Ben and Jerry popular lore is made of and which Ben and Jerry's followers can still quote chapter and verse.

Once the campaign drew to a victorious close and Ben and Jerry's ice cream finally did hit the shelves nationally, the company went through a period of unprecedented growth. "We were growing so fast that one year, we essentially doubled the number of people in the company from 150 to 300," says Greenfield.

This concerned the two mavericks who had always prided themselves on running the company like a big family. Trouble was, not only could the "family" no longer squeeze around the table together, but they were also losing touch with their roots. "We were really concerned about communication and not really having people understand the core values of the company—we were afraid that these would get lost," says Greenfield.

To ensure that this didn't occur, Cohen and Greenfield made a conscious decision to slow company growth. "The idea was that if we spent more energy on developing our people, on developing the company from the inside, that we would be much better able to deal with whatever external situations came up," Greenfield explains.

While it was not easy to turn down business, it was essential, Greenfield notes. The company had to be nimble enough to spring into action in the event of an emergency.

It had to be able to contend with crises like the one that occurred in early 1987 when at Cohen's urging, two new machines were installed in the packing plant: one to produce pints with tamper-resistant seals and another to automate the process of filling the containers with ice cream.

While both were supposed to be up and running in time to handle the summer crunch, no one had counted on just how difficult the new machine would be to master. Trying to coordinate both turned out to be too much, and with summer fast approaching, management eventually decided to forgo the tamper-resistant packaging and concentrate on getting the other machine going.

Even so, at the last minute it became apparent that they were going to come up short of their quota. Over one weekend, everyone, including Greenfield and Cohen, had to pitch in and make up the difference the old-fashioned way: by hand.

Even in this crisis, the staff members were not forgotten. Greenfield, the company Joymeister, hired a masseuse to come in and give workers massages during their breaks.

Such is to be expected at Ben and Jerry's. While Cohen has been particularly pumped up about social issues, Greenfield, likewise, has been the push behind employee concerns. From the start, he has tried to make the company a place where employees would enjoy working.

Among some of the perks here: three pints of ice cream a day, free health club memberships, and a partially subsidized company child care center. Greenfield even went so far as to institute an official "Joy Gang" to help ensure that work would be as pleasurable as possible.

To watch the employees cheerfully yuk it up during a public tour of the pastel-colored Waterbury facility or to listen to the gleeful way the personnel all seem to answer their calls, the Joy Gang seems to be doing its job. And no wonder. Nothing appears out of bounds at this offbeat company. Take the message left on one executive's answering machine where, instead of the typical "at a meeting" fare, the executive mentions that he may not be available to take the call because, among other things, he may be "off doing transcendental meditation."

Neither Cohen nor Greenfield seems to have any pretense either. They come across as casual, friendly—not at all as if they have the weight of a multimillion-dollar company on their shoulders. They are plain and simply who they are: two guys who surely would rather wear jeans and T-shirts any day than button up their act in suits and ties.

Perhaps it's to be expected that instead of Madison Avenue-style advertising, they've resorted more to grass-roots marketing. "We devote marketing dollars toward things and events that the community would find of value as opposed to buying advertising in TV, radio, or newspapers," stresses Cohen. He adds, "Our marketing strategy is really not much different from what our company does."

This year [1991], marketing at Ben and Jerry's means sponsoring peace, music, and art festivals around the country. It also means continuing to draw attention to the many social causes they undertake.

Hot on the agenda are projects like mounting an opposition to the approval of Bovine Growth Hormone, a substance that increases the amount of milk a cow can produce, and that, Cohen and Greenfield worry, will drive a large number of small dairy farms out of the business.

"Small family-owned farms need to be part of our food chain. The goals pursued by family farms go beyond economics—they seek sufficiency, not just efficiency. They are at the heart of a caring, but rapidly disappearing, rural community life," Greenfield wrote in a *Boston Globe* article on the subject.

Despite extensive research on health and safety issues, Cohen and Greenfield are also concerned that the growth hormone might taint the dairy industry's wholesome image. This could, by association, touch Ben and Jerry's as well, since the milk of more than 8,000 cows went into the company's assorted flavors last year.

Another popular undertaking? The Giraffe Project. No, this is not an attempt to spotlight some other very special creatures; the project recognizes people who are willing to stick their own necks out and stand tall for what they believe.

The project is simple. Customers at participating Ben and Jerry's scoop shops receive free information on how to go about nominating local people for a Giraffe Commendation. Also available are posters, flyers, buttons and T-shirts to inspire others to stick their necks out "to make their world a better place."

It's tough to tell where Ben and Jerry's ideals end and their marketing begins. Often, it's their unusual stances that set them apart from their competitors. The customers who buy their super premium product are not kids after their next ice cream treat. They're serious-minded 25- to 45-year-olds who may very likely feel that in some small way they are doing their bit for society when they buy Ben and Jerry's.

If there is a problem in running a company that has actually made it socially responsible to eat ice cream, according to Greenfield, it's in living up to the standards they've set for themselves. "Because we're so vocal about what we believe, we've set up standards that are difficult to maintain," he admits, quickly adding that he wouldn't have it any other way.

Ben and Jerry's is growing up. It has come a long way since the days when Cohen and Greenfield scooped ice cream out of their garage mecca. The company now boasts two manufacturing plants, and is in the midst of building a third. But there have been sacrifices along the way. With a staff of 375 people, gone are the madcap days when anyone could shout out a suggestion at one of the company's frequent meetings.

"We're much more decentralized now," says Greenfield. "We're starting to see ourselves as more branches to a family, with different departments or different sites having monthly meetings, as opposed to everybody trying to get together all the time."

Some things, however, haven't changed. As always, Cohen and Greenfield have new projects in the works. One that both are particularly hopeful about is opening a new scoop shop unlike any other—this one would be located in the Soviet republic of Karelia.

"The whole idea is not to have it be a profit-making venture, but to use the profits from the scoop shop there to help fund cultural exchanges between people in the United States and in the Soviet Union," explains Greenfield.

How will flavors such as Cherry Garcia, Chunky Monkey, Coffee Heath Bar Crunch, and Dastardly Mash go over if this Soviet project takes off? That, of course, is anybody's guess. But if things work out the way Cohen and Greenfield have planned, with Soviets and Americans freely swapping cultural ideas, the end result once again will be sweet success.

SPECULATIONS

1. What is "caring capitalism" and how does it work?
2. Explain why you would or would not choose to work for Ben and Jerry's,

where salaries are limited to a 7-to-1 ratio (top salary can never be more than seven times the lowest salary) and 7.5 percent of the profits go to charity.

3.   Describe the family ethos at Ben and Jerry's when it was a new organization. How has it been forced to change?

4.   Is Lipner too uncritical in her assessment of Ben and Jerry's? Is her method of reporting convincing?

5.   What are the political implications of Ben and Jerry's endorsement of certain environmental issues? How might this political stand affect you as an employee or a customer? What would you do, as an employee, if you disagreed with specific policies?

ASSIGNMENT SEQUENCES

Sequence Number One: Exploring the Values of Work

1. In an essay, describe a work experience—at a fast food restaurant, a convenience store, a supermarket, baby-sitting, doing housework for an allowance—any experience that paid a wage or salary. What did you learn from working? Did working make you more aware of the value of money, more responsible, flexible, cooperative? Did you have a positive or negative experience? What did you learn about employer/employee relations, bosses, the value (or meaninglessness) of an education? Are you glad you worked? Would you recommend it to high school and college students? As you write this essay, describe in rich detail the nature of your work—and reflect on what that work taught you about yourself and others.

2. In an invitation to give a sermon at New York City's Cathedral of St. John the Divine, Monsignor Cielo asks:

> Last week, Wendell Berry delivered a stimulating and thoughtful sermon called "Economy and Pleasure." All 1,200 parishioners in attendance greatly approved of his remarks. But we need to have another point of view, some diversity, a rejoinder of some sort, however great or little it departs from Mr. Berry's own observations.
>
> We understand that you have been reading and thinking about the relationship of work and wealth, work and the common good. Please come to the church on the 15th of November as our guest, where you may deliver your sermon at the 10:00 service.

Write a sermon: serious, satiric, political, or social. In very specific ways respond to the ideas presented by Wendell Berry.

3. In "Economy and Pleasure," Wendell Berry offers the following observations about the tobacco harvest:

> The tobacco cutting is a sort of ritual of remembrance. Old stories are retold; the dead and the absent are remembered. Some of the best talk I have ever listened to I have heard during these times, and I am especially moved to think of the care sometimes taken to speak well—that is, to speak fittingly—of the dead and the absent. The conversation, one feels, is ancient. Such talk in barns and at row ends must go back without interruption to the first farmers. How long it may continue is now an uneasy question; not much longer, perhaps, but we do not know. We only know that while it lasts it can carry us deeply into our shared life and the happiness of farming.

In a reflective essay, describe your own views about the value—or lack of value—of such work. Is Berry being idealistic? Is work such as tobacco cutting meaningful, ritualistic, and healing—or is it exhausting, monotonous, and dreary? Is it both and neither? Do you agree with Berry that we have "removed pleasure from our work in order to remove 'drudgery' from our lives," and that we need to re-examine our values by asking personal questions about the work we actually do: What is the work? For whom is it done? Where and under what circumstances is it done? Without oversimplifying, write about an experience doing a difficult job of manual labor—and the real and ideal effects it had on you.

4. In the excerpt from *The Death Ship*, B. Traven describes how "There were no regulations and rules for the fire-hold. . . . The fire gang had built up among themselves rules which were never mentioned, but, nevertheless, kept religiously. . . . Without this unwritten agreement . . . work would have been nearly impossible." Write an essay analyzing a work situation in which unwritten rules among the workers enabled the work to get done or a goal was achieved through the efforts of a group. Why were these rules unwritten? How did you learn them? How did they benefit you? What was the ethical justification for these rules? In what ways were the rules different from or similar to the unwritten rules and employee bonding that shaped the relationships and values among the workers on the death ship?

5. In the Growing Up section, Lerone Bennett, Jr., wrote about ten myths about the black family. Follow his lead and write "Ten Myths about Work and Wealth." Base your myths on the selections in this section and on any additional reading and research that you do. Offer a short analysis and explanation of each myth, just as Bennett does in his essay.

6. Imagine that you are Lipsha Morrissey in Louise Erdrich's "The Bingo Van." The little horse is tattooed onto your hand by Lewey Koep; you discover the wrecked bingo van in a field, and have fallen asleep on the padded seat. Tell the rest of the story—that is, narrate "Bingo Van, Part 2." What happens to you and to Serena? Write a narrative that is a genuine outgrowth of Erdrich's story.

Sequence Number Two: Work and Individuality

1. One of John McPhee's great gifts as a writer is to describe actions and scenes vividly while somehow implying a greater truth or value beneath the surface. In "Greenmarket," McPhee focuses on the carnivalesque give-and-take at the open-air farmer's market which travels around the New York city area. But what points is he also making about the nature of work and wealth as exemplified by the market?

Why do farmers and consumers choose the market? What values does McPhee seem to be advocating here? What values do these various constituencies represent? What is McPhee saying—if anything— about racial, cultural, and ethnic differences? In an essay, explore the underlying philosophical position(s) that you think McPhee is advocating in this essay.

2. Imagine a conversation between two or three individuals associated with John McPhee's Greenmarket. These individuals might be farmers, casual labor, or customers. They are talking about the market, its good points and bad points, the kinds of values it promotes and stands for. In essence, they are talking about why they work there—or why they shop there. Write the conversation.

3. When talking to Barbara Garson, ex-McDonald's employee Jason Pratt says:

> You follow the beepers, you follow the buzzers and you turn your meat as fast as you can. It's like I told you, to work at McDonald's you don't need a face, you don't need a brain. You need to have two hands and two legs and move 'em as fast as you can. That's the whole system. I wouldn't go back there again for anything.

Pratt may be expressing the point of view of a disgruntled ex-employee or he may be offering a more generalized criticism of the McDonald's working philosophy. In an essay, write an answer to Pratt. What kinds of explanations might an administrator from McDonald's offer after reading this essay? What's *right* about McDonald's? The restaurant chain is a great success story. What positive values, lessons, principles about working at McDonald's may Jason be overlooking?

4. Is Garson right—is McDonald's an "electronic sweatshop"? Is she also correct that a good bit of work in America increasingly exists within an "electronic sweatshop" atmosphere? Support a point of view based on research and observation of local employment practices in your neighborhood. To do this research, interview at least two or three people who work in the food industry. Try to include at least one who works in a fast food environment like McDonald's. Ask questions that specifically develop a picture of the work environment, the employee's attitude, and the kinds of pressures that employees as well as managers face. What inside knowledge do these people have that the public does not see or hear about? Write up profiles of each of the individuals in a paper which includes your analysis, speculations, and conclusions about the main issues, problems, and values represented within the food industry.

5.   Notice how Mike LeFevre's description of his work and Pippip's description of work on the death ship are similar with regard to the oppression and exhaustion that each feels. LeFevre argues that people in power "fear the leisure man" and, like Pippip, he suggests that keeping workers tired is the best way to rule them and keep them in their place. Write an essay that examines, compares, and contrasts what you learned about politics, power, work, and the working class from the perspectives offered in these two selections.

Sequence Number Three: Work and Masculinist Values

1.   In "Disposable Heroes," Donna Gaines describes high school cast-offs, teenagers who seem to have nowhere to go but downward toward drugs, crime, chronic unemployment, and wasted lives. Given what Gaines says about them—and what you know from your own reading and experience—write an analysis which helps to explain what has gone wrong with this group of American teenagers. What has fueled their cynicism and despair? Is the situation as hopeless as Ray and Lenny, for example, believe it to be?

2.   At the very end of her essay, Gaines offers a brief litany of responses that a typical middle-class adult might offer to teenagers like Lenny and Ray: "Just hang in for the new situation. Don't get depressed; be patient. The world is changing. Things will come around; they always do."

Considering the situation of the teenagers described by Gaines and drawing upon your own knowledge, write an editorial response to the problems you see represented in Gaines's essay. In your editorial, identify the problem(s) and then offer some practical solution(s). What can be done? What should be done to turn around the lives of teenagers who have already tuned out? Or is it too late? Should our efforts better be directed elsewhere—toward family counseling, pre-teen education programs, an increase in prisons and detention centers, a change in our laws and governmental policies? Offer your own views.

3.   Gaines writes about the pervasive influence of heavy metal, Metallica, and metal values within the teenage subculture. In an essay, explore the philosophy and values of this teenage subculture as seen in metal lyrics and groups. As you write, consider whether the heavy metal musical phenomenon is a cause or an effect, both, or neither on teen culture.

4.   In "Mike LeFevre, Steelworker," Studs Terkel reports LeFevre as saying: "Picasso can point to a painting. What can I point to? A writer can point to a book. Everybody should have something to point to."

Explore this notion of work in an essay. What does LeFevre want? Why does he want it? Compare his views to those expressed by other workers represented in this section, particularly in selections by Wendell Berry, Donna Gaines, Maxine Lipner, and B. Traven.

5.   Imagine that Terkel's Mike LeFevre meets Diane Joyce, Jan King, and/or Pat Lorance from Susan Faludi's article. Create an appropriate setting for the discussion and offer us a reasonable version of the conversation that you think would occur. Draw upon the material presented in both selections to make your conversation convincing.

6.   One of the themes repeated in the selections by Terkel, Randall, and Traven, who are all men, is *physical strength*. In an essay, consider the value of physical strength in relation to work and wealth. In what ways do Terkel, Randall, and Traven value physical strength? In what ways is that strength perhaps as much a curse as a blessing? Is physical strength valued as well by other writers, such as Grahn, Erdrich, and Faludi? Is this a value that is important to you? In your essay, make explicit reference to at least three of the selections in this section.

Sequence Number Four: The Gendered Workplace

1.   Susan Fraker says that most men and women agree that discrimination is a major problem for women in U.S. corporations, but that the term covers a range of meanings and that most people "often can't define precisely what they mean by the term." After reviewing both Susan Fraker's and Susan Faludi's articles, write an essay that defines and explores the range of meanings associated with sexual discrimination in the workplace. In your essay include the most significant effects on how men and women compete, succeed, or fail in the work place. You may also include personal experiences of discrimination or unfairness which seemed especially meaningful because of your individual perspective as a man or as a woman.

2.   Reread Susan Faludi's essay "The Wages of the Backlash: The Toll on Working Women," paying close attention to the case of Pat Lorance, the woman who went back to school and qualified as a tester at Western Electric. Imagine that you are the male supervisor, whom Pat Lorance trusts and goes to after her demotion and to air the broken promises made by the union and management. As Pat Lorance's supervisor, you have been told to "write her up for a reprimand," an act they hope will discourage her from taking legal action against the company. Decide what you would do in this situation. Your job may be on the line if you do not follow orders. Write one of the following: a) a reprimand of Lorance which deals as fairly as possible with the company's goal and Lorance's complaint; b) a formal letter to Pat Lorance explaining your personal and professional feelings; c) a formal letter to the company explaining your view of the situation and what you recommend should be done now. Write your response as a protest, as a compromise position, as an apology, or as a way of rationalizing the company's position. The goal is to examine the ethics of the situation and to come to a conclusion. Support your opinion or argument with facts from the case, recognizing that whatever is written may be used in a future lawsuit.

3.   As the personnel manager of a large U.S. corporation, you have recently attended a seminar at which the two keynote speakers were Susan Faludi and Susan Fraker, who read their essays from this section. The president of the corporation is sympathetic to Faludi's and Fraker's views and wants the company to promote more women to top management positions. In your company mostly men are in top management positions, and the women are employed largely in clerical positions. A very small percentage of women are in lower management positions, even fewer are in middle management, and none whatsoever are in top management jobs. The president assigns you the job of writing a three-to-five-page analysis and policy statement that will initiate change by stating how women managers should be treated and encouraged in this company. Include a summary of the kinds of discrimination potential women managers have traditionally faced at corporations in general and a description of the changes in perceptions, attitudes, policies, and personnel training that you believe will improve the situation, including policy on pregnancy and family leave. Since several influential men in middle and upper management are uncomfortable with and even hostile toward the changes you have been asked to initiate, write as persuasively as possible to all the employees and managers.

4.   Write an in-depth description of a former boss, a former coworker, or a work situation that typifies at least one aspect of what you think is wrong with the workplace in America. Use specific examples and details about the person or place you describe to argue your case. What assumptions about work, wealth, and personal values lie behind the analysis and critique? Make specific proposals or recommendations to change the situation or the person.

5.   You have been hired by Ben and Jerry's as director of marketing. They are concerned that the public does not know that their product is different from other ice cream. Even worse, people do not realize that Ben and Jerry's operates according to a positive philosophy of

business unlike much of the rest of corporate America. Write a two-
or three-page advertisement that explains their philosophy and the
virtues of their product. Remember that Ben and Jerry's customers
tend to be socially concerned individuals not susceptible to "hard sell"
advertising tactics.

6.   Write an essay which describes the ideal work situation. Consider
the ideas you have read about in this section, including any of the
following: Berry's view of the pleasure that working can provide; Ben
and Jerry's philosophy that work and profit should be socially responsible; or McPhee's idea that "giving good weight" works for people
as well as business. Or you might describe the ideal work situation in
contrast to some of the negative depictions of work in Garson, Traven,
or Faludi. In your essay identify a principle or central idea or specific
examples of what constitutes a career, a job, or a working environment
that makes work worthwhile and valuable.

Sequence Number Five: The Promises and Pitfalls of Competition

1.   Susan Fraker offers many explanations as to why women are not
getting to the top. Interview either a man or a woman who is at or
near the top of an organization. You might want to interview the
president or vice president of a company, a department chairperson
or key administrator within the university—some person who has
risen to a position of considerable influence and power.

In your interview, focus on what it took for that person to rise to
the top. What kinds of educational, social, and political preparation
were necessary? What were the most important attributes or events
that led to that person's rise to the top? Then, in a well-reasoned essay
that draws upon the research Fraker reports, discuss the extent to
which that person's success was dependent on gender. Was that person's rise to the top facilitated or impeded by his or her gender? What
bearing, if any, did gender play?

2.   In "In the Belly of the Death Ship," Pippip describes the brutal
demands placed upon the coal drag, and then with bitter irony justifies the work with the following statement:

> [The work] has to be done by a man whom the company could not
> afford to feed properly on account of the competition with other
> companies. But the company had to stand competition, because it
> was very patriotic, and every company had to go the limit to keep a
> good record in shipping in favor of its country. The country had to
> be first in all things, exportation, importation, production, shipping,
> railroad mileage. All was done for the good and for the glory and for
> the greatness of the country. A company cannot take care of two

things that are contrary each to the other. If the company wants to beat competition, the drag and the fireman have to pay for it. Some way or other. Both the company and the crew cannot win.

In an essay, argue your position in regard to this conflict between the company and the crew, focusing both on the *Yorikke* and on other working situations with which you are familiar. Are you sympathetic to Traven's point of view? Why do such situations exist? Should they? How can a company—or a country—remain competitive without dehumanizing its workers?

3.   Lee Smith presents several portraits of the rural poor in different regions of the country. Go to the library and research urban poverty, street people, and the underclass that populates America's cities. Using Smith's style and method, write up your findings in a profile of the people and places that exemplify the urban poor and their plight. Discuss the reasons behind their situation and what might be done to change it. Give complete references of the books and articles that you use.

4.   In reporting on Ben and Jerry's, Maxine Lipner presents the company as a corporate model. Describe in an essay the central principles of Ben and Jerry's ice cream company that should be implemented by other companies in America. What further recommendations would you make? Examine why adding Ben and Jerry's principles might improve the work environment in many types of companies.

5.   Susan Faludi builds her case by producing considerable research: interviews, research summaries, statistics, expert testimony. Following the Faludi model, investigate a specific economic area which affects women's employment by finding at least three authoritative sources of information—and then produce a report card on women in the workplace. For example, you might want to investigate whether there are more women in the media than there were thirty years ago or the extent to which businesses are providing services such as child care, family leave, and so on. Use library resources and write an assessment of women in a specific work area in the 1990s.

6.   Choosing a character from a selection by Gaines, Erdrich, Terkel, Faludi, or Lipner, write a poem that captures the essence of his or her personality as it relates to work. As a model, use Judy Grahn's "Ella, in a square apron, along Highway 80" or Dudley Randall's "George."

Sequence Number Six: The Working Person Profile

Create a profile of a worker, such as Studs Terkel's based on an interview. To create such a profile, follow the steps below. Refer also to McPhee's process of composing a piece.

1. Choose a profession/job/vocation that you are interested in learning more about. Find someone within your immediate community who works in your specific area of interest. Arrange to have an interview with that person.
2. In small class groups, create a list of questions to ask the individual. Share your questions with other members of the class. Begin the interview with at least 25 questions.
3. Talk over (in small groups and in the entire class) interview procedures. Discuss various options: open vs. closed interview questions, interview style, use of a tape recorder, importance of the interview setting, time constraints, and so on.
4. Interview your subject.
5. Transcribe or paraphrase or summarize the entire interview, omitting useless digressions, and so on.
6. Organize the profile—thinking through what major qualities or points you want to emphasize about your subject and their vocation.
7. Write a first draft, incorporating many quotations. A second interview may be necessary; if so, schedule it right away. If your chosen subject has no time, try for a brief follow-up interview over the phone. Additional library research may provide other relevant information.
8. In a workshop in class, discuss the draft.
9. Complete the profile.
10. Present several profiles by class members, perhaps as a published anthology of essays on work and wealth.

Acknowledgments

JERRY ADLER "The Rap Attitude." From *Newsweek*, March 19, 1990 and © 1990, Newsweek, Inc. All rights reserved. Reprinted by permission. Excerpt from "Fuck Tha Police" (Ice Cube/M.C. Ren/Dr.Dre), Ruthless Attack Muzick (ASCAP), © 1989. Used by permission. All rights reserved. Excerpt from "No More ?'s" (Ice Cube), Ruthless Attack Muzick (ASCAP), © 1988. Used by permission. All rights reserved.

TONI CADE BAMBARA "The Lesson." From *Gorilla, My Love* by Toni Cade Bambara. Copyright © 1972 by Toni Cade Bambara. Reprinted by permission of Random House, Inc.

AMIRI BARAKA "Swing—From Verb to Noun." Reprinted by permission of Sterling Lord Literistic, Inc. Copyright © 1963 by Amiri Baraka.

LERONE BENNETT, JR. "The 10 Biggest Myths about the Black Family." Reprinted by permission of Lerone Bennett, Jr., and *Ebony* Magazine, © 1986 Johnson Publishing Company, Inc. Excerpt from "When Sue Wears Red" from *Selected Poems* by Langston Hughes. Copyright 1926 by Alfred A. Knopf, Inc. and renewed 1954 by Langston Hughes. Reprinted by permission of the publisher.

WENDELL BERRY "Economy and Pleasure." "Economy and Pleasure" from *What Are People For?*, copyright © 1990 by Wendell Berry. Published by North Point Press and reprinted by permission of Farrar, Straus & Giroux, Inc.

TOM BETHELL "They Had a Right to Sing the Blues." © 1991 by *National Review*, Inc., 150 East 35th Street, New York, NY 10016. Reprinted by permission.

LEON BING "When You're a Crip (or a Blood)." Copyright © 1989 by *Harper's Magazine*. All rights reserved. Reprinted from the March issue by special permission.

ALLAN BLOOM "Music." Copyright © 1987 by Allan Bloom. Reprinted by permission of Simon & Schuster.

TRACY CHAPMAN "Fast Car." "Fast Car" by Tracy Chapman © 1988 EMI April Music Inc./Purple Rabbit Music. All rights controlled and administered by EMI April Music Inc. All rights reserved. International copyright secured. Used by permission.

COUNTEE CULLEN "Incident." Reprinted by permission of GRM Associates, Inc., Agents for the Estate of Ida M. Cullen. From the book *Color* by Countee Cullen. Copyright © 1925 by Harper & Brothers; copyright renewed 1953 by Ida M. Cullen.

CLARENCE DARROW "Address to the Prisoners in the Cook County Jail." From *Attorney for the Damned*, edited by Arthur Weinberg, pp. 3–15. Chicago: University of Chicago Press, 1989 [1957]. © 1957, 1989 by Arthur Weinberg. Reprinted with permission from Lila Weinberg.

BARBARA DORITY "The War on Rock and Rap Music." "The War on Rock and Rap Music" by Barbara Dority first appeared in the Sept/Oct 1990 issue of *The Humanist* and is reprinted with permission.

DAVID ELKIND "Childhood's End." From David Elkind, *The Hurried Child*, © 1988 by David Elkind. Reprinted by permission of Addison-Wesley Publishing Company.

LOUISE ERDRICH "The Bingo Van." Copyright © 1990 by Louise Erdrich. Originally published in *The New Yorker*. Reprinted by permission.

GRETEL EHRLICH "Other Lives." "Other Lives," from *The Solace of Open Spaces* by Gretel Ehrlich. Copyright © 1985 by Gretel Ehrlich. Used by permission of Viking Penguin, a division of Penguin Books USA Inc.

SUSAN FALUDI "The Wages of the Backlash: The Toll on Working Women." From *Backlash* by Susan Faludi. Copyright © 1991 by Susan Faludi. Reprinted by permission of Crown Publishers, Inc.

CAROLYN FORCHÉ "The Colonel" from *The Country Between Us* by Carolyn Forché. Copyright © 1980, 1982 by Carolyn Forché. Reprinted by permission of HarperCollins Publishers Inc.

SUSAN FRAKER "Why Women Aren't Getting to the Top." From *Fortune*. © 1984 Time, Inc. All rights reserved. Reprinted by permission.

DONNA GAINES "Disposable Heroes." From *Teenage Wasteland* by Donna Gaines. Copyright © 1990, 1991 by Donna Gaines. Reprinted by permission of Pantheon Books, a division of Random House, Inc.

SHERYL GARRATT "Teenage Dreams." Reprinted by permission of the author.

LINDA RAY PRATT "Elvis, or the Ironies of a Southern Identity." Reprinted by permission of the author.

RAY PRATT "Woodie Guthrie: 'Shakespeare in Overalls.' " Reprinted by permission of Greenwood Publishing Group, Inc., Westport, CT, from *Rhythm and Resistance: Explorations in the Political Uses of Popular Music* by Ray Pratt. Copyright © 1990 by Ray Pratt and published in 1990 by Praeger Publishers.

DUDLEY RANDALL "George." Reprinted by permission of Broadside Press.

RICHARD RODRIGUEZ "Complexion." From *Hunger of Memory* by Richard Rodriguez. Copyright © 1982 by Richard Rodriguez. Reprinted by permission of David R. Godine, Publisher.

THEODORE ROETHKE "My Papa's Waltz." "My Papa's Waltz," copyright 1942 by Hearst Magazines, Inc. from *The Collected Poems of Theodore Roethke*. Used by permission of Doubleday, a division of Bantam Doubleday Dell Publishing Group, Inc.

SCOTT RUSSELL SANDERS "Under the Influence: Paying the Price of My Father's Booze." Copyright © 1989 by *Harper's Magazine*. All rights reserved. Reprinted from the November issue by special permission. Excerpt from "My Papa's Waltz" by Theodore Reothke, reprinted by permission of Bantam, Doubleday, Dell Publishing Group, Inc.

RICHARD SELZER "Imelda." Copyright © 1982 by David Goldman and Janet Selzer. Reprinted by permission of Simon & Schuster.

ROBERT SHERRILL "Murder, Inc." Reprinted by permission of Grand Street Books.

LEE SMITH "The Face of Rural Poverty." From *Fortune*. © 1990 The Time, Inc. Magazine Company. All rights reserved. Reprinted by permission.

BRUCE SPRINGSTEEN "Born to Run." Reprinted by permission.

BRENT STAPLES "Just Walk on By: A Black Man Ponders His Power to Alter Public Space." Reprinted by permission of the author.

ELLEN SWEET "Date Rape: The Story of an Epidemic and Those Who Deny It." Originally appeared in *Ms.* magazine. Reprinted by permission of the author.

AMY TAN "Two Kinds." Reprinted by permission of The Putnam Publishing Group for "Two Kinds" from *The Joy Luck Club* by Amy Tan. Copyright © 1989 by Amy Tan.

RICK TELANDER "Senseless Crimes." The following article is reprinted courtesy of SPORTS ILLUSTRATED from the May 14, 1990 issue. Copyright © 1990, The Time Inc. Magazine Company. Rick Telander, "Senseless Crimes." All rights reserved.

STUDS TERKEL "Mike LeFevre, Steelworker." From *Working* by Studs Terkel. Copyright © 1972, 1974 by Studs Terkel. Reprinted by permission of Pantheon Books, a division of Random House, Inc.

B. TRAVEN "In the Belly of the Death Ship." Reprinted by permission of the author and the author's agents, Scott Meredith Literary Agency, Inc., 845 Third Avenue, New York, New York 10022.

ALICE WALKER "Beauty: When the Other Dancer Is the Self" from *In Search of Our Mother's Gardens*, copyright © 1983 by Alice Walker, reprinted by permission of Harcourt Brace Jovanovich, Inc.

JOHN EDGAR WIDEMAN "The Brother." From *Brothers and Keepers* by John Edgar Wideman. Copyright © 1984 by John Edgar Wideman. Reprinted by permission of Henry Holt and Company, Inc.

ROGER WILKINS "A Modern Story." Reprinted with permission from *Mother Jones* magazine, © 1991, Foundation for National Progress.

JUDITH WILLIAMSON "Urban Spaceman." Reprinted by permission of Marion Boyars Publishers, Inc.

KIMBERLY WOZENCRAFT "Notes from the Country Club." Copyright © by Kim Wozencraft. Reprinted by permission of the author.

MALCOLM X AND ALEX HALEY "Hustler." From *The Autobiography of Malcolm X* by Malcolm X, with Alex Haley. Copyright © 1964 by Alex Haley and Malcolm X. Copyright © 1965 by Alex Haley and Betty Shabazz. Reprinted by permission of Random House, Inc.

Index of Authors and Titles